SELECTED WRITINGS ON CHARIOTS AND
OTHER EARLY VEHICLES, RIDING AND HARNESS

CULTURE AND HISTORY OF THE ANCIENT NEAR EAST

EDITED BY

B. HALPERN, M. H. E. WEIPPERT

TH. P.J. VAN DEN HOUT, I. WINTER

VOLUME 6

SELECTED WRITINGS ON CHARIOTS AND OTHER EARLY VEHICLES, RIDING AND HARNESS

M.A. LITTAUER & J.H. CROUWEL

EDITED BY

PETER RAULWING

BRILL

LEIDEN · BOSTON · KÖLN

2002

This book is printed on acid-free paper.

Library of Congress Cataloging-in-Publication Data

Littauer, M.A.
    Selected writings on chariots and other early vehicles, riding and harness / M.A.
Littauer & J.H. Crouwel ; edited by Peter Raulwing.
        p.   cm.—Culture and history of the ancient Near East; v. 6)
    Includes bibliographical references and index.
    ISBN 9004117997 (alk. paper)
        1.Chariots—History. 2. Horse–drawn vehicles—History. I. Crouwel, J.H. II. Raulwing,
Peter. III. Title. IV. Series.

GT5280 .L57 2001
388.3'41'09—dc21   2001043927

Die Deutsche Bibliothek – CIP-Einheitsaufnahme

Selected writings on chariots and other early vehicles, riding and harness / M. A. Littauer &
J. H. Crouwel. Ed. by Peter Raulwing.. – Leiden ; Boston ; Köln : Brill, 2002
    (Culture and history of the ancient Near East ; Vol. 6)
    ISBN 90-04-11799-7

ISSN   1566-2055
ISBN   90 04 11799 7

PRINTED IN THE NETHERLANDS

CONTENTS

Editor's Preface ix
Glossary of Technical Terms xv
List of Plates xxi
Abbreviations xxxv
Bibliography of the Authors xxxvii

A.
I. *Chariots*

1. Les premiers véhicules à roues, 1983 (M. A. L.)
   [= No. 23][2] 3

2. Kampfwagen B. Archäologisch, 1980 (M. A. L. and
   J. H. C.) [= No. 50] 26

3. The Vulture Stela and an Early Type of Two-Wheeled
   Vehicle, 1973 (M. A. L. and J. H. C.) [= No. 40] 38

4. The Origin of the True Chariot, 1996 (M. A. L. and
   J. H. C.) [= No. 68] 45

5. Chariots in Late Bronze Age Greece, 1983 (M. A. L.
   and J. H. C.) [= No. 53] 53

6. Review of P. A. L. Greenhalgh, *Early Greek Warfare*,
   1977 (M. A. L.) [= No. 18] 62

7. Robert Drews and the Role of Chariotry in Bronze
   Age Greece, 1996 (M. A. L. and J. H. C.)
   [= No. 69] 66

---

[1] M. A. L. = Mary Aiken Littauer, J. H. C. = Joost H. Crouwel, D. C. = Dominique Collon, V. T.-B. = Veronica Tatton-Brown, H. H. = Harald Hauptmann, V. K. = Vassos Karageorghis.

[2] The current numbers and those in brackets indicate the concordance between the Table of Contents and the Bibliography of the Authors as a help for the full bibliographical reference.

8. The Military Use of the Chariot in the Aegean in the
   Late Bronze Age, 1972 (M. A. L.) [= No. 11]   75

9. Fighting on Land and Sea in Late Mycenaean Times,
   1999 (J. H. C) [= No. 39]   101

10. Rock Carvings of Chariots in Transcaucasia, Central
    Asia and Outer Mongolia, 1977 (M. A. L.)
    [= No. 16]   106

11. A 19th and 20th Dynasty Heroic Motif on Attic
    Black-Figured Vases, 1968 (M. A. L.) [= No. 6]   136

12. Chariots in Iron Age Cyprus, 1987 (J. H. C.)
    [= No. 32]   141

13. A Bronze Age Chariot Group from the Levant in
    Paris, 1976 (M. A. L. and J. H. C.; D. C.:
    "The Figurines") [= No. 79]   174

14. A Group of Terracotta Chariot Models – Cypriote or
    Phoenician?, 1991 (J. H. C.) [= No. 35] 190

15. Carts in Iron Age Cyprus, 1985 (J. H. C.)
    [= No. 31]   211

16. Chariots with Y-Poles in the Ancient Near East, 1977
    (M. A. L. and J. H. C.) [= No. 46]   238

17. New Light on the Assyrian Chariot, 1976 (M. A. L.)
    [= No. 14]   246

18. Assyrian Trigas and Russian Dvoikas, 1991 (M. A. L
    and J. H. C.) [= No. 66]   258

19. Metal Wheel Tyres from the Ancient Near East, 1989
    (M. A. L. and J. H. C.) [= No. 62]   261

20. The Origin and Diffusion of the Cross-Bar Wheel?,
    1977 (M. A. L. and J. H. C.) [= No. 45]   272

21. The Earliest Known Three-Dimensional Evidence for
    Spoked Wheels, 1986 (M. A. L. and J. H. C.)
    [= No. 56]   285

22. An Egyptian Wheel in Brooklyn, 1979 (M. A. L. and
    J. H. C.) [= No. 49]   296

23. A Late Bronze-Age Spoked Wheel from Lidar Höyük in Southeast Turkey, 1991 (M. A. L. and J. H. C.; "Introduction" by H. H.)[3] [= No. 81] 314

II. *Other Early Vehicles*

24. Ceremonial Threshing in the Ancient Near East, 1990 (M. A. L. and J. H. C. [= No. 64] 325

25. Early Metal Models of Wagons from the Levant, 1973 (M. A. L. and J. H. C.) [= No. 41] 336

26. Terracotta Models as Evidence for Wheeled Vehicles with Tilts in the Ancient Near East, 1974 (M. A. L. and J. H. C.) [= No. 44] 380

27. A Terracotta Wagon Model from Syria in Oxford, 1990 (M. A. L. and J. H. C.) [= No. 63] 403

III. *Riding*

28. Ridden Horses in Iron Age Cyprus, 1988 (J. H. C. and V. T.-B.) [= No. 76] 411

29. A Terracotta Horse and Rider in Brussels, 1990–91 (J. H. C. and V. T.-B.) [= No. 78] 430

30. Early Stirrups (M. A. L.), 1981 [= No. 22] 439

31. How Great was the "Great Horse"? A Reassessment of the Evidence, 1963 (M. A. L.) [= No. 2] 452

32. After Seeing the Spanish Riding School, 1965 (Revised by M. A. L.) [= No. 3] 460

IV. *Harness and Control*

33. The Function of the Yoke Saddle in Ancient Harnessing, 1968 (M. A. L.) [= No. 4] 479

34. Bits and Pieces, 1969 (M. A. L.) [= No. 8] 487

---

[3] Translation of Prof. Hauptmann's introduction by M. A. L. and the editor.

35. A Near Eastern Bridle Bit of the Second Millennium
    B.C. in New York, 1986 (M. A. L. and J. H. C.)
    [= No. 57] 505

36. A Pair of Horse Bits of the Second Millennium B.C.
    from Iraq, 1988 (M. A. L. and J. H. C.) [= No. 61] 515

37. Slit Nostrils of Equids, 1969 (M. A. L.) [= No. 7] 519

38. An Element of Egyptian Horse Harness, 1974 (M. A. L.)
    [= No. 12] 521

39. Note on Prometopidia, 1969 (M. A. L. and V. K.)
    [= No. 75] 525

40. The Trundholm Horse's Trappings: A 'Chamfrein?'
    Reasons for Doubting, 1991 (M. A. L. and J. H. C.)
    [= No. 65] 530

41. Ancient Iranian Horse Helmets?, 1984 (M. A. L. and
    J. H. C.) [= No. 54] 534

42. New Light on Priam's Wagon?, 1988 (M. A. L. and
    J. H. C.) [= No. 59] 545

Bibliography 550

B. *Indices*

A. Index of Names 591
   1. Historical Persons 591
   2. Scholars 592
B. Index of Places, Areas and Countries 594
C. Index of Subjects 597

EDITOR'S PREFACE

In 1968 Mary Littauer published her first major scholarly article "The function of the yoke saddle in ancient harnessing" in the British journal *Antiquity* (see Bibliography of the Author's no. 4, reprinted here as no. 33). In the same year Joost Crouwel, having graduated in Classical Archaeology at the University of Amsterdam, began research for his doctoral thesis on Mycenaean chariots in Oxford. There, in the next year, the two were introduced to each other by Crouwel's academic supervisor Dr Hector Catling. This meeting marked the beginning of a remarkable and most fruitful collaboration on chariots, other early vehicles, riding and harness, which has now lasted for over three decades.

Over the years Mary Littauer, resident on Long Island near New York, became known as "la grande dame d'hippologie", while Joost Crouwel became Professor of Aegean Archaeology at the University of Amsterdam.

Their bibliography includes two joint books: *Wheeled Vehicles and Ridden Animals in the Ancient Near East*, with its masterly and subsequently much reproduced drawings by Dr Jaap Morel, in the *Handbuch der Orientalistik* series (Leiden-Köln 1979; Bibliography of the Authors no. 48), and *Chariots and Related Equipment from the Tomb of Tutʿankhamūn*. Tutʿankhamūn Tomb Series 7 (Oxford 1985; Bibliography of the Authors no. 55). Both these books, together with the two monographs by Crouwel, *Chariots and Other Means of Land Transport in Bronze Age Greece*. Allard Pierson Series 3 (Amsterdam 1991; Bibliography of the Authors no. 30) and *Chariots and Other Wheeled Vehicles in Iron Age Greece*. Allard Pierson Series 9 (Amsterdam 1991; Bibliography of the Authors no. 36), have established themselves as standard works. In addition, Littauer and Crouwel have published some sixty-five articles for academic journals, mostly written together, though sometimes with other scholars and sometimes individually, as well as various entries for dictionaries, handbooks and exhibition catalogues (cf. Bibliography of the Authors).

A few years ago I suggested to the authors that a selection of their most important papers should be brought out. They readily concurred, and Koninklijke Brill Academic NV at Leiden agreed to publish such a collection. It has been decided to present the papers as originally published and not update them. They are now, however, preceded by an illustrated glossary of technical terms. All the plates are printed at the end, along with a consolidated bibliography and extensive indices. A full bibliography of the authors' work is also included.

Acknowledgements

The editor is grateful to Mary Littauer and Joost Crouwel for their fruitful collaboration in this project. They themselves wish to thank once again all those who agreed to be co-authors, helped with information and advice of various kinds, supplied photographs or allowed them to study material in their care.

Permission to reprint has been generously granted by all copyright owners, as well as by those scholars who collaborated in one or more of the papers: Dr Dominique Collon, Professor Harald Hauptmann, Professor Vassos Karageorghis and Dr Veronica Tatton-Brown.

The editor is most grateful to Dr Mary Moore for her careful proof reading and much other help, to the Netherlands Institute for the Near East in Leiden, to the Thomas J. Watson Library at the Metropolitan Museum of Fine Art in New York, to Koninklijke Brill NV, and in particular Mrs Patricia Radder for encouraging and supporting the ongoing project as well as for her constructive ideas and her endless patience until its final realization of this project.

Further Reading

The *Selected Writings* of Mary Littauer and Joost Crouwel cover the years 1973 to 1997. Following is a brief list of important publications by other scholars that have appeared since 1990 in the same or related fields, and which Littauer and Crouwel either could not yet refer to, or did not have occasion to refer to, in their recent work.

1. *Horses and Chariots*

a). **General overview**. Peter Raulwing, *Horses, Chariots and Indo-Europeans. Founddations and Methods of Chariotry Research from the Viewpont*

of Comparative Indo-European Linguistics. Archaeologingua Series Minor
13. Budapest: Archaeolingua Alapítvány 2000. See also Hans-Georg
Hüttel, "Zur archäologischen Evidenz der Pferdenutzung in der
Kupfer- und Bronzezeit", in: Bernard Hänsel and Stefan Zimmer
(eds.), *Die Indogermanen und das Pferd. Akten des Internationalen Interdisziplinären Kolloquiums Freie Universität Berlin, 1.3-Juli 1992.* Archaeolingua
Main Series 4. Budapest: Archaeolingua Alapítvány 1994 (= *Studies
in Honour of Bernard Schlerath on the Occasion of his Seventieth Birthday*),
197–215.

    b). **Egypt**. Finds of actual remains of chariots and horse gear are
presented by Anja Herold in *Streitwagentechnologie in der Ramses-Stadt.
Bronze an Pferd und Wagen. Forschungen in der Ramses Stadt.... Die Gra-
bungen des Pelizaeus-Museums Hildesheim in Quantir-Pi Ramesse II.* Mainz:
von Zabern 1998; for a summary, see her "Von Pferdeställen und
Wagenteilen. Neuigkeiten über Pferd und Wagen aus der Delta-
Residenz Ramses' II", *Achse, Rad und Wagen. Beiträge zur Geschichte der
Landfahrzeuge* 9, 2001, 4–17. For warfare as represented in Egyptian
art, see Susanna Constanze Heinz, *Die Feldzugsdarstellungen des Neuen
Reiches. Eine Bildanalyse.* Österreichische Akademie der Wissenschaften.
Denkschriften der Gesamtakademie 18 = Untersuchungen der Zwei-
gestelle Kairo des Österreichischen Archäologischen Instituts 17).
Wien: Verlag der Österreichischen Akademie der Wissenschaften
2001. Texts bearing on Ramses II' battle at Kadesh are included in
Kenneth A. Kitchen, *Ramesside Inscriptions Translated and Annotated Translation.* II. *Ramesses II. Royal Inscriptions.* Oxford: Blackwell. 1996. Mili-
tary history is treated by Andrea Maria Gnirs, *Militär und Gesellschaft.
Ein Beitrag zur Geschichte des Neuen Reiches.* Studien zur Archäologie
und Geschichte Altägyptens 17. Heidelberg: Heidelberger Orient-
verlag 1996. See also Alan R. Schulman, "Military Organization in
Pharaonic Egypt", in: Jack M. Sasson (ed.), *Civilizations of the Ancient
Near East* I. New York, Simon and Schuster MacMillan 1996, 289–
301. Transport by chariot and other means is the subject of Robert
Partridge's *Transport in Ancient Egypt.* London: The Rubicon Press
1996. Chariots are discussed by Wolfgang Decker in "Pferd und
Wagen im alten Ägypten", in Hänsel and Zimmer 1994 (see above,
1, a). An overview is given by Peter Raulwing in "Pferd und Wagen
im alten Ägypten. Forschungsstand, Beziehungen zu Vorderasien und
methodenkritische Aspekte", *Göttinger Miszellen. Beiträge zur ägyptologischen
Diskussion* 136, 1993, 71–83. Ian Shaw discusses "Egyptians, Hyksos
and Military Technology: causes, effects or catalysts", in: Andrew J.

Shortland (ed.), *The Social Context of Technology Change. Egypt and the Near East*, 1650–1550 BC. Oxford: Oxbow 2001, 59–71.

c). **Greece**. Chariots feature in Cheryl Diane Fortenberry, *Elements of Mycenaean Warfare* (doctoral thesis, Department of Classics, University of Cincinnati 1990). 'Homeric' and hoplite warfare is the subject of several studies by Hans van Wees: *Status Warriors. War, Violence and Society in Homer and History. Dutch Monographs on Ancient History and Archaeology* 9. Amsterdam: J. C. Gieben 1992, "The Homeric way of war. The Iliad and hoplite phalanx (I and II)", *Greece and Rome* 41, 1994, 1–8 and 133–155, "Homeric warfare", in: Ian Morris and Barry Powell (eds.), *A New Companion to Homer*. Leiden, New York and Köln: Brill 1997, 133–155, and "The development of the hoplite phalanx: iconography and reality in the seventh century", in: Hans van Wees (ed.), *War and Violence in Ancient Greece*. London: Duckworth and The Classical Press of Wales 2000, 125–166.

d). **Other parts of Europe**. A great deal of material is brought together by Christopher F.E. Pare in *Wagons and Wagon-Graves of the Early Iron Age in Central Europe*. Oxford University Committee for Archaeology Monograph 35. Oxford 1992, and in Adriana Emiliozzi (ed.), *Carri da guerra e principi etruschi. Catalogo della mostra Viterbo, Palazzzo dei Papi 24 maggio 1997–31 gennaio 1998*. Rome; "L'Erma" di Bretschneider 1997.

2. *Other early Vehicles*

For an overview see Alexander Häusler, "Archäologische Zeugnissse für Pferd und Wagen in Ost- und Mitteleuropa", in Hänsel and Zimmer (see sub 1, a), 217–257. Jan Albert Bakker, Janusz Kruk, Albert F. Lanting and Sarunas Milisauskas, "The earliest evidence of wheeled vehicles in Europe and the Near East", *Antiquity* 73, 1999, 778–790, discuss the question of the first appearance of wheeled vehicles and their disputed diffusion from Mesopotamia to Europe. In favour of a local development in Europe argue Alexander Häusler, "Der Ursprung des Wagens in der Diskussion der Gegenwart", *Archäologische Mitteilungen aus Nordwestdeutschland* 15, 1992, 179–190, and Markus Vosteen, *Unter die Räder gekommen. Untersuchungen zur Sherratt's 'Secondary Products Revolution'*. Archäologische Berichte 7. Bonn: Holos 1996; see also his article "Taken the Wrong Way: Einige Bemerkungen zu A. Sherratt's Das sehen wir auch den Rädern ab", in: *Archäologische Informationen* 19, 1996, 173–186. See also Andrew Sherratt, *Economy and Society in Prehistoric Europe. Changing Perspectives*. Edinburgh: Edinburgh

University Press 1997 (= collection of, partly revised, articles). A study of a different kind is Jutta Bollweg, *Vorderasiatische Wagentypen im Spiegel der Terracotta Plastik bis zur Altbabylonischen Zeit*. Orbis Biblicus et Orientalis 167. Freiburg/ Switzerland and Göttingen 1997 (see review by Mary Littauer in the forthcoming issue of the *Journal of the American and Oriental Society* no. 121(2) 2001).

3. *Riding, harness and control, domestication and training of horses*

a). **Riding**. Of great interest are the three volumes of Marcus Junkelmann, *Die Reiter Roms* I. *Reise, Jagd, Triumph und Circusrennen*, *Die Reiter Roms* II. *Reitweise und militärische Einsatz*, and *Die Reiter Roms* III. *Zubehör, Reitweise, Bewaffnung*. Mainz: von Zabern 1990, 1991 and 1992 (including sections on chariots).

b). **Harness and control**. Jean Spruytte describes experiments with the harness documented on chariot depictions in Saharan rock art in *Attelages antiques libyens. Archeologie sahariennne expérimentale. Collection Archéologie expérientale et ethnographie des techniques* 2. Paris 1996 (see review by Crouwel, Authors' bibliography no. 38). A major study of early bridle bits by Ute Dietz is *Spätbronzezeitliche Trensen im Nordschwarzmeergebiet und im Kaukasus*. Prähistorische Bronzefunde, Abteilung XVI, Band 5. Stuttgart: Steiner 1998; see also her "Zur Frage vorbronzezeitlicher Trensenbelege in Europa", *Germania* 70, 1992, 17–36. There is also the monograph by Silvia Penner, *Schliemanns Schachtgräberrund und der europäische Nordosten. Studien zur Herkunft der frühmykenischen Streitwagenaustattung*. Saarbrücker Beiträge zur Altertumskunde 60. Bonn: Habelt 1998, with discussions of bridle bits and chariots (see review by Crouwel, in *American Journal of Archaeology* 105, 2001, 545–546). Of note are further papers by Jan Lichardus and Marion Lichardus-Itten, "Das domestizierte Pferd in der Kupferzeit Alteuropas. Eine Betrachtung zur Auswertung der archäologischen Quellen", in: Peter Anreiter, Lazló Bartosiewicz, Erzsébet Jerem and Wolfgang Meid (eds.), *Man and the Animal World. Studies in Archaeozoology, Archaeology, Anthropology and Palaeolinguistics in Memoriam Sándor Bökönyi*. Archaeologia Main Series 8. Budapest: Archaeolingua Alapítvány 1998, 335–365, and Jan Lichardus and Jozef Vladár, "Karpathenbecken—Sintashta—Mykene. Ein Beitrag zur Definition der Bronzezeit als historischer Epoche", *Slovenská Archaeologica* 44, 1996, 25–93. See also Nikolaus Boroffka, "Bronze- und früheisenzeitliche Geweihtrensenknebel aus Rumänien und ihre Beziehungen. Alte Funde aus dem Museum für Geschichte Aiud, Teil II", *Eurasia Antiqua* 4, 1998[1999], 81–135.

See also now M. A. Littauer and J. H. Crouwel, "The earliest evidence for metal bridle bits", *Oxford Journal of Archaeology* 20(4), 2001, 329–338 who reconsider the earliest history of metal driving bits in the ancient Near East.

   c). **Horse domestication**. Overviews are given by Cornelia Becker, "Zur Problematik früher Pferdenachweise im östlichen Mittelmeergebiet", and Norbert Benecke, "Zur Domestikation des Pferdes in Mittel-und Osteuropa. Einige neue archäozoologische Befunde", in Hánsel and Zimmer 1994 (see above, 1, a), 147–177 and 123–144 respectively. See also Benecke, *Archäozoologische Studien zur Entwicklung der Haustierhaltung in Mitteleuropa und Südskandinavien von den Anfängen bis zum ausgehenden Mittelalter. Schriften zur Ur- und Frühgeschichte* 46. Berlin: Akademie-Verlag 1994 (and *Der Mensch und seine Haustiere. Geschichte einer jahrtausendealten Beziehung.* Stuttgart: Theiss 1994).

   d). **Training of chariot horses**. Several recent publications concentrate on the famous Kikkuli treatise. Fundamental is still Annelies Kammenhuber's work on the subject (Hippologia hethitica. Wiesbaden: Harrassowitz 1961). Her interpretation is supported by Valentin Horn, *Das Pferd im alten Orient. Das Streitwagenpferd der Frühzeit in seiner Umwelt, im Training und im Vergleich zum neuzeitlichen Distanz-, Reit- und Fahrpferd.* Hildesheim: Olms 1995. A new interpretation is offered by Frank Starke, *Ausbildung und Trainung von Streitwagenpferden. Eine hippologisch orientierte Interpretation des Kikkuli-Textes. Studien zu den Bogazköy-Texten,* 41. Wiesbaden: Harrassowitz 1995, uncritically adopted by Emilia Masson, *L'art de soigner et d'entraîner les chevaux. Texte hittite du maître écuyer Kikkuli.* Lausanne: Favre 1998, and recently by Birgit Brandau and Hartmut Sickler, *Hethiter: Die unbekannte Weltmacht.* München: Piper 2001, chapter 16). The historial background, as well as the history of research are discussed by Peter Raulwing and Rüdiger Schmitt, "Zur etymologischen Beurteilung der Berufsbezeichnung *aššuššanni* des Pferdetrainers Kikkuli von Mittani", in: Anreiter, Bartosiewitz, Jerem and Meid 1998 (see above, 3, c), 675–706. Critical remarks on new interpretations of the Kikkuli treatise have been made by Raulwing, "Neuere Forschungen zum Kikkuli-Text. Eine kleine Bestandsaufnahme trainingsinhaltlicher Interpretationen zu CTH 284 vier Jahrzehnte nach A. Kammenhubers *Hippologia Hethitica*", in Peter Anreiter and Erszébet Jerem (eds.), *Studia Celtica et Indogermanica. Festschrift für Wolfgang Meid zum 70. Geburtstag.* Archaeolingua Main Series 10. Budapest: Archaeolingua Alapítvány 1999, 352–364.

GLOSSARY OF TECHNICAL TERMS

Note. For frequent lack of precise equivalents, modern terms are often used here to designate ancient elements of harness or bridling. It should be noted, however, that ancient and modern elements of similar function or appearance are seldom identical in every respect, and that the terms are sometimes loosely employed. For the parts of the chariot cf. Fig. 1, and for the more important harness elements Fig. 2.

A-frame cart. This cart has a trapezoidal floor, the side timbers of which continue forward the floor until they meet. This forms a triangular "draught pole" (q.v.), at the apex of which the yoke is attached, the skeleton of the whole resembling a capital letter A.

A-pole. A draught pole (q.v.) in the form of an elongated capital letter A, the yoke being attached at its apex.

Axle. A rod passing underneath the vehicle floor, with the wheels revolving on it, or it revolving with them; in antiquity, always of wood. (Fig. 2)

Backing element. An element of harness (q.v.) that transmits backward movement (as opposed to the unusual forward movement) of the draught animals to the vehicle, at the same time preventing them from backing out of the harness. In antiquity, this element is often lacking and, when present, is relatively inefficient. In the 2nd millennium B.C. it is composed of a strap running either from lower end of yoke saddle (q.v.) or, more effectively, from lower outer end of yoke saddle to draught pole (q.v.) – in either case passing beneath the belly. (Fig. 2)

Bit. A bridle (q.v.) element for control of the horse by the mouth; composed of mouthpiece (q.v.) and cheekpieces (q.v.). Egyptian bronze bits were composed of single or compound (jointed) mouthpieces (cf. Canon) and a pair of cheekpieces. The latter were held in place by divided cheekstraps (q.v.) and the ends of the mouthpieces passed through the cheekpieces. Reins were attached either directly to the mouthpiece ends or to some metal element connecting with them. The action of these bits was closer to that of the modern snaffle than to that of any other modern bit, since they exerted pressure on the corners of the horse's mouth. Their construction, however, was somewhat different, and those with jointed mouthpieces had an added action, unknown in modern bits, from the pressure of the cheek-pieces against the lower jaw.

Blinker. An element attached to the cheekstrap (q.v.) of the head-stall (q.v.), covering the horse's eye and enabling him to see ahead but not to the side. In antiquity it probably also served to protect the eye in battle and/or to prevent harnessed stal-lions from bickering with their team mates or with other stal-lions abreast of them. (Fig. 2)

Body. Used here to designate the floor and superstructure of a vehi-cle. (Fig. 2)

Box. Used here to designate the floor and superstructure of the vehicle.

Breastband. In antiquity, a strap attached to the front edges of a saddle cloth or pack saddle and runnings across the horses's chest. It was designed to hold the these objects in position. Also, on Assyrian chariot horses of 8th and 7th cent. B.C., attached to girth (q.v.) at sides.

Breastplate. In antiquity, protective or decorative element of metal and/or leather, hung across horse's chest.

Breeching. In antiquity, strap attached to rear edges of saddle cloth or pack saddle, running back along the flanks of animal and pass-ing around buttocks, designed to hold cloth or saddle in position.

Bridle. A means of controlling the horse by the head; composed of headstall (q.v.), with or without bit (q.v.), and reins (q.v.).

Browband. The strap crossing the horse's brow and uniting the right and left cheekstraps (q.v.) in this area.

Canon. The mouthpiece of a metal bit, or each single element of a compound ("jointed" or "broken") mouthpiece.

Cart. Always two-wheeled, but with wheels of any construction (q.v.); for carrying stable loads, i.e. goods or seated passengers.

Cavalry. This term may only be properly applied to mounted troops when these are trained to the degree where they can function with precision as a unit – not only advancing on command but changing gaits, turning, deploying and reassembling in their proper positions in the ranks.

Cavesson. Used here for a strong, fitted headstall (q.v.), to which reins (q.v.) were attached.

Chamfron. See Frontlet.

Chariot. A light, fast, two-wheeled, usually horse-drawn, vehicle with spoked wheels; used for warfare, hunting, racing and ceremonial purposes. Its crew usually stood.

Check rowel. The term used here for a slender rod running from the horse's cheek to the area of the yoke saddle (q.v.), with a revolving, spiked disk near its centre. (Fig. 2)

Cheekpieces. In antiquity, two paired elements of a bit, in the form of variously shaped plaques or rods. Lying at the corners of the horse's lips, and attached to the headstall (q.v.) by single or, more often, by multiple cheekstraps (q.v.), the cheekpieces held the mouthpiece in place, and might also expert pressure on the outside of the horse's lower jaw. (Fig. 2)

Cheekstraps. The side straps of the headstall (q.v.), attached to the cheekpieces (q.v.) of the bit, and serving to hold them in place; in antiquity commonly branched to take the cheekpiece. (Fig. 2)

Cross bar wheel. See wheel.

Croup. The part of horse's back lying over the animal's loins and extending to the root of the tail.

Crownpiece. The part of headstall (q.v.) going from side to side over crown or poll (q.v.) of horse's head.

Crupper. In antiquity, strap attached to rear of saddle cloth or pack saddle and running back across centre of croup to pass around root of tail; designed to help keep cloth or saddle in place.

Disk Wheel. See wheel.

Draught pole. In antiquity, the element that connected the vehicle to the yoke (q.v.) of the draught animals. (Fig. 1)

Felloe. One of the sections of the rim of a wheel, into which the outer ends of the spokes are mortised. (Fig. 1)

Frontlet (also nosepiece or chamfron). Protective or decorative element of metal or ivory and leather lying over forehead and nasal bone of horse, sometimes combined with poll crest (q.v.).

Gauge or wheel track. The distance between the two wheels of an axle.

Girth. A band encircling the thorax of an animal.

Goad. A long rod, with pointed (usually metal) tip, for prodding.

Gorget. Smaller, higher-placed form of breastplate (q.v.).

Half noseband. See noseband.

Halter. A simple headstall (q.v.), used for leading an animal or for tying it up by the head.

Harness. The aggregate of the various straps that attach an animal to the traction elements of a vehicle; in antiquity, specifically neckstrap (q.v.) and (often) backing element (q.v.).

Headstall. Part of the bridle (q.v.), made of straps or rope and designed to hold a controlling bit or noseband in place. It composes a crownpiece (q.v.), crossing the crown of the head behind the ear; cheekstraps (q.v.), running down from this to the noseband and/or bit; a throatlash (q.v.), running from side to side under the horse's throat; sometimes a browband (q.v.), running across the forehead; and a noseband (q.v.), encircling the nose or muzzle.

Hogged mane. Mane cut short.

Housing, trapper (or trapping). See Trapper.

Hub. See Nave.

Linch pin. A toggle pin passing through the end of the axle to prevent the wheel from slipping off.

Litter. An open or covered portable conveyance carried by men or animals.

Mouthpiece. The part of the bit lying mainly inside the horse's mouth, composed of one or more canons (q.v.). It was, accordingly, single and solid or "jointed", and the canons might be plain or twisted. At their ends they had loops for attaching reins directly or by means of a metal connecting element.

Nave (or hub). The inner cylindrical element of a wheel, in which the inner ends of the spokes (q.v.) are secured, and through which the axle (q.v.) passes. (Fig. 1)

Nave hoop. A band, usually of metal, encircling each end of the nave (q.v.) to prevent it from splitting.

Neckstrap. A strap passing around the neck and attached at either end to the lower ends of the yoke saddles or to the yoke itself. Its purpose is to hold the yoke in place. (Fig. 2)

Noseband. One of the straps of the headstall. It usually encircles the nose and jaw, but, in the form of a half noseband, may merely run across the nose from cheekstrap (q.v.) to cheekstrap.

Outrigger. Also less accurately called "trace horse". In teams of three or four horses abreast (trigae and quadrigae), a horse not directly under yoke, but connected more loosely with the vehicle.

Pole. See Draught pole.

Pole brace. In Aegean Bronze Age chariots the wooden rod running out horizontally from the top front of the box to the area where the yoke (q.v.) was attached to the draught pole (q.v.) and lying on top of the pole brace (q.v.).

Pole horse (or poler). In antiquity, one of the two horses that flanked the draught pole (q.v.).

Poll. Crown of horse's head.

Poll piece (or poll plume). Decorative and/or protective element on poll (q.v.) constisting of plumes, tassels or helmet crest with horse hair.

Psalion. Greek word for metal element of bridle, separate from bit and having the effect of a muzzle or a rigid noseband. Term often misused for cheekpiece (q.v.) of a bit.

Pulled mane. Mane thinned or even off by hand pulling.

Reins. Straps running back from the bit (q.v.) or cavesson (q.v.) to the driver's or rider's hands.

Spoke. A radial timber of a wheel, set into the nave (q.v.) at one end and into the felloe (q.v.) at the other. (Fig. 1)

Spoked wheel. See wheel.

Spur. In pictures of Aegean Bronze Age Dual chariots (on this term see Crouwel 1981, 63ff.) the projection at the rear of the floor, representing the ends of the floor frame, the protruding end of the draught pole (q.v.), or a conflation of these elements.

Terret. Rings through which reins pass; in antiquity they were fastened to the draught pole or yoke, or to a draught or harness element on the animal's shoulders.

Throatlash. A strap or thong passing under the throat or the rear of the jaw from cheekstrap (q.v.) to cheekstrap and securing the headstall (q.v.); seldom visible in Egyptian representations.

Tilt. A canvas, wicker or wooden canopy or hood for a vehicle.

Trace horse. See outrigger.

Track. See Wheel track.

Trapper, trapping (or housing). A protective or decorative covering for the body of a horse. (Fig. 2)

Tyre. An outer element of the wheel, protecting the tread of the felloe (q.v.); in antiquity, of metal, rawhide or wood. It also helps to consolidate the wheel (q.v.).

Wagon. Always four-wheeled, usually a relatively heavy vehicle.

Wheel.

Cross bar wheel. Wheel with a diametric bar through which the axle (q.v.) passes. Lighter "crossbars" run at right angles to the central bar, between it and the felloe (q.v.).

Disk wheel. Also called "block wheel". Wheel of solid appearance made of one piece of wood or of several – then called "composite disk".

Spoked wheel. Wheel composed of nave (q.v.), spokes (q.v.) and felloe (q.v.), often with a tyre (q.v.). (Fig. 1)

Wheel track. The distance between the centres of the treads of the two wheels of a chariot.

Wings. In Aegean Bronze Age Dual chariots (on this term see Crouwel 1981, 63ff.) the curved extensions at the rear of the box.

Withers. The most prominent area of an equid's or a bovid's spine, formed by the vertebral processes and located between the shoulder blades. The height of an equid is measured from the ground to the highest point of the withers.

Yoke. The wooden element running across the necks of two or more draught animals and connecting them with the draught pole (q.v.). (Fig. 1)

Yoke braces. Two leather thongs branching out from the draught pole (q.v.) and running to either arm of the yoke (q.v.) to prevent the yoke from swivelling on the pole.

Yoke saddle. An element for adapting the yoke to the conformation of equids. Of inverted Y shape, its "handle" was lashed to the yoke and its "legs" lay along the animal's shoulders. (Fig. 2)

Yoke-saddle pad. A piece of leather or fabric, lying beneath the yoke saddle (q.v.). (Fig. 2)

Y-pole. Composite draught pole (q.v.), formed of two poles, one coming from either side of the vehicle, bent inwards and brought together a short distance ahead of the box (q.v.), to run contiguously out to the yoke.

LIST OF PLATES

Pl. 1.   Yoke saddles from the tomb of Tutʿankhamūn. Cairo, Egyptians Museum. (photograph H. Burton, Griffith Institute, Oxford).

Pl. 2.   Ur seal impression, U.13963. (photograph University Museum Philadelphia).

Pl. 3.   Inlay fragment from Nippur 6N-169. (photograph Oriental Institute, University of Chicago).

Pl. 4.   Sintashta, burial 28. Imprints of spoked wheels. After Gening 1977, fig. 3.

Pl. 5.   Wall painting from the Megaron of the palace of Mycenae. After Rodenwaldt 1921, Beilage III, no. 11.

Pl. 6.   Wall painting, same provenance as pl. 5. After Crouwel 1981, pl. 85, no. W8.

Pl. 7.   Wall painting, same provenance as pls. 5–6. After Crouwel 1981, pl. 174.

Pl. 8.   Krater fragment from Livanates. After Dakoroneia, in: Tzalas 1996, 147, fig. 1.

Pl. 9a–b.   Krater fragments, same provenance as fragment of pl. 8. After Dakoroneia in: Tzalas 1995, 148, figs. 2–3.

Pl. 10.   Detail of so-called Aristonothos krater from Cerveteri. After Crielaard 1998, ill. p. 119.

Pl. 11.   Krater fragment from the Dipylon cemetery, Athens. After Grünwaldt 1983, 169, fig. 22, no. 19.

Pl. 12.   Egyptian chariot, showing pole support, yoke braces, yoke saddles and curved yoke ends. Thebes, Tomb of Rekh-mi-Re. New York, Metropolitan Museum of Art facsimile. (museum photograph).

Pl. 13.   Etruscan fragmentary bronze model, showing yoke braces. (photograph Soprintendenza alle antichità, Firenze).

Pl. 14.   Detail of a relief of Ramses III from Medinet Habu. (drawing Oriental Institute of the University of Chicago).

Pl. 15.   Neck amphora showing Ares in a Gigantomachy. London, British Museum B251. (museum photograph).

Pl. 16.   Panathenaic amphora by the Lysippides Painter showing fighting Herakles the giants. London, British Museum B208. (museum photograph).

Pl. 17.   Type B amphora attributed to the Princeton Painter.
              New York, Metropolitan Museum of Art 56.171.9, Fletcher
              Fund 1956 (museum photograph).
Pl. 18a–b.   Stone model from Kourion. New York, Metropolitan
              Museum of Art 74.51.2687. (museum photograph).
Pl. 19.   Stone model. No provenance. New York, Metropolitan
              Museum of Art 74.51.2845. (museum photograph).
Pl. 20.   Stone sarcophagus, detail from Golgoi. New York, Metro-
              politan Museum of Art 74.51.2451. (museum photograph).
Pl. 21.   Stone sarcophagus, detail from Amathus. New York, Metro-
              politan Museum of Art 74.51.2453. (museum photograph).
Pl. 22a–b.   Terracotta model from Ayia Irini. Nicosia, Cyprus
              Museum 2000. (museum photographs).
Pl. 23a–b.   Terracotta model from Ayia Irini. Nicosia, Cyprus
              Museum 1780. (museum photographs).
Pl. 24.   Terracotta model from Ayia Irini. Nicosia, Cyprus
              Museum 1781+798. (museum photograph).
Pl. 25.   Terracotta model from Ayia. Nicosia, Cyprus Museum
              1170. (museum photograph).
Pl. 26a–b.   Terracotta model from Meniko. Nicosia, Cyprus Museum.
              (museum photographs).
Pl. 27a–b.   Terracotta model from Amrit/Marathus(?). Louvre, AO
              25985. (museum photographs).
Pl. 28.   Terracotta model from Ovgoros. Nicosia, Cyprus Museum
              1955/IX-26/1. (museum photograph).
Pl. 29.   Terracotta model from Kition. Larnaca District Museum.
              (museum photograph).
Pl. 30.   Fragmentary terracotta model. New York, Metropolitan
              Museum of Art 74.51.1805. (museum photograph).
Pl. 31.   Terracotta model. Nicosia, Cyprus Museum 1968/V-30/
              635. (museum photograph).
Pl. 32.   Terracotta model. Oxford, Ashmolean Museum 1968.488.
              (museum photograph).
Pl. 33a–b.   Terracotta model. Oxford, Ashmolean Museum 17376.
              (museum photograph).
Pl. 34.   Bronze horse bit from Amathus. Nicosia, Cyprus Museum.
              (museum photograph).
Pl. 35.   Chariot B (our A3), plaster cast of pole support/breast-
              work brace from Salamis, tomb 3. (photograph V. Kara-
              georghis).

Pl. 36a–d.   Bronze chariot model. Paris, Louvre 22265. (museum photographs).

Pl. 37.   Limestone chariot model from Kourion. New York, Metropolitan Museum of Art 74.51.2687. (museum photograph).

Pl. 38a–b.   Figures from the bronze chariot model. Paris Louvre 22265. (museum photographs).

Pl. 39a–b.   Terracotta model no. 1. Oxford, Ashmolean Museum 1974.349. (museum photographs).

Pl. 40a–c.   Terracotta model no. 2 from Marathus (Amrit). Paris, Louvre AO 25985. (museum photographs).

Pl. 41a–b.   Terracotta model no. 3. Paris, Bibliothèque Nationale D 3734. (photographs Bibliothèque Nationale).

Pl. 42a–b.   Terracotta model no. 4 from Dadja. Amsterdam, Allard Pierson Museum 1364. (museum photographs).

Pl. 43.   Terracotta model no. 4 from Salamis (Sal. 3518). (photograph T. Monloup).

Pl. 44a–b.   Terracotta from Salamis (Sal. 3439). (photographs T. Monloup).

Pl. 45.   Terracotta model from Ovgoros. Nicosia, Cyprus Museum 1955/IX-26/1. (museum photograph).

Pl. 46.   Terracotta from Cyprus. Paris, Louvre AM 163. (museum photograph).

Pl. 47.   Terracotta from Cyprus. Paris, Louvre AM 3510. (museum photograph).

Pl. 48a–b.   Terracotta from near Beirut. London, British Museum 136841 (1889.18–17.13). (museum photograph).

Pl. 49.   Terracotta from Naucratis. Oxford, Ashmolean Museum G.70. (museum photograph).

Pl. 50.   Terracotta. Amsterdam, Allard Pierson Museum 6212. (museum photograph).

Pl. 51.   Terracotta model from Tyre. London, British Museum 93092 (1884.10–24.3). (museum photograph).

Pl. 52.   Terracotta from Helalieh. Paris, Louvre AM 1334. (museum photograph).

Pl. 53.   Terracotta from Helalieh. Paris, Louvre AM 1335. (museum photograph).

Pl. 54a–b.   Terracotta from Marathus (Amrit). Paris, Louvre AM 3738. (museum photographs).

Pl. 55.   Terracotta model. Holland, private collection. After *Klassieke Kunst uit particulier bezit*, Leiden 1975, illustration no. 243.

Pl. 56a–b.   Terracotta model from Tyre. London, British Museum 91567. (museum photographs).

Pl. 57a–b.   Terracotta from Marathus (Amrit). Paris, Louvre AO 25986. (museum photographs).

Pl. 58a–b.   Terracotta model. Paris, Bibliothèque Nationale, D 3735. (photographs Bibliothèque Nationale).

Pl. 59a–b.   Cart ("cart/hearse Gamma") from Salamis, tomb 79 (first burial). Catalogue A 4. (photographs V. Karageorghis).

Pl. 60.   Terracotta model from Amathus. (British) tomb 83. London, British Museum A 200. Catalogue TM 5. (museum photograph).

Pl. 61.   Terracotta model from Alambra. New York, Metropolitan Museum of Art 74.51.1792. Catalogue TM 1. (museum photograph).

Pl. 62.   Terracotta model from Alambra, tomb. New York, Metropolitan Museum of Art 74.51.1794. Catalogue TM 2. (museum photograph).

Pl. 63.   Terracotta model from Amathus, (British) tomb 83. London, British Museum A 201. Catalogue TM 6. (museum photograph).

Pl. 64.   Terracotta model from Alambra, tomb. New York, Metropolitan Museum of Art 74.51.1795. Catalogue TM 3. (museum photograph).

Pl. 65.   Terracotta model from Alambra, tomb. New York, Metropolitan Museum of Art 74.51.1793. Catalogue TM 4. (museum photograph).

Pl. 66.   Terracotta model from Amathus, (British) tomb 83. British Museum A 197. Catalogue TM 7. (museum photograph).

Pl. 67.   Terracotta model from Amathus, (British) tomb 88. British Museum A 199. Catalogue TM 8. (museum photograph).

Pl. 68.   Terracotta model from Amathus, (British) tomb 89. British Museum A 198. Catalogue TM 9. (museum photograph).

Pl. 69.   Terracotta model from Amathus, (Cypriot) Tomb 159. Limassol, District Museum M. 652/2. Catalogue TM 11. (museum photograph).

Pl. 70.   Terracotta model from Amathus, (Cypriot) tomb 189/3. Limassol, District Museum M. 703/31 Catalogue TM 12. (museum photograph).

Pl. 71.   Terracotta model from Nicosia, acropolis tomb. Cyprus

Museum CS 2415/14. Catalogue TM 15. (museum photograph).

Pl. 72.   Terracotta model from Tamassos-*Chomazoudia*, tomb II. Nicosia, Cyprus Museum C 36. Catlogue TM 18. (museum photograph).

Pl. 73.   Terracotta model. Nicosia, Cyprus Museum D.106. Catalogue TM 21. (museum photograph).

Pl. 74.   Terracotta model from Amathus, (British) tomb 83. British Museum A 201. Catalogue TM 22. (museum photograph).

Pl. 75.   Terracotta model. Nicosia, Cyprus Museum B 252. Catalogue TM 23. (museum photograph).

Pl. 76.   Terracotta model. Nicosia, Cyprus Museum C 48. Catalogue TM 24. (museum photograph).

Pl. 77.   Terracotta model. Nicosia, Cyprus Museum C 37. Catalogue TM 25. (museum photograph).

Pl. 78.   Terracotta model. Nicosia, Cyprus Museum C 42. Catalogue TM 26. (museum photograph).

Pl. 79.   Terracotta model. Nicosia, Cyprus Museum C 11.742. Catalogue TM 27. (museum photograph).

Pl. 80.   Terracotta model. Nicosia, Cyprus Museum C 40. Catalogue TM 28. (museum photograph).

Pl. 81.   Terracotta model. Nicosia, Cyprus Museum C 46. Catalogue TM 29. (museum photograph).

Pl. 82a–b. Terracotta model. Nicosia, Cyprus Museum C 43. Catalogue TM 26. (museum photographs).

Pl. 83.   Terracotta model. Nicosia, Cyprus Museum C 98. Catalogue TM 33. (museum photograph).

Pl. 84.   Terracotta model. Nicosia, Cyprus Museum C 45. Catalogue TM 32. (museum photograph).

Pl. 85.   Terracotta model. Nicosia, Cyprus Museum C 41. Catalogue TM 31. (museum photograph).

Pl. 86.   Terracotta model. New York, Metropolitan Museum of Art 74.51.1802. Catalogue TM 34. (museum photograph).

Pl. 87.   Terracotta model. New York, Metropolitan Museum of Art 74.51.1796. Catalogue TM 35. (museum photograph).

Pl. 88.   Terracotta model. Oxford Ashmolean Museum 1958.18 (formerly Rugby School). Catalogue TM 36. (museum photograph).

Pl. 89.   Terracotta model. Paris, Louvre N 3305 (formerly

Colonna-Ceccaldi collection). Catalogue TM 37. (museum photograph).

Pl. 90.   Terracotta model. Paris, Louvre AM 223. Catalogue TM 38. (museum photograph).

Pl. 91.   Terracotta model. Paris, Louvre N 3306 (formerly Colonna-Ceccaldi collection). Catalogue TM 39. (museum photograph).

Pl. 92a–b.   Terracotta model from Amrit (Marathus). Paris, Louvre AO 25986. (museum photographs).

Pl. 93a–b.   Terracotta model from Tyre. London, British Museum 91567. (museum photographs).

Pl. 94.   Bronze model. Nicosia, Cyprus Museum 1952/VII-19/2. (museum photograph).

Pl. 95.   Limestone chariot model from Kourion. New York, Metropolitan Museum of Art 74.51.2687. (museum photograph).

Pl. 96.   Bronze chariot model from the Levant. Paris, Louvre 22265. (museum photograph).

Pl. 97a–d.   Terracotta chariot model from Ovgoros (no. 1781+798). Nicosia, Cyprus Museum 1955/IX-26/1. (museum photographs).

Pl. 98.   Relief of Ashurnasirpal II. Berlin, Vorderasiatisches Museum 959. (museum photograph).

Pl. 99.   Layard's interpretation of the Assyrian yoke. After Hrouda 1963, pl. 28, 6–9).

Pl. 100.   Chariot of Ashurnasirpal II, showing yoke end, yoke-saddle finial, sun disk, and shoulder tassel. After Barnett and Falkner 1976, pl. 117.

Pl. 101.   Yoke saddle from a chariot of Tutʿankhamūn. Cairo, Egyptian Museum. After Carter 1927, pl. XLII.

Pl. 102.   Bronze breastplate from Salamis. Nicosia, Cyprus Museum. After Karageorghis 1969, fig. 22.

Pl. 103.   Bronze breastplates from Salamis. Nicosia, Cyprus Museum. After Karageorghis 1973, pl. 128.

Pl. 104.   Chariot horses of Tukulti-Ninurta II. After Hrouda 1963, pl. 28:10.

Pl. 105.   Bronze shoulder pendant from Salamis. Nicosia, Cyprus Museum. After Karageorghis 1969, fig. 21.

Pl. 106.   Chariot of Sennacherib. After Gadd 1936, pl. 13.

Pl. 107.   Chariot of Tiglath-Pileser III. After Barnett and Falkner 1976, pl. 15.

Pl. 108.   Petroglyph from Jamani Us, Mongolian Altai. After Volkov 1972.

Pl. 109a–b. Wall paintings from Til Barsib. After Parrot 1961, pl. 345.

Pl. 110.   Yokes from Tutʿankhamūn's chariots. Cairo, Egyptian Museum. (photograph Griffith Institute, Oxford).

Pl. 111.   Pole and yoke of Ashurnasirpal II's chariot on ferry. (photograph London, British Museum).

Pl. 112.   Standard bearers of Ashurnasirpal II. (photograph London, British Museum).

Pl. 113.   Fitted yoke of Ashurbanipal's chariot curving over neck. (photograph London, British Museum).

Pl. 114.   Relief from Arslan Tash, showing breast plates, yoke saddles and six reins. After Potratz 1966, pl. 45, p. 101.

Pl. 115.   Terracotta model from Ajia Irini. Nicosia, Cyprus Museum 2000. (museum photograph).

Pl. 116a–b. Terracotta model from Ajia Irini. Nicosia, Cyprus Museum 1780. (museum photographs).

Pl. 117a–b. Terracotta model from Marathus (Amrit). Paris, Louvre AO 25985. (museum photographs).

Pl. 118.   Sargon's four-horse fitted yoke. Paris, Louvre. (museum photograph).

Pl. 119.   Senncherib's four-horse fitted yoke. (photograph London, British Museum).

Pl. 120.   Modern Hungarian harnessing, three-a-breast. After Alapfy and Török 1971.

Pl. 121.   Fragmentary bronze model of quadriga from Gordion, with two pole horses under yoke. (photograph Philadelphia, University Museum).

Pl. 122.   Russian *dvoika* showing two gaits. After Anonymous 1823.

Pl. 123.   Russian dvoika, showing attachment of to outrigger. After Atkinson and Walters 1803.

Pl. 124.   Tyre segments A 1–3. Susa, Apadana area. Paris, Louvre Sb 6829. (photograph F. Tallon).

Pl. 125.   Tyre segments B 1–6 Susa, Donjon tomb A 89, originally called 98b. Paris, Louvre Sb 14672–14677 and one unnumbered fragment; Teheran, Iran, Bastan Museum (four segments). (photograph F. Tallon).

Pl. 126.   Tyre segments C 1–2; Tyre segments C 3–5. Holland, private collection. (photograph G. Strietman).

Pl. 127.   Metal linch pin. Susa. Paris, Louvre, SB 9630 (photo-
            graph F. Tallon).
Pl. 128.   Cross-bar wheel in modern Spain.
Pl. 129.   Cylinder seal from Tepe Hissar IIIB. Iran, Bastan Museum.
            (photograph Philadelphia, University Museum).
Pl. 130.   Cylinder seal impression. Paris, Louvre (Collection de
            Clerq 284). (museum photograph).
Pl. 131.   Cylinder seal. Paris, Louvre AO 20.138. (museum pho-
            tograph).
Pl. 132.   Sarcophagus from Vulci, Italy. Boston, Museum of Fine
            Arts 1975.799. (museum photograph).
Pl. 133.   The four wheels from Acemhöyük, with fragmentary
            axles and lugs. (photograph E. Özgen).
Pl. 134.   Face of one wheel. (photograph E. Özgen).
Pl. 135.   View of wheel from tread, showing slightly protruding
            naves and axle, rectangular in section where it ran
            under body of vehicle. (photograph E. Özgen).
Pl. 136.   Pierced lugs, broken off at one end, one with part of
            axle in place. (photograph E. Özgen).
Pl. 137.   T-shaped attachment with loop, arms bent out of posi-
            tion. (photograph E. Özgen).
Pl. 138.   Fragments of sheet bronze body; lower piece riveting
            as well as part of T-shaped attachment in lower right-
            hand corner. (photograph E. Özgen).
Pl. 139.   Egyptian wheel. New York E. 37.1700, Brooklyn Museum.
            (museum photograph).
Pl. 140a–c. a. Egyptian wheel. Detail.
            b. Egyptian wheel. Detail.
            c. Egyptian wheel. Detail. (museum photographs).
Pl. 141.   Pieces of wood accompanying wheel in Brooklyn Museum.
            (museum photograph).
Pl. 142.   Fragmentary wheel of Amenophis III. Oxford, Ashmolean
            Museum 1923.663. (museum photograph).
Pl. 143a–b. Nave of Egyptian wheel. Paris, Louvre E 109. (museum
            photographs).
Pl. 144.   Wheels of a chariot of Tutʿankhamūn. Cairo, Egyptian
            Museum. (photograph H. Burton, Metropolitan Museum
            of Fine Art, New York).
Pl. 145.   Painted wooden chest of Tutʿankhamūn. Cairo, Egyptian

Museum. (photograph H. Burton, Metropolitan Museum of Fine Art, New York).

Pl. 146.   Fragment of Tûna bowl. Boston, Museum of Fine Arts 59.422. (museum photograph).

Pl. 147.   Fragment of a trial relief. Berlin, Ägyptisches Museum 3425. (museum photograph).

Pl. 148.   Drawing on limestone. Hannover, Kestner Museum 2952. (museum photograph).

Pl. 149.   Cylinder Seal. New York, J. P. Rosen Collection. (photograph courtesy of the owner).

Pl. 150.   Threshing sledge (*tribulum*) in Turkey. After Mantran 1959, pl. 70.

Pl. 151.   Winnowing shovel in use in northern Greece. After Theocharis 1973, pl. 163.

Pl. 152.   Pu-abi's sledge from Ur. London, British Museum. (museum photograph).

Pl. 153a–b. Threshing wain (*plostellum poenicum*) in eastern Kermanshaw, western Iran. (photograph C. Kramer).

Pl. 154a–e. Syria no. 1. Bronze wagon model. Paris, Louvre AO 2773. (museum photographs).

Pl. 155a–d. Syria no. 2. Bronze wagon model. Stockholm, Medelhavsmuseet (formerly Statens Historika Museet) 14305. (museum photographs).

Pl. 156a–e. Anatolia no. 1. Bronze wagon model. New York, Metropolitan Museum of Art (formerly Edith Perry Chapman Fund 1966) 66.15. (museum photographs).

Pl. 157a–e. Anatolia no. 2. Bronze wagon model. New York (formerly Pomerance Collection). (photographs L. Pomerance).

Pl. 158a–b. Anatolia no. 3. a. Bronze wagon model. London. (formerly London, P. Adam Collection 358.
b. Scraps of metal acquired with this model. Some may come from other, similar models. (photographs P. Adam).

Pl. 159a–c. Anatolia no. 4. Bronze wagon model. Boston, Museum of Fine Arts 62.678. (museum photographs).

Pl. 160a–b. Anatolia no. 5. Bronze wagon model. Berlin, Stiftung Preussischer Kulturbesitz, Staatliche Museen, Museum für Vor- und Frühgeschichte XLb 1874 A–C/1966. (museum photographs).

Pl. 161.   Anatolia no. 6. Bronze wagon model. France, Collection
                Thierry IV. After Danmanville 1968, 59ff.
Pl. 162.   Anatolia no. 6. Terracotta four-wheeler. Formerly col-
                lection of Mr and Mrs J. Bomford. (photograph Oxford,
                Ashmolean Museum).
Pl. 163.   Anatolia no. 6. Terracotta four-wheeler from Tell Chuēra
                T. Ch. 57/1959. (photograph U. Moortgat-Correns).
Pl. 164.   Anatolia no. 6. Terracotta four-wheeler from Kish,
                Mound A. Oxford, Ashmolean Museum 1925.291.
                (museum photograph).
Pl. 165a–b.   Anatolia a. Bronze wagon model. Private collection.
                (photographs D. Widmer).
Pl. 166a–b.   Anatolia b. Bronze wagon model. Private collection.
                (photographs D. Widmer).
Pl. 167a–c.   Anatolia d. Bronze wagon model. Private collection.
                (photographs D. Widmer).
Pl. 168a–b.   Anatolia d. Bronze wagon model. Private collection.
                (photograph D. Widmer).
Pl. 169a–c.   Anatolia e. Bronze wagon model. Private collection.
                (photographs D. Widmer).
Pl. 170.   Terracotta four-wheeler from Hammam. Oxford, Ash-
                molean Museum 1913.183. (drawing J. Croxall).
Pl. 171.   Terracotta two-wheeler from Cyprus. Oxford, Ashmolean
                Museum 1950.80 (formerly Rugby School). (museum
                photograph).
Pl. 172.   Terracotta four-wheeler from Syria. (photograph cour-
                tesy Mr C. Ede, London).
Pl. 173a–d.   Terracotta four-wheeler from Syria. Oxford, Ashmolean
                Museum 1975.326. (a. drawing G. Strietman, b–d.
                museum photograph).
Pl. 174.   Stone model from Tamassos. London, British Museum
                C 81. (museum photograph).
Pl. 175.   Stone model. London, British Museum C 82. (museum
                photograph).
Pl. 176a–b.   Stone model. Nicosia, Cyprus Museum C 218. (museum
                photograph).
Pl. 177.   Detail of sarcophagus from Amathus. New York,
                Metropolitan Museum of Art 74.51.2453. (museum pho-
                tograph).
Pl. 178.   Stone model. Paris, Louvre AM 210. (museum photo-
                graph).

Pl. 179. Stone model from Golgoi. New York, Metropolitan Museum of Art 54.51.2581. (museum photograph).

Pl. 180. Terracotta model. Amsterdam, Allard Pierson Museum 1881. (museum photograph).

Pl. 181. Stone model from Kythrea. New York, Metropolitan Museum of Art 74.51.2609. (museum photograph).

Pl. 182. Stone model from Tamassos. New York, Metropolitan Museum of Art 74.51.2581. (museum photograph).

Pl. 183. Terracotta model (detail) from Meniko 56+29+77. Nicosia, Cyprus Museum. (museum photograph).

Pl. 184. Terracotta model. London, British Museum 1876.4.9.91. (museum photograph).

Pl. 185. Terracotta model. London, British Museum 1876.4.9.92. (museum photograph).

Pl. 186. Terracotta model from Kurion. New York, Metropolitan Museum of Art 74.51.1778. (museum photograph).

Pl. 187. Terracotta model. Edinburgh, Royal Scottish Museum 1921.354. (museum photograph).

Pl. 188. Terracotta model from Palaepaphos-*Skales*, tomb 52. Kouklia Museum. (museum photograph).

Pl. 189. Terracotta model. Nicosia, Cyprus Museum 1970/XII–8/2. (museum photograph).

Pl. 190a–d. Terracotta model of horseback rider. Brussels, Musées Royaux d'Art et d'Histoire A 1323. (museum photographs).

Pl. 191. Terracotta model of horseback rider reportedly from Tyre. London, British Museum WA93092 (1884.10–29.3). (museum photograph).

Pl. 192. 'Soft' foot stirrup, Mathura (between Agra and Delhi), India. (photograph Boston, Museum of Fine Arts).

Pl. 193. Rope stirrup, Bokhara. After Fitzroy Maclean 1975.

Pl. 194. Rope stirrup, Northeast Iran, of flat-braided camel and horse hair used with a 'soft' saddle on the Iranian Turkoman steppe. (photograph L. L. Firouz).

Pl. 195. Hook stirrup in use. (photograph L. L. Firouz).

Pl. 196. Hook stirrup reconstructed. (photograph J. Spruytte).

Pl. 197a–b. Kushan gem and cast, ca. A.D. 50, width 2.5 cm. London, British Museum. (museum photographs).

Pl. 198. Terminals of torque from Kul Oba Crimea. (photograph St. Petersburg, Hermitage Museum).

Pl. 199. Reconstruction of chariot found in horse burial No. 6 at Liu Li Ko in Honan, China.

Pl. 200.   Detail of wooden chest from Tomb of Tut'ankhamūn. Cairo, Egyptian Museum. (photograph H. Burton, Metropolitan Museum of Art, New York).

Pl. 201.   Amarna relief. Formerly Collection of Mr and Mrs N. Schimmel. (photograph O. E. Nelson).

Pl. 202.   Relief from Tomb of Kha-em-het (photograph New York, Egyptian Expedition of the Metropolitan Museum of Art).

Pl. 203a–b.   'Run-out' bit, showing position when horse is behaving. Mouthpiece width between the cheeks: 11.4 cm. 'Run-out' bit, showing position if horse is pulled to left.

Pl. 204a–b.   Brush 'burr' or 'picker'. Diameter 9.2 cm. Tack 'burr'. Diameter 8.8 cm. (photographs DeLilo).

Pl. 205.   Bronze harness fittings (probably 'burrs') from China. Western Zhou, c. 1000 B.C. Length 6.9 cm. (photograph Royal Ontario Museum, Ontario).

Pl. 206.   'Run-out' bit on simple leverage principle. Mouthpiece between rings 11.4 cm. (photograph New York, Metropolitan Museum of Fine Art, formerly Rogers Fund).

Pl. 207.   Detail of stone relief from Amarna. New York, Metropolitan Museum of Fine Art, formerly Collection of Mr and Mrs N. Schimmel. (photograph Mr and Mrs N. Schimmel).

Pl. 208.   Bronze bridle acessory, often called 'muzzle' or 'cavesson'. (photograph DeLilo).

Pl. 209.   Slit nostrils on a donkey in Iran. (photograph L. L. Firouz).

Pl. 210a–b.   a. Metal bridle bit. New York University, Department of Classics, now on loan to the Department of the Ancient Near East of the Metropolitan Museum of Art, New York L. 1984.85.
                b. Details of the cheekpieces of the bronze bridle bit. (photographs D. Kawami).

Pl. 211a–b.   Pair of metal bridle bits from Tell a-Haddad, Iraq. (photograph D. George).

Pl. 212.   Metal bridle bit. New York Metropolitan Museum of Fine Art L. 1984.85 lent by the Classics Department of New York University. (museum photograph).

Pl. 213.   Donkey with slit nostrils, in Iran. (photographs L. L. Firouz).

Pl. 214.   14th century B.C. Egyptian chariot team showing slit nostrils. Detail from a relief. New York, Metropolitan Museum of Art (formerly Collection of Mr and Mrs N. Schimmel. (photograph courtesy N. Schimmel).

Pl. 215. Four studies of horses' muzzles, with slit nostrils by Pisanello (1395–1455). After Hill 1965.

Pl. 216. St. George and the dragon, by Sodoma (1477–1549). (photograph National Gallery of Art, Samuel H. Kress Collection 1947, Washington, D.C.).

Pl. 217. Pair of head poles from tomb of Tutʿankhamūn. Cairo, Egyptian Museum. (photograph H. Burton, Oxford Griffith Institute).

Pl. 218. Egyptian horse with 'head pole' from Tell-el Amarna. Stone relief. New York, Metropolitan Museum of Art. (museum photograph).

Pl. 219. Salamis, tomb 2. Head of an ass skeleton with bronze gear *in situ*.

Pl. 220. Salamis, tomb 2. Head of a horse skeleton with bronze gear *in situ*.

Pl. 221. Bronze frontlet from Salamis, tomb 2. (photograph V. Karageorghis).

Pl. 222. Terracotta horse head. New York, Metropolitan Museum of Art 74.51.1805. (museum photograph).

Pl. 223. Terracotta chariot group from Tamassos. London, British Museum. (museum photograph).

Pl. 224. Assyrian stone relief with Ashurbanipal shooting at lions. London, British Museum. (museum photograph).

Pl. 225. Assyrian stone relief with Ashurbanipal spearing a lion from the saddle. London, British Museum. (museum photograph).

Pl. 226. Replica of helmet from northwestern Iran on pony stallion's head. (photograph M. A. Littauer).

Pl. 227a–b. Helmet from northwestern Iran. (Amlash region). Edinburgh, Royal Scottish Museum 1969.395. (museum photographs).

Pl. 228a–c. Helmet. Hamburg, Museum für Kunst and Gewerbe 1969.249. (museum photographs).

Pl. 229a–b. Helmet from Iran. Los Angeles, Los Angeles County Museum of Art M. 76.174. (museum photographs).

Pl. 230. Helmet from Amlash, Iran. Formerly Amsterdam. (photograph "Ancient Art").

Pl. 231.   Helmet from Amlash (?). Formerly Amsterdam. (photograph "Ancient Art").

Pl. 232.   Detail of Tut'ankhamūn's bowcase. Cairo, Egyptian Museum. (photograph H. Burton, Griffith Institute, Oxford).

Pl. 233.   Fragmentary chamfron from Hasanlu. (photograph, Philadelphia University Museum).

Pl. 234a–b.   a. Fragmentary bronze chariot from Chianciano. Florence, Museo archeologico 76525. (photograph Alinari).
b. Detail of the yoke and pole. (photograph Soprintendenza alle Antichità d'Etruria).

ABBREVIATIONS

Berlin, VA	Vorderasiatisches Museum
London, BM	Britisch Museum
New York, MMA	Metropolitan Museum of Art
Nicosia, CM	Cyprus Museum
Oxford, Ashm.	Ashmolean Museum

BIBLIOGRAPHY OF THE AUTHORS[1]

Mary Aiken Littauer

1962

1. Review of J. K. Anderson, *Ancient Greek Horsemanship*. Berkeley, California: The University of California Press 1961, *The Chronicle of the Horse*, Vol. 25, No. 36, May 4, 15–16 and Vol. 25, No. 36, May 11, 28. 30–32.

1963

2. "How Great was the 'Great Horse'? A Reassessment of the Evidence", *Light Horse*, Vol. 13, No. 144, 2/6, 350–352. (Reprinted as No. 31).

1965

3. "After Seeing the Spanish Riding School", The Chronicle of the Horse, Vol. 37, No. 24, February 5, 26–27 (Part I), *The Chronicle of the Horse*, Vol. 37, No. 25, February 12, 22–25. (Revised reprint under No. 32).

1968

4. "The Function of the Yoke Saddle in Ancient Harnessing", *Antiquity* 42, 27–31 (pls. 4–5). (Reprinted as No. 33).

5. Letters to the Editor, *Antiquity* 42, 221–224.[2]

6. "A 19th and 20th Dynasty Heroic Motif on Attic Black-Figured Vases", *American Journal of Archaeology* 72, 150–152 (pl. 62). (Reprinted as No. 11).

---

[1] The given number in brackets indicates the current number of the reprinted article in the Table of Contents.
[2] Reply by Charles Green, 224–225 and J. K. Anderson, *Antiquity* 43, 1969, 317–318.

1969

7. "Slit Nostrils of Equids", *Zeitschrift für Säugetierkunde* 34, 183–186. (Reprinted as No. 37).

8. "Bits and Pieces", *Antiquity* 43, 289–300 (pls. 40–41). (Reprinted as No. 34).

1971

9. "The Figured Evidence for a Small Pony in the Ancient Near East", *Iraq* 23, 24–30 (pls. 6–9).

10. "V. O. Vitt and the Horses of Pazyryk", *Antiquity* 45, 293–294.

1972

11. "The Military Use of the Chariot in the Aegean in the Late Bronze Age", *American Journal of Archaeology* 76, 145–157. (Reprinted as No. 8).

1974

12. "An Element of Egyptian Horse Harness", *Antiquity* 48, 293–295 (pl. 35). (Reprinted as No. 38).

13. "Review of Sándor Bökönyi, *The Przewalski Horse*. London: Souvenir Press 1974, *Antiquity* 48, 144–145.

1976

14. "New Light on the Assyrian Chariot", *Orientalia*. Nova Series 45, 217–226 (pls. 1–13). (Reprinted as No. 17).

15. "Reconstruction Questioned", *Archaeology* 29, 212. (Letters to the editor).

1977

16. "Rock Carvings of Chariots in Transcaucasia, Central Asia and Outer Mongolia", *Proceedings of the Prehistoric Society* 43, 243–262 (pls. 18–19). (Reprinted as No. 10).

17. "*Hipposandals* Again. *Plus ça change*", *Antiquity* 51, 235–236.

18. "Review of P. A. L. Greenhalgh, *Early Greek Warfare. Horsemen and Chariots in the Homeric and Archaic Ages.* Cambridge University Press 1973", *Classical Philology* 72, 363–365. (Reprinted as No. 6).

19. "Review of Jean Spruytte, *Études expérimentale sur l'attelage. Contribution à l'histoire du cheval.* Paris: Editions Crépin-Leblond 1977", *Antiquity* 53, 73–74.

1979

20. "Equids at Persepolis", *Antiquity* 53, 218–219.[3]

1980

21. "Horse Sense, or Nonsense", *Antiquity* 54, 139–142.[4]

1981

22. "Early Stirrups", *Antiquity* 55, 99–105 (pls. 21–23). (Reprinted as No. 30).

1983

23. "Les premiers véhicules à roues", *La Recherche* 14, 334–345 (Reprinted as No. 1).

1984

24. "Review of Stuart Piggott, *The Earliest Wheeled Transport. From the Atlantic to the Caspian Sea.* London: Thames & Hudson 1983", *Antiquity* 53, 71–72.

---

[3] A Note on Ahmad Afsahr and Judith Lerner, "The Horses of the Ancient Persian Empire at Persepolis", *Antiquity* 43 [No. 207/March 1979], 44–47; pl. 1–6a.

[4] Comment on Paul Bahn's article "The 'Unacceptable Face' of the West European Upper Palaeolithic", *Antiquity* 52, [No. 206/November], 183–192 (Reply by Bahn pp. 140–142).

Translations by Mary Aiken Littauer

1983

25. Jean Spruytte, *Early Harness Systems*. London: J. A. Allen. (*Études expérimentales sur l'attelage. Contribution à histoire du cheval*. Paris: Editions Crépin-Leblond 1977; 135 pp., 37 pls.).

Joost H. Crouwel

1972

26. "A Chariot Sherd from Mycenae", *Annual of the British School at Athens* 67, 99–101.

1973

27. "Appendix. The Parasol Krater". In: K. A. Wardle, "A Group of Late Helladic IIIB 2 Pottery from within the Citadel at Mycenae", *Annual of the British School at Athens* 68, (297–342) 343–347.

1976

28. "A Note on Two Mycenaean Parasol Kraters", *Annual of the British School at Athens* 71, 55–56.

1978

29. "Aegean Bronze Age Chariots and Their Ancient Near Eastern Background", *Bulletin of the Institute of Classical Studies. University of London* 25, 174–175.

1981

30. *Chariots and Other Means of Land Transport in Bronze Age Greece*. Allard Pierson Series. Studies in Ancient Civilization 3. Amsterdam. 257 pp., 177 figs.

1985

31. "Carts in Iron Age Cyprus", *Report of the Department of Antiquities Cyprus* 1985, 203–221. (Reprinted as No. 15).

1987

32. "Chariots in Iron Age Cyprus, Carts in Iron Age Cyprus", *Report of the Department of Antiquities Cyprus* 1987, 101–118 (pls. 36–39). (Reprinted as No. 12).

1990

33. "A Chariot From Salamis Newly Reconstructed", *Report of the Department of Antiquities Cyprus* 1990, 101–105.

1991

34. "Another Mycenaean Horse-Leader ?", *Annual of the British School at Athens* 86, 65–68.

35. "A Group of Terracotta Chariot Models – Cypriote or Phoenician ?" In: Frieda Vandenabeele and Robert Laffineur (eds.), *Cypriote Terracottas. Proceedings of the First International Conference of Cypriote Studies*, Brussels-Liège-Amsterdam, 29 May–1 June, 1989. Organized by the "Groupe de Contact interuniversitaire d'études chypriotes"/Interuniversitaire contactgroep voor Cyprische Studies, F.N.R.S./N.F.W.O. (Belgium). Bruxelles and Liège, 115–129 (pls. 28–33). (Reprinted as No. 14).

1992

36. *Chariots and other Wheeled Vehicles in Iron Age Greece*. Allard Pierson Series. Studies in Ancient Civilization 9. Amsterdam, 139 pp., 40 figs.

1997

37. "Il mondo Greco" In: *Carri da guerra principi etruschi. Catalogo della Mostra a cura di Adriana Emiliozzi, Viterbo, Palazzo dei Papi, 24 maggio–1997–31 gennaio 1998*. Rome: »L'ERMA« di Brettschneider 1997, 5–7.

38. "Review of Jean Spruytte, *Attelage antiques libyens. Archéologie saharienne expérimentale*. Paris. Collection Archéologie expérimentale et ethnographie des techniques 2", *American Journal of Archaeology* 101, 814.

39. "Fighting on Land and Sea in Late Mycenaean Times", in: Robert Laffineur (ed.), *POLEMOS. Le contexte guerrier en égée à l'âge du bronze*. Actes de la 7ᵉ Recontre égéenne internationale Université de

Liège, 14–17 avril 1998. AEGAEUM 19. Annales d'archéologie égéenne de l'Université de Liège et UT-PSAP. Université de Liège (Histoire de l'art et archéologie de la Grèce antique) and University of Texas at Austin (Program in Aegean Scripts and Prehistory). Vol. II, 455–459 (pls. 85–86). (Reprinted as No. 9).

Mary Aiken Littauer and Joost H. Crouwel

1973

40. "The Vulture Stela and an Early Type of Two-Wheeled Vehicle", *Journal of Near Eastern Studies* 32, 324–329. (Reprinted as No. 3).

41. "Early Metal Models of Wagons from the Levant", *Levant* 5, 102–126 (pls. 32–43). (Reprinted as No. 25).

42. "The Dating of a Chariot Ivory from Nimrud Considered Once Again", *Bulletin of the American Schools of Oriental Research* 209, 27–33. (Reprinted as No. 31).

43. "Evidence for Horse Bits from Shaft Grave IV at Mycenae?", *Prähistorische Zeitschrift* 48, 207–213 (pl. 53).

1974

44. "Terracotta Models as Evidence for Wheeled Vehicles with Tilts in the Ancient Near East", *Proceedings of the Prehistoric Society* 40, 20–36. (Reprinted as No. 26).

1977

45. "The Origin and Diffusion of the Cross-Bar Wheel ?", Antiquity 51, 95–105 (pls. 9–11). (Reprinted as No. 20).

46. "Chariots with Y-Poles in the Ancient Near East", *Archäologischer Anzeiger* 1977, 1–8. (Reprinted as No. 16).

47. "Appendix I. Terracotta Chariot Model" In: Vassos Karageorghis (ed.), *Two Cypriote Sanctuaries of the End of the Cypro-Archaic Period*. Consiglio Nazionale delle Ricerche. Roma, 67–73 (pls. 8, 15, 26).

1979

48. *Wheeled Vehicles and Ridden Animals in the Ancient Near East.* Leiden

and Köln. 185 pp., 85 Figs. (Handbuch der Orientalistik, 7. Abteilung, 1. Band, 2. Abschnitt, Lieferung 1).

49. "An Egyptian Wheel in Brooklyn", *The Journal of Egyptian Archaeology* 65, 107–120 (pls. 12–16). (Reprinted as No. 22).

1980

50. "Kampfwagen (Streitwagen) B. Archäologisch" In: *Reallexikon der Assyriologie und vorderasiatischen Archäologie*, Vol. 5, 344–351. (Reprinted as No. 2).

51. "Appendix. Chariots and Harness in Mycenaean Vase Painting" In: Emily Vermeule and Vassos Karageorghis (eds.), *Mycenaean Pictorial Vase Painting*. Cambridge, Massachusetts: Harvard University Press, 181–187.

1982

52. "A Bridle Bit of the Second Millennium B.C. in Jerusalem", *Levant* 14, 178 (pl. 8).

1983

53. "Chariots in Late Bronze Age Greece", *Antiquity* 57, 187–192. (Reprinted as No. 5).

1984

54. "Ancient Iranian Horse Helmets?", *Iranica Antiqua* 19, 41–51 (pls. 1–8). (Reprinted as No. 41).

1985

55. *Chariots and Related Equipment from the Tomb of Tutʿankhamūn*. Tutʿankhamūn Tomb Series 8. Oxford: Griffith Institute, 118 pp., 78 pls.

1986

56. "The Earliest Known Three-Dimensional Evidence for Spoked Wheels", *American Journal of Archaeology* 90, 395–398 (pl. 23). (Reprinted as No. 21).

57. "Archaeological Notes): 1. A Near Eastern Bridle Bit of the

Second Millennium B.C. in New York", *Levant* 18, 163–167. (Reprinted as No. 35).

1987

58. "Unrecognized Linch Pins from the Tombs of Tutʿankhamūn and Amenophis II.: A Reply", *Göttinger Miszellen. Beiträge zur ägyptologischen Diskussion* 100, 57–61.

1988

59. "New Light on Priam's Wagon?", *Journal of Hellenic Studies* 108, 194–196 (pl. 5). (Reprinted as No. 42)

60. "New Type of Bit from Iran?", *Iranica Antiqua* 23, 323–327 (pl. 1–2). (Reprinted as No. 37).

61. "A Pair of Horse Bits of the Second Millennium B.C. from Iraq", *Iraq* 50, 169–171 (pl. 12). (Reprinted as No. 36)

1989

62. "Metal Wheel Tyres from the Ancient Near East" In: Léon de Meyer et E. Haerinck (eds.), *Archaeologia Iranica et Orientalis. Miscellanea in Honorem Louis Vanden Berghe.* Vol. 1, Gent: Peeters, 111–121. (figs. 1–4, pp. 122–123; pl. 1a–c, pp. 124–126). (Reprinted as No. 19).

1990

63. "A Terracotta Wagon Model from Syria in Oxford", *Levant* 22, 160–162. (Reprinted as No. 27).

64. "Ceremonial Threshing in the Ancient Near East. I. Archaeological Evidence", *Iraq* 52, 15–19. (Reprinted as No. 24). [P. Steinkeller, "II. Threshing Implements in Ancient Mesopotamia: Cuneiform Sources", 19–23] (pls. 1–3)

1991

65. "'The Trundholm Horse's Trappings: A Chamfrein?' Reasons for Doubting", *Antiquity* 65, 199–122. (Reprinted as No. 40).

66. "Assyrian Trigas and Russian Dvoikas", *Iraq* 53, 97–99. (Reprinted as No. 18).

1992

67. "Chariot" In: David Noel Freedman (ed.), *The Anchor Bible Dictionary*. New York et al.: Doubleday. Vol. 1, 888–892.

1996

68. "The Origin of the True Chariot", *Antiquity* 70, 934–939. (Reprinted as No. 4).

69. "Robert Drews and the Role of Chariotry in Bronze Age Greece", *Oxford Journal of Archaeology* 15, 297–305. (Reprinted as No. 7).

70. "Chariot" In: Jane Turner et al. (eds.) *The Dictionary of Art*. New York: Grove. Vol. 6, 477–482.

1997

71. "Antefatti nell'Oriente mediterraneo. Vicino Oriente, Egitto e Cipro" In: Adriana Emiliozzi (ed.) *Carri da guerra principi etruschi. Catalogo della Mostra. Viterbo, Palazzo dei Papi, 24 maggio–1997–31 gennaio 1998.* Rome: »L'ERMA« di Brettschneider 1997, 5–10.

72. "Chariots and Early Horse Equipment" In: David Alexander (ed.), *Furusiyya: The Horse in the Art of the Near East*. Riyadh, Saudi Arabia 1997. Vol. 1, 17–21. [Catalogue of the Furusiyya exhibition of the Saudi Arabian Equestrian Federation planned in Riyadh, Saudi Arabia].

73. "Chariots" In: E. M. Meyers et al. (eds.), *The Oxford Encyclopedia of Archaeology of the Near East*. New York and Oxford: Oxford University Press. Vol. 1, 485–487.

74. "Wheels" In: E. M. Meyers et al. (eds.), *The Oxford Encyclopedia of Archaeology of the Near East*. New York and Oxford: Oxford University Press. Vol. 5, 343–344. (Erroneously the order of the authors has been mixed up in the original publications No. 72–74. It should have been M. A. L. and J. H. C. as given above).

Mary Aiken Littauer and Vassos Karageorghis

1969

75. "Note on Prometopidia", *Archäologischer Anzeiger* 1969, 152–160. (Reprinted as No. 39).

Joost H. Crouwel and Veronica Tatton-Brown

1988

76. "Ridden Horses in Iron Age Cyprus", *Report of the Department of Antiquities Cyprus* 1988, 77–87. (Reprinted as No. 28).

1989

77. "A Horseback-Rider and his Companion", *Report of the Department of Antiquities Cyprus* 1989, 109–110.

1992

78. "A Terracotta Horse and Rider in Brussels" In: C. G. Ioannides (ed.), *ΑΦΙΕΡΩΜΑ ΣΤΟ ΒΑΣΟ ΚΑΡΑΓΙΩΡΓΗ* (Studies in Honour of V. Karageorghis). *Bulletin of the Society of Cypriot Studies*. Vol. ΝΔ′–ΝΕ′ (1990–1991). Nicosia, Cyprus: Anastasios G. Leventis Foundation, 291–295 (pl. 54). (Reprinted as No. 29).

Dominique Collon, Joost H. Crouwel and
Mary Aiken Littauer

1976

79. "A Bronze Age Chariot Group from the Levant in Paris", *Levant* 8, 1976, 71–79. (Dominique Collon: "The Figures", pp. 79–81) pls. 9–11. (Reprinted as No. 13).

Mary Aiken Littauer, Joost H. Crouwel and
Harald Hauptmann

1991

80. "Ein spätbronzezeitliches Speichenrad vom Lidar Höyük in der Südost-Türkei",[5] 1991, 349–358. (Harald Hauptmann: "Einleitung", 349–351). [Here published as No. 23 under "A Late Bronze-Age Spoked Wheel from Lidar Höyük in Southeast Turkey"].

---

[5] The English manuscript has been translated into German for *Archäologischer Anzeiger* by Dr. Ute L. Dietz.

I. CHARIOTS

1. LES PREMIERS VÉHICULES À ROUES*

Les échanges de biens et d'idées entre les populations ont eu une influence fécondante sur le développement des civilisations. Pendant très longtemps, au cours de la préhistoire, le bateau a été le principal moyen de transport et donc d'échange entre régions. Par voie de terre, une quantité impressionnante de biens a été transportée à dos d'animal, jusqu'à nos. jours. Mais les bêtes de somme et leur équipement réduit n'ont laissé que peu de traces archéologiques, leur fonction utilitaire ne suscitant guère la célébration. C'est au véhicule à roues – invention de l'homme – qu'est revenu cet honneur. Dans l'Antiquité, il a joué un rôle éminent dans la vie religieuse, la guerre et le sport et le souvenir de son évolution s'est conservé jusqu'à nous à travers de nombreux documents, textes, œuvres d'art et matériel archéologique, funéraire ou non.

Mais comment est-on passé de la bête de somme au véhicule tiré par des bœufs ou des chevaux? Plusieurs facteurs sont à l'origine de cette évolution intervenue entre le IVe et le IIIe millénaire avant notre ère : la nécessité de transporter des matériaux trop lourds pour des bêtes de somme, l'existence d'animaux déjà domestiqués et capables, par leur taille et leur morphologie, de tirer un véhicule. La traction humaine était déjà utilisée pour tirer des traîneaux ou, quand le terrain le permettait, des plates-formes posées sur des rondins. C'est ainsi, par exemple, qu'ont été transportés les mégalithes. Il restait donc à inventer la roue et à imaginer le moyen d'adapter la force animale à ce nouveau moyen de transport.

L'origine de la roue et du véhicule à roues a toujours fasciné l'homme moderne et nombreuses ont été les théories, souvent contradictoires, proposées pour retracer les premières étapes de son développement. De nouvelles découvertes, le réexamen de données déjà anciennes et pas toujours suffisamment exploitées apportent un

---

* *La Recherche* 14 (No. 142/March), 1983, 334–345.

jour nouveau sur ces questions. On commence à entrevoir par quelles transformations techniques il a fallu passer pour en arriver aux formes que nous connaissons à la fin de l'Antiquité mais également au choix de plus en plus fréquent d'attelages d'équidés, bien que les bovidés n'aient jamais été complètement remplacés.

Une origine controversée

Les plus anciennes représentations de véhicules à roues que nous connaissons actuellement sont des pictogrammes du IVe millénaire inscrits sur des tablettess d'argile venant de la ville d'Uruk (Méso-potamie) (fig. 1a). On trouve sur ces mêmes tablettes des représenta-tions de traîneaux avec et sans patins. Dans ce dernier cas, il s'agit plutôt de plates-formes, de sorte qu'une filiation paraît évidente. La plate-forme, encore utilisée de nos. jours pour le transport des arbres, doit, à tous moments, reposer sur au moins deux rouleaux de façon à rester horizontale et à permettre de replacer à l'avant de la plate-forme les rouleaux arrière au fur et à mesure de l'avancée. Le pas-sage de la plate-forme vers le véhicule à roues se serait fait en maintenant les rouleaux en place à l'aide d'échancrures faites dans le revers de la plate-forme de façon à éviter d'avoir à les replacer sans cesse (fig. 1b). Ceci préfigure le système de l'essieu tournant – sur des crochets fixés sur les côtés – et de la roue fixe. Parallèlement, le diamètre des rouleaux augmente de façon à surélever la plate-forme et diminuer le frottement. L'étape suivante consista à fixer des roues pleines sur un essieu tournant, un type de construction encore utilisé de nos. jours dans la péninsule ibérique, en Anatolie ou en Mongolie (fig. 1c).

Mais d'autres propositions ont été faites concernant l'origine du véhicule à roues. André Haudricourt et Gosta Berg ont proposé une filiation différente pour le char à deux roues qui dériverait non pas d'une plate-forme mais d'un travois.[1] Le travois est composé de deux perches placées de part et d'autre de l'animal, les extrémités avant des perches se croisant devant le garrot de l'animal qui tire. La par-tie arrière, sur laquelle repose le chargement, traîne à terre. Les perches de tente des Indiens d'Amérique en sont un exemple classique

---

[1] Haudricourt 1948; Berg 1935.

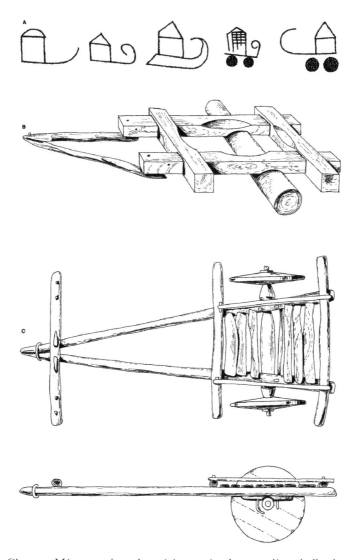

Fig. 1. C'est en Mésopotamie qu'ont été trouvées les premières indications de véhicules à roues. Des tablettes d'argile du IVᵉ millénaire provenant d'Uruk représentent des plates-formes couvertes, dont deux nous intéressent particulièrement. La première est munie de patins tandis que la seconde est montée sur des roues. Ces plates-formes ont été transformées en traîneau ou en plate-forme roulante (a). Le passage de la plate-forme au véhicule à roues s'effectue en deux temps. Le timon triangulaire est fixé de façon à ce que la plate-forme reste horizontale. Ce type de véhicule est utilisé en Géorgie soviétique pour transporter de gigantesques amphores à vin (b). Puis, l'évolution de la plate-forme continue avec l'adoption de roues fixées à un essieu tournant, systéme encore utilisé sur certaines voitures primitives de par le monde (c). (a : d'après Littauer et Crouwel 1979 ; b : d'après Gegeschidze 1956 ; c : d'après Piggott 1968.)

et récent. Mais nous ne possédons aucún témoignage de l'existence de travois au Proche Orient, où l'on trouve pourtant les plus anciennes représentations de voitures. L'arrière d'un travois s'enfoncerait profondément dans le sable et c'est pourquoi les perches des tentes des tribus nomades vivant actuellement dans ces régions sont transportées, à l'horizontale, fixées de chaque côté du bât des bêtes de somme. De cette façon leurs extrémités ne traînent pas sur le sol. Selon Haudricourt, sous le travois aurait été placé un rouleau, donnant ainsi naissance à la voiture à bâti triangulaire puis au char à timon central (fig. 2). Mais on peut objecter que s'il est possible de poser une surface plate (la plate-forme) sur des rouleaux (qui, toutefois «s'échappent» constamment à l'arrière pendant le trajet), il ne serait pas possible de poser des perches sur un rouleau. Elles ne tiendraient pas un seul instant sans être fixées d'une manière quelconque. Enfin, la voiture à bâti triangulaire que Haudricourt présente comme un stade intermédiaire entre le travois et le char à timon central n'est attestée nulle part avant la fin du IIe millénaire alors que la voiture à roues et à timon central était déjà connue en Mésopotamie depuis plus de mille ans à Tell Agrab et Khafajah, par exemple.[2] Les données archéologiques viennent donc contredire la thèse d'Haudricourt, pourtant reprise régulièrement depuis sa publication.

Premier perfectionnement : la roue

À partir des quelques exemples que nous venons de donner, il apparaît que le passage de la plate-forme au véhicule à roues a été conditionné par l'évolution de la roue. Le matériel, découvert à Kish[3] et à Ur[4] en Basse Mésopotamie, à Suse en Elam (sud-est de l'Iran), datant de la première moitié du IIIe millénaire, permet de mieux la comprendre. Parmi les fameuses «tombes royales» d'Ur, fouillées par l'archéologue anglais Léonard Woolley, dans la plus grande tombe – la «tombe du roi» où avait été enterré un souverain accompagné de ses gardes et de ses courtisans avec un faste et une splendeur barbares – deux voitures à quatre roues ont été découvertes. Les tombes de Kiš et de Suse, moins bien conservées, ont livré des restes de

---

[2] Frankfort 1943; Smith 1934, 39, pl. VIII.
[3] Watelin et Langdon 1934.
[4] Woolley 1934.

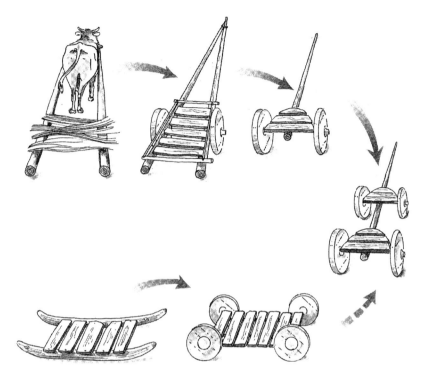

Fig. 2. Haudricourt croyait à une origine différente pour les voitures à deux roues et les voitures à quatre roues. Les premières dérivaient, selon lui, du travois en passant par la voiture à bâti triangulaire, une supposition que les données archéologiques ne permettent pas de retenir. Il convient de remarquer, d'autre part, que la voiture à quatre roues ne comporte aucun élément de traction. Enfin, Haudricourt n'a pas essayé d'expliquer l'origine de la partie la plus importante du système, la roue. (D'après Haudricourt 1948.)

roues. Toutes les roues étaient des roues composites en forme de disque. Elles étaient tantôt cerclées de cuir brut, de cuivre-bronze ou de bois et parfois cloutées. Ces roues, quoique les plus anciennes trouvées en Mésopotamie, témoignent déjà d'un certain perfectionnement technique. Elles sont composées de trois pièces de bois fixées les unes aux autres et non pas, comme on pourrait le penser, d'une seule pièce prise dans l'épaisseur d'un tronc (fig. 3a). A. T. Lucas, qui a étudié les roues actuelles du même type employées en Irlande, a mis en évidence les raisons de ce mode de fabrication.[5] Pour produire une roue d'une seule pièce et d'un diamètre de 60 cm à 1 m

---

[5] Lucas 1952.

comme celles d'Ur, il est nécessaire d'utiliser un tronc d'arbre de 75 cm à 1,15 m de diamètre puisque, même pour une roue d'une seule pièce, il serait nécessaire d'évider le cœur spongieux et tendre de l'arbre. Il paraît peu probable que des arbres d'essence et de dimension appropriées aient existé en Basse Mésopotamie au IIIe millénaire. Lds roues composites étaient surtout consolidées par des tasseaux. Le fait que la roue composite coexiste avec la roue d'une seule pièce dans des régions comme le sud de la Russie, où les arbres avaient une circonférence suffisante pour faire des roues d'une seule pièce, suggère un seul centre d'origine pour la roue dans un pays pauvre en arbres. Les traces de moyeu trouvées dans une des tombes d'Ur indiquent une deuxième étape dans le perfectionnement de la roue. Selon tous les documents de l'époque, les roues tournaient déjà autour d'un essieu fixe, au lieu d'être fixées à un essieu tournant comme dans la phase intermédiaire entre le rouleau et la roue mobile et comme on le trouve encore de nos. jours, sur des véhicules prim- itifs : une autre amélioration est l'utilisation d'un moyeu distinct de la roue et non plus une simple épaisseur dans la roue même (fig. 3b). Ce moyeu, plus long, est aussi plus solide et réduit le ballotte- ment autour de l'essieu. Ceci permettait aux roues de tourner à une vitesse différente et facilitait ainsi les changements de direction.

Les perfectionnements des premiers véhicules à roues varient selon l'attelage utilisé

Des véhicules ni très pratiques ni très maniables

La roue une fois inventée, les perfectionnements ont été fonction des attelages employés pour tirer les véhicules. La traction animale n'é- tait pas vraiment une nouveauté en Mésopotamie puisque, depuis le début du IVe millénaire au moins des bœufs étaient utilisés pour les labours. Ils étaient attelés par paires, avec timon et sous joug, bien que les sols meubles du Proche-Orient ne nécessitent pas une telle force de travail. Mais ce système d'attelage permettait de maintenir le soc de l'araire droit et surtout tenait compte du fait que les bœufs, vivant dans la nature en troupeaux, travaillent mieux à plusieurs, ce qu'on oublie trop souvent. Le système de traction fut adapté aux véhicules à roues : sur les voitures à deux roues, le timon reposait sur l'essieu ou au-dessus, sur les véhicules à quatre roues, il était

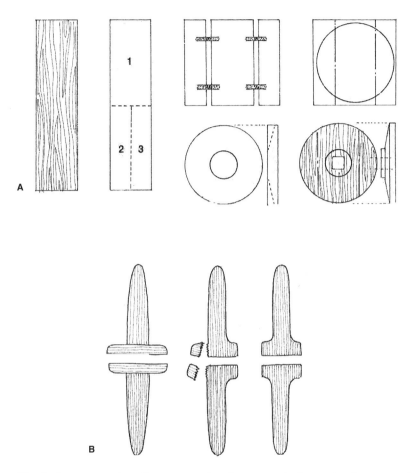

Fig. 3. La construction d'une roue tripartite, reconstituée sur le diagramme (a) permettait d'obtenir une roue d'un diamètre deux fois plus important que si l'on avait utilisé une pièce de bois unique. Au IIIe millénaire, on avait déjà remplacé le moyeu intégral par un moyeu distinct, plus long, ce qui empêchait la roue de ballotter et réduisait les risques de cassure (b). (a : d'après Lucas 1952; b : d'après van der Waals 1964.)

attaché à l'avant du plancher. Bien qu'à l'origine, les attelages aient été constitués exclusivement de bovidés, nous connaissons en Iraq à Tell Agrab et Khafajah des représentations d'équidés attelés au début du IIIe millénaire. Il peut s'agir d'ânes, déjà domestiqués en Égypte et arrivés vers 3 000 ans avant notre ère en Mésopotamie ou bien de produits d'un croisement de l'âne avec l'onagre (*Equus hemionus hemippus*) voire même de ce dernier, ce qui paraît moins probable dans la mesure où il n'existe pas de preuves que cette espèce locale d'équidé ait jamais été domestiquée. On peut même suggérer que c'est l'introduction de l'âne domestiqué qui a stimulé l'amélioration de la roue. Bien qu'à l'époque l'âne n'ait été utilisé que comme bête de somme et non pas comme animal de trait en Égypte, les Sumériens ont saisi la possibilité de le harnacher de la même façon que les bœufs et profiter ainsi de sa vitesse bien supérieure à celle de ces derniers. Quant au véritable cheval, natif des steppes du Nord, il a été utilisé plus tard, mais seulement pour produire des hybrides, selon les textes de l'époque (*La Recherche*, no. 114, p. 919, 1980).

Pourtant, malgré les différences de morphologie, le joug et le timon plus adaptés aux bovidés qu'aux équidés restèrent en usage avec ces derniers encore 3 000 ans. De la même façon on appliqua pendant 1 000 ans aux équidés le système de contrôle utilisé pour les bovidés, l'anneau nasal. L'anneau, renforcé par l'action de la voix et de l'aiguillon, était pourtant parfaitement inadapté à cause de son manque de précision, surtout à grande vitesse. La direction des véhicules tirés par des équidés devait par conséquent être difficilement contrôlable. Un autre facteur, constaté à Ur, limitait aussi la maniabilité des voitures à quatre roues. L'essieu avant était fixé et n'avait pas d'articulation horizontale : pour tourner, la voiture devait donc virer selon un grand arc.

Voitures de cérémonies et voitures de combat

Les voitures à quatre roues étaient assez importantes et prestigieuses pour être enterrées dans les tombes royales des grandes cités sumériennes de Kiš, Ur et de Suse en Elam. Nous possédons même l'«ancêtre» de ces véhicules, découvert dans l'une des tombes royales d'Ur. Il s'agit du traîneau de la «Reine» Pu-abi, tiré par des animaux d'abord identifiés comme des onagres. Dans la «tombe du roi» se trouvaient deux chars, l'un avait peut-être servi de char funéraire, l'autre – dans les vestiges duquel se trouvait un poignard – était peut-être son char de guerre. Toutefois les animaux de trait n'étaient pas les équidés représentés durant cette période, mais des bœufs. De la même façon, l'analyse récente de quelques dents de l'attelage de la Reine Pu-abi a montré qu'il s'agissait de bœufs, également, et non d'onagres. Deux raisons pourraient expliquer l'utilisation de ces animaux pour les chars royaux : les bovins devaient être plus dociles que les équidés non castrés et par conséquent plus faciles à mener lors de la descente dans la tombe; ayant précédé les équidés en tant qu'animaux de trait, les bovins seraient restés traditionnellement attachés au culte et aux grandes cérémonies, tout comme les corbillards tirés par des chevaux ont longtemps survécu à l'arrivée de l'automobile.

La présence d'une voiture à quatre roues utilisée pour la guerre dans la «tombe du roi» à Ur, ainsi que l'existence de figurines en terre cuite représentant des voitures à quatre roues équipées de carquois de javelots permettent de réfuter la théorie développée par le commandant Lefebvre des Noëttes dans son ouvrage intitulé *L'attelage, le cheval de selle*,[6] selon laquelle seuls les véhicules à deux roues participaient aux batailles. Son principal argument était que la représentation des véhicules à quatre roues figurant sur l'une des faces de l'*Etendard d'Ur*, mosaïque d'écaille et lapis-lazuli trouvée dans une des «tombes royales», était due à la maladresse de l'artiste et qu'il s'agissaient en fait de voitures à deux roues (fig. 4a).

Les vestiges de ces véhicules, joints à l'étude de l'*Etendard d'Ur*, nous apprennent qu'il était impossible à deux personnes de s'y tenir côte à côte : le guerrier se tenait derrière le cocher sur une petite plate-forme faisant saillie à l'arrière du plancher et devait se retenir, dans ce véhicule sans suspension, en posant sa main sur l'épaule du conducteur placé devant lui. Les deux autres véhicules à deux roues dc la figure 4, quant à eux, ne peuvent transporter qu'un seul passager. Dans le premier, probablement adapté aux voyages rapides et à la chasse avec des rabatteurs, le conducteur est assis à califourchon et bien calé (fig. 4b). Le second, dont le conducteur se tenait assis sur un banc, les pieds devant lui, devait être moins rapide et probablement utilisé lors de processions ou de courtes promenades (fig. 4c). En effet, on voit mal comment le conducteur aurait pu utiliser ses armes tout en guidant quatre équidés non castrés avec le harnais primitif de l'époque!

Il faut souligner qu'en dépit de l'impact psychologique initial qu'ont pu avoir ces chars sur le champ de bataille, la nouveauté une fois émoussée, les déficiences que nous venons de mentionner les ont rendus à la longue peu pratiques. Toute comparaison de ces chars de guerre avec des tanks modernes serait erronée. Elle a pourtant été proposée par Sir Leonard Woolley, l'archéologue britannique qui a fouillé Ur entre 1922 et 1934, et maintes fois reprise par la suite. Ces voitures étaient fragiles et surtout extrêmement vulnérables : elles

---

[6] Lefebvre des Noëttes 1931.

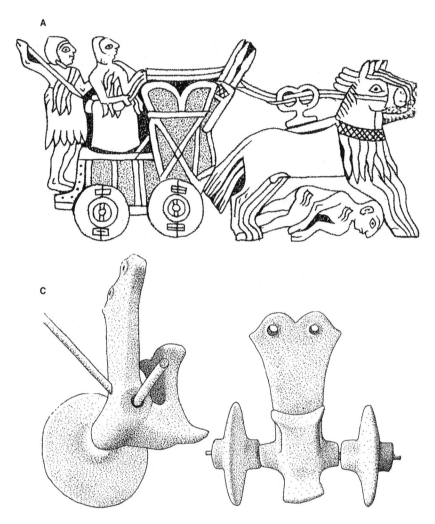

Fig. 4. a) L'une des faces de l'Etendard d'Ur présente des voitures à quatre roues utilisées pour la guerre. L'étroitesse du châssis, attestée par les restes de voitures retrouvées dans les tombes d'Ur, oblige le guerrier à se tenir derrière le cocher. Les quatre équidés sont dirigés par un système d'anneau nasal et de muserolle. Ce type de véhicule va disparaître des scènes de guerre au cours de la seconde moitié du IIIe millénaire. c) La voiture plate-forme, autre modèle de véhicule à deux roues, comporte une banquette placée derrière une haute rambarde. Mais à grande vitesse, le conducteur devait avoir des difficultés à maintenir son équilibre et le véhicule servait plutôt pour des cérémonies ou des promenades. (D'après Littauer et Crouwel 1979, fig. 3, 20 et 7.)

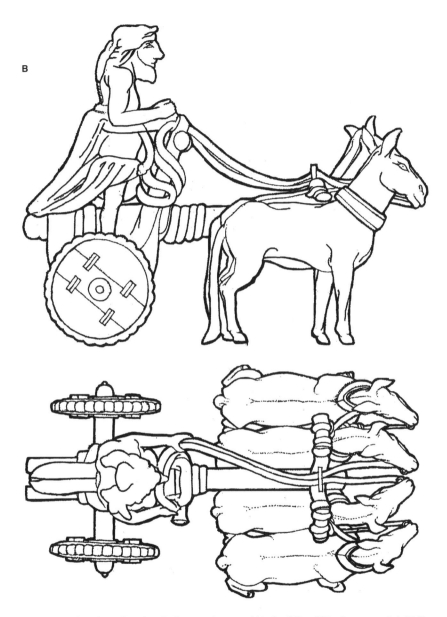

Fig. 4. b) Ce char-chevalet de la première moitié du IIIᵉ millénaire, trouvé à Tell Agrab en Irak, ne peut transporter qu'une seule personne, l'ancien timon, conçu à l'origine pour l'araire, est monté au-dessus de l'essieu. Le conducteur doit se tenir à califourchon, l'essieu fixe étant utilisé un peu comme des étriers, et il peut aussi serrer le timon entre ses jambes pour maintenir son équilibre.

ne pouvaient évoluer qu'en terrain plat et surtout occupants et attelage restaient exposés aux projectiles. Elles étaient donc à tous points
de vue l'opposé des tanks modernes. Il ne faut pas non plus sous-
estimer la fr`gilité des membres et des sabots des équidés qui, à
l'époque, n'étaient pas ferrés. Dans ces conditions, il n'est pas sur-
prenant que durant le reste du IIIe millénaire, pendant les périodes
d'Akkad et d'Ur III (2350–2000 avant J.-C.) au cours desquelles les
Sumériens furent dominés par les Akkadiens, un peuple sémite venu
du Nord, on ne trouve plus de représentation de scènes de guerre
ou même de chasse. Les véhicules tirés par des équidés ne sont
représentés que dans les scènes de culte, transportant une divinité
ou son image.[7] On ne notera plus d'améliorations techniques durant
le IIIe millénaire.

Les chariots en Europe

Que se passait-il au méme moment loin des civilisations urbaines du
Proche Orient, dans les plaines et les forêts d'Europe? Les connais-
sances techniques concernant les véhicules à roues se sont rapide-
ment propagées. En cinq cents ans, la roue tripartite avait atteint le
Danube, les Balkans, les steppes de l'Europe de l'Est jusqu'à l'Oural
et l'Europe du Nord. Cette rapide expansion, et la complexité de sa
structure, mérite bien l'appellation d'«explosion technologique» proposée par l'archéologue britannique Stuart Piggott[8] plutôt que d'être
assimilée à une diffusion ou des innovations indépendantes.

Les rares vestiges des véhicules européens, des roues essentiellement, indiquent que le chariot à quatre roues était plus fréquent que
la voiture à deux roues. Les premiers chariots européens étaient tirés
par des bœufs et leur vitesse devait être trop lente sur les terrains
irréguliers des régions boisées d'Europe pour qu'ils jouent un rôle
déterminant dans le commerce. La plus grande part du commerce
devait se faire par bateau, par porteurs et, là où le cheval avait été
domestiqué, à dos d'animal. Bien que des voies aménagées dans les
régions marécageuses des plats pays nordiques aient pu permettre
l'utilisation des chariots à des fins commerciales ou culturelles, il est
probable que la majorité de ces véhicules ne s'éloignait des habita-

---

[7] Nagel 1966.
[8] Piggott 1979.

tions que lorsque maisons et champs étaient abandonnés après épuisement des sols.

L'usage essentiellement agricole des chariots en Europe est attesté par quelques récipients à boire en terre cuite trouvés en Hongrie à Budaklasz et Szigetszenstmarton entre autres : ils ont la forme de charrettes à hauts bords, inclinés vers l'extérieur et typiques des véhicules qui, encore de nos. jours, transportent du grain, de la paille, du foin et fumier entre les fermes et les champs. Les nombreuses sepultures à véhicules des régions du nord de la mer Noire et du Caucase, datées de 3 000 à 1 500 ans avant notre ère, soulignent l'usage agricole de ces chariots à quatre roues.[9] Attelés à des bovidés, ils se trouvent dans des tombes d'agriculteurs. On a cependant trouvé, au nord du Caucase, une voiture à deux roues et plusieurs figurines de terre cuite représentant des véhicules à deux roues, bâchés, qui pourraient avoir été utilisés par les bergers ou les gardiens de troupeaux lors des transhumances. Il n'y a aucune trace de véhicules attelés à des chevaux, ce qui paraît étrange dans cette région où le cheval était domestiqué depuis au moins un millénaire. L'explication de cette absence tient sans doute, là encore, au fait que pour le chariot de ferme ou l'araire, la vitesse des bovidés était suffisante, qu'ils étaient d'entretien plus économique et qu'ils fournissaient un lait plus riche.

La naissance du char

C'est encore une fois vers l'Est qu'il faut se tourner pour trouver à la fin du IIIe millénaire une nouvelle amélioration de la roue, vers plus de légèreté. Il s'agit de la roue à entretoises attestée pour la première fois à Tepe Hissar en Iran, puis vers 2000 avant J.-C. à Kültepe en Anatolie (fig. 5a). Elle est surtout connue en Méditerranée durant la période classique, toujours associée aux véhicules tirés par des ânes ou des mulets. Elle se trouve encore aujourd'hui dans certaines régions associées à des attelages de bœufs.

Mais c'est également vers 2000 avant J.-C. que naît le véritable char. On a découvert à Kültepe en Anatolie une empreinte de sceau-cylindre représentant un véhicule sans siège, dont chacune des deux roues comportait quatre rais (fig. 5b). Ce char est tiré par deux (et

[9] Häusler 1981.

Fig. 5. A la fin du IIIe millénaire, la roue allégée apparaît. On trouve tout d'abord la roue à entretoises en Iran (a), puis la roue à quatre rais ou plus en Anatolie (b). Les représentations de véhicules munis de roues à rais sont les premières à altester l'apparition d'attelages de chevaux

non plus quatre) équidés qui, bien qu'on ne puisse pas les identifier comme des chevaux, sont assez différents des équidés représentés jusque-là. Seul l'anneau nasal pour les diriger subsiste. Les premières roues à rais ont été trouvées à Acemhüyük en (Anatolie centrale) à la même époque. Elles proviennent d'une figurine en cuivre/bronze représentant un véhicule à quatre roues.[10] À Uruk, au sud de la Mésopotamie, un moule en relief représente un véhicule à deux roues assez proche de ceux des sceaux-cylindres anatoliens.[11] Un péu plus tard, une empreinte de sceau syrien datant du règne d'Hammurabi, le grand législateur de Babylone (vers 1792–1750 avant J.-C.), porte une version modifiée de l'ancienne voiture à banquette dont la rambarde, de forme caractéristique, a été surbaissée.[12] Là encore, les roues ont quatre rais. L'attelage est composé de deux équidés, dont on ne voit que les arrièremains (fig. 5c). Le conducteur de l'attelage tient quatre rênes ce qui suggère un contrôle plus efficace, soit par caveçon avec une muserolle placée bas sur le chanfrein, soit par bridon à filet (embouchure brisée). Cette pièce est extrêmement intéressante dans la mesure où elle présente un attelage de vrais chevaux, identifiés par leur port de queue, haut, alors que les ânes, les onagres et les mules portent la queue basse. Cette particularité a également été retrouvée sur d'autres sceaux-cylindres syriens des xviii–xvie siècles avant notre ère.[13] Des animaux élancés avec des oreilles exagérément petites sont représentés attelés à des chars aux roues à rais et commandés avec des rênes. La structure de ces différents véhicules témoigne de la transformation de l'ancienne plate-forme par élimination du siège, ce qui permet un accès plus facile par l'arrière et l'abaissement progressif de la rambarde avant jusqu'à hauteur de la taille et son extension sur les côtés du char de façon à constituer une caisse.

L'image qui résulte de ces développements progressifs remet en cause plusieurs théories. La plus importante est l'idée reçue, selon laquelle le cheval et le char de guerre seraient arrivés ensembles au Proche-Orient, amenés par les tribus conquérantes dévalant des steppes du Nord. A partir des sceaux-cylindres, nous pouvons suivre la transformation graduelle des véhicules locaux en chars. D'autre part, nous savons que le cheval n'était pas tout à fait un nouveau

---

[10] Mellink 1971.
[11] Ziegler 1962.
[12] Figulla 1967.
[13] Buchanan 1966.

venu au Proche-Orient et qu'il avait eu le temps de s'acclimater et
de se multiplier. La seconde théorie est l'idée reçue selon laquelle
les roues à quatre rais auraient précédé les roues à rayons multiples.
Cette idée était si ancrée qu'elle a été utilisée comme critère de data-
tion pour les œuvres d'art du Proche Orient. Les sceaux-cylindres
syriens représentent des roues à 4, 6, 8 et 9 rais : si les roues à quatre rais étaient le plus souvent représentées, il semble que leur représentation soit due à la petite taille des objets gravés et qu'elle soit là
plus pour la commodité de l'artiste que pour le réalisme. Récemment,
une tombe du xvie siècle avant J.-C., découverte dans les monts
Oural, a livré des roues comportant jusqu'à dix rais et utilisée sur
des voitures légères à deux roues.[14]

L'amélioration du harnais pour les attelages de chevaux

C'est également sur un sceau syrien que nous voyons pour la première fois un véhicule pouvant porter deux passagers côte à côte,
ce qui était d'une grande importance pour la guerre. Pour la première fois aussi un chasseur est équipé d'un arc qui devient l'arme-
ment du char par excellence (fig. 5d). Nous connaissons des versions
perfectionnées de ce char provenant de la XVIIIe dynastie égyptienne (1580–1314 avant J.-C.) et entre autres de la tombe de Tou-
tankhamon : entièrement fait d'un bois léger et solide courbé au
feu et de cuir brut, sans parties métalliques susceptibles de se dé-
tacher sous l'effet des cahots, ces chars sont des merveilles de
robustesse si l'on considère leur légèreté. La plate-forme de lanières
de cuir brut consolide la structure du châssis et assure l'élasticité à
un véhicule autrement dépourvu de suspension. (Ce type de plancher
continua d'être utilisé sur des chars légers, plus tardifs, dans des
régions aussi différentes que l'Italie et la Perse.) Les roues, à six
rayons, ont de longs moyeux pour réduire leurs ballottements et la
voie du char est très large, de façon à accroître sa stabilité.

Un nouveau perfectionnement apparaît au xve siècle avant notre
ère, en Égypte, bien qu'il soit probablement déjà maladroitement
représenté sur les sceaux syriens. Il s'agit du fourchon d'encolure qui
permet d'adapter le joug à la morphologie des chevaux (pl. 1).
Attaché au joug par le manche, ses «jambes» reposent le long des

---

[14] Gening et Ashichmina 1975.

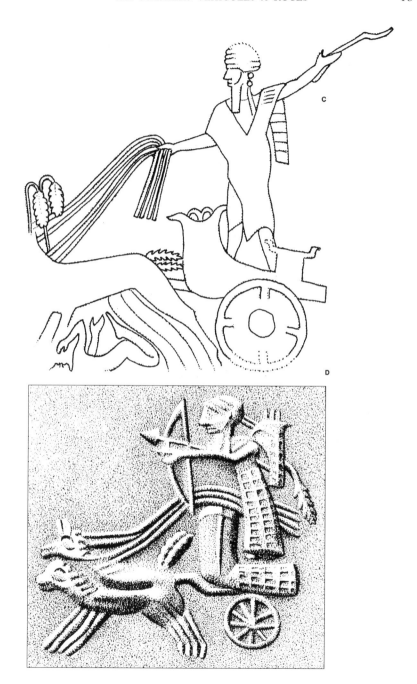

Fig. 5 (c) ainsi que l'usage de l'arc (d). (D'après Littauer et Crouwel 1979, fig. 21. 29. 31. 36.)

épaules du cheval de façon qu'elles supportent la plus grande partie
de la traction. Ainsi, les fourchons fonctionnaient un peu comme le
collier de harnais moderne. Les extrémités inférieures des fourchons
d'encolure sont reliées par une bande de cuir passant devant l'encolure,
mais sans comprimer la trachée artère et la carotide. D'importantes
expérimentations menées par J. Spruytte,[15] qua a reconstitué un harnais avec joug et fourchons d'encolure, ont démontré que les conclusions négatives de Lefebvre des Noëttes étaient sans fondement.
Ce dernier avait tenté d'expliquer que les attelages antiques ne pouvaient tirer que des charges légères parce que les harnais étranglaient
les équidés, les empêchant ainsi d'utiliser leur pleine puissance.

Parallèlement aux progrès des véhicules et du système de traction,
le contrôle des chevaux devient plus efficace et plus précis pour les
attelages. Les premiers mors en bronze sont apparus vers 1450 avant
J.-C. au Proche-Orient, portant pour la plupart des pointes sur la
surface intérieure des barrettes, ce qui renforçait le guidage. Si l'on
n'a pas encore parlé de la monte, c'est qu'elle commence très tard
comme activité militaire ou sportive. Nous avons déjà noté que, dans
les civilisations proche-orientales du moins, les équidés attelés ont
précédé les équidés montés. Pourtant, il est difficile d'imaginer les
hommes élevant ces animaux sans avoir l'idée de sauter sur leur dos,
surtout quand il s'agit d'animaux de petite taille. L'argument selon
lequel le cheval était trop petit au moment de sa domestication pour
supporter un cavalier ne tient pas debout : les premiers chevaux
domestiqués dans les steppes du sud de la Russie avaient une taille
comparable aux chevaux des guerriers scythes de la fan du Ier millénaire avant notre ère, de 1,36 m à 1,44 m. Actuellement, dans
certaines régions du monde comme l'Islande, des adultes montent et
font courir des animaux encore plus petits et récemment encore,
beaucoup de poneys de polo étaient à peine plus grands. Il existe
par contre une autre raison qui devait décourager les cavaliers
éventuels au Proche Orient. Les premiers équidés montés vers la fin
du IIIe millénaire – âne, onagre ou croisement des deux – offraient
une assiette qui avait de quoi les décourager. Ces animaux ont des
garrots et des encolures basses, des épaules étroites qui donnent l'impression à celui qui les monte qu'il va passer par-dessus leur tête,
de sorte que le cavalier recule instinctivement sur les reins de l'animal, l'épuisant à grande vitesse, ou encore plus à l'arrière et alors,

---

[15] Spruytte 1977.

c'est lui qui ressent un maximum de secousses. Cette assiette, assez confortable aux petites allures des autres équidés et à l'usage domestique, ne l'est pas pour une monte plus énergique. Il faut également tenir compte du fait que le poids d'un cavalier armé peut provoquer, quand l'animal est lancé à grande vitesse sur un terrain rocailleux, des lésions aux sabots non ferrés de l'animal plus importantes que celles provoquées par la traction.

Le cheval monté apparaît déjà, mais rarement, vers 2000 avant J.-C., toujours contrôlé à l'aide d'un anneau nasal. Ses premières apparitions dans des scènes de guerre sont gravées sur des monuments égyptiens des xviiie et xixe dynasties mais les cavaliers ne sont encore que des messagers, des éclaireurs ou des fugitifs. Ce n'est qu'au ixe siècle avant notre ère que l'on trouve des chevaux montés par des guerriers et ils ne jouent guère de rôle avant le viie siècle, au moment où les unités montées commencent à remplacer la charrerie (fig. 6). Ce décalage de mille ans paraît significatif. Le cheval, originaire des grandes steppes herbeuses, aurait alors eu le temps de développer le sabot dur et étroit adapté au désert rocailleux, par sélection naturelle et artificielle. Bien que les chevaux proche-orientaux soient ferrés depuis des siècles, leurs sabots sont mieux adaptés aux terrains rocailleux et arides que ceux des autres chevaux. Le char de guerre ou de chasse léger et capable d'une vitesse relativement élevée, le cheval monté de façon sporadique caractérisent le iie millénaire et ce n'est qu'au millénaire suivant que leur importance relative est modifiée.

Le cheval remplace le char

Durant le Ier millénaire, de nouvelles transformations interviennent. Au viiie siècle avant notre ère, apparaît au Proche Orient le char à deux timons. Nous avons vu, jusqu'à présent, des chars avec un timon central, qui passe sous le plancher du char et qui est fixé à l'arrière et à l'avant du châssis. Cette fois, les deux pièces de bois prolongent les côtés du châssis et chaque limon reçoit un joug auquel sont attelés deux chevaux. On utilise aussi, mais plus rarement, un joug à quatre chevaux. Les attelages à quatre chevaux deviennent donc la règle, ce qui permet d'augmenter les chargements. Les chars de guerre portent un équipage de quatre hommes. L'inconvénient de ce nouveau système est une perte de maniabilité qui a dû entraîner des changements dans la tactique militaire.

Fig. 6. Le cheval monté par un cavalier apparaît beaucoup plus tard que le cheval attelé. Il est d'abord contrôlé par l'anneau nasal, comme sur cette plaque de terre cuite du IIᵉ millénaire. Son utilisation par des guerriers armés n'intervient qu'au IXᵉ siècle de notre ère. On trouve alors des représentations sur les bas-reliefs assyriens : l'un des deux cavaliers, répétant le geste du cocher de char, contrôle les deux chevaux pendant que son compagnon tire à l'arc. Il faudra attendre plus d'un siècle encore pour trouver des cavaliers capables de contrôler leur monture tout en maniant leurs armes. (D'après Littauer et Crouwel 1979, fig. 76.)

Le harnais se modifie sensiblement. Au Proche-Orient, le four-chon d'encolure est abandonné au profit d'un joug ajusté avec une place prévue pour l'encolure de chaque cheval. En Grèce, où nos. seuls documents concernent des jougs à deux chevaux, un nouveau type de harnachement est mis au point au début du 1er millénaire avant notre ère. Il s'agit d'un joug dorsal combiné avec une sangle, que l'on retrouvera un peu plus tard, à l'Âge du Fer, utilisé par les tribus celtiques de la période de la Tène. D'après les représentations existantes, J. Spruytte a réussi à reconstituer et expérimenter ce har-nais. Mais il est à noter que les chars de course étrusques et romains étaient inspirés des chars d'Asie Mineure et non pas des chars grecs et l'usage du joug ajusté s'est donc perpétué. Il faudra attendre la période romaine pour trouver un nouveau mode de traction : un cheval entre deux brancards, mais ceci est une autre histoire...

Les guerriers montés commencent à apparaître au ixe siècle avant J.-C. et leur importance militaire augmente avec leur efficacité au cours des deux siècles suivants. Vers 500 avant J.-C., le changement du mors en est le reflet. Pour le cavalier montant sans selle, il est plus difficile de freiner sa monture que de la diriger : le guidage peut se faire par pression de la jambe ou de la main ou par un change-ment d'équilibre mais le freinage est plus difficile surtout si le cava-lier manie une arme au même moment. Pour améliorer son efficacité, le mors est transformé de façon que la partie active concerne non plus les lèvres du cheval mais l'intérieur de la bouche (fig. 7). Un nouveau mors combiné avec un caveçon de métal fait son appari-tion dans les derniers siècles avant notre ère, utilisant la technique du levier, mais il ne s'agit pas encore du mors à gourmette actuel.

Lorsque nous abandonnons l'histoire de la voiture et du cheval au début de notre ère, après 3 000 ans de développement et d'ex-périmentation, le cheval semble prendre le pas sur la voiture. Cette dernière a perdu de son intérêt dans le domaine militaire et, à la fin de l'Empire romain, lorsque l'entretien des routes est pratique-ment abandonné, elle perd aussi de son importance pour le com-merce et les voyages. Dans les régions du Nord, les voitures sont remplacées par le cheval monté ou utilisé comme bête de somme et dans les pays méditerranéens par l'âne et le mulet. Le cheval quant à lui conserve toute son importance militaire.

Il faudra attendre le xvie et surtout le xviiie siècle en Europe pour que la voiture reprenne de l'importance avec l'amélioration du sys-tème routier. Mais il n'en reste pas moins qu'une partie essentielle

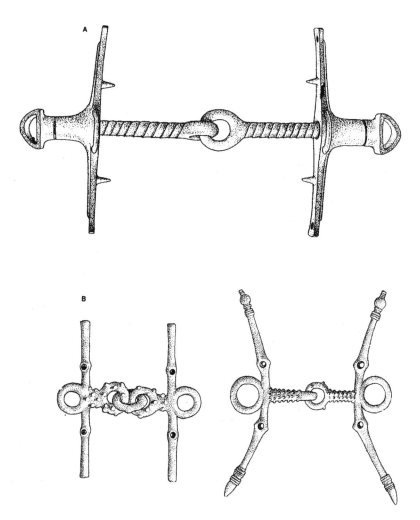

Fig. 7. Un des plus anciens mors en métal qui nous soit parvenu provient de Tell el Amarna en Égypte et date du XIVe siècle avant notre ère. L'usage de pointes sur la face intérieure des barrettes était très répandu et servait à renforcer le contrôle latéral important pour les chars (a). Au Ve siécle avant notre ére, les pointes sont maintenant sur les canons, ce qui permet au cavalier de freiner sa monture plus aisément (b). (D'après Littauer et Crouwel 1979, fig. 49 et fig. 84 a–b.)

de tout ce qui roule sur route ou sur rail, aujourd'hui, repose sur une invention dont le principe était déjà établi au IIIe millénaire avant notre ère : la roue.

Pour en savoir plus:
Karageorghis 1967, p. 337 (tombé à char à Salamine en Chypre); Piggott 1968, p. 266; Piggott 1983; Littauer 1968; Littauer et Crouwel 1979; Spruytte 1977.

2. KAMPFWAGEN (STREITWAGEN) B. ARCHÄOLOGISCH*

M. A. LITTAUER AND J. H. CROUWEL

§ 1. Earlier IIIrd mill. B.C. (to c. 2375 B.C.). The earliest wheeled vehicles used for military purposes appear to have been 4-wheeled wagons of the ED period. Pictorial documents, such as the "Standard of Ur" (fig. 1) show these with a high front breastwork, reinforced by crossed struts and topped by a handrail (elsewhere shown as open) depressed in the centre, by which a driver could steady himself; low sides, and perhaps a seat across the back, the floor projecting behind; disk wheels set closely behind each other and often tripartite. Actual remains of 4-wheelers, not necessarily always military vehicles, yield some details of construction and a range of dimensions: the narrowness of the floors (0.45–0.56 m.) confirms the positions of the two occupants as depicted, one behind the other; axles (length 0.70–1.00 m.) give evidence of being fixed, with the wheels revolving on them; the front axles do not articulate horizontally, thus limiting the manoeuvrability of the vehicle; the wheels (diam. 0.50–1.05 m.) are made of three pieces of wood, the central piece, which also functioned as a nave, being flanked by side pieces, the whole

Fig. 1. Detail of "Standard", Ur. After Littauer and Crouwel 1979, fig. 3.

* *Reallexikon der Assyriologie und vorderasiatischen Archäologie*, Vol. 5, 1980, 344–351.

held together by slats, and consolidated and protected by a tyre of rawhide, metal or wood, with or without hobnails.

The single draught pole may be of two types: one type slants backwards from the yoke to the floor front, where it is probably attached in a manner to articulate vertically; the other rises abruptly in front of the wagon before arching over to run down and forward to the yoke. Traction is supplied by yoked equids – usually four – with two animals under yoke and two outriggers attached by their collars to the yoke animals. They are controlled by single lines to nose rings, which provide only braking, not directional, control. The exact species of equids, illustrated as entire males, is seldom determinable. They could be the native "half ass" or hemione, or the ass (introduced from the southwest) or – perhaps less likely – the horse (introduced from the north), or any of the crosses between these.

The 4-wheeled "battle car" would be primarily a mobile firing platform from which javelins, carried in a sheath attached to a corner of the high front breastwork, could be cast. Recent experiments with a reconstruction of such a wagon show that an expert javelin thrower can cast 30 javelins per min. a distance of up to 60 m. from it while it moves at 16–19.3 km. per hour. The axe that is sometimes also carried would be for use for fighting from a standstill or dismounted. Considering the vulnerability of both animals and vehicle and the strict limitation to open and level terrain, the often-drawn comparison of this wagon with the modern tank is invalid. Poor directional control of the draught team and poor manoeuvrability of the vehicle are also limiting factors.

Of the two types of 2-wheelers illustrated at this time – the "straddle car" and the "platform car" – only the first, in which the driver is astraddle sitting or standing, might be considered a possible candidate for military use, since it is often equipped with a sheath of javelins. It is shown with the same type of disk wheels as the 4-wheeler and, with one exception (the well-known copper model from Tell Agrab, cf. Littauer and Crouwel 1979, fig. 7), has the high, arching type of pole. Draught system and method of control are also the same. Despite its armament, it is never shown in an explicitly military context and, since it cannot properly accommodate a crew of two – driver and warrior –, these arms could as well suggest hunting use, for which it would be more appropriate.

§ 2. Later IIIrd mill. B.C. (c. 2375–2000 B.C.). Although the same types of vehicles continue through the Akkadian and Ur-III periods, there is no evidence for their military use. This may have proved impractical in the long run, owing to the unsuitability of their designs and inefficient control of the draught team. The appearance of the cross-bar wheel at this time (on a seal from Tepe Hissar, cf. Littauer and Crouwel 1979, fig. 21) suggests efforts towards improvement by lightening the wheel.

> *General Discussion*: Childe 1951, 1954; Piggott 1968; Watelin 1934, fig. 3; Woolley 1934, 64, 108f.; de Mecquenem 1922, 137f., figs. 14.16. *Representations*: Amiet 1961, pls. 92–3; Frankfort 1943, pls. 58–60, 65. *Construction and wheels*: Littauer/Crouwel 1973, 101–126, 1977; Zarins 1976.

§ 3. **Earlier IInd mill. B.C.** (c. 2000–1600 B.C.). The traditional type of 4-wheeler, although illustrated only in cult scenes, where it is drawn by four equids still controlled by lines and nose rings, displays both cross-bar and – for the first time – spoked wheels. The latter may well have been devised to lighten a different type of vehicle (2-wheeled). There is evidence in this period for the development in the Near East of a light vehicle with two, spoked wheels and drawn by horses – the true *chariot*. It begins either as a flat car with open railing (Anatolia), as a shallow open-railed vehicle with curving pole (Mesopotamia), or (Syria) as a gradual modification of the old "platform car", itself apparently a 2-wheeled version of the 4-wheeled "battle car". The high front screen and low side ones are replaced by a low screen of equal height at front and sides, the seat is removed, permitting easy access from the rear, and the high, arching pole is reduced to a lower, more mildly curving one (fig. 2). Variety in chariot boxes testifies to experimentation, as does apparent variation in wheel construction and number of spokes – the latter usually four, but six, eight and nine also occurring. Draught teams are composed of two horses, each controlled by a pair of reins running to the sides of a cavesson or perhaps already to the ends of a bit – in either case providing directional as well as braking control.

   To increase stability on the fast turns now made possible by improved control of the team, a wider wheel base would be required. This, in turn, would permit a wider box and, for the first time, we have indications of a vehicle in which a crew of two could stand abreast – an important step in the development of a successful military chariot. While no arms are shown attached to the vehicle, the bow is depicted carried or in use by a charioteer. The motif of the "vanquished enemy beneath the team's hooves", first appearing on

Fig. 2. Syrian seal, Newell Collection 343. After Littauer and Crouwel 1979, fig. 33.

the "Standard" of Ur (fig. 1) and signifying "victory", recurs also (cf. fig. 2), and we may assume that these vehicles are put to military use. They may well represent those mentioned in texts as forming elements of the armies of the time.

> *Representations*: Amadasi 1965, figs. 1, 3; Amiet 1969; Buchanan 1966, nos. 892–895; 1971, pl. II: c-e; von der Osten, 1934, nos. 341 and 343; Özgüç 1965, cat. nos. 9, 24; Porada 1948, nos. 893 E, 971 E; Ziegler 1962, no. 289 – Texts (Old Assyrian and Old Hittite): Kammenhuber 1961, 13, 19, 29ff.

§ 4. Later IInd mill. B.C. (c. 1600–1000 B.C.). Precise material information on chariots of this period is furnished only by Egypt, where they had been introduced from the Levant at some time during the "Hyksos" occupation. Not only are Levantine chariots depicted as similar to Egyptian ones, but it may be assumed that certain basic structural principles would be similar in other Near-Eastern chariots also (fig. 3). To judge from surviving Egyptian examples, the vehicles

Fig. 3. Levantine tribute, Thebes, Tomb of Rekhmire. After Littauer and
Crouwel 1979, fig. 43.

are of light construction, based on the use of heat-bent wood and
rawhide. They have D-shaped floors of interwoven thongs, ca 1.00
m. wide by ca 0.50 m. deep. Chariots of the Hittites and their allies
depicted at the famous battle of Qadeš however, must be deep enough
to accommodate a third man standing behind the normal crew of
two (fig. 4). The approximately hip-high siding, rounded or sometimes rectangular in profile, may consist only of a railing or be partly
or entirely filled in. It extends around the sides and front, leaving
the rear open.

Axles are shown as close to the rear or at very rear of box.
Although loading the necks of the team somewhat, such an axle
position is essential for the stability of a fast 2-wheeler carrying a
shifting and not a stable load. The majority of wheels depicted up
until the late 15th century are 4-spoked and one actual chariot with

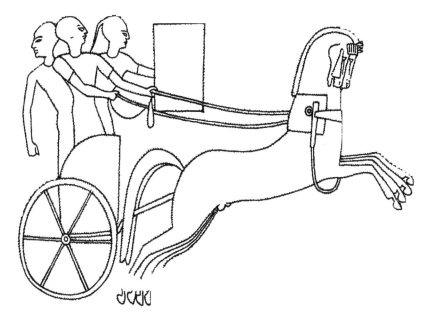

Fig. 4. Hittite chariot at Qadeš Abydos. After Littauer and Crouwel 1979, fig. 45.

4-spoked wheels survives. Six spokes are most common thereafter, and eight spokes are rare. Surviving chariot wheels range from 0.87 m.–1.00 m. in diam., and extant chariots have wide wheel bases of from 1.54 m.–1.80 m.

The draught pole, which runs all the way under the box, is attached in only one place – at the centre front of the floor frame – to which it is lashed. A connection, of thongs or rods, between the top of the chariot front and the pole a short way in front of it, restricts the tendency of pole and floor frame to pull apart in rough going; when rigid, it also gives support to the breastwork. Two thongs (so-called yoke braces) run out from near the centre of the pole, one to each arm of the yoke, and serve to keep the latter at right angles to the pole, as well as to distribute the tractive stress.

Traction is supplied by a pair of horses under yoke. The latter, originally designed for bovids, is adapted to equine anatomy by the use of yoke saddles. These objects, of inverted Y shape, are lashed to the yoke by their "handles", and their "legs" lie along the animals' shoulders, thus placing part of the pull in this area.

While control may sometimes be by cavesson, both organic and metal bits are now attested. The former have cheekpieces of bone or antler and "soft" mouthpieces of thong or sinew. The latters' cheekpieces are circular or bar-shaped, often studded on their inner faces; their mouthpieces may be plain bars or ones jointed in the middle. Both types have "snaffle" action, i.e., they function by exerting pressure on the corners of the horses' lips, and those with bar cheekpieces also exert pressure on the lower jaw. Moreover, the studded inner faces of some cheekpieces exert extra latitudinal persuasion when the rein on the opposite side is pulled.

Chariotry plays an important military role in this period. Although concern for protection indicates that it anticipates exposure to enemy missiles, it is too fragile and vulnerable to be used as modern tanks are. Two-man Asiatic and Egyptian chariots carrying archers are used as mobile firing platforms to run along the face of the enemy so as to soften it up, or to play a flanking and pursuing role. Bowcases and quivers of arrows fixed outside the box provide reserve arms. Asiatic chariots may also sometimes carry a spear at the rear, for use dismounted or from a standing vehicle. Three-man chariots of the Hittite coalition at the Battle of Qadeš, carrying driver, shield-bearer and spearman (quivers are absent) must serve primarily as transports.

> *General Discussion*: Powell 1963; Schulman 1963. *Material Remains*: Botti 1951; Carter 1927, 107–17, pls. 37–44; Carter and Newberry 1904; Quibell 1908; Western 1973. *Representations*: Reade 1975; Wreszinski 1935 (numerous illustrations of chariots, including those of Egypt's enemies). *Texts*: Ebeling 1951; Kammenhuber 1961; Kendall 1975. *Horse Bits*: Foltiny 1967; Boehmer 1972 R.M. – 1216 (see also end of entry).

§ 5. Earlier Ist mill. B.C. (c. 1000–600 B.C.). Evidence of all kinds is scanty at the beginning of this period, but figured documentation becomes plentiful and detailed in Assyrian palace reliefs from the time of Ashurnasirpal II (883–859 B.C.) through that of Ashurbanipal (668–630 B.C.), with the exception of a gap of 75 years between Shalmaneser III and Tiglath-Pileser III, i.e., from ca 824 to 745 B.C.

Ninth-century reliefs show both Assyrian and enemy chariot boxes as having D-shaped floor plans and solid sidings of approximately hip height at front and sides (fig. 5). They usually carry a crew of two abreast; in royal chariots and occasionally in those of officials a 3rd-man shield bearer is shown standing at the rear and holding on by a special loop handgrip. The shield often shown in profile at the rear of the box is suspended from a standing hoop here, as illustrated on a later (7th–6th century) terracotta chariot model from the Levant (cf. Littauer and Crouwel 1979, fig. 60). Cypriot models and actual chariot remains (8th–7th century B.C.) show that this hoop,

Fig. 5. Detail of stone relief of Ashurnasirpal II, Nimrud. After Littauer and
Crouwel 1979, fig. 53.

which was also used as a handgrip in mounting, forms the rear support of an element dividing the box in two, front to rear.

Six- or (in the case of enemy chariots) 8-spoked wheels revolve
on an axle fixed at the rear of the floor. They appear somewhat
smaller and of heavier construction than in the previous period.
Felloes are composite, with what is either a wide second felloe or
wooden tyre in sections forming the exterior element.

Ninth-century Assyrian draught poles appear to be of the Y-pole
type that is documented by some later chariot models from Cyprus
and the Levant. The Y-pole is formed of two poles, one coming
from either side of the vehicle, bent inwards to meet a short distance ahead of the box and run contiguously to the yoke. This construction strengthens the draught system and provides greater support
for the vehicle. The pole support/breastwork brace of the previous
period now appears to have changed to a metal rod. A peapod-
shaped element running from the top front of the chariot box to

the area of pole-and-yoke junction may help to strengthen the draught system, and it perhaps also functions as a case for a spare bow.

Draught teams consist usually of three, but occasionally of two or of four horses – the number clearly indicated by the meticulous rendering of the number of reins. Only two horses are under yoke (still with yoke saddles), the third and fourth animals being outriggers. Control is by bitted bridle, with bits that function largely on the same principles as those of the previous period. The chariot still appears to function as a fast, mobile, firing platform, flanking, harassing and pursuing. Since the extra team horses, when present, are not under yoke, but only outriggers, the vehicle remains quite manoeuvrable. Crossed quivers fixed to the outside of the box con-

Fig. 6. Detail of stone relief of Ashurbanipal, Nineveh. After Littauer and Crouwel 1979, fig. 56.

tain bows, arrows and sometimes axes, and a short spear is carried at the rear, the latter two (close-range) weapons being for use dismounted or from a standing chariot, as is probably the shield carried at the rear. Both crew and horses may wear protective armour.

At least by the time of Tiglath-Pileser III (745–727 B.C.) there is figured evidence of a considerably changed chariot. The box appears now to have a rectangular floor plan and a higher siding and is gradually becoming large enough so that, by the reign of Ashurbanipal (668–630), it will regularly accommodate a 4-man crew (two and two abreast) (fig. 6: detail of stone relief of Ashurbanipal, Nineveh. After Littauer and Crouwel 1979, fig. 56).

Handgrips are added to the upper rear corners of the siding. Axles, as in previous period, are at rear. Wheels are somewhat larger again and are 8-spoked, with an inner felloe and either a wide outer felloe or a wooden tyre in two abutting sections held together by metal clamps.

Draught poles of Assyrian chariots appear to be single once more. From Cyprus there is material and pictorial evidence for the widespread use of two poles, each formed by the prolongation of one side of the floor frame.

Draught teams consist predominantly of four horses – in Assyria under a single 4-horse yoke, while the two poles of Cypriot chariots run out either to a single 4-horse yoke or (more frequently) to two 2-horse ones. Yokes are usually shaped into bays – one for the neck of each horse – and yoke saddles are no longer in use.

Control continues by bitted bridle, the bits have snaffle mouthpieces of varying degrees of severity, and the usually barlike cheekpieces vary also in their size and manner of connection with the mouthpieces. By the time of Tiglath-Pileser III reins are combined in a manner to reduce their number, so that four horses are controlled by only six reins. These pass trough terrets set between the bays of the yoke.

Assyrian chariots of the later 8th and the 7th century B.C. still appear primarily as firing platforms for archers, although less mobile than before as a result of increased size, heavier construction, and the limitations on manoeuvrability imposed by four horses under yoke. Although still shown traditionally launched at speed after a fleeing enemy, we now for the first time (under Ashurbanipal, cf. fig. 6) see archers shooting from stationary chariots, together with slingers on foot and mounted bowmen. Mounted troops are by now largely taking over the traditional role of the light, fast chariotry. The diminished importance of manoeuvrability is reflected in the absence on the cheekpieces of bits of the studs that had once been a means of enforcing directional control.

Quivers are now carried vertically outside either front corner of the box. If other weapons are carried, they are inside it. The chariot box may be armoured (under Tiglath-Pileser III) and crew and horses often wear protective armour. Increased concern for protection is apparent in the presence of *two* shield bearers standing behind driver and archer – first under Sargon II, then regularly under Ashurbanipal (fig. 6).

The chariots of other peoples in the Near East during this time, as illustrated e.g., on Neo-Hittite reliefs, Urartian bronzes or Levantine ivories, often appear to resemble closely the Assyrian ones, and they likewise carry archers. Differences, however, may also be noted, such as the two poles that are found in Cyprus and that would make chariots even less manoeuvrable than the Assyrian single-poled ones with four horses under yoke.

§ 6. Later Ist mill. B.C. (c. 612–330 B.C.). What little information there is concerning unquestionably military chariots during the period between the fall of the Assyrian empire and that of the Achaemenid one comes mainly from classical (i.e. Greek and Latin) texts. There are no actual remains, and much of the pictorial evidence is ambiguous.

No Persian war chariot of the type described by classical authors (very highsided, armoured and with scythed axles and wheels) is anywhere depicted, and what is shown may be rather traditional hunting and processional chariots. Cypriot terracotta models (at least one of which is from a firm 6th-century B.C. context) show a somewhat different type of war chariot.

We may assume the rectangular floor plan indicated for other chariots, as well as solid sidings strengthened sometimes by visible struts, and a handgrip of some kind (raised, reserved or a hanging loop) at each rear corner.

Axles appear in various positions, from fully rear to beneath centre of box – the latter only on small surfaces where the position may be dictated by exigencies of space. Wheels show 6 to 12 spokes, often decoratively carved near their centres. Felloes are composite, with either an outer felloe or wooden tyre forming the exterior element, and treads may be hobnailed.

Models in the round attest the use of both the Y-pole and 2 poles. On two-dimensional representations the type of pole is uncertain. Draught teams consist of 2 or 4 horses. Quadrigae with 2 poles have either a single 4-horse yoke or two-2-horse ones – both arrangements documented on two gold models from the Oxus Treasure and on terracotta models from Cyprus – either system severely limiting manoeuvrability.

Control continues by bitted bridle – the usual type of bit now emphasizing braking rather than directional control.

Classical authors suggest a changed role for the war chariot under the Achaemenids. It is no longer a mobile firing platform but rather, with its scythed axle and wheels and its high armoured box, an engine launched directly against enemy lines. Only Cypriot terracotta chariot models carrying driver and archer with one or two shield-bearers standing behind them continue the traditional role of chariots as firing platforms. That the objectives of the new military chariots in the Near East – to terrify and break up the enemy's battle formation – were only partly successful seems proven by history. The new – and final – role of the military chariot was the result of the steadily increasing importance of mounted troops. These, with their superior mobility, their ability to function in rugged terrain and their economy in man and animal power and material, had not only assumed the functions of the old light chariotry, but had surpassed it in these respects.

Representations: Dalton 1964, fig. 21, pl. IV; Frankfort 1939a; pl. XXXVII: d, n; Littauer and Crouwel 1977c (terracotta model from Meniko); Schmidt 1953, pls. 53, 32: A–B, 48: A–B. *Texts (and use)*: Xenophon, *Anabasis* I, 7. 10–12, 8. 10, 20. Arrian III, 8.6, II. 6–7, 13.5–6; Vigneron 1968, 227ff. – *General surveys*: Hančar 1955 – Littauer and Crouwel 1979; Nagel 1966; Nuoffer 1904; Spruytte 1977; 1983; Studniczka 1907; Yadin 1963. *Texts*: Salonen 1951; 1956. – *Horse bits*: Potratz 1966.

3. THE VULTURE STELA AND AN EARLY TYPE
OF TWO-WHEELED VEHICLE*

M. A. LITTAUER AND J. H. CROUWEL

This note is to reconsider points in the restoration of the mythological scene in Mme Marie-Thérèse Barrelet's very stimulating discussion of the Vulture Stela in JNES 29, 1970, 233–258: the interpretation of the vehicle, and the resulting position and proportions of the figure therein, as well as the nature of the team (p. 255, fig. 15).[1] We are led to do this because we believe that these were founded on a mis-understanding of the basic form of the vehicle in use.

A charioteer's garment overlapping the breastwork and touching the pole, as in fig. 15, is unique in Mesopotamian iconography. Mme Barrelet has, however, argued convincingly (249–251) that the smooth curved area that we see to the left of the pole on the mythological side of fragment F (p. 15, fig. 2f) represents a dress similar to that worn by the large figure on fragments D and E; and it would indeed be very difficult to see in it any part of a front breastwork – the only alternative. The diagonal line running across this garment, however, represents, it seems to us, not the handle of a lance, as suggested by Mme Barrelet, but of a goad, such as is aimed at the rump of the draft animal in fig. 9d, and as is carried by the drivers of the two forward wagons in the lower register of the Ur "Standard."[2] We shall later return to this point.

Mme Barrelet is also surely correct that the presence of this gar-ment in this position is more apt to indicate a two-wheeler than a four-wheeler. And it would be likely to be a variant of the most common type of two-wheeler depicted in this period. This is the "char chevalet" of des Noëttes,[3] Nagel's "Deichselbockwagen,"[4] and

---

* *Journal of Near Eastern Studies* 32, 1973, 324–329.
[1] All references herein to figures or plates without further qualification should be taken as referring to those in Mme Barrelet's article.
[2] Strommenger and Hirmer 1964, pl. 72.
[3] Lefebvre des Noëttes 1931, 28.
[4] Nagel 1966, 3 and 5. Of Nagel's four types listed on p. 5, nos. 1. 3. 4 are all

Fig. 1. Drawing of a straddle car from Tell Agrab. After Frankfort 1943, pl. 60d.

what the present writers would like to call a "straddle car." On this, the driver sits astride or stands astride the pole or pole casing, with a foot on either side, as he does in fig. 14b. This fact is confirmed by two circumstantially detailed models in the round – one early and one late – the Early Dynastic copper model from Tell Agrab (our fig. 1)[5] and the Elamite bronze model from Susa in the Louvre.[6] Despite the fact that the later model must have had a curved, instead of a straight pole, that it has a different breastwork, and a rear upright totally lacking on the earlier example, these vehicles functioned on the same principle. This was a most ingenious conveyance, which required a minimum of superstructure (although later, more "luxurious" examples may have added it), and which combined the advantages of central and rear axle. The driver's feet were place on two treads just in front of the axle (our fig. 1). At slow gaits or in smooth going he could sit, thus keeping his weight over the axle

constructed on the same principle and vary merely in the superstructure and the angle of the pole.
[5] Frankfort 1943, 12f., pls. 58–60.
[6] Contenau 1931, figs. 609f.; Salonen 1951, pl. 20. (Contenau's and Salonen's two views of this vehicle illustrate this peculiar feature better than some larger and more recent photographs.)

and off the team; at fast gaits or in rough going, or to cast a javelin, he could stand – and in a position that placed his weight ahead of the fulcrum, thus increasing the stability of the vehicle. At speed, he would not only stand, as he did in other springless vehicles, to absorb the shocks of locomotion in the springs formed by his ankle, knee, and hip joints, but also to grip the shaft between his calves or knees to strengthen his position in turns or rough going. At the same time, of course, because his weight had been transferred from the seat to his feet, the center of gravity of the vehicle was lowered, and the latter became more stable. To stand on the seat of such a vehicle would be to negate all its advantages. This would be a rather precarious tour de force on cars with flat seats, such as those mentioned, and this type of car often has a deep saddle seat, on which it would be even more difficult to stand (fig. 9a).[7] It was these considerations that led us to doubt whether the original mythological side of the stela could have depicted a charioteer in the position in which he is shown in fig. 15.

Mme Barrelet, however, believes that the area on which the figure is standing in fig. 15 is the floor of the car. This is partly because she did not take into consideration the construction of this type of vehicle, and partly because she based her restoration on a misleadingly erroneous drawing of the sealing from Ur (fig. 9d). A comparison of the drawing with a photograph of the sealing (our pl. 2) shows that the modern draftsmen who drew the interpretation (reproduced also in Salonen[8] and Nagel[9]) not only did not comprehend the vehicle he was trying to render, but also was so careless that he reproduced a chip in the sealing in the wrong place. He created a horizontal floor to the car, where there was none, decorated this with imagined verticals, hung an incomprehensible loop under the front of it, and placed two invisible feet on top of it. He added two vertical lines to the center of a charioteer's garment, made incorrectly wide. A more accurate, although still not perfect, drawing is in Amiet,[10] which is copied by Potratz.[11] The inaccuracy in the latter, crucial for our subject, is dropping the saddle seat too low, in an area that on the original is covered by the lower skirt of the

[7] Frankfort 1939b, pl. 109c.
[8] Salonen 1951, pl. 13, 1.
[9] Nagel 1966, fig. 9.
[10] Amiet 1961, pl. 96, no. 1260.
[11] Potratz 1966, fig. 5c.

driver. He is standing *athwart* a low saddle seat. This is simply another example of the straddle car. The rider's feet, although invisible, would be slightly above and ahead of the axle, and his proportions accordingly would be quite different from those shown on fig. 9d.

The driver of the winged felid in fig. 14b is also standing athwart a straddle car and his feet are about halfway between the axle and the rim of the wheel.

The possibility that the vehicle shown on the stela was the other type of two-wheeler – the platform car – seems unlikely. This type, so familiar from the numerous fragments of Old Babylonian votive models,[12] is represented only twice in the Early Dynastic period: once on the fragment of a steatite vase found in Sin Temple IX in Khafajah,[13] and once on an Early Dynastic I or II terra cotta group from Kiš.[14] While the relief on the vase does show the feet of the driver, and in this constitutes an exception among Early Dynastic representations of two-wheelers, it is an extremely primitive piece of work, in which the artist may well be showing what he knew was there rather than what would actually be visible to the eye. The model in the round from Kiš shows that the floor was not raised high above the axle on this type, and that in a true profile view the feet would have been obscured by the wheel.

The space left above what seems to be the figure's waistline on fragment F (pl. 15, fig. 2f) sets a limit on how far his feet can be dropped to place them nearer the axle. With a vehicle on a ground line as low as that in fig. 15, the necessary lengthening of the lower body would entail considerable departure from the proportions proposed by Mme Barrelet. A raising of the ground line, however, combined with a slight increase in stature in *both* figures in fig. 15 might result in setting the facing figure on the ground line, which would make it more consistent with what is known of other figures on the stela, none of which are standing on a void. We wonder if Mme Barrelet would consider this possibility. In such circumstances, however, the felid's wings would be raised to a height level with, or above, the arch of the pole, and they would appear on fragment F, which they do not – a fact to which we shall return.

---

[12] Barrelet 1968, pl. 11, figs. 115–118; pl. 52, figs. 549–553; pls. 58 and 59, figs. 614–627; pl. 71, figs. 740–742.
[13] Delougaz and Lloyd 1942, fig. 63.
[14] Langdon and Watelin 1934, pl. 14.

A "normal" position of the driver also brings up the question of the location of the wheel in fig. 15. On the cylinder from Ur (fig. 14b) Mme Barrelet has, of course, a good example for a wheel placed far forward, but this is not the position on any of the known Early Dynastic reliefs of the straddle car (fig. 9a)[15] or even on the Ur sealing from that period (our pl. 2 and fig. 2). In the circumstantial models in metal, the position of the wheel is immediately behind the rider's feet, in both early and later periods. These would be safer examples to go by than a later, Akkadian seal, and we would therefore like to suggest moving the wheel further back.

We now come to the nature of the team. Mme Barrelet bases her argument for non-equid draft animals (251–54) on the fact that the *timon avec courbe* "en epingle à cheveux" (pl. 15, fig. 2f) would be impossible "entre un char et un attelage d'animaux hauts sur pattes" (such as equids) since, if continued forward and down at the angle here visible, the pole would run into the croups of such a team. In her tentative reconstructions in figs. 10a and 10b she shows how she envisages this. Had she backed the teams up somewhat, with their croups under the pole and their tails touching the wheel, as they appear on such originals as those illustrated in figs. 9a, 9b and 9h, the situation would already be partly remedied. Moreover, our pl. 3 shows that the curve of a pole might change its course; here it swings forward again to reach to the necks of a team of animals which are undeniably equids.

Mme Barrelet concedes that the winged felid that she feels would fit better under the pole is not evidenced as a draft animal before

Fig. 2. Drawing of the straddle car from the seal impression, Ur. Drawing by Mary B. Moore.

---

[15] Frankfort 1939b, pl. 192; 1943, pl. 65.

the Akkadian period. She lists four documents for fabulous animal draft at that time (p. 253). Two of these are seals (figs. 14a, 14b) showing winged felids; the third, a neo-Sumerian relief in Berlin,[16] shows animals too fragmentary to identify, and they are not winged. The fourth document probably belongs to the same relief as the third, and shows no animals, but only the lower part of a vehicle with the beginning of a pole. Because it is a double, bound pole, such as that on the mythological side of the Vulture Stela (pl. 15, fig. 2f), the author offers it as evidence for continuity of content over the centuries. But since we do not even know whether the animals on the Berlin relief are fabulous or not, and since there is not enough remaining of the pole on the historical side of the Vulture Stela (fig. 13b) to prove that it too was not double (with surely a team of equids), this would not seem to be a very strong argument.

Attention may be called to a third Akkadian document showing a winged feline draft animal, a seal in Berlin (VA 242).[17] This, like fig. 14a, shows tall wings reaching well above the highest part of the pole. Even on fig. 14b the tip of the wing is level with the crest of the pole. There is no evidence of such a thing on fragments F and C (pl. 16), and the reconstruction in fig. 15 accordingly keeps the wings lower in relation to the pole than on the originals. (On two of these documents – figs. 14a and 14b – the winged felid is surmounted by a standing goddess, for whom there would be no room at all on the stela.) All three drivers of winged felids brandish whips held high in the air, but the driver on the stela carries a goad pointing diagonally downward across his dress, as discussed above. Nor do the three examples with feline draft animals show a quiver, yet the vestiges of such seem to appear above the terret ring on fragment F (pl. 15, fig. 2f).

We feel that attention should also be called to the fact that the Early Dynastic period has furnished us with a large number of representations of draft animals; even a cursory list yields twenty-three examples: nine seals or sealings,[18] six shell or bone inlays,[19] six reliefs,[20]

---

[16] Moortgat 1967, p. 72, figs. 192f.

[17] Strommenger and Hirmer 1964, pl. 113 (third row from top).

[18] Barrelet 1970, 242, fig. 9, a-h; Amiet 1961, pl. 92, nos. 1212 and 1214; Strommenger and Hirmer 1964, pl. 64.

[19] Barrelet 1970, fig. 9b; Langdon and Watelin 1934, pl. 24, 3; Parrot 1953, pl. 69; 1956, fig. 88; Crawford 1959, 79.

[20] Barrelet 1970, fig. 9a; Frankfort 1943, pls. 65 and 67d; Frankfort 1939b, pl. 107, no. 187 and pl. 108, no. 188; for the privilege of seeing photos of a sixth

one copper model,[21] and one vase painting.[22] Is there no significance to the fact that not one of these is a winged felid?

As to the composition of the team, it may be suggested that on as important a work as this, and one on this scale, it would be accurately shown as consisting of four, or at least two, animals. All the reliefs and the shell or bone inlays, the copper model, and the vase painting depict full teams. Paired draft was essential to the pole-and-yoke system of harnessing. It is only in the miniature technique of the seals that we find the *pars pro toto* formula of the single animal. It seems likely, therefore, that whatever species pulled the stela car would have been represented as a team.[23] A glance at figs. 9a and 9b will show that the manner of indicating this – by closely overlapping figures – took up singularly little room, and would be possible in the space available on the stela – particularly if the wheel and the team were moved back somewhat.

These suggestions were inspired by Mme Barrelet's extremely careful and thought-provoking restoration of the Vulture Stela, and we hope that they may contribute something to one particular aspect of this.

---

plaque, excavated by the Oriental Institute of the University of Chicago in level VII B of the Inanna temple at Nippur, and now in Baghdad (Cat. no. 7N 104), we are indebted to the kindness of Dr. Donald P. Hansen.

[21] Frankfort 1943, pls. 58–60.

[22] Delougaz 1952, pls. 62 and 138.

[23] In n. 4, p. 254, Mme Barrelet suggests as prototype a large model "sacred chariot" with fabulous draft, kept in a temple. She cites Civil 1968, 3, for evidence. Yet Civil himself on p. 7 translates this passage relating to the draft as "donkeys" under a "yoke"—which means at least a *pair* of *nonfabulous* animals.

4. THE ORIGIN OF THE TRUE CHARIOT*

M. A. LITTAUER AND J. H. CROUWEL

Early spoked wheels in the steppes

The spoked wheel, together with horse draught and the bitted bridle, are usually considered the essentials of the war, hunting and
(later) racing chariot, but it can be shown that these features alone
are not enough.[1] The recent calibrated radiocarbon dating to c. 2000–
1800 B.C. of light, horse-drawn vehicles from Sintashta and Krivoe
Ozero, in northern Kazakhstan just east of the Urals, has revived
the claim that the chariot originated in the steppe area rather than
somewhere in the Near East (Gening et al. 1992; Kuzmina 1994,
163–457; Anthony 1995, 561f.; Anthony and Vinogradov 1985). The
burials from which the northern datings come contain the remains
of horses and the bone cheekpieces of soft-mouthed bits; of the vehicles there are in most cases only the impressions of their two, spoked
wheels as placed standing in the graves (pl. 4). The earliest southern documentation is provided by cylinder-seal impressions from the
time of Kārum II at Kültepe, central Anatolia, usually dated to the
early 2nd millennium B.C. (fig. 1), and by a terracotta plaque from
Uruk in southern Mesopotamia, possibly of slightly later date (Littauer
and Crouwel 1979, figs. 28–30; Garelli and Collon 1975, no. 46).
The latter show equid drawn vehicles with two spoked wheels.

We do not know what superstructure the Ural vehicles had. The
soil impressions of the wheels, placed vertically in especially made
slots in the bottom of the burial chamber, when combined with the
dimensions of the chamber, give two basic measurements: the wheel-
track or gauge (the distance between the wheels, 120 cm.) and the
maximum length of the nave (20 cm.). As explained later, these
dimensions would render the vehicle impractical at speed and limit

---

* *Antiquity* 70, 1996, 934–939.
[1] The chariot may be defined as a light, fast, usually horse drawn vehicle with
two spoked wheels; its crew usually stood.

Fig. 1. Karum II, Kültepe, detail of cylinder seal impression. After Littauer and
Crouwel 1979, fig. 29.

its manoeuvrability. These cannot yet be true chariots. The Anatolian
seal impressions and Uruk plaque show small passenger vehicles with
light railings.

Such a vehicle would have had many limitations and, in the majority of cases, been inferior to a mount. It would have been ineffectual
in herding free horses, the speed and agility of which it could not
equal; for the same reason, it would have been of little use in hunting, unless the game were driven by beaters into nets or confined
in a park, as later in the Near East and Egypt (Littauer and Crouwel
1979, 63, 95, 133). In many types of terrain such a vehicle would
have had difficulty: thick woods, soft sand, deep mud, freshly ploughed

ground, standing grain, high-grass prairie, steep or rocky terrain, bog, snow, ice. Its virtues of speed and lightness would have had no value on migration, where pack animals could have carried a bigger load. For travel, it would have been more comfortable to sit on a mount than to stand in a springless vehicle, and it would surely have been easier to replace individual horses than a team en route.

The chariot, moreover, was costly to make and to maintain, and draught teams had to be especially trained and to be matched in height and stride (Piggott 1992, 42–48). While chariotry eventually would enhance the conspicuous display of the great powers, such as Egypt or the Hittite empire, it was an adjunct of the greater military (Hofmann 1989; Schulmann 1979; Beal 1992; Littauer and Crouwel 1979, 90–94. Robert Drews [1988, chapters 5, 7; and particularly 1993, chapters 10–14] – incorrectly – assumes a prime role for chariots in the armies of Egypt, the Near East and Greece in the Late Bronze Age, eventually to be superseded by that of infantry). For warfare on the steppe, the mount would have been more suitable, as it was more comfortable for travel, and with a greater range than any vehicle of the time. If we may assume – what seems most likely in a region where the horse had been domesticated for many centuries – that the mount was well known, we may wonder what could have inspired the invention of the chariot; a stimulus other than necessity must be found.

Early wheeled vehicles in the Near East

The 3rd-millennium B.C. Near East, in contrast, had no conveyance comparable to the mounted horse, yet needed fast personal transport. Sumer, in southern Mesopotamia, consisted of a number of city-states, with a common language, religion and shrines. Industry and commerce were highly developed, as were the arts and crafts; architecture was ambitious. Literacy fostered written laws and litigation and facilitated trade. Although transport of all kinds could come downstream by river, it had to go upstream by land, and land travel was encouraged by the level terrain (Postgate 1994).

Neither local equid was (for different reasons) a successful mount. The hemione is no longer considered ever to have been domesticated beyond the degree sufficient to get hybrids with the donkey, which its greater speed and stamina made desirable (von den Driesch 1993; Postgate 1986; Zarins 1986, 180–189). The domestic donkey, because his withers are lower than his croup and because he has a low head-and-neck carriage, is a very imperfect mount: to counter the sensation of sliding forward – especially unpleasant when riding bareback – the rider retreats to the rear, near or over the croup. At slow gaits this is tolerable for rider and animal, but at speed the shocks of locomotion from the hind legs, which provide the propulsion, are uncomfortable for the rider, and the rider's pounding on its kidneys is abusive of the mount (Littauer and Crouwel 1979, 66–68).

Although pictographs representing primitive four-wheeled vehicles are known from Uruk of the later 4th millennium B.C., it is not until c. 2800 B.C. that detailed representations of both two- and four-wheeled vehicles appear in Mesopotamia (Littauer and Crouwel 1979, chapters 4–6; Nagel 1966, 1–10). Of particular interest is the type of two-wheeler that was clearly designed as a substitute for a mount – the 'straddle car', where the single rider sits astride, as if riding an animal (fig. 2). In this case, it seems, necessity was indeed the mother of invention!

The 3rd-millennium teams shown were always of four: two equids under yoke, and two loosely attached outriggers. The outriggers would have had little pulling power and, despite their disc wheels, these small vehicles would not have needed it, the bodies being of bent wood and osier or reed – used in the making of many things in southern Mesopotamia. It would seem as if the rewards of conspicuous expenditure were already being recognized. Wheeled vehicles flourished: the 'straddle car' developed a more comfortable, saddle seat, padded by a leopard skin. Four-wheelers appear in military contexts. Wheeled vehicles are also represented as conveyances of the gods; later texts refer to 'sacred vehicles' and their 'carriage houses' as having existed already by the middle of the 3rd millennium (Civil 1968). The processional sorties of these sacred vehicles are listed, as is the food brought to them as offerings. As status symbols, wheeled vehicles were buried in rich tombs (Zarins 1986, 164–171; Littauer and Crouwel 1979, 16).

The issues: progress vs invention

The steppes also had burials with wheeled vehicles, in the Pit-Grave culture of the late 4th and 3rd millennia B.C. – ox-drawn wagons with four disc wheels. A re-examination of all the pertinent documents

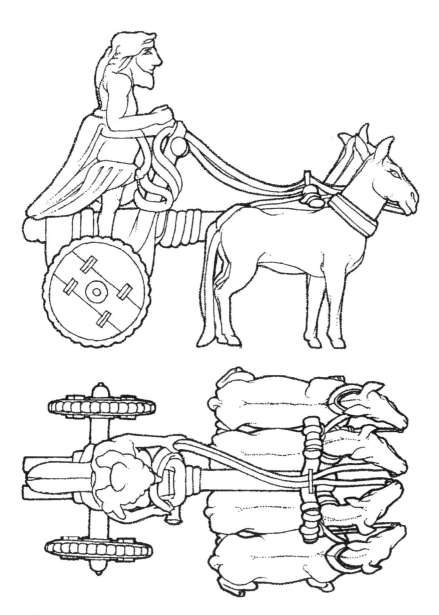

Fig. 2. Tell Agrab, copper model. After Littauer and Crouwel 1979, fig. 7.

and material forms the basis of a recent doctoral dissertation for the
Institute of Archaeology of St Petersburg by Yelena Izbitser (1993).
Several new facts have emerged. Wherever the superstructure can
be deduced, it has turned out to be rather light, and for a seated
passenger. But these vehicles would not have been fast, and their
range even more limited than that of two-wheelers. A second conclusion is more significant. Hitherto, when an irregular number of
wheels (beyond four) have been found in a few graves, it has suggested the presence also of two-wheelers. Dr. Izbitser's examination
has shown that these wheels belonged to other four-wheelers. If she
is correct in her readings, it means that no early tradition of fast
transport by two-wheeler existed on the steppe. Yet it is inconceiv-
able that the steppe tribes would not have needed fast transport and
have found a solution. The obvious one would have been the ridden horse, whether he was bridled with a bit or without one. There
is every good reason to believe that the steppes had a mount well
before the Sintashta-Petrovka vehicles appeared (Anthony 1994; 1995,
559, 561).

What also seems to emerge from Dr. Izbitser's work is that many
of the four-wheeled vehicles buried with seated passengers would
have been more suitable for processions and for burial rites than for
workaday use. These must have been ceremonial, status-conferring
vehicles.

In the Near East, however, by the later 3rd millennium B.C., fast,
single-person, equid-drawn two-wheelers had been in use for many
centuries. The domestic horse is depicted there by the 23rd–21st
centuries B.C., to judge particularly from the terracotta figurine of
a stallion recently found at Tell es-Sweyhat in Syria (Holland 1993–94,
283, fig. 111). This animal's muzzle was pierced in an area that
could only be for a bit (not a nose-ring) and he was associated with
models of wheeled vehicles. When the horse was ridden, it was still
with the 'donkey' seat, and horse-back riding continued to be considered unsuitable for the élite (Moorey 1970; Littauer and Crouwel
1979, 45–46, 65–68; Owen 1991). But an animal faster, stronger
and handsomer than the native donkey soon found his appropriate
role – in draught with that traditionally prestigious conveyance – the
wheeled vehicle.

Does it not seem more likely that the horse's introduction to draught
in the Near East stimulated the local wheelwrights to invent a lighter
wheel for the already long-existing two-wheelers than that people
without a history of two-wheeled vehicles and with an already superior

personal conveyance – the mounted horse – should find reason suddenly to invent such a vehicle in its entirety? The scenarios are one of improvement and development out of an established and very useful artefact versus one of the new creation of a superfluous artefact.

We should like to suggest that it was the prestige value of the Near Eastern two-wheelers that inspired imitations on the steppes. A Near Eastern and a steppe origin has been previously argued by the authors (Littauer and Crouwel 1979, 68–71) and by Piggott (1983, 103f.) respectively. Piggott later adopted a more cautious view (1992, 48f.; cf. also Moorey 1986). The idea of the war chariot originating on the steppes has recently been revived, chiefly on the basis of the calibrated radiocarbon dates from Sintashta and Krivoe Ozero (Anthony and Vinogradov 1995, 40f.).

'Proto-chariots'

Let us consider what is actually known of the Sintashta and Krivoe Ozero vehicles. At Sintashta, there remained only the imprints of the lower parts of the wheels in their slots in the floor of the burial chamber (fig. 1); Krivoe Ozero also preserved imprints of parts of the axle and naves. At Sintashta, the wheel tracks and their position relative to the walls of the tomb chamber limited the dimensions of the naves, hence the stability of the vehicle. Ancient naves were symmetrical, the part outside the spokes of equal length to that inside. Allowing enough room for the end of the axle arm and linch pin on the outer side of the nave and for a short spacer on the inner side of the nave end to keep it from rubbing on the body of the vehicle, we are left with no more than 20 cm. for the entire length of the nave. The shortest ancient nave of which we know on a two-wheeler is 34 cm. in length, and the great majority are 40–45 cm. (Littauer and Crouwel 1985, 76, 91). The long naves of ancient two-wheelers were required by the material used: wooden naves revolving on wooden axles cannot fit tightly, as recent metal ones do. The short, hence loosely fitting nave will have a tendency to wobble, and it was in order to reduce this that the nave was lengthened. A wobbling nave will soon damage all elements of the wheel and put all parts of the vehicle under stress. If the vehicle should hit a boulder or a tree stump, the wheel rim would lose its verticality and, so close to the side of the body, could damage that as well as itself.

The present reconstructions of the Sintashta and Krivoe Ozero vehicles above the axle level raise many doubts and questions, but one cannot argue about something for which there is no evidence (fig. 3). It is from the wheel-track measurements and the dimensions and positions of the wheels alone that we may legitimately draw conclusions and these are alone sufficient to establish that the Sintashta-Petrovka vehicles would not be manoeuvrable enough for use either in warfare or in racing.

Acknowledgements

We are grateful to Dr. D. W. Anthony and Dr. Y. Izbitser for help and information, and to Antiquity's reviewers for valuable comments and suggestions.

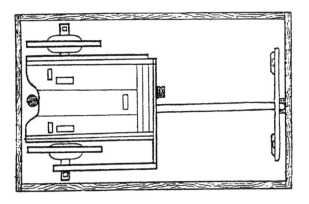

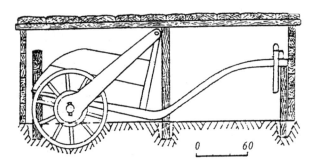

Fig. 3. Sintashta, burial 12, reconstruction of vehicle. After Gening et al. 1992, fig. 80.

5. CHARIOTS IN LATE BRONZE AGE GREECE*

M. A. LITTAUER AND J. H. CROUWEL

The long-standing debate on the military use of chariots in Late Bronze Age Greece was joined in 1973 by P. A. L. Greenhalgh. In his provocative book, he argued that Mycenaean warriors using thrusting spears had fought at speed from massed chariots. At the same time he rejected as unrealistic Homer's descriptions of chariots as conveyances for warriors who dismounted to fight on foot. These opinions were recently briefly restated in antiquity, where Dr Greenhalgh reaffirms his theory, using the well-known metal panoply from chamber tomb 12 at Dendra as additional evidence (Greenhalgh 1980). In doing so, he disregards the objections that have been raised against his position (Littauer 1977b; Anderson 1973; 1975).

To begin with the spear – since Greenhalgh rejects the throwing spear, we must consider whether a thrusting spear used 'at speed from massed chariots' is practicable. A thrusting spear is a confrontational weapon, hence would necessarily have been used directly against either enemy chariotry or foot soldiers. The absurdity of a head-on attack of chariot against chariot becomes apparent when one considers that upon contact they will not only be brought to a dead stop (thus making them no better than the despised 'taxis' to the battlefield), but that the shock could break yokes and poles and injure horses which it may have taken many months to train – one's own as well as the enemy's. And if there is a second rank of speeding chariotry, it will, of course, pile up on the rear of the first, thus being rendered useless and increasing the number of damaged vehicles and teams.

Moreover, we see that a 10-foot thrusting spear – a length suggested by Snodgrass (1967, 16f.) on the basis of the sixteenth-century Lion-Hunt dagger from a Mycenae Shaft Grave (Marinatos and Hirmer 1973, pl. L: below) – could not possibly reach an enemy in a directly facing chariot (fig. 1a). All it could do, if skillfully enough

* *Antiquity* 57, 1983, 187–192.

aimed, would be to pierce the forehead of one of the horses of the opposing team − but not soon enough to prevent collision. Even were we to postulate that a spear the length of the 18-foot Macedonian *sarissa* existed in the Late Bronze Age, it would not solve the problem; Markle's experiments with a reconstruction of this weapon have shown that it had to be held near its centre to prevent its being overbalanced to the front (Markle 1977, 324, 333).

In a confrontation of chariotries the vehicles, in order to avoid collision, would have to be spaced a chariot's width apart, which means far enough so that their wheels would not interlock with those of the opposing chariotry or their projecting axles shatter each other, and with a margin for error. The dimensions of extant late bronze age chariots found in Egypt reveal the wide track (averaging c. 1.75 m.), designed to increase the stability of such light vehicles, and the long naves (averaging c. 0.40 m.), essential to reduce the wobbling of the wheels on the wooden axles. Fig. 1 is a scale drawing based on these dimensions and those of poles, and assuming chariot animals of c. 13 hands at the most. It shows that there would have to be a distance of about 1.60 m. between the *boxes* of the two opposing chariots at their closest, i.e. when the platforms were roughly parallel (fig. 1b). But the thrusting spear is a piercing, not a slashing, weapon and is not used for sideswiping; the more direct the thrust, the more effective it is, and the more frontal the target, the more easily the latter is hit. As a result, a chariot-borne spearman would try to strike his opponent from as close to right angles as possible. The Mycenaean thrusting spears had heavy heads (Snodgrass 1964, 115ff.), and the long ones would have been two-handed. As shown on the Lion-Hunt dagger from Shaft Grave IV at Mycenae, in order to counterbalance the head, a section of the shaft protruded behind the wielder, thus diminishing the effective reach. As we see in fig. 1c, the optimum angle obtainable with a spear of this length would still not have permitted more than a glancing blow. But even these problems remain academic when we consider the difficulties in wielding (and accurately aiming) a two-handed spear in an open-backed Bronze Age chariot that is swaying and bouncing across a field of battle. (Because the draught pole was rigidly attached to both box and yoke, every up-and-down movement of the team would have been transmitted to the chariot, which would have rocked with the motion of the gallop even on level terrain.) Even without the jolt received when his spear struck home, the warrior who had no hand free to steady himself would tend to lose his balance to the rear.

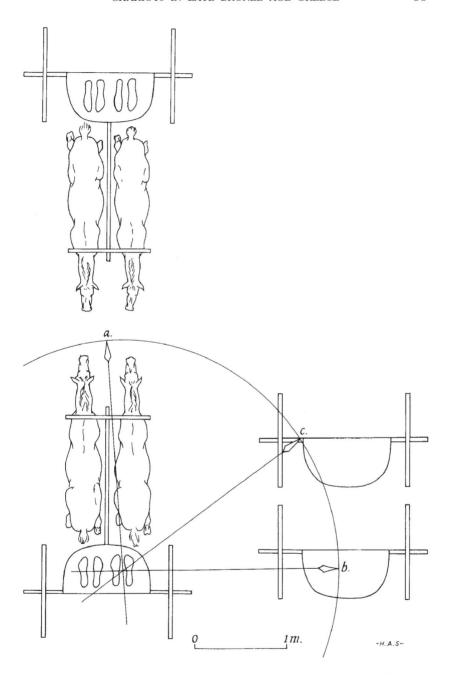

Fig. 1. Scale drawing based on the dimensions of a Late Bronze Age chariot from Egypt. See p. 54 for explanation of a, b, c.

The problem is very clearly illustrated by the example of the Egyptian two-man chariots in which the warrior is a bowman, hence also has no hand free to steady himself. The bridged reins pass around his hips and can thus prevent his sudden unintentional exit to the rear; the charioteer holds a small shield high in his left hand to protect the face and throat of the archer and steadies *himself* with his right hand on the reins ahead of the latter, in a position where he can exert directional control (Yadin 1963, 335–337; Littauer 1972, 146f.). The alternative – that chariots charged infantry – would, of course permit the use of a shorter, one-handed spear. Had the infantry panicked and run, some of it might be run down and speared from the chariot when it was alongside. Had the ranks separated to let the chariot pass through (either in panic or with foresight, as the Greek ranks separated for Darius Codomanus's scythed chariots at Arbela), the foot soldiers might also often be within striking distance. But again we have the problem of the 'speeding chariot'. If it is not to stop dead and is to speed on, the spearman will be disarmed; he will have no time to withdraw the spear from the body it has pierced (Littauer 1972, 149; Markle 1977, 334). And if he is using a two-handed spear, the shock of impact will even unsteady him enough so that his feet will be pulled out from under him by his forward-speeding chariot and he will fall backwards out of the open rear. What we know of late bronze age warfare in Egypt and the Near East tells us that the effective chariot weapon was the bow and that chariotry avoided confrontation, being used as a mobile platform from which to fire missiles, and as a fast, flanking and pursuing arm (Littauer and Crouwel 1979, 90–95).

In his article, Greenhalgh adduces the Dendra panoply's heavy metal collar or neck-guard as a 'specialized piece of equipment for chariot-borne warriors who needed neck armour in battle precisely because they could not use shields' (202). In support, he claims that the Egyptians used high-collared corselets in two-man chariots, but fails to note that these are rarely represented in actual battle scenes, while the small head shield is consistently shown. Although a neck guard appears in the scene on the chariot box of Tuthmosis IV, it is worn by an enemy charioteer whose scale corselet is transfixed by one of the arrows of the also chariot-borne pharaoh (Yadin 1963, 192, 196). Indeed, neck armour, when worn in Oriental chariot warfare, would have been a protection against volleys of arrows rather than against a single long spear. As we pointed out above, it would

have been extremely difficult for a spearman in a speeding, swaying chariot to aim with precision at a chariot-borne opponent's neck
and to reach his target with consistency. When spears are depicted
in the three-man chariots of the Hittites and their allies in Ramses
II's battle at Kadesh, it seems much more likely that they are to be
used from the ground than from moving vehicles. The spears are
never shown poised for action, and the chariot teams and crews
would be vulnerable to the arrows of the Egyptian chariot bowmen
long before they reached their ranks (Sandars 1978, fig. 10; Littauer
and Crouwel 1979, 91 with n. 74).

From Late Bronze Age Greece, Greenhalgh offers two representations as evidence of the use of thrusting spears from speeding chariots in warfare. One of these, on the fifteenth-century B.C. lentoid
seal from the Vaphio *thólos*, shows a chariot with a long-robed driver and a bare-chested spearman. (Incidentally, more is preserved of
the spearman than is shown in Greenhalgh's fig. 3; see Christopoulos
1974, ill. p. 261; Crouwel 1981, pl. 11, no. G 3.) The long spear
is held high in both hands, one arm stretched backwards to thrust
it and the other forwards to steady it, in a manner standard among
depictions of warriors and hunters on foot in Aegean art at this time.
It seems here to be merely a dramatic manner of indicating its future
use from the ground – but whether in battle or in the hunt is uncertain, since neither an enemy nor a quarry is depicted. It is unwar-
ranted to read as much into this seal as Greenhalgh does (1978, 24).
He writes of 'a chariot thundering into battle [the horses are merely
trotting] with a lancer preparing to thrust out with his long spear
as his driver closes with the enemy.' Greenhalgh's other piece of
figured evidence for the use of the spear from a chariot in battle is
on a later thirteenth to twelfth-century B.C. vase fragment from
Tiryns. The single, unarmed figure, his left hand extended to grasp
the reins and a rod-like object carried by its very butt in his right
hand, is much more suggestive of a racing driver with a goad than
of a chariot-borne spearman, who would not hold his weapon in
such a manner and who would require a driver (Schliemann 1886,
fig. 155; Crouwel 1981, pl. 64, no. V 48). The possibility of a racing driver here is reinforced by the recent publication of an indubitable racing scene on a fragmentary vase from Tiryns (Kilian 1980;
Crouwel 1981, pl. 66, no. V 51), in which the goad is indeed held
by its very end.

In connexion with spears in chariots, yet another vessel from Tiryns should be considered. This crudely drawn scene on a fragmentary krater was recently cited by Dr Kilian in this journal in a brief reaction to Greenhalgh's paper (Kilian 1982, 205 with pl. XXVI b). According to him, this thirteenth-century B.C. chariot carries 'driver, shield-bearer and armed lancer'. In fact no shield appears here (nor any other defensive or offensive arms) and what he interprets as an upright lance head is not carried by any of the three schematized humans of similar height and shape to this 'lance head' that precede it; it could as well be another passenger in whom the eye was overlooked. (Indeed, when spears are *clearly* carried in a different type of chariot in the following century, they are not held vertically, but always obliquely, and a thrusting spear that, when vertical, reached only the same height as the humans' heads, would be much too short.) Or this lance head may represent, as suggested by Rutter 1975, 378, the shaft of a parasol, the shade of which extended over the heads of all the occupants, and which would also counterindicate a military scene.

In Antiquity Greenhalgh states (203f.) that 'a lancer who is going to thrust out with a spear from a moving chariot is not going to have a free hand to manipulate a shield (and in fact none of the chariot-borne warriors on the LH III representations do carry shields as they would have done if they had been going to dismount to fight on foot in the Homeric fashion)'. The second part of this assertion overlooks the fragments of four later thirteenth to twelfth-century B.C. vases on which shields − most of them carried by spearmen − do appear in chariots (Crouwel 1981, pl. 53, no. V 18; Kilian 1982, pl. xxvii a and b). The fourth vase was illustrated by Greenhalgh in his article as fig. 2 (Crouwel 1981, Pl. 60, no. V 43; Kilian 1982, pl. xxvi a, b). Noting the corselets of the chariotborne warriors and the neck armour of one of them, Greenhalgh overlooked the shield carried by the other.

None of the warriors depicted on these or other Late Mycenaean sherds, and who carry spears, is shown fighting from the vehicles. Since there is no indication of bows, bowcases or quivers, the chariots could hardly have constituted mobile firing platforms such as the contemporary chariots in Egypt. It is more likely that these Mycenaean vehicles served merely as conveyances for warriors who would dismount to fight. This assumption is supported by representations on later thirteenth to twelfth-century B.C. vases, such as that on the famous Warrior Vase from Mycenae, of similarly armed war-

lacks verisimilitude for another reason: one does not breach the defences of a walled city with chariots, as Yadin cogently pointed out (1963, 69).

Despite the claims made by Greenhalgh, there is no convincing evidence that chariots in late bronze age Greece ever played an active role in battle, with warriors fighting *from* them, as they did in Egypt and the Near East. The only illustration of the use of the bow in a chariot – on the gold ring from Shaft Grave IV at Mycenae – is invalid as a military document, since it shows a hunting scene (Crouwel 1981, 121f., pl. 10, no. G 2). And the problems shown to be involved in attempting to use the thrusting spear from a speeding chariot would discourage such use of that weapon. On the other hand, there is no evidence that chariots were *not* used as military conveyances for warriors armed with spears and swords and/or daggers, who fought on foot in hand-to-hand combat.

6. REVIEW OF P. A. L. GREENHALGH, *EARLY GREEK WARFARE: HORSEMEN AND CHARIOTS IN THE HOMERIC AND ARCHAIC AGES*. CAMBRIDGE AND NEW YORK: CAMBRIDGE UNIVERSITY PRESS, 1973 (PP. XVI + 212; 78 ILLS. IN TEXT)*

M. A. LITTAUER

P. A. L. Greenhalgh is to be commended for having chosen controversial subject matter that still needs to be discussed, and for pursuing it with energy. He compares the Homeric use of the chariot with its "realistic" use, suggests that the chariots in Geometric art are all really racing chariots and that the chariot in Homer regularly disguises a pair of riders (knight and squire), and interprets the functions of mounted warriors as depicted on vases of the seventh and sixth centuries B.C.

The initial premise (upon which much else is built), that the thrusting spear was an appropriate weapon for massed chariot attacks at speed, cannot, in this reviewer's opinion, be sustained. Such a spear can be used only from a standing or slowly moving chariot if one hs to pull it out again after it has struck home. And at speed, if the spear were not immediately dropped, it would knock the wielder out of the shallow, backless chariot. The warrior would be particularly vulnerable with both hands engaged, as on the long Mycenaean spear; this is clearer on good photographs of the Vaphio sardonyx than in G.'s figure 2. This gem may be significant in being the only representation after the Shaft Graves of a weapon being *used* in a chariot. The spear is tilted upward, as if about to be thrown. Not only is the angle inappropriate for a thrusting spear, but too little of the shaft extends in front of the warrior's hand for the point to reach a chariot-borne opponent. It is noteworthy that the team here is only trotting, and that it trots or walks or stands in all subsequent representations, with the exception of one chariot *kratér* and of

* *Classical Philology* 72, 1970, 363–365.

Rodenwaldt's doubtful restoration of the fragmentary Mycenae mural. The Hittite spears at Kadesh seem not always even "seven feet long" (10) and, in the few cases where they are shown in use, they are held horizontally at eye level or above the head by one hand near the butt – proof that they can be neither very long nor heavy, and are there used as throwing spears. The Hittites' second spears (and there may have been more, since most spears seem not to have been incised but to have been painted in) might then be intended for use either again as throwing spears, or as thrusting spears, when and if the chariots were brought to a standstill. Yadin 1963, 109 suggests that the Hittite chariot crew was virtually a "transported or mounted infantry unit." This conclusion about Hittite practice makes one wonder about G.'s interpretation of Nestor's speech as revealing an earlier "realistic use of chariotry" (p. 7) in Greece. Certainly the statement, "Thus of old, men sacked cities and walls," is not realistic, as Yadin has elsewhere pointed out.

In chapter 2 G. persuasively sustains von Mercklin's interpretation (1909) that what look like four-wheeled vehicles in Geometric vase painting are in fact two-wheelers. But there are factual errors here. Where is the evidence for a chariot of the type G. designates as G2 (figure 6, which is represented not by "one" but by two Late Geometric sherds from Attica) in the Near East in the late eighth century? The Orient by this time had heavy closed chariots. There were *no* Egyptian chariots with "flaps" (i.e., the wings of the "dual" chariot). Again, in dismissing the type as "optimistically reconstructed" (31f.), G. overlooks the most recent and most explicit illustration of it on a sherd from Tiryns (Verdelis 1967, Beilage 34, no. 3). How "exclusive and . . . precious an object" (43) need a chariot be? Surely the noble who could afford the luxury of the three- or four-horse racing chariots postulated for the third quarter of the eighth century might have afforded a military one – and might even have granted it priority. The presence of three- and four-horse teams at this period need not be proof only of racing; they already pulled war chariots in the Orient.

The author's new contribution is the theory that the "Homeric *Hippēes*," consistently represented by Homer as chariot warrior and driver, actually consisted in the Dark Age of mounted pairs, a warrior (who dismounted to fight) and a squire. G. presents abundant pictorial evidence for such pairs from the late seventh century on, but this evidence does not extend to the Geometric period. To support his thesis, he cites the appearance of horseback riders (the majority already noted in papers by M. S. F. Hood and A. R. Schulman) in the Bronze Age. But these are casual and sporadic riders, such as one would expect to find wherever horses were used for any purpose. Even as late, however, as the thirteenth-century Egyptian reliefs which show great professional armies of the Near East, the only riders depicted are scouts, messengers, or fugitive chariot warriors, sitting sideways and recognizable by their long mail tunics that prevent them from sitting astride. Isolated armed riders need not even be military; in insecure times the privileged class has usually traveled armed. The position of the majority of these riders, seated well back on the croups of their mounts, betrays familiarity chiefly with the backs of mules or asses, where the low neck-carriage and flat withers induce one to retreat to the rear. This position is suitable for the mule's easy traveling gait, but, at a gallop, a rider on horseback would receive unsettling shocks of locomotion from the hindquarters of the animal, and the horse's kidneys would soon suffer from the pounding of the rider's weight. G.'s example of the rider on the Tell Halaf relief does show a horseman's seat, but the relief is now dated to about 900 B.C., not to the time of the "eleventh and tenth centuries" (44); and the armored rider holds the reins in his right hand and a short stick in his left, so that it is not clear what weapons he has or how he will use them. The weaponry is clear in the case of Assyrian mounted warriors of the ninth century – though these are not in fact a "very important arm alongside chariotry" (44), but still greatly inferior in numbers. These warriors always go in pairs, translated directly from the chariot: the bowman and the driver, who still holds the reins of both horses, both riders with cramped and unhorsemanlike seats. These Assyrians use the weapon they used in the chariot and, no matter how awkwardly at first, they persist in fighting mounted, thus continuing their chariot-fighting tradition. The Greek warriors shown on seventh-century vases carry light spears and do not attempt to fight from horseback, any more than did their chariot-borne ancestors of the Bronze or Iron Age who are illustrated in art and literature. And a warrior with as much armor as the Greek warrior carries was more apt to have come out of a chariot than to have started mounted.

Yadin's suggestion that the spear-armed Hittites may have functioned partly as chariot-borne infantry has already been mentioned. He also offers textual evidence that the Philistines introduced individual combat and the combat of selected groups of champions into Palestine, and suggests that they brought the custom from the Aegean (1963, 265–267). As a seasoned soldier no less than an archaeologist, he may be worth listening to.

G.'s bibliography has surprising lacunae. The omissions include such important works as Ridgeway 1905; des Noëttes 1931; Vigneron 1968; Catling 1968; Nagel 1966. For anyone using oriental chariot warfare as a criterion of Bronze Age practice, Schulman 1963 and Yadin 1963 are indispensable.

Greenhalgh's book has well-selected and plentiful illustrations, but their scale is unsatisfactorily small. It also supplies useful vase references for the material cited. It is, however, disproportionately expensive.

7. ROBERT DREWS AND THE ROLE OF CHARIOTRY IN BRONZE AGE GREECE*

M. A. LITTAUER AND J. H. CROUWEL

The ancient chariot was properly a light, fast vehicle with two, spoked wheels, drawn by horses that were yoked on either side of a draught pole, and it carried one or more standing riders. This type of vehicle continues to exercise the imagination of linguists, historians and archaeologists alike, especially in the context of the renewed interest in the Indo-Europeans, their 'homeland' and movements. The chariot has been made responsible for fundamental changes, not only in warfare but also in the socioeconomic and political organization of societies in many parts of the ancient world, extending from northern Europe and Greece to China and from the Russian steppes to Egypt. Here we shall concentrate on the role of chariots in the Bronze Age of Greece and the eastern Mediterranean, in the light of two recent books by Robert Drews: *The Coming of the Greeks. Indo-European Conquests in the Aegean and the Near East* (Princeton 1988) and *The End of the Bronze Age. Changes in Warfare and the Catastrophe ca. 1200 B.C.* (Princeton 1993).

Drews and other scholars have observed that the Shaft Graves of Mycenae, dated roughly to the 16th or 17th centuries B.C., provide the first direct – pictorial – evidence for the presence of the chariot in Greece.[1] Scholars have also pointed out the Indo-European origin of terms relating to the chariot and its parts that are reported in Linear B tablets from Knossos, written in Greek in the earlier 14th century B.C. or, alternatively, at some time during the 13th century. In the view of these scholars, the terms demonstrate that the Indo-European Greeks did not enter Greece before the chariot.[2] Indeed, Drews in chapter 8 of *The Coming of the Greeks* takes the

---

* *Oxford Journal of Archaeology* 15, 1996, 297–305.
[1] For the absolute chronology of the Shaft Graves (late MH–LH I, and extending into LH IIA), see recently Warren and Hankey 1989, 138–144, 169 (table); Butter 1993, 756 (table 2); Cline 1994, 5f. and table 2.
[2] See Wyatt 1970; Messerschmidt 1988 (cf. Raulwing 1995).

chariot to be the military means by which Indo-European invaders established themselves and their language as the first Greeks – at the time of the Shaft Graves. The hypothetical link, however, between the 'arrival of the Greeks' and that of the chariot is unsustainable on the basis of the terms in the Linear B tablets: axle, wheel and yoke were not only essential to the chariot but also to all other types of wheeled vehicle of the time.[3] At least one such type – the slow-moving four-wheeled wagon, which would have been drawn by a team of oxen, was actually known in Greece before the time of the Shaft Graves.[4]

Some of the scholars who support the theory that the Indo-Europeans brought the chariot to Greece assume they came from the north.[5] Drews would have them originate in Transcaucasia – an area which he and others regard as the 'homeland' of the Indo-Europeans.[6] But the origin of the Greek chariot is rather to be sought elsewhere in the Near East, which already had more than one type of equid-drawn two-wheeler. There we can observe a series of modifications in the construction of the body and wheels of earlier wheeled vehicles, and in the methods by which the draught teams were controlled. These modifications resulted in the establishment – early in the second millennium B.C. at the latest on present evidence – of the spoke-wheeled, horsedrawn chariot.[7] The earliest archaeological sources for the latter come from east-central Anatolia, Syria and Mesopotamia, while the first texts refer to the new type of vehicle among the Amorites, Hurrians and Hittites, the latter speaking an Indo-European language.[8] It may be noted that there is no compelling evidence for a special or unique role of Indo-European or other linguistic groups in the early development of the chariot.[9]

---

[3] See Hooker 1989, especially 63–66; cf. also Wyatt 1970, 106f. For recent discussion of the vehicular terms in the Linear B tablets, see Plath 1994a; also 1994b, 107–109.

[4] Crouwel 1981, 54–58 no. T 52 with pl. 49 (terracotta model of MM IA from Palaikastro in east Crete). Cf. the remains of terracotta groups of yoked bovids of EH II date from Tsoungiza in the northeast Peloponnese; these were probably used to pull ploughs rather than wheeled vehicles, Pullen 1992, 49–54 with figs. 1–4; Rutter 1993a, 767 with fig. 4.

[5] Nagel 1987, 174–177; Messerschmidt 1988.

[6] Following the linguists Gamkrelidze and Ivanov 1995 (and other publications); see also Renfrew 1987.

[7] Littauer and Crouwel 1979, 68–70; Moorey 1986.

[8] For early (Hittite) textual references, see Houwink ten Cate 1984, especially 57–60; Beal 1992, especially 143f., 147f., 279–282.

[9] Littauer and Crouwel 1979, 68–71; Moorey 1989; Raulwing 1995. For the

From the Near East the use of the chariot spread to Egypt, some time during the Second Intermediate period, and to other parts of the ancient world, including Greece.[10] Why was this piece of equipment so widely adopted and why did it remain in use for so long? The answer to this question has mainly to do with the vehicle's military possibilities and its prestige value. In warfare, horse-drawn chariots combined speed with manoeuvrability, provided the terrain of operation was level and open. Both the chariots and their teams of horses were susceptible of lavish decoration, thus catering to the love of display of an élite class.

There is ample documentation, particularly from the Near East and Egypt, that — under the right circumstances — the chariot (which was capable of carrying reserve arms) could perform a variety of military functions, primarily as a mobile firing platform for an archer, to run along the face of the enemy, so as to soften it up, or to play a fast flanking and pursuing role (fig. 1).[11] The chariot, however, was not only limited in its field of operation but, despite the use of scale armour by its crew as well as on its body and harness team, remained extremely vulnerable. The wounding of one horse or its laming from an obstacle-strewn field could bring the entire equipage to a standstill, thereby eliminating most of its effectiveness and making the elevated crew an easy target.[12] The chariot — a vehicle costly to manufacture and maintain, with a team and crew requiring extensive training — would of necessity have been kept for limited use: in warfare, hunting (with beaters) or in processions. It was far too light and small for goods transport, which was served by boat, pack animal or ox- or mule-drawn cart or wagon.

Drews' greatest weakness lies in his claim that chariotry became an army's primary force, and tactics then required a furious rush of massed chariots against the chariots of the enemy. Were such a manoeuvre to take place, one's own chariotry would be destroyed as well as that of the enemy. The charge would immediately result in a melée of broken legs and wheels since axles projected as much

---

contrary view, stressing the role of Indo-European groups, see recently Nagel 1987, especially 170–175; 1992, 67–81 (critically reviewed by Raulwing 1994).

[10] For a recent overview of the spread of chariots, see Piggott 1992, chapter II. For Egypt, see most recently, Hofmann 1989; Decker 1994.

[11] Littauer and Crouwel 1979, 63f., 90–94; Moorey 1986.

[12] For the limitations and risks, see Powell 1963, 159, 163f.; Littauer and Crouwel 1979, 92; 1983; Schulman 1979, 114–144. See also Piggott 1992, 45–48 (logistics of chariot-keeping).

Fig. 1. Detail of stone relief of Ramesses III from Medinet Habu. After Littauer
and Crouwel 1979, fig. 44.

as 25 cm. beyond the wheels. The chariots of both sides would have
to be very accurately spaced and able to maintain that spacing. This
would be very difficult: as soon as any horse on either side went
down, would the succeeding ranks be able to open up to avoid the
fallen and yet maintain their formation? This stricture would apply
to the open country of the Near East and Egypt and would have
been even more applicable to Greece, where the often broken terrain would have severely limited the movements of chariotry.

Drews' theory of Indo-European chariot warriors coming from
eastern Anatolia and making their way by land and sea to Thessaly
whence they continued to Mycenae, where they – as the first Greeks –
founded the Shaft Graves dynasty – is unsubstantiated. What would
have motivated a people with a large chariotry and consisting (by
Drews' estimate) of some 75,000 men, women and children (*sic*) to
leave their homes and migrate by land and sea from eastern Anatolia
to mainland Greece is never discussed. Neither are the logistics considered nor the effects on the local populations and régimes in the
areas the migrants passed through.[13]

---

[13] See also the critical comments by Hooker 1989; Dickinson 1994, 295.

The Shaft Graves of Mycenae themselves do not mark a new dynasty imposed from outside, as Drews and other scholars would have it; nor do they represent a sudden clear break with the Middle Helladic past.[14] The tombs indicate the rise of vigorous local chieftains who became a warrior élite. This rise is still not fully understood but can be observed not only at Mycenae in the northeast Peloponnese but also in other parts of mainland Greece, notably in Messenia in the southwest. The ruling families not only had close links with each other but also with the Cycladic islands, and particularly with Crete, whence much of their remarkable portable wealth and prestige goods came.[15]

If the chariot was not introduced to Mycenae by conquerors, how did it first appear there? One of us has argued in 1981 that this piece of equipment came from the Near East, quite possibly first to Crete and thence to Mycenae and elsewhere on the Greek mainland.[16] Unlike the mainland's simple communities, the Minoan palaces had long-standing peaceful contacts with their eastern counterparts. The first chariots, perhaps together with their harness teams, may well have come to the island as valued gifts between royalty, a common practice at the time. From Crete the chariot may in turn have been passed on to mainland Greece in the same way as various other pieces of military equipment: certain types of swords and daggers, thrusting spears with socketed heads, and probably also helmets and shields.

The vehicle was appropriate to the early Mycenaean warrior society, which had itself portrayed on the stelae that crowned some of the richest Shaft Graves. Apart from serving as military transport (see below), the chariot lent status to its owner, raising him literally above his fellows in a manifestation of conspicuous consumption.

Chariots were a prominent feature of the Mycenaean palace states of the 14th and 13th centuries B.C. According to the Linear B tablets, the vehicles were under the supervision of palace authorities. The latter were also responsible for the construction and maintenance of roads and bridges that were specially built to facilitate chariot circulation. The remains of such 'public' works can still be seen, particularly around Mycenae and in Messenia.[17]

---

[14] Contra Drews, and Muhly 1980: Diamant 1988.
[15] See especially Dickinson 1977, 107–110; 1989; Dietz 1991, 325f.; Graziadio 1991; Rutter 1993a, 785–797.
[16] Crouwel 1981, 148f.; cf. discussion by Piggott 1992, 58–63.
[17] Crouwel 1981, 29–31, 150. For recent studies of the roads and bridges around

How was the chariot used in warfare in Late Bronze Age Greece? According to Drews, in chapters 9 and 10 of his most recent book *The End of the Bronze Age*, it was in the same way as that described in his earlier book and discussed by us above, i.e. massed chariots charging each other – a manifestly catastrophic manoeuvre for both sides.[18] In Greece, there is no evidence for the association between the military chariot and the bow so well documented in the Near East and Egypt. Instead, chariots here functioned as a means of transport for warriors who fought not from the vehicle but on the ground with close-range weapons – a role determined to a large extent by the nature of the terrain.[19] This role, it may be noted, is exactly that described in several passages of Homer's *Iliad*, where again the bow is notably absent from the chariot.[20] In *The End of the Bronze Age* Drews argues that the dominant role of the chariot came to an end – in Greece and further east – at the time of what he calls 'the Catastrophe'. This term refers to the series of destructions by fire that struck the Mycenaean and Hittite centres and other ones in the Levant and on Cyprus in the later 13th and earlier 12th centuries B.C.[21] Rejecting other possible causes of these widespread disasters, Drews attributes them invariably to 'barbarian' raiders coming from different directions, overland or by sea. Among these invaders are the notorious 'Sea Peoples', mentioned in Egyptian royal inscriptions of the time. Drews provides hardly any discussion of the local political and socio-economic background to the various supposed invasions but concentrates on the reasons for their success: the possession

---

Mycenae and in the nearby Berbati area, see preliminary notices in *Archaeological Reports* for 1991–92 16f., for 1992–93, 18, and for 1994–95, 12; Wells, Runnels and Zangger 1990, 223–227.

[18] Following the present authors, Drews does reject the theory advanced by others that Mycenaean warriors fought with thrusting spears from moving chariots; see Greenhalgh 1973; 1980; also Kilian 1982; Höckmann 1980, 283–286; 1987, 380. 340f.

[19] Crouwel 1981, 119–145; 1992, 54f.; also Littauer 1972, 145–157; Littauer and Crouwel 1985, 190f. The only illustration of the bow in a chariot in the Aegean Bronze Age – on the gold ring from Shaft Graves IV at Mycenae – is invalid as a military document, since it shows a hunting scene (Crouwel 1981, 121f., no. G 2 with pl. 10). It may possibly point to the practice of a prepared hunt or battue in which game was driven in front of privileged individuals. It is also possible that the ring depicts no more than an attractive motif borrowed from the east.

[20] Crouwel 1981, 119–145; 1992, 54f. Cf. the view of Van Wees 1994, 9–13 and 137, 140f.

[21] In addition to Drews, see, recently, the various contributions to Deger-Jalkotzy 1983, Musti 1990, Ward and Joukowski 1992, and Karageorghis 1994; also Lehmann 1985; Liverani 1994 (correctly criticizing Drews' detailed reconstruction as being 'too mechanical and too simple, more akin to a war game than to true historical writing' – p. 242).

of superior infantry weaponry. With its help the invaders were able to overturn the balance of power and put an end to the supremacy of the chariot on the battlefield.

Changes in military equipment can indeed be observed in Greece and the eastern Mediterranean at the time.[22] They affected both offensive and defensive weaponry, including swords and spears, body armour and shields. But at least some of the new weaponry, notably the formidable Naue II cut-and-thrust sword and the smallish round shield, are already attested before the destructions – in Greece at any rate. Drews does not mention the replacement of the standard type of chariot in Greece by a new, lighter type, a change again already documented before the destructions of the palaces there.[23]

In Greece, after the collapse of the palace organization, chariots continued to be used for military purposes, albeit probably on a smaller scale. There is no evidence for a clear break in military practices due to the arrival of invaders with superior infantry weaponry. This point is well illustrated by comparing two late Mycenaean vase paintings, both probably dating to around 1100 B.C. One is the well-known Warrior Krater from Mycenae which shows files of soldiers on the march, wearing body and leg armour and helmets, while carrying shields and single spears (fig. 2).[24] The other vase painting is a fragmentary krater from nearby Tiryns, where similarly armed men are seen riding in light chariots (fig. 3).[25] All these armed men would have fought on the ground, as they had before in Greece, the chariot-borne warriors presumably being the higher-ranking ones.

Further east, Egyptian temple reliefs of the earlier 12th century B.C., followed by Assyrian palace reliefs and other Near Eastern representations of the 9th–7th centuries B.C., show chariots playing the traditional, active role in warfare, i.e. as mobile firing platforms for archers. It is from the 9th century B.C. onwards that figured and textual documents in the Near East testify to a new arm: mounted troops. With their obvious advantages in accessibility to different

---

[22] Apart from Drews, see also Rutter 1992, especially 67f. (referring to discussion in a doctoral thesis by Fortenberry 1990).

[23] The so-called Rail type replacing the 'Dual' type of chariot; see Crouwel 1981, 140, 150; 1992, 54; Karageorghis 1992, 54.

[24] Vermeule and Karageorghis 1983, no. XI. 42; Sakellarakis 1992, no. 32.

[25] See Vermeule and Karageorghis 1983, no. XI. 16; Crouwel 1981, 140f.; 1992, 54 (discussion).

Fig. 2. Detail of the Late Mycenaean Warrior Krater from Mycenae. After
Furtwängler and Loeschke 1886, pl. 42.

Fig. 3. Detail of Late Mycenaean krater from Tiryns. After Crouwel 1981, pl. 60.

kinds of terrain and in economy of man and horse power, they were increasingly to take over the military role of the chariot.[26]

Neither of Drews' two main theses can sustain close scrutiny. In his first he postulates the establishment of new rulers at Mycenae at the time of the Shaft Graves, that these came by land and sea from eastern Anatolia and that their conquest was made possible by the new and superior arm they brought with them — the chariot. His other thesis is that the 'Catastrophe' in the Aegean and further east in the decades around 1200 B.C. was caused exclusively by groups of raiders, this time equipped with new infantry weaponry. As far as we know, there was no clear and decisive break in warfare at this time, with chariotry dominant before and infantry afterwards, as Drews tries to demonstrate. Clearly, he has not realistically thought through the role of the chariot in Late Bronze Age Greece and the Near East and its consequent influence on the history of the region.[27]

---

[26] Littauer and Crouwel 1979, 128–133 (chariots), 134–139 (mounted troops); Crouwel 1987; Spruytte 1983b.

[27] We are most grateful to P. Raulwing for comments on a draft text.

8. THE MILITARY USE OF THE CHARIOT IN THE
AEGEAN IN THE LATE BRONZE AGE*

M. A. LITTAUER

Recent discoveries of representations of Cretan and Mycenaean chariots in various media have stimulated new interest in this vehicle.** Most notably, a chariot mural has been discovered at Pylos,[1] and the fragments of one from Knossos have been recognized and joined together;[2] an LH III C krater fragment, with the rendering of a chariot almost intact, has been found at Tiryns (fig. 1).[3] But no one has contributed more to our understanding than Dr. Catling.[4] Besides summarizing and setting in order much of the evidence, he has joined together two long-familiar LH III C krater fragments from Mycenae, one now in Athens[5] and the other in Nauplion,[6] and has given us something new and perhaps revealing. While most of the finds merely repeat well-known conventions, these two fragments (Catling's "No. 19"), which largely complement each other, together constitute the most circumstantial and complete picture we yet possess of the armament of the crew of that rarely depicted object – the late Mycenaean war chariot (fig. 2).

This armament is singular enough to give pause; it is, as far as the present writer knows, unique in chariot iconography. Although it would be a mistake to read too much into this single piece of

* *American Journal of Archaeology* 76, 1972, 145–157.

** The author is indebted to Professor J. K. Anderson for reading this paper in an early stage and for giving encouragement and suggestions; to Mr. Joost Crouwel (the subject of whose forthcoming dissertation is "Bronze Age Chariots in the Aegean" [cf. Crouwel 1981]) for invaluable advice and criticism and for his generosity in contributing important references; to Miss Mary B. Moore for her careful reader's eye. They are not responsible, however, for opinions expressed or errors occurring herein. Thanks are also due to Miss Moore for preparing the figures.

[1] Lang 1969, 44. 73. 74. 97, pls. 18: 26 H 64. 123: 26 H 64.
[2] Alexiou 1964 and Cameron 1967.
[3] Verdelis 1967, 26–28, suppl. 34: 3, pl. 2: 2; Vermeule 1968, fig. 37.
[4] Catling 1968.
[5] Lorimer 1950, pl. 11: 3.
[6] Wace 1949, pl. 71c; Snodgrass 1964, pl. 20.

Fig. 1. After Verdelis 1967, Beilage 34:3.

Fig. 2. After Catling 1968, pl. 23: 19–19.

evidence, and one that is, in certain respects, highly schematized, the realistically rendered, knobby, bent knees which, as Miss Lorimer noted, "suggest that the chariot is in rapid motion and that they are trying to counteract the jolting,"[7] testify to a directness and freshness of observation that gives us confidence in the "truth" of the subject matter. Moreover, the implications of this armament, considered in conjunction with some of the other Aegean chariot material, are so interesting that they may be worth considering even

---

[7] Lorimer 1950, 316.

before we have sufficient evidence to justify definitive conclusions.

Both the shields and the spears here are of great interest in connection with the chariot. What may be especially significant is that our only other example of a shield (and only one this time) being carried by the occupant of a Mycenaean chariot is also from LH III C, on the new krater sherds from Tiryns (fig. 1). The shields in figure 2, if one may judge by the charioteer, whose two arms show, are carried on telamons, but may have a handgrip, as Miss Lorimer suggested for those on the Warrior Vase.[8] Unfortunately, we know nothing of the complement of the chariot on the Shield-Bearer Vase,[9] but the warriors walking before it carry handgrip shields, as does a warrior in a fragment illustrated by Schliemann.[10] Could the telamon-slung shields in figure 2 have been carried in this manner, too? They look larger also, but size may have varied with the artist's eye.

Even more significant is the fact that two shields are not shown carried by the crews of any other Bronze Age chariots anywhere, or in any other two-man chariots at all, except those occasionally depicted much later – again in Greece – in geometric and archaic art.[11] In Egypt and the Near East, Bronze Age chariot crews wore extensive body armor;[12] only a single small or medium-sized handgrip shield was carried, held high to protect the face, for helmets were not always worn and, when they were, were open-visaged (fig. 3).[13]

---

[8] Lorimer 1950, 147.

[9] Lorimer 1950, 149, fig. 9; Åkerström 1953, 12, 13, figs. 1. 2; Benson 1961, pl. 107.

[10] Schliemann 1885, 353, fig. 153.

[11] Examples in the Geometric are rare: Davison 1961, fig. 136, and A. Snodgrass 1964, pl. 27. It seems possible, however, that both crew members may have worn shields more often than shown, but that it was difficult for the geometric artist to depict two "Dipylon" ones in the cramped space of the chariot. It may be significant that in the first of these examples both occupants are made to carry the rather rare rectangular shield, and in the second the artist squeezes both onto the chariot by making the warrior carry the rectangular shield although the charioteer wears a "Dipylon" one. Miss Lorimer mentions two warriors with Dipylon shields in a chariot on a sherd from Vrokastro (supra n. 5) 161. The archaic artists at least seem to have heard of a time when both wore shields, and they may sling a "Boeotian" one over the charioteer's back, although they give most of their chariot-borne warriors the hoplite shields of their own day: CVA Gr. Brit. IV, pl. 144: 1g; CVA U.S.A. XII, pl. 36: 2; and two important figurines: Richter 1969, pl. 326 and Mollard-Besques 1954, B 104, pl. 13.

[12] Wreszinki 1923, pl. 56a; Wreszinski 1935, pl. 104; Starr 1937–39, 475–480, 540f., pl. 126; Pritchard 1954, pl. 161; Yadin 1963, 84, 85, 196, 197, 241; Lorimer 1950, 197–199.

[13] Wreszinki 1923, pl. 56a; Wreszinski 1935, pl. 36. 104. 169; Pritchard 1954, pls. 314f., 330; Yadin 1963, 5. 88. 192f., 237. 239.

Fig. 3. After Powell 1963, fig. 39.

There is, moreover, no evidence that the Greeks ever attempted to cope with the difficulties seemingly encountered further east in *using* (as opposed to merely carrying) even one shield in a chariot. The problems arising from handling a small or medium-sized shield in a fast-moving vehicle are clearly illustrated in the figured documents. The Egyptian shield, for instance, is held up in the hand of an inactive archer advancing into battle (fig. 4) but, during the actual fighting, it is transferred to the hand of the charioteer. He sometimes merely guides the reins, which may be tied around the archer's waist or hips, the driver thus steadying himself with his right hand on the reins, while the bowman does so by being able to lean back against them (fig. 5).[14] The Hittite and allied chariots at Kadesh, whose weapons are not bows, but javelins, carry the burden of a third-man shield bearer (who holds a hand shield high up in front); thus the javelin thrower could use his spare hand to steady himself, as the shield bearer would also be able to do.[15] Even in the Iron Age, Neo-Hittite and Assyrian documents show no shields in use in *two-man* chariots. The only ninth-century Assyrian chariots to show this are *three-man* chariots, usually royal, where a special shield bearer

[14] Wreszinski 1935 pl. 137. 176; Smith 1965, fig. 120; Schulman 1962–63, 88; Littauer 1968b, 151, n. 23; Yadin 1963, 334.
[15] Gurney 1954, pl. 3; Yadin 1963, 239; Smith 1965, fig. 120.

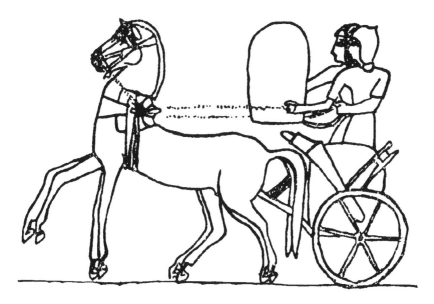

Fig. 4. After Yadin 1963, 5.

Fig. 5. After Yadin 1963, 334.

holds a shield up in front of the king's face — and this absence obtains despite the fact that the Assyrian chariotry at this period did not wear helmets.[16]

These were all shallow-bodied chariots, open at the rear, in which it cannot have been easy to maintain one's balance while moving at speed, perhaps with abrupt stops and over uneven terrain. This is testified to by the changes in design that were clearly introduced to cope with such a problem. One of these, in the Orient, was the switching of the axle to the rear. Despite the fact that this placed more weight on the horses (not less, as has sometimes been asserted), it had the advantage of giving more fore-and-aft stability to the vehicle, and reduced the danger of the occupants being thrown out by centrifugal force on turns. Another modification was the insertion on Neo-Hittite and Assyrian chariots of a front-to-back partition down the center of the body. This not only prevented the crew members from jostling each other in rough going or on turns, and gave them an extra wall to brace against, but it made it possible to attach a shield as a partial closure in the middle of the rear (fig. 6).[17] On the three-man Assyrian royal chariots of the ninth century a hanging loop is provided at the front of the chariot for use as a handhold by the shield-bearer who stands in the rear.[18]

---

[16] Barnett (n.d.), pls. 25, 142.

[17] The presence of this partition is attested on the remains of two late 8th or early 7th century chariots found in the *dromos* of Tomb 79 at Salamis in Cyprus: Karageorghis 1967b, 339, fig. 140; 1969, 80f., pls. 36 and 11. The chariots are Assyrian in type but seem to be old-fashioned, since they resemble the shallow, open Assyrian vehicle of the 9th century rather than the contemporary square, closed one. On chariot *beta* this partition was terminated at the rear by a vertical loop made of bronze tubing 50 cm. high, which formed a handhold (as appears also on many Cypriote clay models). This loop is wide enough so that a shield hung on it would rest flat against it, not swivel loosely, as it would if hung on the narrow end of one of the sides. The remains of a round shield ca 55 cm. in diameter were found near the rear of the chariot, and may well have hung on this loop, effecting a partial closing of both sides of the chariot, not merely one side. A clay model of a chariot found at Marathus in Syria, now in the Louvre, shows a round shield with a lion's head hung on the rear of this partition (Studniczka 1907, 169, fig. 17; Heuzey 1933, pl. 5). Such shields are shown in profile at the rear of chariots on early first-millennium Neo-Hittite reliefs (Bossert 1951, no. 488; Frankfort 1958, pl. 161; Pritchard 1954, no. 172), and ones with toothed projections on Assyrian chariots under Ashurnasirpal II (Barnett (n.d.), 15. 24f.; Yadin 1963, 386f.; Meyer 1965, pl. 3). The appearance of a shield in this place may be taken to indicate the presence of a back-to-front partition, although the strict profile view prevents the partition itself from appearing on the reliefs.

[18] Barnett (n.d.), pls. 14. 25; Barnett and Falkner 1962, pls. 116f. On the first of these the loop is fully seen, grasped by the shield-bearer; on the latter three the

Fig. 6. After Evans 1935, fig. 794.

The telamon-slung shields of figure 2 might seem at first glance to answer this problem of security by leaving the hands free, but, as worn, they fail to protect the face (and Mycenaean helmets were open) – one of the reasons for carrying shields in other chariotries – and, since they do not extend below the waist, they cannot protect the upper legs, which would be especially vulnerable in this peculiarly open chariot. It also seems possible that on really gusty days a pair of such shields, worn in this way, could have offered wind resistance out of all proportion to a light vehicle, such as that in figure 2, and overturned it, or at least slowed down the team.[19]

---

knuckles and thumb of the shield-bearer's right hand appear grasping a loop just above the top of the right-hand quiver.

[19] "For it [the wind] not only did many other violent things, but when he [Cleombrotus] had left Creusis with his army and was crossing the mountain ridge which runs down to the sea, it hurled down the precipice great numbers of pack-asses, baggage and all, while very many shields were snatched away from the soldiers and fell into the sea. Finally many of the men, unable to proceed with all their arms, left their shields behind here and there on the summit of the ridge, putting them down on their backs [i.e., upside down] and filling them with stones . . . on the following day they went back and recovered their shields." Xenophon, *Hellenica* 4.17–18, trans. C. L. Brownson. I wish to thank J. K. Anderson for supplying me with this reference.

The single spear is also curious. To the author's knowledge, spears appear in chariots unequivocally only three times elsewhere in Aegean art, and doubtfully twice more – always in ambiguous contexts. There is the spear that is poised and about to be thrown by the naked, apparently helmetless, figure in the trotting-horse chariot on the sardonyx from the late Shaft-Grave-period tholos at Vaphio;[20] a spear is carried horizontally over the shoulder of the charioteer himself on one and possibly on two, fragments of LH III fresco from Tiryns, which will be discussed later. An LH III terracotta chariot group from Marcopoulo in the Louvre[21] shows the second occupant of a chariot carrying what appears to be a short, thick rod across his extended arms. It is impossible to tell whether this is meant to be a lance, shortened and thickened by the exigencies of the medium, or a sword, or a *kentron* clumsily rendered – probably the latter. The one other possible LH III C example, on a sherd from Tiryns, was already identified by von Mercklin as a *kentron*. Not only does this object seem to be too light and short to be a spear, but no spear of any kind is wielded, or even carried, as this is, by its very end.[22] And we see the lower end of a spear on our also late chariot in figure 1.

The Egyptian chariot weapon was the bow (fig. 5), although javelins might be carried as auxiliary arms.[23] Two to four spears are shown carried in three-man Hittite and allied chariots in the earlier drawings of the reliefs of the battle of Kadesh.[24] Modern black-and-white photographs give very little information in this respect. The few spears to be distinguished on the Ramesseum relief seem to be both light and short – more of casting than of thrusting ones, but they may have been used for the latter purpose if the chariot was brought to a standstill.[25] On the later Neo-Hittite reliefs of two-man chari-

---

[20] Xenaki-Sakellariou 1964, no. 229; Marinatos and Hirmer 1960, pl. 211.

[21] Mollard-Besques 1954, no. Al, pl. 1.

[22] Schliemann 1885, 354. n.*, fig. 155; von Mercklin 1909, 29; Catling 1968, pl. 23, no. 22. Schliemann calls this a "couched lance," probably because it is held level, but the leveled lance was held either in two hands, as the Sassanian cataphract held it, or with the butt under the armpit (and usually on a rest) as the later medieval knight held it, and there is no evidence that it was ever used in a war chariot. Ramses III is shown using an exaggeratedly long thrusting spear when hunting the wild bull, but it is not held by the end (Breasted and Allen 1930, pl. 130).

[23] Carter and Newberry 1904, pls. 10f.; Wreszinski 1935, pl. 1. 2. 137; Pritchard 1954, nos. 314f.; Yadin 1963, 235. 240. 334f.; Schulmann 1962–63, 88.

[24] Nuoffer 1904, pl. 4; nos. 17f.

[25] Wreszinski 1935, pl. 104; Yadin 1963, 239.

ots an archer has consistently replaced the spearman, and a short, thick, thrusting spear is relegated to a sheath at the side or rear of the chariot (fig. 6),[26] as it is on Assyrian chariots, where it and the shield are presumed to be in readiness should it be necessary to fight either from a standing vehicle or dismounted.

The weapon used perforce from a fast-moving chariot is the bow or the cast spear or javelin. The short, stout, thrusting spear is practical only in a slow-moving or stationary vehicle, for once it has struck home there is no time to pull it out again if the chariot is moving on, and the user is then disarmed for fast fighting. And, as noted above, the chariots on figure 2 seem to be moving on. If this is so, their thrusting spears cannot be "poised," as suggested by Catling. As a matter of fact, the angle at which they are shown is very close to that of the shouldered spears on the Warrior Vase, while the actually poised spears in the hands of the warriors on the other side of that vase have a quite different inclination.[27] Moreover, although charioteers must be able to fight from a disabled or obstructed chariot brought to a standstill, stationary fighting is never shown as the primary method in Bronze-Age warfare.[28] A standing chariot does appear in the Iron Age in late seventh-century Assyrian battle scenes, but archers are using it as a platform from which to shoot, and it is a heavy vehicle, closed behind, with a team wearing protective housings.[29] The wide-open LH III C model would seem as unsuitable for this stationary type of fighting or for countering a wild beast attack as its armament would seem for fast, mobile work.

Beginning with the vehicles on the Standard of Ur, with their attached sheaths of javelins, most Oriental chariots conspicuously carry crossed bow-cases and quivers, lance or javelin holders. Surely one of the reasons why the costly chariot retained its role so long against cavalry was its superior ability to carry these sinews of war. Although no vehicle in the Aegean displays these,[30] it is particularly

---

[26] Bossert 1951, pl. 488; Frankfort 1958, pl. 161; Pritchard 1954, no. 172.

[27] Lorimer 1950, pl. 3: 1a, 1b; Bossert 1937, nos. 134, 135.

[28] For the use of the Bronze-Age Egyptian chariotry see Schulmann 1962–63, 84ff.

[29] Gadd 1936, pls. 34. 44; Salonen 1951, pls. 39. 41; Yadin 1963, 452; Meyer 1965, pl. 161.

[30] A quiver-bearing chariot represented on a relief band on a pot from Cyprus and classified by Catling (1968, 43, no. 7) among Minoan-Mycenaean examples, does not fall in this category, despite the Aegean character of other elements of the scene Catling and Karageorghis 1960. Kenna is surely correct here in considering the chariot, with its quiver and its rear axle, with its solitary archer-charioteer with the

surprising to find them absent from chariots manned by warriors, as on ills. 1–2, and from those in the Mycenae battle scenes.

When all these factors are taken into consideration, the question arises: if neither the chariots nor their complements here seem prepared to fight in the Oriental manner, what are they doing? Is it possible that officers are merely being transported to the forefront of battle, hence that "Homeric practice" antedated the Dark Age, to which it is often relegated – although rejected even for that period by some? If this is so, when did the "right, true use" of the war chariot in Greece cease?[31]

Dr. Catling remarked on the singular absence of weapons-bearing chariots on LH III A and B vases.[32] This circumstance is particularly curious in view of the fact that the scenes on these vases are usually considered to have been inspired by wall painting. Was the martial theme, so popular later with geometric and black-figure pot painters, for some reason taboo here? Or did the chariots as depicted in military scenes not lend themselves to vase decoration? A reexamination of the possible military chariot frescoes, which Catling did not consider in detail, and the inclusion of new material in this field may shed light on the general subject.

Our understanding of murals with chariots in possible military contexts has been based largely upon Rodenwaldt's work on the material from Tiryns and Mycenae.[33] To this we may now add Miss Lang's on that from Pylos.[34] The chariot on the Knossos mural studied by Alexiou and Cameron seems,[35] however, to have been bound on a peaceful errand. The earlier murals at Tiryns show charioteers

---

reins around his waist and something very like a Pharaonic crown on his head, as an intrusive Egyptian motif. Kenna questions only the position of the horse, remarking that Egyptian ones are always "stretched out in a stylistic gallop." Although this is the more frequent pose, we find, as early as the 18th Dynasty, examples of horses at the pace or trot in positions very similar to the one on this pot from Cyprus (Pritchard 1954, nos. 322. 328). The rear axle would place the motif no earlier than the 15th century and, if taken direct from Egypt, the 4-spoked wheel would probably put it not later than ca 1400 B.C. But 4-spoked wheels and horses at this pose are found on Egyptianizing scarabs of Palestine through to the 20th Dynasty (Amadasi 1965, figs. 6: 1. 7: 4). On this relief see also Buchanan 1966, 175f.

[31] See Anderson 1965 for late evidence of "Homeric practice," and Delebecque 1951, 86–109, Kirk 1964, 22f., Snodgrass 1964, 159–163 for the argument contra.

[32] Catling 1968, 46.

[33] Rodenwaldt 1912, 8–12. 97–106, pl. 1: 3. 4; 11: 1. 4, 6; xi: ii. xii; 1921, 24–33. 41–44. 55f., suppl. I. II. IV.

[34] Lang 1969, 44. 73. 74. 97, pls. 18. 123.

[35] Alexiou 1964 and Cameron 1967.

carrying lances – but whether for military or hunting purposes is uncertain. The murals from the Megaron at Mycenae show chariots in a war scene, but only one of these vehicles *may* be in actual action, and there is no evidence that arms were carried in any of them.

Of the two fragments from Tiryns that may depict lances carried in chariots, only the first shows enough to identify the subject; the interpretation of the second fragment as showing the same subject is based only on its similarity in other details to the first; the section where the vehicle would be is missing. In the first, the composition is unusual in that it shows the reins and *kentron* held in the right hand, while the spear is carried horizontally balanced over the left shoulder and steadied by the left hand.[36] A spear held thus over the left shoulder is not only not in a position for use (as Rodenwaldt himself remarks), but finds no parallel in either Greek or Oriental scenes. There is, of course, no shield here and, although Rodenwaldt believed he saw indications of the ends of helmet cheekpieces in the pointed chins of these men, these could as well represent beards. Thus the purpose of this armed errand is uncertain; all that is clear is that the chariots are not going into immediate action of any kind.

At Mycenae Rodenwaldt found three groups of fragments from which he was able to reconstruct chariot scenes. Among the first were pieces showing parts of an unhitched pole-and-yoke system and of three horses. Accordingly, he postulated two chariots: an unhitched one, plainly evidenced by the horseless yoke, and to which a team was perhaps being brought up (a "harnessing scene"), and because of the third horse, a second chariot – either in the same condition or already hitched.[37] Greaves on two of the standing figures here, a helmet, and sections of what are apparently lance shafts indicate a military context.

The only chariot of which there may be evidence in the siege scene proper was suggested to Rodenwaldt by the presence of a patch of reddish-brown paint along the top edge of a fragment that shows a palace roof below.[38] A warrior with bent legs appears to hurtle down between the two, and Rodenwaldt believed he was supposed to be falling from a chariot passing above (or beyond) the

---

[36] Rodenwaldt 1912, 8f., pl. 1: 3, 4.
[37] Rodenwaldt 1921, 24–29.
[38] Rodenwaldt 1921, 32f. 55f., suppl. II; Sakellariou 1957, pl. Da–b; Vermeule 1964, pl. 31A.

palace tower – the patch of red paint being part of the belly of a horse (fig. 7). But W. Stevenson Smith has pointed out that in the Abu Simbel relief of the battle of Kadesh, where Rodenwaldt thought he had found the model for this group, the warrior was actually being tossed out *upward* from a chariot, not falling headlong *down* from one.[39] His chariot had been forced to an abrupt halt (by Egyptian *arrows*), which accounts for his having been pitched out forward. A body falling from an object moving at speed, however, as the chariot at Mycenae must be doing if Rodenwaldt's inference (based on the line of a galloping horse's belly) is correct, falls *behind* it, not in front, as on this reconstruction. Such a rendering would imply on the part of the artist a lack of the most elementary sense of how moving bodies function.

It was the fact that the curving lower edge of the fragment of reddish paint recalled to Rodenwaldt the lines of the belly of one of the horses at the "flying gallop" on the gold ring from Shaft Grave IV that led him to assume that here, too, were horses in this position and, by inference, pulling a chariot. But *horses* at the true flying gallop are singularly rare in the Aegean. They occur, harnessed to a chariot, on the gold ring mentioned, and, running at liberty, on the blade of a dagger from Shaft Grave V – both of an earlier period.[40] They may also appear on a part of the Boar Hunt mural at Tiryns. These Tiryns fragments, which show what may be the tails and hindquarters of horses at the flying gallop are, on Rodenwaldt's own admission, a very garbled rendering of this subject – if that is what it is. The "hindlegs" and chariot pole appear on one side of a tree trunk, the "tails" on the other. Rodenwaldt believed that a fragment with horses' heads belonged with these, and, on the basis of the angle of the necks to the reins, he judged the heads to be stretched out, as are the heads and necks of horses at a gallop. His standing horse at Mycenae, however, shows the same

[39] Smith 1965, 84, fig. 120. If one must find an Egyptian inspiration for such a scene, the Siege of Tabor by Ramses II on the Ramesseum at Thebes offers more plausible parallels, with men falling from the central tower: Evans 1921–35, 87, 104, fig. 58; Wreszinski 1935, 107–109; Yadin 1963, 229.

[40] Karo 1930, pls. 24, no. 240; 86, no. 748. The horses on the grave stelai at Mycenae are not moving at the flying gallop but at the much commoner *calabré allongé*, Reinach's position g: Reinach 1901, 6f., fig. 1. The ivory gaming box from Enkomi that does display a team at the flying gallop is not considered to be of true Aegean manufacture: Barnett 1939, 11; Kantor 1947, 93.

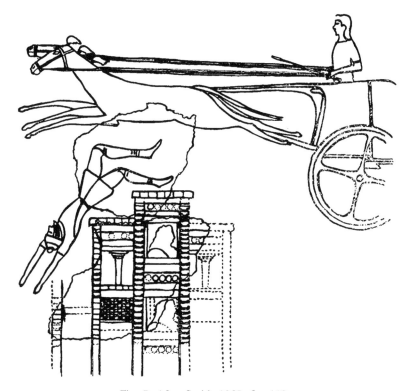

Fig. 7. After Smith 1965, fig. 118.

relation of neck to reins in the reconstruction, and the telling angle, that of the head to the ground, remains unestablished at Tiryns.[41]

Rodenwaldt admits being puzzled by the absence of any girth in the tower scene, although precisely that area of the belly where there should have been one was preserved. This is the more curious in a mural that elsewhere shows many details of harnessing (pole, pole-stay and yoke). Rodenwaldt's explanation – that the horses on the Shaft-Grave ring displayed no girth either – shows how strongly he was under the influence of that much earlier object, which, however, gives no details of harness at all.[42]

Careful examination of the original remains of the palace-tower scene leads to the conclusion that, at least today, there is nothing beyond a fragmentary contour to suggest a horse.

[41] Rodenwaldt 1912, 104f., pl. 41f.; 1921, Suppl. I. The reins in the Mycenae group are not actually present on the remaining fragments.
[42] Rodenwaldt 1921, 33.

Fragments of fresco with two other chariots in a military context were found at Mycenae.[43] The first is sufficiently intact to indicate a chariot at a standstill or moving slowly. Of the charioteer only enough remains to show an unbelted chiton. As he is placed, there would seem to be no room for another occupant, and the group has been reconstructed with one figure. Of the second chariot, much of the wheel and of the lower part of the box, as well as the two hind legs of the team remain. The vehicle is at a standstill. There is no clue to its crew. Immediately behind it, however, appear the greaved legs of a crouching figure facing in the opposite direction. Rodenwaldt interprets this figure as a warrior who had just jumped down from the chariot, hence he reconstructs the vehicle with only a driver.

In conclusion, Rodenwaldt suggests that "Zwei verschiedene Kampfwesen treten uns entgegen: man kämpft entweder vom Wagen herab oder man springt herab und lässt den Wagen halten."[44] The first of these conclusions is based on the, as we have seen, very questionable interpretation of a swiftly moving chariot in the Siege Scene. Of the second Rodenwaldt himself suggested that it illustrated fighting in the "Homeric" manner.[45] This premise would be easier to accept if the figure who, according to Rodenwaldt, has just stepped from the chariot, had not been restored by him as a virtually unarmored archer. Not only does the bow play hardly any role in Homer but, as a long-distance arm, it is the weapon *par excellence* of the chariot fighter, whose mobility and elevated position gives him an advantage in the use of it. Why should he prefer to fight "dismounted"? Moreover, there is no evidence of bows or quivers on any of the Mycenae fresco fragments. Rodenwaldt explained that he restored this figure as an archer because the only parallel that he could find in Aegean art for the position of the legs was in that of the bowman on the Lion-Hunt dagger.[46] But is not this reading this object a bit too meticulously? The forward legs of the spearmen here are bent in a similar manner at the knee, and this bending of the front knee involves a bending of the rear one – whether it is depicted thus on the Hunt dagger or not; one has only to try for oneself. If we could give this figure a spear instead of the postulated bow, he would

---

[43] Rodenwaldt 1921, 41–43, suppl. IV.
[44] Rodenwaldt 1921, 43.
[45] Rodenwaldt 1911, 246.
[46] Karo 1930, pl. 44, no. 394; Rodenwaldt 1921, 42; Marinatos and Hirmer 1960, pl. 36.

be more in line with "Homeric" and/or actual practice, as well as using a weapon of which there is evidence in the murals themselves and which does appear in the hands of warriors in the chariots of ills. 1 and 2. Greaves are shown on the man's legs, and it seems unlikely that he should be wearing this accessory armor without any more basic protection. If we restore the figure with a helmet and a spear, like the "standing officer,"[47] we shall have something more in the nature of either a Homeric "hero" or a real Mycenaean officer. And now his chariot, already headed towards the rear and waiting to convey him to safety should he be wounded, makes more sense.

Among the newly-published murals from Pylos we are fortunate to have a chariot in a military context. It serves only to reinforce the impression of the static role of the Mycenaean war chariot.[48] There seems to be no question of a second occupant in the vehicle, and the team is either moving slowly or standing still. Miss Lang comments on the very poor state of preservation of the fragments. Hence it may be wondered whether two unusual features of de Jong's restoration – a charioteer's chiton so short it ends somewhat above the chariot's side, and upward billowing reins are accurate. These would not, however, alter the interpretation of the scene.

Thus the only solidly substantiated military function of the chariot in any of these murals is "standing by." Although the Tiryns charioteers with lances over their left shoulders may be setting out to war, they may also be setting out to hunt, which is more likely if they are alone, as they appear to be, in their chariots. We have, unfortunately, only a tiny fraction of the Mycenae and Pylos battle scenes, but the chariots that we do see on them are behaving in a manner unparalleled in scenes of eastern warfare. This must mean either that they, were actually used in this fashion in mainland Greece or that chariots were not in military use there at the time but that tales in which they were used in a "Homeric manner" were already potent legends.

The Knossos and Pylos tablets give the lie to the second alternative. Chariots were in use and, at Knossos anyway, were associated with corselets, which are a type of protective armor probably devised especially for chariotry.[49]

---

[47] Rodenwaldt 1921, suppl. 1, 7.
[48] Lang 1969, 73f., 74, 97. pls. 18, 123.
[49] Evans 1935, 786–806; Ventris and Chadwick 1971, 361–375.

The corselet, as we know it from the Dendra tomb,[50] from the Knossos and Pylos ideograms,[51] and from the number of plates listed, is neither the sleeveless, waist-length, close-fitting, body armor that went by that name for archaic and classical times and for our rather recent European past, nor the very long, flexible, short-sleeved, fitted tunic, made up of many small scales, that was worn by the chariotry of Egypt and the Near East.[52] It is a cumbersome, tubular garment, composed of wide segments of bronze, which almost looks as though it could have been inspired by Minoan flounced skirts. It probably extended to the knees. Greaves, which seem to have been an Aegean invention, may perhaps be seen as its complement.[53]

This clumsy armor cannot have been designed for infantry, and points clearly to the use of the chariot – but whether for large-scale fast deployment in the Oriental manner, or simply for bringing officers or nobles to the forefront of battle is not indicated by its form. The sheer numbers of chariots recorded at Knossos (over 500)[54] would indicate the former (if they were to be used all at once, which seems doubtful), although still not on a scale comparable to that of much Near Eastern warfare. But in the absence of any confirmation of this use in the fourteenth and thirteenth centuries, we may tentatively suggest an alternative for this latter period. Not only is much of Greek terrain highly unsuitable for chariot manoeuvres in the Oriental manner, but an area like the Peloponnese which, as we now know, had a fairly dense population in LH III times,[55] might have found it difficult to support the numbers of non-meat-and-milk-producing animals required for this. Yadin has noted that, although the Bronze Age chariot teams were bigae, the proportion of horses to chariots captured was often 3:1;[56] reserve horses may have accompanied the chariotry. Would not the hundreds of horses required to

---

[50] Vanderpool 1963, 280f., pl. 62; Snodgrass 1967, 24, pl. 9; 1965. Verdelis 1967, 8–16, suppl. 10–17.

[51] Evans 1935, 803–806; Ventris and Chadwick 1971, 375–381.

[52] See supra n. 12.

[53] Lang 1969, 45 suggests that because greaves appear also to be worn in non-military contexts, they may be thought of more as a defense "against the ferocity of the Greek undergrowth . . . than as a defensive armour." But what was invented to serve a military purpose might have been adopted by civilians; this seems to be a chicken-or-egg problem.

[54] Ventris and Chadwick 1971, 371.

[55] McDonald and Hope Simpson 1961.

[56] Yadin 1963, 88f.

be kept in fighting condition, as well as those in breeding and training, have laid a heavy burden on the plains of Argos and Sparta, Messenia and Elis – a burden perhaps unwillingly borne except in times of necessity?

On the other hand, such has always been the convenience and also the prestige of a vehicle or a mount, that it is not readily relinquished by the class that has become accustomed to it. The wearer of such armor as the Dendra corselet, although he might actually fight on foot, almost certainly needed a vehicle to convey him any distance, once he was armed. This might have become so traditional that, even with the change to lighter protective armor that is evidenced for LH III B and C, the custom persisted. A pertinent parallel may be furnished by the infantry officer of the eighteenth and nineteenth centuries A.D. who, because gentlemen were once always mounted, continued to go mounted – except in action.

This would help to explain the passive role of the military chariots at Mycenae and Pylos. And, if we may judge from the fragments showing warriors, the longish, heavy body armor is already obsolete. The short, fitted tunics that the figures wear could be of leather alone or of leather or linen with small scales sewn into it, or they may be linen surcoats covering briefer, tighter corselets.[57]

We may now tentatively answer the question asked several paragraphs back as to why the chariots on kraters are not in military scenes. It may simply have been that a chariot standing by, as the mural battle chariots appear to be doing, is not an inspiring motif. Moreover, the single charioteer in these would not fill up the space over the chariot body as well as the extra one or two passengers usually present in the LH III A and LH III B krater chariots do.

Figure 2 not only displays a new style of krater painting and depicts a type of chariot which, although it may not be brand-new in itself, is fresh to the pot painter's repertory, but it chooses to represent a different moment of action. Here it is no longer a chariot standing by, as on the Mycenae frescoes, but a chariot carrying a warrior into battle. As one who expects to fight on foot, the latter carries a large shield and a stout spear and, probably because his armor is no longer so effective, the charioteer wears a shield too. By late geometric times, when human figures are again represented,

---

[57] Rodenwaldt 1921, suppl. 1. 7. III. 10. 11; Lang 1969, pls. 122: 18 H 43, 123: 26 H 64.

the shield will have been cut out into a wasp-waisted "dipylon" one. (Was this an attempt to answer the problem of air resistance – no small one in as breezy a land as Greece?)[58]

What does the position of the axle tell us, if anything, of the use of the chariot in LH III? While the central position is unvarying prior to this period, there are some surprisingly rarely-noted exceptions at this time. These are on the chariots at Mycenae and Tiryns.[59] Fragments of fresco from the pertinent areas have survived to show that at least one chariot at Tiryns and two at Mycenae had axles placed very close to the rear.[60] On the other hand, the Pylos chariot seems to show a central axle.[61] The chariot on the mural from Knossos is not in a military context, and its reconstruction with an almost central axle has been arbitrary, since the crucial parts of the fresco are missing.[62] The chariots on typical LH III A and LH III B kraters are too sketchy to read literally, but they show a variety of positions, from central to full rear, with all stages in between (fig. 8).[63] Regrettably, figure 2 does not show this part of the vehicle, nor do any of the other LH III C sherds except that in figure 1. This appears to show a wheel somewhat rear of center, but the drawing is too schematized to be reliable. In the late Geometric, when the chariot is again depicted, it has a central axle. But does this mean that the LH III C chariot had it? There is no answer. Moreover, this may be merely a convention in an art that is full of conventions, for it is followed also in black-figure at a period when we know that the axles of at least some racing chariot models found at Olympia were in the near rear or rear position.[64]

It should, however, be stressed that the switching of the axle from a near central to a near rear or rear position was not the unqualified improvement it has often been considered. It was an improvement only for a certain type of harnessing *used under certain conditions*. Because the pole was rigidly fixed to the chariot floor, any increased seesaw

---

[58] See supra n. 19.
[59] Powell 1963, 161 calls attention to the near-rear position of the axle on the Tiryns mural.
[60] Rodenwaldt 1912, pl. 40, pl. 14. 9; 1921, Suppl. IV, 15f.
[61] Lang 1969, pl. 123: 26 H 64.
[62] Alexiou 1964, Abb. 3; Cameron 1967, fig. 12.
[63] Furumark 1941, 333: motif 39.
[64] Lorimer 1950, 318f.

Fig. 8. After Furumark 1943, motif 39.

movement of the chariot, caused by driving over an obstacle or by
the rapid switching of the load consequent upon active fighting,
would be immediately transmitted to the yoke. The slackness of the
girth on Bronze Age harnessing would only increase this tendency.[65]
A switch of the load to the rear of the axle, for instance, would
cause a raising of the yoke and increase of upward pressure on the
draught animals' throats; a sudden switch to the front would cause
the yoke to bang down on the backs of their necks. With the fulcrum at the rear instead of under the center of the box, this see-
saw movement would be largely eliminated. The change of position
also reduced the stresses and strains on the areas where the chariot
floor was attached to the pole, and on the pole itself. The chariot
occupants would have a smoother ride and would be in less danger
of being tossed out to the rear by centrifugal force on rapid turns.
That these advantages applied primarily to the yoke-and-pole hitched
chariot when used in fast fighting is clear from the fact that it was
on Egyptian and Near Eastern war and hunting chariots that the
rear axle position particularly obtained. Ninety percent of all other
two-wheeled vehicles, from farm carts to the light, fast roadsters of
nineteenth-century England and America, have had a central axle.
The advantages of the latter are that, with a properly balanced and
stable load on reasonably smooth and level going, there is a minimum of weight on the draught animal, while for uphill or downhill
work the load may be adjusted either before or behind the axle,
respectively, to facilitate the draught.[66]

---

[65] Littauer 1968a, 30.
[66] See Powell 1963, 158ff. for a recent discussion of this question.

But if the Greeks did, in the long run, keep to the central axle (a fact of which, as just pointed out, we are not sure), it may have been because the advantages of the rear axle, which were for fighting at speed, were of less importance to them than the greater facility the central axle offered for negotiating mountainous terrain on campaign. The determination of the most advantageous location for a fulcrum (which is all the axle is) is a simple empirical matter; we need not invoke diffusion to account for it. We may stop to ask ourselves how the chariot was used between battles. That charioteer and warrior stood up all day in a jolting, springless vehicle, even though the roads were graded and, in some areas surfaced,[67] seems unlikely. Standing is more tiring than walking, and would be particularly so when the chariot itself was moving at a slow pace and the exhilaration of speed was lacking. And this would occur on every upgrade and downgrade – which, in Greece, would mean frequently. Even with modern harnessing, the occupants of a vehicle may get out and walk on a grade to relieve the animals; in ancient times the limitations of the harnessing would have made this the more imperative. On upgrades, pressure on the throat would have increased; on downgrades the absence of a brake would have had to be countered by attaching a drag. With a central axle the switching of the load could somewhat offset these disadvantages, provided this load was not too heavy. Such a panoply as the Dendra one would not have been worn traveling. Was it carried by pack animal, by cart, or in the chariot itself? If the latter, the chariot would in this foreshadow the knight's charger, which often carried his master's armor on the march, the latter riding a more comfortably gaited animal, while the destrier's burden was reduced.

There is another modification in the construction of the chariot in the Aegean that may be worth considering. This is the bracing or widening of the spokes as they approach the felloe. Our first evidence of it is from fifteenth-century B.C. Crete, on the gem from Avdu (fig. 9),[68] and it remains an almost constant feature of Greek wheels straight through classical times. That it probably originated in the Levant is suggested by at least three cylinder seals in Old

---

[67] McDonald 1964.
[68] Evans 1935, 823, fig. 803; Lorimer 1950, 312, fig. 40; Kenna 1960, 133, no. 308, pls. 12, 23.

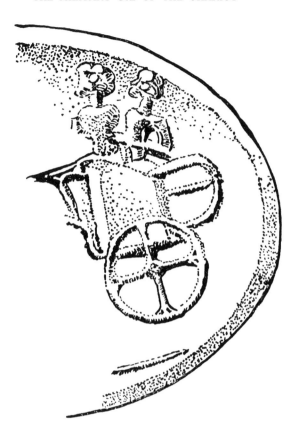

Fig. 9. After Evans 1935, fig. 803.

Syrian style,[69] which show a chariot with it. The final Oriental solution, however, to strengthening the wheel, was to use a greater number of spokes. Egypt and the Levant were experimenting with this earlier than is generally realized – certainly early enough to have transmitted such techniques to the Aegean along with the spoke bracing. Powell has discussed the early evidence for Egypt,[70] and I am indebted to Mr. Joost Crouwel for pointing out two Old Syrian cylinder seals, one displaying a chariot wheel with six spokes, the other, one with eight.[71] The merely abortive essays at bracing and the

[69] von der Osten 1943, pl. 23: 343. Amiet 1969, figs. 4f.
[70] Powell 1963, 154–158.
[71] Buchanan 1966, pl. 56, no. 895; Ward 1910, 312f., fig. 981; Amadasi 1965, fig. 2, no. 4.

prevalence of the six-spoked wheel in the Orient from ca 1400 B.C.
on would indicate that additional spokes proved the more efficient
strengthening method for the type of warfare conducted in this area.
But ideas on techniques of chariot construction were not hermeti-
cally sealed off in each region. If the Aegean world chose to keep
to a modified four-spoked wheel, it was not necessarily from any
great conservatism but because, for some reason, this model of wheel
was adequate to her purposes. One may again suggest that Greek
chariot use did not correspond exactly to that of the eastern Mediterranean. The "primitiveness" of the four-spoked wheel is often remarked
for the late Geometric and subsequent periods, but what does not
seem to be appreciated is that it is not as surprising for these late
periods, when the chariot no longer played a big role, as it is for
the fourteenth and thirteenth centuries, when it is usually presumed
to have been in strenuous action.[72]

The half-round extension or "wing" on either side at the rear of
the Aegean chariot is another feature that distinguishes it from its
contemporaries further east, and that led to Evans' naming it the
"dual chariot" (fig. 8). While it is possible that the original function
of these wings was to protect the occupants' legs during action, the
absence of anything like them from the very active Oriental military chariots, which were sometimes even partly open at the sides,
makes this doubtful. Nor does their earliest appearance, which is on
the peaceful goat chariot on the gem from Avdu bespeak a military
origin (fig. 9).[73] The seemingly plausible suggestion has often been
made that these wings formed a handgrip for mounting. They extend
unnecessarily far to the rear of the floor, however, for this, nor is
there any opening in the wall that would facilitate a handhold. Two
other explanations have recently been offered: that the wings served
as racks on which game or trophies could be brought home,[74] and

---

[72] To this it may be objected that racing was also strenuous practice – which it
must have been, but in a very different way from military use. On the track, wheels
were not abused by the necessity to support two men and their armament over
perhaps uneven or obstacle-strewn terrain at rapid and unforeseen changes of pace
dictated by circumstance; the danger lay in interference with the wheels of other
chariots. Wheels must frequently have been wrenched off the axles and smashed. Racing
wheels had only to be strong enough to support the light one-man chariot on
smooth ground; if they had four spokes rather than six or eight, they would have
been more economical to replace – a consideration that must have played some role.
[73] See supra n. 68.
[74] Vermeule 1964, 202.

that they acted as a counterpoise to the extra weight in front caused by the pole stay.[75] But their rounded profiles would preclude the first possibility, and the negligible amount of weight added by the pole-stay could easily be counteracted by the position of the occupants or a slight change in the position of the axle. Moreover, the pole-stay appears on the Vaphio and Knossos gems without any wings. They may have served a very different purpose. They could have been "mudguards," protecting against the flying stones and gravel which would have been kicked up by the wheels. This again would point to the softer, civilian use of the vehicle.

Schachermeyr and Nagel have noted that in Aegean harnessing the reins go straight from the horses' mouths to the charioteer's hands without passing through rein guides that would break the direct line of action.[76] They certainly appear to do this on the Vaphio gem, as well as on those from Avdu[77] and Knossos[78] and on the sealings from Hagia Triada and Slavokambos.[79] The Tiryns and Mycenae murals show reins crossing the neck high up, apparently without passing through guides.[80] While the Pylos fresco does not show this section of the reins,[81] their angle would indicate the same thing. Only the LH III A and LH III B chariot kraters sometimes show what might be interpreted as rein rings. But this material, with its schematic distortion of many elements, is very shaky evidence. Moreover, the "rein rings" are always placed suspiciously high on the horses' necks.[82] By contrast, at the same period the reins of the chariot teams of Egypt and her enemies passed through rein guides placed on the shoulder (apparently at the junction of the yoke-saddle end and throat strap), in such a way as to break the line of action in favor of the driver.[83] This broken line was of no significance when the reins were slack, but when they were taut the driver had the distinct advantage of having the longer line of the pulley on his

---

[75] Wiesner 1968, 49.
[76] Schachermeyr 1951, 728; Nagel 1966, 48.
[77] See supra no. 20 and 68.
[78] Walters 1926, pl. 1: 39; Evans 1935, fig. 795; Lorimer 1950, fig. 41.
[79] Marinatos and Hirmer 1960, pl. III; Betts 1967, fig. 5.
[80] Rodenwaldt 1912, Abb. 41; Mycenae, suppl. IV, 1–5 (actual neck area destroyed, but position of reins above pole indicates this).
[81] Lang 1969, pl. 18: 26 H 64.
[82] CVA GR. Brit. I, pls. 19: 4. 8, 20: 12, 22: 8, 23: 13.
[83] Yadin 1963, 192f.

side. The horses had only to raise their heads, or the driver his hands, to increase this still further. This system obtained also in the Assyrian chariotry until the eighth century.[84] Could the Aegean's failure to adopt this practice at a period of active contact with the East indicate that she was not using the chariot so strenuously and did not need this added power of control? Her bits, as far as we know them, were similar to, and certainly not more powerful than, those in use further east.[85]

The absence in the Aegean of chariots in real military action – or at least of the evidence of these – in LH III A and B is the more peculiar in view of the fact that these were periods of active contact with Egypt and the Levant. Yet the typical signature of the battle chariot of these areas is conspicuous by its absence. This is the fallen enemy beneath (or, more precisely, beside) the hooves of a team represented at a bounding gallop – a motif that in the east appears first in Early Dynastic times and occurs with frequency right down through the Neo-Hittite reliefs (fig. 6).[86] Were the Greeks already using the military chariot in a different manner?

Hector's rather garbled memories of massed chariotry would then be accounted for as an Asia Minor theme misplaced in the mouth of a mainland Greek.[87]

To return briefly to the LH III C chariot; what does its completely open breastwork tell us, if anything? Dr. Catling suggests that it may indicate an army "that had to travel far and travel rough before committing its equipment to battle."[88] Could it not also speak of the shortages of a period when, owing to widespread devastation or drought, or both, cattle and crops suffered, hence hides and linen were scarce, and imports were difficult?

As for the entirely naked model on a sherd from Lefkandi, this remains an enigma (fig. 10). Where, for instance, is the pole, which should be showing because it comes out from directly under the

---

[84] Barnett (n.d.), pls. 26f.

[85] Potratz 1966, fig. 45; compare Mycenaean bit "g" with Egyptian bit "f."

[86] For selected examples from various periods see Frankfort 1958 pls. 36, 161; Wiseman 1962, pl. 26f.; von der Osten 1943, pl. 23: 343; Amadasi 1965, fig. 7, nos. 1, 3. (The entire problem of the Shaft Grave stelai – where many consider such a motif to exist – is purposely not considered in this paper.)

[87] *Iliad* 4.297–309. For the impracticality of actually attacking fortified cities with chariotry see Yadin 1955.

[88] Catling 1968, 46.

Fig. 10. After Catling 1968, pl. 21:1.

chariot floor? And the peculiar straps around the driver's calves (if that is what they are) must soon have been abandoned as more a liability than an asset.[89] Any attachment fixed less than halfway up on a vertical body serves only to trip it once the state of balance is upset, unless that body's base is fixed or weighted. And such a strap would prevent the charioteer from jumping or falling free of the vehicle, and, once he was fallen, would drag him – a dangerous business.

---

[89] Catling 1968, 49.

9. FIGHTING ON LAND AND SEA
IN LATE MYCENAEAN TIMES*

JOOST H. CROUWEL

This paper will concentrate on military practices in LH IIIC Middle (ca. 1150/40–1100/1090 B.C.). It was a brief period of increased prosperity and contacts in the Aegean, well after the break-up of the Mycenaean palace system at the LH IIIB/IIIC transition (end of 13th century B.C.).[1]

Important sources of information on land warfare in LH IIIC Middle are the so-called Warrior Krater from Mycenae and other, mostly fragmentary, pictorial kraters from different parts of mainland Greece and Euboea. These vase paintings show armed men, either on foot or riding in chariots. Their equipment includes helmets, corselets and greaves, shields, spears (single or in pairs) and swords. All these men would have fought on the ground, the chariots presumably serving as prestigious means of transportation for higher-ranking warriors.[2]

In fact, however, the most explicit illustrations of fighting involving foot soldiers and chariots are found not on the krater of mid-LH IIIC but on wall paintings from the Megaron of the palace of Mycenae dating before the great fire destruction at the end of LH

---

* Published in: Robert Laffineur (ed.), *POLEMOS. Le contexte guerrier en égée à l'âge du bronze*. Actes de la 7e Recontre égéenne internationale Université de Liège, 14–17 avril 1998. AEGAEUM 19. Annales d'archéologie égéenne de l'Université de Liège et UT-PSAP. Université de Liège (Histoire de l'art et archéologie de la Grèce antique) and University of Texas at Austin (Program in Aegean Scripts and Prehistory), vol. II, 1999, 455–459. (See also the discussion reprinted on pp. 461–463 in that volume).
[1] See especially Deger-Jakotzy 1991; 1994; Mountjoy 1993; Rutter 1992; S. Sherratt 1981. For the relative chronology of the various destructions in southern and central Greece, see recently Mountjoy 1997.
[2] Crouwel 1981, 140f.; Crouwel 1992, 54. For the Warrior Krater from Mycenae and other contemporary (fragmentary) kraters with military scenes, mainly from Mycenae and Tiryns but also from Athens, Kalapoidi in Phocis, Volos in Thessaly and Lefkandi on Euboea, see Vermeule and Karageorghis 1983, no. XI.42 and chapter XI; Sakellarakis 1992, no. 32 and others; also Crouwel 1991b. For finds from Kalapodi, see Felsch 1981, 84. 86, fig. 7; Jacob-Felsch 1987, 28f., figs. 50–51.

IIIB. Fragmentary through they are, these wall paintings include battle scenes, depicting spearmen running and falling (pl. 5). At least some of the fighting centered around a building complex representing a palace or city (pl. 6). Chariots are also shown – not actually taking part in battle but as conveyances for warriors who dismounted to join the fighting on the ground (pl. 7) where the warrior may be restored as another spearman).[3] This particular form of chariot use was determined to a large extent by the broken nature of Greek terrain which prevented the vehicles from being employed in the same active way as on the flat expanses of the Near East and Egypt, where they functioned as elevated mobile firing platforms for archers.[4]

It has often been observed that changes in military equipment took place in Greece in the 13th and 12th centuries B.C. These changes affected both offensive and defensive weaponry, including swords and spears, body armour, shields and helmets, as well as chariots, with the lighter Rail type replacing the standard Dual chariot. But these changes, some of which are first documented before the destruction of the Mycenaean palaces and others after them, did not mark a fundamental break in military practices, as has recently been claimed by Robert Drews.[5] Chariots too continued to be used for the same military purposes, albeit exercised control over large stretches of land.

So far we have been concerned with fighting on land in late Mycenaean times. Remains of pictorial kraters of LH IIIC Middle have recently been found at Pyrgos Livanaton, a hill-site near the modern village of Livanates on the coast of east Lokris opposite Euboea. These vase paintings illustrate similarly-armed men – not on land but on board ships (pls. 8 and 9).[6] The ships are basically

---

[3] Rodenwaldt 1921; Immerwahr 1990, 123–125. 192 (My no. 11); Littauer 1972; Crouwel 1981, 129–132. 170f. (no. W1–12), both arguing against Rodenwaldt's interpretation of two sets of fragments as showing an archer jumping off a chariot (our pl. 6) and a team of galloping horses above a falling warrior (our pl. 7). For these and other Aegean battle scenes, see Döhl 1980; also Fortenberry 1990.

[4] Crouwel 1981, 119–145; Crouwel 1992, 54f.; Littauer and Crouwel 1983 and 1996 taking issue with Drews' ideas of massed chariots, carrying archers and charging each other, in Greece as well as further east, as expressed in his books *The coming of the Greeks: Indo-European Conquests in the Aegean and the Near East* (1988) and *The End of the Bronze Age: Changes in Warfare and the Catastrophe ca. 1200 B.C.* (1993).

[5] Drews 1993. For changes in weaponry see, in addition to Drews (174–208), Fortenberry 1990; Rutter 1992, 67f.

[6] Dakoroneia 1990 with figs. 1–3; 1995, 147f., figs. 1–3; 1996, 162 with fig. 9. See also Lenz 1995, 123–125. 182f. (nos. 13–14) figs. 67–69; Wachsmann 1996, 542, fig. 42:C–E; Wedde 1996, 581. These and other krater fragments are on display in

oared galleys with a shallow hull, a tall prow, sharply curved forward and upward at the top, and with a straight tall stern. Sometimes
a mast is shown, along with a raised platform at the prow and stern.
A helmsman at the rear is seen holding a steering oar with tiller.
Other men, apparently standing on a deck, are wearing 'spiked' helmets, while brandishing spears and holding up shields. The latter
may be round and concave, or shaped rather like an hour-glass, with
fringes above and below. Some of the armed men are wearing short
fringed tunics or a kind of corselet with loops at the top, or perhaps rather a combination of these. Most of the equipment can be
matched on pictorial kraters of similar date from elsewhere in Greece
illustrating land-based warriors.[7]

Of one Livanates krater enough survives for us to see that two
ships are shown opposing each other, with shield-bearers brandishing spears while standing on the platform at the front (pl. 9a–b).
There can be no doubt that these and the other warriors on board
are engaged in battle at sea rather than readying themselves for
combat on land. One man, standing at the front of a ship on another,
more crudely painted krater, may well be an archer rather than a
spearman, to judge from the position of his arms (pl. 8).[8]

The new pictorial vase paintings of late Mycenaean date from the
coastal site of Livanates provide the first explicit evidence for sea
battles in Greece. There are several, earlier figured documents illustrating ship-borne warriors, sometimes combined with drowning
figures. These mostly fragmentary scenes in different artistic media
come from mainland Greece as well as the islands of Crete, Therea
and Aegina. They date to the Middle Bronze Age of, more often,
to the early part of the Late Bronze Age, and include such well-
known documents as the silver Siege Rhyton form Shaft Grave IV

---

the Museum at Lamia. Two more of them have so far been illustrated in print:
Dakoroneia 1987, 234, pl. 135d (part of land-based human figure) and 1991, 194f.,
pl. 83:d (part of shield-bearer on board ships; sherd erroneously illustrated upside
down). The dating of these ceramic finds is confirmed by details of the krater shape,
such as the slashed ridge below some of the rims, as well as by details of the painted
decoration – all of which have parallels from dated context elsewhere in Greece.
For the site, identified with Homeric Kynos by the excavator, see Dakoroneia 1996.

[7] See particularly the fragments of a warrior krater from the coastal site of Volos
in Thessaly, which illustrate a spear, "spiked" helmets, and parts of an hour-glass
shield and a corselet; Vermeule and Karageorghis 1983, no. XI.57; Immerwahr 1985.

[8] Cf. the archer, possibly standing in a similar position in the bow of a ship,
seen on a krater fragment from Volos: Vermeule and Karageorghis 1983, no. XI.58;
Immerwahr 1985, 92f. and fig. 3.

at Mycenae and the miniature wall paintings from the West House at Akrotiri on Thera.[9] The general theme seems to be land attacks carried out by raiders from the sea. Although the combination of ship-borne warriors and drowning figures suggest prior naval engagements, there is no sign of vessels actually engaged in battle, such as those depicted on at least one of the late Mycenaean kraters from Livanates.

In the Near East, land attacks by sea-borne raiders are mentioned in the Amarna letters and then in the correspondence bearing on the final years of the kingdom of Ugarit.[10] Actual naval engagements are first recorded in a text of the last Hittite king Šuppiluliuma II: "The ships of Alashiya met me in the sea three times for battle, and I smote them; and I seized the ships and set fire to them in the sea."[11] No information is provided on details of these engagements, which were followed by one on land in Alašiya itself – a kingdom most probably to be identified with Cyprus or part of it.

The first figured documents from the east which are relevant here are large-scale stone reliefs on the walls of the mortuary temple of the Egyptian pharaoh Ramesses III at Medinet Habu, illustrating the navel battle against the so-called Sea Peoples in the eighth year of his reign. This battle, which is described in the accompanying inscriptions, in fact took place not on the high seas but in the Nile delta close to the shore, the Egyptians attacking the vessels of the Sea Peoples with ship-borne fighters as well as land-based archers.[12] After bombarding the enemy ships with arrows, javelins and slings tones, the Egyptians came close enough with their ships to engage in hand-to-hand fighting.

---

[9] Most of these figured documents are discussed and illustrated by Morgan 1988 especially 150–154. 159f., also 104–115, pls. 189–194; see also Döhl 1980, 21–26; Fortenberry 1990, 257–259. The earliest representation of armed men on board a ship may be a painted fragment of a Middle Helladic pithos from Kolonna on Aegina; see Siedentopf 1991, 25, 62 no. 162, pl. 38, cf. 18f., 24f., 55 no. 158, 62 no. 158, fig. 4 Pls 35–37; Hiller 1984, 28, fig. 1, cf fig. 2; Rutter 1993b, 780, fig. 14b, cf. fig. 14c For the miniature wall paintings from the West House at Akrotiri, see now Televantou 1990, especially 315–321 (North Frieze) and 1994.

[10] See a.o. Linder 1973; Astour 1965; Yon 1992, 115–117. Earlier, Tuthmosis III recorded seizing two ships and their cargo at sea while returning to Egypt from his fifth Syrian campaign; see Sethe 1961 par. IV.686; Breasted 1927, 196, par. 460 (I owe these references to M. H. Wiener – see this edition – and W. M. van Haarlem).

[11] See especially Güterbock 1967 (tablet KBo 12.38); Hoffner 1992, 48f.

[12] See Nelson 1943; Yadin 1963 (II) 251f., ills pp. 250–252, 340f.; Raban 1995.

Similar tactics are suggested by the vase painting form Livanates: the warriors with their spears, helmets and corselets would eventually proceed to attempt board the enemy ships. The depictions of two confronted ships, facing each other and each carrying a group of warriors again basically equipped for fighting on land, is strongly reminiscent of the so-called Aristonothos krater from Cerveteri. This pot, dating to the 7th century B.C., bears the signature of a Greek, Aristonothos, but was probably made in Etruria (pl. 10).[13] The warriors standing on the deck and in the bow are hoplites depicted in fighting stance, with their spears raised. One of the ships on the Aristonothos krater has a (theriormorphic) ram, a feature absent from the much earlier Livantes ships. The ram, possibly first explicitly illustrated on a bronze fibula from a Middle Geometric I grave in the Kerameikos at Athens (ca. 850 B.C.), seems to have developed out of a projection of the bow to facilitate beaching. Its presence indicates a change in naval tactics, with purpose-built warships maneuvering in order to incapacitate and sink enemy vellels.[14] Before then naval engagements in the Aegean appear to have been confrontations of infantrymen placed on the ships' decks and bow platforms. Such tactics are illustrated first on the late Mycenaean krater fragments from Livanates and then on the large Attic kraters of Middle Geometric II and Late Geometric I (ca. 800–735 B.C.) that served as grave markers. The ships on the latter are shown engaged in battle at sea and also beached, with the fighting taking place on and around them (pl. 11).[15] Similar naval tactics are implied by a pyxis of Sub-Protogeometric II–III (ca. 850–825 B.C.) from Lefkandi in Euboea, where a group of spears is shown inside the stern of an otherwise unmanned ship.[16] As a matter of fact, the practice of stack-

---

[13] See Schweitzer 1955, pls. 34–35; Gray 1974, 26 no. H.7, 70, 72; Basch 1987, 233f., fig. 482; recently, Coldstream 1993, 101–103, figs. 2–5.

[14] For the early history of the ram, see especially van Doornick Jr. 1982; Basch 1987, 150f. 198. 201 etc.; also M. Wedde in this edition. The earliest sea battle recorded in a Greek written text – between Corinthians and the Corcyraeans – is said to have taken place probably in the second quarter of the the 7th century B.C. (Thucydides I.13). The first recorded use of ramming tactics relates to the battle – between the Phocaeans and the allied forces of Etruscans and Carthaginians – of Alalia on Corsica ca. 535 B.C. (Herodotus I. 166).

[15] For these representation, see especially Kirk 1949 Morrison and Williams 1968, chapter 2; Ahlberg 1971b, especially 25–38; Gray 1974, especially G 57–61. 84–90. 130; Grünwaldt 1983; Basch 1987, 163–201; recently Coldstream 1996–97, 8–10 (discussing aspects of the earliest, Middle Geometric II karter showing fighting centered on beached ship: New York, Metropolitan Museum of Art no. 34.12.2).

[16] Popham 1987; Calligas 1995.

ing spears aboard ships is also illustrated on the Aristonothos krater and several of the Attic Geometric kraters, as well as on the much earlier miniature wall paintings from Akriotiri on Thera.[17]

The ships seen on the late Mycenaean krater fragments from Livanates belong to a type that is also depicted in other Mycenaean vase paintings of the later 12th century B.C. and which seems to be first illustrated on a LM IIIB (13th century B.C.) painted larnax from Gazi in Crete.[18] In the latter representations this type of ship is not shown in a military setting, and its use may indeed have been multi-purpose. The type of ship remained in use into the Early Iron Age, its representations including the 9th century pyxis from Lefkandi in Euboea and the 8th century Attic kraters.[19] Our sources then provide clear evidence for continuity in ship building form the Bronze Age to the Iron Age in Greece.

In the light of the Livanates krater fragments, we can say that there was also continuity in the kind of military use that was made of such ships: as carriers for warriors who fought on land but as sea too, as the need arose. Indeed, these late Mycenaean vase paintings provide glimpses of the fighting that was to be so graphically illustrated on Attic Geometric kraters and on the Aristonothos krater from Etruria. At the same time, they recall the activities of the seaborne raiders who figure frequently in the Homeric poems and later Greek literary texts and inscriptions.[20] We may end by quoting one such inscription, a three-line hexameter on a grave stela of ca. 600 B.C. from Corcyra: "This is the tomb of Arniades whom flashing-eyed Ares destroyed as he fought beside the ships in the streams of Arathos. He was the bravest by far in the wretchedness of war."[21]

[17] Popham 1987, 358 with n. 13; Morgan 1988, pls. 189, A (North Frieze, the spears shown inside a platform at the bow) 9–12, B (South Frieze, the ships not only carrying spears but also helmets and shields); see also Musee imaginaire, 131f.
[18] Mycenaean pyxis from tholos tomb at Tragana: Korres 1989, ills. pp. 200–202; Vermeule and Karageorghis 1983, no. XI. 92; Sakellarakis 1992, no. 255; Basch 1987, 141–146, figs 297–298. Mycenaean stirrup jar from Asine in the Argolid: Vermeule and Karageorghis 1983, no. XI. 94; Basch 1987, 146, fig. 309). Cf. a 12th century krater fragment, preserving part of a "horned" fringed ship's prow, from Enkomi in Cyprus: Dikaios 1969–71, 264. 593 no. 5549/3 (identified as hedgehog), pls. 72:8.307:199 (Area I, Level IIIA, Room 26, between floor III-II); Lenz 1995, 233f. no. 196, fig. 70. Larnax from chamber tomb at Gazi, Crete: Alexiou 1973, pl. 1; Basch 1987, 144–146, figs. 303–304. 306.
[19] 19 For the type of ship and its history, see especially Basch 1987, 141–148. 159–162.196; Dakoroneia 1989, 118–120; also M. Wedde in this volume.
[20] See, recently, van Wees 1992, 207–217. 244–258. Still fundamental is Ormerod 1924.
[21] Hansen 1983, 80 no. 145; Lang 1991, 75 (quotation).

10. ROCK CARVINGS OF CHARIOTS IN TRANSCAUCASIA, CENTRAL ASIA AND OUTER MONGOLIA*

M. A. LITTAUER

Petroglyphs of light, spoked-wheeled chariots have recently been discovered in Armenia, in the Central Asian republics of Kazakhstan and Tadzhikistan and in the western Gobi. These will have to be considered in any future general surveys of chariotry. Although some have not yet received full publication, and although not all publications have been accessible to the author, the carvings seem too important to wait longer before being brought to the attention of the West. Lacking archaeological contexts, most of them have been dated only roughly by their publishers on the basis of typology. We shall not attempt here to appraise these datings, but by pointing to differences or similarities between these chariots and ones east or west, in both manner of rendering and in what is known of the actual construction of extant vehicles, we may provide greater means for doing so.

The Sites

Transcaucasia

In the Syunik region of Armenia, at some 3300 m. above sea level, in a transhumance area, thousands of rock carvings have been found (Karakhanian and Safian 1970), the majority representing animals (both wild and domestic) and men. A small number, however, depict wheeled vehicles. While ox-drawn four-wheelers greatly predominate, seven chariots have been published by the authors (figs. 1–7). These all come from Oughtasar. The carvings as a whole are considered to cover a period from the fifth through the second millennium B.C., and the chariots as belonging towards the end of this period.

* *Proceedings of the Prehistoric Society* 43, 1977, 243–262.

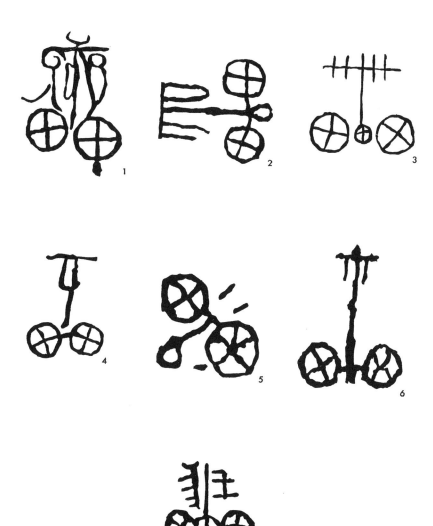

Fig. 1. Syunik. After Karakhanian and Safian 1970, fig. 82.
Fig. 2. Syunik. After Karakhanian and Safian 1970, fig. 107.
Fig. 3. Syunik. After Karakhanian and Safian 1970, fig. 117.
Fig. 4. Syunik. After Karakhanian and Safian 1970, fig. 198
Fig. 5. Syunik. After Karakhanian and Safian 1970, fig. 205.
Fig. 6. Syunik. After Karakhanian and Safian 1970, fig. 276.
Fig. 7. Syunik. After Karakhanian and Safian 1970, fig. 315.

Central Asia

In southern Kazakhstan, in the northwestern foothills of the Karatau range, which lies to the north of the Syr Darya (ancient Jaxartes), appears another large area of rock carving (Kadyrbaev and Marjash-chev 1972 and 1973). Again we find animals and men – often com-bined in hunting scenes – and again a few vehicles, by comparison insignificant in number. These are concentrated in the region of Kojbagar at about 700 m elevation. Here, light two-wheelers pre-dominate (figs. 9–14), with the few wagons being camel-drawn. While the large group of petroglyphs is considered to extend from the mid-dle of the second millennium B.C. to the end of the first millen-nium A.D., the authors have dated the chariots to the end of the second millenium or beginning of the first millennium B.C.

The Pamirs

In Tadzhkistan, on the right bank of the North Akdzilgi river (north-ern slopes of the Alichur range), at an altitude of 3800 m. (!), a large group of rock carvings was found by the geologist V. P. Bulin and has been given brief notice by Zhukov and Ranev 1972. The five chariots found here (fig. 15) once more represent only a fraction of a long series of grafitti that are estimated as extending from the late second or early first millennium B.C. right up to recent times. No attempt has been made to date the chariot petroglyphs themselves.

Outer Mongolia

On the western slopes of the Mongolian Altai, on almost inaccessi-ble cliffs over the narrow gorge of Jamani Us, or 'Goat Water', now passable for pack animals only at certain seasons, but until recently an important caravan route leading to a pass through the main Altai range, was found another extensive area of rock art. Once again, the representations of vehicles (figs. 16–21; Volkov (1972) constitute exceptions among the very numerous petroglyphs of animals (pri-marily ibex) and men. Volkov 1972, a co-discoverer, and the pub-lisher of the vehicles, places four of these at the end of the second or beginning of the first millennium B.C., and the two others in the Han period (206 B.C.–220 A.D.), or even later.

At Kobdo Somon in the southern Gobi, a large basalt boulder carries a carving of one or two vehicles (fig. 22) (Okladnikov 1964; Kozhin 1968; Dorzh 1968 [in Mongolian]; Volkov 1972. Yet again, this occurs in an area rich in petroglyphs – primarily of ibex and men. The number of vehicles (one four-wheeler or two two-wheelers) here is differently interpreted by different authors, and the dates assigned to this subject vary widely – from before 1400 B.C. (Kozhin) to the last centuries B.C. (Dorzh reported by Volkov 1972, 84).

Besides the sites mentioned above, Kadyrbaev and Marjashchev 1973, 139 note other sites with chariot petroglyphs in Kazakhstan. One was found in the Dzhambulsk region, another southwest of Lake Balkash, and several in central Kazakhstan. These are all unpublished. Two carvings from Tamgaly have been published by Maksimova 1958 and two more from Kopala by Makhmudov 1971 in publications that I have not seen. These carvings are not discussed, except to mention that the one from the Dzhambulsk region resembles those at Kojbagar.

Volkov 1972 also describes briefly, without illustrating it, another chariot petroglyph on a 'stag stone' set beside a large kurgan at Darvy Somon in the Kobdo region, and published by Rintchen (1968).

The Chariot Representations

A distinction should be made between 4-wheeled wagons, 2-wheeled carts and chariots. The first, from the early second millennium on, were used primarily for the transport of men and/or goods, and, when covered, sometimes served as habitations. The second, with solid or spoked wheels, were confined to the same uses; they usually had a central axle, and the passengers normally sat in them. Chariots had spoked wheels, and with certain notable exceptions, a rear axle; the occupants stood in them, and they were used for military, sporting, or ceremonial purposes.

All the representations discussed here are assumed to be of chariots proper, unless this status is specifically questioned. All, with the exception of the two late ones at Jamani Us, show vehicles and animals in the same schematized convention. The chariots are for paired draught, with animals on either side of a pole and beneath a yoke – as were all true chariots.

All the chariots at Oughtasar (figs. 1–7) are schematically, as well as crudely and often carelessly, rendered, and sometimes incomplete. The wheels are 4-spoked, with one exception, where one of the pair is 5-spoked (fig. 5). On the four examples where a box is shown (figs. 2, 3, 5, 7), it is twice depicted as quartered by the pole and axle, which (if read literally) would indicate a central axle, and twice (improbably) as behind the axle. Only in two cases do draught animals seem to be included, and they appear to be oxen (figs. 1 and 7). Among the well over 300 crowded plates in Karakhanian and Safian we find representations of 33 ox-drawn wagons, a few ox-drawn travois, numerous individual, or even paired, oxen. There is only one recognizable figure of a horse, and this is bridled (fig. 8) and, although unfinished, does not appear to have been a harness animal. It is executed in a technique different from that of any of the other animals illustrated (cf. figs. 2–7), and its 'crenellated' mane would point to a much later date. Maenchen-Helfen 1957 has shown that this type of mane cut is associated only with the ridden horse, and is first documented in the Pazyryk tombs. The yokes here are shown as straight, without upturned ends, and where yoke fittings occur, these are long loops (figs. 2) or verticals (figs. 3 and 6). Individual wheels are found here too, mostly with four spokes, but

Fig. 8. Syunik. After Karakhanian and Safian 1970, fig. 274.

some with five and even with seven spokes (Karakhanian and Safian 1970, figs. 148 and 312).

In the Karatau, 19 chariot carvings were found at three sites (labelled by the authors Kojbagar I, II and III, but apparently without chronological implications) and a single petroglyph at Kokbulaka (Kadyrbaev and Marjaschev 1972 and 1973). We reproduce here some of the best preserved ones (figs. 9–14). The subjects are drawn in the same convention as those from Syunik. All chariots, including, according to the authors, ones they do not illustrate, have 4-spoked wheels. In two cases (figs. 10 and 12) a circular box is situated centrally between the wheels, and quartered by pole and axle. In two cases (figs. 9 and 14), it is insignificant in size but placed (improbably) behind the axle; in fig. 11 it is D-shaped, with the axle at its rear edge and the pole probably running back to the latter; and in fig. 13 this was probably also the intention. Two chariots (figs. 9 and 11) show teams of horses harnessed to the yoke and as if lying back to back. In fig. 9 two pairs of reins run back from the horses' heads to the box. In fig. 11 two extra lines run back part way from the yoke. Fig. 10 shows an unharnessed chariot. The yoke ends are upturned and from the yoke depend the forked yoke saddles (Littauer 1968). In fig. 13 a pair of Bactrian camels are yoked to the chariot and shown as if lying face to face. Fig. 14 shows an unharnessed chariot; the camel to the right and ibex to the left of the yoke do not seem directly associated with it. The yoke has upturned ends and fixtures of some sort (saddles or neck rods?) to attach it to the draught team's necks.

The Pamirs site contains five chariot petroglyphs. The one example illustrated by Zhukov an Ranev 1972, 540 shows a biga (fig. 15) represented in the same manner as the previous ones, but with more detail. The axle supports the rear edge of a box with D-shaped floor plan and flooring of interwoven thongs, and the pole runs under the floor all the way back to the axle. One wheel shows seven spokes, the other nine, but the odd 'spokes' look more like axle ends. Supports, either of leather straps or of wood or metal rods run between the front of the box and the pole a short way before it, and yoke braces run out from the pole to the thick yoke on either side. The yoke shows neither yoke saddles nor neck embrasures, but either of these was probably beyond the ability of the artist to depict on a yoke in use. The two draught animals are ithyphallic, and from them reins run back to the hands of an ithyphallic driver, who is walking behind

Fig. 9. Karatau. After Kadyrbaev and Marjaschev 1972, fig 5:1.
Fig. 10. Karatau. After Kadyrbaev and Marjaschev 1972, fig. 5:2.
Fig. 11. Karatau. After Kadyrbaev and Marjaschev 1972, fig. 8:2.
Fig. 12. Karatau. After Kadyrbaev and Marjaschev 1972, fig. 9.
Fig. 13. Karatau. After Kadyrbaev and Marjaschev 1972, fig. 7:2.
Fig. 14. Karatau. After Kadyrbaev and Marjaschev 1972, fig. 8:1.

15

Fig. 15. Pamirs. After Zhukov and Ranev 1972.

the vehicle carrying what looks more like a goad than a whip. According to the text, the five chariots, each with a similar driver (two of the chariots are unfinished) are in a line; in front and behind them are three human figures, apparently rendered in the same manner, but with outstretched arms and conspicuously defined ribs. These, the authors suggest, may be the dead, in whose honour the procession is being held.

Figure 16, from the group of petroglyphs at Jamani Us in the Altai, depicts a quadriga with a roughly oval or D-shaped box, an axle shown as somewhat rear of centre, and wheels with eight spokes. Random, oblique lines on the floor of the box probably stand for a woven thong flooring. The pole runs under the floor to the rear, and yoke-arm braces, starting a little more than half-way out the pole, are clearly defined. The two pole horses are yoked and the right-hand trace horse is connected by a trace leading back to the chariot box. The left-hand horse was probably intended to be attached in a similar manner, and the carving (as often seems to have been the case) may not have been completed. This may also account for the fact that no reins are shown. The driver, a schematic figure, with arms akimbo, is depicted as if lying on his back with feet touching the rear edge of the box, in which he is certainly supposed to be standing. According to Volkov 1972, loose horses appear in front of the chariot and the impression is given that the charioteer is chasing or following a herd of horses.

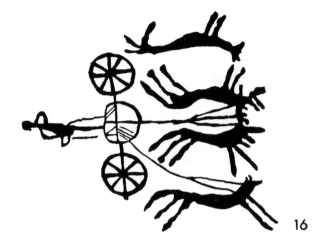

Fig. 16. Jamani Us, Mongolian Altai. After Volkov 1972, fig. 1.

A second, rather similar, vehicle (fig. 17) is even less explicit. While the position of the box, if read literally would indicate a central axle, the box itself is so schematically rendered (like a third, somewhat oval, 8-spoked wheel) that it is impossible to interpret it realistically. The wheels are 8-spoked. The pole is probably meant to run under the box to the rear. The yoke is shown as a straight bar with sharply upturned ends. This carving is particularly interesting in representing a triga (unless it is an unfinished quadriga?). There are two horses under the yoke, and the trace horse is again connected directly with the box. What are probably intended to be yoke braces, but which reach to the pole horses' necks rather than to the yoke, run out from the pole on either side. No reins are shown. The rendering of the driver is very similar to that of figure 16.

A third chariot in this series (fig. 18) has neither horses nor driver, although a curtailed line running forward obliquely from the left corner of the box may indicate that a triga or quadriga was planned. The box is subrectangular and is quartered by the pole and axle. The wheels are 8-spoked. There are yoke braces running to an unrealistically short yoke with upturned ends.

Across, on the opposite side of the gorge, a fourth chariot representation – a biga – was found (fig. 19). The box is rendered as an oval, quartered – presumably by axle and pole end. The author states that, because of the poor condition of the surface, it is impossible to determine the number of spokes to the wheels. Traction system and driver are lacking. The horses are back to back.

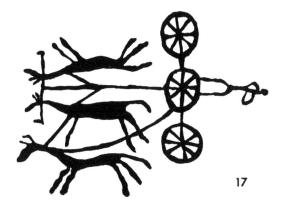

Fig. 17. Jamani Us, Mongolian Altai. After Volkov 1972, fig. 3.

Fig. 18. Jamani Us, Mongolian Altai. After Volkov 1972, fig. 2.

Fig. 19. Jamani Us, Mongolian Altai. After Volkov 1972, fig. 4.

Two more petroglyphs of vehicles were found in this area, rendered in a different convention, with both vehicles and draught animals in profile (figs. 20 and 21). They are carts with elaborate canopies, and each shows a single, seated occupant. In both cases the wheels are shown as 8-spoked. In fig. 20 the cart is drawn by a team of two or three; Volkov 1972 suggests a triga, but from the illustration it would also seem possible to interpret this carving as showing two horses on either side of a high, arching pole. Fig. 21 shows a cart with a single horse, probably in shaft harness. The first cart is accompanied by two riders – one before and one behind – the front horseman with bowcase slung on his back. The second vehicle is preceded by a single (apparently unarmed) rider.

Fig. 20. Jamani Us, Mongolian Altai. After Volkov 1972, fig. 5.
Fig. 21. Jamani Us, Mongolian Altai. After Volkov 1972, fig. 6.

A description of the 'Gobi Quadriga' (fig. 22) depends on whether one sees it as a 4-wheeler or as two 2-wheelers. Thus, it could be described as a wagon or carriage with a triangular flooring at the rear and a circular one in front, with four wheels, the number of their spokes varying from seven to eight, and with a pole and yoke. There are two pole horses and two trace horses (all ithyphallic), the latter connected by traces running back to the front edge of the box. What looks like a rod topped with two eyelets and a perhaps zoomorphic finial, extends on the left, half-way between rear and front wheels and may be intended to be upright. There is no occupant in the vehicle, but a human figure, carrying a drawn bow, strides towards the right trace horse. At the rear of the vehicle a human figure which, because of its position head-downwards, seems to be lying on the ground, is connected with the left rear wheel by a wide curving line, while a straighter line goes from one hand to a bushy-tailed quadruped.

Viewing the scene as two 2-wheelers, the forward one might be described as having a circular box quartered by pole and axle. The rear vehicle could perhaps be an A-frame cart, with the yoke running across the apex of the A, and a zoomorphic 'standard' rising at their junction.

Fig. 22. Kobdo Somon, Outer Mongolia. After Okladnikov 1964, pl. 16.

Volkov 1972, 85f. describes the representation of a chariot on a 'stag stone' at Darvy Somon as being drawn in a perspective similar to those discussed above. It is pulled by two horses, has a circular box, a pole and yoke, and lines leading from the pole to the withers of the horses. The only striking difference between this and others is that its wheels show no spokes.

Comparisons

In order to interpret these representations we may go to actual extant chariots or fragments thereof from Egypt (Quibell 1908, 65–67; Carter 1927, 109–117; Botti 1951, 192–198); Cyprus (Karageorghis 1973, 68–75); Soviet Armenia (Mnatsakanian 1957, 151f.; 1960, 143; Piggott 1974, 1624) and China (von Dewall 1964, 127, 207–253); to representations (the richest sources for these being Egyptian and Assyrian paintings and wall reliefs) and to some models in the round. Besides these, since a relationship with western rock art (Althin 1945, 102–106; Anati 1960, 53f.; Hagen 1967, 110) has been emphasized

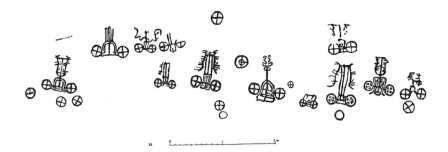

Fig. 23. Frænnarp, Sweden. After Althin 1945, figs. 70–72.

Fig. 24. Begby, Norway. After Hagen 1967, pl. 38.

Fig. 25. Val Camonica, Italy. After Anati 1960, figs. 6 and 7.

Fig. 26. Early Chinese pictogram. After Hančar 1955, fig. 9:3.

by Okladnikov and Kozhin and repeated by Kadyrbaev and Mar-jaschev 1972, its vehicles (figs. 23–25) and the oddly similar schema-tization in Shang pictographs (fig. 26), must both be considered. African petroglyphs largely repeat the same conventions, but some also reveal a different type of draught system. They are too exten-sive to be discussed at this time and, fortunately, the conventions of African rock painting are sufficiently different to permit its exclusion here also.

The perhaps seemingly arbitrary description above of the floors of several chariot petroglyphs as being 'quartered' by pole and axle may first need an explanation. On all extant chariots, with the pos-sible exception of the Lchaschen ones, where this feature seems to have been uncertain, the pole runs through, underneath the floor, to the rear of the chariot, no matter where the axle is located. These two elements form the floor support.

In our description we have noted axle positions and number of spokes per wheel – but just how reliable are these as criteria (although often used) for dating? To cite some examples: an early first millennium B.C. cist grave at Berekej in Daghestan (Hančar 1943, 26f.; 1956, 154–155) shows a schematic carving of a chariot with 4-spoked wheels and, next to it, an 8-spoked wheel – this in a closed context (fig. 27). The petroglyphs at Oughtasar depict chariots with 4-spoked wheels and one with both a four- and a five-spoked wheel, as well as four unattached wheels, two with five and two with seven spokes, respectively. Yet, nearby, in the Lchaschen tombs, dated by their discoverer, Mnatsakanian, to c. 1300–1100 B.C. (Piggott 1968, 280) actual light two-wheelers with 28 spokes to a wheel have been found and these 28 spokes cannot have arrived overnight. Three bronze model chariots, one with 8-spoked and two with 6-spoked wheels, were found in the Lchaschen tombs. Had the wood in these tombs not been accidentally preserved by flooding, we would be inclined to conclude that the maximum number of spokes for the place and time was eight. In China, Shang pictographs (fig. 26) continue to show 4-spoked wheels at a time when we already have material evi-

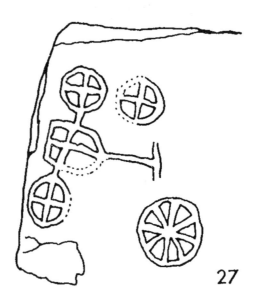

Fig. 27. Berekej, Daghestan. After Hančar 1943, fig. 1.

dence from tombs for wheels with 18 spokes (von Dewall 1964, 220). We may take a warning also from the remains of two-wheeled vehicles recently discovered in a Bronze-Age cemetery in the central Urals (Gening and Ashikmina 1975). The imprint of the wheels in the earthen sides of the channels dug for them in the tomb floor revealed that they had been 10-spoked. Objects found in the cemetery date it to an early Sejma horizon of the Abashevo culture, which would probably put it not long after the middle of the second millennium B.C. We may suggest that in such contexts as pictograph or rock art, where the intention seems to be merely to *indicate* a chariot with (certainly in the first instance and perhaps also in the second) an economy of means, a 4-spoked wheel (presumably the earliest true spoked wheel) simply came to stand for any spoked wheel – the number of spokes unspecified. There are, however, other types of representations which seem to be more reliable. Not only do the Egyptian reliefs attempt to reproduce with a certain amount of circumstantiality actual scenes, but many details of chariots in them have been corroborated on the chariots found. Assyrian reliefs are even more realistic, and at least some of the chariot or harness parts depicted in them have been confirmed by finds of such elements in peripheral regions (Littauer 1976, 217–226). We may therefore feel justified in discriminating between the reliability of one type of figured evidence and another.

The same observation may be applied, with reservations, to axle position. The vast majority of Egyptian representations, from c. 1400 on show chariots with rear or very close to rear axles, and this is all we find on extant examples. Yet even in Egypt the exigencies of space may move some axles to the centre, as may be noted, for instance, on the painted box of Tutʿankhamūn (Yadin 1963, 214–215), where some of the chariots in his suite have rear axles and some have central ones – the latter clearly in an attempt to show the whole of the wheel in front of the second team's legs. While all Egyptian chariots found have had rear axles, the two chariots from a little later from Lchaschen had, if the reconstructions are correct, central axles. The best location for an axle, which on two-wheelers is simply a fulcrum, must have been quickly arrived at by trial and error; it could hardly have been a 'discovery' in a period as advanced technically as the Late Bronze Age. Axle position would vary less with the period than with the manner in which the chariot was used. For instance, a stable load properly balanced over a central axle would have relieved the team of most of the weight, while a shifting load, such as a fighting complement, would, under such circumstances, have caused the chariot to bucket back and forth. This is when the rear axle would give stability – at the price of weighting the team.

Hence the position of the axle has little diagnostic value for dating, except within a given culture. Even there, its representation may be governed more by artistic or spatial considerations in certain media where the area is limited, as for instance, seal stones or orthostats.

The two-wheelers at Syunik (figs. 1–7) are too abbreviated to permit of much interpretation. The only two shown with teams seem to be harnessed to oxen (figs. 1 and 7), and the yoke fittings in figures 2 and 3 look more like ox-yoke than equid-yoke fittings. All the 4-wheelers here are ox-drawn and, as noted above, there is only one representation of a horse, and it is not in harness. Are these two-wheelers carts rather than chariots? The only known representation of a true chariot pulled by bovids is that in the eighteenth-Dynasty tomb of Huy (Smith 1958, pl. 144A). All the vehicles, both 4-wheelers and 2-wheelers, illustrated from Syunik are rendered in the conventional petroglyph perspective. The depiction of the box on some of the 2-wheelers as roughly a circle conforms with that on some of the other rock carvings both east and west, as well as on Chinese pictographs (figs. 10, 12, 17, 19, 23f., 26).

At Kojbagar in the Karatau, figures 10 and 12 show the box in the same convention as those just mentioned. This is not only common in Eurasian rock art, where it has often been interpreted as representing the sun disk rather than a 'transparent' chariot floor (a subject to which we shall return), but it exactly repeats the Shang pictographs, where the chariot floor is indeed represented by an almost perfect circle, quartered by pole and axle (fig. 26) and which are from a land in which there was no solar cult, as Kozhin notes. At least two Shang graves contained chariots with oval floor plans (von Dewall 1964, 211, 214), which would easily lead to such a convention. Moreover, such chariots may once have had a wider diffusion than we know. In figure 11 the box has the D-shaped floor plan known from actual eighteenth-Dynasty chariots (Carter 1927, pl. XXXVII B; Quibell 1908, pl. LV) and still attested on some Cypriot terracotta models of probably the sixth and fifth centuries B.C. (Myres 1933, 35, n. 25; Ohnefalsch-Richter 1893, pl. CXCVI; Studniczka 1907, 187, fig. 32). The closest that we seem to find to this in China is the box of an Early Chou chariot, basically rectangular in shape, but with chamfered front corners (fig. 28B).

Four-spoked wheels are not particularly informative, as discussed above. Kadyrbaev and Marjaschev 1972 note, without specifying which, that some of the chariot petroglyphs from other areas in Kazakhstan show 8-spoked wheels, and they would consider this difference as chronologically significant. While the earliest spoked wheels have four spokes, there are brief appearances of eight spokes in the Bronze Age. Syrian seals dated before the middle of the second millennium show some (Buchanan 1966, no. 895E; Amiet, fig. 9) and in Egypt they appear once in a relief attributed to the reign of Tuthmosis III (1504–1450), (Bruyère 1952, pl. IV), and once, notably but briefly, on the chariot of Tuthmosis IV (1450–1425). And from Lchaschen we have material evidence of 28 spokes three to five hundred years before eight spokes begin to appear on Assyrian reliefs.

No attempt is made to give any shape to the yokes themselves here, yet we know that Egyptian and Near-Eastern equid yokes were roughly bow-shaped until at least the eighth century B.C. (Carter 1927, pl. XLI A; Barnett n.d., pl. 19) and that thereafter they were shaped with individual bays for the horses' necks (Yadin 1963, 426). The earlier yokes were very slender, with strongly recurving ends; on the later ones the ends seem shorter and cup-shaped (Barnett n.d., pls. 59 and 121). Four petroglyphs at Kojbagar (figs. 10. 12–14) seem to show upward curving ends. They look most of all like the simple metal yoke ends actually found in Cyprus on a chariot dated to c. 700 B.C. (Karageorghis 1973, pl. LXXIX) and illustrated on a fifth-century relief on a stone sarcophagus in the Metropolitan Museum (Myres 1933, 3f) and on a very explicit unpublished terracotta model in the Royal Ontario Museum (cat. no. 958.61.309). But this may be reading too much into them. What they differ distinctly from are the horizontal Shang and Chou yoke ends, with their bronze leaf-shaped or lanceolate terminals (von Dewall 1964, pl. 14:3 and 4, pl. 21:2). The earlier type of yoke, however, was associated with yoke saddles, of which we find a clear example here in figure 10. Since yoke saddles, although apparently abandoned in the west sometime in the eighth century B.C., were found with the fifth–fourth century B.C. carriage from Kurgan V at Pazyryk (Rudenko 1970, pl. 131) and in Late Chou tombs in China (Needham 1965, pl. CXXXVIII), it would be unsound to use them as a dating criterion for Central Asia. Fig. 14 may also show yoke saddles, or it may show the pairs of wooden rods used on some ox yokes. The presence of a camel in close proximity (although apparently not attached) to the yoke might suggest camel draught, as in figure 13, hence a different yoke from that used for equids.

Fig. 11 shows seven lines running back from the horses' heads or the yoke area. The central one of these certainly represents the pole, and the two outside pairs would be the reins. There remains a single, shorter line on either side of the pole inside the reins. The right one of these joins the pole about two thirds of the way back, while the left one (probably erroneously drawn) joins the inside rein of the left-hand horse. These seem to represent yoke braces – a largely overlooked element of equid-yoke harnessing, probably because, being of perishable material, they have not survived. We find them as early as the eighteenth Dynasty (pl. 12) and as late as the third century B.C. (pl. 19) and they are evidenced in between in ninth-century Assyria (Barnett n.d., pl. 13). These straps seem to have served more than one function. Since the yoke and pole were attached to each other only by a pin and lashings at their junction, the yoke would have a tendency, when under lateral pressure, to swivel on the pole. This meant that on sharp turns the hind quarters of the inside animal risked colliding with the pole. I have also been informed by J. Spruytte, who has experimented with equids under the ancient type of pole-and-yoke hitch, that, without the braces, the faster horse of an unevenly matched team will pull ahead of the other, thus producing a bias pressure on their necks. He also tells me that the braces help to transfer some of the pull further back on the pole and to distribute it on the yoke, thus relieving the main area of attachment of some strain.

In figure 12, do the two lines running from yoke to box on either side of the pole also represent yoke-arm braces? Some of these in the Egyptian chariot-workshop scenes are shown as joining the pole very far back, and that may be what is intended here (Yadin 1963, 202). The 'harnessing scene' is unique in its composition. Most of those known to us from the ancient civilizations follow an established pattern: either one or two pole horses are already hitched, while the second pole horse or a trace horse is being led up alongside or being backed up to the chariot (Cooney 1965, pl. 31; Barnett n.d., p. 59; Buschor 1969, pl. 132).

We have already mentioned western evidence for the D-shaped box that we find at Akdzilgi in the Pamirs (fig. 15). The flooring here is apparently of interwoven thongs. Actual chariots found in Egypt in eighteenth-Dynasty contexts have such floorings (Carter 1927, 109; Quibell 1908, pl. LV; Botti 1951, fig. 2), and it is now believed that the light two-wheelers found at Lchaschen also had them (Piggott 1974, 16). A probably fifth-century B.C. terracotta model from Cyprus (Ohnefalsch-Richter 1893, pl. CXCVI; Studniczka 1907, 187, with fig. 32) has such a floor painted in, and we find it engraved on the gold models from the Oxus Treasure (Dalton 1964, p. XL). A thong flooring is postulated for one of the buried chariots from the Western-Chou site of Changchia-p'o (pl. 30B and von Dewall 1964, 227), and evidence of its existence on many others may be lacking merely due to the perishability of both wood and leather.

The pairs of oblique lines running to the pole on either side from the box can be interpreted as representing the supports connecting upper box front and pole on actual Egyptian chariots and illustrated in Egyptian paintings and reliefs. These sometimes look as though they were no more than a pair of leather straps (pl. 18), but we know from the Tut'ankhamūn chariots exhibited in Cairo that they might also consist of pairs of wooden rods. In view of the fact that the yoke braces in figure 15 are shown as double lines, although they probably were meant to indicate single, wide straps, the quadruple support at the box front might also be interpreted as merely a pair.

The chariots in the petroglyphs at Jamani Us again fall into the convention of the other rock carvings illustrated and of Chinese pictographs. The roughly oval boxes in figs. 16, 17 and 19 could be pure schematization or could stand, with varying degrees of approximation, for the different types of rounded floor plans: the D-shaped boxes of western Asia – probably prevalent there until the eighth century B.C. – or the apparently more oval ones of which we have remains from Shang China. The small rectangular box, with slightly rounded corners that appears in figure 18 is extraordinarily reminiscent, both in shape and proportions, of a Shang chariot found at An-yang (fig. 34). The central or near central axle position on the Jamani Us chariots, if it can be read literally, echoes that of Chinese pictographs (fig. 26) and actual Chinese chariots (figs. 28, 30 and 34).

The yokes in figures 17 and 18, however, show the turned-up ends that are characteristic of western rather than of Chinese chariots. We have here also, in figures 16 and 18 (and perhaps in figure 17) the yoke braces recorded in the west but thus far unnoted as

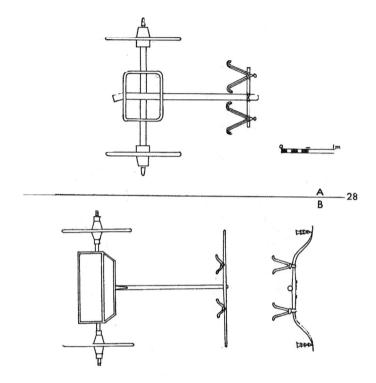

Fig. 28. Ch'ang-an, Chou period. After von Dewall, Taf. 19B.

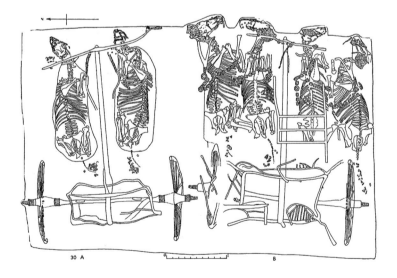

Fig. 30. Ch'ang-an, Chou period (same burial as 28). After Wang, Chung and
Chang, fig. 94.

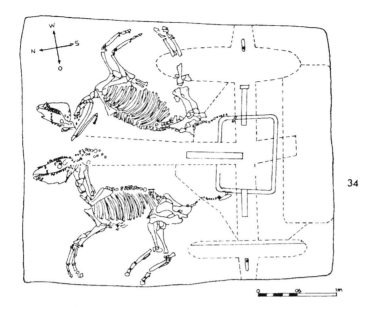

Fig. 34. Anyang, Shang period. After von Dewall, Taf 5B.

such by Chinese archaeologists. In figure 30A, however, of a Western Chou chariot burial at Chang-chia-p'o, for which I am indebted to Mrs Barbara Stephen, one may see lines running back from the yoke on either side of the pole. These are decorated with shells for only a short distance, where, if they were yoke braces, they might show above the horses' necks; behind that they are plain. Although they are not shown as connecting with the pole at their rear ends, it seems possible that they could have done so; certainly they must have been attached somewhere. In other burials, undecorated leather straps may have disintegrated completely. That these rather essential elements of yoke harness did in fact exist in China may also be indicated in figure 26, where, even in the abbreviation of a pictograph such braces are shown.

Fig. 16 probably shows a quadriga (although a triga cannot be completely ruled out). When a team appears on western petroglyphs, it consists of only two animals: the Chinese pictographs show none. The four-horse team, once thought evidenced in a Shang tomb at An-yang (von Dewall 1964, pl. 4B), does not, as Miss von Dewall has established (138), occur in China before the Western Chou (i.e. late eleventh century B.C.). In western Asia it is not securely documented before the ninth century B.C., although teams of four equids, harnessed to very different vehicles, were usual in third-millennium Mesopotamia. Fig. 17 depicts either a triga or it is an incomplete representation of a quadriga. The triga was common in ninth-century B.C. Assyria (Barnett n.d., pls. 26 and 27) and, although we have no evidence of it from Shang or Chou China, a team of three appears (with collar harness?) on a moulded brick attributed to the Han period (Needham 1965, fig. 565).

As for figures 20 and 21 – they are clearly carts, not chariots, and are too late to concern us here. The condition of the rock surface already indicates a later date and Volkov 1972 notes the profile view, the canopies, the cortege compositions, the technique of sunken relief, and the rendering of one wheel as slightly ahead of the other (fig. 20), and finds their closest parallels in Han (206 B.C.–220 A.D.) tomb reliefs, but suggests that they could be even later. We may note in passing still another feature typical of the Han but over-looked by Volkov 1972: the gait – a trot or pace – at which the horses are moving.

The 'Gobi Quadriga' (fig. 22) has received far more attention than any of the other petroglyphs discussed. Okladnikov, who originally published it, considered it a 4-wheeler. He gave it no specific date, remaining vague on the subject. Noting that the carvings of ibex in its vicinity were very similar in style to those in other parts of Central Asia, he suggested the Bronze Age and the ubiquitous Indo-Europeans. The vehicle he considered a Chariot of the Sun because of the disk between two of the wheels, and he compared it to the six-wheeled bronze model of the so-called Chariot of the Sun from Trundholm, Denmark, of the late second millennium B.C. (Powell 1961, pl. 27). On the other hand, Okladnikov believed he found in the composi-tion a 'standard' with a finial in the form of a goat, which he com-pared to Scythian standards of the seventh–fifth centuries B.C. Kozhin sees the composition as showing two chariots. While not denying the possibility that a solar chariot may be represented here, he notes the similarity in the rendering of the 'front' two-wheeler to the chariots on Shang pictographs (fig. 26), and, citing the absence of a sun cult in China, suggests that the quartered disk between the two wheels is merely the chariot floor, as in the pictographs. Although recog-nizing the fact that the number of spokes in representations may not always be read literally, he still bases his dating on this factor. Pointing out that the earliest Shang chariots found in tombs have a large number of spokes (a minimum of 18: von Dewall 1964, 124), he suggests that this carving, with its 8-spoked wheels, which to him appears Chinese in inspiration, must have been made some time after the formation of the pictographs but before the earliest Shang chariots from the graves at An-yang. This, according to him, would be before 1400 B.C., although western sinologists would place it rather before c. 1200 B.C.

Dorzh (as reported by Volkov 1972, 84) accepts the vehicle as a 4-wheeler and one that, in his opinion, is similar to the 4-wheeled carriage from Kurgan 5 at Pazyryk (Rudenko 1970, pl. 131), hence he attributes it to the last centuries B.C. Volkov 1972 (82–87) also sees a 4-wheeler here, and gives it roughly the same dating as he does the earlier Jamani Us petroglyphs, i.e. the end of the second or first half of the first millennium B.C.

The 'Gobi Quadriga', as a possible (and rather unusual) 4-wheeler, should first be compared with other petroglyphs of wagons with pole-and-yoke hitch shown in the same perspective. None exist among the Shang pictographs. The nearest area to show them in rock carving is Syunik, where we find a large number of 4-wheelers (fig. 29). These, however, have rectangular wagon beds and with one exception solid wheels; they are ox-drawn, and (again with perhaps one exception) have no more than two draught animals. They are rarer in Scandinavia (fig. 31) and, although we do find spoked-wheeled wagons here (with four spokes), they are still pulled by only a pair of oxen. These are called 'Middle Bronze Age' and given a range of c. 1200–800 B.C. by Stenberger (98ff.). There are a few examples in the Italian Alps, where again some of them are solid-wheeled and ox-drawn (fig. 32A), as well as horse-drawn (Anati 1960, 145).

Fig. 29. Syunik. After Karakhanian and Safian, fig. 177.

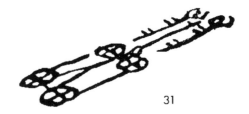

Fig. 31. Bohuslan, Sweden. After Treue 1965, p. 181.

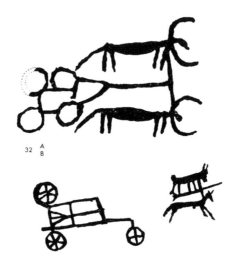

Fig. 32A, 32B. Val Camonica, After Anati 1961, pp. 144 and 146.

Here, however, we also find horse-drawn wagons with spoked wheels (fig. 32B and Anati 1960, 104). Anati, dating stylistically, places the solid-wheeled examples in the period 1400–800 B.C., and the spoked ones c. 800–550 B.C. Fig. 316 shows both 4- and 6-spoked wheels on the same vehicle.

Despite these differences, it is tempting to see in the irregular triangle between the rear wheels of the Gobi vehicle (if they are rear wheels) something similar to the triangular brace shown at the rear of all these wagons except those from Syunik and the earlier ones from Camonica. This indicates an undercarriage i.e. the floor of the wagon box is elevated above the axles. If such a deduction were correct, this (as well as the 4-horse team) would probably place a *terminus ante quem* of at least the early first millennium B.C. on the

Gobi carving. This still would not solve the problem of the quartered disk between the front wheels here, which corresponds to nothing in ancient representations of 4-wheelers that are shown in this perspective. While it does suggest a certain part of a modern forecarriage that limits the swivelling of a front axle, we have no evidence of such a thing even on those ancient vehicles that do have articulating forecarriages (Klindt-Jensen 1950, figs. 59f.). Material remains of 4-wheelers from western Asia are scanty, and even the latest of the wagons from the Caucasus area discussed by Piggott (1968, 280) – those from Lchaschen, dated by him 1300–1100 B.C. – had a floor resting directly on the axles, solid wheels, and a triangular draught pole. Later and closer to hand is the carriage found in Kurgan 5 at Pazyryk, which Rudenko (1970, 307) dates to the fifth century B.C. Although there is neither a triangular nor a circular part to the framework of its box, and it is crowned by a high rectangular canopy, the wheels are spoked (34 spokes would surely have been too many for a rock artist!), it had a straight pole and a team of four horses, the outsiders being trace animals (Rudenko 1970, 189ff. with pl. 131). Moreover, the Pazyryk carriage, which seems to betray Chinese influence (although probably not actual Chinese manufacture) and which was found in the same tomb with Chinese embroideries, suggests an explanation of the peculiar disk between the two front wheels. This is not rendered in the same manner as the wheels, i.e. if what we see are four 'spokes' the areas between them appear as solid, not open. Even schematically rendered chariot floors are not shown thus. We have evidence from the Han period in China, if not earlier, of circular baldachins or parasols carried in carts (Needham 1965, figs. 394, 541, 543–4). Parasols are shown on Assyrian reliefs of the eighth and seventh centuries B.C. (Madhloom 1970, pls. III: 2, IV: 2, VI: 1, 3 and 4). Chinese influence, however, would seem to be the one to look for in this region, and Needham (1965, 70–1) even cites a textual reference in the Han to a very large parasol that was made for a 4-wheeler. We might then perhaps interpret the Kobdo Somon vehicle as a 4-wheeler with a triangular rear undercarriage and a circular baldachin over the front axle, the long side beams of the floor having been omitted in the carving. Although in western Asia the parasol is an attribute of royalty, in Han China it may be carried in a number of vehicles in procession. Hence it might be rash to suggest a special significance to the one on the Gobi vehicle.

On the other hand, we must remember Kozhin's objections to the interpretation of this vehicle as a 4-wheeler (1968, 35, n. 3). He notes that the front and rear wheels are neither on axles of equal length nor in line, and that the front pair of wheels is larger than the rear pair. The possibility of two 2-wheelers must be considered. In this case the front one would either show the parasol postulated above and evidenced on 2-wheelers east and west, or this disk would be an eccentric rendering of the convention of the nearly circular box quartered by pole and axle. We would find here the 8-spoked wheels and 4-horse team with two trace horses already observed at Jamani Us (fig. 16). A new and extremely interesting feature appears in the harnessing of these animals: there is a marked upward projection at the base of each neck. Unless they are hump-backed cattle (which seems highly unlikely in this region and with a quadriga), this may represent the top or finial of a yoke saddle (Littauer 1968). The yoke saddle, which seems to have been abandoned in western Asia in the eighth century B.C., appears in China from the beginning (figs. 26. 28. 30. 34) and it continues in use right down to Han times. The upper end of this wishbone-shaped object in China was sometimes quite prominent and might even be capped with rattles (von Dewall 1964, pl. 7:1 and 2; pl. 16:5 and 6). Large yoke saddles were still used on the carriage team in Kurgan 5 at Pazyryk. Now the interesting thing is that at Pazyryk and on all western Asiatic quadrigae (Barnett n.d., pls. 16 and 18), these yoke saddles were used only on the pole horses – at least Rudenko, who calls them 'primitive horse collars' (1970, 191), records no more than the two attached to the yoke, although he himself is not certain about all the details of harnessing. But, if the curious humps on the Gobi animals do represent yoke saddles, *these are on the trace horses here as well.* This does not seem to make practical sense, since the function of this saddle is to adapt the yoke (invented for oxen) to equids' necks. But perhaps in the interests of symmetry, yoke saddles may sometimes have been placed also on trace horses' necks. Unfortunately, in the later Chinese burials with chariots and horses, the animals were unharnessed and buried separately. We do, however, have one example of an early Chou burial at Chiang-chia-p'o, which may shed light on the matter. Miss von Dewall (40) writes of all four horses here as having been under the yoke, and they all wore yoke saddles. Fig. 30B, however, illustrating the burial, shows the two pole horses under a short yoke and the other two outside it. Were the two yoke ends broken off? If they were not, this harnessing would be very similar to that shown on the Gobi rock, and the evidence of each would tend to reinforce that of the other, suggesting that such a practice did at one time exist in the east.

The ithyphallic character of these animals reminds one of the Pamirs chariot team (fig. 15) and is found again on some of the Swedish carvings (fig. 23). Curiously, while western Asiatic, Greek, and Etruscan representations are usually careful to indicate that chariot animals are not only males, but whole males, it is only the mount of Dionysus (mule) that is shown as ithyphallic. On horses in Chinese art the sex is never directly indicated, although the secondary sexual character-istics of stallions are often markedly present or markedly absent.

But, while the 'front chariot' at Kobdo Somon might be thus explained, it is more difficult to interpret the 'rear chariot'. Although it is true that unharnessed chariots are found with harnessed ones in Syunik, at Jamani Us and at Frannarp in southern Sweden (fig. 23), none are in such close proximity to each other as would be those on the Gobi scene. The triangular floor plan is not near to that in any chariot petroglyphs, but could suggest a different type of 2-wheeler: the A-frame cart. We have an example of one with spoked wheels at Oughtasar in Syunik (fig. 33). While the axle here is advanced, actual carts of this type with rear axles were found in the burials at Lchaschen (Piggott 1968, fig. 8). Although similar carts

Fig. 33. Syunik. After Karakhanian and Safian, fig. 45.

in Anatolia today have solid wheels (Piggott 1968, fig. 9), a spoked-wheeled example was photographed at Tbilisi (Lane 1935, pl. II) and the A-frame cart of India has spoked wheels. The rod with the zoomorphic finial above a pair of eyelets that runs up from what would here be the front end of the pole may now perhaps be interpreted as a type of object found in conjunction with vehicle burials at Lchaschen. This is apparently a descendant (now nonfunctional) of the Near-Eastern third-millennium terret rings with zoomorphic finials (Calmeyer 1964, 76 with fig. 19; Mnatsakanian 1957, 149–50, fig. 8, 13, 14). The former seem to have been found near the junction of pole and yoke and they merely have hooks on the sides for attachment; the rein holes of the real terrets have gone. Whether any of these were found directly associated with A-frame carts here is not clear from the excavator's reports, but since they existed so close together, this seems possible. In conclusion, a very different sort of suggestion may be offered, but again very tentatively, by the author. After a survey of so many petroglyphs one begins to wonder if such a variety of vehicles – 4-wheelers and 2-wheelers of different shapes, with different draught animals – oxen, horses and camels – can all be solar chariots. Was the god drawn by both horses and camels in the same region (*e.g.* figs. 13 and 14)? And in the genre-like scene of harnessing here would it be the god himself, or his groom, who is leading up the team? In the apparently processional scene at Akdzilgi in the Pamirs (fig. 15) does the god have several chariots, and what would be the connection of the dead men here with them? Are D-shaped (figs. 11 and 15) and rectangular (fig. 18) and bell-shaped (fig. 23) chariot boxes solar symbols, as well as the circular ones (figs. 3, 10, 19)?

Kozhin 1968, 42 suggests that the schematic rendering of the equipages resembles a view from below or above, hence of a vehicle crossing the sky. An objection to the former perspective is that the animals are not seen as they would be in life if viewed from below, but on their sides, usually back to back or nose to nose. The wheels also, if read literally, would seem to have been dismounted and to be lying at the ends of the axles. The view from above seems closer to being a possibility, but not as connected with the sky. What the so-called schematic rendering does bring to mind is an actual scene and one that we have been made more familiar with by recent discoveries (*e.g.* Vermeule 1964, pl. XLVII B; Karageorghis 1967b, fig. 144). This is the tomb or the dromos in which vehicles and draught animals were buried together. When the animals were symmetrically disposed after slaughter and have been undisturbed by subsequent burials, they are often found lying back to back or nose to nose (fig. 34). While wheels are less often dismounted, they sometimes are. One cannot help wondering if, no matter what other ends it may eventually have served, this type of rendering of a vehicle was not first suggested to the artist by looking down into a tomb and if, in some instances, such as at Akdzilgi in the Pamirs, it did not remain associated with the funerary cult.

Acknowledgements

The author is greatly indebted to Dr K. Jettmar, who first informed her of the existence of these petroglyphs and who generously supplied her with copies of published material difficult to obtain in the United States, to Dr E. Porada for going out of her way to provide her with the Armenian literature, and to Professor S. Piggott for kindly sending her the report on the Urals chariot. She is also most grateful to Dr M. B. Moore, whose friendship was equal to the patience with which she executed a long series of drawings of an alien subject.

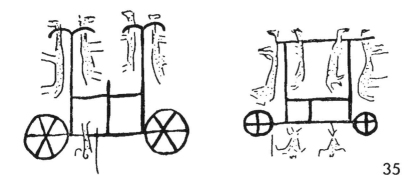

Fig. 35. Uad, Zigza. After Graziosi 1942, fig. 11.

11. A 19TH AND 20TH DYNASTY HEROIC MOTIF ON ATTIC BLACK-FIGURED VASES?*

M. A. LITTAUER

While reviewing the figured evidence for various ancient chariots, the author came across a peculiar pose of the chariot warrior, found on 19th and 20th dynasty monumental reliefs and on Attic black-figured ware, which may be called "the-foot-on-the-chariot-pole."** The chariot warrior stands astraddle the front breastwork of the vehicle, one foot on the pole just in front of the breastwork. Since the pole here is already slightly higher than the chariot floor and since the figure leans forward, the forward leg is bent at the knee, while the other remains straight. The Egyptian warrior or hunter (who is always the Pharaoh) may wield a bow, a spear or a sickle sword; his Greek counterpart (who may be Ares, Herakles or an anonymous παραιβάτης) may use a bow, spear or sword.

There are Egyptian representations of the theme at Karnak: Sethos I charging the Libyans,[1] and Ramses II conquering the towns of Sabat and Akat;[2] at Medinet Abu: Ramses III fighting the Syrians and storming a city (pl. 14)[3] and the same king hunting the wild bull;[4] and at Beit-el Weli in Nubia: scenes of foreign conquests of Ramses II.[5]

Even a relatively cursory glance at the Greek material yields eighteen examples of this motif. The earliest seems to occur on a fragmentary dinos by Lydos in Athens, showing Herakles in a Gigantomachy.[6] Group E contributes a warrior in a fight on a type B amphora

* *American Journal of Archaeology* 72, 150–152
** My warmest thanks are due to Professor J. K. Anderson, without whose encouragement and very kind help this note would neither have been undertaken nor completed. Its defects, however, are entirely the author's.
[1] Wreszinski 1935, pl. 50.
[2] Wreszinski 1935, pl. 56.
[3] Wreszinski 1935, pl. 151; Breasted and Allen 1932, pl. 88.
[4] Schaefer and Andrae 1925, pl. 394.
[5] Wreszinski 1935, pl. 164.
[6] Beazley 1956, 107, no. 1, from the Acropolis.

in Copenhagen,[7] and another one, perhaps driving into battle, on a neck amphora in Berlin.[8] Herakles fights with Geryon on a Near Group E, type B amphora in the Vatican.[9] The same group gives us two examples of Ares in a Gigantomachy on neck amphorae in the British Museum[10] (pl. 15), and a hoplite on a similar vase in Copenhagen.[11] Another neck amphora, in the manner of Exekias, in Tarquinia, displays Herakles in a Gigantomachy again.[12] The same hero appears in a different context on a volute krater made by Nikosthenes in London.[13] This yields both an orthodox example and an interesting variant: Herakles faces forward but Kyknos, who flees before him in another chariot, has assumed the pose in reverse, after swiveling around with his legs still athwart the breastwork, and is facing backward to launch a parting shot. The Elbows Out Painter (Painter of Louvre E 705) decorated a band cup in Naples with a hoplite in a fight;[14] and Herakles fights the giants again on a small Panathenaic amphora by the Lysippides Painter in London[15] (pl. 16). A type B amphora in New York, which has been attributed to the Princeton Painter, depicts a hoplite[16] (pl. 17); but Herakles comes right back again in a Gigantomachy on a type A amphora in the Vatican by the Painter of Vatican 365.[17] He occurs in the same role on a fragmentary "self-made" kantharos in Athens,[18] as well as on a Leagros Group hydria in the Vatican.[19] Three examples apparently not in Beazley are all of warriors in fights: on a volute krater in Copenhagen, where the style has been compared to that of the manner of the Antimenes Painter;[20] on an amphora, also in Copenhagen;[21] and on a vase of the same class in Tarquinia.[22]

---

[7] Beazley 1956, 135, no. 33, from Vulci.
[8] Beazley 1956, 137, no. 62, from Orvieto.
[9] Beazley 1956, 138, Group of Vatican 347 no. 1, from Cerveteri.
[10] Beazley 1956, 139, no. 1 and 2, both from Vulci.
[11] Beazley 1956, 139, no. 3, from Vulci.
[12] Beazley 1956, 147, no. 2.
[13] Beazley 1956, 229, no. vi.
[14] Beazley 1956, 250, no. 28.
[15] Beazley 1956, 260, no. 29, from Vulci.
[16] Beazley 1956, 299, no. 15, from Vulci.
[17] Beazley 1956, 311, Painter of Vatican 365 no. 1, from Cerveteri.
[18] Beazley 1956, 347, from the Acropolis.
[19] Beazley 1956, 363, no. 45, from Vulci.
[20] CVA Denmark 8, pl. Denmark 325, 1a and 1b.
[21] CVA Denmark 3, pl. Denmark 103.
[22] CVA Italia 25, pl. Italia 1148.

The motif evidently persisted for at least half a century, and Herakles occurs as frequently in the role at the end of the period as at the beginning, although his popularity is shared throughout by the unidentified hoplite.

The pose in Egypt may simply have been the result of removing the typical striding, conquering Pharaoh of the period from the ground and placing him in a chariot. There is, however, nothing essentially superhuman about this feat, despite the fact that it is usually the Pharaoh who is depicted executing it. The front breast-work of the Egyptian chariot is often shown as low enough for the leg to pass over it, and its body was so shallow from front to back that it allowed little room for the spread stance of vigorous action; it is easy to see why someone wielding a weapon would have been tempted to assume such a position. But to do so he would have had to stand in the center of the chariot in line with the pole and this would have necessitated that he occupy the chariot alone. The weight of a second, now necessarily off-center occupant (even were there room enough for him on one side, which seems doubtful) would badly upset the lateral equilibrium of this light and easily overturned vehicle.[23]

Hence the fact that all Attic black-figured vases with this motif show two persons in the chariot – warrior and charioteer – is already a strong argument against the Greeks ever having attempted this

---

[23] This is not the place to bring up the whole vexed question of whether the Pharaoh did or did not ever drive alone with the reins tied around his hips. Suffice it to say that this is not an impossible feat under proper conditions with properly trained horses. As Bronson 1965, 97–99 has pointed out, it was a usual practice of Etruscan and, later, of Roman racing drivers. And the fact that one of the early Egyptian representations of the motif depicts merely a royal scribe would seem evidence that it was not invented solely to enable the artist to portray the Pharaoh without an inferior being beside him; Wreszinski 1923, pls. 1 and 26. Moreover, an illuminating scene occurs in the next-to-lowest register of the relief of Ramses III fighting the Libyans, at Medinet Abu; Wreszinski 1935, pl. 137. The Egyptian chariots here, which are charging the enemy, carry, as usual, a complement of only two men, but the drivers bear shields in their left hands. The control of the horses seems to be effected by a curious cooperative effort, in which the reins are tied around the archer's hips, but only after passing through the right hand of the shield-bearer-charioteer. Obviously, it was the bowman who provided the strong braking power when needed, while the shield-bearer exercised directional control. The problem of the latter, plus the danger of being fouled up in one's own reins should the chariot overturn, for which see Bronson 1965, 99, is what makes it seem highly unlikely that the Pharaoh ever risked his life alone in this position on the battlefield. What it did do was to provide the artist with a convenient way to display him in solitary glory.

position in actual practice. It did not appear in Greece at a time when the chariot might still have been used in warfare (there is not a hint of it before the sixth century), nor did it conform with what tradition tells us of that warfare. That it was not even worked out independently by the Greeks as an artistic convention seems evidenced by another aspect that is never plausibly presented on the black-figured examples. The front breastwork of the usual archaic chariot was too high to be straddled; but there is no attempt on the part of the artist to resolve this problem by reducing its height, which remains inalterably silhouetted against the center of the warrior's body up to his waist. Neither does the performance appear to have been associated with any particular Greek legendary hero, since there are a variety of protagonists.

It looks far more like a borrowed theme, and one not hard to come by. The Egyptian examples were not hidden away in tombs, but were on monumental reliefs, all, with the possible exception of that at Beitel-Weli, well within the sightseeing range of a Greek craftsman visiting relatives in the Delta. The pose is a dashing one and it provided the artist with a strong diagonal with which to emphasize the movement and excitement of his subject. It is easy to understand why it would have been seized upon.

But it may be worth noting that, although the black-figure artist seemed willing to borrow the motif without worrying overmuch about how it could have been implemented on the archaic chariot, he borrowed no other part of this scene from the Egyptian repertory. He apparently did not feel free to vary his own known form of chariot by changing the shape of the breastwork, adding more spokes to the wheel, or shifting the axle to the rear in the Egyptian manner. And as for the most striking element in the Egyptian composition – the isolated Pharaoh with reins tied around the waist – he evidently found it too conspicuously far from Greek practice to be tempted by it.

One wonders also if these thrusting Pharaohs did not cast an even longer shadow across time and space. With out scanty evidence on the origins of certain aspects of Celtic chariot warfare, it is idle, but nonetheless tempting, to speculate upon a possible connection. A black-figured vase, of almost any of the classes to which those cited above belonged, finding its way north of the Alps, would have constituted an important enough possession to become an heirloom. Years later Gallic chariot warriors, gathered in some house where such a vase was treasured, might well have been fired by the scene

upon it. They might even have dared each other to go one step further – which would have put them completely out on the chariot
pole.[24] In a society where individual physical skill and prowess played
an important role, it is not difficult to see how such a feat, however
negligible its real military value, would have proved attractive.

Let southeast Asian specialists tell us how this theme reached
Angkor Wat in the twelfth century A.D.[25]

---

[24] Caesar, *De Bello Gallico* 4, 33. It is to be noted that the Celts *could* practice a
form of this feat with two people just because it was so exaggerated. With one of
the participants entirely out on the pole, both could remain in the central axis of
the chariot-and-pole complex. And if we are to believe what seems to be the only
early illustration we have of this accomplishment, the coin of Sasserna of ca 50
B.C. (Piggott 1952, 87ff., pl. 1), it was the charioteer who went forward. (Caesar
is not specific about this.) Thus neither would the reins be interfered with nor would
they interfere with the warrior.

[25] Groslier and Arthaud 1957, pls. 134f. This relief, from the west-wing gallery,
south section, depicts a scene from the Mahābhārata – the fight between the Pandava
and the Kaurava. The hero, who is a deity, is in a poled chariot, neither Egyptian
nor Greek in type, and has one foot on the pole. That the small figure whose neck
is pierced with an arrow may not be supposed to be on the ground on the far side
of the team (which is collapsing) but may represent a charioteer entirely out on the
pole is indicated by a relief from Bapuon illustrated in Couchoud 1928, 191, fig.
17. Here a small figure in a similar position is unmistakably the charioteer squat-
ting forward on the pole. This would tend to confirm the Celtic version.

12. CHARIOTS IN IRON AGE CYPRUS*

J. H. CROUWEL

In *RDAC* 1985 I discussed evidence for the use of a particular type of wheeled vehicle – the cart – in Cyprus during the Iron Age.** A cart may be described as a two wheeler, designed to carry a stable load, i.e. goods or seated passengers. The present paper is concerned with another type of two-wheeler – the chariot – which was suitable for carrying a less stable load of one or more persons who usually stood. As noted in the earlier paper, a third type of vehicle – the four-wheeled wagon – is not attested in Iron Age Cyprus. (For definitions of chariot, cart, wagon and other technical terms used here, see the glossaries in Littauer and Crouwel 1979, 3–7, and Crouwel 1981, 23–27).

Chariots in Cyprus have received a good deal of attention but no attempt at a systematic study has so far been published.[1] The sources are extensive, deriving both from representations and from remains of actual vehicles. The representations are mainly terracotta models in the round, most of them dating to the 7th and 6th century B.C. but also including later ones;[2] there are also several 5th century models made of stone,[3] as well as two-dimensional representations, such

* *Report of the Department of Antiquities Cyprus*, 1987, 101–118.

** I am most grateful to Miss A. Caubet, Dr V. Karageorghis, Mrs S. Lubsen-Admiraal, Dr J. R. Mertens, Dr P. R. S. Moorey and Dr V. Tatton-Brown for information and assistance of various kinds. I am also much indebted to Mrs M. A. Littauer for comments upon most of a draft text, to my wife for help with the English, and to Mr M. Bootsman for assistance with the illustrations. Most of the photographs appear by courtesy of the Ashmolean Museum (Oxford), the Department of Antiquities (Cyprus), the Metropolitan Museum of Art (New York) and the Musée du Louvre (Paris).

[1] The best surveys appeared in unpublished doctoral dissertations: Tatton-Brown (nee Wilson) 1972, chapter V; Törnqvist 1970, 87–95. I am grateful to both authors for letting me have copies of their work. Studniczka 1907, 160–188, is still valuable.

[2] No list is attempted here but individual examples are mentioned in the text when relevant. The largest excavated collections are from Ayia Irini (Gjerstad 1935, 642ff. with pls. CCXXXIV–CCXXXV; 1963, 10–4; Törnqvist 1970, 87–103), Kourion (Young and Young 1955, esp. 216f., 228–30; Buitron 1983, 230f.) and Salamis (Monloup 1984, esp. 54–72, 161–4).

[3] Cesnola 1894, pl. LXXX: 520 (= Studniczka 1907, no. 30; from Kourion; our

as two stone sarcophagi with relief sculpture of similar date,[4] vase paintings of the 8th but mostly 7th century,[5] embossed gold plaques[6] and seal engravings of the 7th–6th centuries.[7] (The time span covered by this material is known in local terms as Cypro-Geometric III, Cypro-Archaic I–II, Cypro-Classical I–II and Hellenistic).[8]

In addition, chariots as well as carts have been identified among the remains of actual vehicles buried along with their draught teams and their harness in tombs of the 8th–7th century B.C. (Cypro-Geometric III to Cypro-Archaic I/II) at Salamis.[9] The wooden parts of the vehicles had decayed but had left at least partial impressions in the soil and some metal parts were preserved *in situ*, together with metal bits and other horse gear. In some cases the identification of the vehicles as chariots is in part based on the absence of iron bearing shoes for revolving axles which are typical of many carts but not of chariots.[10] Finds of similar metal gear from funerary contexts at Tamassos, Amathus and Palaepaphos, dating to the 8th–6th century B.C. (Cypro-Archaic I and II), suggest that such burials were not confined to one site.[11]

---

pl. XXXVI: 1–2), 515–517 (Golgoi); Myres 1914. no. 1016 (our pl. 19): Hermary 1981, nos. 45–47 (Amathus; for no. 47 see also Ohnefalsch-Richter 1893, pl. CXCVI: 3); Pryce 1931, no. C 84; Young and Young 1955, 175, esp. nos. St 228. 214 (Kourion; recent finds mentioned in Buitron 1983, 230).

[4] Amathus sarcophagus (our pl. 21): see esp. Myres 1909–11, 1f.: Studniczka 1907, no. 29; Tatton-Brown (née Wilson) 1972 and 1981. Golgoi sarcophagus (our pl. 20): see esp. Myres 1909–11, 3f.; Studniczka 1907, no. 28; Tatton-Brown (née Wilson) 1972.

[5] Karageorghis and des Gagniers 1974, nos. II.1 (Tamassos), II.2, II.3 (Palaepaphos), II.6; 1979, no. SI.1 (= Karageorghis 1973b: White Painted III krater of Cypro-Geometric III; from Khrysokhou; our fig. 3); Karageorghis 1966, 109 with fig. 9 (Morphou).

[6] Kapera 1981, 110f. nos. 7–9 with pls. XIV: 3, XV: 1–2 (Amathus); Ohnefalsch-Richter 1893, pl. CXCIX: 3 (Kourion); Karageorghis 1967a, 61f. nos. 67/2 and 61/29 with pls. LX–LXI (Salamis, Tomb 31); 1967b, 243 nos. 2–7 with fig. 22 (Palaepaphos, Tombs 7 and 8).

[7] Scarabs and scaraboids, see Gjerstad 1935, pl. CCXLIV: 8 (Ayia Irini no. 1148); Amadasi 1965, figs. 21: 2 (Idalion), 4 (Amathus), 5, 25: 1 (Lapithos), 5: 4 (attributed by Furumark 1950 to the Late Bronze Age, but probably also of Archaic date, see Boardman *apud* Crouwel 1981, 155 with n. 26).

[8] For chronology, see Karageorghis 1982b, 9f., table A. At Kourion terracotta chariot models apparently continued to be made into Roman times, see Young and Young 1955, 228–230.

[9] General survey of tombs in Karageorghis 1969, chapter III. For dating, see also Coldstream 1985, 54.

[10] This criterium is particularly important in the case of the highly fragmentary vehicle, probably a chariot (our A 6), from Tomb 50, see Crouwel 1985, 203 n. 3.

[11] Tamassos, "royal" Tomb IV (Cyprus-Archaic 11): see esp. Buchholz 1973, 330–7; 1974, 598 with fig. 59; 1978, 191–195 with fig. 41. Amathus, shallow pit

The following text is organized along the same lines as that dealing with Cypriot carts: it treats of the construction of the chariots, according to their constituent parts (body, axle, wheels, traction system), their draught animals, the ways in which the latter were harnessed and controlled and the use to which the vehicles were put. Concluding remarks will assess possible local, Cypriot characteristics and foreign elements. Reference is made throughout to the catalogue of actual chariot remains from Salamis that follows upon the main text.

Note. It is often difficult to decide whether chariot representations from Cyprus reflect vehicles that were actually used in the island. This is the problem, for instance, with the illustrations on some of the silver bowls of the so-called Cypro-Phoenician class of the 7th century B.C.; even if Cypriot manufacture can be demonstrated, the iconography of these bowls is strongly oriental in character.[12] Another example is an incomplete, restored terracotta chariot group of the 5th century B.C. from Mersinaki showing the goddess Athena mounting a quadriga. Here the chariot and harnessing are very Greek in appearance and have no parallels in Cyprus.[13]

Body

The actual chariots of the 8th–7th century B.C., buried at Salamis, include both bigae with a single, central draught pole, and quadrigae with two poles.

We have information on the bodies of two out of a total of five single-poled chariots. One (A 8, fig. 2: 1) was described by the excavator as having a more or less rectangular floor, 0.90 m. wide by 0.72 m. deep, its siding preserved to a height of only 0.25 m. A wooden partition ran front-to-back through the centre and at the rear there was a vertical wooden board, 0.18 m. high. The body of the other chariot (A 3) was found crushed but its depth could be measured as 0.60 m. Its siding, 0.60 m. high, was described as "convex . . ., the upper edge and flanks curved."[14] Brown stains of leather suggested siding screens of this material and a flooring of interwoven straps.

---

306 (near Cypro-Archaic II tomb): see Karageorghis 1980b, 1018 with figs. 120f. Palaepaphos (Cypro-Archaic I tombs): Karageorghis 1963a; 1967b (Tombs 7 and 8).

[12] See most recently Markou 1985; cf. Crouwel 1985. 204 n. 5.

[13] Westholm 1937, 364f. no. 814 etc. with pls. CXLVI–CXLVII: 1; Karageorghis, Styrenius, Winblath 1977, 43 with pl. XXIII: 1.

[14] Karageorghis 1967a, 50.

The dimensions of both bodies indicate rather small vehicles, the first chariot (A 8) offering room for two persons to stand abreast separated by the central partition.

The description of the second chariot (A 3) suggests a floor plan in the shape of a capital D, with one or two timbers forming the front and sides joined at the rear by a straight bar. The D-shaped floor plan was standard on the single-poled chariots of the Late Bronze Age in the eastern Mediterranean. In the Near East it can still be recognized on Assyrian reliefs of the 9th century B.C.,[15] while in Cyprus firm evidence is provided by a group of 7th century terracotta models of central-poled chariots (pl. 32).[16] According to extant chariots of the 15th–14th century B.C. from Egypt, the floor frame, c. 1 m. wide by 0.50 m. deep, was held together by inter-woven rawhide thongs, recalling the suggested flooring of Salamis chariot A 3.[17]

The single-poled chariots from Salamis, like the earlier Egyptian ones, had axles fixed under the rear floor bar. The poles must similarly have run all the way under the centre of the floor, to be anchored between the rear floor bar and the axle. In Egypt the chariot was supported at four points: by the pole – at the front and rear – and on two blocks that were placed between the ends of the floor bar and axle to accommodate the thickness of the pole end. A similar arrangement may be assumed for the Salamis chariots, where such details of construction have not been preserved.

The floor plan of the single-poled chariot A 8 from Salamis, described as more or less rectangular, may not have been D-shaped but composed of four timbers meeting at right angles, as were those of the three two-poled chariots from the site; one of these was sufficiently well preserved to allow for its reconstruction (A 7; fig. 1). The two poles could have been prolongations of the sides of the floor or they might simply have been rivetted to these.[18]

---

[15] Littauer and Crouwel 1979, 76f., 103.

[16] Brown and Catling 1980, no. 91 (our pl. 32); Studniczka 1907, nos. 13–14; Megaw 1954, 173 with fig. 2; *CVA* British Museum 2 IICc, pl. 9: 13 = Walters 1912, no. C 1004; *CVA* Cambridge 2, IIIA, pl. V1: 4; Karageorghis 1973c, no. 70; 1974, 836 with fig. 16; Karageorghis and des Gagniers 1974, 354 no. XXVd = Tatton-Brown 1979, no. 271.

[17] For these chariots, see Littauer and Crouwel 1985, esp. "Commentary".

[18] See experiments with reconstruction of two-poled chariots, based on Cypriot and other evidence, by Spruytte 1978–79, 54ff. with figs. 20–30.

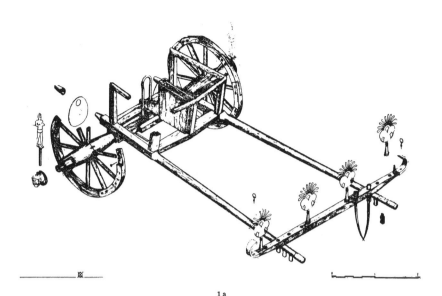

1 a

1 b

Fig. 1.

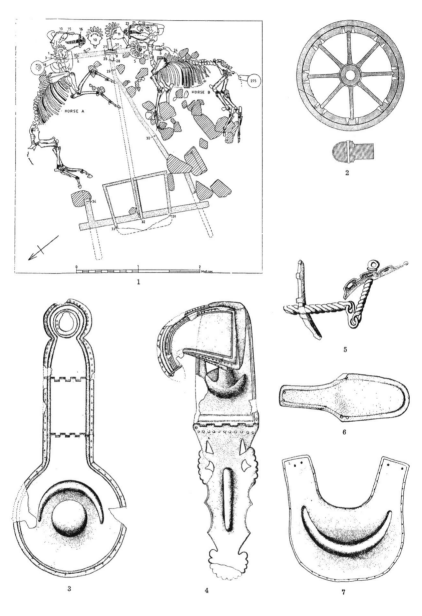

Fig. 2.

As reconstructed, chariot A 7 has a rectangular floor, 0.85 m. wide by 0.68 m. deep, formed by the two poles which are joined fore and aft by two cross timbers by means of mortise-and-tenon; the front timber presents a slightly convex front edge, as does the corresponding siding, which is only 0.44 m. high. This siding has been reconstructed with vertical posts at all four corners, but the excavator suggested that the rear edges may have been somewhat rounded. According to his report, the sides were screened in plaited osiers. As on the single-poled chariot A 8, the body was divided by a central partition: "The wooden partition, which extended about 2/3 of the way back, was double, 0.09 m. thick and 0.40 m. high; the rear part was a single, low-shaped board, 0.04 m. thick, dropping to the back".[19] The vertical bronze loop, 0.50 m. high and made of tubing, found near the rear edge of the floor (fig. 1), must have been fitted at the centre rear, quite possibly over the lower part of the partition.[20] (Both partition and loop appear on many terracotta chariot models from Cyprus, see below).

The two-poled chariots represented by numerous terracotta and some stone models from the island must have had rectangular floors too (e.g. 22 a–b–25). The several instances where the floor appears to be more or less D-shaped cannot be taken literally. The construction of a two-poled chariot requires a rectangular floor and this indeed attested elsewhere by two gold models of Achaemenid date from the so-called Oxus Treasure and by several north African rock carvings.[21] In the Near East such floor plans can be recognized on Assyrian reliefs of the 8th and 7th century B.C., but they are associated with a single central pole or possibly with a so-called Y-pole (see s.v. Traction system).

An interesting detail of one of the Cypriot stone models of a two-poled chariot, repeated on one of the Oxus gold models, is the indication of a flooring of interwoven thongs;[22] clearly, this type of taut and at the same time resilient flooring was used with both D-shaped and rectangular floors.

---

[19] Karageorghis 1973a, 73.

[20] Karageorghis 1973a, 73, 29 no. 220/2 with figs. VII, 10 (our fig. 1a–b) and pls. C, CCXLVI.

[21] Dalton 1964, XXXVII, 3f. no. 7 with fig. 20 and pl. IV (with four-horse yoke), 4 with fig. 21 and "additional plate" (with two-horse yokes); Littauer and Crouwel 1979, 145–148 with fig. 82 (Oxus Treasure); Spruytte 1978–79, 54ff. with fig. 7 (after Graziani 1942, fig. 11, cf. pls. 37–39), 17–18.

[22] Hermary 1981, no. 45 = Studniczka 1907, no. 32; Dalton 1964, fig. 21 and "additional plate".

The bigae and quadrigae depicted in the figured documents from Cyprus carry up to three occupants – two abreast – thereby suggesting chariots that were often rather deeper than those buried at Salamis. The positions of the crew are clear from the terracotta and stone models where one person appears to stand behind the other. Three occupants are common on terracottas of the 7th–6th century B.C. (pls. 23a–b–25, 26a–b); they also appear in one of the four chariots illustrated on the 5th century Amathus sarcophagus (21) and on seal engravings of the Archaic period.[23] There is also evidence for four-man crews, in the form of a small, homogeneous group of terracotta quadriga models presumably of 7th century date. One of these, was apparently found in Phoenicia (pl. 27a–b) and the group may be of Levantine manufacture, although a Cypriot origin is perhaps more likely.[24]

In the Near East chariot crews of the earlier first millennium B.C. normally consisted of two or no more than three men, the third standing behind the other two. Four man complements are only seen on Assyrian reliefs of the later 8th and 7th centuries and on one ivory carving from Nimrud.[25]

The three-dimensional representations from Cyprus illustrate chariots with a solid siding, usually rising to approximately hip height. On several of the terracotta and stone models – of bigae and quadrigae alike – the breastwork does not extend to the very rear of the floor, thus creating a platform (pls. 18, 26a–b).[26] This is a feature also of the chariots depicted on the two sarcophagi (pls. 19–20) and cannot be paralleled on Assyrian reliefs or other Near Eastern representations.

The siding seen in the figured documents from Cyprus presents a variety of profiles, not all of which need to be read literally. It may be strictly rectangular or combine a horizontal top edge with a rounded profile at the rear (pl. 29). It may rise towards the front,

---

[23] *Supra* n. 7; Amadasi 1965, figs. 21: 4 and 5: 4.

[24] Heuzey 1923, no. 187 = Studniczka 1907, no. 17 = Littauer 1976a, 221 with fig. 20 = Littauer and Crouwel 1979, 102f. with fig. 60 = Cassimatis 1986, 181f. with pl. XXXVIII: 2–3, 5 (reportedly from Marathus/Amrit; our pl. 27a–b); Catling 1971, no. 99 = Brown and Calling 1981, no. 82 (formerly Collection de Clercq); Poulson 1912, 62f. with figs. 60f. These models and their place(s) of manufacture are to be discussed in a later article.

[25] See Littauer and Crouwel 1979, 103f.

[26] See terracottas, Littauer and Crouwel 1977a, 7f. with figs. 3–6 (Ovgoros; our pl. 28); 1976, 68 with pl. XXV (Meniko; our pl. 26a–b).

the rear edge being more or less vertical or rounded. More frequently, the top edge of the breast-work rises towards the rear corners before dropping down vertically or in a curve. This rise may be gradual (pl. 33) or rather abrupt (pl. 22a–b), which recalls the "humped" rectangular profile of the chariots on Assyrian reliefs of the 8th and 7th centuries.[27] In one case, the Amathus sarcophagus, an open handgrip is reserved in the raised upper rear corner of the siding (pl. 21). In the Near East, though not in Assyria, open handgrips of varying type are illustrated in this position.[28]

Many of the Cypriot terracotta and stone models, from the 7th century onwards, illustrate the front-to-back partition inside the body that is materially attested on chariots from Salamis. Often, but not always, it appears together with the upright loop at the centre rear – a bronze example of which was also found at Salamis. Some models show that the tubular object had a solid lower part, against which the partition may well have abutted. The latter would have strengthened the fabric of the chariot body, by bracing the front breastwork. At the same time the partition would have prevented crew members from jostling each other in rough going or on turns, while giving them an extra wall against which to brace and to maintain balance.[29] The loop at the centre rear of the body would have served as a handgrip in mounting (see pl. 28),[30] or to carry a shield, as is clearly illustrated on one of the terracotta models of a four-man chariot cited above as apparently found in Phoenicia (pl. 27a–b). The shield is of a type that is also depicted in Near Eastern art of the earlier first millennium B.C.: round and with a lion-headed central boss.[31] It may be noted that the remains of a round shield, 0.56 m. in diameter, were found near the rear of chariot A 3 at Salamis; it may have hung on such a loop – although no traces of the latter were found – effecting a partial closing at both sides of it.[32]

The presence of a loop, and quite possibly of the central partition as well, may be assumed on many chariots in two-dimensional art where a shield, sometimes with a lion-headed boss, is seen in

[27] See Littauer and Crouwel 1979, 104.
[28] See Littauer and Crouwel 1976, 75; 1979, 105. 146.
[29] See Littauer 1976a, 221; Littauer and Crouwel 1979, 103.
[30] Gjerstad 1935, pl. CCXXXV: 3 (Ayia Irini no. 1781 + 798; our pl. 24).
[31] For such shields, see Madhloom 1970, 56.
[32] Karageorghis 1967a, 33. 36 no. 25, 46 with fig. XVI, pls. XLIV, CXXIX.

profile in this position. Representations include Assyrian reliefs of the 9th century, Neo-Hittite reliefs and Nimrud ivories as well as a vase painting and an incomplete terracotta model from Cyprus itself.[33]

One or two Cypriot terracottas illustrate an "apron" hanging from the front breastwork (pl. 26a-b).[34] Of cloth or leather, this would have protected the crew from mud, flying stones or gravel kicked up by the draught team's heels. Some of the stone models seem to indicate a cloth draped in swags over the siding, at the front or sides (pl. 19).[35] On the Golgoi sarcophagus such a cloth is shown over the rear part of the side only (pl. 20).

Axle

The actual chariots found at Salamis had axles placed at the full rear of the floor (figs. 1–2: 1). In the case of the figured documents, whether two – or three – dimensional, there is no such consistency: axle positions vary from central to full rear (see pls. 22a-b–29).

A central axle acts as a fulcrum and would be unsuitable for standing occupants switching their weight rapidly in fighting or hunting, which would cause the vehicle to see-saw back and forth. For the same reason mounting and dismounting would put extra stress on the area of pole attachment and on the traction and harness system. An axle located beneath or near the rear floor bar would eliminate these inconveniences. Consequently, it is a matter of doubt whether the central axle illustrated on several of the profile representations from Cyprus is realistic or simply a convenience – in order to create a composition as compact as possible – or to make economical use of the available space. The same problem, it may be

---

[33] See Littauer 1976a, 221f.; Littauer and Crouwel 1979, 103; Karageorghis and des Gagniers 1974, no. II.6 (Cypriot vase); Cesnola 1894, pl. LXVIII: 627 (terracotta from Amathus; animal-headed boss confirmed by personal examination). Interestingly, this loop, in combination with a rod-like horizontal partition, also occurs on some metal chariot models, associated with vehicle burials of the later 2nd millennium B.C. at Lchashen in Transcaucasia, see Barnett 1964, 12 with figs. 10, 12; Piggott 1983, 97; Littauer and Crouwel 1979, 75 with n. 16 (further refs.); also personal information M. A. Littauer.

[34] Littauer and Crouwel 1977b, 69 with pl. XXV (Meniko; our pl. 26a–b); Gjerstad 1935, pl. CCXXXIV: 6 (Ayia Irini no. 1046).

[35] Hermary 1981, no. 45 (Amathus); Pryce 1931, no. C 84.

noted, is posed by numerous chariot representations on small-scale surfaces from the ancient Near East. On the other hand, full rear axles are consistently depicted on the Assyrian reliefs and near rear axles on the later Achaemenid ones from Persepolis – walls offering the space necessary for realistic rendering.[36] As regards the Cypriot terracotta and stone models, the varying axle positions may simply reflect carelessness on the part of the makers.

The long axles on some terracottas, which project considerably beyond the edges of the vehicle body, probably reflect reality (pl. 26a–b). They allowed for the long wheel naves which were essential if the wheels were not to wobble on the wooden axles. Long axles would also permit a wider wheel track and improve stability in rough going or on fast turns.[37]

The axles of the Salamis chariots were fixed rigidly to the rear floor bar, the wheels revolving on them. The wheels in turn must have been secured on the axles by linch pins. While these are never shown in the figured documents from Cyprus, a pair of very long (0.56 m.) and elaborate bronze ones was found with chariot A 7 at Salamis. These linch pins pierced ornate bronze caps on the axle ends (fig. 1).[38] Other evidence for the use of metal axle caps in Cyprus is absent. Bronze examples of different design are known from Urartu and certain details of Assyrian reliefs suggest that they were also used with Assyrian chariots in the earlier first millennium B.C.[39]

Wheels

Cypriot chariots were equipped with spoked wheels. A notable exception is the quadriga depicted in relief on a stone base of Hellenistic date, which has cross-bar wheels, otherwise associated only with carts.[40] The wheels of terracotta and stone models are often shown

---

[36] See Littauer and Crouwel 1979, 53. 78. 105. 147.
[37] See Littauer and Crouwel 1979, 54. 78.
[38] Karageorghis 1973a, esp. 70. 80f. nos. 188 +220/4+4+4A and 129+220/5+5A with fig. V11, pls. CI–CV, CCLVI–CCLVII. There is also an actual, decorated bronze linch pin (L. 0.135 m.) from Nimrud, see Mallowan 1966, 208f. with fig. 142. The axle caps are of the "hat-shaped" type also known from Late Bronze-Age vehicle burials in Central Europe, see Piggott 1983, 112–114 with fig. 66.
[39] See Özgen 1984, 114f. with figs. 43–45; Haerinck and Overlaet 1984, 62f.; also infra, n. 49; Littauer and Crouwel 1979, 105f. (Assyrian reliefs).
[40] Cassimatis 1976, 178f. with pl. XXX; Crouwel 1985, 209.

as disks, with and without raised centres to indicate the nave. When no spokes are indicated, in paint or relief, it cannot be assumed that solid disk wheels were intended (pl. 32).

The wheels of two actual chariots from Salamis (A 3, A 7), with estimated diameters of c. 0.85 m. and 0.90 m. respectively, have been reconstructed with long naves into which eight or ten spokes were mortised.[41] As reconstructed, the rim of a wheel from chariot A 3 consists of two concentric elements – the felloe into which the outer spoke ends were mortised and the wooden type, lying flush with it (fig. 2: 2). It has been suggested that these elements, each made of overlapping segments, were held together by a tongue-in groove construction, in which a tongue on the inner surface of the wooden tyre lay in a groove in the perimeter of the felloe. The actual metal U-shaped clamps, with a nail joining both terminals, found on either side of the outer spoke ends, helped to hold felloe and tyre together.[42] Now it would be very difficult to hold a flush tyre firmly in place by these means, particularly in rough going, and a separate rawhide tyre, put on wet and allowed to shrink, would have been a great help. Rawhide binding may also have been used to hold the felloe and tyre segments together.[43]

For comparison, Assyrian reliefs consistently show the rims of six- and eight-spoked chariot wheels as composed of two concentric elements, the outer one wider than the inner. By the 8th century B.C. two pairs of large metal champs are depicted joining both parts of the rim of eight-spoked wheels, hereby confirming the tongue-and-groove construction suggested for the wheel of chariot A 3 from Salamis.[44]

---

[41] The recorded lengths of the impressions left by the naves in the soil of A 3 and A 7 (c. 0.70 and 0.68 m.) are suspect, since they fall far outside the norm of ancient naves which runs between c. 0.35 and 0.45 m. The recorded diameters of the wheels of chariot A 2–1.40/1.50 m. – are also very large by comparison.

[42] Karageorghis 1967a, 40, 49f. nos. 152. 159–195 with pls. CXXI–CXXII; 1973a, 68 n. 1; Kossack 1971, 155–159 with fig. 34 (our fig. 2: 2). What are probably the remains of similar iron clamps (previously interpreted as pole fittings) have been found in the dromos of "royal" tomb IV at Tamassos, which also produced bronze blinkers and frontlets along with horse bones, see Buchholz 1978, 193 with fig. 43; also *supra* n. 11 Metal U-shaped clamps for wheel rims have also been found in Iron Age Europe, see Kossack 1971, figs. 28a–b, 29, 31, 33: 3.

[43] In the published reconstruction drawings the segments seem to be held together only by two metal nails, 0.06 m. in length (Karageorghis 1967a, 40. 49 no. 158 with pls. XLIX, CXXI). For the use of rawhide on ancient spoked wheels, see Littauer and Crouwel 1985, 76–78, 93f.

[44] For Assyrian wheels, see Kossack 1971, 157–159; Littauer and Crouwel 1979, 107f.

The metal U-shaped clamps, associated with the wheel rims of chariot A 3 at Salamis are absent from the ten-spoked wheels of chariot A 7 at the side. Instead, there were "twenty pairs of iron doubleheaded nails around the rim, each pair fixed horizontally across at the end of its corresponding spoke". The reconstruction of the rims, consisting of "ten pieces of broard, with straight cut terminals over-lapping on the sides and fitting in a stepped lane" and held together by these nails, may be questioned (fig. 1: a).[45] It is based on modern Cypriot cart wheels which have no parallels among ancient wheels, except possibly among the carts from Salamis itself.[46]

Figured documents from Cyprus illustrate chariot wheels with a widely varying number of spokes – from four to ten or more. As in the case of the axle positions, these numbers may not always reflect those of the spokes of actual chariot wheels. On the other hand, the material remains from Salamis demonstrate that eight- and ten-spoked wheels were used in the island in the 8th–7th centuries.

In the Near East, Assyrian reliefs illustrate only chariots with six- and eight-spoked wheels, the latter number becoming standard in the 8th century B.C. On non-Assyrian chariots of the time, the numbers of spokes varies from four to eight, with a tendency to become fixed at eight. Later on, Achaemenid chariot representations show wheels with six to twelve spokes.[47]

Traction System

Traction was provided by teams of two or four horses under a yoke or yokes, connected with the vehicles by means of one or two draught poles.[48] The Salamis burials preserve the remains of both bigae – with the yoke fastened to a single pole – and quadrigae – with one or two yokes fastened to two poles. The single pole was central, running all the way under the floor of the vehicle. The double poles,

---

[45] Karageorghis 1973a, 68 with n. 1, cf. 30, 32 nos. 220/14–32 with fig. 4 (nails).
[46] See Karageorghis 1967a, 24 no. 68 with pls. XVII and CXVI (similar nails belonging to reconstructed cart from Tomb 2, pl. CXV).
[47] Littauer and Crouwel 1979, 106, 147.
[48] There is as yet no evidence for the three-horse hitch in Cyprus. The remains of our chariot A 7 at Salamis, identified by Chamoux (1975) as those of a triga, were actually those of a quadriga. His objection that the space between the poles at the front (1.15m., see Karageorghis 1973a, 73) was too small for the two inner animals has been disproven experimentally by Spruytte (1978–79, 55 n. 6).

as discussed above (see under "Body"), seem to have been formed by projections of the side timbers of the floor frame. On the reconstructed two-poled chariot A 7 (fig. 1) they extended 0.10 m. beyond the rear floor bar, with decorated ovoid bronze disks hung over the rear ends. At either end these poles had metal caps.[49] On this chariot, as on others, the poles would have run diagonally upwards to the yoke and not horizontally as in the reconstruction, to allow for even small animals under yoke. (At Salamis, horses stood from 1.32 to 1.53 m.; see s.v. Draught animals). Numerous Cypriot figured documents do, in fact, illustrate poles rising to the yoke at an oblique angle, as do those on the Assyrian reliefs and other representations from the Near East.

The terracotta and stone models confirm the use in Cyprus of both single- and two-poled chariots (pls. 18ff.).[50] The poles, however, are often shown attached to the vehicle body in unlikely places and running out at unlikely angles, due to ignorance or convenience of the modellers. Outside the island, the use of two draught poles is explicitly documented only by the two gold models of Achaemenid date belonging to the Oxus Treasure and by north African rock carvings.[51]

A terracotta and stone model dating to the 7th and 5th century respectively illustrate a third type of pole (pls. 18, 28).[52] This is the so-called Y pole, formed of two timbers, one from each corner of the vehicle which come together to run contiguously out to the two-horse yoke. Something similar is suggested by the profile views of chariots on 9th–8th century Assyrian reliefs; an incomplete Levantine bronze model, probably dating to the 6th–4th century B.C., illustrates this more explicitly.[53]

There is figured documentation and one element of material evidence for the use of a pole support/breastwork brace with Cypriot

---

[49] Karageorghis 1973a, 73. 81 nos. 220/6–7, 9 (pole caps) and 220/1, 3 with pls. CCLIV, CCLXXIX. Note the recent discussion on the distinction between pole and axle caps among Urartian bronzes; see Seidl 1980 and 1982; Haerinck and Overlaet 1984, 64f. with fig. 5 and pls. VI–VIII.

[50] For single-poled chariots, see terracottas listed *supra* n. 16; also Heuzey 1923, pl. X: 2; Breitenstein 1941, pl. 2: 12; Karageorghis 19696, 462 with fig. 46a–b (our pl. XXXIX: 2).

[51] See *supra* n. 21.

[52] Littauer and Crouwel 1977a, 7f. with figs. 3–6 (Ovgoros; our pl. 28), 2 with fig. 1 (Kourion; further refs., *supra* n. 3; our pls. 18, 19).

[53] Littauer and Crouwel 1976, esp. 75–78; 1977a; 1979, 109f.; Seeden 1980, no. 1725. The use of Y-poles in Assyria has been disputed by Jacobs 1984–85, 157.

chariots. A 6th century terracotta model appears to show two braces joining the central pole of a biga to the lower front of the body, one on either side (pl. 33).[54] By comparison, the Levantine model, just mentioned, has such a brace to each arm of the Y-pole; this type of brace is shown also with single-poled chariots on Iron Age vase paintings of mainland Greece.[55]

A group of 7th century Cypriot terracotta models of single-poled chariots illustrate a pole support/breastwork brace dropping from the front breastwork to the central pole at an almost vertical angle (pl. 32).[56] A similar brace may be intended on the Amathus sarcophagus, which illustrates bigae (pl. 21), and it is a standard feature of the chariots depicted on Assyrian reliefs and many other profile representations from the Near East during the earlier first millennium B.C. On the Assyrian reliefs, the brace, sheathed in metal or an actual metal rod, forks near its attachment to the pole.[57]

Some other Cypriot figured documents portray yet another type of pole support/breastwork brace, the most explicit being a recently found terracotta quadriga model of c. 500 B.C. from Kition; here each of the poles, rising towards the pole at a slant, is joined to the top of the front breastwork by two horizontal braces; screens with curved lower edges cover the junctions of braces and poles (pl. 29).[58] Something similar is indicated, albeit less explicitly, on a few terracottas of the 7th–6th centuries, on embossed gold plaques and on the 5th century Golgoi sarcophagus which illustrates a quadriga (pl. 20). In these cases the braces, shown naked or covered by screens, drop down obliquely to the poles.[59]

Material evidence for a single such brace was found with a central-poled chariot at Salamis (A 4; pl. 35).[60] The plaster cast made

---

[54] Karageorghis 1967a, 49 with fig. 8; *Ancient Cypriote Art* (exhibition catalogue. Athens 1975) 78 with ill.

[55] Crouwel 1981, 96 with pls. 143. 147.

[56] See *supra* n. 16.

[57] Littauer and Crouwel 1979, 110.

[58] Karageorghis 1980a, ills. on cover and 38f.; 1980b, 790 with fig. 81.

[59] Littauer and Crouwel 1977b, 70f.; for gold plaques, see esp. Karageorghis 1967a, pl. LXI, 67/2 (also *supra* n. 6). An incorrect interpretation of the covered brace of the chariot on the Golgoi sarcophagus as part of the vehicle's siding has found its way into a reconstruction of a two-poled chariot, see Spruytte 1978–79, 55 with figs. 22–25. 27–30.

[60] Karageorghis 1967a, 50f. with pl. XXXVIII: 3; Littauer and Crouwel 1977b, 77f.

during the excavation shows that the horizontal brace (L. 0.50 m.) formed a triangle with the pole (L. of its preserved part 0.73 m.), in the same way as seen on the two-poled chariot of the Kition terracotta model; leather thongs, of which traces were found, would have held pole and brace together. Since this brace would not be high enough above the original level of the pole to have sprung from the top of the front breastwork, it may have been attached lower down, where a vertical centre post would have afforded solid anchorage. Outside Cyprus, pole supports/breastwork braces of this type are attested only on the Levantine metal model: it shows one brace to each of the arms of the Y-pole, dropping down from part-way up the front breastwork.

Draught Animals

Chariot teams were exclusively composed of horses. The paired equid skeletons found with the remains of actual chariots at Salamis have been identified as only those of horses, those belonging with the carts as both horses and asses. The dimensions obtained from some of the horse skeletons show a wide range, from 1.32 to 1.53 m. at the withers.[61] Horse bones or teeth have also been reported from tombs at Tamassos, Amathus and Palaepaphos, quite possibly originally forming part of similar vehicle burials.[62]

Harnessing

As stated earlier, bigae with a central pole or Y-pole had a two-horse yoke. Quadrigae with two poles had either a single four-horse yoke or two two-horse yokes.

The single four-horse yoke is explicitly shown on some 7th–6th century terracotta models and on stone ones of the 5th century (pls. 19, 26a-b); it is probably to be assumed for the actual two-poled

---

[61] Ducos 1967; 1980, esp. table I.
[62] Tamassos: Buchholz 1978, 191 with fig. 41 ("royal" Tomb IV). Amathus: Karageorghis 1980b, 1018. Palaepaphos: Karageorghis 1963a, 285–288, 299 with figs. 28f. 31–32; 1967b, 244 with fig. 27 (Tomb 8).

chariots from Salamis (cf. fig. 1). Outside the island this yoke is attested on one of the gold models of the Oxus Treasure and on some of the north African rock carvings.[63] Assyrian reliefs of the later 8th and 7th century B.C. sometimes illustrate unharnessed chariots with a single four-horse yoke but always with one rather than two poles.[64]

The combination of two-horse yokes with two poles is documented in Cyprus by some other terracotta models of the 7th–6th centuries (pl. 22a-b) and it is standard on the later ones from Kourion.[65] Explicit information on the use of this harness system outside the island is furnished by the second of the Oxus models and by north African rock art.

It has been shown experimentally that a single four-horse yoke linking the two poles presents a stronger, more compact unit (with the vehicle) than two two-horse yokes and two poles would. At the same time, it requires four animals of exactly the same height which is not always easy to obtain. An advantage of the two-horse yokes is that they do not need four perfectly matched horses and they also allow for some flexibility in the poles.[66]

Several Cypriot terracotta and stone models suggest that the yokes were shaped to lie across the necks of the draught animals, just ahead of the withers. The yokes often have upturned ends, which are also marked on the two stone sarcophagi and recall the bronze terminals of the yokes of chariots A 7 and A 8 at Salamis (figs 1–2: 1; pls. 18, 20, 21).[67]

The yoke of quadriga A 7, 1.55 m. long and apparently in one piece, has been reconstructed rather like an ox-yoke, with a straight beam and long rods piercing it and supposedly holding it in place on either side of the neck of each horse (fig. 1: a). No evidence for these rods, which are similar to those on modern ox-yokes in Cyprus, was actually found with this chariot. The excavator based his reconstruction on impressions left in the soil by pairs of wooden rods associated with the two-horse yokes of chariot A 4 and of a cart, also

---

[63] See *supra* n. 21.
[64] Littauer and Crouwel 1979, 110, 114.
[65] Young and Young 1955, figs. 15–17.
[66] Spruytte 1978–79, 56 with figs. 22–30.
[67] Karageorghis 1973a, 30, 73 no. 220/8 and 38, 75 no. 320/1–2 with pls. LXIX, CXXIII, CCLIV, CCLXII.

from Salamis.[68] The latter may be interpreted as the remains of yoke saddles. Of inverted Y-shape, these harness elements, which were lashed to the yoke, their legs lying along the animal's shoulders, were used with two-horse yokes in the Late Bronze Age in the Eastern Mediterranean. In the Near East they survived into the 9th and probably 8th century B.C., at which time the new, fitted yoke with bays for the neck of each horse was introduced.[69] There is no figured evidence for the use of yoke saddles with chariot harnessing in Iron Age Cyprus. As mentioned above, several documents clearly illustrate the fitted neck yoke, sometimes with yoke pads – pieces of fabric or leather protecting the horses' necks from being bruised or chafed (pl. 21).

The yokes were attached to the poles, near the ends of the latter, by lashings. Clay pellets over the areas of junction of pole and yoke on some terracotta models may suggest the presence of so-called yoke pegs to reinforce their connection (pl. 28).[70]

The yokes were kept in place by a neck strap passing in front of the neck of each animal, and a girth. On terracottas a loop sometimes marks the place where these straps were tied to the yoke (pl. 26a–b).

At Salamis two types of bronze harness elements were associated with some vehicles, including both chariots (A 7, A 8) and carts. One is the so-called shoulder pendant, which consists of a decorated disk, hinged to a tongue with a suspension loop at the top (fig. 2: 3).[71] The disk is pierced, probably to take a backing and fringe of tassels, as is often seen on 9th century Assyrian reliefs and other figured documents from the Near East, as well as on a few 7th–6th century terracottas from Cyprus itself (pl. 33).[72] Actual bronze shoulder pendants, differing somewhat in detail, are also known from

---

[68] Karageorghis 1967a, 78 (A 4), 62 (cart from Tomb 3); 1973a, 74 with fig. 16: 1–2 (modern ox-yokes): cf. Littauer 1976b.

[69] Littauer and Crouwel 1979, 60. 85. 113 (yoke saddles), 114 (fitted yoke).

[70] At Salamis the lashing of yoke to pole was sometimes facilitated by the presence of three wooden attachments to the pole, see Karageorghis 1973a, 78 (A 8); cf. 1967a, 51 with pls. XLIX, CXIX (cart from Tomb 3).

[71] Karageorghis 1973a, 76, 83–6 nos. 155+162. 189. 320/18. 24. 135 and 275 with esp. pls. CCLXXII-CCLXXVI (A 7, A 8 and cart from the same tomb; no. 320/18, from A 8 = our fig. 2: 3); cf. 1967a, 49 nos. 23, 114 with pls. XLVI, CXXVIII (cart from Tomb 3). One such object found its may to Olympia in Greece, see Philipp 1981 (incorrectly dated to 6th cent. B.C.).

[72] See also Gjerstad 1935, pl. CCXXXV: 6 = 1963, 10 with fig. 10 (Ayia Irini no. 249+115).

Urartu.[73] Combining the material evidence from Salamis with the pictorial information, there appear to have been only two such objects to a harness team, each hanging on the outside shoulder of the outer horse. Clearly too small (diam. c. 0.20–0.30 m.) to have afforded protection, they seem to have had no other obvious functions than as decorations and fly chasers.[74]

The other bronze harness elements are the palmette-shaped objects belonging with the yokes of some chariots (A 7, A 8) and carts (figs. 1: a, 2: 1).[75] Such yoke standards are never seen on figured documents from Cyprus but they are reminiscent of the fan-shaped yoke ornaments shown with later, Achaemenid chariots on the Persepolis reliefs; four of these adorned the four-horse yoke of one of the gold models of the Oxus Treasure. Nearer in time is the fan-shaped object that appears in the yoke area of Assyrian chariots depicted on reliefs of the 9th century and on some later ones. Two actual examples of this, of decorated bronze, were found at Zinjirli and they may well have been fixed to the centre of the yoke, possibly as a finial to a yoke peg, facing forward.[76] Finally, there is the possible yoke decoration from Urartu, in the form of disks with tongue-shaped extensions, known from actual finds and representations.[77]

Control

The draught teams were controlled by bridles, each composed of a headstall, usually with a bit, and reins.

Bits. Surviving horse bits from Cyprus, often of iron but sometimes of bronze, all belong to a single type of snaffle, with a jointed mouthpiece and long, narrow, flat cheekpieces. The type is documented chiefly by finds associated with the buried chariots and carts of the 8th–7th centuries at Salamis, some of them lying *in situ* on

---

[73] Haerinck and Overlaet 1984, 57–61 with fig. 3 and pls. II–V.

[74] See Littauer 1976a, 220f.; Littauer and Crouwel 1979, 117.

[75] Karageorghis 1967a, 68, 75–77. 79 nos. 138–140. 320/9–12. 238f. 240. 119f. 113–134 with esp. pls. CCLXIV–CCLXVI (A 7, A 8 and two carts from the same tomb); cf. 1967a, 52 nos. 17–19 with pls. CXIX, CCXXIII (cart from Tomb 3).

[76] Littauer and Crouwel 1979, 115, 150; Andrae 1943, 79–85 with figs. 90f., pls. 40c–d (Zinjirli).

[77] Seidl 1980, 76f., 79 with fig. 12 and pls. 14: 2–17; Özgen 1984, 117 with figs. 46–48.

the harness animals (fig. 2: 5).[78] In addition, there are some from disturbed burials at Palaepaphos, and a pair from Amathus (pl. 34).[79] The two canons of the mouthpiece are almost always made of heavy wire, looped directly together in the middle or by means of a separate link. They pass through holes, sometimes collared, in the centres of the cheekpieces and end in loops or rings to take the reins or rein attachments. The cheekpieces are usually roughly rectangular but sometimes curved and carry three loops or apertures for attachment to the headstall. The action of these bits could be severe, depending on whether the mouthpieces were very long – as they often were – in which case they would have great leverage on the cheekpieces to squeeze the lower jaw, and the joint in the middle would press painfully against the roof of the horse's mouth.

This type of snaffle bit goes back to the Late Bronze Age in the eastern Mediterranean. In the first millennium it can be seen on Assyrian reliefs of the 9th and 8th century; there is also an actual specimen from Ashur.[80] In Cyprus itself the most explicit illustrations of bits are on the 5th century Amathus sarcophagus; it shows curved cheekpieces fastened at three points to the cheekstraps (pl. 21). Similar cheekstraps, implying a bitted bridle, are seen on the Golgoi sarcophagus (pl. 20). They further appear on a large terracotta horse head (Ht. 0.103 m.) of a chariot group of the 6th century, clay pellets marking the ends of the mouthpiece, as seen on some other terracottas (pl. 30).[81] Other representations are too summary to give details of the bits. Several of them simply illustrate cheekstraps and a band encircling the nose, suggesting a bit incorporated into a noseband (pls. 23a–b, 24).[82]

Headstall. Apart from cheekstraps and noseband, illustrated headstalls in Iron Age Cyprus always comprise a browband – sometimes

---

[78] Dikaios 1963, 160 with fig. 17 (A 2); Karageorghis 1967a, 21 (cart, Tomb 2). 49 (cart, Tomb 3). 77–79. 86 (A 4 and A 5), 105 (A 6) with esp. pls. CXIV, CXXVIII, CXLI; 1973a, 76 (cart), 82 (A 7), 86 (A 8) with esp. pl. CCLXIII (no. 320/122, from A 8 = our fig. 2: 5); Donder 1980, nos. 5–20. 22–6.

[79] Palaepaphos: Karageorghis 1963a, 280. 294 no. 22 (cf. no. 22a) with fig 20; 1967b, 202. 212. 242 nos. 49–51 with fig. 21 (Tombs 7 and 8); Donder 1980, nos. 21. 27–29. Amathus: Karageorghis 1981, 1018 with fif. 121. There are also two single bits, not from controlled excavations, see Donder 1980, nos. 30 (Kourion), 31 (with decorated cheekpieces).

[80] Littauer and Crouwel 1979, 88 (type 4), 119 (type 2) with fig. 66 (Ashur bit).

[81] Karageorghis 1967a, 48 with fig. 10 = Littauer and Karageorghis 1969, 153 with fig. 5 (our pl. 30).

[82] A good example is the terracotta horse head, Tatton-Brown 1979, no. 273.

in conjunction with a brow cushion – and occasionally a half nose-band or a throatlash.

Several of the terracotta models show a quilted or padded object that lies across the brow and must have been attached to the brow-band. In some cases this cushion is shown as lying beneath what is probably a hinged metal frontlet (see below), thereby cushioning the parietal bones against the metal (pl. 30). In the Near East the brow cushion appears, with and without an hingeless frontlet, on Assyrian reliefs of the 8th and 7th centuries and on some ivories.[83]

Some terracotta models from Ayia Irini illustrate two straps run-ning from the noseband to the browband and crossing each other in the middle (pls. 23a–b, 24). This so-called half noseband is also known from Assyrian reliefs of the 8th and 7th century B.C., and explicitly illustrated on a stone horse head from Zinjirli.[84]

The use of a throatlash is attested on the Amathus sarcophagus (pl. 21).

Reins and terrets. At Salamis metal rings, placed along the yokes of the actual chariots and carts, acted as terrets for the reins to pass through (cf. fig. 1: a).[85] There is no other explicit evidence for the use of terrets in Cyprus but they can be seen with two and four-horse yokes on Assyrian reliefs.[86]

In Assyria there may have existed a method of reining, leaving the drivers of quadrigae during the later 8th and 7th centuries with only three reins in each hand.[87] Evidence for some such arrange-ment in Cyprus is yielded by the Golgoi sarcophagus, which shows a quadriga and six reins, including one running to the outside of the near horse, and by a terracotta model from Ayia Irini (pls. 20,

---

[83] See Littauer and Karageorghis 1969 (cf. fig. 6: terracotta from Frangissa near Tamassos); The Kition model (pl. XXXVIII: 4) seems to show a browband cov-ered with disk-shaped, possibly metal appliques, such as are known from the Near East; see Littauer and Crouwel 1979. 127.

[84] Gjerstad 1935, pis CCXXXIV: 3 (no. 1780; our pl. 23a–b), 6 (no. 1046), CCXXXV: 3 (inner horses only; no. 1781+798; our pl. 24); Littauer and Crouwel 1979, 118 with fig. 63 (Zinjirli head).

[85] See esp. Dikaios 1963, 153f., 159; Karageorghis 1967a, 77–79. 105; 1973a, 75, The numbers of terrets found with chariot yokes at Salamis – 1 (biga A 6), 2 (biga A 1), 4 (bigae A 4 and A 8, quadriga A 2), 6 (quadriga A 5) – surely do not always reflect the original ones. Two iron rings from disturbed tombs at Palaepaphos (7 and 8), which also yielded horse bits, may well be terrets in view of their par-allels at Salamis, see Karageorghis 1967b, 212, no. 52 with fig. 21.

[86] Littauer and Crouwel 1979, 124.

[87] For Assyrian reining, see Nagel 1966, figs. 71–75; Littauer and Crouwel 1979, 123f.; Jacobs 1984–85, 156.

23a–b).[88] On the latter the noses of all four horses are joined by straps or rods. Experiments have shown it to be likely that such connections between the horses' heads obtained wherever there were two poles and two yokes, as otherwise the poles might be pulled apart and the vehicle damaged.[89]

Bridle accessories. These include blinkers, frontlets, varying types of poll decoration, tassels and bells.

1. *Blinkers.* Pairs of bronze blinkers, either plain or decorated, have been found *in situ* on buried harness animals of both chariots and carts at Salamis. They are spade-shaped, as are the few examples made of ivory or covered with gold foil from the same site[90] and bronze ones from tombs at Tamassos, Amathus and Palaepaphos and from non-funerary contexts at Idalion (fig. 2: 6).[91] Blinkers, presumably of similar shape, are illustrated on many terracotta models of the 7th–6th centuries (pls. 28, 30); they still appear in the 5th century, on stone models and the Amathus sarcophagus, but no later (pls. 18, 21).

Bronze and ivory blinkers of similar or D-shape are known from Assyria and other parts of the Near East, apparently dating no later than the 8th–6th century B.C. They are also shown on contemporary figured documents, though never explicitly on Assyrian reliefs.[92]

2. *Frontlet.* Like blinkers, these are well-known from actual specimens and representations. Bronze examples have again been found *in situ*, lying over the forehead and nasal bone of harness animals

---

[88] Gjerstad 1935, pl. CCXXXIV: 3 (Ayia Irini no. 1780).

[89] Spruytte 1978–79, 56. The six terrets associated with the yoke of a two-poled chariot A 5 at Salamis suggested to the excavator that the heads of the inner horses were linked together by a rope, see Karageorghis 1967a, 78f.

[90] Dikaios 1963, 152f. (A 1), 160 nos. 162. 155. 158 with figs. 21. 31 (A 2); Karageorghis 1967a, 87 (A 5), 87f. nos. 72. 88. 91. 93 (ivory; A 4), cf. 21. 48 (carts from Tombs 2 and 3). 87 (gold leaf; cart from Tomb 47) with esp. pls. CXIV, CXXVII, CXXXIX, CXL; 1973a, 81 (A 7). 86 (A 8). cf. 76f. (carts) with esp. pls. CCLVII–CCLXVIII (no. 320/20, from A 8 = our fig. 2: 6); Donder 1980, nos. 122f. 127–137. 144–157. 168–177. 180–189. 192. Blinkers were worn fastened in the corner of cheekstrap and browband and not hanging from the browband, as seen in the reconstruction drawing, Tatton-Brown 1979, 71.

[91] Tamassos: Buchholz 1974, 598 with fig. 59; Donder 1980, nos. 126, 158–161. Amathus: Karageorghis 1981, 1018 with fig. 120; Palaepaphos: Karageorghis 1963a, 289 no. 28 with fig. 33; Donder 1980, nos. 178–179. Idalion: Donder 1980, nos. 138–143. 162. 164. 190f. Note also two unprovenanced blinkers, Donder 1980, nos. 166–167.

[92] Littauer and Crouwel 1979, 125 (with refs.); Özgen 1985, 99f. with figs. 22f. 49 (bronze examples from Urartu).

of both chariots and carts. Most but not all of these are hinged to an arched poll crest (see below) or to a plate covering the poll (fig. 2: 4). They are often highly decorated. There are also a few frontlets made of ivory or covered with gold foil.[93] Elsewhere in the island hinged bronze examples have been found in tombs at Tamassos and Palaepaphos.[94]

Frontlets often appear on terracotta models of the 7th–6th centuries, but of no later date. They are also absent from the stone models and the two sarcophagi of the 5th century, most of which still illustrate blinkers. On the more detailed of the terracottas a distinction can be made between frontlets suspended from the browband and those continuing over it (pls. 27a–b, 28). The latter must have been hinged, like most of the actual metal frontlets from Cyprus. Decoration is often marked by incision. One terracotta horse head in addition shows a knob and its lower end is shaped like a rosette, a feature also found at Salamis (pl. 30).

Frontlets were also well-known in the Near East during the 9th–7th centuries, *viz.* actual finds and representations. Numerous examples – of bronze, ivory and a few of silver – have survived from different areas varying considerably in design; the bronze ones are not hinged as in Cyprus.[95]

3. *Poll decoration.* The majority of bronze frontlets from Salamis have an arched crest. This is channeled, presumably to take a back-to-front horse hair fan fig. 2: 4). Such fans are illustrated on Assyrian reliefs of the later 8th and 7th centuries, though not together with hinged frontlets.[96] In Cyprur the presence of such a crest, with and without a frontlet, may be suggested by some terracottas.

---

[93] Dikaios 1963, 193 nos. 159. 168 with fig. 20 (A 1 or A 2); Karageorghis 1967a, 87 (A 5). 87f. nos. 89. 92 (ivory; A 4). cf. 21. 48 (carts from Tombs 2 and 3), 87 (gold leaf; cart from Tomb 47) with esp. pls. CXXXIX, CXL; 1973a, 81f. (A 7). 86 (A 8). cf. 76f. (carts) with esp. pls. CCLXVIII–CCLXXI (no. 320/19, from A 8 = our fig. 2: 4); Donder 1980, nos. 204–209. 211f. 227–232. 234–243. The term front band, used by Karageorghis and in Tatton-Brown (1971, reconstruction drawing, 71) should be avoided as there is no. question of *binding* something.

[94] Tamassos: Donder 1980, nos. 210. 215f. 244. Palaepaphos: Karageorghis 1963a, 270 no. 14A–B with fig. 9a–c; Donder 1980, nos. 213f.

[95] Littauer and Crouwel 1979, 125f. (with refs.); Özgen 1985, 92–8 with figs. 6–18. 49–50 (Urartu; his type A recalls some of the hingless frontlets illustrated on 6th century Cypriot terracottas, see Karageorghis 1978, no. 196 with pl. XLVIII – horse head from Kazaphani; 1977b, no. 15 with pls. VII–IX – ridden horse from Meniko.

[96] Littauer and Crouwel 1979, 126.

Other forms of arching metal crests, holding fans of hair, appear on a 8th century vase painting (fig. 3) and on the Amathus sarcophagus (pl. 21). The figured documents from Cyprus also illustrate yet other kinds of poll decoration.[97]

4. *Tassels and bells.* Horses in Cyprus are often shown with up to three decorative tassels, stacked in a tier, apparently suspended froth the front of the neck strap (pl. 26a–b). On more explicit representations, however, such as the two sarcophagi, they hang from a separate strap below the neck (pls. 20, 21). Similar decorative tassels appear frequently on Assyrian reliefs and other contemporary representations from the Near East.[98]

Some bronze bells from Tomb 79 at Salamis may well have belonged with the harness animals buried there. They have good parallels in the Near East and recall the groups of bells hung from a strap passing around the neck, as illustrated on Assyrian reliefs of the 7th century B.C.[99]

Chariot use

Chariots in Iron Age Cyprus up to the 5th century B.C. usually had a military appearance. This is amply demonstrated by the weapons carried and the evidence for the protection of both the crew and the draught team.

Our main source of information are the terracotta models from Ayia Irini and other sites of the 7th–6th century B.C. (see pls. 22a–b–29).[100] These show two- and four horse chariots, often carrying a crew of three – driver and archer standing in front, with the driver usually on the right, and a shield bearer at the rear; the latter is

---

[97] See Gjerstad 1935, pl. CCXXXV: 6 = 1963, 10 with fig. 10 (Ayia Irini terracotta no. 249Z + 115, showing tassels stacked on top of each other and thereby recalling 8th century Assyrian reliefs, see Littauer and Crouwel 1979, 126).

[98] Littauer and Crouwel 1979, 127.

[99] Karageorghis 1973a, 83 nos. 142 and 163 with pl. CCLIV (from A 7 or cart), cf. 87f. with pl. CCLV (six bronze straps from which such bells – or tassels – may have been suspended, belonging with A 7 and cart. The reconstruction drawing shows the bells hanging from an imaginary vertical strap, see Tatton-Brown 1979, 71); Littauer and Crouwel 1979, 127 (with refs.); Özgen 1985, 109–111 (Urartu).

[100] See esp. Gjerstad 1935, pls. CCXXXIV–CCXXXV; 1963, 10–14; Törnqvist 1970, 88–91; Littauer and Crouwel 1977b, 72f.; cf. also Young and Young 1955, no. 1055 (remarkable fragmentary terracotta from Kourion); Cassimatis 1986, no. 6 (Tamassos).

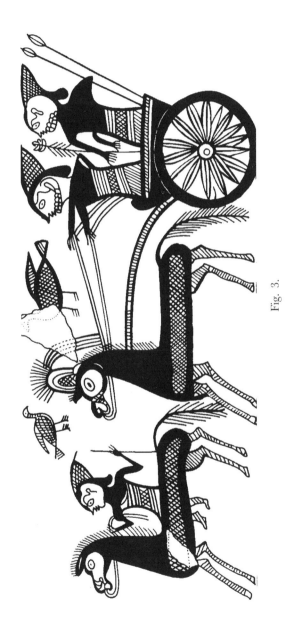

Fig. 3.

sometimes seen protecting the archer with his round shield (pls. 23a–b–25).[101] Bowcases and quivers of arrows, attached to the outside of the vehicle body or placed inside, provided the archer with reserve arms. The archer may be replaced by a man brandishing a spear, though bowcase and quiver are still shown, or the shield bearer may at the same time be wielding a spear (pl. 22a–b).[102] On a vase painting of the 8th century a pair of spears is fixed at the rear of the vehicle body (fig. 3). Swords, suspended from a baldric, are sometimes carried by crew members (pl. 26a–b).[103] It may be noted that a sword, spear and round shield as well as bunches of arrowheads and traces of quivers and possibly a bow were found associated with the remains of a two-poled chariot (A 3) at Salamis, dating to c. 600 B.C.[104] The crew often wore helmets of varying design. They may also have worn armour of some kind but few traces of this – presumably in paint – if any remain.

All this military equipment can be matched among chariots in the Near East during the earlier first millennium B.C.[105] Similarly armed crews of three first appear on Assyrian reliefs of the 9th century, when shields are often seen hanging at the rear of the chariot body. In the late 8th and 7th centuries we find four-man crews, including two shield bearers protecting the driver and archer from the rear. (Such four-man complements, unarmed except for the shields with central bosses carried on the backs of the two men at the rear, form part of a group of terracotta models of possibly Cypriot manufacture, see pl. 27a–b).[106] In addition to the bow, weapons associated with Near Eastern chariots included single spears, probably for thrusting and fixed at the rear, as well as swords and axes. Quivers and bowcases are attached to the outside of the chariot body, but carried inside from the 8th century onwards in Assyria. For protection the crew may wear scale armour Helmets are often shown.

---

[101] Gjerstad 1935, pls. CCXXXV: 4 and CCXXXIV: 3 (Ayia Irini nos. 1170 and 1780; our pls. 25, 23a–b).

[102] Gjerstad 1935, pl. CCXXXIV: 5 (Ayia Irini no. 2000; Karageorghis 1969, 462 with fig. 46a–b (our pl. XXXVII: 1).

[103] Littauer and Crouwel 1977b, 72 with pl. XXV: 3 (Meniko; our pl. XXXVIII: 1); Gjerstad 1935, pl. CCXXXIV: 2, 4 (Ayia Irini nos. 1166, 1715).

[104] Karageorghis 1967a, 33. 43. 50f. nos. 95 (sword), 123 (spear), 25 (shield), 110 and 173 (bundles of arrowheads) with fig. XVI and pl. CXXIX.

[105] For what follows, see Littauer and Crouwel 1979, 128–33.

[106] See *supra* n. 24.

Chariot horses in Cyprus, as seen particularly clearly again on the terracottas, also wore protective armour of varying forms. It may consist of a bib-shaped gorget or breastplate, with a fringe of tassels along the bottom edge (pl. 33). The gorget may have been of boiled leather or of metal; actual bronze specimens of similar form, both plain and decorated, have been found with the 8th–7th century vehicle burials at Salamis (fig. 2: 7)[107] and also at Hasanlu in N.W. Iran, the latter in a context of c. 800 B.C. Such breastplates are seen worn by chariot and ridden horses of Assyrian reliefs of the 9th and 8th centuries but no later, and on non-Assyrian representations of the time. Bronze gorgets of related type, with two hinged parts, are known from Urartu.[108] The fringe, which is a constant feature, may have helped to keep flies off, besides being decorative (cf. the tasseled fringe of the shoulder pendants, see s.v. Harnessing).

Other Cypriot terracottas seem to suggest a long, rectangular chest protection, sometimes with a fringe too (pls. 22a–b, 24). In one case this protection extends along the forward sides of a quadriga's outer horses – a form of armour not illustrated in the Near East.[109]

Yet another Cypriot terracotta model shows a trapper covering the front and entire sides of the outer horses, held in place by straps over their backs (pl. 25). This recalls the trappers seen on 7th century Assyrian reliefs which extend all the way up to the necks of the horses.[110] Embossed gold plaques from Cyprus seem to illustrate trappers armoured with scales, such as appear on Assyrian reliefs of the 8th century and on some other Near Eastern representations.[111]

Finally, the blinkers and frontlets worn by many horses in the earlier first millennium B.C. – in Cyprus and the Near East – may have had a protective function, depending on the materials used and the degree of decoration.

---

[107] Karageorghis 1973a, 84–6 (A 7). 86 (A 8). cf. 76 and 78 (carts) with esp. pls. CCLXXV–CCLXXVIII (nos. 320/17, from A 8 = our fig. 2: 7); cf. 1967a, 49 with pl. CXXVIII (cart from Tomb 3).

[108] For gorgets, see Littauer and Crouwel 1979, 129 (with refs.); Haerinck and Overlaet 1984, 56f. with figs. 1f., pl. I; Seidl 1986 (Urartu).

[109] Gjerstad 1935, pl. CCXXXV: 5 = 1963, 10 with fig. 9 (Ayia Irini no. 1998); cf. Blinkenberg 1931, nos. 1982a–b with pl. 88 (Cypriot terracotta chariot horses with rather short chest protection found in Rhodes).

[110] Littauer and Crouwel 1979, 131.

[111] See esp. Karageorghis 1967a, pl. LXI, no. 67/2; cf. Littauer and Crouwel 1979, 131 (Near East).

The Cypriot sources, in particular the 7th–6th century terracottas rendered in circumstantial detail, strongly suggest the actual use of chariots in warfare in the island. This is supported by the disappearance of the military accoutrements in the 5th century B.C.[112] Active, presumably military use is also implied by the presence, from the 8th century onwards, of two poles – a feature apparently peculiar to Cypriot chariots at this time. These poles would have given greater tractive efficiency to the animals than the single pole with four horses under yoke attested in Assyria; besides, the lateral stress on turning would have been taken by two areas rather than one. Though a more rigid equipage, experiments have shown that two-poled chariots could take a turn by describing a sweep of no more than about ten meters.[113] Unfortunately, there are neither figured nor textual references to actual battles involving chariots in Cyprus, as there are in Assyria. Herodotus, however, in a passage which may be significant (V: 113) mentions military action by chariots in the island in the early 5th century B.C.

We know, primarily from Assyrian reliefs of the 9th–7th centuries, that chariots in Assyria and other parts of the Near East were mainly used as elevated, mobile firing platforms for an ancher standing beside the driver. The close-range weapons also carried were used should it be necessary to fight from a slow-moving or immobilized chariot or on the ground. Although concern for the protection of crew and draught team indicates that chariots came within reach of enemy missiles, they remained too vulnerable to be used as a shock force against a well-prepared enemy line.

The many similarities in military equipment between the Cypriot chariots and those in the Near East imply a similar use in warfare in the island, on whatever scale.

As said above, the military function of chariots in Cyprus seems to have been abandoned in the 5th century B.C., from which time onwards representations show only civil vehicles. There is nothing military, for instance, about the chariots represented by the stone models and on the sarcophagi of the 5th century (pls. 20, 21). The file of vehicles, including one with a parasol inside, and horsemen seen on the Amathus sarcophagus, suggests a procession of some kind.[114]

---

[112] Littauer and Crouwel 1977b, 73; Tatton-Brown (née Wilson) 1972, 187f.

[113] Spruytte 1978–79, 56f.; cf. Littauer and Crouwel 1977a, 6.

[114] Tatton-Brown 1981, 79f., 82. For stone models, see *supra* n. 3; see also the terracotta from Kition, *supra* n. 58 with pl. XXXVIII: 4).

The demise of military chariots in Cyprus can be paralleled, although at a somewhat earlier date, in the Near East and may perhaps be explained likewise, with reference to the development of mounted troops. In the Near East, by the late 8th and 7th centuries, mounted troops had improved their horsemanship to a degree that enabled them to take more effective use of their weapons (bow and spear) and thus exploit more fully their advantages over chariotry as regards mobility in different types of terrain and in economy of material.[115] The later scythed chariots of the Achaemenid and other armies represent the final and degenerate stage of the military chariot in the Near East.[116] In Cyprus scythed chariots are not attested. As for ridden horses with a military appearance, these are illustrated in various media, beginning in the 8th century B.C. (see fig. 3).[117] However, no development in riding techniques can be observed and there is no significant increase in the number of representations from the 5th century onwards.

Another use of chariots in the Near East – in hunting – is not explicitly documented in Cyprus, although the animals carried in a few of the 7th–6th century terracotta chariot models may represent hunting trophies.[118] At the same time these animals may represent offerings, since most of the terracottas served as ex-voto's in sanctuaries.

Chariots in Cyprus also had a funerary function. We see this reflected not only in a few terracotta models found in tombs, such as one from Kition (pl. 29), but also in the actual vehicles buried at Salamis and other sites.[119] At Salamis eight single and two-poled chariots were discovered with their draught teams of two and four horses respectively in six tombs out of a total of well over a hundred. In the case of chariot A 7 from Tomb 79 the animals must have been removed to make room for the second burial. There may be one chariot associated with a burial (A 1, A 2, A 6 from Tombs 1 and 50) or a pair (biga and quadriga A 4 and A 5 belonging with the second burial in Tomb 47). In Tomb 79 the individuals buried during the two phases each had two vehicles of different type and

---

[115] Littauer and Crouwel 1979, 130f. 137–139; Spruytte 1983.

[116] Littauer and Crouwel 1979, 153.

[117] See esp. numerous terracottas, Young and Young 1955, 211–216; Tatton-Brown 1982a, 177f.; Monloup 1984, 37–54.

[118] Littauer and Crouwel 1979, 133 (Near Fast). Gjerstad 1935, pl. CCXXXV: 1 (Ayia Irini no. 1125); Studniczka 1907, no. 16 = Cassimatis 1986, 181 with pl. XXXVIII: 7 (boar with bound feet).

[119] See refs.; *supra* nn. 9. 11; also Coldstream 1985, 53–56 (Salamis).

purpose – a chariot (A 7 and A 8 respectively) and a cart; the same combination of chariot (A 3) and cart accompanying a single burial occurs in Tomb 3.[120] During the funerary ceremonies chariots and carts alike were taken into the wide dromoi of the tombs, where their draught animals were killed while still under yoke. They were then left behind and subsequently covered by the earth used to fill in the dromoi.

The draught animals of both chariots and carts wore iron bits along with blinkers and frontlets, the latter mostly of plain or decorated bronze but sometimes of ivory and covered with gold foil. Other, yet more striking differences can be observed in the degree to which the team's harnesses and yokes as well as the vehicles themselves were decorated. Thus both chariot teams from Tomb 79 (A 7 and A 8) had bronze breastplates and shoulder pendants, highly decorated in the case of A 7, while the yokes of these vehicles were embellished with bronze standards, exactly like the cart teams and yokes from this tomb and from Tomb 3.

Chariot A 7 is an outstanding specimen: its two poles have bronze caps at either end with decorated ovoid disks hung over them at the rear, and its axles are fitted with finely worked bronze caps pierced by highly ornate linch pins. Surely a vehicle like this would have been restricted in its use to parades or (funerary) ceremonies (cf. also the low siding, recorded as only 0.44 m. high). It is no coincidence that the same, first burial in Tomb 79 also contained a highly decorated cart of some kind as well as splendid bronze vessels and furniture decorated with ivory – "a splendid corpus of luxuries apropriate to a local despote".[121]

The single-poled chariot A 8 from the second burial in this tomb, although the decoration of its team's harness and yoke is less conspicuous, seems to have been suitable for similar ceremonial purposes.

Other chariots at Salamis, as far as can be ascertained from their often poor remains, may have been put to more active use, including warfare. The military equipment associated with chariot A 3 from Tomb 3 is particularly suggestive in this respect.

---

[120] Note that Tomb 2 had only a cart, as had the first burial in Tomb 47. For these and the other carts from Salamis, see Crouwel 1985, esp. 212–214.
[121] Quoted from Coldstream 1985, 54; see also Karageorghis 1973a, esp. 81. 86.

Concluding remarks

We have seen that chariots are first attested in Iron Age Cyprus in the 8th century B.C. and are documented down to Hellenistic times. In addition there is some evidence for their use in the island at a much earlier date, in the Late Bronze Age.[122] When chariots reappear, it is clear that many elements have been adoped from the Near East, not only with regard to the construction of the vehicles, the harness and means of control of the animals and their decoration but also in respect of the equipment carried and the – military – use to which these equipages were put. This is not surprising in view of Cyprus' proximity to and close connections with its eastern neighbours in the earlier first millennium B.C., including a period when the island was actually under the domination of Assyria (709–c. 669 B.C.).

It is well worth noting, however, that the chariots buried at Salamis during the 8th and 7th centuries and the terracotta models of the 7th–6th century are not identical with the chariots seen on 9th–7th century Assyrian reliefs or other contemporary figured documents from the Near East. To some degree the Cypriot vehicles reflect the vehicles depicted on Assyrian reliefs of the 9th century rather than later ones. They may also combine elements seen on Assyrian reliefs of different dates.[123]

At the same time there are possible local features, such as the platform at the rear of the floor, the use of the two poles, sometimes in conjunction with two two-horse yokes, the occurrence of wheels with ten or more spokes and hinged frontlets with attached poll crests. To some extent these and other apparently Cypriot traits, including the partition down the centre of the chariot body and the loop at the rear, may, however, have to do with the nature of our

---

[122] See Vandenabeele 1977. (She was incorrect in including Mycenaean vases and terracottas found in the island among evidence for the use of such vehicles in Cyprus, since they were quite probably imported from mainland Greece).

[123] For instance, the group of terracottas of possibly Cypriot manufacture (*supra* n. 24) recalls chariots seen on late 8th and 7th century Assyrian reliefs in having a four-man complement, including two shield bearers at the rear; at the same time it is reminiscent of 9th century reliefs on account of the shield with lion-headed boss suspended from the loop at the centre rear, shown with one model, pl. XXXVIII: 2. Partition and loop both occur at an earlier date in Transcaucasia, see *supra* n. 33. The bench down the centre of the body, seen on one of the later Oxus models (*supra* n. 21), may have developed out of the partition.

evidence: in the island we have remains of actual chariots and their draught teams' gear as well as detailed models in the round of terracotta and – in the 5th century – of stone, whereas in the Near East we have to rely mainly on two-dimensional representations, albeit often large scale and detailed as on the Assyrian reliefs.

What seems to be a local trait is the burial, over a period of two hundred years or more, of chariots – and carts – with the harness teams and their gear in the tombs of what must be the local élites in the island. This practice is not documented in the Near East at this time, but only much earlier and with different types of vehicles – in third millennium Mesopotamia and Elam. It also occurs in China, from the Shang period onwards. Elsewhere, we have examples of people buried either with their chariots, as in New Kingdom Egypt, or with their draught animals, as sometimes seen for instance in Greece in the Late Bronze Age and early Iron Age.[124]

In this connection it is important to note that there is nothing to suggest a connection between Cypriot and Greek chariots in the Iron Age. In Greece, chariots were no longer used in warfare by the Archaic period and its heroizing art represents chariots and crews that are very different from the Cypriot ones and that already reflect obsolete practices.[125] Chariot racing, so popular in Greece at this time, is not documented in Cyprus.

Cypriot chariots and their military use in the earlier first millennium B.C. firmly belong within the Near Eastern orbit, well documented by figured and textual sources pertaining to Assyria, the Levant and Urartu.

In Cyprus itself we have no one standard type of chariot. Bigae and quadrigae, the latter with a single four-horse or two-horse yoke, occur side by side over a long period. No clear structural development can be observed, but there is an important functional change: from the 5th century B.C. onwards we witness the demise of the military chariot, while its civil use continues.

---

[124] See Littauer and Crouwel 1985, 97f. (with refs.). For Greece, see Crouwel 1981, 34 (Marathon, tholos tomb); Popham, Touloupa and Sackett 1982, 171 (Lefkandi, "Heroon"; two of the four horses had iron bits in their mouths, according to the information kindly provided by M. R. Popham).

[125] See Anderson 1970, 159 with n. 35; Crouwel 1981, 144.

Catalogue of Chariot Remains from Salamis

A 1. Single-poled chariot with two horses (4 and 5). Tomb 1 (first burial). Cypro-Geometric III. Dikaios 1963, 152–4 with fig. 26; Karageorghis 1969a, 27.

A 2. Two-poled chariot, found with three horses (1–3). Tomb 1 (second burial). Cypro-Archaic I. Dikaios 1963, 156–61 with figs. 4, 17, 19, 21, 26, 28–31; Karageorghis 1969a, 27 with fig. 2 and pl. 8.

A 3. Single-poled chariot ("chariot B") with two horses (B and D) (fig. 2: 2–wheel). Tomb 3. Cypro-Archaic I/II. Karageorghis 1967a, 31, 33, 49–52 with fig. XVI and pls. XXVIII: 1, XXX–XXXIII, XXXVIII–XLIX, CXX–CXXI; 1969a, 68–70 with fig. 15.

A 4. Single-poled chariot with two horses (A and B). Tomb 47 (second burial). Cypro-Archaic I. Karageorghis 1967a, 77f. with fig. XXIX and pls. LXVII: 3, LXVIII–LXIX, LXX: 11–2; 1969a, 53f. with figs. 5, 7 and pl. 16.

A 5. Two-poled chariot with four horses (C-F). Tomb 47 (second burial). Cypro-Archaic I. Karageorghis 1967a, 77–9 with fig. XXIX and pls. LXVII: 3, LXVIII–LXX, LXXI: 3–4; 1969a, 58 with figs. 8, 10.

A 6. Single-poled chariot with two horses. Tomb 50 (first burial). Cypro-Archaic I/II. Karageorghis 1967a, 105f., 115, 118 with pl. XCVI; 1969a, 58 with figs 8, 10.

A 7. Two-poled chariot ("chariot *Beta*") (fig. 1). Tomb 79 (first burial). Early Cypro-Archaic I. Karageorghis 1969a, 78–80 with fig. 20 and pls. 36–27, 45–46; 1973a, 12, 68–74, 78–86 with figs. IV, V11, 10–13 and pls. XXI–XXIII, CCLVIII, also LXXIX, LXXXI–CVIII.

A 8. Single-poled chariot ("chariot *Delta*") with two horses (fig. 2: 1). Tomb 79 (second burial). Cypro-Archaic I. Karageorghis 1969a, 81, 83 with pls. II–III; 1973a, 12, 74f. with figs. VI, IX and pls. XXVIII–XXX, CCL, also CXXIII–CXXVIII.

13. A BRONZE AGE CHARIOT GROUP FROM THE LEVANT IN PARIS*

D. COLLON, J. CROUWEL AND M. A. LITTAUER

Editorial Note. In a discussion of this interesting bronze group in the Louvre, Mrs. Littauer and Mr. Crouwel on the one hand, and Dr. Collon on the other, found themselves in marked disagreement over its dating, although agreeing that the chariot and its figures appear to have been made at one and the same time as a single group. It has therefore seemed best to present their respective arguments in two parallel papers.

A. *The Chariot*

M. A. Littauer and J. H. Crouwel

The Bronze group, comprising the chariot and two figures, was described as early as 1905 by A. de Ridder, when it still formed part of the well-known collection of L. de Clerq. It had been acquired for this collection by Péretié, chancellor of the French consulate in Beirut, and was said to have come from "Phoenicia". The model, together with other selected pieces from the de Clercq collection, was donated in 1967 to the French State and deposited in the Louvre, where it is now on display (inv. no. 22265 figs. 1–2, pl. 36a–d).[1] The piece, which is undoubtedly genuine, deserves more detailed study.

Description

Material and technique: Metal said to be of bronze rich in copper (no analysis reported). Probably cast in one piece by lost-wax process, except for the wire-like band running up the sides and along the

* *Levant* 8, 1976, 71–79. Dominique Collon, "B. The Figures", 79–81 (see pp. 185–189).
[1] For this gift see Parrot 1967 and Parrot 1968.

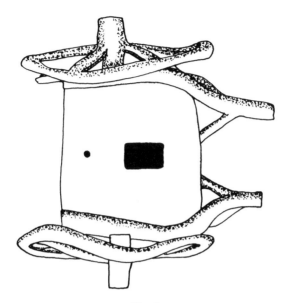

Fig. 1.

Fig. 2.

top of the box and forming loops at the top rear corners, which was probably soldered on separately.

Condition: Some dried earth still adhering, as the model was not cleaned down completely after casting. Metal in good condition. Even, dark, green to slighly bluish patina. One loop at top rear on left side broken off, as are both draught poles just in front of box. Wheels bent out of shape.

Acknowledgements

The authors are most grateful to Dr. P. Amiet for permission to study and publish the chariot group. In addition they wish to thank Miss A. Caubet for her cooperation and for supplying photographs; Dr. D. von Bothmer for permission to examine the Kourion model and for providing a photograph; Dr. V. Karageorghis for enabling them to study the Ovgoros model; and Dr. P. R. S. Moorey for several references. Miss Collon would like to thank Mr. W. Graham for help with photographs.

Dimensions: Overall. L: 0.0675 m.; W: 0.108 m.; H: (excluding loops) 0.065 m.
Box. D: (front to rear) 0.042 m.; W: 0.072 m.; H: 0.04 m.
Floor. Thickness: 0.0025 m.
Hole in floor. L: 0.011 m.; W: 0.0075 m.; distance from front: 0.012 m.
Wheels. Diam: 0.055 m.

Rectangular floor, wider than deep, with very slightly rounded front corners. Rectangular hole in centre of floor and, in line with it, a tiny round hole towards rear. Solidly walled front and side screens rising to the same height. No screen at rear. Vertical at front corners and at rear edges, and horizontal bands along top of screens. These form loops at the upper rear corners and rise from them at a slightly oblique angle. On outer side of front screen a pair of cross braces applied saltirewise, not completely filling the rectangle. Similar braces on outside of side screens, here touching the corners. In each side screen, a small round hole in the forward angle of these cross braces.

No axle marked under floor. Two six-spoked wheels fixed to sides of box, extending somewhat beyond front and back. Their naves, set just behind the centre of the floor, project at either side and are

round in section. The shorter projections on the inside run somewhat under the two draught poles. The latter run directly under the
floor, one along each side, and end at rear of floor. Immediately in
front of the box the poles bend inwards and upwards. Both round-
sectioned poles are broken off; the stump of one pole rises slightly
higher than the other (probably being bent out of shape). Each pole
is joined to the front of the box by two round-sectioned supports.
One of these is short and straight, running back almost horizontally
to near the centre of the front screen just above its lower edge. The
other is longer and bent, joining the front screen about halfway up,
near the outer edge.

Bibliography of Group

de Ridder 1905,129f., 134f., no. 209 with pl. XXXII.
Przeworski 1928, 277.
Müller 1929, 188 with pl. XXVI:372.
Forrer 1932, fig. 19:1 (caption incorrect).
Barnett 1964, 62 with fig. 8.
Barnett 1969, 410 with pl. VI:B, C.
Amiet 1968, 304 with fig. 4.
Wilson 1972, 132f., 138, 141, 145 with fig. 10:1.

The following discussion will concentrate solely on those features of
the chariot model that imply a first- rather than a second-millennium B.C. date: the rectangular floor plan in combination with the
rigid loop hand-grips at the top rear corners of the box, and the traction system, involving probably a Y-pole. Other aspects of the chariot,
interesting though they may be, will not be considered. Some features, such as the position of the axle, the six-spoked wheel and the
angular outline of the box for instance may be paralleled both in
later second- as well as in first-millennium B.C. chariots.

The Floor Plan

A rectangular box is not documented by any actual second-millennium chariots. Those that have survived, preserved in Egyptian New-
Kingdom tombs,[2] have floor plans rather like a capital D, with one

---

[2] Actual chariots found in Egypt: Florence, Museo Archeologico. Cf. Botti 1951.
Cairo, Egyptian Museum. 1. Cf. Carter and Newberry 1904, 24ff.; 2. Cf. Quibell
1908, 65ff.; 4–9. Cf. Carter 1927, 107ff., particularly pls. XXXVII and XXXVIII.

or two heat-bent timbers forming the front and sides of the floor-frame and a straight member joining the ends of these across the rear. The many chariots depicted in strict profile view on Egyptian walls during the New Kingdom appear to conform closely in type with the specimens actually found. They have the same rounded line at the rear, indicating the bent wood rail that frames the sidings on the actual chariots and that would structurally be a more logical accompaniment of a D-shaped floor plan than of a rectangular one.[3] Exceptions are some three-man enemy chariots appearing in the reliefs of the Battle of Kadesh,[4] where the sharply rectangular siding makes one suspect the possibility of a rectangular floor plan. At Abu Simbel, one of these appears among chariots of other shapes in the forefront of battle in the famous scene of confrontation.[5] The preserved chariot of Yuaa and Thuiu, however, which does have squared-off rear upper corners, possesses a D-shaped floor plan.[6] The enemy is generally shown on Egyptian reliefs as employing what appears to be a variant of the Egyptian chariot, usually with solid, rather than fenestrated side screens, but with a curving profile that suggests the use also of heat-bent wood.[7] Moreover, New Kingdom representations of tribute chariots from the Levant[8] and the (by comparison) scanty representations from that area itself[9] show a curving profile. While there seems to be evidence of an open-sided rectangular chariot box in Cappadocia at the beginning of the second millennium,[10] and of a closed one on some Syrian cylinder seals,[11] such a thing appears in very limited contexts in the *later* part of the millennium, and at least two features of the Louvre model were lacking on it: the upright handgrip and (see below) the Y-pole.

The latter chariots will be described in a forthcoming publication of the Griffith Institute, Oxford, by M. A. Littauer and J. H. Crouwel [cf. Littauer and Crouwel 1985].

[3] Useful selections of illustrations in Yadin 1963; for more comprehensive coverage see Wreszinski 1935.

[4] Wreszinski 1935, pls. 21–23, 96–97, 169–174.

[5] Wreszinski 1935, pls. 169, 170, 176; Bossert 1942, no. 752.

[6] Quibell 1908; Yadin 1963, 190.

[7] Bossert 1942, 746, 748f.; Yadin 1963, 239.

[8] Yadin 1963, 189, 194.

[9] E.g. patera from Ras Shamra (*supra*, n. 3), 187; box from Enkomi: Lorimer 1950, pl. XI: 1.

[10] E.g. Özgüç 1965, 28, with pl. VIII: 24 a, b (Inv. No. Kt. a/5 200); Amiet 1969, 2f., figs. 1, 2 (Louvre AO 8306).

[11] E.g. Amiet 1969, fig. 3; von der Osten 1934, 53, no. 343, pl. XXIII; Buchanan 1966, 174, no. 892, pl. 56.

The early first millennium gives evidence of what seems to be a continuation of the second-millennium D-shaped floor. Assyrian reliefs of the ninth century show a low-sided, shallow box, with rounded rear corners, and a siding that dips towards the front.[12] The quivers attached to the box are depicted in a convention that seems to imply that they do not lie flat against the side but hang at the front corners of the D. Cypriote chariots display many Assyrian features, although often with considerable provincial time lag, and it is possible to suggest that certain sixth- and fifth-century limestone models of chariot groups with D-shaped boxes hark back to the Assyrian chariots of this type.[13]

Chariots with a rectangular box appear in Assyrian reliefs of the eighth to seventh centuries B.C. They seem deeper than the ninth-century chariots and have sharp front corners.[14] Similarly, rectangular boxes are seen in profile view on other eighth-century representations, such as some eighth-century ivories from Ziwiyeh,[15] two Achaemenid cylinder seals,[16] and several fifth- to fourth-century coins from Sidon.[17] The chariots of the King at Persepolis[18] and on the famous mosaic of the Battle of Issus show the same sharp corners and deep box.[19] Again, Assyrian profile views of assumed rectangular boxes may be confirmed by Cypriote models in the round,[20] while the Achaemenid ones are supported by the two gold models from the Oxus Treasure.[21]

The rather limited evidence available suggests that the prevalent D-shaped floor plan of the later second and earlier first millennium was largely replaced in the course of the first half of the first millennium by a rectangular one, better capable of accommodating the four-man complement now often seen.[22]

---

[12] Barnett (n.d.), pls. 25, 26.
[13] Myres 1914, 145, no. 1016; Studniczka 1907, 187 with fig. 32.
[14] Cf. Yadin 1963, 420f. 452.
[15] Godard 1950, figs. 83–85.
[16] Frankfort 1939a, pl. XXXVII: d (BM) and n (Boston, MFA).
[17] Cf. Franke and Hirmer 1964, pl. 195; Hill 1932, pl. 20, nos. 56–57; Studniczka 1907, 189ff.
[18] Schmidt 1953, pl. 52.
[19] Cf Nuoffer 1904, 61ff., no. 47; Rossi 1970, pl. 6.
[20] E.g. limestone model in MMA: Myres 1914, 145, no. 1017; terracotta models: Gjerstad 1963, 10, fig. 10; also a very explicit unpublished model in the Royal Ontario Museum, Toronto (no. 958.61.309).
[21] Dalton 1964, xxxviiff. with figs. 20, 21; pl. IV and "Addition" pl.
[22] E.g. Yadin 1963, 452; Strommenger and Hirmer 1964, pls. 248, 254.

The Handgrips

The loops at the upper rear corners of the side screens of the model can be explained as handgrips. Although we find handgrips reserved in these corners,[23] soft handgrips,[24] and handgrips formed by a rigid standing loop at centre rear of the chariot box,[25] only rigid loops rising above the corners of the screens at the rear need concern us here. A solid form of this raised handgrip first appears in Assyria under Tiglath-Pileser III (745–727 B.C.)[26] and continues there into the next century.[27] The first example of its modification in hollow form is also probably eighth century, on a Nimrud ivory, perhaps from Zinjirli.[28] It is, however, under the Achaemenids that this type of handgrip is especially prominent. We see it on royal chariots on cylinder seals,[29] on the reliefs at Persepolis,[30] and on the mosaic of the Battle of Issus.[31] A chariot on an Egyptian drawing on stone, showing strong Persian influence, also displays it.[32] Closest of all to that on our chariot seems to be the handgrip on the chariot on the seal in the British Museum,[33] where the straight top line of the side screen and the external braces in saltire extend the resemblance.

---

[23] The only handgrips illustrated in the second millennium are of the reserved type, and we know of only two objects showing these: the famous gold bowl from Hasanlu, dated by (Porada 1964, 34, with pl. 23 and figs. 63, 64) to the thirteenth or twelfth centuries B.C., and a related, unprovenanced metal vase from north-west Iran published by Amiet (1965, 235ff. with pls. XVI–XVII and fig. 2). These chariots, however, are very different in appearance from ours. The first millennium provides more examples, *e.g.*: Barnett 1957, 195 with pls. XXXIII–XXXIV; Bossert 1942, no. 886 (relief from Sakçagözü); Myres 1909–11, 1f. (sarcophagus from Amathus, Cyprus); Dalton 1964, "Addition" plate.

[24] E.g. Barnett (n.d.), pl. 14 (relief of Ashurnasirpal II); Parrot 1961, pl. 345 (wall painting from Til Barsib); Schmidt 1953, pl. 32B (relief from Persepolis).

[25] This loop occurs on many Cypriote terracotta models of the seventh century B.C. and later, *e.g.* Gjerstadt 1963, figs. 11, 13; its presence in Cyprus has been confirmed by an actual example of just such a bronze loop at the rear of a late eighth-century chariot (B) from tomb 79 in Salamis 1973a, 73 and 121 with pl. CCXLVIII). A terracotta model from Marathus (modern Amrit) in the Louvre has a similar loop at the rear (Studniczka, 1907, 169ff., no. 17). The presence of such a loop may probably be deduced on ninth-century Assyrian chariots, cf. Littauer 1972, 147, n. 17.

[26] Barnett and Falkner 1962, pls. IX, LXXI, LXXXIII.

[27] Strommenger and Hirmer 1964, pls. 248. 253.

[28] Mallowan 1966, 538f. with fig. 462.

[29] Frankfort 1939a, pl. XXXVII: d, n.

[30] Schmidt 1953, pl. 52.

[31] Rossi 1970, pl. 6.

[32] Brunner-Traut 1956, 101f. with pl. XLVIII (Hannover, Kestner Museum 2952). For a corrected dating of this drawing see Littauer and Crouwel [1979].

[33] Frankfort 1939a, pl. XXXVII: d.

The Traction System

At first sight, the remains of the two poles would seem to indicate a two-poled chariot, such as we know existed in the first millennium, but of which we have no evidence of any kind from the second millennium B.C. This new traction system is documented by the remains of actual eighth- to seventh-century chariots from Salamis in Cyprus,[34] by many terracotta[35] and two limestone models[36] from that island, all dating from the seventh century onwards, by a terracotta model from Phoenicia,[37] and by the two gold models from the Oxus Treasure.[38] In every case, traction is provided by teams of four horses – two between the poles and two outside them, either under a single four-horse yoke or under two separate two-horse ones.

But whereas, in these examples, the two poles run straight forward to the yoke or yokes, on the Louvre model they bend inwards. Under such circumstances, unless the chariot were of exceptional width, there would have been no room for the two inner animals of a quadriga to be placed between the poles. One might suggest a triga, with a single animal between the poles, as an alternative. Nowhere, however, do we have any certain evidence of anything but two pole horses and one trace horse in triga hitch. And it is late Roman times before single animals between shafts begin sporadically to appear.[39] The other, more likely, alternative is that the poles not only converged but actually came together. Such an arrangement is clearly documented by two first-millennium B.C. chariot models from Cyprus: one, of limestone, possibly dating to the fifth century B.C., from Kourion, is now in New York (pl. 37),[40] the other, of terracotta, and dating to the seventh to sixth century B.C., from Ovgoros, is in Nicosia.[41] On the more circumstantial of the two, the model in New York, the poles bend inwards and meet, not to merge, but to run alongside each other to the yoke. We thus have not a

---

[34] Dikaios 1963, 156ff. (tomb 1, second burial); Karageorghis 1967a, 49ff. (tomb 3, Chariot B); Karageorghis 1973, 78ff. (tomb 79, chariot B).

[35] E.g. Gjerstad 1963, 10, 13 with figs. 9, 14; Studniczka 1907, 167 with fig. 15.

[36] Studniczka 1907, 187 with fig. 32; Myres 1914, 145, no. 1016.

[37] Studniczka 1907, 169ff. with fig. 17 (mentioned *supra*, n. 25), and also Heuzey 1923, 53f., no. 187 with pl. V: 1.

[38] See Dalton 1964.

[39] For shaft harness see Piggott 1968, 267 and des Noëttes 1931, 83f., 123f.

[40] New York, MMA acc. no. 74.51.2687. Myres 1914, 145, no. 1017; Studniczka 1907, 185, no. 30.

[41] Nicosia, CM inv. no. CM1955/IX–26/1. Spiteris 1970, ill. p. 93; Megaw 1955, 43 with pl. II: d.

single, forking pole, but a composite construction of two poles.[42] This is also supported by the less obvious evidence of ninth and early eighth century B.C. Assyrian reliefs, on which the pole, where it curves upwards and forwards from floor level, impinges on the lower side of the chariot box as it could not were it a central pole. The suspicion that this indicates two poles (one at either side of the box) is reinforced by the fact that the partial outline of a second pole actually appears just beneath the near pole in several instances.[43] Since these appear to be trigae, this would suggest that the two poles converged somewhere behind the animals to form a Y-shaped pole, as on the two models.[44]

The Y-pole may be interpreted as an effort to produce a stronger chariot for the three-man team that appears occasionally on royal chariots under Ashurnasirpal II and more frequently under Shalmaneser III.[45]

Piggott has suggested that the Y-pole developed directly from the A-frame cart of Transcaucasia (fig. 3).[46] It seems quite possible that Assyria's campaigns in the north brought her into contact with the A-frame cart (for which there is no evidence in Mesopotamia) and suggested to her a way of making a stronger chariot with a stronger traction system. The Metropolitan Museum model, with its preservation of the two individual poles seems, indeed, to point to such an origin.

Under the old system, the single pole was only a separate element, running under the chariot floor. If that floor was, as we have reason to believe, still of interwoven thongs, as it had been in Egypt,[47] the pole could have had only two points of attachment to the box – in the places where it ran under the floor frame, front and rear. On the other hand, two poles, formed by extending the side beams of the floor, or attached securely to these, would have supplied both

---

[42] This is not to be confused with the *vertically articulating* Y-pole of four-wheelers that probably existed as early as the third millennium B.C., and which was a separate element, supporting no weight. Cf. Littauer and Crouwel 1973b, 116f.

[43] E.g. Barnett (n.d.), pls. 24f.; Budge 1914, pl. XXII (below). This hitherto unnoticed detail was pointed out to me by J. K. Anderson several years ago (M.A.L.).

[44] This interpretation was also independently arrived at by M. J. Spruytte whose long practical experience in driving led him to draw the same conclusion from the Assyrian figured evidence alone.

[45] Barnett (n.d.), pls. 25, 148, 169, 172; Yadin 1963, 455.

[46] Piggott 1968, 289ff., esp. 295.

[47] Karageorghis 1973a, 73 and 1967a, 50; Dalton 1964, xi.

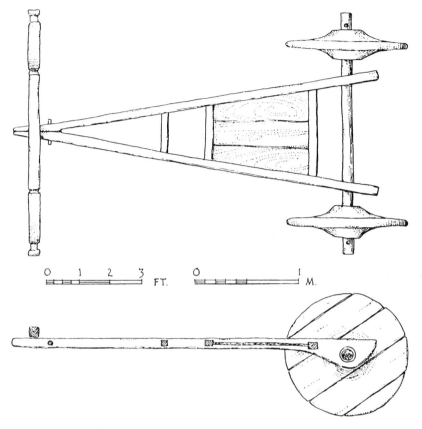

Fig. 3.

greater support and greater tractive strength. From the old habit of heat bending the single chariot pole vertically it would be but a step to bending the two poles horizontally as well, or at a combined upward and inward angle. Although the A-pole of the cart had been suitable for slow moving oxen, it would have placed a team of horses too far ahead of the box and too far apart for efficient control, and have reduced the compactness of the unit, hence the conversion to the Y-pole.

The true two-poled chariot, with its poles running straight to either the two two-horse yokes or a single four-horse yoke[48] may

---

[48] Yadin 1963, 426; Gadd 1936, pl. 18 (above). On the latter the part of the relief with the left outer bay of the four-horse yoke has been broken off.

probably also be seen as a development from the A-frame, achieved this time by pushing the poles apart, rather than running them together. It would maximize the pulling power of the four horses for the four-horse teams of the big four-man chariots we see in the late eighth and seventh centuries B.C.[49] Although we have no direct evidence of Assyrian use of the actual two-pole chariot, the existence of such to her west in Cyprus and the Levant, and later, to her east, in Oxiana, would indicate that she knew it.

It has often been suggested that the travois was the ancestor of wheeled transport, particularly of the two-wheeler, and that the A-frame cart provides a "missing link". Piggott[50] gives references and discusses some of the pros and cons. We have, however, no evidence of the A-frame cart before the later second millennium B.C., whereas two-wheelers with a central pole are known from the early third millennium in Mesopotamia. The A-frame cart occurs in the vicinity of mountainous territory, where we also have evidence of the travois[51] in the second millennium, and it easily could derive from the latter. But these travois are pulled by *paired draught under a yoke*. The basic travois or slide car consists of two poles dragged on either side of a *single* animal, held up and united by a support over the back and kept forward by a line across the chest, which also takes the pull. It is already essentially shaft-and-breaststrap harness. It is hard to see, if the travois was the ancestor of wheeled vehicles, why this far more efficient and economical system of draught did not obtain from the beginning. What would be the reason for using a yoke and paired draught with a travois where (given the shape of the platform) the widely spaced animals would make the equipage very awkward? Such use implies the prior existence (and already powerful tradition) of the yoke system – a system required by the single pole. This method must go back to oxen yoked on either side of a plough pole – a means of traction thereafter applied indiscriminately for millennia to a variety of vehicles and draught animals.

Date and Origin of the Model

The features discussed above – the rigid, raised handgrip loops and the traction system, in combination with the rectangular floor plan –

---

[49] See *supra*, n. 22.
[50] Piggott 1968, 292.
[51] Karakhanian and Safian 1970, pls. 52, 96, 148.

point on present evidence to the chariot being of first- rather than second-millennium B.C. date. A more precise attribution of the model in time and space is rendered difficult by several factors. Firstly, there is no single piece of more or less firmly dated and provenanced evidence (remains of actual chariots, models, or two-dimensional representations) that compares with it in all details. Secondly, several of the features displayed by the model are found over a wide area, ranging from Persia to Cyprus and Egypt, and over a period covering several centuries. This is in itself not surprising, as there was obviously much interchange of ideas, stimulated by war or trade.

Despite this, it is nonetheless possible to date the model within a broad span of years – eighth to fourth centuries B.C. – and to locate it in the Levant, as its history and workmanship indicate. Considering its particularly close parallels with Achaemenid documents, we might even suggest a date of manufacture during Persian domination.[52]

B. *The Figures*

Dominique Collon

It should first be emphasized that although the figures are separate from the chariot, yet they form an integral part of the group. I believe the two parts were made at the same time and would favour a date in the fourteenth to thirteenth centuries B.C., as suggested by Amiet. The patina and similar state of preservation of the two parts would support this view. There is a possibility, however, that the chariot was made at a later date (the view held by the writers of the first part of this article). In that case it must have replaced an earlier chariot, since one of the figures seems to have been designed specifically as a charioteer and the figures cannot, therefore, have been freestanding. The chariot group may have formed part of a standard and would, in that case, have been set on a small platform at the top of a pole and have been fixed in position by means of the tenon beneath the stand which supports the figures (pl. 38a–b).

This stand measures 4.5 × 1.9 cm. and is 0.35 cm. thick. Two of the angles on one of the long sides have been rounded off so that

---

[52] P. Amiet mentioned a fourteenth-century date (Amiet 1968, 304). Is it completely impossible that the "smiting god" figures continued into the first millennium B.C.? See the piece in the Louvre (no. AO 3932) attributed by several scholars to the Persian period; cf. Dr Collon's paper, n. 54, no. 32.

it fits into the chariot. Beneath this stand, and set back from the centre, is a tenon which is 2 cm. long in its present state of preservation. A quarter of the way down it is pierced by a small lateral perforation and where the tenon is broken there was probably another similar perforation. If the tenon was originally fitted into the end of a pole, then it must have been fixed in position by means of small pegs or nails driven through these perforations. The length of the tenon and the possible existence of the lower perforation are arguments in favour of this use of the chariot group. A pin through the upper perforation would have fixed the figures securely in position in the chariot. The tenon fits exactly into the hole cut for it in the bottom of the chariot (tenon = 1.08×0.74 cm. and chariot slot = 1.1×0.75 cm.).

There are two figures fixed to the stand and most likely cast in one piece with it, probably by the *cire perdue* process. The quiver-strap of the smaller figure was applied to the basic wax model according to the method described by Henri Seyrig in connection with another group of Syrian figures which, unlike our figure, were cast in copper.[53] This is interesting since the same technique seems to have been adopted for the manufacture of the wirelike band which runs up the sides and along the top of the box of the chariot and forms the hand-holds. This again would be an argument in favour of the contemporaneous manufacture of the two parts of the group.

Both figures appear to be male and the larger of the two stands with the smaller on his right. He is 12.8 cm. high (excluding the base-plate) and stands with his right hand raised in the "smiting" gesture.[54] His right forearm is fixed to the back of the other figure's head, thus giving the group additional solidity. His right fist is clenched – presumably round some weapon which has now disappeared and which must have been held horizontally. His left arm is bent and his fist clenched so that he must have held a weapon vertically before him.

This larger figure wears the Egyptian White Crown with *maat* feathers, one of which is slightly broken, surmounted by a disc and with ram's horns extending horizontally on either side. A small perforation immediately above each horn may have served for fixing

---

[53] Seyrig 1953, esp. 30ff.
[54] Collon 1972, esp. 130.

the *uraei* which are normally associated with this type of headdress. The twisting horns and feathers are indicated by incisions only on the front of the figure. There is no trace of any form of decoration on the front of the White Crown. An incised line round the base of the headdress is indicated on the back of the figure, however, and below it hang double horizontally hatched, fringed bands extending half way down the back.

The features are clearly indicated and well-modelled with the line of the eyebrows running into the nose (see fig. 2 where the same convention is used). Both the ears are double-pierced. The figure is clean-shaven.

The upper part of the body is naked. The figure has a plain belt low round his waist and below this he wears a closely fitting, ankle-length garment, the hem of which is indicated by a single line. The separations of the feet and toes are also indicated by incised lines.

The second figure, which measures only 10.5 cm. in height (excluding the base-plate), is bent slightly forwards, almost certainly intentionally, and holds both arms out at an angle. His right arm is broken just above elbow level but his left arm is complete and ends in a fist which obviously held something – probably the reins in view of the position of the figure and the fact that he is riding in a chariot. These reins would have been made of bronze wire, of which a fragment survives in the perforation of his left fist.

This "charioteer" wears a strange variant of the Egyptian White Crown which is crested in profile and has a ridge down the front decorated with transverse incised lines. Two horns are applied to the lower part of the headdress and arch over like giant eyebrows. There is no line to indicate the lower edge of the headdress at the back (see fig. 2).

The features are clearly indicated according to the same conventions as those of the larger figure (see fig. 2). Both ears, here again, are double-pierced, but since the larger figure's right arm is attached behind the charioteer's left ear, the holes through this are blind. The figure is clean-shaven.

The charioteer is bare-chested and has a quiver slung from his right shoulder. The quiver strap was probably, as mentioned above, applied separately to the basic wax model. The quiver is simply a bar of metal with rounded ends; no details are shown. Round his waist he wears a belt which is knotted in front and which has two ends, decorated with horizontally incised lines and ending in fringes, hanging down in front. The ankle length garment and feet of this figure resemble those of the larger figure exactly.

The figures are well preserved and the metal is in good condition but certain details would be clearer if the piece were cleaned, since dried earth still adheres. There are filing marks on the sides of the tenon and just in front of the feet of the two figures. This may well have been done when the piece was discovered in the last century.

We can be virtually certain of the Levantine origins of the piece since it was obtained from Péretié, who was chancellor in the French consulate in Beirut throughout the time that de Clercq was building up his collection. He obtained many objects for de Clercq.

The identification of the figures poses a problem. They have been variously called a king and Amon (?) (de Ridder), a king and god (Müller, who misinterpreted the photograph he had of the group and thought that the "god" was resting his arm in the "king's" shoulder), an attendant god and Reshef (?) (Barnett 1964) and a charioteer and Anath in her capacity as goddess of chariotry (Barnett 1969). Amiet suggests a deity such as Baal with a minor deity in attendance. The present writer would prefer not to hazard a precise identification but believes, in the absence of any female characteristics, that both figures are male, while their horned headdresses show them to be divine, though one is noticeably the more important. The deities represented are almost certainly Levantine, since the piece was probably made in the country in which it was found. Gods in headdresses resembling that of the larger figure occur frequently on Syrian seals of the eighteenth century B.C. or later.[55] Furthermore, the larger figure stands in the "smiting" posture – a posture which originated in Egypt but was adopted in Anatolia and the Levant at the beginning of the second millennium B.C. as part of the iconography of the Weather-god.[56] The smaller figure is presumably the Weather-god's divine charioteer. This is an unusual iconographical representation, although we do have a representation of the storm-god driving a team of bulls across deified mountains from *Imamkulu*

---

[55] E.g. Collon 1975, nos. 137. 138. 141. 143.

[56] Op. cit. in n. 54, esp. 130–131. The following work should also be consulted since it gives an exhaustive list of bronzes of the same type, but was unfortunately overlooked: Roeder 1956, 35–41, paragraphs 60 and 61, esp.; but see also the following paragraphs up to 45.

and the same scene is shown on the Malatya reliefs.[57] Since our group is Syrian and not Anatolian, however, we cannot necessarily make the deduction that it was a team of bulls which our bronze charioteer was driving.

There is the final problem of date. There are no exact parallels among the bronze figures in a smiting posture discussed by the present writer (see n. 54). A figure from Byblos[58] wears a similar headdress but is so badly preserved that the features cannot be distinguished. Furthermore, the Byblos figure cannot be closely dated but it does belong to the second millennium B.C. The facial features, with the line of the eyebrows running into the nose, are paralleled by an undated example from the Borowski collection.[59] (It should perhaps be noted that, unlike so many other bronzes of this type, our chariot figures were never intended for inlay or gold plating.) All the bronze figures wear short kilts except for an undated bronze of probable Egyptian origin.[60] Although none of the Ras Shamra examples provides a close parallel for our figure, nevertheless several of the bronzes from this site are of the same high quality of execution and we have here a context into which our bronze would fit without any difficulty. The Ras Shamra bronzes can be dated, for the most part, to the fourteenth to thirteenth centuries B.C.[61] The distinctive double-pierced ears of both figures in our group appear again on a series of frit masks of which one example, from Tell el Rimah, has been dated to the thirteenth century; the others are probably contemporary.[62]

None of the points listed above can be called more than an indication of a possible date. In the present writer's view, one of the main arguments in favour of a date in the fourteenth to thirteenth centuries B.C. is the fact that the group then fits into a convincing technical and cultural context.

---

[57] Contenau 1947, Akurgal 1962, pl. 105.
[58] Collon 1972, fig. 2, no. 11.
[59] Collon 1972, fig. 8, no. 2.
[60] Collon 1972, fig. 7, no. 6.
[61] Collon 1972, fig. 1, nos. 5 and 9 from Ras Shamra and no. 10 from Miner el Beida.
[62] Parrot 1969, 409–418.

14. A GROUP OF TERRACOTTA CHARIOT MODELS – CYPRIOTE OR PHOENICIAN?*

J. H. CROUWEL

This paper discusses four terracotta models of chariots in different public collections.** They have many features in common, such as an – unusual – four-man crew, and are also very close in fabric and technique of manufacture. In fact, their similarities are so great as to suggest the same area of manufacture – either in Phoenicia, where at least one of them is reported to have been found, or in Cyprus, the source of so many terracotta chariot models. This group of models in turn raises the question of the place of manufacture of a whole range of other, related terracottas, including chariots, carts, riders on horseback and men on foot – all made at some time during the first half of the first millennium B.C.

Catalogue

1. (pls. 39a–b). Oxford, Ashmolean Museum 1974.349; formerly colls. L. de Clercq and J. Bomford.
L. (base) ca 0.085; W. (base) 0.06–0.09; Ht. ca 0.15.
Complete, except for most of right-hand man in front, one yoke end and one shield boss. Surface weathered and incrustated in places.

* In: Frieda Vandenabeele and Robert Laffineur (eds.), *Cypriote Terracottas*. Proceedings of the First International Conference of Cypriote Studies, Brussels-Liège-Amsterdam, 29 May–1 June, 1989. Organized by the "Groupe de Contact interuniversitaire d'études chypriotes"/Interuniversitaire contactgroep voor Cyprische Studies, F.N.R.S./N.F.W.O. (Belgium). Brussels/Liège, 1991, 115–129.
** I am most grateful to all those who have helped with information and assistance of various kinds: Miss A. Aghion, Dr. M. Amandry, Dr. H. W. Catling, Miss A. Caubet, Dr. J. R. Curtis, Mrs. S. Deluy, Mr. H. E. Frenkel, Dr. A. Hermary, Dr. V. Karageorghis, Mrs. M. A. Littauer, Dr. R. A. Lunsingh Scheurleer, Dr. Th. Monloup, Dr. P. R. S. Moorey, Miss A. Tamvaki, Dr. V. Tatton-Brown, Prof. F. Vandenabeele and Dr. H. Whitehouse. The photographs appear by courtesy of Dr. Monloup, the Ashmolean Museum (Oxford), the Bibliothèque Nationale (Paris), the British Museum (London) and the Musée du Louvre (Paris).

Rather coarse, reddish yellow clay (5 YR 6).[1] Roughly oval hole near rear of base. Heads of men made in same mould, the rest hand-modelled with rather roughly finished surfaces. Traces of black, red and yellow paint.

Bibliography (select): de Ridder 1909, no. 187; Heuzey 1923, no. 187; Bossert 1951, fig. 136; Catling 1971, no. 99; Brown and Catling 1980, 129 no. 92; Monloup 1984, 113, 162, 174f.; Crouwel 1987, 104 n. 24.

Note: de Ridder 1909, 92, in a discussion of the 'Syrian' terra-cottas in the de Clercq collection (nos. 187–195) which mostly come from M. Péretié (see below, nos. 2–3), supposed that all are from a necropolis at Antaradus (modern Tartous) in northern Phoenicia, except for no. 188 and perhaps no. 187 (our chariot model).

2. (pl. 40a–c). Paris, Louvre AO 25985 (formerly S 9; acquired from M. Péretié, chancellor in the French consulate in Beirut c. 1850). According to the memory of Guillaume-Rey (see Heuzey 1923, no. 187), from a necropolis at Marathus (modern Amrit) in north-ern Phoenicia.

L. (base) 1.11; Ht. 0.18; Diam. wheels 0.052.

Incomplete. Missing are (wooden) axles and (terracotta) wheels for base, most of one chariot wheel and adjacent chariot body, head of one horse, almost all of the two men in front and most of head of right-hand man in rear. Surface chipped in places.

Red clay (2.5 YR 4/6), light brown at surface (7.5 YR 6/4). Technique as no. 1, with men's heads made in same mould.

Bibliography (select): de Longperier 1871, pl. XX:2; Heuzey 1883, 4 with pl. 5, middle; Heuzey 1923, no. 187; Perrot and Chipiez 1885, 202 with fig. 145; Huish 1900, 45 with pl. VII; de Ridder 1909, no. 187; Studniczka 1907, 169–171 with fig. 17; Ohnefalsch-Richter 1915, 60 with figs. 1–2; Littauer 1976a, 221 with fig. 20; Littaucr and Crouwel 1979a, 102 with fig. 60; Monloup 1984, 113, 162, 164, 174f.; Cassimatis 1986, 181f. with pl. XXXVIII:2–3; Crouwel 1987, 104 n. 24 with pl. XXXVIII:2a–b.

3. (pls. 41a–b). Paris, Bibliothèque Nationale D 3734 (formerly 5912; acquired in 1855 from M. Péretié, through a Parisian auc-tioneer, M. Bonnefonds de Lavialle).

---

[1] *Munsell Soil Color Charts* (Baltimore 1973).

L. (base) 0.112; W. (base) 0.095; Ht. 0.146.
More or less complete, except for arms of men in front. Surface
chipped and incrustated in places.
No information on clay (model not personally examined). Technique
as nos. 1–2, with heads of men made in same mould.
   Bibliography: de Ridder 1909, no. 187; Poulsen 1912, 62f. with figs.
60–61; Ohnefalsch-Richter 1915, 60f.; Heuzey 1923, no. 187; Monloup
1984, 113, 162; Crouwel 1987, 104 n. 24.

   4. (pl. 42a–b). Amsterdam, Allard Pierson Museum 1364 (acquired
in 1934); formerly colls. Pozzi (Paris) and C. W. Lunsingh Scheurleer
(The Hague). From near the modern village of Dadja, Knidos penin-
sula, south-western Turkey (information A. Hermary).
Ht. 0.163; W. (ex.) ca 0.085; Diam. wheel ca 0.065.
   Fragmentary. Preserved are part of hindquarters of one horse, most
of one wheel and all four men, except for right arm of right-hand
man in front.
Rather coarse, red clay (2.5 YR 4/6), light brown at surface (7.5
YR 6/4). Technique as nos. 1–3, with men's heads made in same
mould. Small round firing hole in plank-like back.
   Bibliography: Collection S. Pozzi (deuxième partie). Art antique, cat. vente
25–27 juin 1919, galerie Georges Petit (Paris), no. 266; *Algemeene Gids
Allard Pierson Museum* (1937) no. 186; Lubsen-Admiral and Crouwel
1989, no. 177; Hermary 1990.

Discussion

Chariot body

The models represent actual chariots large and strong enough to
accommodate a four-man crew – two standing abreast. Unfortunately,
the coroplasts provide little information on the shape and construction of the floor and siding. However, the presence of two draught
poles points to a rectangular floor frame, with four timbers meeting
at right angles, rather than one shaped like a capital D, with one
or two heat-bent timbers forming the front and sides. Both types of
floor were used in the Near East and Cyprus in the first millennium
B.C. In the Near East chariots with rectangular floor plans can first
be recognized on Assyrian palace reliefs of the 8th and 7th century

B.C., where they are associated with a single, central draught pole.[2] In Cyprus the rectangular floor plan is attested on an actual, two-poled chariot of the late 8th century B.C. found buried at Salamis, and then on terracotta models of the 7th–6th centuries and later.[3] From both areas there is some evidence to indicate that the flooring of the two-poled chariots consisted of interwoven thongs.[4]

On our models the chariot siding is only very sketchily rendered, with screens at front and sides rising to approximately hip height.

One of the models (no. 2) illustrates an upright loop at the centre rear of the body (pl. 40c). This loop is a feature of many Cypriote terracotta chariot models, often in combination with a back-to-front partition through the middle of the body. An actual bronze loop, 0.50 m. in height, was found near the rear edge of the actual chariot from Salamis just mentioned. Here it was also associated with a back-to-front partition, which would have prevented crew members from jostling each other in rough going or on turns while giving them an extra wall against which to brace and to maintain balance.[5] The rigid loop itself would have served as a handgrip in mounting or to carry a shield, as is clearly illustrated on our model no. 2. There the shield is round and convex, carrying a lion-headed central boss (pls. 40b and 40c). It may be noted that the remains of a round shield, 0.56 m. in diameter, were found near the rear of another actual chariot from Salamis; it may have hung on such a loop – although no traces of the latter were found – effecting a partial closure at both sides of it.[6] On our model no. 2 some form of closure may be indicated by the pair of horizontal lines running on either side of the loop;[7] alternatively, these lines may belong with the two men standing in the rear part of the chariot – perhaps as belts.

The presence of a loop, and quite possibly of the central partition as well, may be assumed for many chariots in two-dimensional

[2] Littauer and Crouwel 1979a, 103f.

[3] Karageorghis 1973, esp. 68–74 with figs. 10–12, 13: 1–2 and VII (tomb 79, chariot *Beta*); Crouwel 1987, 102 (chariot A 7).

[4] Crouwel 1987, 104 with n. 22.

[5] Karageorghis 1873, 29. 73 no. 220/2 with figs. VII, 10 and pl. CCLXXVI; Crouwel 1987, 102. 104.

[6] Karageorghis 1967a, 33. 36. 46 no. 25 (tomb 3, chariot B); Crouwel 1987, 104f. (chariot A 3).

[7] The possibility of a double door was considered by Studniczka 1907, 171. Rear doors were present on royal chariots of Ashurbanipal and on later Achaemenid ones, see Littauer and Crouwel 1987, 104. 146.

art where a shield, sometimes also with a lion-headed boss, is seen in profile in this position. Representations include Assyrian reliefs of the 9th century, Neo-Hittite reliefs and Nimrud ivories as well as a vase painting and an incomplete terracotta model from Cyprus.[8] The round shield with convex profile and a boss in the form of a lion head, its tongue hanging from a gaping mouth, is clearly of Near Eastern origin. In addition to being shown in conjunction with chariots, such a shield is seen, for instance, carried by Assyrian foot soldiers on reliefs of Ashurnasirpal II (883–859 B.C.) and among the loot from an Urartian temple carried off by Assyrian soldiers of Sargon II (721–705 B.C.).[9]

Axle and wheels

The position of the wheels on the models seems to indicate an axle placed at the rear of the floor or a little ahead of it. The original chariots may well have had a full rear axle, like those found at Salamis and the ones illustrated on Assyrian reliefs of the 9th–7th century B.C.[10]

Information on the wheels is supplied by models nos. 1 and 4. Both have eight-spoked wheels, on no. 4 rendered in relief and on no. 1 in paint (the spokes of nos. 2 and 3 must originally have been painted too). Eight-spoked wheels are common in the first part of the first millennium B.C. On Assyrian reliefs they appear in the 9th century, to become standard in the 8th and 7th. In Cyprus eight-spoked wheels are documented by one of the actual chariots from Salamis and by terracotta models and two-dimensional representations.[11]

Our model no. 4 shows groups of incised lines across the spokes some distance away from the raised nave (pl. 42b). These lines may indicate a (rawhide) spoke binding, attested on Egyptian and some Near Eastern chariot wheels of the second half of the second millennium B.C. but apparently no. later.[12] Alternatively, the lines may suggest the nave was metal-sheathed, with short metal sockets through which the spokes passed before being mortised into the wooden core of the nave. Such a construction is documented on some Iron-Age (late Hallstatt) wheels in Europe and has been suggested for Assyrian

---

[8] Crouwel 1987, 105 with n. 33.
[9] For such shields, see Madhloom 1970, 56, type 1c (iv).
[10] Crouwel 1987, 105.
[11] Karageorghis 1967a, 49f. (tomb 3, chariot B); Crouwel 1987, 105f. (chariot A 3).
[12] Littauer and Crouwel 1985, 76. 78.

and other Near Eastern wheels of the 9th century B.C. and later.[13]

On the same chariot model no. 4 the rim of the eight-spoked wheel is shown as composed of two concentric elements, the outer one wider than the inner. This may indicate a tongue-in-groove construction, in which a tongue on the inner surface of the outer wooden element lay in a groove in the perimeter of the inner one. Such a construction has indeed been suggested for an actual eight-spoked chariot wheel (c. 0.85 m. in diameter) from Salamis and also for the six- and eight-spoked wheels depicted on 9th–7th century Assyrian reliefs.[14] Our chariot model no. 4 preserves several groups of incised lines running across the outer element of the wheel rim. These lines recall the metal, U-shaped clamps, with a nail joining both terminals, found on either side of the actual eight-spoked wheel from Salamis where they helped to hold the two concentric rim elements together. For comparison, Assyrian reliefs of the 8th and 7th centuries show two pairs of large clamps joining both parts of the rim of eight-spoked wheels, thereby confirming the tongue-in-groove construction.[15]

Traction system

Traction is provided by four horses under a yoke, connected with the vehicle by means of two draught poles. The latter are explicitly indicated only on model no. 2 (pl. 40a). Here, as on other, Cypriote chariot terracottas, the poles are attached to the vehicle body in unlikely places and running out at unlikely angles, due to ignorance or convenience of the modellers.

Two-poled quadrigae are first attested on the late 8th century chariot buried at Salamis. They also occur on many Cypriote terracotta models, ranging from the 7th–6th century to Hellenistic times, and on some 5th century stone models from the island.[16] Firm evidence from the Near East is lacking until the Achaemenid period, when their use is suggested by two gold chariot models belonging to the Oxus Treasure.[17]

---

[13] Littauer and Crouwel 1979a, 107 with n. 35.

[14] Kossack 1971, 155–159 with fig. 34; Karageorghis 1973a, 68 n. 1; Littauer and Crouwel 1979a, 107f.; Crouwel 1987, 106.

[15] Crouwel 1987, 106.

[16] Crouwel 1987, 102. 104. 106f.

[17] Dalton 1964, fig. 20 and pl. IV (with four-horse yoke), fig. 21 and "additional plate" (with two two-horse yokes).

Harnessing and control

The horses are harnessed under a single yoke. The combination of
a four-horse yoke with two poles is documented in Cyprus by some
of the 7th–6th century terracottas and on stone models of the 5th
century. It is probably to be assumed for the actual two-poled chariot of the late 8th century from Salamis.[18] In the Near East the
arrangement with a four-horse yoke and two poles is only suggested
by one of the Achaemenid gold models of the Oxus Treasure. Assyrian
reliefs of the later 8th and 7th century sometimes illustrate unharnessed chariots with a single four-horse yoke but always with one
rather than two poles.[19]

On our chariot models the four-horse yoke is shown as a straight
beam with upturned ends. While the latter are a realistic feature,
present on the Salamis chariots and those illustrated in Cyprus as
well as in the Near East, the actual yoke must have been shaped
into bays to lie across the neck of each animal. This so-called fitted
yoke is most clearly indicated on Assyrian reliefs of the later 8th and
7th century B.C.[20]

The yoke is kept in place by a neck strap (not explicitly rendered
on the models), passing in front of the neck of each horse, and by
a girth going around the belly behind the forelegs. On model no. 2
a loop marks the place where the straps were tied to the yoke, as
was the standard arrangement of the time (pl. 40b).

The horses wear a bib-shaped gorget or breastplate, with a fringe
of tassels along the bottom edge. The gorget may have been of
boiled leather or of metal. Actual bronze specimens of similar form,
both plain and decorated, have been found with the 8th–7th century vehicle burials at Salamis and also at Hasanlu in north-west
Iran, the latter in a context of ca 800 B.C. Such breastplates are
seen worn by chariot horses on some of the 7th–6th century Cypriote
terracottas, by draught and riding horses on Assyrian reliefs of the
9th and 8th century but no later, and also on other Near Eastern
representations of the time.[21]

---

[18] Crouwel 1987, 107f. Other Cypriote terracottas feature a combination of two
poles with two two-horse yokes.
[19] Littauer and Crouwel 1979a, 110. 114f.
[20] Littauer and Crouwel 1979a, 114; Crouwel 1987, 108.
[21] Littauer and Crouwel 1979a, 129; Winter 1980, esp. 3–6; Crouwel 1987, 112f.;
Crouwel and Tatton-Brown 1988, 82.

The horses are shown with a decorative tassel, hanging over the gorget. Such tassels are a common feature of chariot – and ridden – horses in Cyprus and the Near East. On more explicit representations, such as the Assyrian reliefs, they hang from a separate neck strap.[22]

The animals must have been controlled by bridles, composed of a headstall and reins. All models show cheekstraps, running to the corners of the horses' mouths and thereby suggesting the presence of bits which were commonly used at the time.[23] Model no. 1 illustrates a flat browband, while nos. 2 and 3 instead show a so-called brow cushion. This padded or quilted object is well-known from Cyprus and the Near East and must have been attached to the browband.[24] In the case of our models the cushion is probably meant to be lying *beneath* a metal frontlet, thereby cushioning the horse's parietal bones against the metal.

The frontlets, seen on models nos. 1–3, appear to be hinged to a forward-arching poll crest. Bronze examples of these have been found at Salamis, some of them in *situ* on buried harness animals. They are hinged and channeled, presumably to take a back-to-front horse hair fan. In Cyprus the presence of such a crest, with a hinged frontlet, is suggested by several terracotta chariot models of the 7th–6th century B.C. Here, as on our models (best preserved on no. 1), decoration is sometimes marked by incision, recalling the highly decorated bronze examples from Salamis.[25] In the Near East arched poll crests and frontlets are illustrated on Assyrian reliefs of the later 8th and 7th century, though not hinged together. Actual frontlets, again hingeless, of bronze or other materials, are also known from different parts of the Near East, dating to the 9th–7th centuries.[26]

In addition to frontlets and poll crests, the horses of our models wear blinkers, of which only some now remain. Blinkers are shown on many terracotta models and other figured documents from Cyprus, dating to the 7th–6th and 5th century B.C. but no later. As in the

---

[22] Littauer and Crouwel 1979a, 127; Crouwel 1979a, 112; Crouwel and Tatton-Brown 1988, 81. See also the terracotta model of a ridden horse (our pl. 51).

[23] For – metal – bits, see Littauer and Crouwel 1979a, 118–123; Crouwel 1987, 109; Crouwel and Tatton-Brown 1988, 77f.

[24] Littauer and Crouwel 1979a, 127; Crouwel 1987, 109.

[25] Karageorghis 1967a, esp. pl. CXXVII: nos. 116f.; Karageorghis 1973a, esp. pls. CCLXVIII–CCLXX: nos. 320/13–19. 192. 165. 178f.; Crouwel 1987, 111f.

[26] Littauer and Crouwel 1979a, 125f.; Crouwel 1987, 111f.; Crouwel and Tatton-Brown 1988, 79.

case of frontlets, actual examples, mainly of bronze, have been found at Salamis, again sometimes *in situ* on buried harness animals. Bronze and ivory blinkers are known from Assyria and other parts of the Near East, apparently dating no later than the 8th–7th century B.C. They are also shown in contemporary figured documents, though never explicitly on Assyrian reliefs.[27]

Chariot crew

Our chariot models carry a crew of four – two standing abreast. Of the two men in front the one to the right must be the driver, his (never completely preserved) arms bent forward as if holding reins. The man beside him has his right arm folded across the chest, his left hand holding on to the chariot siding. On model no. 1 this passenger is turned somewhat to the outside.

The two men in the rear are shown with a shield very high on their backs and surely suspended from a (not shown) baldric. The shields are round and have a central conical boss, the markings sometimes visible on the inside possibly reflecting a wickerwork construction. Round shields with such a boss are well-known from Cyprus and the Near East in the first half of the first millennium B.C.[28]

In addition to our models, four-man chariot complements are documented only by Assyrian reliefs of the reigns of Sargon II (721–705 B.C.) and Ashurbanipal (668–630 B.C.), and by one of the North Syrian ivory plaques found at Nimrud, presumably dating to the 8th century B.C.[29] Again the men must be standing two abreast, with the driver to the right in front. On earlier Assyrian reliefs – of the 9th to mid-8th century – and on other Near Eastern chariot representations of the time, the crews consist of no more than three men, the third standing behind the others. The same is true for the many

---

[27] Littauer and Crouwel 1979a, 125f.; Crouwel 1987, 111f.; Crouwel and Tatton-Brown 1988, 79.

[28] See Madhloom 1970, 55f. (for wickerwork shields, see 55, 57: types 1b and 3);Törnqvist 1970, esp. 64–66.

[29] Littauer and Crouwel 1979a, 104f., 130 n. 109; Crouwel 1987, 104. For Sargon II's four-man chariots, see Botta and Flandin 1849–60, esp. pl. 58 (= Madhloom 1970, pl. IV: 1; Albenda 1986, pl. 116). For those of Ashurbanipal, see ills. in Barnett 1975 and 1976. For the Nimrud ivory, see esp. Mallowan and Hermann 1974, pl. III; Littauer and Crouwel 1973), 27–33; Winter 1976, 52 with n. 108 (dated to time of Tiglath-Pileser III, 745–727 B.C.).

terracotta chariot models and other documents from Cyprus, where four-man complements are not in evidence.[30]

The men riding in our chariot models have strikingly similar heads, their faces made in a mould and their backs only roughly flattened. The facial features include rather almond-shaped eyes, a prominent nose and a mouth with straight, fleshy lips and folds on either end. While their lips are clean-shaven, the men wear a long, vertically grooved beard. A fringe of hair, grooved like the beard, is visible below a conical cap. The latter has long ear-flaps from which two thongs (see below) depend to the men's shoulders. The two chariot riders in front, who are rendered in more detail than those in the rear, wear the same type of garment, apparently a long mantle enveloping both arms down to the wrists.

The men belong to a well-known class of terracottas, recently described as "personnages barbus de type assyrien".[31] Under this heading a variety of terracotta figurines can be grouped, sharing the same technique of manufacture which involves a combination of hand-modelling and a mould-made face which was subsequently retouched by hand. These male figurines have very similar facial features and a long beard, usually with vertical grooves. They often wear a conical cap and a mantle with a fringed border over a tunic. Their right arms may be held across their chests and wrapped in the mantle, exactly as seen on our chariot models.

The representatives of this class of terracottas are widely distributed over the eastern Mediterranean, as the following brief survey shows.

Most are from Cyprus, particularly Salamis (fig. 1; pls. 43, 44a–b, 45 and 46, 47).[32] Few of the examples found in the island are

---

[30] Crouwel 1987, 104. Monloup 1984, 162 n. 64 is incorrect in assuming that one of the several terracotta chariot models from the sanctuary at Ayia Irini illustrates a four-man crew (Ayia Irini no. 1781 + 798, personally examined); ills. in Gjerstad 1935, pl. CCXXXV: 3; Spiteris 1970, 134; Crouwel 1987, pl. XXXVII: 3.

[31] Monloup 1984, 173–179; cf. Karageorghis 1978, 186.

[32] Monloup 1984, nos. 644–649 (Salamis; Ht. 0.083 and 0.079) and p. 174 with nn. 16–17. 20–22 (refs.). Add : an unprovenanced chariot model in Athens, its worn three-man crew possibly of this class (Karageorghis 1967, 49 with fig. 8; Crouwel 1987, pl. XXXIX: 4); some unprovenanced, incomplete figurines in Paris (Louvre AM 163 and AM 3510–0.08 and 0.092 in height, our pls. 46, 47); another, reportedly from Larnaka and now in Oxford (Ashm 1875.6B; given by G. J. Chester); and a complete figurine, unprovenanced, also in Oxford (Brown and Catling 1980, 127 no. 93, very similar to Cesnola 1984, pl. IX: 70 from Kouklia-Palaipaphos). Somewhat related to our class are the crew of a four-man chariot model from Frangissa near Famagusta (Ohnefalsch-Richter 1915, 54ff. with pl. IX; Bossert 1951,

Fig. 1.

complete, an exception being the man leading a two-horse chariot team from Ovgoros near Famagusta (pl. 45).[33] It may be noted that the driver and archer inside the chariot have rather different, bearded faces with hollow eye sockets, strongly resembling an archer from Salamis and a head said to be from near Beirut (pl. 48a–b).[34]

There are fragmentary figurines like ours from the sanctuary of Athena at Lindos in Rhodes (fig. 2).[35] Others may derive from sanctuaries near the village of Dadja on the Knidos peninsula, the supposed source of our chariot model no. 4 (fig. 3).[36] A single head was found at the Heraeum in Samos,[37] while another incomplete example comes from Naucratis in the Nile Delta (pl. 49).[38]

---

fig. 139) and an unprovenanced, beardless warrior on foot Karageorghis 1973, 606 with fig. 17.

[33] Spiteris 1970, ill. p. 93; Littauer and Crouwel 1977b, 7f. with figs. 3–6; Monloup 1984, 182 no. 662, 164 with fig. 11; Crouwel 1987, pl. XXXVIII: 3.

[34] Monloup 1984, 181f. no. 662 (from a Cypro-Archaic context); Walters 1903, no. A 458 = Culican 1975–76, 51 with fig. 5: F (Ht. ca. 0.08; our pl. 48a–b).

[35] Blinkenberg 1931, 485–487, esp. nos. 2009f. (Ht. 0.102 and 0.063; our fig. 2), cf. nos. 1994–1999 (with and without, separately modelled, beards); Monloup 1984, 174.

[36] Blinkenberg 1931, 484–486 with fig. 55 (our fig. 3); Mendel 1908; nos. 3488–3489, cf. nos. 3490–3493; Hermary 1990 cf. SCE IV: 2, 332.

[37] Samos VII, 23. 25. 75f. no. T 1195 with pl. 35 (Ht. 0.064); Monloup 1984, 174.

[38] Gutsch 1898–99, 95 no. 290 with pl. XII (Oxford, Ashm G.70; Ht. 0.083). Another fragmentary example, bought in Cairo in 1931–34, is without provenance (Amsterdam, Allard Pierson Museum 6212; Ht. 0.127; our pl. 50).

Fig. 2.

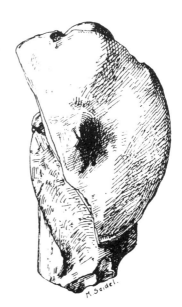

Fig. 3.

With regard to the Levant, a rider on horseback of this class has
been reported from Tyre (pl. 51).[39] Interestingly, the accoutrements
of his mount are the same as those of the draught teams of our
chariot models: breastplate, frontlet (though without crest), blinkers
and a tassel in front suspended from a neck strap with incised chevron
pattern. In addition, there are some incomplete terracottas of the
class from Helalieh near Sidon (pls. 52, 53).[40] Related figures can
be seen reclining on two cart models, one said to be from Tyre, the
other, like our chariot model no. 2, reportedly from a necropolis at
Marathus (Amrit) (see Appendix, nos. c, a; pls. 56a–b and 57a–b).
The latter terracottas in turn recall a head and torso, again from
Marathus (pl. XXXII, c–d), and two fragmentary figurines from
Salamis, reclining and seated respectively.[41]

It is unfortunate that most of these terracottas have been incompletely preserved, thus impeding the reconstruction of their original
appearance – whether standing in a chariot or on the ground, seated
on a horse or on a chair, or reclining on a cart or couch. Several
of them may well have been chariot occupants, particularly three
incompletely preserved men – one from Dadja, the others from
Helalieh – carrying a round shield on their back, as seen on our
chariot models (fig. 3; pls. 52, 53). There is also a charioteer, belonging to a fragmentary chariot model without provenance (pl. 55).[42]
The model preserves the back-to-front partition wall (see s.v. Body),
but no remains of other crew members.

This class of terracottas has been called "de type assyrien" because
of its eastern appearance. However, most of its characteristics have
excellent parallels in Cyprus. For instance, the rigid, hieratic attitude
of most of the men, with the right arm bent inside the enveloping
mantle, recurs in Cypriote coroplastics and stone sculpture. The mantle is again often shown with a fringed border and as worn over a
tunic.[43] The cap-like, conical headdress is also well attested in the
island. Its material must have been fabric or leather rather than

---

[39] London, BM 93092 (1884.10–24.3). Ht. ca 0.145; L. (base) 0.078; W. (base)
ca 0.03.

[40] Paris, Louvre AO 1134 and 1135. Ht. 0.055 and 0.058.

[41] de Longperier 1871, pl. XX: 3 = Heuzey 1923, no. 189 (Paris, Louvre AM
3738. Ht. 0.094; our pl. 54a–b); Monloup 1984, nos. 660f.

[42] Stoop 1975, 16f. with figs. 29–31; *Klassieke kunst uit particulier bezit* (exhibition
Rijksmuseum van Oudheden, Leiden 1975), no. 243.

[43] Monloup 1984, 174f.; cf. Myres 1914, nos. 2170–2174. For mantles in Cyprus,
see Törnqvist 1970, 7–9. For such stone sculptures, see o.a. di Cesnola 1885, esp. pl.
VVII: 393 (from Golgoi), and pls. VI. XXXIV. XLII. XLV–XLVIII. LI, LIV–LV.

metal, to judge from the long ear-flaps and the "tail" that is often – though not on our group of chariot models – seen falling back from the top. The cap could be tied under the chin by thongs depending from the ear-flaps. These thongs are often indicated and sometimes – though again not on our models – end in tassels.[44]

Chariot Use

Most of the elaborate horse gear – breastplates, frontlets and blinkers – associated with our chariot models is basically a protection against enemy missiles, while presumably also enjoying an ornamental purpose. The presence of shields too points to a potentially military role for the chariots and their crews, as do the conical caps with their long ear-flaps protecting the backs of their heads and cheeks.

The four-man chariots depicted on Assyrian reliefs of Sargon II and Ashurbanipal are often actually engaged in warfare. They function as firing platforms for an archer (including king Sargon himself), standing beside the driver. The two men in the rear hold up round shields to protect those in front. The chariot occupants have conical helmets of metal and, under Ashurbanipal, both crew and draught animals wear armour.[45] It may be noted that on other reliefs of Ashurbanipal four-man chariots appear in hunting scenes, the king stretching a bow and his attendants in the rear thrusting spears against lions. A lion hunt is also illustrated on the ivory carving from Nimrud mentioned above.[46]

An active, presumably military use of the four-man chariots represented by our chariot models is also implied by the two draught poles – a feature apparently shared only with Cypriote vehicles of the time. These poles would have given greater tractive efficiency to the horses than the single pole with four animals under yoke attested in Assyria. Besides, the lateral stress on turning would have been taken by two areas rather than one. Though a more rigid equipage, experiments have shown that two-poled chariots could take a turn by describing a sweep of no more than about ten meters.[47]

---

[44] Monloup 1984, 174f. For conical caps in Cyprus, see Törnqvist 1970, 42ff.; cf. Bossert 1951, fig. 133 (thongs tied under chin). The thongs may also have been used to fasten the ear-flaps when these were in a raised position, as is sometimes illustrated in Cypriote stone sculpture; see Törnqvist 1970, 45.

[45] Littauer and Crouwel 1979a, 130–132.

[46] Littauer and Crouwel 1973c, 27–33; Littauer and Crouwel 1979a, 131, 134.

[47] J. Spruytte 1978–79, 56f.; Crouwel 1987, 113.

In Cyprus a military role of two-poled chariots is strongly suggested by the 7th–6th century terracottas. As stated above, these illustrate an armed crew of no more than three-driver and archer in front and a shield bearer in the rear, the latter sometimes seen protecting the archer with his round shield.[48]

The lack of offensive weapons and the way in which the shields are carried by the two riders in the rear suggest that our chariots are depicted as if engaged in some peaceful activity. This is supported by the crew's distinctly non-military dress. Quite possibly, the models portray an important dignitary standing beside his charioteer and with his bodyguards at the back.

Function of the Chariot Models

One of our models (no. 2) is reported to come from a cemetery in northern Phoenicia; another (no. 4) may derive from a sanctuary on the Knidos peninsula. Yet other terracottas "de type assyrien" have been found in tombs or sanctuaries but also at settlement sites. This points to different possible functions, as the need arose.[49]

Yet another use, as a toy, may be suggested for chariot model no. 2 which was originally mounted on four wheels, in contrast to the others of our group which were immovable on similar, slab-like bases. There are other terracotta models that originally rolled on four wheels. They include a chariot from Ovgoros in Cyprus and a cart reportedly from Marathus (Amrit), both mentioned above, and another cart, presumably also from Phoenicia (Appendix, no. b; pl. 58a–b). Also mounted on four wheels are a three-man chariot model and a horseback rider, probably from Cyprus, and other fragmentary models from the settlement site at Salamis.[50]

Chronology and Place of Manufacture

Relatively few of the terracottas discussed above have known, let alone closely datable find contexts. The examples from the sanctu-

---

[48] Crouwel 1987, 113. The archer maybe replaced by a man brandishing a spear, though bowcase and quiver are still shown attached to the outside of the vehicle or placed inside, or the shield bearer may at the same time be wielding a spear.
[49] Monloup 1984, 18–22.
[50] *Supra* n. 32 (chariot model); Crouwel and Tatton-Brown 1988, pl. XXV: 3 (horseback rider); Monloup 1978, 169–176; Monloup 1984, 161–165.

aries in Rhodes and Samos, along with other dedications with Cypriote affinities, are assumed to date no later than about the middle of the 6th century B.C. The single fragment from Naucratis ranges within the time span between the later 7th century and the invasion by Cambyses in 525 B.C.[51] Some of the examples from Salamis – found in the settlement and in the Cellarka cemetery – have contexts varying from Cypro-Archaic 11 to Cypro-Classical 11, i.e. from ca 600–475 to 400–325 B.C.[52]

It has been claimed that the figures belonging with the terracotta chariot model from Ovgoros (pl. 45) are clearly in the so-called Proto-Cypriote style which may date to ca 650/640–590/580 B.C. (the later part of Cypro-Archaic I to the beginning of Cypro-Archaic II).[53] This may well be as close as we can get, pending new finds of this class of terracottas with good find contexts.

Other, general dating information may be yielded by the size of the crews and the accoutrements of the draught teams of our chariot models. We have seen that the four-man complement can be paralleled only in Near Eastern art of the 8th and 7th century, though it should be noted that our main source of information – the Assyrian palace reliefs – ends with the reign of Ashurbanipal (668–630 B.C.). The accoutrements of our chariot horses, and of the related ridden horse from Tyre (pl. 51), have close parallels among the actual metal finds from the Salamis tombs of the late 8th and 7th century. Figured documents illustrating such objects range from the 9th to the 7th century in the Near East, while in Cyprus they extend into the 6th century B.C.

With regard to the place of manufacture of this class of terracottas, we have already referred to its wide distribution in the eastern Mediterranean. The question is whether the terracottas derive from one or more production centres in a particular area or from different places, using the same or closely similar moulds for the human faces.

The majority of finds appear to come from Cyprus, including pieces from controlled excavations. At the same time, these terracottas

---

[51] See esp. Wriedt Sørensen 1978. For Samos, see Samos VII, 93–98 (the fragmentary figurine of our class, cited *supra* n. 37, comes from pre-Second World War excavations of the "Schuttschichten" east of the Rhoikos altar, Schmidt's area B 5a).

[52] Monloup 1984, 174; Karageorghis 1970, 181f., no. Q.16 with pl. XXVII (pyre Q), 184f. no. T.1, 4 with pl. XXXI (pyre T 1), cf. 85 no. Ch. 10 with pl. CXXIV (tomb 54).

[53] Tatton-Brown 1982a, 179f. and 1985, 60f.

have been described as non-Cypriote and as of eastern appearance, chiefly because of their type of face.[54] The class may indeed have originated in Phoenicia, where several examples seem to have been found, though not during controlled excavations. Of our group of four chariot models, the one in the Louvre (no. 2) reportedly comes from a necropolis belonging to the important site of Marathus (Amrit) in northern Phoenicia, along with some related pieces – a cart model (Appendix, no. a), a head and torso (pl. 54a–b) and a god seated on a throne.[55] This provenance can probably be accepted, as it is based on information from A. E. Guillaume-Rey, a French scholar who was active in the Levant and Cyprus in the 1850s and 1860s.[56] Two other chariot models (nos. 1, 3) may also be from Phoenicia: like no. 2 they were acquired for French collections from a Mr. Nretié, counsellor in the French consulate in Beirut around the middle of the nineteenth century.[57] Other terracottas of our class have a Phoenician provenance too, including a cart (Appendix, no. c) and horseback rider (pl. 51) from Tyre, both in the British Museum and acquired in 1884 from the G. J. Chester collection, as well as some fragmentary figurines from Helalieh near Sidon, now in the Louvre (pls. 52, 53).

This class of terracottas may then have been introduced in Cyprus from Phoenicia at some time during the later 7th century B.C.[58]

It is, however, unlikely that the finds from Cyprus – and those from elsewhere (Rhodes, Samos, the Knidos peninsula and Naucratis) – were all made in Phoenicia. Instead, some at least may well have been produced in Cyprus, using imported moulds or copies of these for the human faces.[59] Unfortunately, the clay fabrics do not, for the

---

[54] Monloup 1984, 174f.; Catling 1975, no. 99 (our chariot model no. 1); Brown and Catling 1980, no. 92 (same model).

[55] *Supra* n. 41 (head and torso); de Longperier 1871, pl. XXIII: 3 = Heuzey 1923, no. 190 = Vandenabeele 1986, 354 with pl. XXXI: 2 (god on throne). For the site, see *I Fenici* (exhibition Venice, 1988) 149f.

[56] For this man, see Caubet 1984; also letter of 26 October 1989.

[57] See esp. Heuzey 1923, 41f. and no. 187; Archaeologische Zeitung XI in *AA* 60 (1853), 403; Winter 1903, p. LXXXXVI; also information supplied by the Bibliothèque Nationale, Paris.

[58] For eastern influences on terracottas from Cyprus, see Vandenabeele 1986 and 1985.

[59] See Karageorghis, *Terracottas*, 1f.; Vandenabeele 1986, 352 n. 15 (a mould for terracottas of Phoenician type found at Kition). Note the case of the closely similar, mould-made, bearded heads from Ovgoros, Salamis and Beirut, *supra* nn. 33–34 (pl. XXX, e and XXXI, c–d). For comparison, an incomplete mould for a female

moment, shed much light on this matter. Visual examination, backed by the *Munsell Soil Chart*, suggests both similarities and differences between the various terracottas. A program of chemical and petrological analyses of the clays, against the background of a large database, would be helpful, though it cannot be ruled out that clays travelled from one area to another.

As for the moulds used for the men's faces, the same ones were clearly employed for the crews of the individual chariot teams of models nos. 1–4. In the case of the faces of some fragmentary figurines from single find places – Salamis and Lindos – the use of the same mould has been assumed (see pls. 43, 44a–b).[60] It would be significant if this could also be established for the terracottas of the class found at different places, such as our chariot models. However, as we have said, it is quite possible that moulds travelled and were copied.

Finally, the terracottas of this class found outside Phoenicia and Cyprus, including chariot model no. 4 from the Knidos peninsula, may well have been exported from Cyprus or made by Cypriote coroplasts working on the spot. This is supported by the presence at the same sites of other terracottas as well as limestone sculptures with clear Cypriote and not Phoenician affinities.[61]

Addenda

Since this paper went to press two important publications by the late A. M. Bisi (1982 and 1989) have come to my notice. In these studies she argued that our chariot model no. 2 from Amrit and other terracottas of the same class found in Phoenicia are Cypriote imports. I hope to take up this matter again in an article on the terracotta model of a horseback rider, reportedly from Byblos and now in Brussels (*Les Phéniciens et le monde méditerranéen*, exhibition Brussels 1986, no. 41; *I Fenici*, exhibition Venice 1988, no. 30 and ill. p. 133) [see article no. 28 below, PR]. Two more, fragmentary "personnages

---

head from Corinth is reported to be of local clay but of eastern type; it is one of the oldest moulds from Greece, its context dating to the 7th cent. B.C.; see Newhall Stillwell 1948, 87f. no. 1; Dunbabin 1957, 137.

[60] Monloup 1984, 173 (caption to fig. 12, nos. 644–655 = our pl. XXX, a–c); Blinkenberg 1931, no. 2012, cf. also nos. 1995–1996, 2000 (?), 2001f.

[61] See esp. Wriedt Sørensen 1978, SCE IV: 2, 318–322. 327–335; Blinkenberg 1931; Samos VII.

barbus de type assyrien", both unprovenanced, have been recently published by Decaudin 1987, 82f. no. 89 with pl. XXXIV (Lyon, Musée Municipal 37637), 113 no. 67 with pl. XLV (Lyon, Musée des Beaux-Arts E 366).

Appendix

Three terracotta models representing carts, drawn by two horses and carrying reclining or seated passengers, deserve a few special comments. Two of them have already been referred to, as they are quite closely related to our chariot models and other terracottas of the same class – in both technique of manufacture and style, while also sharing the same provenances.

a. (pl. 57a–b). Paris, Louvre AO 25986 (formerly S 10). Provenance and history as chariot model no. 1. L. 0.124; Ht. 0.098. Bibliography: de Longperier 1871, pl. XX:1; Heuzey 1883, 4 with pl. V:top; Heuzey 1923, no. 188; Monloup 1984, 164, no. 605, 179, no. 661; Crouwel 1985, 204 with pl. XXXIV:1–2.

b. (pl. 58a–b). Paris, Bibliothèque Nationale D 3735 (formerly 5913). History as chariot model no. 3. L. 0.135; Ht. 0.14. Bibliography: Poulsen 1912, 63f. with figs. 62–63; Heuzey 1923, no. 188; Crouwel 1985, 204.

c. (pl. 56a–b). London, BM 91567 (acquired in 1884 from G. J. Chester). From Tyre. L. c. 0.13; Ht. c. 0.12. Bibliography: Crouwel 1985, 204 with pl. XXXIV:3–4.

These cart models form a closely-knit group. All three illustrate a man walking between the draught animals and leading them by the head, as is also seen on the two-horse chariot model from Ovgoros, mentioned above (pl. 45), and on a two-horse stone model of a covered cart from Amathus, also in Cyprus.[62] The animals, though worn, still show tassel pendants in front, like our chariot horses. The carts themselves are open, without any superstructure. Two of them (nos. a and c) carry single, reclining men who support themselves on one elbow; the men are bearded and dressed in long garments,

---

[62] *Supra* n. 33 (Ovgoros model); Crouwel 1987, 211f., 216 no. SM 1 with fig. 1 (stone model).

their feet extending beyond the floor of the carts. The third model (no. b) carries a female figure seated on a chair placed sideways, with a high back-rest and lower arm-rests.

While the latter subject is unparalleled, the first is well-known from Cypriote terracotta models of the 6th century B.C., illustrating one, rarely more, reclining persons. In some cases the passengers are seen resting with their elbows on a cushion.[63] The same subject, here involving horse-drawn carts with two persons reclining side by side, can be seen on a poorly preserved silver bowl of the so-called Cypro-Phoenician class, probably dating to the 7th century B.C.[64]

All these cart passengers, including the ones of models nos. a–c, may be regarded as important or wealthy people, travelling slowly to, for instance, parties or religious gatherings. Indeed, the reclining attitude of most, supporting themselves on one arm, is the same as that portrayed in banquet scenes from Cyprus, the Near East and elsewhere.[65]

The three cart models nos. a–c all probably come from Phoenicia. Two of them (nos. a and c) are reported to have the same find places – a necropolis at Marathus (Amrit) and Tyre – as chariot model no. 2 and other terracottas of the same class. As stated above, the cart models have much in common with the chariot models and other terracottas of the same class discussed in this paper. They are hand-modelled, apart from the human heads which are again made in moulds. The head and conical headdress of the man on foot of cart model no. c, though worn, may have been similar to those of our chariot terracottas. The other two men leading teams of horses have different, beardless faces and wear bonnet-like headdresses. At the same time all three are shown with the same short garment, ending in a point at about knee level, exactly like that of the man in a similar position – and with a head of our class – belonging to the model from Ovgoros in Cyprus (pl. 45).

The worn facial features of the reclining passenger of cart model no. c, from Tyre, may have been similar to those of our class. He wears a broad-rimmed conical headdress, just like the incomplete figurine reportedly from Marathus (Amrit) (pl. 54a–b).[66]

---

[63] Crouwel 1985, esp. 212 and ills.

[64] Markoe 1985, 181f. no. Cy 13; Crouwel 1987, 204 with n. 5, 212.

[65] For this theme, which also became popular in Greek and Etruscan art, see esp. Denzer 1982; Crouwel 1987, 212. 216.

[66] *Supra* n. 41.

Two of the cart models (nos. a and c) originally rolled on four wheels, recalling our chariot model no. 2.

The seated female passenger of cart no. b wears a veil over her comb-like hair. The rendering of the hair can be matched on the figure of a bearded god, similarly seated on a high-backed but more elaborate chair, from Marathus (Amrit).[67]

---

[67] *Supra* n. 55.

15. CARTS IN IRON AGE CYPRUS*

J. H. CROUWEL

This paper presents evidence for a particular type of wheeled vehicle – the cart – which was used in Cyprus during the Iron Age.** A cart may be described as an animal-drawn two-wheeler, designed to carry a stable load, i.e. goods or seated passengers. In contrast, the other type of two-wheeled vehicle that was used at this time in the island – the chariot – was designed to carry a less stable load of one or more persons who usually stood. Interestingly enough, a third possible type of vehicle – the four-wheeled wagon – is not attested in ancient Cyprus. (For definitions of cart, chariot, wagon and other technical terms used here, see the glossaries in Littauer and Crouwel 1979, 3ff., and Crouwel 1981, 23ff. and the Glossary above; see p. XV).

While chariots in Cyprus have received a good deal of attention, the more humble and less well-documented carts have not. What we know of carts derives both from representations and remains of actual vehicles. The representations are mainly terracotta models in the round; there are also some models of stone or lead as well as a vase painting. All these range from the 8th/7th to the 4th century B.C. (the periods known in local terms as Cypro-Geometric III, CyproArchaic I–II and Cypro-Classical I–II).[1]

In addition, carts as well as chariots have been identified among the remains of actual vehicles buried along with their draught teams and their harness in tombs of the 8th–7th century B.C. at Salamis.[2]

* *Report of the Department of Antiquities Cyprus*, 1985, 203–221.

** I am most grateful to Miss A. Caubet, Mrs P. Jacobs, Dr V. Karageorghis, Dr M. Loulloupis, Mrs S. Lubsen-Admiraal, Dr J. R. Mertens, Dr P. R. S. Moorey, Dr V. Tatton-Brown and Mr R. L. Wilkins for information and assistance of various kinds. I am also much indebted to Mrs M. A. Littauer for comments upon a draft text, to my wife for help with the English, and to Mr J. Morel and Mr G. Strietman for most of the drawings of Figs 1–2. The photographs appear by courtesy of the Ashmolean Museum (Oxford), the Trustees of the British Museum (London), the Department of Antiquities (Cyprus), the Metropolitan Museum of Art (New York) and the Musée du Louvre (Paris).

[1] For chronology, see Karageorghis 1982, 9f., table A.
[2] A general survey of these tombs in Karageorghis 1969, chapter III.

The wooden parts of the vehicles had decayed but had left impressions in the soil and some metal parts were preserved *in situ*. The identification of the vehicles as carts is based primarily on the iron bearing shoes of their axle brackets, which are typical of carts but not of chariots (see below, s.v. Axle).[3]

Both the figured documents and remains of actual vehicles impose severe restrictions on our knowledge, the first because of the often summary rendering of the carts, the second due to poor preservation and/or disturbance by later burials or other activities. Given these limitations, comparative material from outside Cyprus is adduced when appropriate.[4]

The following text deals with the construction of the carts, according to their constituent parts (body, axle, wheels, traction system), their draught animals, the ways in which the latter were harnessed and controlled and the use to which the vehicles were put. Concluding remarks will assess possible local, Cypriote characteristics and foreign elements. Reference is made throughout to the catalogue of representations and actual remains that follows upon the main text.

Body

A lead model from Salamis (LM 1, fig. 1), incomplete though it is, shows the basic framework of the cart floor as composed of three timbers joined by three cross-pieces. The length-wise timbers project slightly at the rear and in front, the central one actually continuing as the draught pole (see below, s.v. Axle and Traction System). Although the model is undated, it reveals the simple, rectangular framework that is characteristic of many carts, ancient and modern. The same framework is probably indicated on several of the Cypriote terracotta cart models, by projections on either side of the floor, at the rear and sometimes also in the middle (TM 5–6, 8, 10–12, 18, 24, 27–28, 31–32, 34–36, 38, pls. 59a–b–91), while it appears too in the reconstruction of the actual cart from Tomb 2 at Salamis (A 1, fig. 1).

---

[3] The absence of these objects would favour a chariot rather than a cart in the case of a highly fragmentary vehicle from Tomb 50, see Karageorghis 1967, 105f. 115. 118 with pl. XCVI; 1969, 58 with figs. 8, 10.

[4] Much relevant information in Tarr 1969; Littauer and Crouwel 1979, especially 99ff., 144ff.; Höckmann 1982, chapter III; Piggott 1983 (index s.v. cart).

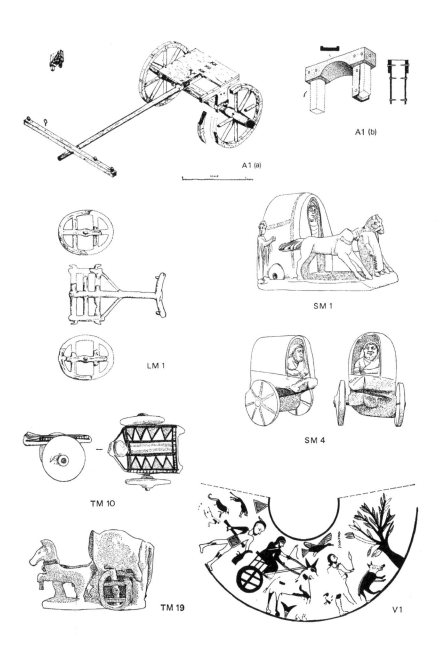

Fig. 1.

Whereas on the lead model the floor frame was left open, the ter-racottas show a solid, presumably plank flooring. (The lines, some-times painted on the floors, may reflect such a wooden flooring, see TM 5, 8, 12, 14, 28, 30, 37, pls. 59a–b–91; cf. TM 10, fig. 1). A plank flooring is also implied by other, schematic terracottas show-ing carts carrying a large jar with a wide opening at the top (TM 7, 9, 15, 20, 22, 39, pls. 59a–b–91).

As reconstructed, one of the actual carts from Salamis too has a plank flooring, fastened on to the framework by cross-headed iron nails (A 1, fig. 1). The floor seems to have been small, c. 0.60 m. long by c. 0.75 m. wide. In the reconstruction, the wheels, set at the middle of the floor, are c. 0.90 m. in diameter and therefore extend beyond the floor at front and rear. (The recorded measure-ments of the floors of the two carts from Tomb 79 – A 4 and A 5 – also indicate rather small vehicles, with a length of 0.51 m. and 0.90 m., and a width of 0.71 m. and 0.80 m.).

The Cypriote figured documents seem to illustrate carts of vary-ing dimensions, the wheels extending beyond the floor or *vice versa*. Welcome information on the proportions is furnished by the stone and terracotta models of carts carrying passengers, either seated, reclining while supporting themselves on one elbow, or lying down lengthwise on the floor. There is usually only one such passenger (SM 1, 3–4, fig. 1; TM 1–4, 12, 21, 23–26, 34, pls. 59a–b–91), but one terracotta model (TM 1, pl. 62) indicates that there could be sufficient floor space to accommodate two persons reclining side by side; on this model a third person, a boy playing a double flute, is seen perched on the laps of the two adults, one of them holding him with an arm around his waist. Carts with two persons reclin-ing side by side are shown on a poorly preserved silver bowl of the so-called Cypro-Phoenician class. Without provenance, it probably dates to the later 7th century B.C.[5]

The Cypriote carts are shown with and without a superstructure. An entirely open platform appears on some terracottas which are either empty or carrying passengers (TM 5, 8, 10, 25, 27, fig. 1,

---

[5] This vessel – New York, MMA (Cesnola coll.) 74.51.4555 – is not included in the Catalogue as its Cypriote manufacture has not been universally accepted; besides, its iconography is oriental in character and does not reflect actual life in Cyprus. See Myres 1914, no. 4555; Gjerstad 1946, 8ff. with pl. IV; Alexander 1963, 247f. with fig. 7; Stream 1971, 119 n. 222, 122; Fehr 1971, 22ff. no. 4; Dentzer 1971, 237ff. with fig. 6; 1982, 72f. with fig. 104.

pls. 59a–b–80). The cart of the lead model (LM 1, fig. 1) shows no superstructure, but here the hooks on the side timbers of the floor may have served to fasten a (removable) siding of some kind. The reconstructed actual cart from Salamis (A 1, fig. 1) also has an entirely open platform. The same is true for the carts seen on the Cypro-Phoenician silver bowl and for those represented by three closely dated terracotta models of 7th/6th century B.C. date from Phoenicia. Two of these, from a necropolis at Marathus (modern Amrit) and from Tyre, carry an incompletely preserved reclining man (pls. 92a–b–93a-b); the third, its find-place unknown, supports a female figure seated on a chair which is placed sideways.[6]

The carts represented by the majority of terracotta models from Cyprus have a low or very low siding, usually leaving the front and rear open. This siding may have a horizontal top edge or one that curves down towards the rear (TM 1–3, 6, 13–14, 23–24, 29–30, 34–35, 37, pls. 59a–b–91). On most of these terracottas the painted decoration of the siding is unfortunately not explicit enough to indicate structural details. One model, however, has an arched siding, sloping slightly outwards (TM 28, pl. 80); this may well reflect the construction of actual carts, in the same way as the painted vertical lines on the arched siding, which suggest an open railing with vertical supports.[7] In contrast, the groups of painted vertical lines alternating with clay pellets on the siding of another model (TM 1, pl. 62) would seem rather to be purely decorative.

Still other terracottas have a siding of equal height, extending all around. This siding is usually straight and set within the edge of the floor (TM 11, 26, 31–33, 38, pls. 69–91). In one case there is enough space for a figure to sit at the junction of the floor and the draught pole, while holding on to the siding with one outstretched arm (TM 26, pl. 78).

Some stone and terracotta models illustrate carts with an arched tilt (SM 1–2, 4, fig. 1; TM 18–19, 21, 36, fig. 1, pls. 69–91). One of the actual carts from Tomb 79 at Salamis (A 5) was reported to

---

[6] These models may well be of Levantine manufacture, but a Cypriote origin cannot be excluded. *Marathus* (Paris, Louvre AO 25986), see Heuzey 1923, no. 188 with pl. V: 2; Monloup 1982, s.v. no. 661. *Tyre* (London, BM 91567), unpublished. *Find place unknown* (Paris, Cabinet des Médailles 5913), see Poulsen 1912, 63f. with figs. 62–63; Heuzey 1923, s.v. no. 188.

[7] An arched, railwork siding is shown with Elamite carts on Assyrian reliefs of Ashurbanipal, see Barnett 1975, pls. 155. 160.

have a tilt (or canopy) as well, but no evidence was provided to support this.[8] Although the models yield only limited information on this form of superstructure, we may assume that the tilts were composed of some kind of fabric or wickerwork on hoops.[9] The painted vertical and horizontal lines on SM 1 (fig. 1) suggest that the framework of hoops could be strengthened by horizontal slats. On TM 36 (pl. 87) the lower part of the tilt is painted differently from the rest; its zigzag pattern, unless it is purely decorative, could suggest thongs securing the covering material of the tilt. According to our evidence, the tilts could be open or closed at front and rear. Interestingly, some stone models show one or two partly drawn curtains at the front (SM 1–2, 4, fig. 1).

The known models of tilt carts never show more than one passenger who is always facing forward and probably meant to be leaning on his or her elbows. The single passenger corresponds with those seen in most models of open carts. Quite probably we have to do with similar vehicles, to which a siding or tilt was added, as the need arose, depending on the use to which they were put or on the weather.

The vase painting of a cart seems to show a rather different vehicle from those discussed so far (V 1, fig. 1). It looks very small, with only a seat, supported by vertical struts, for the driver, his feet resting on the floor projecting at the front.

What looks like a wheeled throne is illustrated by a terracotta model where a person is seated on a chair with back and arm rests and is facing forward (TM 4, pl. 65). This small conveyance, its axle unusually placed at the rear and with a central pole, recalls the two-wheeled platforms, bearing either a throne or a chariot box, that are illustrated on Assyrian stone and bronze reliefs and on wall painting from Til Barsip and are also mentioned in Assyrian texts (fig. 2:1 illustrates an example on a stone relief of Sargon II).[10] These royal "rickshaws" also have a rear axle and a central pole and were pulled by men. What seem to be wheeled thrones, but drawn by

[8] Karageorghis 1973a, 75.

[9] For construction of tilts, see Littauer and Crouwel 1974, 27.

[10] For representations, see Hrouda 1965, 68 with pl. 17: 1 (Til Barsip), 2 (our fig. 2: 1), 3; Littauer and Crouwel 1979, 134 with n. 121; Oates 1983, 44, fig. 5 (newly published bronze gate of Ashurnasirpal II from Balawat). For texts, see Salonen 1951, 64ff.

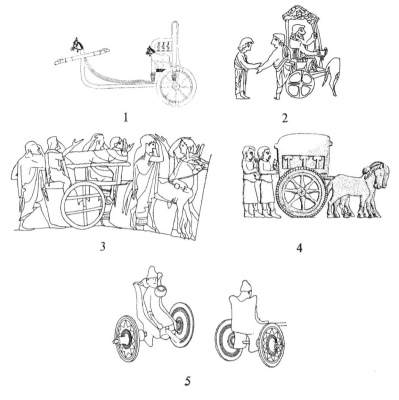

Fig. 2.

teams of animals, are also attested elsewhere in the Mediterranean world during the 1st millennium B.C.[11]

A parallel from Cyprus itself may conceivably be found in the partly reconstructed "hearse" Alpha from Tomb 79 at Salamis (A 4, pl. 59a–b). This vehicle is related to the cart from Tomb 2 (A 1) by the two iron bearing shoes for the axle brackets, while its floor dimensions (0.51 m. long by 0.71 m. wide) also correspond quite well. There is evidence to show that the vehicle had a central pole

---

[11] See Höckmann 1982, especially 136f. nos. G 14 (Thraco-Macedonian silver coins of c. 480 B.C.; see also Franke and Hirmer 1964, pl. 126: bottom, left) and G 20 (incomplete terracotta plaque of similar date from Locri, S. Italy; see also Zanciani Montuoro 1955, 283ff. with pls. I–III). It may be noted that the "wheeled throne" seen in a Lycian tomb painting is, in fact, a chariot with a separate throne placed inside it, as is also seen on a relief from Heroon G at Xanthos, see Mellink 1973, 298ff. with pls. 45: 7, 46: 9–10 (Karaburun, tomb 2); Metzger 1963, pls. XXXIX: 1, XLI: 1.

too and was likewise pulled by animals. It appears, however, to have
been far more complex and ornate, with a footrest at the front,
made up of two wooden boards hinged in the middle, and with a
tilt or canopy supported on vertical posts. The presence of the latter is based on the discovery of five bronze lion heads with sockets
at the back which would have been attached at the four corners of
the floor, the fifth one decorating the rear end of the draught pole.
As reconstructed, this vehicle may have been a wheeled throne, such
as is represented by the simple terracotta model mentioned above,
with a canopy to protect its occupant.

The reconstruction with a canopy finds unexpected support in the
illustration on a small Attic Red-Figure jug of c. 400 B.C. (fig. 2:2).[12]
It belongs with the special class known as choes and shows children
imitating an episode from a ceremony during the Anthesteria festival,
namely the sacred wedding procession of the wife of the Archon Basi-
leus and Dionysos. We see an open-sided, equid-drawn cart, with a
canopy raised on four tall posts. The god is already seated on a chair
in the vehicle, while the best man prepares to help the bride mount.

Axle

On our figured documents the axle is usually shown as centrally
placed under the floor. Only on the wheeled throne of T 4 (pl. 61)
is it located at the rear, as it is on the royal "rickshaws" in Assyria
(see s.v. Body). At Salamis the axle position of the actual carts is
uncertain, while the chariots had axles at the rear. A central axle is
characteristic of ancient and more recent carts and is suitable for
stable loads.

As to the shape and manner of attachment of the cart axles, the
figured documents are not really informative. The pierced loops or
tubular sheaths below the floors of the terracotta and stone models
respectively, meant to carry a wooden axle rod, were merely a convenience for the artists. The round axle ends, seen on the cross-bar
wheels of TM 19 (fig. 1), may indicate an axle rigidly fixed to the
vehicle floor, with the wheels revolving on it; the roughly oval axle
ends of LM 1 (fig. l) may point to an axle revolving with the wheels.
While a fixed axle and revolving wheels are desirable for fast vehi-

---

[12] Bieber 1949, 34f. with pls. 5: 1A–B (New York, MMA 27.97.34).

cles, the revolving axle with fixed wheels requires far less skill to make and is useful for slow transport; as a result, it is in use in certain areas even today.[13]

The revolving axle is definitely attested on actual carts buried at Salamis, whereas the chariots there had fixed axles. On the Salamis carts the axles revolved in a pair of thick, T-shaped wooden brackets (also called axle blocks), concave on the under face, one on either side of the floor and fastened to it by iron nails (see fig. 1: A 1).[14] The excavator made an exception for the decorated conveyance A 4 where the axle was fixed by metal nails to the brackets and to a separate, wooden "case" between them (pl. 59a-b). The presence here of axle brackets and of iron bearing shoes (for these, see below), as on the other carts, suggests that we have to do with an originally revolving axle which was subsequently converted into a fixed one.[15]

Axle brackets are a feature of many carts, ancient and more recent, and not only served to keep the revolving axle in position but also to raise the floor of the vehicle to the required height.[16] On carts, the draught pole usually formed an integral part of the vehicle floor, running out horizontally or at a moderate angle to the yoke area (see s.v. Traction system). In order to keep the floor in a horizontal position rather than tilting, axle brackets were used to raise it, their height depending on the size of the wheels and that of the draught team. (This system contrasts with that of ancient chariots where the pole was made of a separate timber, lying directly above the axle and below the floor and curving upwards rather more sharply in front of of the vehicle to reach the necessary yoke level).

The axle brackets, open as they are at the bottom, permit the cart and pole to be lifted off the axle at any time for convenience – when in store, for instance. On the Salamis carts a ∏-shaped iron bearing shoe on the concave underside of the wooden brackets protected the latter from wear by the revolving axle. (fig. 1: A1).[17] Such a metal bearing shoe is illustrated with a hand-pulled cart on an

---

[13] Littauer and Crouwel 1979, 16f.; Wegener Sleeswyk 1982, 478f.; Piggott 1983, 191.

[14] The narrow faces of the axle brackets were apparently studded with numerous metal nails, see Karageorghis 1967, 23 (A 1); 1973a, 61 (A 4), 67 (A 5).

[15] Karageorghis 1973a, 61.

[16] See Lorimer 1903, 136; Höckmann 1982, 31.

[17] See Catalogue s.v. Actual cart remains.

Assyrian wall painting of the 8th century B.C. at Til Barsip,[18] and
it is still used with carts in Portugal today.[19]

Wheels

The documents indicate that both spoked and cross-bar wheels were
in use on Cypriote carts; there is no good evidence for solid disk
wheels.

The wheels of the stone and terracotta models, where preserved,
are usually shown as disks, with and without raised centres, to indicate the nave. (In the case of terracotta models it is not always certain if the wheels are in fact the original ones). These model wheels
are often painted with lines radiating from centre (SM 4, fig. 1; TM
1–4, 18, pls. 59a–b–91). The lines, rendered in one colour or alternately black and red, vary from four to eight or more, and must
indicate spokes. We may wonder whether their numbers always reflect
those of actual cart wheels. (The painted or plastically rendered
spokes of the wheels of chariot models also range substantially, from
four to ten or more.)[20]

The reconstructed actual cart from Tomb 2 at Salamis (A 1, fig. 1)
has eight-spoked wheels. As reconstructed, these wheels have a diameter of c. 0.90 m. and resemble fairly closely the reconstruction of the
ten-spoked wheels of a chariot from Tomb 79 at the site.[21] They share
the long, barrel-shaped nave in two uneven sections – the outer longer
than the one – apparently joined in the area of the sockets to accommodate the inner ends of the spokes, and they both have felloes in
overlapping segments into which the outer spoke ends are morticed.

The reconstruction of the cart wheels raises more than one question. Barrel-shaped naves are unusual for the period, as far as is
known, and to construct them in two parts, joined just at the point
where the spoke ends would have erected maximum pressure to forge
them apart, must be considered to be structurally unsound. Besides,
we have seen above that the axles of this and most other carts buried

---

[18] Parrot 1961, pl. 117; Littauer and Crouwel 1979, 100.
[19] Galhano 1973, especially 138 with figs. 16. 18. 21f.
[20] See Littauer and Crouwel 1977c, 69.
[21] Karageorghis 1973a, 68 with n. 1 and figs. 10f. (chariot Bèta). As reconstructed,
the eight-spoked wheel from Tomb 3 (chariot B) is rather different, see Karageorghis
1967, 49f. with pls. CXXf.; also Kossack 1971, 151ff. with fig. 37.

at Salamis were not fixed like those of chariots but revolved within iron-clad brackets (see s.v. Axle). As reconstructed, the wheels of cart A 1 revolve on an axle that itself revolves within its brackets. Now wheels revolving on revolving axles would be technically unsound, creating extra drag and friction. And indeed, the iron bearing shoes point rather to the presence of a revolving axle and fixed wheels. (It may be noted that, according to the excavator himself, the wheels of cart A 5 from Tomb 79 were fixed on a revolving axle, whereas the originally revolving axle of A 4 from the same tomb had been converted into a fixed one, see s.v. Axle.)

The other, cross-bar type of wheel can be seen on vase painting V 1 (fig. 1), while the openwork wheels of lead model LM 1 (fig. 1) and of one terracotta model with a tilt (TM 19, fig. 1) are also of this type. The cross-bar wheel is characterized by a diametric bar through which the axle passes, with lighter "cross-bars" at right angles to the diametric bar, between it and the felloe. This type of wheel has a long history, going back to the later third millennium B.C. in the Near East, and has existed into recent times in different parts of the world. In antiquity it was normally associated with carts – in the Near East as well as in Greece and Italy – but not with chariots.[22] A notable exception from Cyprus is the quadriga depicted in relief on a stone base of Hellenistic date.[23]

Cross-bar wheels are usually fixed on a revolving axle but may also revolve on a fixed axle. In the later case they require a nave and are secured by linch pins. In Cyprus both systems appear to be documented, viz. the roughly oval, or round axle ends respectively, seen on the lead and terracotta models mentioned above (see also s.v. Axle). The Cypriote representations of cross-bar wheels show straight "cross-bar" rather than crescent-shaped ones, and in this they resemble Greek examples of the 6th and 5th century B.C. as well as an actual, fragmentary wheel of this type from Olympia and another from Gordion, with find contexts dated to the 6th and 5th century B.C. respectively.[24]

---

[22] Littauer and Crouwel 1977a; Hayen 1980–81; Wegener Sleeswyk 1982, 490ff. (called H-spoked wheel); Piggott 1983, especially 97f.; Boehmer 1983, 36ff.

[23] Vessberg and Westholm 1956, 95 with pl. XIII: 1–2 (from Vitsada); Cassimatis 1976, 178f. with pl. XXX.

[24] Hayen 1980–81, 153ff. with figs. 10–13. 20 (Olympia); Kohler 1980, 69 with fig. 32 (Gordion).

Traction System

Traction was provided by teams of animals under a yoke which was connected with the vehicle by means of a single, central draught pole. In the one case where single draught is seemingly illustrated (V 1, fig. 1), it is merely a simplification of the artist (cf. the six reins shown here!). There is no evidence for carts with two poles and four animals, such as there is for many, though not all, chariots from the island.[25]

The great majority of figured documents yield no information on the shape of the pole or its attachment to the body. Most terracottas, for instance, simply have a tube with a hole in the centre of the front for the insertion of a wooden pole. Most explicit is the – undated – lead model (LM 1, fig. 1) where the pole is formed by a continuation of the central lengthwise timber of the cart floor. This construction is characteristic of many carts, ancient and recent. The lead model also shows two short pole braces to restrict its sideways motion and strengthen its connection with the vehicle body, something that can be paralleled on ancient chariots from outside Cyprus.[26]

On the lead model the pole runs out horizontally, as it does on the reconstructed actual cart from Tomb 2 at Salamis (A 1, fig. 1). On the latter, however, the pole must have run out at a slant and not horizontally, to allow for even small animals under the yoke.[27] A stone and a terracotta model (SM 1 and TM 19, fig. 1) do, in fact, illustrate a pole rising to the yoke area at an oblique angle, while on the vase painting (V 1, fig. 1) it rises at an impossibly sharp angle. Whether these poles were also an integral part of the vehicle's floor or separate, bent timbers that ran under the floor as on contemporary chariots, is uncertain.

---

[25] See Littauer and Crouwel 1977c, 70f. Neither is there evidence for Cypriote carts with the so-called Y-pole, formed of two timbers, one coming from each corner of the vehicle to run contiguously to the yoke. This pole is attested on some Cypriote chariot models with two-horse teams, see Littauer and Crouwel 1977b.

[26] Littauer and Crouwel 1977b, 2f. with fig. 2 (Levantine bronze model); Crouwel 1981, 96 (Greek vase paintings).

[27] Cf. Karageorghis 1967, 22.

Draught Animals

In the few representations where draught animals are associated with carts, they are equids. In one case asses or mules were probably intended, the ears appearing longer than those of horses (V 1, fig. 1). In the other cases – stone and terracotta models of carts with tilts (SM 1–2, TM 19, fig. 1) – the animals may well be horses; at any rate, they do not differ from the horses shown with chariots on many other models. The carts depicted on the Cypro-Phoenician bowl and those of the terracotta models from Phoenicia are also horse-drawn (pl. 92a–b–93a–b).

The paired equid skeletons found with the remains of actual carts at Salamis have been identified as both assess (A 1) and horses (A 2 and A 3), those belonging with the chariots buried there only as horses.[28] It may be noted that outside Cyprus carts in antiquity were normally drawn by oxen, mules or asses, not by horses.

Harnessing

The draught animals were harnessed under a yoke, on either side of the central pole. Three cart models show two-horse teams (SM 1–2, TM 19, fig. 1), and similarly-sized teams of horses or asses were associated with the Salamis cart burials. For comparison, the chariot burials there had teams of two or four horses, which corresponds well with the evidence of the chariot models.

The yokes were attached to the poles, near the end of the latter, by lashings.[29] Cart and chariot models suggest that the yokes were shaped to lie across the necks of the draught animals, just ahead of the withers.[30] The reconstructed actual cart from Salamis (A 1, fig. 1) shows the yoke not shaped but as a straight, rather heavy beam,

---

[28] Ducos 1967, 156. 158. 181. 1980, especially table I.

[29] The pole and yoke were sometimes protected at their junction by iron plaques, see Karageorghis 1967, 23 nos. 59a–b (A 1), 51 no. 102 (A 2).

[30] It has been claimed that the yoke of A 2 was used in conjunction with yoke saddles, like the yoke of chariot Beta from Tomb 79, see Karageorghis 1967, 52; 1973a, 74; for yoke saddles in general, see Littauer and Crouwel 1979, 85. 113. The yoke of A 5 from Tomb 79 appears to have had horn-shaped bronze terminals similar to those of the chariots from the tomb, see Karageorghis 1973a, 68. 73. 75f.

rectangular in section – something highly improbable as a neck yoke for equids.

The yokes were kept in place by a neckstrap encircling the neck of each animal and attached at either end of the yoke, as on chariots. While TM 19 (fig. 1) shows only a neckstrap, SM 1 (fig. 1) also illustrates a second harness strap, passing under the belly just behind the forelegs. This strap (often called girth) is characteristic of ancient harnessing, in Cyprus and elsewhere, and often acted as a backing element.[31] Outside the island it is usually absent on cart harness and it was obviously not essential for such vehicles.

Control

None of the persons seen in the cart models is concerned with controlling a draught team, whether it is represented or not. These vehicles, their passengers reclining, lying down or seated, must have been led by someone on foot, as is indeed seen on a stone model of a tilt cart (SM 1, fig. 1) as well as on the three terracotta models from Phoenicia (pl. 92a–b–93a–b). The incomplete noseband that remains on the broken head of one of the animals of SM 1 may have belonged to a halter – a simple headstall for leading animals or for tying them up – rather than to a bridle. The latter, composed of a headstall, with or without a bit, and reins, was invariably used with chariots. A bridle, however, is implied by V 1 (fig. 1), which shows a man seated in a cart and actually driving his single ass or mule with six reins and a whip, the headstall unfortunately effaced. The cart, with its unrealistic number of animals and reins, is shown in a hunting setting where a bridle would give welcome directional as well as braking control to a driver.

The animals that pulled the actual carts buried at Salamis were also controlled by bridles, including metal bits identical to those of the chariot teams buried there. As on the chariots, pairs of metal rings, placed along the yoke, acted as terrets for the reins to pass through.[32] We may doubt, however, whether this method of control was standard on Cypriote carts. In the ancient Near East, Greece and Italy cart teams of oxen, asses or mules were usually controlled

---

[31] See Littauer and Crouwel 1979, 116f.
[32] Karageorghis 1967, 24, 52, 79 (A1–A3); 1973a, 68 (A 5).

simply by a stick, goad or whip in combination with the human voice, while equids in addition often wore a halter.

Use

Carts in ancient Cyprus appear to have been used exclusively for civil purposes. In this they differ from chariots, which until the later 5th century B.C. usually had a military appearance, presumably reflecting their use in war. From that time onwards we no longer see military chariots, only examples of civil ones.[33]

Most of our evidence concerns the role of carts – open or covered with an arched tilt – as conveyances for human beings. As we have seen earlier, these men and women are not concerned with driving and they must have had somebody to lead the draught team at a slow pace. This is actually illustrated by an interesting stone model of a covered cart which carries a female figure and is accompanied by a second attendant on foot (SM I, fig. 1).[34] A similar group consisting of a cart pulled by two yoked horses with a man at their head is found on the three terracotta models from Phoenicia. These show open carts, one carrying a female figure seated on a chair which is placed sideways, the others a reclining bearded man supporting himself on one elbow (pl. 92a–b–93a–b).[35] The latter position is quite often portrayed on terracotta models of definite Cypriote manufacture. It also appears on one fragmentary stone model (SM 3), while another illustrates a male figure lying on his stomach and supporting himself on both forearms (SM 4, fig. 1). On some terracottas the passengers are resting with their elbows on a cushion (TM 1–3, 25, cf. also 24, pls. 59a–b–80). Such a cushion, rendered by a pellet, recurs in a similar position near the front, on terracotta models of empty carts, open or covered, thus implying that the vehicles were used for a similar purpose (TM 5–6, 8, 10, 13–14, 18, 28–30, 33, 35, 37, cf. also 24, fig. 1, pls. 59a–b–91).

This purpose is quite likely to have been various forms of travelling over longer and shorter distances, presumably by important or

---

[33] Wilson 1972, 187ff.; Littauer and Crouwel 1977c, 72f.
[34] There is also at least one Cypriote terracotta chariot model with a man at the head of the two-horse team, see Littauer and Crouwel 1977b, 7f. with figs. 3–6 (from Ovgoros); also Monloup 1982, s.v. no. 605.
[35] See above, p. 204.

wealthy people. We may note that the Cypro-Phoenician silver bowl, mentioned earlier, illustrates a journey made by people in a horse-drawn cart and a chariot from a walled city to a palm grove and back.[36] While the chariot occupants are shown standing, those in the cart are reclining on what seem to be mattresses. And Greek texts tell us that in the orient, at the time of the Achaemenid empire, women and grandees travelled in carriages, which were covered as a protection against the elements and for privacy.[37] Such covered carriages, with partly drawn curtains are well illustrated by our SM 1–2, 4 (fig. 1).

One particular use of carts in Cyprus seems to have been for going to such gatherings as parties or religious ceremonies. Indeed, the reclining attitude of several passengers, supporting themselves on one elbow with a cushion, is the same as that portrayed in con-temporary banquet scenes.[38] Such a use for carts is supported by a terracotta model depicting two adults reclining side by side in an open vehicle, with a boy playing a double flute perched on their laps, his waist encircled by the free arm of one of the adults (TM 1, pl. 61). And there is also another model showing a reclining man in an open cart, holding up what seems to be a drinking cup (TM 34, pl. 86). We may note that in Iron-Age Greece the use of carts, by men and women alike, at wedding parties and other ceremonies, religious and funerary, is well documented by figured as well as tex-tual evidence. Similar usage is documented for Iron Age Italy.[39]

These Cypriote cart models clearly illustrate activities of the living. Is this also true of the crudely rendered and/or incompletely preserved persons lying stretched out on the floors of two other terracotta mod-els of open carts? It has been suggested that these figures are not the living but the dead being transported on hearses (TM 23–24,

---

[36] See above, p. 210.

[37] Lorimer 1903, 141; Vigneron 1968, 166f.; Fehr 1971, 22f.: Höckmann 1982, 133 with n. 705, 148. For earlier use of tilt vehicles in the Near East, see Littauer and Crouwel 1974. There is only little evidence for the use of such vehicles in Greece itself, see Newhall Stillwell 1952, 130ff. no. XVII.36 with pls. 26–27 (ter-racotta model from Corinth). On the other hand, they appear to have been quite common in Italy in late Etruscan and Roman times, see Vigneron 1968, 170; Weber 1978, 106ff.; Höckmann 1982, 145 no. E 18, 148f.

[38] See Dentzer 1982, 155ff. 212f. 279ff.; Monloup 1982, s.v. nos. 612 (our TM 16) and 661.

[39] See especially Höckmann 1982, 131ff. (Greece), 141ff. (Etruria).

pls. 75–76).[40] However, another similar, but well preserved figure is lying with one hand at his mouth, the other arm bent across his belly, which does not suggest his being a corpse (TM 12, pl. 70). Indeed, it is more likely that these terracottas simply show an alternative pose to the reclining one considered above.

This takes us to the use of the actual carts that have been found in funerary contexts at Salamis. The excavator believed that these carts served as hearses, carrying the dead in coffins to the tombs.[41] In assessing the use of these vehicles as hearses or otherwise, it may by useful to review briefly their find circumstances, to see if these shed any light on the matter.[42]

The carts were buried with their draught animals. In the case of A 4 the animals must have been removed to make room for the second burial. There is never more than one cart associated with a burial. The carts may be alone (A 1 and A 2 from Tombs 2 and 3) or accompanied by a chariot with its draught team of two or four horses (A 4 and A 5 from the two burials in Tomb 79). In contrast, Tomb 1 contained two chariots, but no cart. The animals of carts and chariots alike wore iron bits, bronze blinkers and frontlets. In addition, the cart teams from Tombs 3 and 79 (A 2, A 4, A 5) had bronze breastplates and shoulder ornaments, and the yokes of these vehicles were decorated with bronze standards, exactly like the chariot teams and yokes. Such elaboratedly decorated harness would be most unusual for cart teams and is presumably to be explained by their being part of the pompous obsequies of important individuals. In the funeral ceremonies, carts and chariots alike were taken into the dromoi of the tombs, where their animals were killed while still under yoke. They were then left behind and subsequently covered by the earth used to fill in the dromoi.

Differences can be noted in the degree of decoration of the cart teams' harnesses and yokes as well as in the vehicles themselves. While the cart from Tomb 2 (A 1, fig. 1) is quite plain, that from the second burial in Tomb 79 (A 5) reportedly had a canopy or

---

[40] Karageorghis 1967, 119. This interpretation has already been questioned by Höckmann 1982, 148 n. 764.

[41] Karageorghis 1967, especially 118f.; 1973a, 60. 66f.

[42] For the find circumstances of the vehicles, see Karageorghis 1967, 9f., 22 (Tomb 2), 31ff. (Tomb 3), 77ff. (Tomb 47), 105f., 115 (Tomb 50), also 117ff.; 1973a, 10ff. (Tomb 79); also Dikaios 1963, 152ff. (Tomb 1).

tilt.[43] The vehicle from the very rich first burial in this tomb (A 4, pl. 59a–b) was originally designed as an elaborate conveyance for a seated person under a canopy, his feet resting on a support in front. As we have seen above (s.v. Body), it recalls the open "wheeled throne" illustrated by a terracotta model (TM 4, pl 65: 8, where the seated person is holding on his lap a flat, rectangular object, unfortunately unidentified) as well as by the royal Assyrian "rickshaws" and some other representations from outside Cyprus.[44]

There seems to be no compelling reason to assume, with the excavator, that this elaborate conveyance was converted into a hearse for the funeral.[45] With the canopy supported on five posts arranged around the edges of the floor (itself only 0.51 m. long by 0.71 m. wide) there would have been little room for a coffin, whether placed sideways or lengthwise. The excavator found evidence to show that the canopy was in place, which would argue against the possibility of it having been removed for the purpose of accommodating a coffin. What is more, the canopy of this vehicle and the canopy or tilt reported with the cart of the second burial in the tomb (A 5) are not immediately suggestive of hearses but indicate rather protection for living persons from the sun etc. (The floor dimensions of A 5–0.90 m. long by 0.80 m. wide – suggest a seated passenger and not a reclining one, as is depicted on several cart models). In Tomb 79 we may then have to do with conveyances that had been used by the dead during their lifetime, like the chariots buried with them. The individuals buried during the two different phases in the tomb would each have possessed two vehicles – a cart and a chariot – for different purposes. The same combination of a cart and a chariot accompanying a single burial occurs in Tomb 3 at Salamis, but not in any of the others.

Apart from the two carts from Tomb 79, it is only the one from Tomb 2 (A 1, fig. 1) that provides information relevant to its use. This vehicle has no superstructure, its floor measuring c. 0.60 m. in length and c. 0.75 m. in width. While these dimensions would afford room for a seated person, they would not easily allow for a reclining one. A coffin might have been placed across the floor, with

---

[43] Karageorghis 1973a, 75.
[44] See above, p. 212.
[45] Karageorghis 1973a, 60. 76. This interpretation has also been doubted by Höckmann 1982, 29 n. 191, who pointed to the foot support as being intended for a living person.

both ends extending beyond it towards the wheels. Since, however, the wheel track was only 1.25 m. (cf. cart A 2 from Tomb 3 with a wheel track of 1.30 m.), it could only have taken a short coffin with a corpse in a contracted position. Were the coffin to have been carried lengthwise on the cart, it would have required careful balancing and would have had to be fairly short so that the overhang at the front would not have interfered with the hind legs of the draught team.

Looking for two-wheeled hearses from outside Cyprus, an Attic Black-Figure vase painting surely indicates a wider and longer platform than that of the Salamis carts (fig. 2:3).[46] It carries a bier on legs placed lengthwise, with female mourners seated on either side. On the other hand, two-wheelers depicted in several Graeco-Persian funerary representations from Anatolia and Phoenicia may have had floors of similar dimensions to those of the Salamis carts (fig. 2:4 shows a detail of a stela from N.W. Anatolia).[47] They do not extend beyond the wheels at front and rear and carry lidded chests, which have often been regarded as coffins. These chests may have contained either a corpse in a contracted position or cremated remains or, perhaps more likely, grave goods.

The entirely open cart buried in Tomb 2 at Salamis would have afforded room for a chest or short coffin, but not for a bier. Until more evidence comes to light, the actual function of the carts at Salamis, perhaps with the exception of these buried in Tomb 79, must remain uncertain.

A different use of carts – in hunting – is apparently illustrated by V 1 (fig. 1). Here the vehicle, its seated driver controlling his mule or ass with reins and a whip, is shown with huntsmen on foot, one of them holding a dead animal, along with three dogs and what is probably a boar by a tree. The function of the cart in this context is obscure. It certainly differs from what we know of the role of vehicles – always chariots – in hunting in the orient at this time: they

---

[46] Beazley 1956, 346 no. 8 (Paris, Cabinet des Médailles 355: one-handled kántharos from Vulci); also Zschietsmann 1928, 26. 44 with suppl. XV: 92.

[47] Borchardt 1968, 192ff. nos. 2–4 with pls. 40f., 47: 2 (our fig. 2: 4), 48, 50 (three stelai from the Daskyleion area near the Hellespont); *The Anatolian Civilisations* II (exhibition, Istanbul 1983) no. B 141 (stela from Sultaniye, Karacabey); Mellink 1973, 298ff. with pl. 45: 7, and 1974, 356f. with pl. 67: 12 (painting in tomb 2 at Karaburun, Lycia); Fleischer 1983, 19f., 44ff. with pls. 1–5, 36–38 (so-called Sarcophagus of the Mourning Women from Sidon). For discussion, see also Weller 1970, 223ff., Metzger 1975; Littauer and Crouwel 1979, 145ff.

were used not merely as conveyances but were also equipped with bows or hand weapons for royal or other hunters accompanied by their drivers and (sometimes) hunt attendants.[48]

Some Cypriote terracotta models give us a glimpse of carts being used for transporting goods or liquids rather than people. Most obvious are the carts, however schematically rendered, carrying large jars for oil or wine TM 7, 9, 15, 20, 22, 39, pls. 59a–b–91). The jars have a wide opening at the top and what may be a tap low down at the back; at least, this is one explanation of the small projection at the centre back seen on TM 20 and apparently also TM 39.[49] Two other models, TM 7 and 9, have two or three of these projections, one in the middle and one at each side – perhaps indicating rather the ends of the lengthwise floor timbers (see s.v. Body).

Carts in Cyprus could clearly be adapted to different usage. This is well illustrated by a model which shows both the pellet-like cushion at the front and a siding all around (TM 33, pl. 83: 4). The latter also appears on other models (TM 11, 26, 31–32, 38, pls. 59a–b–91) and was quite probably designed for transporting farm produce or other bulky material. Indeed, in present-day Cyprus ox-carts can still be seen in the fields.[50]

Concluding Remarks

We have seen that carts are first attested in Cyprus around 700 B.C., i.e. well into the Iron Age, and are documented until the 4th century B.C. (To this century belong two terracotta cart models, TM 21 and 25, if we may judge from the style of their passengers).

At a much later date, in the 3rd century A.D., a cart is illustrated on a floor mosaic from the so-called House of Dionysos at Nea (Kato) Paphos.[51] This ox-drawn cart, mounted on solid disk wheels and loaded with wine skins or sacks of grapes, appears in a mythological scene and does not necessarily reflect vehicles in actual use at the time in Cyprus. There is also an interesting, unprovenanced bronze model of a cart with four-spoked wheels and a female figure

---

[48] See Barnett 1975, pls. 32ff. 102ff. (reliefs of Ashurnasirpal II and Ashurbanipal); Parrot 1961, pl. 345 (wall-painting from Til Barsip); Littauer and Crowel 1979, 133.
[49] See Karageorghis 19736, s.v. no. 69 (our TM 20).
[50] Karageorghis 1973a, 79 with fig. 16: 1–4.
[51] See Vermeule 1976, 101ff. with pl. IV: 2; Karageorghis 1982, 183 with fig. 132.

seated sideways. This model cannot be earlier than the late Roman period, because of the shaft-and-breastcollar harness of the single draught animal, quite probably a horse (pl. 94).[52]

Chariots, in comparison, are also documented from about 700 B.C. onwards, lasting well into Hellenistic times, while in addition we have some evidence for their use in the island at a much earlier date, in the Late Bronze Age.[53]

These differences in the dating of our records for carts and chariots respectively surely do not reflect an actual situation. No doubt carts were used in Cyprus before and after the time of their documentation by representations and actual remains. They could have played an important role in transport, of course, depending on the nature of the terrain. One thinks in particular of their use in conveying bulky and/or heavy goods, such as agricultural produce or building materials.

Nevertheless, carts are only rarely illustrated explicitly in these functions, viz. in particular some terracotta models of vehicles carrying large oil or wine jars (cf. also the models of carts with a siding all around). In Cyprus, as in the Near East, Greece and Italy, wheeled vehicles are usually depicted carrying people rather than goods, thereby reflecting the interests of the artists and their patrons.[54] The vehicles are mostly chariots with standing occupants, but carts with seated or (in Cyprus and Phoenicia) reclining passengers are also shown, albeit much less frequently.

The evidence available for Cypriote carts does not allow us to trace a clear development in their construction. All we can do is to try and assess local and foreign elements.

Let us look first at the carts that were buried, over a period of c. 200 years, in tombs at Salamis, in most cases together with chariots.

---

[52] See Megaw 1953, 135 with n. 14 and pl. IV: a (Nicosia, CM 1952/VII–19/2). This new harness system is first attested in 3rd cent. B.C. China, to be introduced into the west from late Roman times onwards, see Littauer and Crouwel 1979, 9f.; Piggott 1983, 26. 242; Raepset 1982.

[53] For Iron-Age chariots, see Wierner 1968, 72ff.; Wilson 1972, 120ff.; Littauer and Crouwel 1977c. For Bronze Age chariots in the island, see Vandenabeele 1977. (She was incorrect in including Mycenaean vases and terracotta models found in the island among evidence for the use of such vehicles in Cyprus, since they were quite probably imported from mainland Greece). Wheelmarks at the Late Bronze Age sites of Kition and Sinda may be attributed to either chariots or carts or both, see Karageorghis 1976, 61 (Kition, outside city wall); Furumark 1965, 113 s.v. fig. 4 (Sinda, inside city gate).

[54] Cf. remarks by Crouwel 1981, 55.

There is no doubt that the latter were strongly influenced by Near Eastern chariots, both as regards their construction and the harness and means of control of their draught animals.[55] At Salamis the same metal harness parts – bits, blinkers, frontlets, breastplates and shoulder ornaments – were found with the carts. This raises the question of whether the carts themselves were also indebted to oriental prototypes. The multi-spoked wheels, apparently resembling those of the chariots, and the iron bearing shoes for the axle brackets, which can be paralleled in an Assyrian wall painting at Til Barsip,[56] may well suggest influences from that direction. Such influences may perhaps also be assumed in the case of the decorated conveyance for a seated person from the first burial in Tomb 79 (A 4). Its foot support, however, seems to have no parallels in the orient, although something similar is illustrated in 6th century B.C. Greece.[57] Apart from this feature, there is nothing in the carts and chariots from Salamis that is reminiscent of Greek vehicles or harness.

As for the carts illustrated by Cypriote figured documents, the crossbar wheels of some of them can be matched both in the east and west. The use of an arched tilt on carts, either as a protection against the elements or for privacy, is not well documented in either Greek or Near Eastern art of the time. Greek authors, however, refer to covered vehicles in the Achaemenid empire, and the idea may also have come to Cyprus from the east.[58]

We may end by mentioning the unusual position in which passengers are depicted in several Cypriote cart models as well as on a Cypro-Phoenician silver bowl and two terracotta models from Phoenicia – reclining and supporting themselves on one elbow. It is the same pose as that assumed by dinners on a couch – a theme of oriental origin that is often illustrated in Cypriote art.[59]

---

[55] See Littauer and Crouwel 1979, 102ff.

[56] Parrot 1961, pl. 117.

[57] See Lorimer 1903, 144; von Bothmer 1960, 73f. with pl. 7 (lekythos by the Amasis painter).

[58] Höckmann (1982, 148) has suggested that the covered carts in late Etruscan and Roman Italy also derived from the east.

[59] For this theme, which also became popular in Greek and Etruscan art, see especially Fehr 1971; Dentzer 1971 and 1982.

Catalogue

The material in this catalogue, which is not meant to be exhaustive, is categorized as follows:

A   — Actual cart remains
LM — Lead model
SM — Stone models (always limestone)
TM — Terracotta models
V   — Vase-painting

A 1. Cart with two yoked asses ("horses" A and B) (fig. 1). From Salamis, Tomb 2 (first burial). Cypro-Geometric III or early Cypro-Archaic I (find context). Karageorghis 1967, 9ff., 22ff., 118f., 181 (asses, not horses) with figs. II, VI and pls. XVIII, CXV, also 22f. nos. 57–58 with pls. XV, CXVI (iron axle bearing shoes); 1969, 31f. with fig. 4 and pls. 9–12.

A 2. Cart ("chariot A") with two yoked horses (C and A). From Salamis, Tomb 3. Cypro-Archaic I/II (find context). Karageorghis 1967, 31, 33, 51f. with pls. XXXI, XXXV, also 31, 35 no. 11 with pls. XLIX, CXXII (iron axle bearing shoe); 1969, 70f. with fig. 15; Ducos 1967 and 1980 (horses).

A 3. Cart with two yoked horses (G and H). From Salamis, Tomb 47 (first burial). Cypro-Archaic I (find context). Karageorghis 1967, 79, 86, 118 with figs. XXVI–XXVII, XXIX and pls. LXXII–LXXIV, also 80, 86 nos. 4 and 23 with pls. LXXXV, CXLIII (iron axle bearing shoes); 1969, 53 with figs. 5–6 and pls. 17–18; Ducos 1967 and 1980 (horses).

A 4. Cart ("cart/hearse Gamma") (pl. 59a–b). From Salamis, Tomb 79 (first burial). Early Cypro-Archaic I (find context). Karageorghis 1969, 80f. with pls. 37–39; 1973a, 12, 60ff., 76ff., 120ff. with figs. VIII, XI, 5–9 and and pls. XXXVIII–XL, CCXLIX, also 34f. nos. 221/42 and 76 with pls. CIX, CX, CCLX (iron axle bearing shoes).

A 5. Cart ("cart/hearse Alpha"). From Salamis, Tomb 79 (second burial). Cypro-Archaic I (find context). Karageorghis 1969, 85; 1973a, 12f., 66ff., 75f., 120ff. with figs. IX–X and pls. XIX–XX, CCXLVII, also 44f., 67 nos. 416/25 and 42 with pls. LXXIII and CCLII (iron axle bearing shoes).

LM 1. Incomplete cart without siding (fig. 1). From Salamis. Palma di Cesnola 1882, pl. VI: 1a–c; Lorimer 1903, 136.

SM 1. Horse-drawn cart with tilt and female passenger (fig. 1). Vienna, *Kunsthistorisches Museum* I, 635. From Amathus, necropolis; von Schneider 1891, 171f. with ill.; Ohnefalsch-Richter 1983, 479 with pl. CXCVI: 1; Lorimer 1903, 141 (incorrectly said to be of terracotta); Hermary 1981, no. 43 with pl. 10.

SM 2. Horse-drawn cart with tilt. Provenance as SM 1. Ohnefalsch-Richter 1893, 476; Hermary 1981, no. 44 (no ill.).

SM 3. Fragmentary cart without siding carrying reclining male passenger. From Amathus, settlement (French excavations, 1976). Aupert 1977, 792 (no. 76.790.1) with fig. 28.

SM 4. Cart with tilt and male passenger, facing forward leaning on his elbows (fig. 1). From Mersinaki, sanctuary. Westholm 1937, 368 no. 879, 381 with pl. CXVI: 1–2; Bossert 1951, fig. 57.

TM 1. Cart with siding down long sides carrying two reclining passengers, a third one perched on their laps (pl. 61). New York, MMA (Cesnola coll.) 74.51.1792. From Alambra, tomb. Doell 1893, pl. XIV:15 (940); Colonna-Ceccaldi 1882, 132ff. with fig. 4; Cesnola 1894, pl. XIV: 108; Myres 1914, no. 2110 with ill.; Höckmann 1982, 148 with n. 764 and pl. 68:5; Monloup 1984, 158 s.v. no. 600 (= our TM 16).

TM 2. Cart with siding down long sides and reclining male passenger (pl. 62). New York Metropolitan Museum of Art (Cesnola coll.) 74.51. 1794. Provenance as TM 1. Doell 1873, pl. XIV:14 (939); Cesnola 1894, pl. XIV: 113; Myres 1914, no. 2112.

TM 3. Cart with siding down long sides and reclining passenger (pl. 64). New York, MMA (Cesnola coll.) 74.51.1795. Provenance as TM 1. Doell 1873, pl. XIV:16 (941); Colonna-Ceccaldi 1882, 134 with fig. 6; Cesnola 1894, pl. XIV: 112; Myres 1914, no. 2113; de Borghegyi 1970, 21 (ill.).

TM 4. Cart with seated passenger (pl. 65). New York, MMA (Cesnola coll.) 74.51.1793. Provenance as TM 1. Doell 1873, pl. XIV: 13 (938); Colonna-Ceccaldi 1882, 134 with fig. 5; Cesnola 1894, pl. XIV: 110; Myres 1914, no. 2114.

TM 5. Cart without siding (pl. 60). London, BM A 200. From Amathus, (British) Tomb 83. Smith 1900, 113 to 21 with fig. 164; Walters 1903, no. A 200.

TM 6. Cart with siding down long sides (pl. 63). London, BM A 201. Provenance as TM 5. Walters 1903, no. A 201; Wilson 1972, pl. 7:2.

TM 7. Wine or oil cart (pl. 66). London, BM A 197. Provenance as TM 5. Smith 1900, 113 no. 15 with fig. 164; Walters 1903, no. A 197.

TM 8. Cart without siding (pl. 67). London, BM A 199. From Amathus, (British) Tomb 88. Walters 1903, no. A 199.

TM 9. Wine or oil cart (pl. 68). London, BM A 198. From Amathus, (British) Tomb 89. Walters 1903, no. A. 198.

TM 10. Cart without siding (fig. 1). From Amathus, (Swedish) Tomb 9. Cypro-Archaic 11 (find context). Westholm 1935, 57 nos. 8 + 9 + 70 with pls. XVII and CLVII: 20.

TM 11. Cart with siding all around (pl. 69). Limassol, District Museum M. 652/2. From Amathus, (Cypriote) Tomb 159. End of Cypro-Archaic II (find context). Karageorghis 1979a, 44 with fig. 46; 1979b, 681 with fig. 24.

TM 12. Cart without siding carrying passenger, lying down (pl. 70). Limassol, District Museum M. 703/31. From Amathus, (Cypriote) Tomb 189/31. Cypro-Archaic II (find context). Karageorghis 1981, 1008 with fig. 76.

TM 13. Cart with siding down long sides. Amathus, settlement (French excavations, 1976). Mixed find context. Aupert 1977, 792 (no. 76.815.27) with fig. 29.

TM 14. Cart with siding down long sides. Philadelphia, University Museum MS 157. From Amathus. Betancourt 1969, 5 with fig. 2.

TM 15. Wine or oil cart (pl. 71). Nicosia. Cyprus Museum CS 2415/14. From Nicosia, acropolis, tomb. Cypro-Classical I (find context). Karageorghis 1978, 43 with fig. 43.

TM 16. Incomplete cart. From Salamis, settlement (French excavations). Cypro-Archaic II (find context). Monloup 1984, no. 600 (no ill.).

TM 17. Incomplete cart without siding carrying reclining passenger. Provenance as TM 16. Monloup 1984, no. 612 with pl. 30.

TM 18. Cart with tilt (pl. 72). Nicosia, CM C. 36. From Tamassos-*Chomazoudia*, Tomb II. Find context attributed to 6th–5th century B.C. Karageorghis 1973a, 75 with fig. 17; Buchholz 1978, 187 no. 26 with figs. 36: i and 37.

TM 19. Horse-drawn cart with tilt (fig. 1). Athens, National Museum. Provenance unknown. Lorimer 1903, 140f. with fig. 7.

TM 20. Wine or oil cart. Larnaca, Pierides Collection Provenance unknown. Karageorghis 1973b, no. 69 with ill.

TM 21. Cart with tilt and female passenger (pl. 73). Nicosia, CM D. 106. Provenance unknown. Unpublished.

TM 22. Wine or oil cart (pl. 74). Nicosia, CM 1970/IV–16/4. Provenance unknown. Karageorghis 1971, 25 no. 18 with fig. 55.

TM 23. Incomplete cart with siding down long sides and passenger, lying down (pl. 75). Nicosia, CM B. 252. Provenance unknown. Karageorghis 1967, 119 with fig. 21.

TM 24. Cart with siding down long sides and passenger, lying down (pl. 76). Nicosia, CM C. 48. Provenance unknown. Karageorghis 1967, 119 with fig. 22.

TM 25. Cart without siding carrying reclining male passenger (pl. 77). Nicosia, CM C. 37. Provenance unknown. Dikaios 1961, 204 n. 36.

TM 26. Cart with siding all around and passenger, seated at front (pl. 78). Nicosia, CM C. 42. Provenance unknown. Unpublished.

TM 27. Cart without siding (pl. 79). Nicosia, CM (neg. no. C. 11.742). Provenance unknown. Unpublished.

TM 28. Cart with siding down long sides (pl. 80). Nicosia, CM C. 40. Provenance unknown. Unpublished.

TM 29. Cart with very low siding down long sides (pl. 81). Nicosia, CM C. 46. Provenance unknown. Unpublished.

TM 30. Cart with siding down long sides (pl. 82a–b). Nicosia, CM C. 43. Provenance unknown. Unpublished.

TM 31. Cart with siding all around (pl. 85. Nicosia, CM C. 41. Provenance unknown. Unpublished.

TM 32. Cart with siding all around (pl. 84). Nicosia, CM C. 45. Provenance unknown. Unpublished.

TM 33. Cart with siding all around (pl. 82). Nicosia, CM C. 98. Provenance unknown. Unpublished.

TM 34. Cart with siding down long sides and reclining male passenger (pl. 86). New York, MMA (Cesnola coll.) 74.51. 1802. Provenance unknown. Myres 1914, no. 2111.

TM 35. Cart with siding down long sides (pl. 87). New York, MMA (Cesnola coll.) 74.51.1796. Provenance unknown. Myres 1914, no. 2115.

TM 36. Cart with tilt (pl. 88). Oxford, Ashm 1958.18 (formerly Rugby School). Provenance unknown. Littauer and Crouwel 1974, 26 with pl. I: below.

TM 37. Cart with siding down long side (pl. 89). Paris, Louvre N 3305 (formerly Colonna-Ceccaldi Collection). Provenance unknown. Unpublished.

TM 38. Cart with siding all around (pl. 90). Paris, Louvre AM 223. Provenance unknown. Unpublished.

TM 39. Wine or oil cart (pl. 91). Paris, Louvre N 3306 (formerly Colonna-Ceccaldi Collection). Provenance unknown. Caubet 1975–76, no. 87 with ill.

V 1 Ass- or mule-drawn cart with seated occupant (fig. 1). Nicosia, CM 1951/XI-17/4. From Nicosia, Old Municipality, Tomb 4. Bichrome IV jug. Beginning of Cypro-Archaic I (find context). Karageorghis 1966, 108ff. no. 4 with figs. 4–8; Karageorghis and des Gagniers 1974, vol. 1, 16, vol. II, no. 11.4; Flourentzos 1981, 126ff. no. 13 with pl. XII: 10.

Addendum

After the above was written, another Cypriote terracotta model of a "wheeled throne" came to my notice, see Forrer 1932, 94 with figs. 5:3 and 6:3 (here fig. 2:5). Formerly in Forrer's own collection, its present whereabouts are unknown. The object was only briefly mentioned and illustrated in two drawings., its provenance given as "Chypre, fouilles Piéridies-Fossard, 1873" but without reference to a site. As Prof. O. Masson kindly informs me (letter of March 16th 1985), Piérides is almost certainly Dimitrios Pierides of Larnaca (1811–1895), founder of the well-known Pierides collection (see Masson 1961 with nn. 3–4; also Karageorghis 1973b, 9f.).

The model is probably genuine, though the wheels associated with it may not be the original ones. It recalls the "wheeled throne" of TM 4 (pl. 65) but has a high back support. The seated male figure, wearing a conical headdress and holding a cup and a mace, was identified by Forrer as a deity.

16. CHARIOTS WITH Y-POLES IN THE ANCIENT NEAR EAST*

MARY AIKEN LITTAUER AND JOOST H. CROUWEL

The tractive power for all ancient wheeled vehicles was supplied by paired animals under a yoke and on either side of a pole that connected the yoke to the vehicle and transmitted the pull.** The pole also served to turn the car as the animals turned. These were its functions on both four-wheelers (wagons) and two-wheelers (carts or chariots), but on the latter it played another essential role: when the animals were harnessed, a rigidly connected pole, being supported at its far end by the yoke, kept the vehicle upright. Four-wheelers, however, required no support to stay upright, and with a fixed pole there would have been undesirable stress on wagon, pole, and team when the long rigid unit was on uneven ground, with front or rear wheels often in momentary suspension. A vertically articulating pole (not to be confused with the horizontally articulating front axle of later times) would eliminate much of this strain by allowing pole and wagon to tilt independently. Evidence that such a pole existed at least as early as the later third millennium or the beginning of the second millennium B.C. is supplied by metal models of wagons from the Levant.[1] These poles were a type of Y-pole that forked shortly in front of the wagon, the prongs of the fork probably articulating on a bar attached across the wagon front. The double attachment would have been desirable because of the inherent weakness of an

* *Archäologischer Anzeiger* 1977, 1–8.
** We are most grateful to Mr J. Spruytte for discussing the Assyrian chariots and to Dr V. Karageorghis for permission to study and publish the Ovgoros model and its photographs (figs. 3–6); also to Professor J. K. Anderson for first alerting us to certain peculiarities of the chariots of Ashurnasirpal II. The other photographs appear by courtesy of Dr D. von Bothmer and the Metropolitan Museum of Art, New York (pl. 95), of Dr P. Amiet and the Louvre (pl. 96), and of Dr G. R. Meyer and the Staatliche Museen zu Berlin (pl. 98). Finally, we are indebted to Dr Mary B. Moore for the drawing (fig. 1).
[1] Littauer and Crouwel 1973a, 116ff.

articulating connection. This would have been aggravated by the weight of the four disk-wheels and by the fact that metal was sparingly used by the cartwrights of the time.

Another type of articulating pole, an A-pole, the two parts of which only meet at the yoke, is attested also on four-wheelers from Transcaucasia towards the end of the second millennium B.C.[2]

Articulating poles, however, of necessity ended at the front of the vehicle. The rigidly fixed poles on all extant examples of light, spoked-wheeled chariots (two-wheelers) of the Late Bronze Age were single, and were heat-bent at the front of the chariot so as to be able to run all the way under the floor (of woven thongs) and support it at front and rear of the frame.[3]

In the first millennium B.C. the chariot with single pole continues, but is supplemented by the two-poled chariot. Actual remains of such,[4] as well as limestone models[5] and numerous terracotta ones[6] are known from Cyprus. At least one terracotta model comes from the Levant,[7] and two metal models from as far east as Transoxiana.[8] Rock carvings in the Fezzan, south of Cyrene, also show such vehicles very plainly.[9] These chariots were pulled by four horses, under either a single four-horse yoke or two two-horse ones.

It is now of interest to find evidence of the use of still another type of pole on Near-Eastern chariots in the first millennium B.C. – and particularly because it may throw light on some hitherto puzzling details of Assyrian reliefs. Although this is also a Y-pole, it differs considerably from the Y-pole of four-wheelers, and probably has a different inspiration.

Documentation is still very limited, consisting of only three chariot-model groups – two from Cyprus and one from the Levant. The most explicit example is a limestone model said to be from Kourion in

---

[2] Mnatsakanian 1960, 145, fig. 9; Piggott 1968, 193f. fig. 12.

[3] Carter and Newberry 1904, 25; Quibell 1908, 66 pl. 55; Carter 1927, 109; Botti 1951, figs. 1. 2.

[4] Dikaios 1963, 156ff. (tomb 1, second burial); Karageorghis 1967a, 78 (tomb 47, second chariot); Karageorghis 1973a, 73 (tomb 79, chariot B).

[5] Studniczka 1907, 186 with fig. 32; Myres 1914, 145, no. 1016.

[6] Gjerstad 1935 pls. 234. 235; Gjerstad 1963, 10. 13 figs. 9. 4; Studniczka 1907, 167 fig. 15.

[7] Heuzey 1923, 53, no. 187 pl. 5, 1.

[8] Dalton 1964, p. XXXIXf. pls. 4 and 'additional'.

[9] Lhote 1953, fig. 7. 8.

Cyprus (pl. 95). This biga, carrying two occupants, and dating probably to the fifth century B.C., has long been in New York.[10] Its Y-pole is clearly formed of two poles, one coming from each side of the chariot, which converge in front of the box and run forward together to the yoke. It is not a single forking pole, but a composite pole.

Among the numerous terracotta chariot groups from Cyprus, dating from the seventh century B.C. onwards, there is an example with a Y-pole from a sanctuary at Schionia near Ovgoros, in the Famagusta district, presently in Nicosia, which we are privileged to publish here, owing to the kindness of V. Karageorghis (97a–d). The Ovgoros model, which is described in detail in the Appendix, conforms in most respects to the usual Cypriote terracotta models of its period, although it is one of the more explicitly rendered examples of its kind. What is unusual about it, apart from the Y-pole, is the 'squire' leading the team.[11]

The third (bronze) model, although unprovenanced, must have been made in the Levant (pl. 96).[12] Its date is disputed but, in our opinion, falls within the eighth to fourth centuries B.C., and possibly not before the period of Achaemenid domination. This model, formerly in the Collection de Clercq and since 1967 in the Louvre, is unfortunately incomplete as far as its traction system and draught animals are concerned. A Y-pole construction is, however, suggested by the two poles that run under the entire depth of the floor, one along each side, and bend inwards and upwards immediately in front of the box before being broken off. Interestingly, each pole is joined to the front of the box by two supports. One of these is short and straight, running back almost horizontally to near the centre of the front breastwork just above its lower edge. The lack of similar or differently shaped pole supports on the two Cypriote models may be due to the different materials (limestone and terracotta) of which they are made. Some kind of pole support would have been necessary.

---

[10] MMA. 74. 51. 2687. Cesnola 1885, LXXX 520; Myres 1914, 145 no. 1017; Studniczka 1907,185 fig. 30; Littauer, Crouwel and Collon 1976, 76 pl. 10.

[11] This is unusual only for terracottas of war or hunting chariots. Some Phoenician parallels for the squire motif exist with terracotta models of unarmed vehicles; cf. Poulsen 1912, 63 figs. 62. 63; Heuzey 1923, 54f. no. 188 pl. 5, 2. The squire motif with war chariots is found, however, on Assyrian reliefs. Cf. a.o. Barnett (n.d.), pls. 143, 145. 149 (Shalmaneser III, 858–824 B.C.); Barnett and Falkner 1962, pls. 43. 71. 82.

[12] Littauer, Crouwel and Collon 1976, 71ff. pl. 9.

Most important is the light these poles may throw on chariots in Assyrian reliefs of the ninth century B.C. Several years ago the attention of one of the authors was called to two peculiarities of some of the chariots of Ashurnasirpal II (883–859 B.C.).[13] The first is that the draught pole, as it rises from beneath the chariot floor, is shown as impinging on the lower near side of the box.[14] The second is that on several of the same reliefs the pole is doubly outlined on its underside (visible in the area between the chariot front and the horses' buttocks, pl. 98).[15] The first characteristic has, to our knowledge, never otherwise been noted, while the second has only occasionally been remarked but never satisfactorily explained.[16] One explanation for the two features that suggested itself was that they indicated a two-poled chariot. This, however, seemed unlikely. Not only is there no undisputed evidence for such before the late eighth century,[17] but the apparently prevalent trigae of Ashurnasirpal II would not lend themselves to such a traction system. And when we see the rare four-horse chariots of the king being ferried across a river, it is plain that they have but single poles.[18] Moreover, in two-poled harness all four animals were yoked (four to one or two to two yokes). In the ninth century the yoke saddle was still in use,[19] and the number of horses actually under the yoke may be deduced from the number of saddles (as on the ferried chariots) or their reel-shaped finials.[20] Never more than two of these finials are shown (pl. 98), which means that the extra third (and sometimes fourth) horse was a trace horse and that we have to do with a single pole of some kind.

It was only recently, on becoming acquainted with an experiment in making a scale model of a chariot of Ashurnasirpal II by J. Spruytte, a practical driver, that a satisfactory explanation of the two peculiarities became apparent. Without knowledge of the existence of the Y-poled chariot models considered above, and purely as a

---

[13] Personal communication of J. K. Anderson.

[14] This peculiarity is visible on almost all the chariots on reliefs of Ashurnasirpal II, including those being transported on ferries. Cf. Barnett (n.d.) pl. 20.

[15] Meyer 1965, pl. 109. Cf. also Barnett (n.d.), pls. 22 (rear chariot). 25. These peculiarities appear as late as the early 8th century B.C. on a provincial relief: Thureau-Dangin 1931, pl. 7.

[16] Nuoffer 1904, 39 ("reserve pole"); Madhloom 1970, 14 ("subsidiary pole or brake"). A brake would be impossible in this position.

[17] Cf. supra nos. 4–9.

[18] Barnett (n.d.), pl. 20.

[19] Littauer 1968a, 27ff. pls. 4. 5.

[20] James 1974, 31ff.

result of analysing the reliefs on the basis of practical knowledge and experience, Spruytte had arrived at the conclusion that the chariots of this king must have been Y-poled. One pole does indeed rise from the near floor edge of the chariot, and the double outline indicates the presence of a twin pole coming from the opposite floor edge. Were the outline beneath the pole merely to represent a reinforcement of the latter, both would emerge from under the centre of the box.

As to the precise construction of these particular Y-poles — the reliefs of Ashurnasirpal II show each pole as rising almost vertically from the chariot floor before being bent over to run obliquely forward. This sharp angle would seem to exclude the possibility that the two poles are simply heat-bent continuations of the side beams of the floor frame. We may, rather, have to do with poles fitting into what appear to be metal sockets at the front edges of the floor frame. More likely even, if the floor plan was roughly D-shaped as seems to have been the case with Assyrian chariots of this period, the poles may have been set into metal sockets at the front ends of separate straight beams running underneath or alongside the sides of the floor frame but not curving with these at the front.

This type of Y-pole may have been inspired by the A-frame cart of Transcaucasia, with which Assyria must have become acquainted during her campaigns to the north (fig. 1), since it was unknown in Mesopotamia.[21] The pole of such a cart is formed by the continuations of the side beams of the frame, which run forward to join just before the yoke — a type of construction both simple and strong. The limestone model from Kourion (pl. 95), with its clear preservation of the two individual poles, although later than the reliefs, may still indicate such an origin.

Under the earlier system, the single central pole could support a woven-thong floor only at its front and back edges. There seems to be evidence that such floorings continued into the later first millennium B.C.[22] In this case, two poles, formed by the continuation of the side beams of the floor or attached securely thereto, would have given both better support for the vehicle and greater tractive efficiency to the animals, and the lateral stress in turning would have been

---

[21] Piggott 1968, 290, fig. 8.
[22] Cf. a.o. Studniczka 1907,186 fig. 32; Dalton 1964, p. XXXIXf.; Karageorghis 1967a, 49ff.

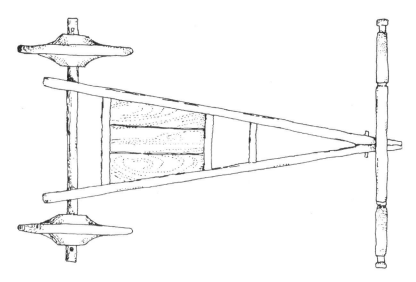

Fig. 1. A-frame cart from Lchaschen, Armenia.

taken by two areas rather than one. These advantages would have been valuable on the heavier-wheeled chariots that appear in the ninth century, with their sometimes increased complement of three men. The unmodified A-pole, although suitable for ox draught, would have spread the horses, thus reducing the compactness and efficiency of control desirable in a chariot. To remedy this, the poles would be bent inwards as well as upwards. The Y-pole in use on Near-Eastern chariots during the first millennium B.C. might well have been devised in this manner.

One might suggest that the true two-poled chariot may equally have had its origin in the A-frame cart, the change in this case consisting in pushing the two poles apart until they ran parallel, rather than bringing them closer together. Such a system would increase the tractive efficiency of the teams in the big four-horse chariots we see in the late eighth and seventh centuries and distribute the yoke pressure equally over all four animals. While there is, as yet, no direct evidence of the two-poled chariot in Assyria herself, the existence of such both to the east and to the west[23] suggests that she would have known it.

---

[23] Cf. *supra* notes 4–9.

Appendix

Description of the terracotta model from Ovgoros, Cyprus (pl. 97a-d). Nicosia, CM, 1955-IX-26/1. Dimensions: max. height: 16,5 cm.; plat-form length: 11,5 cm., ditto, width: 9,5 cm.

Coarse reddish-buff clay, partly handmade, partly moulded (cf. men's heads); roughly finished surface shows signs of original polychromy.

All four wheels originally carrying rectangular platform are now missing; left arm of archer and head of shield-bearer missing. Chariot box subrectangular, with floor apparently extending somewhat beyond siding at rear (cf. New York, MMA example pl. 95). Siding, which reaches to about waist level, has rounded upper rear corners. Vertical division through centre of box, front to back, with vertical loop at back, the latter indicated by horizontal and vertical incisions. Wheels, set somewhat rear of centre, have slightly projecting hubs. Thick Y-pole. Yoke, slightly shaped, has recurving ends; clay pellet at its centre may represent top of pole peg. Yoke pads showing above and below yoke. Each neckstrap of yoke (applied strips) carries an incised tassle at front. Immediately below each yoke end, a disk with pendant strap. Applied, incised strips of clay mark cheekpieces of bits and the cheekstraps that hold these on. Applied oval pieces indicate blinkers. Long strip with incisions in chevron pattern indicates chamfron. Chariot carries complement of three men: driver right front, with archer to his left, shield bearer behind them. The driver's arms are stretched forward, his fists pierced for reins. The archer's right arm is bent, as if to draw a (missing) bow. Both men are bearded and wear high narrow helmets or caps. The shield bearer stands astride the central partition, which may thus have afforded him extra stability. Leaning to the left, he carries on his left arm a shield with spiked central boss, with which he protects the archer. His wide belt is vertically incised and he wears a kind of loin cloth with incised hem. In front, between the horses, strides a man holding each horse by its rein or headstall. He is bearded and wears a conical cap or helmet with long ear flaps extending down to his chest. He is dressed like the shield bearer.

Traces of black and red paint: solid support underneath chariot, black with vertical red stripes; siding of box, black with horizontal red stripes, four on sides and two at front; lower part of loop at rear of box, red; wheel spokes, red (number now uncertain); Y-pole, black with red stripes; yoke, horses' tails, black; black stripes on legs – vertical on hind and horizontal on fore; traces of red on much of harness; men's beards black; chariot complement have alternating black and red vertical stripes on their upper bodies; vertical red stripes on belt of shield bearer; shield, black; upper body of footman painted like those of driver and archer; his beard black, and helmet black with red stripes.

17. NEW LIGHT ON THE ASSYRIAN CHARIOT*

MARY AIKEN LITTAUER

Although details of construction of Assyrian chariots and of the harnessing of their teams may seem very remote from the religious theme of the XXIème Rencontre Assyriologique, it is thanks to cult practices – to that of burying worldly goods with the dead, and that of offering up votive models – that we are better able to interpret Assyrian chariots.** For, despite the fact that these chariots are among the most frequently and most circumstantially represented, the strict profile view in which they, with rare exceptions, appear leaves many things open to doubt, and Assyria herself has yielded neither material remains nor models in the round to help solve this problem. Fortunately, other areas of the Near East are able to furnish us with comparative evidence of this type – some of it come to light only recently.

Egyptian documents, although long- and well-known, have been insufficiently consulted in attempts to understand the parts of Assyrian harness, and they are the earliest for this purpose. The yoke found in a Theban tomb with the 18th-Dynasty chariot now in Florence, and those of the chariots of Tutʿankhamūn (pl. 110)[1] help to interpret the yokes of four unharnessed chariots shown in a 9th-century relief in the British Museum (pl. 111).[2] This is the scene of the river crossing of Ashurnasirpal II and is the only one of this period in which the yokes are not completely distorted, as they are when the

* *Orientalia.* Nova Series 45, 1976, 217–226.
** The author's warm thanks go to Dr. E. Porada, who read this paper in its original form and made valuable suggestions, to Dr. V. Karageorghis who generously permitted examination of the Cypriote material and contributed photographs of the Ayia Irini models, and to Professor J. K. Anderson and Mr. J. H. Crouwel for helpful discussions of the contents.

[1] Carter 1927, 112. 117, pl. XLI; Fox 1951, 15 with pl. 5; Botti 1951, 197 with figs. 1 and 2; Bossert 1942, no. 736. While profile scenes of harnessed chariots do not reveal the shape of the yoke, it is clearly shown in some tomb paintings with workshop scenes: e.g., Wreszinski 1923, pl. 41.
[2] Barnett (n.d.), pls. 16–20; Yadin 1963, 388f. (top register).

artist attempts to show them on a harnessed chariot in side view. It is essentially the same yoke as the Egyptian one, slender and curving, shaped rather like a composite bow. Layard deduced a variety of yokes (pl. 99) – all of them unworkable – from the variety of renderings of the object by different relief artists. If the 9th-century Assyrian yoke is so close to 14th-century Egyptian ones, we may safely extrapolate backwards – if this is necessary for the White Obelisk – and suggest that the yokes shown on that monument would have been the same.[3] A painting in the 15th-century tomb of Rekhmire[4] shows an unharnessed chariot brought by Orientals as tribute. On this the same type of yoke appears; if faithfully oriental and not merely drawn after the Egyptian, it indicates that this sort of yoke was in use at this period further east.

Egypt also explains the two small projections, sometimes likened to dagger hilts,[5] that rise from Layard's yokes (pl. 99) and that appear, doubly or singly, above the yoke area on harnessed horses (pls. 100 and 112). They agree very closely in form with the finials of the yoke saddles found with the six chariots of Tut'ankhamūn (pl. 101) and the chariot in Florence.[6] Such yoke-saddle finials appear frequently (if inconspicuously) on Egyptian representations, although no attempt is made to show more than one of them.[7] They are shown with the saddles on the unharnessed tribute chariot from the tomb of Rekhmire mentioned above.[8] The saddles are documented also for the Aegean region by Linear-B tablets, and were evidently a widely-used means of adapting the ox yoke to equids before the fitted yoke was developed.[9]

Failure to recognize these objects on Assyrian harnessing may have been due to the fact that on harnessed horses the artist shows only the finials, not the legs of the fork. This could be because the horse nearest the viewer was a trace horse – a supposition supported by the circumstance that in the 9th century the end of the yoke is never shown as coming down over the neck of the outside horse (pl. 100),

---

[3] Unger 1932, pl. VIII.
[4] Wreszinski 1923, pl. 337 = Yadin 1963, 189.
[5] Madhloom 1970, 14, 16.
[6] Carter 1927, pl. XLII; Botti 1951, 197 with figs. 1 and 2 (where the saddles are hung on upside down).
[7] E.g. Smith 1958, pl. 110A = Aldred 1961, pl. 93.
[8] Cf. *supra* n. 4. The finial is quite clear on some Neo-Hittite chariots (e.g. Bossert 1942, no. 862 = Yadin 1963, 366). See also James 1974, 31ff.
[9] Littauer 1968a, 27–31.

as it does in the late 8th and 7th centuries B.C., when we have the fitted, 4-horse yoke (pl. 113). We always see it, in a peculiar attempt at foreshortening, entirely *above* the horse's neck, which seems to indicate that this horse is not under it and must be a trace horse.

The forks of the yoke saddles do appear, however, on the yokes of the unharnessed chariots being carried on ferries (pl. 111). The apparent absence of the finials here is likely to have been due to the artist's inability to depict both these and the fanlike decoration that is placed in the same area.

We must go to a provincial draughtsman to find both the finial and the leg of a fork represented – although he has admittedly had a hard time with the yoke end (pl. 114). This is at Arslan Tash,[10] and may indicate that the method of harnessing with yoke saddles existed – in this area at least, as late as the reign of Tiglath-Pileser III. This left-facing equipage, although showing only two horses, has six reins, which points to a three-horse team. If so, then we would suggest that what we see here is one of the pole horses, since he is under the yoke saddle, and that the trace horse must have been the outside horse on the right. Is it pure coincidence that what we seem to see on chariots in Assyria proper is always the trace horse? The great majority of these chariots face right, and we see the right outside horse. True, the yokes on the few left-facing chariots are rendered in the same way, with no yoke-saddle leg visible and, because the six reins on these also indicate a team of three, one would expect in these cases to see the saddle, as at Arslan Tash.[11] Assyrian artists, however, had developed a formula for dealing with chariots, and it is very possible that they found it easier, in the rare cases when they showed left-facing chariots, to use a mirror image of the right-hand horse rather than to copy from life. To the vexed question of the size of the team at various periods and to the methods of harnessing and control we shall return later.

A less functional object that may appear in connection with the pole under Ashurnasirpal II is an engraved disk (pls. 99 and 100).[12] This

---

[10] Thureau-Dangin 1931, 78–80 with pl. 8. We find what is apparently the saddle leg on Neo-Hittite reliefs, where no attempt is made to render the yoke, cf. *supra* n. 8.

[11] Barnett (n.d.), pl. 14; Strommenger 1964, pl. 206 (bottom) = Moortgat 1967, pl. 267 (bottom right).

[12] See also Barnett (n.d.) pls. 26, 27 = Strommenger 1964, pl. 202 (top and center) = Moortgat 1967, pls. 264f.

seems to occur only on royal chariots, which would be the proper place for it if it represents the sun disk, as did that which adorned the Pharaoh's chariot pole in the same area.[13] Both plain and engraved examples from Tut'ankhamūn's tomb were supported on the heads of figurines of hawks, and figurines and disks faced forward,[14] while the Assyrian one was apparently affixed to a vertical rod. It is impossible to tell from the Assyrian documents whether this disk was attached to the yoke itself, as Layard reconstructed it (fig. 1), or sat independently on the pole, as did the Egyptian. The Egyptian examples were made of wood, covered with gesso, and gilded.[15]

From Cyprus comes light on other elements of horse gear, some of which first appear on 9th-century B.C. Assyrian reliefs. Tomb 79 at Salamis has two burials with horses and relatively well-preserved material. The first burial (with a chariot and a 'hearse') was in the late 8th century, and the second (with a similar combination) soon after.[16] Tomb 3 at Salamis, which also contained similar elements of horse gear, has been dated to c. 600 B.C.[17]

In all these burials were found breastplates (pls. 102 and 103) of a shape resembling that of the 'bibs' shown on chariot horses under Tukulti-Ninurta II (pl. 104) and Tiglath-Pileser III (pl. 114) and on ridden horses under Ashurnasirpal II and Shalmaneser III.[18] These were of bronze,[19] with holes along the edge for fastening them onto a leather or cloth backing, from which would depend the fringe that always appears on them in representations. The metal would suggest that they originated for protection. It may be significant that they are regular equipment on the numerous votive models of military chariots from the Cypriote shrine of Ayia Irini (dated roughly

---

[13] Pritchard 1954, pls. 322, 323, 327; Yadin 1963, 192f. 213f. 216. 235.

[14] Carter 1927, 113. 116 with pl. XLIV. The Egyptian artist apparently makes no. attempt to render these hawks.

[15] Three of these hawks were found with the chariots of Tut'ankhamūn. They stood 0.19 m–0.21 m, and were set on concave bases which fitted over the pole. I am indebted to the kindness of Dr. G. E. Mouktar and Dr. H. Riad for permission to examine the objects in Cairo; also to the Griffith Institute, Ashmolean Museum, Oxford for access to H. Carter's notes in the preparation of J. H. Crouwel's publication of the chariots, in which I am collaborating [cf. Littauer and Crouwel 1985].

[16] Karageorghis 1967b; 1969a, 76–98; 1973a.

[17] Karageorghis 1966b; 1967a, 25–54.

[18] Budge 1914, pls. XIV, XV; Barnett (n.d.), pls. 143. 161; Yadin 1963, 384f. 456.

[19] Karageorghis 1967b, fig. 147; 1969a 1. 12. 23ff. 36. 39f. 76. 78. 84–86, with pls. LXXII, LXXVI, XC–XCVII, CXXII, CXXVIII, CCLXXVI, CCLXXVIII; Karageorghis 1966b 33, 35, 38, 49 with pls. XXVIII: 3, XXIX: 3, XLVI: 22, 111, CXXVIII: 111, 22.

625–500 B.C.),[20] but do not appear on 7th- and 6th-century models of purely civilian chariots.[21] Arms too were found associated with
the chariot in Tomb 3, where the breastplates look more functional
than the ones in Tomb 79. In the latter the horses pulling the
'hearses' also wore them, but these were elaborate ones (pl. 102)
that might have constituted a kind of 'parade uniform' – particularly
in a royal funeral. Two similar breastplates of bronze from the other
side of Assyria were found in Burnt Building V at Hasanlu, and are
now on exhibit in the University Museum at Philadelphia, although
not yet published (HAS 72–143a and HAS 72–147a).

Another piece of Assyrian harnessing conspicuous from the time
of Tukulti-Ninurta II to that of Sennacherib (pls. 104, 100 and 106)
has also materialized at Salamis. This is the shoulder disk (pl. 105),[22]
originally hung with tassels. These objects (two to a team) were
of bronze, and ranged from 0.21 to 0.30 m in diameter, with total
lengths of 0.44 m to 0.58 m. Their weight indicates that they could
not have been suspended from the outside rein, as has been suggested.[23] The uneven downward pull on the horse's mouth and the
weight in the driver's hands would have been too great. This is also
clear from such a well-defined and well-preserved relief as that
of Ashurnasirpal II's lion and bull hunt.[24] In this respect, our figure 6 is incorrectly drawn. The disk seems to have hung from the
attachment of the throatband and, since the latter had an unfortunate tendency to rise and press on the horse's windpipe, a pull here
would have done no harm. The object is too small to have afforded
protection, and its original purpose remains unclear.

The earlier chariots from Salamis (those from Tomb 79) were the
only ones found sufficiently preserved to yield information on some
of their structural details. At least the earliest and best-preserved box
of the two, that of chariot *beta*,[25] was not large, and seems to have

---

[20] E.g. Gjerstad 1963, figs. 10–12. 15. On some models the horses are wearing
much larger and more elaborate protection, cf. ibid.
[21] Studniczka 1907, figs. 30, 32; Myres 1914, 145, nos. 1015 and 1017; Reinach
1924, 277, no. 3.
[22] Karageorghis 1969a, 85 with pl. 49; 1973a, 12. 20–24. 36–40. 76f. 82f. 86
113 with pls. LXXVI LXXXIX. CXXI CXXVIII, CCLXXII–CCLXXIV.
CCLXXVI. CCLXXVII.
[23] Karageorghis 1969a, 49 with n. 4; Madhloom 1970, 12. 17 with n. 5. These
conclusions are based on drawings inaccurately interpreting the originals.
[24] Cf. *supra* n. 12.
[25] Karageorghis 1967b, 339–340 with figs. 140. 141; 1969, 78–80 with pl. 36;

resembled in its proportions (hence perhaps in construction) Assyrian 9th-century chariots, rather than the bigger higher-sided ones of its own day.[26] On both it and chariot *delta*[27] a partition divided the box from front to rear. Against this each occupant could brace his inside leg to maintain balance and prevent him from jostling his companion, and it may also have helped to strengthen the construction of the box. At the rear of this partition was found an upright loop of tubular bronze, 0.50 m high. The partition and loop appear on the vast majority of Ayia Irini models (pl. 115a–b)[28] and one of them shows a warrior grasping it as he mounts. A model of a war chariot from Marathus, now in the Louvre, shows that this loop not only formed a handhold for mounting, but served here to carry a lion-head-decorated shield (pl. 117a–b).[29] The loop is wide enough so that a shield hung on it would not swivel loosely, as it would if hung on the narrower end of one of the sides, as has sometimes been suggested. May we not deduce that the appearance of a shield at the rear of Assyrian chariots in the 9th century (pl. 115)[30] (and on 8th-century neo-Hittite ones as well?)[31] indicates a similar loop – even if the strictly profile view prevents this from showing on the reliefs? And was there a partition in these also? It seems very possible. Cypriote

---

1973a, 68–74 with figs. 10–13 and pls. XXI–XXIV, CCXVIII. The box and wheels of this chariot were better preserved than the poles and yoke. The chariot has been unfortunately reconstructed (ibid. figs. 10–11) with straight poles which, with a wheel diameter of 0.90 m and a level floor (such as one sees on all chariots except some in late Roman racing and mythological scenes), would only fit draught animals ca 0.45 m high. The yoke, too, is reconstructed as a heavy ox yoke, rectangular in section. It is neither the earlier Assyrian horse yoke discussed above (cf. our pls. 99, 110 and 111) with proper yoke saddles (our pl. 100), nor the later fitted yoke (our pls. 118–119). Nor would the spacing of the animals be proper as shown on the reconstructed yoke.

[26] Hrouda 1965, pl. 26, compare fig. 3 with fig. 4.

[27] Karageorghis 1969a, 81–85 with pl. II; (3) 74f. with pls. XXVIII–XXXI. CCL–CCLI.

[28] Gjerstad 1963, figs. 11 and 13, where the loop is visible. Both loop and partition have been confirmed by autopsy of the large collection of models from Ayia Irini in the Nicosia Museum.

[29] Heuzey 1923, 53 with pl. V: 1; Studniczka 1907, 168, no. 17.

[30] For the shields: Hrouda 1963, pl. 23: 22f. For the toothed shield on chariots: Barnett (n.d.), pls. 24f. = Yadin 1963, 386f. = Moortgat 1967, 267 (upper register), see also lower register here. For lion-headed shields on chariots: Barnett (n.d.), 160 (bottom reg.). 161 (top reg.). 164. 169. 170 (top reg.); for combination of teeth and lion's head: Budge 1914, pl. XXV = Yadin 1963, 455.

[31] For shields on neo-hittite chariots: Bossert 1951, no. 488 and Bossert 1942, 886 = Meyer 1965, pl. 90. A shield with simple boss appears on the well-known reliefs from Charchemish: Bossert 1942, 862 = Yadin 1963, 366.

horse gear in general shows a strong Assyrian influence, not only as noted above, but in details of bridling and head protection as well.[32] The partition on some Cypriote models seems rather wide (pl. 116a–b), and one may suggest that it may also have been sometimes used as a temporary (and welcome) seat. On both of the gold models from the Oxus Treasure there is such a narrow seat running from front to back.[33] If we are correct in assuming that the partition obtained under Ashurnasirpal II, its existence both east and west of Assyria at later periods would suggest that it is likely to have continued there in the 8th and 7th centuries B.C., when the larger chariots would have afforded it ample room.

The shield, moreover, would have acted as a partial closure and leg protection behind. This may well have been replaced by a door on the high-sided, rectangular boxes that we find from Tiglath-Pileser III on.[34] There is no shield here any more (it may be inside the chariot) and the thick mounting tassels attached to the rear corners of the box (pls. 106 and 107) argue for the absence of the loop as a handgrip. Although we have no evidence of this from models or remains, such a door would help to brace the new, high sides, and the toggle-fastened strap that appears on the left side of chariot boxes under Ashurbanipal may point to such, while Xenophon writes of closed chariots in Persian times.[35]

The finds in the Salamine tombs,[36] as well as the Cypriote models and the model from Marathus, amply confirm the existence of four-horse teams in the 7th century – a fact already clear from three different representations of unharnessed four-horse fitted yokes, one under Sargon in the 8th century (pl. 118) and two under Sennacherib in the 7th (pl. 119).[37] This raises the still-vexed question of how these quadrigae, as well as the three-horse teams, were harnessed, and of how early the four-horse team first appeared.

Under Ashurnasirpal II six reins and three heads largely prevail, yet we occasionally see eight reins (pl. 112),[38] and the four horses

---

[32] Littauer and Karageorghis 1969.

[33] Dalton 1964, XXXVII–XL with figs. 20. 21 and pls. 4 and "addition".

[34] See also Barnett and Falkner 1962, pls. XVI, LXXXIII; Meyer 1965, pl. 161; Potratz 1966, pl. XXV: 57. XXVIII: 63. VIII: 14 = Yadin 1963, 452.

[35] Strommenger and Hirmer 1964, pl. 248; Xenophon, *Cyropaedia*, VI, iv. 9.

[36] Chariot *Beta* in Tomb 79 was a quadriga.

[37] The relief in this illustration is broken off just where the outer arch of the left side of the yoke would come. For the second chariot see Yadin 1963, 430.

[38] Barnett (n.d.), pls. 24. 25 = Yadin 1963, 386–387 = Moortgat 1967, 267 (top register).

being swum behind the king's ferried chariot point to a quadriga.[39] It has been suggested that the yokes seen on the ferried chariots were rendered in a clumsy manner that made them look shorter than they were, and that they actually extended over the necks of the four horses, the 'fittings' (i.e., the yoke saddles) being only for the pole horses.[40] But we have seen how closely these yokes resembled the Egyptian ones in detail and proportions. The yoke saddles of Egyptian yokes were also attached near the ends of the yoke arms, as they are shown on the ferried chariots (pls. 110 and 111).[41] Moreover, nowhere do we have evidence of such a hybrid yoke as that postulated, in which part of the team would be under yoke saddles and the other part under shaped embrasures of the type seen on Sargon's and Sennacherib's yokes (pls. 118 and 119). Nor would the slender Egyptian yoke, roughly round in section, be suitable for such a purpose. If three or four horses were sometimes used at this period, the outer animals may have been connected with the yoke horses at the girth and/or there may have been some connection such as that seen on recent Hungarian equipages (pl. 120), although these are not under yoke harness. The failure in such a circumstantial art as the Assyrian to show a trace going back to the box, as we see on even the most stylized of Greek black-figured vases,[42] surely indicates that this was not the manner by which the outside animals were attached. That these outside horses, whether one or two, were not under the yoke is also suggested by the fact, noted above, that the yoke is never shown as coming down over the side of the nearest horse's neck in the 9th-century reliefs.

This premise is supported by incontrovertible evidence from western Asia, furnished us again as a result of cult practice. It is that of a bronze model found in Tumulus P at Gordion[43] and now in Ankara, the tomb dated to c. 700 B.C. (pl. 121). It clearly shows that the yoke terminates on the outside of the pole horse and is not broken off.[44] Note that the wheels of this fragmentary model, in both design

---

[39] See *supra* n. 2.
[40] Madhloom 1970, 16 with pl. X: 3.
[41] The bearing parts of the Tutʿankhamūn saddles were bound with leather, the remains of which can be seen in fig. 13; the bound parts near the yoke ends were for the attachment of the yoke saddles.
[42] E.g. Arias and Hirmer 1962, pl. XI, figs. 36f. (top), 100 (top).
[43] Kohler 1964, 59f. with pl. XVIII: 2.
[44] While the right part of the yoke has been broken, the left part is intact and extends only over the left pole horse. This is confirmed by autopsy. See also Kohler 1964, pl. XVIII: 2.

and proportions, and in their number of spokes, resemble Assyrian wheels of the 9th century.

Although we have no material evidence or documents in the round from the Near East itself to testify to three-horse hitches, it was probably a triga of Asia Minor that Homer described.[45] Trigae are represented in Late Geometric art in Greece proper and at least once in the 7th century B.C.[46] They are more popular in Etruscan racing scenes in the 6th and 5th centuries, and there is some evidence of them even later.[47] At the other end of the world, in the Mongolian Altai, we find a representation of a triga (pl. 108), and a religious motive may have inspired the rock art in which it appears.[48] Here the third horse seems to be connected by its neck to both the girth of a pole horse and, in the Greek manner, to the chariot. This carving is not directly datable, but Volkov, who discovered and published it, places it at the end of the second or beginning of the first millennium B.C.

What could have been the purpose of such a hitch where the extra horse added little or no pulling power? Yadin noted the count of three horses to one chariot in records of booty taken in the Late Bronze Age.[49] Considering the fragility of horses' limbs and digestive tracts under stress, even without the factor of battle wounds, and what must have been the frequent difficulty of replacing such especially trained animals locally, it is only natural that reserve horses would accompany the chariotry. There seems no evidence, however, before the 9th century, of their having been driven with the team. And although they would indeed have been more vulnerable if attached when in action, that is also when they would be most needed.

For the king's chariot and those of a few important individuals, such as the standard bearers, two spare horses, rather than one, might have been added; and it is on just such chariots that we see the eight reins, rather than the usual three, meticulously depicted (pl. 112).[50]

The comparatively small, low chariots seen under Ashurnasirpal

---

[45] Iliad XVI, 145–154. 467–476.

[46] E.g. Davison 1961, figs. 21. 23. 26. 35. 36; Kübler 1950, figs. 39–40.

[47] Bronson 1965, with pls. XIV and XV, see particularly 102–104; Brown 1974.

[48] Volkov 1972, 78f. (In Russian). The author is indebted to the kindness of Dr. K. Jettmar for this reference.

[49] Yadin 1963, 88f.

[50] See *supra* n. 2.

II which, with few exceptions save that of the royal vehicle, carried only two people, and the relative scarcity and awkward horsemanship of the mounted troops suggest that, at this time, at least part of the chariotry was still a light, fast, flanking and pursuing arm. This would require considerable manœuvrability, a manœuvrability still possible if the extra horses were attached only by traces, as they were on Greek and Etruscan racing chariots, which were required to make many turns at high speed. All four horses under the yoke would have created a highly rigid equipage, and one that would have been a particular liability in the campaigns into the mountainous north and east.

Eight reins handled in the manner in which they are so carefully depicted (pl. 112),[51] with a rein passing individually between each pair of fingers and between forefinger and thumb, would be very awkward to handle. It never seems to have occurred to the Assyrians to knot them into two bundles, as did Greek quadriga drivers.[52] Neither did they combine them in the modern way, in which only half the actual number of reins reach the driver's hands, and the majority of them are always held in the left hand, giving the right hand the possibility of adjusting them. This situation would encourage efforts to diminish the number of reins as quadrigae became more frequent. We may suggest that a method still known today in primitive driving was employed then. Nagel already postulated such an arrangement,[53] but was evidently not aware that there was documentary confirmation from close by. A Cypriote terracotta model from Ayia Irini (pl. 116a–b) may perhaps shed light here also. This shows straps joining the noses of four horses, bit end to bit end. On most of these models the reins have been broken off and lost, and on some examples even the applied strips of clay representing the headstall have been lost. It is impossible to tell how many other models (if any) may once have had similar connecting lines. Textual references to the use of six reins for controlling four horses occur in the Western Chou period (1027–771 B.C.) in China.[54] The manner in which this reduction might have been effected is illustrated by an

---

[51] See also *supra* n. 12.
[52] E.g. Beazley 1951, pl. 9 (center); Richter 1949, figs. 107 and 111; Arias and Hirmer 1962, pl. XI.
[53] Nagel 1966, pl. 73.
[54] von Dewall 1964, 44. 180.

engraving on a bronze vessel from late in the Eastern Chou period (probably 5th–4th centuries B.C.).[55] The noses of each pair of horses on either side of the pole are joined and the only real rein on each outside horse is the outer one.

We would like to suggest here the possibility that the line we see behind the yoke in 7th-century Assyrian scenes (pls. 106, 109a and 113), which has so often been explained as the continuation of the outside rein running back not to the driver's hands, but to the box, may not be a rein at all, but something quite different, i.e. a yoke brace. This element of harnessing consisted of a pair of straps, running out diagonally from the pole to either arm of the yoke inside the horses. Very long braces are visible in representations of unharnessed chariots in Egyptian tribute-bringing or workshop scenes,[56] shorter ones on Ashurnasirpal's chariots being ferried across the river (pl. 111); they are found as far afield as Central Asian petroglyphs,[57] and in China are attested on Shang pictographs, as well as on engraved bronze vessels of the late Eastern Chou period.[58] In the west we still find them in Etruria in the 3rd century B.C. on the remaining pole and yoke from a life-sized bronze chariot in Florence.[59]

The purpose of these yoke braces was to prevent the yoke from swivelling on its pin, as it would if one horse of the team went considerably faster than the other (as on turns), which would either cause the yoke to assume an undesirably oblique position across the horses' necks or force the slower of the pole horses' hind legs up against the pole, with the consequent danger of the latter being kicked to pieces. At the same time, the braces took some of the pull off the area of junction of pole and yoke and transferred part of it to an area further back on the pole, as well as distributing it to two other areas on the yoke.[60]

These evidently essential elements of the yoke-and-pole harness are not shown on the four-horse yokes of Sargon and Sennacherib (pls. 118 and 119), yet these longer, hence proportionately weaker,

[55] Weber 1968, fig. 69: f.
[56] E.g. Yadin 1963, 189. 194. 202; Wreszinski 1923, 269. 337.
[57] Volkov (post) 1969, figs. 3 and 5.
[58] Hančar 1956, Abb. 9: 3; Weber 1966, figs. 26d and 27d.
[59] Alberti-Parronchi and Piccardi 1950–51, fig. 1.
[60] I am greatly indebted to Mr J. Spruytte, who has experimented with reconstructing and driving ancient pole-and-yoke harness, for confirming this empirically by driving both without and with the yoke braces.

yokes would sustain considerable strain if the outside horses did not keep pace with the pole ones, and would particularly need support near their ends. It would be difficult, however, to run braces back from the ends of a four-horse yoke to the pole, since the pole lay lower than the backs of the horses, which would thus be in the way of the braces. An alternative would be to run the braces at a height where nothing would interfere with them, which would mean having to run them back to the chariot itself, rather than to the pole. The bowknot at the yoke end in pls. 106 and 109a would indicate the brace's manner of attachment there. In the famous relief of Ashurbanipal's lion hunt this bow appears on those chariots already harnessed and in motion,[61] while in the preliminary harnessing scene (pl. 113) the bow is not yet tied. There is a slip knot at the chariot end in what seems an intention to make the line easily adjustable. On turns, for instance, it might be desirable to slacken the brace on the outer side of the turn – although within distinct limits, for the reasons pointed out above.

If we look at some of the chariots of the preceding century – of Tiglath-Pileser III (pl. 107), for instance,[62] we may perhaps see a stage in the conversion of this element. Here an effort is made to indicate the second line, as well to record the well-observed fact that at each bound of the gallop there would be a slight slackening of the line as the horses' heads came up, since the pole would have been somewhat limber. The yoke braces do not seem yet, however, to be attached at the yoke ends, but nearer the center, as on earlier yokes. That their attachment to the box was near its center rather than at its corners even in the 8th century seems illustrated by a comparison of pls. 109a–b, from the mural of the lion hunt at Til Barsib. The element is present on all chariots, but on those of the hunt attendants, with dead lions hung over the front, the attachments to the box are obscured by the animal, which lies between them and the corner quiver.

If Assyria herself refuses to oblige with further information about her chariots, let us hope that peripheral regions will continue to yield the type of material that can bring indirect light to bear on this very important element of her warfare and prestige.

---

[61] Strommenger and Hirmer 1964, pls. 248 and 253.
[62] See also Barnett and Falkner 1962, pls. XLIV and LXXXIII.

18. ASSYRIAN TRIGAS AND RUSSIAN DVOIKAS*

M. A. LITTAUER AND J. H. CROUWEL

Much has been written about chariots with three-horse hitches in antiquity. Although the triga's use in racing is generally accepted, its suitability for the battlefield is more often questioned. Greek evidence for its use is found in the *Iliad* and in a few figured documents of the 8th century B.C. and later (Wiesner 1968, 20–2, 66; Chamoux 1975).[1] In Italy the triga was known to both the Etruscans and the Romans (Bronson 1965; Humphrey 1985, 16f.). In the Near East more controversial evidence is found in 9th century B.C. Assyrian reliefs of war and hunting chariots, for which its "asymmetrical" hitch has been considered impractical (Bronson 1965, 102; Nagel 1966, 54; Jacobs 1984–85, 157). This note is to point to the possibility that Ashurnasirpal II's chariots may *not* have been unbalanced despite the asymmetrical harnessing (fig. 1).

All ancient harness systems were based on the use of paired animals on either side of a *central* pole and under a yoke. Consequently, a third horse, added to one side or the other would, by apparently increasing the pull on one side, seem to throw the equipage out of balance; it should move in a circle, like an insect with a broken wing. Indeed, in the racing chariot this has been interpreted as intentional and as helping to cope with the sharp 180° turns of the ancient circus. But it must have been possible to keep the one-sided extra power in reserve for the turns, for the outrigger cannot have affected the movement of the chariot on the straightaways that constituted the many laps of the ancient chariot race.

The possibility of the practical functioning of an asymmetrical hitch may be demonstrated by a recent traction system, although it is not the same as the triga. While everyone knows the Russian *dvoika*, with

* *Iraq* 53, 1991, 97–99.

[1] There is yet no evidence for trigas in Cyprus. The remains identified by Chamaux as those of a triga in royal tomb 79 at Salamis were actually those of a quadriga. His objection (i.e. that the space between the poles of this two-poled chariot was too small for two inner animals) has been disproved experimentally by Spruytte (1978–89, 55, n. 6).

Fig. 1. Assyrian chariot of Ashurnasirpal II, Nimrud, Berlin, Vorderasiatisches Museum 959. After Littauer and Crouwel, 1979, Fig. 53.

its trotter between the central shafts and the outriggers, was the more common, particularly in the early 19th century (pl. 122). It has been far less often illustrated in recent times than the more spectacular *troika*.

The dvoika points rather clearly to the origin of this Russian draught system in the need to bring along reserve or spare horses. Distances were great and the Russian roads were notorious for their deep mud and potholes during the long spring thaws and under the autumn rains. In this system, whether it was a *troika* or a *dvoika*, the fast trotter between the shafts did the work, while the outrigger or outriggers were kept at an easy canter. The shafts went directly to the axle just inside the front wheels (these were four-wheelers: they were reinforced by heavy ropes and/or steel cables that went to the axle *ends*, outside the wheels. The front wheels were kept small enough to place the shafts at an angle that helped the shaft horse to pull them out of potholes. The galloper or gallopers, on the other hand, were attached to swingle trees suspended from wooden "cranes" hanging out much higher up from the sides of the quite narrow vehicle (pl. 123). The only assistance they really gave was in helping to pull the larger, back wheels out of the holes in an emergency.

The unusual use of two different gaits was based on the fact that the trot is the smoothest gait for the passengers, jerking the vehicle much less than the gallop. A fast trot, however, is more tiring to the horse than a canter or an easy gallop. The spare horse (or horses), moving at athe latter gait and taking no part in the normal traction, would be fresh when transferred between the shafts.

Although the case of the *dvoika* may demonstrate that it is possible for a single outrigger to be attached so that it has no effect on the movement or direction of the vehicle, other arguments have been advanced against the use of such a horse with the war chariot. Bronson (1965, 102) protests that "being on the outside, it would be the first to be killed". We are not certain whether it was on the "outside" (i.e. the side exposed to the enemy), but this would surely be the better place for it. Were it killed, it would be easy to cut it loose and leave it behind, whereas a slaughtered pole horse would stop the chariot entirely.

The outrigger that seems to appear on the Assyrian battle and hunting fields in the 9th century B.C. (fig. 1) was obviously even more loosely connected than was that of the Russian *dvoika*.[2] It must have been attached either directly to the pole horse next to it or to the end of the yoke on that side. The first would be more likely to interfere with the pole horse's movement and to disturb it. A connection to the yoke, however, finds an early – although neither close nor continuous – parallel in the harnessing of the four animals of the 3rd-millennium B.C. Tell Agrab metal model, where the collars of the outriggers are attached to the ends of the yoke.[3] Among the numerous straps and fittings of the 9th century B.C. Assyrian outrigger that are securely fastened in the area just in front of the withers (i.e. in a line with the yoke) (Littauer and Crouwel 1979, 115f.), there is certainly one by which the even less direct effect on the vehicle than had the asymmetric hitch of the Russian dvoika.

Although the Russian reserve horse originated for travel, a reserve horse in battle would ideally be to replace one injured by weapons or disabled by hoof or leg injuries, to which horses are particularly suceptible (Littauer and Crouwel 1979, 128). Prior to the invention of horseshoes, this would have caused a special problem on an obstacle-strewn field. From the later 8th century B.C. onwards, however, as Assyrian chariots become bigger and heavier and carry larger crews, we see only quadrigas with *all* four horses under yoke.[4]

---

[2] Outriggers may perhaps also implied on the earlier White Obelsik, see Littauer and Crouwel 1979, 86, n. 27. 113, n. 59.

[3] Littauer and Crouwel 1979, 86, n. 29 with fig. 7.

[4] The latter harness system is shown, together with elements of 9th-century type, on two unprovenanced, provincial (?) fragments of sheet bronze, see Seidel 1986.

19. METAL WHEEL TYRES FROM THE ANCIENT NEAR EAST*

MARY A. LITTAUER AND JOOST H. CROUWEL**

Within recent years several more pieces of a puzzle in early wheel construction have come to light or have been re-examined. This material consists of segments of copper or bronze tyres of a distinctive design.

In 1955 A. Haller and W. Andrae listed three broken fragments from a hoard beneath a temple at Ashur simply as "Beschläge". In 1984 M. H. Pottier reported fourteen such fragments from the Afghan market; these may possibly have come from the Bactrian area. In 1987 F. Tallon reconsidered the early metalwork excavated at Susa, among it two groups composed of six and twelve "bandages de rue" respectively. In the same year four fragments of a tyre and a fragment of a fifth appeared in a private collection in Holland, ostensibly from Iran. The new material and the re-examination of the old provide us with the occasion to re-appraise the role of these metal objects in the history of wheeled vehicles.

Catalogue

A 1–6. Paris, Louvre Sb 6829, pl. 124.

Provenance: Susa, Apadana area. Found on floor above skeleton of equid, together with pair of linch pins and other metal object.

Condition: segments more or less complete.

Bibliography: Mecquenem 1922, 137f., fig. 14; 1924, p. 111; 1943, p. 90, fig. 74:1; Salonen 1951, 114f., fig. 7; Littauer and Crouwel 1979, 39[10] (incorrectly attributed to tomb K); Tallon 1987, (I) 301, 305f., 351, (II) p. 127 and ill. p. 337 (no. 1304).

* In: *Archaeologia Iranica et Orientalis. Miscellanea in Honorem Louis Vanden Berghe*, edenda curaverunt L. de Meyer et E. Haerinck. Vol. 1, Gent, 1989, 111–121.
** This article has been revised by M. A. L.

B 1–12. Paris, Louvre Sb 14672–14677 and one unnumbered fragment; Teheran, Iran Bastan Museum (four segments); pl. 125.

Provenance: Susa, Donjon tomb A 89 (originally called 89b). Found with human skeleton, together with cylinder seal, three metal vases, three metal arrow heads, dagger and axe.

Condition: segments varying from complete to fragmentary.

Bibliography: de Mecquenem 1943, p. 89f., fig. 74: 2f.; pl. X:1; Littauer and Crouwel 1979, p. 39, 69, fig. 19; Tallon 1987, (I) 302, 305f., figs. 45f., (II) p. 128 and ill. p. 336 (no. 1305–1307).

C 1–5. Holland, private collection; fig. 1; pl. 126.

Provenance: probably Iran (acquired on Teheran market in early 1960's).[1]

Condition: four segments more or less complete, the fifth fragmentary. Unpublished.

D 1–3. Berlin, Vorderasiatisches Museum VA 5027, 5024, 5020; fig. 2-right.

Provenance: Ashur, beneath Temple of Ashur. Part of a hoard of metal objects contained in a terracotta vessel.

Condition: fragmentary.

Bibliography: Haller and Andrae 1955, p. 12, pls. 26:f, 27:e (our fig. 2-right), s; Tallon, 1987, (I) 306.

E 1–14. Present whereabouts unknown. fig. 2-left.

Provenance: seen on Afghan market in 1970's or early 1980's; reputedly from a tomb in Bactria (northern Afghanistan).

Condition: not reported (the one illustrated almost complete).

Bibliography: Pottier 1984, 49, 110, fig. 44 and pl. XLIV, (no. 326); Tallon 1987, (I) 306.

---

[1] Two of these objects (C 4–5) bear the number '683' in red paint on their interiors. This might simply be the dealer's stock number, though in Teheran we would perhaps expect that to be in Arabic numerals. In might also represent an excavation number and it may not be entirely coincidental that the objects excavated at Susa in the 1890's also have numbers painted in red. This number, is, however, occupied by an inscribed brick in de Morgan's inventory (information F. Tallon). Moreover, no finds of metal tyre segments were recorded in the published account of his excavation (de Morgan 1900).

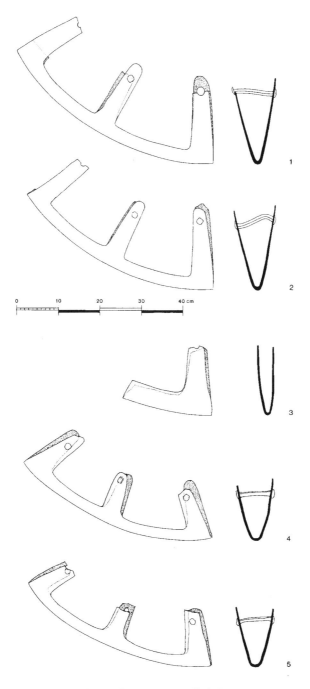

Fig. 1. Tyre segments C 1–5.

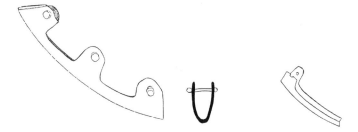

Fig. 2-left Tyre segments E 1, "Bactria".   Fig. 2-right Tyre segment D 1, Ashur.

Discussion

The metal – copper or bronze – the technique, dimensions and form of these tyre segments are so similar that they all must belong to the same clearly defined type. In two cases the find contexts help to date them:

1. The segments from tomb A 89 in the Donjon area at Susa (B 1–12) were found together with an axe of so-called *Attaḫušḫu* (or *Addaḫušḫu*) type, named after a ruler of Susa (c. 1900/1800 B.C.), who left examples with votive inscriptions bearing his name.[2] This type of axe has, however, a longer history than his reign, covering also the Ur III and Isin-Lars periods.[3]

2. The tyre fragments from Ashur (D 1–3) formed part of a hoard of metal objects which had a *terminus ante quem* of the reign of Šamši-Adad I. (c. 1812–1781 B.C.), who founded the temple of the god Ashur overlying it.[4] The hoard has been placed at the end of the third millennium B.C., though two human figures in it have been variously described as "Early Dynastic" or "Akkadian".[5]

Dating information of a different kind is yielded by the illustration of a wheel of somewhat similar type on a fragment of a stone stela of Gudea of Lagaš found at Girsu (Tellō) (fig. 3).[6] There are

---

[2] Calmeyer 1969, 46–48.
[3] Carter and Stolper 1984, 26 and 28.
[4] Calmeyer 1969, 39.
[5] Braun-Holzinger 1984, 14f. nos. 43f.; cf. Haller and Andrae 1955, 12 (end of Early Dynastic period).
[6] Boese 1975, 202, pl. 111: b; for other fragments of this stela (in Berlin, Paris and Istanbul) and a tentative reconstruction, see ibid. 199–202, fig. 36: a–b; cf. also Littauer and Crouwel 1979, 39, fig. 18: b (= our fig. 3).

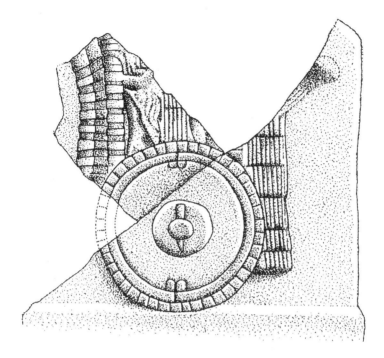

Fig. 3. Fragment of stela of Gudea of Lagash, Girsu (Tello).

also texts of similar Ur-III date that may refer to metal wheel tyres.[7] The tyre segments are V-shaped in cross-section. Each has three pairs of clamps or lobes that extended inwards on the wheel – a pair at either end and another in the center. The clamps have holes near their rounded ends, through which a stout rivet passed. Thus each segment was secured at three points to the fabric of the wheel. Traces of the latter's wood remain inside some tyre segments belonging to B 1–12 as well as inside C 4; the grain can be seen to run with the tyre segments.

The material of these objects has usually been described simply as "copper" or "bronze". Metal analyses are now available for the

---

[7] CAD s.v. *ḫuppu* D. AHw s.v. *ḫūpu(m)*; Limet 1955, 82; 1960, 128f., 213 no. 52; cf. Salonen 1951, 114–147. Dr. F. A. M. Wiggermann (personal communication) regards the interpretation of *ḫuppu* as a tyre possible in the texts where the term is associated with a wheel (*dubbin*, now read as *umbin*) or a vehicle. Doubts are, however, raised by the low weight of the copper *ḫuppu* recorded (varying from c. 0.17–1.8 kg.; one actual tyre segment, C 4, weighing as much as 2.4 kg.) and the fact that there is never a hint of it having been made in more than one piece.

examples from Susa and those in Holland. A 1–6 from Susa are of copper, with a little tin (varying from 1.35 to 1.85%) and arsenic (varying from 0.61 to 1.1). The one analysed fragment belonging to B 1–12, also from Susa, is a tin-bronze, containing 1.85% tin.[8] Tyre fragments C 2 and 3, now in Holland, are also tin-bronze, with 6.27 and 8.23% tin respectively; in contrast, the one analysed bolt of C 2 is of copper, with 0.72% arsenic (see Appendix II).

According to the cuneiform texts that possibly refer to such metal wheel tyres, they are not of "bronze" (*zabar*) but of "copper" (*urudu*). It has recently been suggested that the latter does not indicate pure copper but an alloy with arsenic.[9]

With regard to their technique of manufacture, the tyre segments were probably cast directly into shape. Bending of metal sheets into the required shape should well lead to their breaking. The rivets were inserted after the tyre segments had been fitted around the wheel rim.[10]

The dimensions of the segments all fall within the limited range but, at the same time, no example exactly duplicates any other – even within the same group (see Appendix I).

Although spoked wheels begin to appear in the Near East in the early second millennium B.C.,[11] these tyre segments are unlikely to have been used with them. The clamps project inwards by up to 0.175 m. with holes not far from their ends. All early spoked wheels so far documented had slender, heat-bent felloes of little depth. Even the one set of wheels of Tut'ankhamūn that incorporated a wooden tyre reached only a total depth of 0.083 m.[12]

Impressions of the grain of the wood remaining inside one of the segments of B 1–12 from Susa show the same piece of timber extended to full depth of the clamps, i.e. it would have been some 0.153–1.666 m. thick.[13] As G. Kossack has shown, there are distinct limitations to the degree to which a length of timber of a certain thickness can be heat-bent to form a felloe. He suggests that a thickness of some-

---

[8] Tallon 1987, (II), 127f.
[9] See Waetzold and Bachmann 1984, especially 16. For the texts possibly referring to metal wheel tyres, see *supra* n. 7.
[10] For recent reviews of early metallurgy in Mesopotamia and Iran, see Moorey 1982a (cf. 87f. on Susa) and 1982b.
[11] Littauer and Crouwel 1979, 48ff.; also 1986.
[12] Littauer and Crouwel 1985, 27 (chariot A 4).
[13] Tallon 1987, (I), 305 (no. 1306).

thing like 0.065 m. for a wheel of 0.80–1.00 m. in diameter.[14] The alternative, with a spoked wheel, would be for the clamps to be riveted though the spokes. This, however, would tend immediately to split the spokes. It would therefore seem that these tyres must have been used on disc wheels. Moreover, as J. Spruytte has kindly pointed out to us, the tyre, which is V-shaped in cross-section, would require a V-shaped folloe, quite unsuitable for receiving the ends of the spokes.[15]

Disc wheels were the usual type of wheel in the Near East before the turn of the third millennium B.C. Some sort of tyres is documented by both actual remains and representations of wheels and, indeed, would be predicated by necessity. The solid wooden wheels, which were normally made of three rather than a single piece, would often have required more than external slats or internal dowelling to hold them together, to cover the joins at the rim where dust or pebbles could easily penetrate to damage the fabric, and in general to protect the running surface of the tread. (On tripartite disc wheels, the tread, if unprotected, would quickly wear differentially because part of it ran with the grain and part across the grain.)[16]

Tyres were present on some disc wheels belonging to vehicles which were buried in graves of the Early Dynastic period, traces of a substance that may have been a leather or rawhide tyre were noted at Ur. At Susa a wooden tyre, 0.045 m. in depth and flush with the faces of wheel (c. 0.83 m. in diameter), was pierced by metal hobnails. Similar nails were found on a wheel at Kiš.[17]

Narrow tyres, with and without hobnails, are often shown in contemporary or later (Akkadian and Ur III) figured documents of both four- and two-wheelers.[18] These tyres may have been of wood, rawhide or metal. The latter material is certainly represented on the fragment of the king Gudea of Laga, mentioned above (fig. 3). Here we see in detail a tyre made in two segments, with clamps like ours at either end but not in the middle, encircling a single-piece disc wheel. This tyre, perhaps showing a transitional arrangement, is combined

---

[14] Kossack 1971, 144, 146.
[15] Cf. the cross-sections of the felloes of spoked wheels from the tomb of Tutʿankhamūn, Littauer and Crouwel 1985, pls. XXXI, LIX.
[16] Littauer and Crouwel 1977c, 98f.; 1979, 19.
[17] Littauer and Crouwel 1977c, 98; 1979, 19; Tallon 1987 (I), 297f., fig. 42, cf. fig. 43 (two other wheels from Susa, tomb Donjon B 280).
[18] Littauer and Crouwel 1977c, 98; 1979, 19. 38, figs. 7–8, 13.

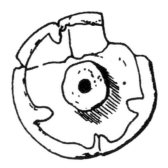

Fig. 4. Terracotta wheel model, Susa.

with hobnails which must have pierced it and helped to secure it to the wheel. The tread must have been flat, unlike that of our tyre segments. Metal tyres, again made in segments with clamps and, like ours, without hobnails, can be seen on a damaged terracotta wheel model from Susa (fig. 4).[19] Unfortunately, there is no precise indication of the number of segments (surely more than two) or clamps. Metal tyres, as we have seen, may be mentioned in the Ur-III texts, but without details of their type.

One may wonder on what type of vehicle these tyres were used and whether it was two-wheeled or four-wheeled. On the fragment of Gudea's stela enough remains to show that the wheel with its two tyre segments and hobnails belonged to a well-known type of two-wheeler. This so-called straddle car is here apparently illustrated in aceremonial setting.[20] The wheel seems to be of small diameter, which may account for its being a single-piece disc and having only two tyre segments; it shows a round axle and nave and a plain lynch pin, implying a wheel revolving on a fixed axle.

In at least one case (A 1–6 from Susa), our metal tyre segments can be assumed to have also belonged to revolving wheels of a two-wheeler, of uncertain type. This is because the segments were found together with a pair of metal linch pins, their heads shaped as hedge-hogs (pl. 127).[21] These six segments with only minor variations in

---

[19] de Mecquenem 1943, 125, fig. 91: a 2 (= our fig. 4); Littauer and Crouwel 1979, 39, n. 10; Tallon 1987, (I), 306 (five segments assumed).

[20] See Boese 1975. For the straddle car, see Littauer and Crouwel, 1979, 20–22, 39.

[21] de Mecquenem 1922, 138, fig. 16; Tallon 1987, (I), 306, (II), ills. 337 (nos. 1308–1309). For these and other decorated metal linch pins from the ancient Near East, see Calmeyer 1980.

dimensions, have been combined into one tyre, making for a fairly large wheel, 0.97 m. in diameter.[22] The fairly large size may well suggest a tripartite rather than a single-piece disc wheel. (For comparison, the remains of the tripartite disc wheels from Early Dynastic tombs at Ur, Kiš, and Susa gave diameters ranging from 0.50 to 1.00 m.).[23] The diameters of the wheels to which the other groups of metal tyres belonged have been calculated as varying from 0.67 m. to 1.02 m.; (see Appendix II); they may also have been tripartite discs.

A look at figs. 1 and 2 further reveals that the original wheels were convex in section, their fabric varying quite considerably in thickness. It is of note that segments B 1–12, from one tomb at Susa, have been divided into three groups of four, each forming a complete tyre, indicating one wheel 0.67 m. and two 0.70 m. in diameter.[24] On the other hand, segments E 1–14 have been taken to represent two complete sets of tyres of seven segments each, making for a pair of wheels of equal diameter (c. 80–0.85 m.). We seem than to have variations in the number of segments forming a tyre, ranging from four to seven. In addition, there is the related tyre in only two segments studded with hobnails, illustrated on the fragment of Gudea's stela. The latter wheel would have had a flat tread, while the actual metal tyres discussed here show a very narrow tread, more suitable for rocky ground than soft or sandy terrain.

The distribution area of these objects is very wide, extending from Ashur in the west through Iran to "somewhere" in Afghanistan. Whereas the Ashur and Susa examples were found in controlled excavations, we should perhaps be cautious of the Afghan finds (E 1–14). Under present conditions in Iran, many antiquities found there are apparently clandestinely removed to neighbouring countries that are more inviting to the foreign collector. While it is possible that the tyres for sale in Afghanistan came from a tomb in the area north of the Hindu Kush that was once known as Bactria, as H. M. Pottier

---

[22] Tallon 1987 (I), 305, (II), 127, revising the diameter of 1.05 m. proposed by Mecquenem 1922, 137.

[23] Woolley 1934, 64, 108 (Ur, tombs PG 789 and 1232); Watelin 1945, 30 (Kiš Tomb Y 356); de Mecquenem 1943, 103, 122–126, and Tallon 1987, (I), 298, 300 (Susa, Donjon Tomb B and "Ville Royale"). See also Littauer and Crouwel 1979, 17, 19.

[24] Tallon 1987, (I), 302f.; Mecquenem 1943, 87f. had estimated the wheel diameters as 0.647 and 0.825 m

suggests, it cannot be excluded that they were brought to Afghanistan from Iran.[25]

Widely distributed though they may have been, this form of wheel tyre apparently did not remain long in use. The amount of metal would have made it unusually costly as well as adding considerably to the weight of wheels. (Even an individual tyre segment, such as C 4, weighs as much as 2.3. kg.).

These metal tyres are important to us as one piece of evidence of active development in wheel construction that was taking place during the later third and earlier second millennium B.C. This development, characterized by the appearance of the cross-bar wheel and then of the spoked wheel, was an essential factor in the successful emergence of the light, fast, horse-drawn war and hunting chariot in Late Bronze-Age.[26]

Acknowledgements

We are most grateful to the owner of the tyre segments in Holland for permission to publish them and to have their metal analysed. We are also indebted to Dr. J. Kragten and Mr. G. Feenstra (Institute of Analytical Chemistry University of Amsterdam) for the analyses. Many thanks are due to Dr. F. Tallon, Dr. F. A. M. Wiggermann, Dr. P. R. S. Moorey and Mr. H. E. Fraenkel for information and assistance of various kinds. The drawings of figs. 1–2 and the photographs of pl. IIa–b are by Messrs. G. Strietman and M. Bootman respectively.

---

[25] Pottier 1984, 5–8. For "Bactrian" antiquities, see also Amiet 1987, 16–24 (with references).
[26] Littauer and Crouwel 1979, esp. 68–71; Moorey 1986.

Appendix I

Chart of Comparative Dimensions (in meters)

Tyre segments	Length across chord	Length clamps	Depth tyre	Max. Spread (tyre edges)	Max. Spread (clamp edges)	Diameter wheel
A 1–6	0.495–0.59	0.115–0.12	0.022	0.012	0.036	0.097 (1x)
B 1–12	0.49–0.498, 0.46	0.126, 0.136, 0.127	0.027, 0.026	0.015, 0.019	0.037, 0.039	0.70 (2x), 0.67 (1x)
C 1–5	0.48–0.49, 0.502–0.545	0.108–0.12 0.145, 0.175	0.02–0.025, 0.02	0.025, 0.0033	0.082– 0.085, 0.09–0.097	0.92(2x), 1.02 (2x)
D 1–3	—	—	—	—	—	—
E 1–14	0.40	0.095–0.10	0.029	0.023	0.05	0.80– 0.850 (2x)

Appendix II

Elemental Composition (% by weight)

Sample Element	C2 (clamp) %	RSD*	C 3 (tyre edge) %	RSD	C2 (bolt) %	RSD
Cu**	91,6		88,9		96,7	
Sn	6,27	1,6	8,23	1,3	0,13	15,4
As	0,29	6,8	0,009	18,3	0,72	4,2
Pb	0,97	0,6	1,10	1,5	1,11	0,5
Zn	0,30	0,7	0,30	0,7	0,34	0,9
Fe	0,31	2,3	0,15	2,2	0,29	1,4
S	0,16	4,1	0,13	4,9	0,08	3,2
Si	0,004	7,4	0,028	5,8	0,006	1,3
Ni	0,26	1,9	1,01	0,5	0,54	0,8
Ag	0,04	0,7	0,05	1,6	0,03	0,8
Sb	0,05	2,2	0,05	3,8	0,04	11,7

* RSD is relative standard deviation in %.
** Copper has been determined by comlexometric titration. The sum of all elements, including copper, does not deviate from 100% within the errors of determination. The copper content in the table has been calculated by substraction from 100%.

20. THE ORIGIN AND DIFFUSION OF THE CROSS-BAR WHEEL?*

M. A. LITTAUER AND J. H. CROUWEL

The cross-bar wheel has never been completely legitimized in the history of draught, being alternately declared in direct line of descent or merely collateral. This wheel (pl. 128 and fig. 7) is characterized by a single diametric bar, thick enough to accommodate the nave, and by two slender 'cross-bars' on either side of the nave which traverse the central bar at right angles to it, and the ends of which are mortised into the felloe. There may alternatively be four (or more) shorter cross-bars in similar relation to the central bar, but with their inner ends mortised into it. This type of wheel has long been recognized in Greek and Italic civilizations from the Archaic period on (Lorimer 1903; Mötefindt 1918). It has existed into recent times in areas as far afield as Spain (pl. 128), Mexico (Eggenhofer 1961, 73f.), England (Pyne 1806, pl. 55; Fenton 1973, 165), Outer Mongolia (Andrews 1932, pl. lxxviib), and China (des Noëttes 1931, figs. 134f.).

It was Lorimer 1903, 145–147 who, on the basis of the two wheels from Mercurago near Arona in northern Italy (Déchelette 1910, 289 with fig. 110) (fig. 1a and 1b), first derived the cross-bar wheel from the tripartite disk wheel with lunate perforations. She dated these Terramare wheels simply 'Bronze Age of Northern Italy' and suggested that the light, barred example had survived in the cross-bar wheel of humble vehicles familiar from classical antiquity. Since ancient western Asiatic tripartite disk wheels were then still unknown, she suggested that, 'For the origin of an object common to Northern Italy, Thrace and the mainland of Greece, it is natural to look to some European locality.' Mötefindt 1918, in an exhaustive typological paper which, however, took little account of either chronology or the actual construction of wheels, placed the origin of the cross-bar wheel in central or southern Italy.

* _Antiquity_ 51, 1977, 95–105.

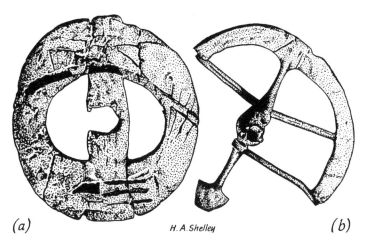

(a) H.A.Shelley (b)

Fig. 1. a and b: Wheels from Mercurago. After Déchelette 1910.

When Childe in 1951 wrote his famous paper on the diffusion of wheeled vehicles, the tripartite disk wheel was already well documented in the third-millennium Near East, and he was able to trace its diffusion thence. The cross-bar wheel, however, was unrecognized in this region and, since he considered the dating of the barred wheel from Mercurago to be Late Bronze (i.e. late second millennium B.C.), when spoked wheels were already known, he suggested that this was not a cross-bar wheel at all, but simply the result of an attempt to make a six-spoked wheel by someone who had seen the latter but 'had not learned the proper method of constructing one'. He again twice dismissed the Mercurago wheel as a sport (Childe 1954a, 3–5. 10; 1954b, 213f.).

In the light of some new evidence, however, and of a new assessment of some of the material already known to Childe, it may be possible to reinstate Miss Lorimer's technological, if not her geographical, conclusions, and at the same time to accord the cross-bar wheel a more venerable position in the history of draught than before.

Before discussing the possible genetic connexion between early tripartite disk wheels and crossbar wheels, it may be well to summarize briefly the construction of the former. Actual remains or traces thereof have been found at Kiš (Watelin 1934, 30–33), Ur (Woolley 1934, 64. 108), and Susa (de Mecquenem 1943, 103f.). They have been found in Transcaucasia, on the Kalmyk steppe, in southern Russia (Piggott 1968, 266–318) and in the Netherlands (van der

Waals 1964, 103–156), as well as in Scotland, Denmark and Germany
(Piggott 1957, 238–241). Such wheels have recently been in use in
the Iberian peninsula and in Sardinia (Suffern and Hemp 1929,
340–342), in Great Britain (Fox 1931, 197–199; Fenton 1973, 160–
166), Ireland (Lucas 1952, 135–414), Anatolia (Koşay 1951, pls. xv
and xvi), the Caucasus (des Noëttes 1931, fig. 185), China (Needham
1965, 79f.) and India (Mackay 1929, pl. II fig. 2). We thus have
considerable information to go by. In comparing ancient with modern examples, however, two circumstances must be borne in mind:
1) recent wheels of this type belong to very primitive carts and often
are *fixed* on a *revolving axle*, while the wheels on ancient vehicles considered worthy of burial or representation often appear to have *revolved*
on a *fixed axle* (see below); 2) when recent disk wheels do revolve on
a fixed axle, modern technology has often intervened to provide axles
or nave tracks of iron and a tubular iron nave, which can frequently
be bought ready made. This considerably simplifies the construction,
as well as strengthening the fabric.

   We are fortunate to have an account of the actual process of construction of a recent Irish tripartite disk wheel which, although turning *with* the axles, has an integral half nave (Lucas 1952, 135–144;
Piggott 1968, 268–270). Because the wheel was fixed on the axle it
did not require the full nave that prevents a revolving wheel from
wobbling on the axle, and it is only two-thirds of the thickness needed
for a proper revolving tripartite disk wheel of this type of construction (compare figs. 2*a* and 2*b*). Because the face of a disk wheel runs
with the grain of the wood, not across it, all types of disk are made
from planks, not cross-sections of trunk. The tripartite disk wheel
may be constructed from a plank only half the width required for
a solid disk; thus timber from a tree of smaller girth may be used.
A central plank as long as the diameter of the finished wheel and
half as wide is flanked by two planks half its width. The latter may
be cut from either a continuation of the first plank or from a similar cut from the same section of trunk but on the opposite side of
the weak heart wood which, anyway, cannot be utilized. The two
narrower pieces are placed on either side of the central plank, with
flush surfaces, and secured to it by internal dowels. Thus a square
is formed, the sides of which are roughly equal in length to the
diameter of the future wheel. The corners are cut away and the
edges rounded to form a disk. The nave is made by cutting a hole

of the desired diameter in the centre of the disk and then adzing away the excess surface from the rest of the wheel, leaving the nave (of whatever shape) standing proud. Note that the original plank had to be as thick as the finished nave length (figs. 2a and 2b).

This is a very simple method of making a wheel, and the proportions of some early tripartite disk wheels suggest that it was indeed known in ancient times; but it has certain drawbacks. While it may seem an economical way of using timber (when compared to a solid disk), the integral nave makes it wasteful. To produce a wheel of this sort required a plank at least three times as thick as that needed to make the wheel without the nave. Moreover, the integral nave has two other disadvantages. When it stands out as a thin-walled cylinder at right angles to the wheel surface, as it did on the solid disk wheels from the Netherlands and from Storezhvaja Mogila on the Pontic steppe, the projecting part, because it goes with the grain of the wood, is weak and liable to break off, as described by van der Waals (1964, 127f.) (fig. 3). Although this problem may be coped with, as it was on second-millennium tripartite disk wheels found at Trialeti in Armenia and on the recent Irish wheels described above, by sloping the faces of the wheel up gradually towards the nave and thus giving the latter broad support, or by making the nave thick and barrel-shaped, as at Trialeti, this would have kept the wheel at its maximum weight (Piggott 1968, figs. 7 and 11). Under the system of ancient harnessing, this would have been particularly undesirable wherever equid draught was used.

It may be taken as axiomatic that a round axle end indicates a wheel revolving *on* the axle and a rectangular axle end a wheel that revolves *with* the axle. It would have been very difficult to have fixed a round-ended revolving axle firmly in a round-holed nave. The ability of wheels on the same axle to revolve independently of each other, hence at different speeds, considerably facilitates the turning of the vehicle by eliminating the skidding of the outside wheel. A nave, being relatively closed, can be oiled, and this reduces the friction and noise that go with the revolving axle.

These advantages must have been recognized very early. The round axle ends shown on third-millennium monuments and the traces of such found in tombs indicate that the revolving wheel was already in use. In Mesopotamia, too, a further refinement seems to have been reached. This was the separate, inserted nave. Woolley

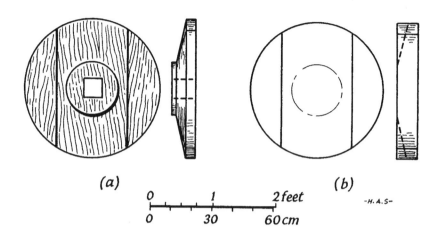

Fig. 2. a and b: Formation of modern tripartite disk wheel. After Lucas.

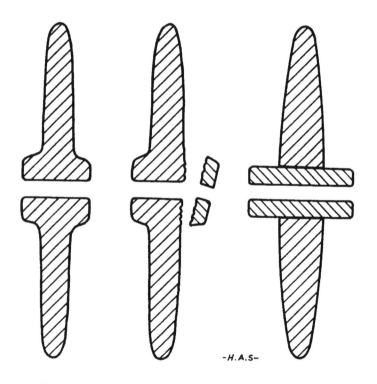

Fig. 3. Integral and inserted naves. After van der Waals 1964.

believed he found evidence of this at Ur in PG/1232, where a small wooden 'felloe' that projected 0.04 m. beyond the axle hole fell off the wheel (Woolley 1934, 64). Piggott has suggested that the external bonding slats evidenced from both soil stains and representations of third-millennium Mesopotamian and Elamite vehicles (figs. 4 and 5) may indicate wheels of thinner fabric than those put together with internal dowels (Piggott 1968, 270). The external slats indicate also that the disks were flat, as the sloping faces of wheels with raised naves would not have afforded the level surfaces needed for such slats. The central plank, whether straight-sided or lentoid, as so common in Mesopotamia, must have been flush with the flanks in the areas where the slats crossed both centre and flanks (figs. 4 and 5).

In third-millennium Mesopotamia and Elam we also find frequent indications of the use of some sort of tyre. In PG/789 at Ur Woolley noted a 'white substance' encircling the tread of the wheel, which fell to dust with excavation. To him it seemed to have been of leather (Woolley 1934, 64). At Kiš and Susa the treads were studded with

Fig. 4. Wheel with crescentic side pieces. After Woolley 1934.

hobnails, which may have pierced a rawhide tyre (Watelin 1934, fig. 3; de Mecquenem 1943, 122ff.). De Mecquenem even found at the latter site a tyre 0.045 m. deep of wood under the nails (fig. 5). The stone reliefs found at Ur and Khafajeh distinctly show a rigid band encircling the wheel (Frankfort 1939b, pl. 109: c; 1943, pl. 56, no. 318; 1958, pl. 33). This does not look like hide, which would be pliable and overlap the edges, but like metal. And, by the end of the third or beginning of the second millennium B.C., there is evidence from Susa of bronze tyres (de Mecquenem 1922, 137f.; 1924, IIIf.; 1943, 89f.).

Such tyres would have had more than one function: (1) to protect the running surface of the wheel which, because part of it ran with the grain and part against the grain, would quickly wear differentially. This was a factor perhaps more serious in fast military or courier vehicles. The uneven wear of the perimeter of such wheels when lacking tyres was described by a traveller who saw them in use in eighteenth-century Scotland (Haddon 1898, 138); (2) to prevent dirt and pebbles working their way into the join ends where these touched the ground, and wedging them apart; (3) to assist to an important degree the action of the bonding slats in consolidating the three parts of the wheel. There is no record of such tyres on the Armenian, Russian or European specimens, but iron ones are common today on disk wheels.

A further refinement, and one that must have required considerable skill on the part of the wheelwright, took place in Mesopotamia. This was the wheel formed with a lentoid central plank flanked by crescentic ones (fig. 4). This halved the number of joins in the running surface and reduced the tendency for the parts of the wheel to separate.

All these improvements were in the direction of making a stronger and lighter wheel, more appropriate for equid draught. The conformation of these animals is less well adapted to the pole-and-yoke hitch than is that of bovids. And the greater speed and more strenuous use of military or courier's vehicles would put a premium on both factors.

These refinements had all been adopted in Mesopotamia, if not in Elam, by Early Dynastic III (2600–2350 B.C.), while the Early-Dynastic II Tell Agrab copper model still had the vertical-sided central plank (Frankfort 1943, pl. 60a). After this, there is both a drop in frequency of representations and no sign of change in wheel structure until late in the third millennium B.C. We again, however, find innovations on a cylinder seal from Tepe Hissar in northeast Iran, now in Teheran. This was attributed by the excavator (Schmidt 1937, 199) to level IIIB (mostly dated to the last quarter of the millennium), and shows a two-wheeled vehicle with a wheel that has been taken as an example of a spoked wheel (Childe 1951, 188; 1954a, 12) (pl. 129). If correct, this would make it the earliest known representation of a spoked wheel. Dyson, however, has used this seal, with its supposed spoked wheel, as an argument to lower the terminal dating of Tepe Hissar level IIIB to the eighteenth century B.C. or slightly earlier (1965, 240; 1973, 688). Moorey (1968, 430–432) challenged this interpretation, pointing out certain resemblances between the wheel on the Hissar cylinder and tripartite disk wheels that could place it in the latter category. Comparing it with wheels from Susa (fig. 5), he saw the single crosspiece as representing the central plank, and those at right angles to it as the external bonding slats of the disk wheel. One may add to this that these do not *radiate* as do spokes and that, if these were spokes it would make this a six-spoked wheel, while early representations of the spoked wheel consistently show only four spokes. We would like to suggest here a third interpretation: that the Hissar seal shows indeed an effort towards lightening the old disk wheel, but in the form of a cross-bar wheel and not a spoked one (Dr Moorey now concurs in this interpretation: letter of 6 August 1969). On all representations, for instance, of tripartite disk wheels that make any effort to show the construction, the transverse slats that join the three planks *cross* the joins (figs. 4 and 5). It would seem far easier for the far-from-skilful artist who executed the Hissar cylinder to cut two pairs of transverse lines running straight across the central plank than for him to suppress them as carefully as he clearly did in this area. They run *into* or *through* the central plank rather than across it, and it in itself is exceptionally narrow when compared with tripartite disk wheel central planks (figs. 2, 4, and 5). If, however, one were to narrow the central plank of a tripartite disk wheel and reduce the thickness of the flanking ones (the Mesopotamian examples already suggest the crescentic form), to increase the thickness of the former external slats (or internal dowels) and to make them abut in the central piece or run straight through it, one would have a cross-bar wheel. In this way all the elements of the tripartite disk wheel are retained; they are merely transformed.

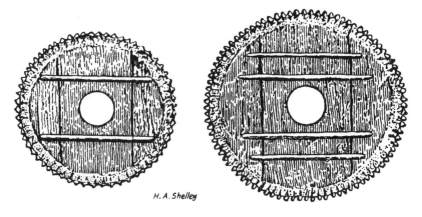

H.A.Shelley

Fig. 5. Wheels from Susa. After Childe.

That the wheel shown on the Hissar cylinder was not merely an isolated and abortive attempt in the Near East may be shown by some subsequent figured documents. The stylistic homogeneity of Cappadocian seals of the beginning of the second millennium B.C. underlines the differences between some of the wheels depicted on them or their impressions on tablets. It is clearly a four-spoked wheel that is shown on Morgan Collection 893E (Porada 1948, 112, pl. cxxxiv), and apparently the same is on a quite worn sealing from level II of the Assyrian merchant colony at Kültepe, the seals of which are traditionally referred to as 'Cappadocian' (Özgüç 1965, 67, pl. III:9), while on the impression on de Clercq 284 (Frankfort 1939a, 248–250, pl. xln) the parallel, paired, crosspieces suggest cross-bar rather than spoked wheels (pl. 130). Other seals show what look like garbled attempts to depict either crossbar or spoked wheels (e.g. Frankfort 1939a, pl. xlm. The actual cylinder of this impression is also preserved, cf. Smith 1928, pl. vii, b).

A little later we again find a telling juxtaposition of cross-bar and spoked wheels that emphasizes that the cross-bar here is intentional, and not an artist's unsuccessful attempt to depict a spoked wheel. This occurs on an unprovenanced stamp cylinder (Louvre AO.20.138), usually called 'Hittite', but diverging in style from the typically Hittite stamp cylinders, although probably made in Anatolia. It is usually dated to around the middle of the second millennium B.C. (pl. 131). There is here a strong contrast between the cross-bar wheels of the bovid-drawn chariot with its divine driver in the upper register and the 4-spoked wheels of the apparently horse-drawn chariots in the lower register, with their presumably mortal drivers (Parrot 1951, 180–190; for further references see Littauer and Crouwel 1973b, 125 with n. 108).

The contrast here between the natures of the drivers with the two different types of wheels suggests that the cross-bar, as the one associated with the deity, might have been the more venerable. This argument is supported by another probable appearance of a deity in a vehicle with a cross-bar wheel. This is represented on a recently published fragment of a relief vase from Boğazköy in central Anatolia (fig. 6), dated to the seventeenth or sixteenth centuries B.C. (Bittel 1970a). Here a god seems also to be mounting a bovid-drawn cart with cross-bar wheels of a type similar to ones in use in the British Isles as late as the last century (fig. 7, Pyne 1806, pl. 55; cf. also Fenton 1973, fig. 20). In this, the diametric bar and crescentic 'felloes' are heavy, and the cross-bars numerous and very slender. (The fact that these are engraved only on one half of the wheel on the vase is probably to be attributed to the fact that the artist did not leave himself as much room for them in the other.) While the examples previously discussed do not show how the wheel was attached, their lighter construction may indicate a fixed axle. The relief vase, however, shows a rectangular axle end, as did its recent British counterpart. This implies a fixed wheel on a revolving axle. Bittel notes

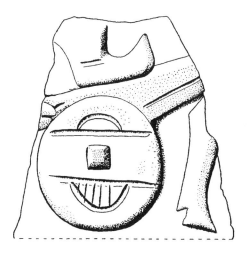

Fig. 6. Hittite relief vase. After Bittel 1970a.

that this would be appropriate to what looks, from its open, upward-slanting platform, like the A-frame carts still in use in Anatolia although these have disk wheels (Koşay 1951, pl. xvi).

Another example of the light type of cross-bar wheel turns up on an Egyptian scarab bearing the cartouche of Tuthmosis III (first half of fifteenth century B.C.) (Hayes 1959, fig. 66, centre row, left-hand seal). After this, we have no further evidence of this type of cross-bar wheel in these regions. The ox carts of the 'Sea Peoples' had disk wheels, and the Hittite four-wheeled baggage waggons at Kadesh rolled on spoked ones – both recorded only because they played a part in historic events. The humble vehicle to which the cross-bar wheel must have been relegated, as the spoked wheel was taken over by the finer and faster ones, was not of interest to Near Eastern art. It is only when the later Assyrian kings of the eighth and seventh centuries B.C. choose to celebrate their victories and achievements in circumstantial detail that we again see simple carts. The Assyrian carts show a type of cross-bar wheel that may have superseded the type with double cross-bars in this area. It was made with a thick felloe and only two heavy bars crossing at right angles (Salonen 1951, pl. xliv). It would have been simpler to make than the earlier type, and must have answered the needs of mass production for vast public works. If the spoked wheel had originated *before* the cross-bar wheel, however, one would expect this simple Assyrian form to be the earliest and most widespread type of cross-bar wheel, since the four spokes crossing at right angles would suggest it, rather than the more complicated version that covers so much more time and space. There seems to be no evidence of this Assyrian wheel in antiquity outside of its own area and in the Neo-Assyrian period, although a wheel of rather similar construction is illustrated on a recent Yemeni ox cart (Bulliet 1975, fig. 95). The other carts recorded on these reliefs, of lighter type, and belonging to conquered peoples, already have multiple-spoked wheels (Strommenger and Hirmer 1964, pls. 218, 236). There is no further evidence of the cross-bar wheel in south-west Asia.

The first known European example is the wheel from Mercurago (fig. 1*b*), which comes from either the Early- or the Middle-Bronze phase of this site, i.e. from somewhere between 1800 and 1100 B.C. (Barfield 1971, 74). It recalls the lighter of the eastern wheels in its general proportions and in the closeness of the lateral bars to each

Fig. 7. Cross-bar wheel in England, early nineteenth century. After Pyne, 1806.

other at the centre. The spade-shaped ends of the diametric bar, which actually form part of the felloe, betray a genetic link with the tripartite disk wheel. That the Mercurago wheel was not merely an unsuccessful imitation of a spoked wheel, as Childe thought, is suggested by what look very much like its direct descendants in Italy. These are represented on a sixth-century B.C. Etruscan gem in the Museum of Fine Arts, Boston (acc. no. 27.663; Richardson 1966, pl. xxxiii), on an Etruscan coin of the fifth century B.C. (Franke and Hirmer 1964, pl. III), on grave stelae of the fourth century B.C. in the Museo Civico, Bologna (Ducati 1910, 602 with figs. 18, 50, 51, 52) and on an important third-century B.C. sarcophagus from Vulci (pl. 132) now in Boston (acc. no. 1975. 799; Chase and Vermeule 1963, 192). These also have the relatively slender members, with the lateral bars curving away from the diametric bar, as on the Mercurago example. The difference in these is that the ends of the diametric bar form no part of the felloe, but are mortised into it and that, at least in the case of the Boston sarcophagus, the wheel clearly revolves with the axle (but we found this construction already at Boğazköy). Since a sixth-century B.C. bronze model of a cart from Bolsena, now in the Villa Giulia (Moretti and Maetzke 1970, pl. 88), has crescentic bonding slats on its disk wheels, it could be argued that this particular type of cross-bar wheel was a local Italic development, independent of other cross-bar wheels. A Thraco-Macedonian coin of the Ichnaeans, however, dated 520–480 B.C., carries a wheel with crescentic lateral bars, and the ends of the diametric bar, although they form no part of the felloe, widen suddenly in a manner reminiscent of the Mercurago wheel (Franke and Hirmer 1964, pl. 124).

In Greece proper there appears to be no actual or figured evidence for disk wheels (although this certainly does not prove their absence). Our earliest cross-bar ones are first depicted in the sixth century B.C. when one appears on a mule cart on a Panathenaic vase, and others in the scenes from daily life that now occasionally creep into the pot painter's repertoire (Lorimer 1903, 136ff. with figs. 3–6 and 8). To this may be added an Athenian coin from the same century (Franke and Hirmer 1964, pl. 114) and a relief of the classical period (Catling 1971–72, 3 with fig. 1). In Cyprus, cross-bar wheels are first recorded possibly a century earlier (Karageorghis 1966a, 108f. with figs. 4, and 8). These all have straight lateral bars rather than curved ones and, in this and in the slenderness of their fabric, resemble the early Near-Eastern examples – with the exception of the Boğazköy-sherd wheel. Despite an apparent chronological hiatus in the evidence, it seems likely that the cross-bar wheel was introduced into Cyprus and Greece directly from the Near East.

There is, to our knowledge, only one document for the cross-bar wheel in northern Europe in ancient times, and it is pictorial: a petroglyph of a solitary, unattached wheel at Solberg in Ostfold, southeast Norway (Marstrander 1963, 283 with fig. 701: 1), attributed to northern Bronze Age V or VI. While we have no material survivors of these, as we have of disk wheels (Piggott 1957; van der Waals 1964), their flimsier fabric may have made them more perishable.

To return to the possible genetic role of the cross-bar wheel in the formation of the spoked wheel – we have noted that there are indications that the most advanced disk wheels of third-millennium B.C. Mesopotamia and Elam may have had separate inserted naves and that they show some kind of tyre – at Susa apparently of wood 0.045 m. in depth. The separate nave is already an essential component of the spoked wheel, and an independent circumferential element – particularly a wooden one, would have been capable of suggesting the future felloe. What was missing were the spokes. The conversion, in the cross-bar wheel, of the external bonding slats or internal dowels into lateral bars with their outer ends mortised into a felloe could have suggested these. The Hissar seal (pl. 129), the Cappadocian (pl. 130) and the Anatolian stamp cylinder (pl. 131) appear to show cross-bar wheels, the slender lateral bars of which are very close together. Were these to be combined to form single bars of the same thickness as the diametric bar and were their inner ends mortised into a nave inserted into the diametric bar (as it must have been where the wheels revolved on the axle), we would have two spokes at right angles to the diametric bar. The next step would be to convert the latter itself into two spokes mortised also into the nave. This done, we would have a full-fledged four-spoked wheel. This reasoning would only obtain, of course, were the early spoked wheels in this area made with spokes mortised into a cylindrical nave. Were they to have been assembled in the much more complicated fashion attested in actual chariot wheels found in Egyptian eighteenth-dynasty tombs, they could hardly have evolved in this manner (Western 1973, 91–94 with figs. 1 and 2 and pl. xxxiv). The recent evidence, however, of wheels with ten spokes from graves in the central Urals, attributed to around the middle of the second millennium B.C. (Piggott 1975, 289f.), indicates mortised spokes, as such a number could not have been achieved with the method known from Egypt.

Chronologically there seems to be no serious problem. The seniority of the cross-bar wheel is suggested by the Hissar III seal and by the early occurrence of the wheel on vehicles carrying deities. This seniority, however, cannot have been of more than a few centuries. It could also represent an independent attempt, roughly contemporary with the first spoked example, to make the lighter wheel that was evidently demanded by events at this time.

What we would like to suggest here is that the cross-bar wheel is much more ancient than hitherto recognized, that it is indeed old enough to have perhaps played a role in the evolution of the spoked wheel, that because it was lighter than the disk wheel, yet simpler to make than the spoked one, it may have enjoyed diffusion in its own right. That the cross-bar wheel continued to be diffused is suggested by examples in Mexico and Britain, which may have migrated from the Iberian peninsula in relatively recent times. Mexico cannot have had cross-bar wheels before the Conquest, and the most likely source then would have been Spain. And although, as noted above, the cross-bar wheel is attested at least once among Scandinavian Bronze Age petroglyphs, there is no subsequent documentation of it from northern Europe while, when we find it in Great Britain, it is only in the late eighteenth or early nineteenth century A.D. There was a direct sea route from Iberian Atlantic ports to west British ports, and the 'Spanish jennets' (light, easy-gaited horses) of the later Middle Ages must have come this way, as well as the 'Irish' donkey. At a later period, soldiers returning from the Peninsular Wars could have brought back with them the idea of the cross-bar wheel.

Ancient cross-bar wheels are depicted, with the exception of the Boğazköy example, as of light construction. If such wheels were devised, as we have suggested, in an effort materially to lighten the load for equid draught (although bovids might still be used with them in ceremonies) this early lightness is not surprising. In later antiquity the wheel is shown with light carts or, occasionally, chariots, where it was probably a substitute for a spoked wheel and would imitate the latter's lightness. While recent cross-bar wheels are usually heavy, they still vary in details of construction, as did their ancestors. They may either be fixed on a revolving axle (Vulci and recent Yorkshire) or revolve on a fixed one (Mercurago and modern Spain); the ends of the diametric bars may form sections of the felloes (Boğazköy and modern Mexico), or they may be mortised into them (Vulci and modern China); they may have only pairs of lateral bars, as on the majority of ancient and recent specimens, or more numerous very fine ones (Boğazköy and recent England).

It has often been postulated that the apertures that are found in some later disk wheels indicate an effort to lighten the wheels that may correspond to some actual transitional stage between the disk and spoked wheels. What chronology we have today, however, does not support this. Early Near-Eastern cross-bar wheels are considerably earlier than any wheels with lunate openings from western Europe (which are not attested until after 1300 B.C.). Moreover, the only example we have of some such thing from the Near East itself is on a Neo-Hittite relief from Malatya attributed to the tenth century B.C. (Frankfort 1958, pl. 133b), where a pentepartite disk wheel shows minute circular openings. Van der Waals (1964, 123) has plausibly suggested that the apertures were the means of getting a hand-hold on an object otherwise awkward to grasp. It may be significant that these apertures first appear on wheels primarily in areas where the soil might have been soft and damp, and the vehicle could easily have become bogged down. The Mercurago, Blair Drummond (Scotland), Dystrup (Denmark), Buchau (Germany) and Ezinge (Holland) wheels all were found at least in the vicinity of boggy areas. And certainly such narrow crescentic slits as those in the last four wheels are too insignificant greatly to have reduced the weight (Piggott 1957, fig. 13; van der Waals 1964, fig. 25). Recent disk wheels have also sometimes been fenestrated, as we see in examples from the British Isles and the Iberian and Indian peninsulas (Fenton 1973, figs. 21:1, 39; Suffern and Hemp 1929, pl. II; Mackay 1929, fig. 2).

This suggestion of the origin and diffusion of the cross-bar wheel cannot be proved without more evidence – both from the late third millennium B.C. and later – that would provide some of the missing links in the chain. All we can offer here is a model for future research to bear in mind, in order either to substantiate or to refute it.

Acknowledgements

We are grateful to Dr P. Amiet and the Louvre for the photograph of AO 20.138 (pl. 131), and for permission to photograph an impression of de Clerq 284 (pl. 130). The drawing of the Hittite relief vase was kindly prepared by Miss P. Cullen.

We wish to thank Dr P. Amiet and Dr P. R. S. Moorey for their dating of the Susa bronze tyres.

Addenda

As this article was about to be sent off, we received, through the kindness of Professor Piggott, A. T. Lucas's important article (Lucas 1972). This also discusses at length the wider background of the disk wheel, including many European examples. Had we been acquainted with it before, the present paper would have been composed rather differently. We are happy to find that we share Dr Lucas's recognition of a similarity between the Hissar-III seal wheel and the cross-bar one from Mercurago, and we hope that we have been able perhaps to supply missing links in the chain between Hissar and Mercurago.

In the matter of lunate openings, we find our contention that these cannot have lightened the wheels materially supported by Dr Lucas and illustrated by further pertinent examples. His suggestion of the possible origin of these apertures as a result of the shrinkage of the crescentic side pieces of Mesopotamian tripartite disk wheels is interesting, although we have little evidence for this. His suggestion of one function of the holes being to permit the passage of a pole through opposite wheels, to lock them, is most attractive.

We are also grateful to Professor Piggott for calling our attention to an Iberian bronze votive model of probably late Hallstatt or early La Tène date, which seems to show cross-bar wheels. It is in the museum at Guimaraês, as from Vilela, Paredes de Douro and has been published in Forrer 1932, and in the *Archivo Español de Arqueologia*, xxx, 1946, 1–28.

21. THE EARLIEST KNOWN THREE-DIMENSIONAL EVIDENCE FOR SPOKED WHEELS*

M. A. LITTAUER AND J. H. CROUWEL

For Machteld J. Mellink

During the 1970 excavations at Acemhöyük, due south of Ankara in Anatolia, Prof. Nimet Özgüç found the remains of a copper/bronze vehicle in one of the corridors of the Burnt Palace (level III).** Bullae from the same level provide evidence for its synchronization with the Karum B1 level at Kültepe, i.e., the first half of the 18th century B.C. by the so-called middle chronology.[1]

The material is at present stored in five wooden boxes in the Museum of Anatolian Civilization in Ankara. It consists of four complete, four-spoked, cast metal wheels; four incomplete, pierced lugs; numerous broken rods; three "T-shaped" attachments riveted to sheet metal, and one that is no. longer attached; and over 100 fragments of badly corroded sheet metal (pls. 133–138).

The wheels are of exceptional interest. Components of an unusually large model or trolley, they are the earliest three-dimensional spoked wheels yet recorded from a securely dated context. The earliest known two-dimensional representations of spoked wheels are found on Anatolian cylinder seals and in seal impressions, some of which come from the Kārum II level at Kültepe, usually dated to the late 20th or early 19th century B.C. The majority show the traditional Mesopotamian four-wheelers with a seated driver, drawn by a team of four equids, but there are two examples of two-wheelers

* *American Journal of Archaeology* 90, 1986, 395–398.
** We are most grateful to Prof. N. Özgüç for permission to examine the objects in the Museum of Anatolian Civilization in Ankara in September 1971. We owe special thanks to Prof. E. Özgen for taking the photographs for us and for comments and suggestions on the material, which we would not have been able to publish without his generous assistance. We are also indebted to Dr. P. R. S. Moorey for comments on a draft of the text.
[1] Mellink 1971, 165 ("bronze wagon"); Littauer and Crouwel 1979a, 49, 54 n. 7; 1973b, 122 n. 88. For dating, see esp. Özgüç 1980.

with a new, rail-type superstructure and a team of two equids (probably horses), controlled by a standing driver.[2]

The metal wheels (pls. 133–135), ranging in diameter from 0.17 to 0.177 m., reveal details of construction impossible or very difficult to depict in two dimensions and in a very small space, such as is available on cylinder seals. The naves project slightly on both sides. The axles appear to have been round in section as they passed through the naves, but rectangular in section between them, indicating revolving wheels on a fixed axle (pl. 135).

The wheels (two with axle fragments still in their naves), the other axle fragments, and the four lugs are stored in one box, apart from the other material. It seems likely that these objects were found in a position suggesting their interconnection. Moreover, a fragment of a rod remaining in one of the lugs (pl. 136) corresponds in thickness to the axle fragments in the naves.[3] It therefore seems reasonable to suggest that the axles were attached to the superstructure by means of the lugs. While there is no indication of how the lugs were attached, they must have hung below the sides of the vehicle floor. This arrangement is often found on model vehicles – particularly terracotta ones – and probably does not reflect the carriage-building practice of the day, but was for the convenience of the modeler.[4]

The spokes appear to widen slightly as they approach the felloes and the felloes themselves at this junction seem to thicken, producing a rounded angle. Binding of the rims or felloes on either side of the spoke might account in part for this effect, and would be a logical precaution to take to reduce the tendency of a rim to split under pressure of the spoke ends. A binding of the spoke itself near the felloe would suggest a wheel construction similar to that documented on actual four- and six-spoked wheels in New Kingdom Egypt. At least one set of chariot wheels from the tomb of Tutʿankhamūn – the best preserved – has gilt bronze wire bindings on the spokes and felloes in these areas.[5] The bindings are also illustrated on the royal chariot in scenes on the body of the chariot of

---

[2] Littauer and Crouwel 1979a 48–51, figs. 25, 28, 29.
[3] Communication of E. Özgen, November 1984.
[4] Littauer and Crouwel 1974, pl. 1 below (terracotta model).
[5] Carter 1927, pl. 40; Desroche Noblecourt, ill. p. 242; Crouwel 1981, 81–90; full discussion in Littauer and Crouwel 1985.

Tuthmosis IV[6] and on Tut'ankhamūn painted box,[7] as well as on the Levantine chariot in a tomb painting which also shows the "swollen joints."[8] The latter feature only, without the detail, is depicted in at least two Egyptian chariot-workshop scenes in Theban tombs.[9] The combination of bindings and thickenings is found also in representations of Bronze Age Aegean chariots.[10]

It is possible that these rounded angles at the felloes in the Acemhöyük wheels, as well as those where the spokes join the nave, simply facilitated casting. The angles of the spokes with the naves, however, like the outer angles, may reflect an actual technique, similar to that documented on several extant chariot wheels of Dynasty XVIII in Egypt. In this type of construction, a single piece of wood, half-oval in section, is bent halfway along its length to form a V and glued back-to-back to the complementary half of the adjacent spoke. The angle at the apex either forms an integral part of the nave[11] or nestles in bays in the nave.[12] Thus there are no spoke ends inserted into mortises in a barrel nave, but the whole is consolidated by a rawhide binding applied in a wet state and allowed to shrink. The hide extended for a short distance from the nave along each spoke, and on some chariots was covered with birch bark – which has waterproofing properties – or, on parade chariots, by gilded gesso, which also had the effect of rounding the nave-spoke angles. This technique of wheel construction appears to have obtained in the second half of the second millennium B.C. in Egypt and in (at least parts of) the Near East. It now is materially attested in the latter area by the remains of a six-spoked wheel found at Lidar Höyük in the Euphrates salvage excavations in eastern Anatolia.[13] As noted above, rounded angles and spoke and felloe bindings illustrated in the Aegean in the Late Bronze Age seem to point to the

---

[6] Yadin 1963, 192f.

[7] Davies and Gardiner 1963, pls. 1–4.

[8] Yadin 1963, 189.

[9] Those of the vizier Hepu: Davies 1962, pl. 8, and of Puy-em-re: Davies 1922 pls. 23–24.

[10] For spoke and rim binding, see Crouwel 1981, pl. 95 (Wa6); for thickening, pls. 32a–b, 85 (W8).

[11] On a fragmentary wheel of Amenophis III, see Western 1973, 91–94, pl. 34.

[12] For chariot wheels of Tut'ankhamūn, see Littauer and Crouwel 1985.

[13] For the Lidar wheel, not yet published in full, see Mellink 1983, 433; information and illustrations were generously provided by the excavator, Prof. H. Hauptmann, who has revised the original tentative eighth century B.C. date upwards.

same construction technique there.[14] The remains from Acemhöyük may now indicate that spoked-wheel production had already reached a certain sophistication by the 18th century B.C. in central Anatolia.

A different, simpler, and far more familiar wheelwright's technique may be documented by our earliest evidence of actual full-sized spoked wooden wheels. This is constituted by impressions in the soil of buried two-wheeled vehicles at Sintashta in the central Urals, dated to around the middle of the second millennium B.C.[15] These wheels were 10-spoked and, while the construction method already described cannot be ruled out, the sharper angle (36° instead of the 60° for six-spoked wheels) at the apex of the spokes would seem to render that method more difficult; hence the simpler drum or barrel nave with mortised-in spokes would appear more likely. Ceramic models of four-spoked wheels from Slovakia, however, considered approximately contemporary with the Sintashta vehicles, may indicate a wheel design similar to that of the wheels from Acemhöyük.[16]

The Acemhöyük wheels (two with diameters of 0.177 m., one of 0.173 m. and one of 0.17 m.) formed part of a larger vehicle than those of a group of copper/bronze four-wheelers, unprovenanced but presumably from Anatolia, dated to the later third or early second millennium B.C.[17] These models have disk wheels and (with one exception) a superstructure of rods or wire and sheet metal. In type they appear to derive ultimately from the traditional Mesopotamian four-wheeler with double-hooped high front. They are usually pulled by pairs of cast metal figurines of bovids under yoke. Wheel diameters, measured on 12 of the models, range from 0.038 m. to 0.11 m., with only three at 0.08 m. or over and the majority under 0.06 m. Not only are the Acemhöyük wheels — with diameters of 0.17–0.177 m. — much larger, but the fragmentary remains of the superstructure contain no pieces similar to the double-hooped fronts

---

[14] It is also possible that the widening of the spokes may represent wedges placed on either side of them where they join the felloes — something we suggested in 1979 in connection with chariot wheels shown on 18th and 17th century B.C. Syrian cylinder seals, but of which we are no longer so certain. Such wedges were indeed widely used on chariot wheels in Iron Age Greece; see Littauer and Crouwel 1979a, 54, fig. 33, and Crouwel 1985, 82.

[15] Piggott 1974; 1983; 31f., fig. 47.

[16] Piggott 1983, 92f., fig. 49.

[17] Littauer and Crouwel 1979a, 37f., fig. 15; full discussion in Littauer and Crouwel 1973a. Add Muscarella 1979, no. 125; Nagel 1984/85.

of the other vehicles, nor any draft animals, nor evidence of a yoke or a draft pole – and this despite the fact that they were found in a controlled excavation. Moreover, the loose "T-shaped" attachment with a curled loop and what appear to be the fragments of three similar attachments still riveted to the sheet metal (pl. 137) are elements not found with any of the "Anatolian metal models." Özgen has suggested that this type of attachment functioned as a lug, with the one riveted at the center front of the vehicle used for attaching a chain or cord to pull it along. The difficulty with this attractive suggestion is that there were apparently three more of these pieces. This problem disappears, however, if the attachments were placed in pairs at the front and rear of the vehicle. Pulling from two lugs permits greater control of direction than pulling from only one, and parallels may also be found among early terracotta model vehicles.[18] The terracotta vehicles, however, do not have lugs at the rear.

The placement of lugs at both front and rear may indicate a ceremonial trolley, as proposed by Özgüç, a movable brazier, or a practical carrier that could be pulled in either direction.[19] Two possible parallels present themselves. The nearest in time is a trolley carrying a solar model boat, from the tomb of Queen Ahotep at Thebes, associated with the Pharaoh Kamose on the eve of Dynasty XVIII.[20] The trolley had four, four-spoked wheels of copper/bronze, 0.093 m. or 0.095 m. in diameter, and projecting naves, but the wheels revolved on wooden axles. An object from a site closer to Acemhöyük – Toprakkale – had four six-spoked bronze wheels that revolved on iron axles and were comparable in size (0.16 m. in diameter) to the Acemhöyük wheels. The object is considered Urartian,[21] however, and it is thus later than the Acemhöyük material. It has a lug at the front, suggesting not a model but a functional vehicle, such as a cult trolley, movable brazier or the like (ill. 1).

In closing, it may be noted that the wheels from Acemhöyük are strikingly similar to wheel-shaped cheekpieces of copper/bronze horse bits of the second half of the second millennium B.C. from eastern

[18] Littauer and Crouwel 1974, fig. 2, pl. 2.
[19] Letter from N. Özgüç, 17 June 1971.
[20] See von Bissing 1900, 21f., pl. 10; Vernier 1927, no. 52668, pl. 41; Smith 1958, pl. 84A–B. Porter and Moss 1964, 602. These wheels, however, show no rounded angles where the spokes join the felloes.
[21] See Scheil 1914, 179f.; Salonen 1951, pl. IX.

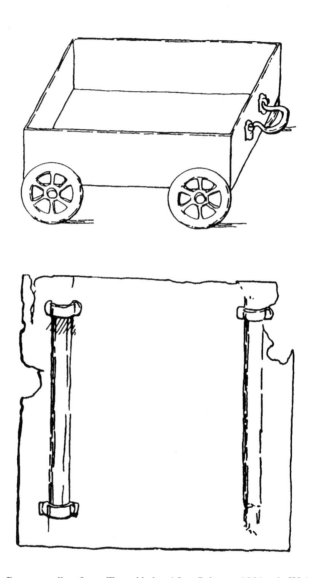

Fig. 1. Bronze trolley from Toprakkale. After Salonen 1951, pl. IX:1, 2.

Anatolia and the Aegean. This type of wheel construction,[22] once considered confined to Egypt, thus appears to be widely distributed. Convenience in casting (provided it existed) might account for the similar design of both types of object, but a bit is now known with wheel cheekpieces and, apparently, composite spokes, like those of actual Egyptian wheels.[23]

---

[22] Bittel 1975, 303f., figs. 4f., pl. 56: 1–2 (reportedly from Sarkisla, eastern Anatolia); Crouwel 1981, nos. B 1–2, 5–6, pls. 1, 5 (Mycenae and Thebes). These bits belong to a larger category of circular bits, documented from Egypt to Transcaucasia, which seem also to have been inspired by the wheel but which, with their often decorated and fanciful spokes, appear to be further removed than these from the original inspiration: Potratz 1966, type II, figs. 46b. d–f, pls. 115. 118. 119; see also Littauer and Crouwel 1982, 178, pl. 127A–B.

[23] Unprovenanced bit, recently identified in New York, now on loan from the Classics Department of New York University to the Metropolitan Museum of Art, New York (see Littauer and Crouwel 1986b).

22. AN EGYPTIAN WHEEL IN BROOKLYN*

M. A. LITTAUER AND J. H. CROUWEL

This paper is concerned with a wheel from Egypt in the Department of Egyptian and Classical Art of the Brooklyn Museum (acc. no. E. 37.1700, Charles Edwin Wilbour Fund).** The object was purchased by H. Abbott, an English physician, some time between 1832, when he presumably went to Egypt to practise, and 1843, when his collection was first catalogued by J. Bonomi.[1] In 1852 the Abbott collection was brought to New York, where it was eventually acquired by the New York Historical Society.[2] In 1937 the wheel went to the Brooklyn Museum on loan with the Abbott collection, and it was acquired by the museum in 1948.[3] Although already discussed – particularly by J. G. Wilkinson and C. R. Williams – the wheel deserves more detailed study.[4] This is the more important since it is in many

** The *Journal of Egyptian Archaeology* 65, 1979, 107–120.*

** We are grateful to B. von Bothmer for permitting us to study and publish the wheel and accompanying material; to R. Fazzini for his patience during the necessarily tedious examinations of these, and for generously contributing new comparative evidence; to Al Mellilo, also of the Brooklyn Museum, for practical suggestions; to Miss E. Riefstahl for commenting upon an earlier version of this paper. We are indebted to the late J. Vandier for permission to publish the Louvre nave, and to J.-L. de Cenival, who made it available for study. We wish to thank P. R. S. Moorey for his advice and for enabling us to examine the fragmentary wheel in the Ashmolean; P. Munro for providing us with a photograph of the drawing in the Kestner Museum, Hanover, and Miss N. Scott and J. R. Harris for help with the figured evidence. We wish to express our thanks to the Committee of Management of the Griffith Institute, Oxford, for permission to study the documentation of the chariots of Tutʿankhamūn, and to G. E. Mukhtar and H. Riad for authorizing us to examine these in the Egyptian Museum Cairo. Finally, we are indebted to Mrs N. Einhorn for the scale drawings of the wheel (fig. 1), and to Miss M. Moore and D. Laub for their assistance in examining the wheel.

[1] Bonomi (n.d.). According to Williams 1920, Bonomi wrote the catalogue in 1843, although it was not published until 1846.

[2] Abbott 1915, 25.

[3] Brooklyn Museum Quarterly 24, 1937, 89ff.; New York Historical Society Quarterly and Annual Report for 1948, 120.

[4] Wilkinson 1878, 234f.; Williams 1923 with cover plate. Cf. also Nuoffer 1904, 15.

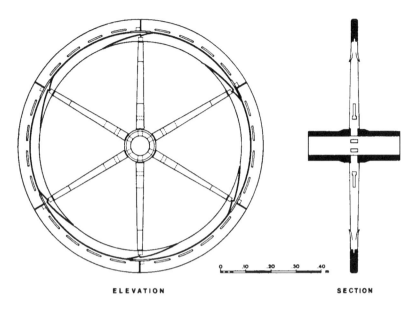

ELEVATION   SECTION

Fig. 1

respects unique among extant Egyptian wheels, all of which are of
the Eighteenth Dynasty. As we shall see, it may in fact be attributed to the Late Period (950–332 B.C.), a time span from which we
have little evidence of wheeled vehicles.

Description

The wheel is c. 0.96 m. in diameter. Each of the six spokes is tenoned
at one end into the nave and, at the other end, into the felloe (see
pls. 139–140a–c; fig. 1). They are elliptical in section and taper from
the nave outwards. As they approach the felloe they are carved on
their narrower faces so as to appear barbed when viewed from the
wider faces (see pl. 140b).

The nave (see pls. 139–140a and fig. 1), 0.37 m. long, is formed
from a single cylindrical piece of wood but, although the diameter
of the interior is constant throughout (0.072 m.), the exterior is slightly
thicker in the central area, where the spoke-end mortices are located.
Numerous fine parallel lines (see pl. 140a) indicate that it was turned
on a lathe.

The felloe is composed of six pieces of artificially bent(?) wood, rectangular in section, 0.03 m. wide by 0.035 m. deep, overlapping each other in sequence, and mitred (with a little 'jog' in the mitre) at the overlaps (see pls. 139, 140c and fig. 1). Outside this is a wooden tyre composed of six lengths of artificially bent(?) wood, rectangular in section, 0.03 m. wide by 0.04 m. deep, butt-ended, and joined by mortice-and-tenon at the ends (see pls. 139, 140b–c). We call this a tyre, rather than a second felloe, because the spoke-ends do not penetrate it. Near the inner edges of the tyre sections, and at approximately equal intervals, are four slots, 0.06–0.07 m. long (see pls. 139, 140c and fig. 1). Through these evidently passed wide rawhide bands that went entirely around the adjacent sections of the felloe. These were probably put on green, so as to shrink in drying. No trace of hide remains today, but Wilkinson's drawing (see fig. 2), made in Egypt, shows bindings in five places, and he states that the felloe and tyre were held together by rawhide bands,[5] of which there were perhaps still traces when he saw the wheel. Any possibility that bands of metal were used for this purpose is eliminated by the fact that there is no trace of the holes that would necessarily be left by the nails securing the ends of such bands.

The joins of the tyre-ends are at present located directly over the areas in the felloe where the spoke-ends are morticed. The extra outward pressure here would tend rather to force the tyre-ends apart than to keep them together. It is in these areas, moreover, that the slots are widest apart, hence where the rawhide bands would be of the least benefit in consolidating the overlapping felloe-ends. In Wilkinson's drawing (see fig. 2) the tyre-joins are shown as just over the end of each felloe-join, which would permit two bands, rather than one, as now, to pass around each felloe-join, but would still place some extra pressure on the area of the tyre-join. The optimum position for the joins would seem to be half-way between each felloe join. The wheel has clearly been reassembled at least once, and probably twice or more. There is nothing in its basic construction that would require the tyre-ends to be originally positioned as they now are. Modern steel plates screwed across the tyre-ends (on the reverse side from that photographed) probably belong to the most

---

[5] Wilkinson 1923, 234f., with fig. 66. Williams 1923, 8 also suggests restoring the "leather bands, . . . for the passage of which the twenty-four slits in the tire . . . were originally employed".

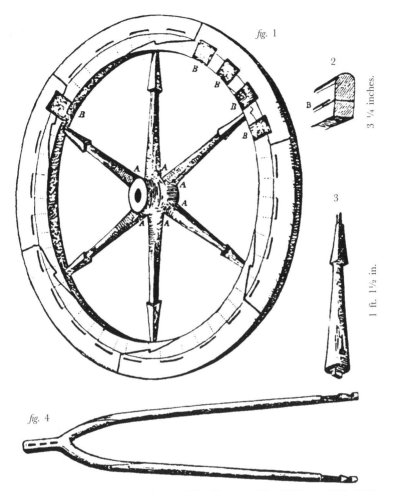

Fig. 1. Wheel; 3 ft. 1 in. diameter. After Wilkinson 1878, 243f.
4. Shafts; 11 feet in total length.

Fig. 2

recent reassemblage. Single holes or pairs of them near the tyre-joins on the opposite side of the wheel (see pls. 139, 140c) must have been for nails that held cruder metal strips or rawhide that at one time served the same purpose. Their erratic positions, however, bespeak hasty and makeshift work, and it is unlikely that they date from the origin of this otherwise metalless wheel. They were either not present when Wilkinson made his drawing (see fig. 2) or he did not consider them original; for they do not appear on it.

There is no sign of there ever having been a second tyre of hide or metal and, while we cannot rule out the former,[6] the wear on the tread seems to indicate that for at least part of its active life the wooden tyre was without protection. The surface of the tread is worn in a peculiar manner (see pl. 140b); instead of being flattened with wear, it has a narrow wavering ridge in the centre, from which it slants down on either side. This suggests that the tread was originally quite high-crested, and that the wheel wobbled from side to side on a loose-fitting nave, so that it was seldom absolutely vertical, hence received its wear on the bias. The graining of the wood may also have had something to do with the differential wear, as is particularly obvious at the knot near one tyre-end (see pl. 139, top).

A few worm holes are present in the spokes and nave (see pls. 139 and 140a–c).

A unique feature of this wheel is the T-shaped aperture cut out of the wider face of each spoke near the nave (see pl. 140a and fig. 1), the head of the T lying towards the nave. The flimsy, (relatively) modern wire that passes through these slots suggests their original purpose; they must have been for the passage of a reinforcement that helped to hold the spokes tightly in the nave. It seems likely that this was of rawhide rather than of metal, as there seem to have been no other metal parts to the wheel. If it were rawhide put on green, it would shrink as it dried and have a considerable constricting effect, an effect usually produced on nave-morticed spokes such as these by strong, tight-fitting felloes and tyres, and one probably lacking here owing to the numerous parts of which the felloe and tyre consist. Such a band just outside the nave is not exemplified on any wheel, past or present, known to us either from material or representational evidence. All that would show, of course, in the strict profile view that is the usual one in early art, would be, in proportion to the rest, a mere line and, as a matter of convenience,

---

[6] At least two chariots of Tut'ankhamūn (those found in the treasury) had rawhide tyres, as did the chariot of Yuaa and Thuiu (Quibell 1908, 67), although in the latter case a decorative dressed leather tyre covered two of rawhide. That rawhide tyres may not be as impractical as they might seem is demonstrated by their use in recent times. The American pioneer 'Red-River cart', in which no metal was used, had a rawhide tyre 'shrunken' on, i.e. put on green. This cart was intended for rough country and carried a far heavier load than the Egyptian chariot. The chief defect of the rawhide tyre appeared to be that, if it became wet again and remained so for too long, it became 'unshrunk' (Eggenhofer 1961, 80). This problem would hardly arise in Egypt.

this might have been omitted in representations. The reason for the shape of these apertures, however, is still not explained; for the stem of the T would seem to have no functional purpose. Perhaps the slot was made in this shape to render it more decorative – if not to the observer on the side lines, then to the vehicle occupants, a stipulation that applies also to the 'barbs' near the outer ends of the spokes.

Discussion

In attempting to determine the type of vehicle (chariot, cart, or wagon) to which the Brooklyn wheel may have belonged and its possible date, its reported provenance – 'a tomb near the pyramids of Dashour', according to Bonomi, or a 'mummy pit near Dashour', according to Abbott,[7] – is of no help. No mention is made anywhere of the other wheel or wheels that must originally have belonged with it. Nor is the interpretation of some accompanying pieces of wood as 'shafts of a chariot' valid (see pl. 141).[8] The periods during which the cemetery at Dahshûr was in use seem to have been largely confined to the Old and Middle Kingdoms, with the exception of a few later remains, including Roman tombs.[9]

Although the wood of the wheel is too contaminated to be dated by radio-carbon, internal evidence points to a date no earlier than

---

[7] Bonomi (n.d.), 4f.; Abbott 1862, 29.

[8] The 'shafts' as illustrated by Wilkinson are composed of a wishbone-shaped piece of wood with three slots in the 'handle' and two apparently identical extensions to the 'legs', the joins being mitred. The over-all length is given as 11 ft (3.352 m.). Of this object, however, only the first element now remains and none of the other miscellaneous pieces of wood accompanying the wheel would fit as extensions or even as parts thereof. Not only is the harnessing of a single horse between shafts considered a late development, still experimental and sporadic in Roman-Imperial times (Spruytte 1977, 132, with pl. 35), but there is no record then or subsequently of shafts splaying outwards from a single attachment to a vehicle, as these 'shafts' would. Not only would the shape and dimensions of the wishbone's 'handle' make it unsuitable for attaching to any vehicle, but the shallow slots, which do not pierce it, would not furnish any means of attachment. When we subtract from the complete object as seen by Wilkinson the length of the 'handle' (0.265 m.), there would still be more than 3.0 m. left in front of the vehicle. This would make the 'shafts' extend over 1.0 m. further ahead of the vehicle than any known chariot-pole.

[9] Porter and Moss 1964, 239 n. 18; for Dahshûr in general see 229ff., for Roman tombs see 233.

well into the Late Period, yet there is no reason to believe that it is (relatively) modern. The evidence is primarily furnished by the type of marks encircling the nave, which indicate the use of the true lathe. While most authorities favour an introduction of this tool into Egypt not earlier than the Hellenistic or even the Roman period,[10] another relatively late Egyptian adoption may help us to place an upper limit on the manufacture of the Brooklyn wheel. Cole has suggested that the lathe was not in common use until iron cutting-tools were available,[11] and this would certainly apply to anything as relatively thick and heavy as the nave of our wheel. According to Lucas and Harris, iron-ore was not worked in Egypt before the sixth century B.C., although it may have been worked a little earlier in Nubia, and iron objects in small quantities had, of course, appeared in Egypt over a long period of time.[12]

Unfortunately, by far the greatest amount of comparative material-evidence for Egyptian wheel-construction is too early to be very illuminating. It may be noteworthy, however, that both nave- and spoke-construction of extant Eighteenth Dynasty wheels are very different from those of the Brooklyn specimen. This construction, with each spoke consisting of two sections glued back to back, the angles at their heads forming integral parts of the nave, is more explicit in pl. 142 than many words could make it. This shows exactly these parts of a wheel of Amenophis III, now in the Ashmolean Museum, Oxford.[13] The same parts of the wheels of two chariots of Tut'ankhamūn that were sufficiently disassembled to be completely examined were constructed on a variant of this pattern.[14] The area of nave- and spoke-junction on the other Eighteenth Dynasty wheels shows a surface-profile identical to that of the Amenophis III nave or the Tutʿankhamūn examples referred to above, and very different from that of the same area on the Brooklyn wheel.

Other material evidence for Egyptian wheel-construction is confined to the small, solid disc wheels of a four-wheeled trolley of the Ptolemaic

---

[10] Lucas and Harris 1962, 449f.; cf. also Aldred 1957, 222f.

[11] Cole 1954, 518.

[12] Lucas and Harris 1962, 237–243.

[13] Western 1973 with figs. 1 and 2 and pl. xxxiv.

[14] This is apparent on H. Carter's drawings of the wheels of chariots, nos. 332 and 333, now preserved in the Griffith Institute of the Ashmolean Museum, Oxford, for whom the authors are publishing the Tutʿankhamūn chariots. They were also able to confirm this by autopsy in Cairo.

period from Medînet Mâdî[15] and to a hitherto unpublished, damaged, lathe-turned nave now in the Louvre,[16] (see pl. 143a–b). The
latter is constructed on the same principle as the nave of the Brooklyn
wheel and also had its spokes tenoned into it. It has, by a curious
coincidence, a recent history rather similar to that of the Brooklyn
wheel. It comes also from a collection formed in Cairo at about the
same time as the Abbott collection, by another amateur collector
and medical man, the French surgeon, Antoine-Barthélemy Clot
(called Clot Bey), and brought back to France around 1860, probably reaching the Louvre only after having belonged to the city of
Marseilles.[17] The only suggestion as to its provenance is that it is
likely to have come from the region of Thebes, since that is where
Clot Bey acquired much of his collection.[18]

> This nave is also basically cylindrical, formed from a single piece of
> wood and 0.322 m. long. The diameter of the interior passage is con-
> stant throughout (0.08 m.) and, like the Brooklyn nave, it is thicker-
> walled at its centre, where the spoke-end mortices are located. It varies
> from the Brooklyn example in having mortices for eight, rather than
> six, spoke-ends, and in that the exterior walls thicken again towards
> their ends, giving them a rather trumpet-like profile. The spoke-
> mortices are stepped, being 0.047 by 0.03 m. at their outer openings,
> and 0.04 by 0.02 m. at their inner ones, with vertical walls 0.005–0.01 m.
> deep between. Roughly in the centre of each space between two mortice-
> holes there is a small round hole, c. 0.004 m. in diameter and c. 0.018 m.
> deep. All but one of these holes are still plugged with the remains of
> wood, the purpose of which is unknown. As on the Brooklyn nave,
> numerous parallel incisions indicate that this nave was also turned on
> a lathe.

On what type of vehicle might the Brooklyn wheel have been used?
We shall distinguish between chariots, which are two-wheeled; carts,
which are also two-wheeled; and wagons, which are four-wheeled,
discussing the less likely candidates first. It is a striking feature of an
art so rich in circumstantial scenes of daily life as the Egyptian that
representations of true carts are so rare that one is forced to conclude that they were little used.

---

[15] Dittmann 1941 with figs. 1 and 3.
[16] Louvre E 109.
[17] We have, however, looked in vain through Maspero 1889 for any listing of
this nave.
[18] Personal communication of J.-L. de Cenival.

We know of only two figured documents from the Late Period with carts, neither of which shows the wheels in sufficient detail for comparison with the Brooklyn wheel:

1. Relief on wall of pyramid temple at Bergerauieh near Meroë, Nubia (Twenty-fifth Dynasty), depicting a funerary procession in which a stela is carried on a shallow two-wheeler pulled by two men, the wheel of which is shown as eight-spoked.[19]

2. Fragmentary relief on wall of temple at Sanam, Nubia, built by Taharqa (Twenty-fifth Dynasty), showing part of the felloe and of one spoke of load-carrying vehicle. (A cart, rather than a wagon, is suggested by the position of the mule behind it.)[20]

Late Period evidence for wagons, apart from the actual low trolley with small, solid wheels mentioned above (diam. 0.31 m.),[21] consists of several figured documents. On reliefs from the temple of Taharqa mentioned above we see at least three – perhaps four – four-wheeled wagons and one that is apparently six-wheeled.[22] They all have six-spoked wheels, the spokes and felloes of which are noticeably thicker than those of the eight-spoked chariot wheels also depicted there.[23]

All other representations of four-wheelers from the Late Period known to us show floats supporting a papyrus bark, in the centre of which is placed a funeral shrine or the shrine of a deity – the continuation of a practice documented as early as the Thirteenth Dynasty by a painting in the tomb of Sebeknakhte[24] and in the Eighteenth Dynasty by the model from the tomb of Queen ʿAhḥotpe.[25] At least seven Late Period examples are known, five of which were discussed by Dittmann:

---

[19] Lepsius 1913, fig. 41a; Dittmann 1941, 67 with fig. 6. It should be noted that the drawing in Dittmann is taken from Lepsius, who is not always reliable in the matter of spokes. For instance, the drawing of the relief of the battle of Kadesh on the second pylon of the Ramesseum, so frequently reproduced in the earlier literature, erroneously shows eight-spoked wheels instead of six-spoked ones on all but the royal chariot.

[20] Griffith 1922, 94 with pl. xxiv, 3.

[21] Dittmann 1941, 60–4 with figs. 1 and 3.

[22] Griffith 1922, 99 with pl. xxxii, 3 and 7.

[23] Griffith 1922, pls. xxiv, 2 and xxxii, 1. The wheel of the only other chariot here (pl. xxiv, 4) is effaced.

[24] Tylor 1896, pl. II; Dittmann 1941, 65 with fig. 4.

[25] Vernier 1927, pl. xlix; Smith 1958, 125 with pl. 84 (a.). A wooden model of a boat on wheels found in a Nineteenth Dynasty tomb at Gurob (Brunton and Engelbach 1927, pl. lii) is not considered to belong in this category, but perhaps

1. Relief on wall of pyramid temple at Bergerauieh (already mentioned);[26]

2. Relief on east wall of chapel of tomb of Petosiris at Hermopolis (dated by Lefebvre to the end of fourth or beginning of third century B.C.);[27]

3. On a mummy-cloth painting, illustrated by Wilkinson, of unknown date and provenance, but attributed by Dittmann to the same period as the Petosiris tomb;[28]

4. On a relief on a limestone block found at Kôm el-Fakhry near Memphis, attributed to the Twenty-sixth Dynasty, now in the Cairo Museum;[29]

5. On an Alexandrian coin.[30]

To these may be added the following:

6. On the north wall of the tomb of Si-amùn in the Sîwa Oasis, dated by Fakhry '400–200 B.C.';[31]

7. On a second Alexandrian coin.[32]

No. 1 has ten-spoked wheels; on nos. 2, 3, and 6 the wheels are eight spoked, nos. 2 and 6 having carved papyriform spokes; no. 7 is spoked, but the number of spokes is uncertain, and nos. 4 and 5 have solid, disc wheels. On nos. 2 and 6 the felloes appear to be studded. Although dimensions deduced from figured documents are unreliable, where human figures are present for comparison these wheels all appear smaller than the Brooklyn specimen, which is 0.96 m. in diameter. They also seem heavier. Our wheel really does not fit this picture.

Finally, when considering the possibility of the use of the Brooklyn wheel with a chariot, it may be worth while briefly to compare its dimensions and construction with other surviving chariot wheels,

---

to represent a warship; the wheels, which are solid, are painted in an unintelligible manner.

[26] Dittmann 1941.

[27] Lefebvre 1923–24, 1. 129. 111, pls. 30. 34; Dittmann 1941, 68f. with fig. 7.

[28] Wilkinson 1878, 237 with fig. 69; Dittmann 1941, 69 with fig. 8.

[29] Cairo, no. 2434. Mariette 1889, pl. 35a; Dittmann 1941, 67; Drioton 1949, pl. 192.

[30] Dattari 1901, no. 3557, pl. 27; Weber 1914, 255f. with fig. 127; Dittmann 1941, 68.

[31] Fakhry 1944, 144 with fig. 24.

[32] Dattari 1901, op. cit. no. 1158.

although these are much earlier (fourteenth century B.C.). There is
a striking accord in certain dimensions. For instance, the heaviest of
Tutʿankhamūn's chariot wheels[33] (see pl. 144) have diameters of
c. 0.97 m., which is close to the Brooklyn wheel's diameter of c. 0.96 m.;
the depth of the perimeter (from inside to outside), in both cases
composed of a felloe and a wooden tyre, is 0.083 and 0.085 m.
respectively. The spokes are elliptical in section on both wheels, and
taper towards the felloe; on the older one they are 0.042×0.02 m.
at the nave, tapering to 0.02×0.018 m. at the felloe; the corresponding measurements on the later wheel are 0.045×0.035 m. and
0.025×0.018 m. The nave-length of the earlier wheel is 0.405 m.,
and that the later one 0.37 m. The most appreciable difference is
in the interior diameter of the nave, that of the Eighteenth Dynasty
nave being 0.048 m. and that of the Brooklyn nave 0.072 m. This
indicates an axle half again as thick.

Although, as mentioned above, the construction of nave and spoke
is based on quite different principles in the two wheels, the felloe
and tyre in both cases are made on essentially the same principles,
if differing in execution. The overlapping sections of felloe on the
first wheel are two, those on the second six; the butt-ended sections
of tyre are four on the first and six on the second. Moreover, the
tyre-sections are attached to the felloe by differing methods: in the
first only at their ends by narrow bronze thongs, in the second at
close intervals throughout their length by wide leather bands. Despite
these last differences, the Brooklyn wheel would thus seem a possible candidate for a chariot wheel.

If this wheel should belong to a chariot, then to what sort of chariot? What were the Egyptian chariots of the Late Period like? With
the chariots of her enemies developing rather rapidly during the first
millennium, would Egypt have kept hers unchanged? This is a question that, so far as we know, has never been raised. However, before
discussing possible changes, it is advisable to review briefly the 'classic' Egyptian chariot. This, as seen in profile in New Kingdom reliefs
and wall-paintings and exemplified materially by Eighteenth Dynasty
survivals, is a very light, shallow vehicle, just wide enough (c. 1.0 m.)
for two to stand abreast, and about half as deep from back to front

---

[33] Chariot no. 161. Dimensions obtained from Carter's drawing in the Griffith
Institute, see above n. 14.

(see pls. 145 and 144 right).[34] The floor-plan is like a capital D and the large fenestrations so often present in the side of the box lighten it. The railed edge of the box is normally very rounded as it drops to the floor at the rear on either side. When equipped for war or hunting, a long bowcase is attached at one side of the chariot-box, projecting conspicuously in front. Quivers for arrows are shorter and are attached at the sides at less of an angle.[35] By the time of Sethos I, a pair of knobbed javelins with tassels are added to the quivers and project considerably beyond the arrows.[36] The axles of all but a few of the earliest of these chariots are set under the rear edge of the box. Four-spoked wheels prevail until near the end of the fifteenth century B.C., when six-spoked wheels become the standard, with occasional eight-spoked exceptions.

There is no material evidence of chariots from the Late Period, and the figured documents are neither always very precisely dated nor very informative. They consist of three faience relief vases, a scarab, some stone reliefs, and a drawing on stone.

The last Egyptian representations that we have of wheels with six spokes (the number of the Brooklyn wheel) come probably at the beginning of this list. They are on a faience relief chalice from Tûna at Eton College and from a fragment of a similar chalice in Berlin – both attributed to the Twenty-second Dynasty (c. 950–817 B.C.).[37] They are most unsatisfactory documents, however. Beyond the facts that the wheels are six-spoked and that the chariot-box on the first chalice may be interpreted as deep and rectangular (that on the second is incoherent), little can be deduced.

Probably to be considered with these (although Smith has suggested a date as late as the seventh century B.C.) is the fragment of a Tûna bowl in Boston.[38] This shows not only a wheel with more spokes (nine) but a chariot-box that is quite different from those on

---

[34] Dimensions obtained from Botti 1951, 197, and from A. C. Mace's notes and Carter's drawings preserved in the Griffith Institute (see above n. 14), supplemented by personal examination of chariots in Cairo.

[35] Carter and Newberry 1904, pls. 10 and 11 = Wreszinski 1935, pls. 1 and 2 = Pritchard 1954, nos. 314 and 315 = Yadin 1963, 192–3.

[36] Wreszinski 1935, pl. 36a = Pritchard 1954, no. 322.

[37] Tait 1963, no. xix (Eton 72), 117–19 with pl. xix, no. xxxviii (Berlin 16024), p. 126 with pl. xxii. Nagel 1966, 34 and 66 with fig. 22) mistakenly places the Twenty-second Dynasty representation in the seventeenth century B.C.

[38] Boston, MFA no. 59.422; Boston, MFA Annual Report (1959), 114; Tait 1963, 129 with pl. xxiii, 7; Smith 1965, 47, with fig. 73.

the chalices (see pl. 146). Its actual date would be particularly pertinent; for it indicates that by the time it was made familiarity with
the classic, New Kingdom chariot type had disappeared – at least in
regions where the great temple-reliefs were not immediately accessible to refresh the memory. On it we apparently see a misunderstood and deformed version of the old chariot, for its ultimate
inspiration is a Nineteenth Dynasty scene at Karnak: Sethos I striding towards his chariot with armfuls of prisoners.[39] In the original
scene the chariot is the standard New Kingdom fenestrated type
described above. On the bowl fragment, the thick, obliquely set shafts
at front and back are evidently misinterpretations of bowcases and
quivers. The siding of the anomalous box shows a rectangular pattern reminiscent of chariot-sidings of a type first recorded in Assyria
in the eighth century B.C.[40] The feet of the driver are shown as
level with the top of the siding.

A scarab of Shoshenk IV is more securely dated, but the picto-
graphic rendering of the chariot tells us only that its wheel was eight-
spoked.[41]

Fragmentary wall reliefs from Taharqa's temple at Sanam provide
somewhat more revealing glimpses of three chariots.[42] One of these
had enough of the wheel left to deduce eight spokes.[43] Two others
seem to show vertical quivers at the front of the box,[44] as on eighth-
and seventh-century B.C. Assyrian chariots,[45] but an obliquely fastened sheath of some sort projects in front, as did the bowcases on
the old chariots.[46] The box seems to have a different top-line from
that of the traditional Egyptian chariot.

Two scenes, considered to be consciously archaizing, offer dubi-
ous evidence. A relief in the tomb of Ebe (period of Psammētichus
I) shows an eight-spoked wheel in a workshop-scene, but in a field-
scene from the same tomb the classic chariot, even down to the old

---

[39] Wreszinski 1935, pl. 36a.
[40] Thureau-Dangin and Dunand 1936, pl. xlix and Madhloom 1970, 18, pl. xii,
1; Barnett and Falkner 1962, pl. xliv; pls. lxxi and lxxxiii and Madhloom 1970,
pl. III 2 and 1.
[41] Berlin no. 14427. Newberry 1906, 166 with pl. xxviii, 18.
[42] Griffith 1922, 94 and 99 with pls. xxiv, 2, 4 and xxii, 1, 2.
[43] Griffith 1922, pl. xxxii, 1.
[44] Griffith 1922, pls. xxiv, 4 and xxxii, 1.
[45] See above n. 40.
[46] See above n. 35.

four-spoked wheel, appears.[47] Another workshop scene from a tomb relief now in Florence, also dated to the Twenty-sixth Dynasty, provides another example of the old-fashioned chariot with four-spoked wheels.[48] These are from Theban tombs, where the artist would have had representations of the old chariots before his eyes.

A fragment of a trial relief in Berlin is assigned to a later period (Ptolemaic) (see pl. 147).[49] This is another example of misinterpretation of the Sethos I motif already noted on the Tûna relief bowl in Boston. The chariot-box siding is here shaped like a sugar loaf and appears unrealistically open at front and back. The eight spokes are papyrus-headed and the felloe is studded with large nails − both features reminiscent of the wheels on the funeral wagons of Petosiris and Si-amūn.

A relief of lion-headed Astarte driving a quadriga, from the Great Temple of Edfu and dating to the reign of Ptolemy XVI,[50] supplies us with a no less atypical Egyptian chariot, and one whose type seems to derive from the Orient, possibly from Phoenicia. Although the floor of the vehicle is represented as level with the upper edge of the box, and there is an unexplained 'lip' at the front of the latter, this relief testifies either to the recent presence at this time in Egypt of a type of chariot evidenced on fourth-century B.C. coins of Sidon,[51] or to the artist's acquaintance with its representation − on coins or otherwise. The well-preserved coins of this type show a chariot box with vertical panelling similar to that on the Edfu vehicle and an eight-spoked wheel that has similarly carved spokes.

So far these are only hints (negative or positive) that the Egyptian chariot was following the trend of other chariots in the Near East in the first millennium B.C. In Assyria, for instance (from which we have the most extensive documentation), the small, fast, two-man chariot was going out in the eighth century B.C., its role being taken over by mounted troops (which had already begun to appear in the ninth century). The chariot was becoming larger and heavier, with an apparently rectangular floor-plan, and it might carry three or

---

[47] Wreszinski 1923, pl. 137.
[48] Florence, Museo Archeologico, no. 31124; Wreszinski 1935, pl. 36.
[49] Berlin, VA 3425. Borchardt 1935, 40; Wreszinski, op. cit. 11 36a; Brunner-Traut 1956, pl. xlviii.
[50] Naville 1870, 17 with pl. xiii, Leclant 1960, 54ff. with pl. iva and b.
[51] Head 1887, 672 with fig. 354; Babelon 1893, pl. 30, 11 = Nuoffer 1904 frontispiece = Studniczka 1907, 191 with fig. 35.

four men; by the seventh century it had conspicuously larger wheels and was drawn by four horses.[52]

From Egypt we do have one much more explicit example of one of the new chariots than any of those cited above. This appears in a drawing on a limestone block of unknown provenance now in the Kestner Museum, Hanover (see pl. 148).[53] Although it has been dated variously to the Eighteenth or Nineteenth Dynasty, the simple fact that it is a *quadriga* would place it much later. The first appearance anywhere of the four-horse chariot occurs in the ninth century B.C.,[54] but it does not become prevalent until the eighth or seventh century B.C.[55] The convention used in the Kestner drawing, which shows four nose- and four chest-profiles of the horses, though only two sets of legs, is similar to one sometimes obtaining in eighth-century B.C. Assyria, where a pair of horses may have two facial profiles and only one set of legs.[56]

The chariot-box in this study is without the old Egyptian fenestration, and is deeper from back to front than the earlier chariot. Its general profile not only does not resemble those of New Kingdom chariots but is reminiscent of that of a chariot on an eighth-century-B.C. Neo-Hittite relief from Sakçagözü,[57] of those of fifth-century Persian and Syrian chariots at Persepolis,[58] and even of those of the

---

[52] Parrot 1961, pls. 65 and 345; Strommenger 1964, pls. 248 and 253; Gadd 1936, 204 with pl. 44 = Yadin 1963, 452. Although the teams in these are depicted as only one animal, the four reins (the outside reins being attached by slip knots to the chariot front corners) indicate four horses, as do the four-horse yokes shown with unharnessed chariots: cf. Gadd 1936, 187 with pl. 18; Yadin 1963, 426 and 430 (lower ill.). For possible rein arrangement cf. Paterson 1915, 107–8.

[53] Hanover, Kestner Museum no. 2952. Baud 1935, 55f.; Brunner-Traut 1956, 101f. with pl. xlviii; Woldering 1958, fig. 38; 1961, pl. 12; 1967, 129 with pl. 23. Hoping to find another means of limiting the time-range for this piece, through the kindness of Professor J. R. Harris, we asked Professor Iversen of the University of Copenhagen, who has been working on canons of proportion, if the grid on this sketch could give us any lead to its dating. Unfortunately, while this drawing is made under the first canon of proportion, this canon continued in use even after the second canon was introduced in the Twenty-sixth Dynasty. We wish to thank both Dr Harris and Professor Iversen for this information.

[54] Barnett (n.d.), pls. 18. 20. 24. 25. In the first two instances two pairs of horses are being swum after a single chariot transported by boat, and in the latter two instances the four pairs of reins carefully rendered indicate four-horse teams.

[55] See above n. 52.

[56] Barnett and Falkner 1962, pls. xliv, lxvii, and lxxxiii.

[57] Bossert 1942, no. 886; Meyer 1965, pl. 90; Madhloom 1970, pl. xiii, 1.

[58] Schmidt 1953, pls. 32a and b and 52.

yet later gold models from the Oxus Treasure.[59] There is no evidence for a small, *attached*, open handhold at the rear upper corner of the box in the second millennium B.C. and, indeed, this appears primarily (in a slightly different shape) on Persian chariots of the fifth and fourth centuries B.C.[60] The pole-support that drops down from the top of the front breastwork at a far sharper angle than the Egyptian ones (see pl. 145) is very typical of Assyrian chariots.[61] What appears to be a fringe hangs from the lower edge of the chariot side. Such a thing is never shown on New Kingdom chariots, but sometimes appears on oriental chariots in the eighth and seventh centuries B.C.[62] The horses are not moving at the high *cabré allongé* by which New Kingdom artists rendered the gallop (see pl. 145), but at the low one by which the Assyrians and the Persians depicted this gait.[63] The chariot-box shows no arms, and the driver is unarmed, flourishing merely a whip. There is no indication that this is a battle scene and that this might be a fleeing enemy chariot. The charioteer is clearly an Egyptian, and we may suggest that this represents an Egyptian chariot of its period, and one that has developed along oriental lines. Since, however, it combines features of different Asiatic chariots over a fair range of time (late eighth to fifth and even fourth century B.C.) and place (Syria to Persia and beyond) it is impossible to date it precisely or to establish that it was the product of any particular influence. Was it the result of the seventh-century B.C. Assyrian invasions under Esarhaddon and Ashurbanipal, or of the Persian dominations of the sixth and fourth centuries B.C.?[64]

We may, therefore, ask if the Brooklyn wheel may not have belonged to an Egyptian chariot influenced by Asiatic types. The lathe-turned nave of our wheel firmly places it in a time (well within

---

[59] Dalton 1964, xxxix–xli with figs. 20. 21, pl. IV and 'additional' pl. at end. Ghirshman 1964, pl. 301.

[60] Cf. Persepolis relief (Schmidt 1953, pl. 52) and seals (Frankfort 1939a), pls. xxxvii d and n; Terrace 1962, pl. 57; Ghirshman 1964, pl. 329).

[61] Barnett (n.d.), pls. 24–5; Strommenger 1964, pls. 248 and 253.

[62] Bossert 1942, no. 886; Meyer, op. cit. pl. 90; Strommenger, op. cit. pl. 248; M. Mallowan, Nimrud and its Remains (New York, 1966), pl. 387; Madhloom 1970, pl. xiii, 1 and 2; Karageorghis 1966a, 105f. with fig. 3; 1967a, fig. 7.

[63] Strommenger 1964, pls. 206 (above), 248 and 253; Frankfort 1939a, pl. xxxvii d; Ghirshman 1964, pl. 329.

[64] Sennacherib (704–681 B.C.), during his invasion of Palestine, records capturing 'Egyptian charioteers' in the battle in the plain of Eltekeh: cf. Pritchard 1955, 287.

the first millennium B.C.) when this would have been very probable. We have already seen that there is little, if any, reliable evidence for the use of the classic, second-millennium type of Egyptian
chariot at that time. Apart from the two apparently consciously
archaizing scenes in the Ebe tomb reliefs and the relief in Florence,[65]
all we have are some misunderstood renderings of it,[66] and we may
be justified in wondering if such chariots were still in use. The
Brooklyn wheel, by its slightly heavier build than the heaviest surviving chariot wheels of Tut'ankhamūn (see above), and by its pro-
vision for a thicker axle, would be suitable for one of these generally
larger and heavier first-millennium B.C. oriental chariots. On the
other hand, certain details of construction give reason to believe that
this wheel did not belong merely to an imported oriental chariot,
but to an Egyptian one built under oriental influence. The rim, made
up of felloe and wooden tyre, is only slightly deeper (0.02 m.) than
that on the Eighteenth Dynasty chariot mentioned above, but not
nearly as deep in proportion to the total diameter as those consistently depicted on Assyrian chariots.[67] The difference in relative proportions of felloe and tyre and the manner of joining these two seems
even greater. While in the New Kingdom chariot wheel and the
Brooklyn wheel the felloe and tyre are of almost equal depth, the
wooden tyres of Assyrian and Persian wheels are shown as at least
twice as deep as the felloes.[68] In both Egyptian examples the outer
surfaces of the felloe and the inner surfaces of the tyre are smooth,
and merely lie flush with each other, but those of Assyrian and
Persian chariot wheels were apparently tongued and grooved into
each other.[69] However, the wide bands that bind tyre to felloe in
the Brooklyn wheel (see fig. 1) look as if they might have been
inspired by examples of similar appearance on Assyrian chariot
wheels,[70] although in the latter case they were fewer in number and
probably of metal.

In contrast to royal Assyrian chariot wheels of the seventh century and to Persian examples of the fifth and fourth centuries

---

[65] See above nn. 47 and 48.
[66] See above nn. 37. 38. 49. 50.
[67] Barnett (n.d.), pls. 24 and 25; Strommenger 1964, pls. 248 and 253.
[68] Barnett (n.d.), pls. 24 and 25; Strommenger 1964, pls. 248 and 253; Schmidt 1953, pl. 52.
[69] Kossack 1971, 155–9.
[70] Strommenger 1964, pls. 248 and 253.

B.C.,[71] the Brooklyn wheel has no studded tyre. It is interesting to note that the wheel on the chariot of Asiatic type in the Kestner-Museum drawing is also unstudded. In Egypt studded wheels are only seen on some representations of the Ptolemaic period.[72]

The number of spokes, i.e. six, in the Brooklyn wheel would be rather unusual in both Egypt and other parts of the Near East from the eighth century B.C. onwards, when the prevalent number becomes eight or more. Six are still sometimes found, however,[73] and our wheel may be one of the exceptions.

More significant may be the minimal carving on the narrower faces of our spokes. While these carvings would hardly be visible in a strict profile view, it may be worth noting that at least by the beginning of the fifth century B.C. Persian chariot-wheel spokes show slight decorative carving near their centres.[74] Yet this carving is quite different from the heavy carving we have seen on the spokes of Ptolemaic funeral floats and garbled renderings of chariots and which was apparently popular in that period.[75] The Brooklyn wheel may thus bear early witness to the modest beginning of carved spokes in Egypt, perhaps under Persian influence.

---

[71] Strommenger 1964, pls. 248 and 253; Schmidt 1953, pl. 52; Frankfort 1939a, pls. xxxvii d and n; Ghirshman 1964, fig. 301; Dalton 1964, pl. IV.

[72] Cf. nn. 27, 31, and 49.

[73] E.g. New York MMA, acc. no. 74.51.2451: relief of end of fifth century B.C. Cypriote limestone sarcophagus from Golgoi, Studniczka 1907, 182 with fig. 28; Myres 1909–11, 5f.; Athens 17376: terracotta chariot model, Karageorghis 1967a, fig. 8.

[74] Schmidt 1953, pl. 52; Frankfort 1939a, XXXVII n; Terrace 1962, pl. 57.

[75] Cf. nn. 27. 31. 49. 50.

23. A LATE BRONZE-AGE SPOKED WHEEL FROM LIDAR HÖYÜK IN SOUTHEAST TURKEY*

HARALD HAUPTMANN

*Introduction***

The second millennium B.C. in the region of the middle Euphrates belongs to the insufficiently studied periods of Old Syria. The excavations in Carchemiš at that time had not reached the second millennium level, except for a sondage on the main Tell. Thus, it was not possible to evaluate the archaeological background of this north-Syrian center during the Middle Bronze Age Ammorite dynasty and during the following Hittite domination in the Late Bronze Age.[1] According to texts from Ebla, Carchemiš already by the middle of the 3rd millennim B.C. played a leading role in Syria,[2] and retained this position as the seat of the Hittite *Sekundogenitur* in Syria until the fall of the central power in the Anatolian plateau.

For the first time a sequence of strata at Lidar Höyük allows us a glimpse of a Middle and Late Bronze Age settlement (fig. 1).[3] Lidar Höyük is situated on the left bank of the Euphrates; from here an important trade route leads 9 km. upstream to the loftily situated settlement of Samsat and to an important pass in the Taurus mountains of Commagene. Thus, Lidar Höyük provides one of the con-

---

* Published as "Ein spätbronzezeitliches Speichenrad vom Lidar Höyük in der Südost-Türkei", *Archäologischer Anzeiger* 1991, 349–358. (H. Hauptmann, "Einleitung", 349–351.)
** Translated by M. A. Littauer and the editor.
  Sources of figures: fig. 1: K. Messmer.—fig. 2: Lidar Excavation (Archive). Fig. 3: Th. Stern.—fig. 4. 5 after Littauer Crouwel 1985, pl. 71, 55.
  [1] Woolley and Barnett 1952, 214.
  [2] Astour 1988, 143 N. 29; 235f. n. 15, 17.
  [3] Hauptmann 1983, 254f. 35, 1985, 204. 37, 1987, 204f. Mellink 1983, 433. 88, 1984, 448f. pl. 58: 7; 89, 1985, 555 pl. 63; 91, 1987, 8f. figs. 2, 8; 92, 1988, 110f. figs. 5–9; 93, 1989, 114f. fig. 4; 94, 1990, 135 figs. 10–12.

Fig. 1. Map showing location of Lidar Höyük.

nections between Syria and Anatolia. Excavations at Lidar Höyük
in the province of Urfa were part of the Lower-Euphrates-Salvage
Project between 1979 and 1987. Due to the rising of the water level
of the Atatürk reservoir, further excavations were not possible.

Within Lidar Höyük's history of settlement – covering a period
from the Early Bronze Age (3rd millennium B.C.) to the Islamic
Middle Ages in the 13th century A.D. – the Middle Bronze Age is
of particular importance. The settlement covered four large con-
truction periods displaying Syrian and Hurrian elements in its architectural design. This settlement was destroyed by a fire which may
have been connected with the campaign of the Hittite king Ḫattušili
to Northern Syria around 1650 B.C. In the following Late Bronze

Age the settlement consisted of two smaller levels and there was no longer as spacious as the previous Hurrian buildings.[4]

Levels of the late Bronze Age were – with the exception of a *Stufengrabung* on the Northern slope – discovered on a large area in the southern and eastern part of Lidar Höyük. On the eastern slope (area M/N 49) in 1982 (stratum 7) parts of a badly burned building were investigated. The remains of this sun-dried bricked building yielded a room 14 m. by 5 m. with hearth and post holes. This room ended with 1 m.-wide limestone wall. This wall formed the border of a 3 m.-wide corridor floored with large flagstones. From this corridor a 1.10 m.-wide stair led down to the main room. Another flag-stoned entrance lay at its northwest end and behind a smaller room which contained numerous loom weights and pithoi.

In the debris from fire which filled the main room among the remains of charred beams – belonging to a part of the ceiling – finds came to light which proved a relationship to the 125-km., Carchemiš situated upstream. Before the southern stone wall two pithoi were placed, one of which bore an incised design. Next to a hunting scene there was a Hieroglyphic-Luvian royal sign. This was again repeated on the front of a limestone sculpture of a lying ibex.[5] On the fire-hardened floor numerous ibex horns were found, as well as the charred remains of a wheel (figs. 2 and 3). It was preserved as a thin layer of charred wood, thus permitting interpretation by M. A. Littauer and J. H. Crouwel.[6]

The dating of the building to the end of the Late Bronze Age is established by numerous vessels, among which there was a characteristic field flask and a bull's head rhyton. This dating was confirmed by two identically sealed clay bullas found in 1985 in a room south of the corridor. Both impressions show the seal of a king of Carchemiš called Kuzi-Teššup, Son of Talmi-Teššup.[7] As thus far known, this king was the last of a dynasty of Carchemiš, covering four generations, inaugurated 1325/22 B.C. by Šuppililiuma I. According to con-

---

[4] Hauptmann 1987, 205.
[5] Hauptmann 1983, 254; Mellink 1983, 433, pl. 58, 10.
[6] M. A. Littauer and J. H. Crouwel offered to publish this find seperately. We are indebted to R. Neef, Biologisch-Archeologisch Instituut of the University of Groningen, for the interpretation of the wheel and S. Bottema and M. N. van Loon for the transfer of the analysis. fig. 2 shows—in contrary to the drawing of the wheel as found (fig. 3)—the final stage of the excavation.
[7] Sürenhagen 1986, 183ff.; Hawkins 1988, 99ff.

temporaneous data, he also could be synchronized with Šuppililiuma II. of Ḫatti and Ḫammurapi, the last king of Ugarit, who can be dated at the end of the 13th century B.C. Kuzi-Teššup is mentioned in Hittite cuneiform records from Ḫattuša as a contemporary of Šup-pililiuma II. – but without a title. And it is likely that Kuzi-Teššup as 5th king of Carchemiš survived the collapse of the Hittite empire attributed to around 1200 B.C., because of his title "King of the land of Carchemiš".[8] The destruction of the building level does not indicate an important break in the history of the settlement since, in the following rebuilding and in the Early Iron age levels, a clear continuation of the Hittite Late Bronze Age architecture and par-ticularly the in the ceramics is to be observed. A lower limit for the destruction of Lidar Höyük, situated on the eastern border of the vice-kingdom of Carchemiš in the 12th century by the growing power of the Assyrians under Tiglathpilesar I. (1114–1076 B.C.) conquer-ing towards the west, cannot be excluded. A dating of the building with the wooden wheel to the period Kuzi-Teššup, the founder of the 'late Hittite' dynasty of Malatya,[9] and thus to the first quarter of the 12th century, to the beginning 'Dark Ages' following the 'inva-sion of the Sea Peoples' seems likely.

The Spoked Wheel

Mary Aiken Littauer and Joost H. Crouwel

The wheel was partly preserved as a thin layer carbonized in the fire that destroyed the building in the Late Bronze Age. Three whole spokes and part of a fourth are well preserved, while two further ones are recognizeable only by impressions and a slight discoloura-tion. Only small parts of the rim of the wheel are preserved as a thin layer of charcoal. The remainder, however, is clearly distinguishable as a dark-coloured impression. Most of the nave is missing. Enough remains, however, to establish the special construction of the wheel. It was made according to a technique that is materially documented only by surviving four- and six-spoked wheels of Egyptian chariots of the 18th Dynasty. At the same time, this construction is familiar

---

[8] Hawkins 1988, n. 100.
[9] Hawkins 1988, 102f., fig. 1.

Fig. 2. Lidar Höyük. Photograph of the spoked wheel as found.

from representations of chariots not only in Egypt but also else-where.[10]

The Lidar wheel was six-spoked, with a diameter of 0.86 m. In wheels of this construction from Egypt, the spokes are composed of lengths of wood that are flat on one side and half elliptical on the other. Each length is bent at its center to form an angle (of 60° in the case of a six-spoked wheel).[11] The individual V-shaped pieces were

---

[10] See Littauer and Crouwel 1985.
[11] The angle was obtained by bending under heat or possibly by influencing the growing process of the wood.

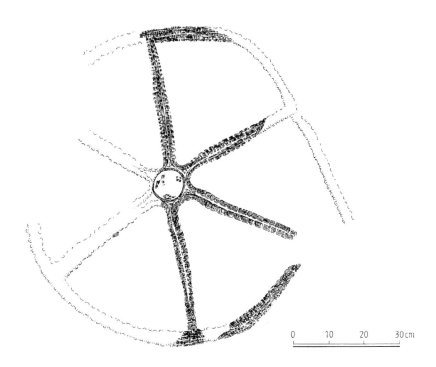

Fig. 3. Lidar Höyük. Drawing of spoked wheel as found.

then glued back to back along their length to form complementary
halves of sister spokes elliptical in section. In some Egyptian wheels
the apices of the spokes are joined together so as to form the nave
of the wheel (fig. 4);[12] in others they nestle in a separate, cylindrical nave (fig. 5).[13] The charred remains of the spokes of the Lidar
wheel clearly betray the "Egyptian" construction, and the nave appears
to belong to the second type described. Its length is not known; its
inner diameter (ca 8 cm.) is quite large by comparison with the naves
of Egyptian wheels (5.8–7 cm.) and would indicate a thick (and cor-
respondingly heavy) axle. The wheels would seem to have wobbled

---

[12] See Western 1973; Littauer and Crouwel 1985, 67f. (no. 4a), 76.
[13] Littauer and Crouwel 1985, 76–78 with pls. 55, 59.

considerably. However, the leather lining of the nave, present on Egyptian wheels, has certainly perished and this fact, as well as carbonization, may account for this apparent anomaly. The diameter of the Lidar wheel (ca 0.86 m.), on the other hand, is small by comparison with that of normal Egyptian chariot wheels which vary from ca 0.90 to ca 1.00 m., the majority falling in between.[14] Again, it may be the carbonization which accounts for the difference. The depth of the felloe (4 cm.) is within the range of that of the Egyptian chariot wheels (4–5.1 cm.). If the wheel resembled Egyptian chariot wheels in every respect, the felloe or rim would be of two unequal lengths of heat-bent wood, mitred where they overlapped. The outer ends of the spokes were inserted into the felloe. The remains are not sufficient, however, to confirm all these details.

Two samples of the wood, one from a spoke, the other from a part of the felloe, were identified as elm (*Ulmus*).[15] The spoke showed a little plane (*Platanus orientalis*.) which must have come from contact with the beam of this material that had fallen on it. The use of elm is materially confirmed in Egypt at this time: in the composite spokes and nave of the chariot of Amenophis III and in the felloes of one chariot of Tut'ankhamūn (fig. 4).[16]

The Lidar wheel is the first actual example of this construction that has been found outside Egypt and the only one to come from a settlement site and not a tomb where the wheels were deposited together with the chariot to which they belonged. The question arises whether it is a regular Egyptian wheel of a chariot that was captured in battle or acquired in diplomatic exchange, whether it was of local manufacture or made somewhere in Western Asia. Any of these suggestions seems quite possible.

Detailed Egyptian New-Kingdom representations in bas-relief or painting of Near Eastern chariots – either in battle scenes or as tribute – suggest that they basically resembled in all important respects the Egyptian chariot. At the same time, several sources indicate that the light, spoked-wheeled, horse-drawn chariot, in which the occupants stood, was not developed in Egypt but, like the horse, was

---

[14] The small idiosyncratic two-wheeled vehicle from the tomb of Yuia and Thuiu has wheels only 0.74 m. in diameter; see Littauer and Crouwel 1985, 67 (no. 3), 76, 100f.

[15] As determined by R. Neef, Groningen.

[16] Western 1973, 67f., 76; Littauer and Crouwel 1985, 92f.

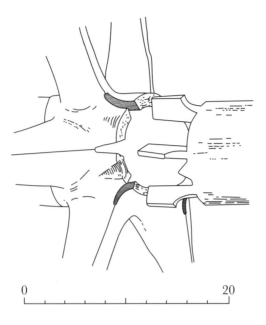

0   20

Fig. 4. Thebes. Detail of wheel from tomb of Amenophis III. Oxford, Ashmolean
Museum 1923.663

introduced from Western Asia.[17] It may be noted that Near Eastern
inspiration may also be assumed for the contemporary Late Bronze
Age chariots in the Aegean.[18] Figured documents clearly show that
the four-spoked wheels of these vehicles had the "Egyptian" nave-
and-spoke construction. The origin of this wheelright's technique is
probably to be sought in Western Asia where we now finally have
material evidence from the Middle Euphrates area. This technique
may be traced back to the 18th century B.C., if one is to judge
from the four-spoked cast bronze wheels of a large model or trolley from the so-called Burnt Palace at Acemhöyük in central Anatolia.[19]

The use of elm also points to a Near Eastern origin. Certain vari-
eties of this wood grow today in the "crescent formed by the foothills

[17] Littauer and Crouwel 1985, 96f.; see also Schulman 1979, 105–153.
[18] Crouwel 1981, 81f., 148f.
[19] Littauer and Crouwel 1986a.

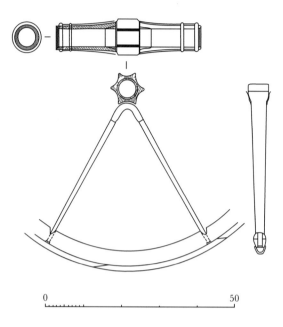

Fig. 5. Thebes. Details of wheel from tomb of Tutʿankhamūn. Cairo, Egyptian Museum 2321.

and mountains that run through Anatolia, northern Syria and north-eastern Iraq", and elm is likely to have grown there also in the Bronze Age.[20] Its use in the construction of wheels in Egypt, where elm did not naturally occur but had to be imported, would also point to the original discovery of its value for this purpose in a region where this timber was native. The rawhide which held the naves and spokes together, was put on wet and as it shrank in drying became an effective binding material, except if exposed to moisture when it tended then to stretch; it was frequently covered with birch bark. Birch does not grow in Egypt but is found in Anatolia and Armenia and must have been imported thence.[21] Its water-repellent properties were far less necessary in the dry climate of Egypt than during Egyptian military campaigns towards the north in the Levant.

---

[20] Western 1973, 93 with references. Elm is mentioned as wood of chariot wheels in Linear B tablets from Knossos; see Crouwel 1981, 87; it may be noted that later wheelwrights had a preference for this timber; see Piggott 1983, 28.
[21] Littauer and Crouwel 1985, 92f. (with references).

Thus the use of birch bark points to the origin of this form of wheel in an area where this variety of wood was easily obtainable and its properties known.

A comparison of these spoked wheels with those made according to a simpler method, in which the inner ends of the spokes are simply inserted in a cylindrical or barrel nave, is illuminating. The earliest available evidence of wheels made in this manner comes fron the site of Sintashta in the southern Urals where two-wheeled vehicles have been found in graves dated c. 2000–1800 B.C.[22] To be sure, there is yet no certain evidence of their construction, but impressions in the soil indicate ten spokes. These, if bent, would form an apex angle of only 36°, which would be more difficult to achieve by bending than the 45°–90° of the four- to eight-spoked wheels such as are actually preserved or represented in figured documents from Egypt and the Near East. The earliest known wheels unquestionably testifying to this simpler construction come from the burials of light, two-wheeled vehicles at Lchaschen on the shores of Lake Sevan in Armenia, and have been dated to the middle of the second millennium B.C.[23] Here, the 28 spokes in a wheel with a diameter of ca 1.00 m. are clearly inserted in a cylindrical nave, the diameter of which increases at its center in order to be able to receive them all.

In the late third millennium B.C. there must have been a strong drive towards the development of a lighter wheel. A different (and perhaps the first) attempt in this direction is illustrated by a cylinder seal from Tepe Hissar in northeastern Iran that was assigned by the excavator to level IIIB (usually dated to the last quarter of the third millennium B.C.). Just such a "cross-bar wheel" appears on Anatolian seal impressions of the early second millennium B.C.[24] This was an essentially lighter wheel than the tripartite disk wheel from which it appears to have derived, the latter being the earliest wheel of which we have material evidence. From its later history, however, it is clear that the cross-bar wheel did not suffice for regular use at speed. In antiquity it was limited to good carts and

---

[22] Piggott 1983, 91f. with fig. 47; Häusler 1984, 664 with pl. 2: 1–2. Gening, Zdanovich and Gening 1992; Antony 1995, 561f.; Antony and Vinogradov 1995; Littauer and Crouwel 1996; Raulwing 2000, Chapter V.

[23] Littauer and Crouwel 1979, 77f.; Piggott 1983, 95f. with fig. 51

[24] Littauer and Crouwel 1977c.

travelling wagons which were usually drawn by donkeys or mules or sometimes by oxen, the draught animals today used exclusively with them. Further search for a lighter construction eventually led to the two types of spoked wheel described above. It is possible that the Egyptian wheel was suggested by naturally forking wood, a possibility experimentally demonstrated by J. Spruytte.[25] On the other hand, the cross bars of the cross-bar wheel could have inspired the inserted spokes of the other construction.[26]

Both types of wheel had their strengths and weaknesses which depended on usage and the climate. While the familiar type of wheel, with its spokes set directly in the nave, was substantially the easier to make, it had certain defects. Before the appearance of the sweated-on iron tyre – considered to be the invention of Celtic wheelwrights in the La Tène period – it was not easy to prevent spokes from being shaken loose. A rawhide tyre had been the main means of constricting the wheel, which was not only sensitive to precipitation but also to so common an occurrence as the passage of a ford. Also under conditions of extreme aridity the individual parts of the wheel would shrink and come loose. The problem is well illustrated by the apparent attempt in a wheel from the later period in Egypt to correct it: notches on the front and rear faces of the spokes about 4 cm. from the nave can only have been for strengthening the fabric by means of a strap or strap-and-wedge arrangement close to the nave which could be drawn tightly so as to reinforce or replace the action of a rawhide tyre and hold the spokes in place.[27]

The "Egyptian" wheel, on the contrary, was a refined and complex product that required the skills of a number of experienced craftsmen, such as could be supplied by a palace or the economy of an oriental city state. The remarkable construction of the nave and spokes strengthened by glue and by rawhide which shrunk in drying, was substantially stronger and better for speed and over uneven terrain. The spokes could not be shaken loose, as they could with the other type of wheel, unless moisture penetrated the rawhide. In most of the remaining examples the latter was protected either

---

[25] Spruytte 1977, 116ff. (= 1983, 113ff.).
[26] Littauer and Crouwel 1985, 102f.
[27] Littauer and Crouwel 1979, 107–120. We are indebted to A. Wegener Sleeswyk for the discussion of the wheel; see his Pre-stressed wheels in ancient Egypt (Wegener Sleeswyk 1987).

by gypsum and sheet gold or by birch bark, the latter being the more practical and more suitable for military use. Thus the passage through a shallow ford which could temporarily loosen a rawhide tyre would not have too negative an effect, provided the nave itself were not soaked. Chariots in Egypt itself, with an extremely low annual precipitation, would be in need of little protection from dampness; in the campaigns to the north and east, however, this would be more needed.

The wheels from Lake Sevan, with their numerous inserted spokes, were the answer to the different conditions, both environmental and economic. Here it was mountainous and forested country with easily obtained timber and high precipitation. Although it was already stratified and included a prosperous elite, society in this area cannot have had a level of organisation or wealth such as those of Egypt or the oriental city states. We do not know the purposes for which the light two-wheelers from Lake Sevan were intended. According to their present reconstruction, it does not appear to have been military. On the other hand, their lightness, their poor accessibility (mounting from the front) and the small dimensions of the body suggest transport at speed for seated occupants. In such a climate the "Egyptian" wheel would be unsuitable. But with not less than 28 inserted spokes, the loss of a few en route would not necessarily entail a breakdown and could easily be remedied, since timber was available.

In this connection, it may be noted that the 16 spokes of the wheels of the chariot of the Prince of Elam represented in Assyrian reliefs of the 7th century B.C. must have played the same role as the more numerous spokes at Lake Sevan, and that the easily obtainable timber in Elam permitted this construction.[28] This wheel in other respects, such as felloes, felloe clamps and axle caps, resembles that of the Assyrian chariot. The 18 to 20 or more spokes of the chariot wheels of the Western Zhou period in China (1027–771 B.C.) were surely the result of the same technique and associated with insufficient means of keeping the spokes in place.[29]

Numerous spokes bring up another factor: weight carrying. The long-bodied Elamite carts which are represented in the role of troop

---

[28] Barnett (n.d.), pl. 121.
[29] von Dewall 1964, 227f., 244–246.

transports on Assyrian reliefs of the 7th century B.C. are usually shown with 12 spokes, although 14 and 15 also appear; some (usually smaller) carts may have eight spokes.[30] Speed and large distances were not required of these means of local transport which were mostly drawn by mules, so that the replacement of a lost spoke did not present an immediate necessity. These carts, however, were likely often to have carried goods that were heavier than the human occupants that are depicted. Added weight required stronger and/or more spokes. In either case the "Egyptian" type of wheel would not have come under consideration, even if its high costs had not precluded its use on this type of vehicle.

The Assyrian chariot of the late 8th and 7th centuries B.C. was heavier than the Bronze Age one and often carried as many as four occupants. Its wheels, which seem to have been made in the "Egyptian" manner – although this has never been proven – show eight spokes.[31] The latter number would appear to be the minimum for a chariot of this weight and probably also the maximum that can be made by this technique. Were the Assyrian wheel actually of the "Egyptian" type, it would seem to be the last time that such a wheel saw military use.[32] At least by the middle of the first millennium B.C. it was obsolete.[33] The reason is not far to seek. A type that had apparently been excellently adapted to a combination of circumstances (climate, terrain and type of warfare) in Bronze Age Egypt and the Near East, did not necessarily continue to obtain as these circumstances changed. Egypt's might sank, the arena of war in the Near East now included mountainous regions to the north and east, and mounted troops began largely to supplant chariotry. Due to its sensitivity to moisture and its complicated construction, the "Egyptian" wheel was unsuitable for other climates, terrains and economies. Thus, even knowledge of its construction was lost for some 2500 years until surviving Egyptian chariot wheels were found earlier in this century.

---

[30] Barnett (n.d.), pls. 129, 133, 135.

[31] Barnett (n.d.), pl. 96.

[32] It should be noted that, according to the excavator, the remains of actual eight- and ten-spoked wheels of Cypriot chariots of the 8th–7th centuries B.C. were of the simpler construction with inserted spokes, while the vehicles were otherwise heavily influenced by Assyrian prototypes; see Karageorghis 1967a, pls. 32: 5, 121; 1973a, figs. 10–11.

[33] In Archaic and Classical Greece the "Egyptian" wheel appears still to have obtained for light, racing chariots; see Crouwel 1991a, 35f.

II. OTHER EARLY VEHICLES

24. CEREMONIAL THRESHING IN THE ANCIENT NEAR EAST*

M. A. LITTAUER AND J. H. CROUWEL

I. *Archaeological Evidence*

Although well-known from Roman times on, and still in use today in parts of the Near East and North Africa, two early threshing implements – the *tribulum* or threshing board and the *plostellum punicum* or threshing wheel[1] – appear now to be documented in ceremonial contexts in the ancient Near East. The first may be identified on three figured documents of the Uruk and Jemdet Nasr periods and the second in cuneiform texts of the Early Dynastic period. A recently published cylinder-seal impression,[2] an unpublished cylinder seal[3] and a long-known, small stone plaque in the British Museum[4] provide early illustrations.

The seal impression, of Uruk style, from recent excavations at Arslantepe, near Malatya in southeastern Anatolia, preserves the greater part of a scene centering around what has been described as "a regular figure in a sledge vehicle" (fig. 1). The figure is on a seat with short legs and beneath an arched baldaquin. Roughly rounded projections at front and rear of the seat suggest litter-pole terminals, an interpretation supported by two early documents from

---

* *Iraq* 52, 1990, 15–19. This paper is dedicated to Edith Porada.

[1] White 1966, s.v. *Tribulum*, 152 and 156, s.v. *Plostellum Poenicum*, 152 and 156.
[2] Palmieri 1981, 106–107 and pl. XVa; Palmieri 1985, 90 and fig. 11.11; Palmieri and Frangipane 1986, 42 and fig. 5a (our fig. 1); Sürenhagen 1975, 230–232 and fig. 1; Collon 1987, 14, no. 10.
[3] Seal in collection of Mr. J. P. Rosen, New York. Made of black chlorite; two holes on top which communicate by meeting at an angle below the surface. H. 2.34 cm., diam. 2.28 cm. Professor Porada informs us that the means of suspension is characteristic of Syrian cylinder seals of the late 4th and early 3rd millennia B.C. (Our pl. 149).
[4] London, BM 12885 (formerly Collection Ernst Herzfeld); Sürenhagen 1975, 231f. and fig. 2; Amiet 1961, 92 and pl. 47; Littauer and Crouwel 1979, 13f. and fig. 2 (our fig. 149).

Fig. 1. Seal impression from Arslantepe. After Palmieri and Frangipane, *Dialoghi di Archeologia* 3rd series 4, (1986), fig. 5a.

Egypt. One is king Narmer's macehead (fig. 2) which illustrates a figure seated in an arched litter, the latter's legs set on the ground and its carrying poles – with terminals – shortened to conform to the available space. The other is the reconstructed open litter of queen Hetepheres, showing actual pole terminals reminiscent in profile of those mentioned above.[5] On the Arslantepe sealing a driver stands between the litter and the upturned "prow" of the sledge; in one hand he holds a large ring to which the line of control seems to be attached, and in other hand a goad. The draught animal is bovine. Two attendants on foot follow the sledge, the forward one appearing to steady the canopy with one hand. From near his waist, a wide object, like a hand with extended fingers, protrudes at an oblique angle. Of the second figure only the body from the waist down and the legs remain, but a similar hand-like object protrudes from behind him also.

The striking resemblance of this scene to that on the British Museum plaque has already been noted elsewhere.[6] The plaque, unprovenanced but possibly bought in Baghdad, can be dated on stylistic grounds to the later 4th millenium B.C. (fig. 3). The relief clearly shows a sledge-bearing male figure on a seat with stout legs, a diagonal stretcher between them, and beneath an arched canopy or baldaquin. The structure is open at the sides except for a single

---

[5] Moorey 1970, 19 and fig. 2 (our fig. 2) = Vandier 1952, 602–605 and fig. 394; Reisner and Smith 1955, 33f., fig. 34 and pls. 27–29 = Kayser 1969, 277 and fig. 249 (litter of Hetepheres, mother of king Cheops). For a scene from the Near East itself, roughly contemporary with the Arslantepe sealing and showing someone being carried in a litter with arched covering and short legs, see Amiet 1972, no. 691 and pls. 18 and 85; Collon 1987, 158, no. 711 (sealing from Susa).

[6] Sürenhagen 1975.

Fig. 2. Covered litter on Narmer's macehead from Hierakontopolis. Oxford, Ashm 1896–1908 E. 3631. After P. R. S. Moorey 1970, fig. 2.

rail. What seem to be carrying poles, directly beneath the seat and shortened to fit the space, project slightly at front and rear show characteristic stops at the ends; they strongly suggest a litter. The figure in the litter is bearded, he wears his hair in a bun, and he has the thick, rolled headband of the so-called priest king frequently shown on Uruk-style seal impressions.[7] A driver stands between him and the upturned "prow" of the sledge, a line of control to the draught bovid in one hand and what is probably meant to be a goad in the other.

The complete and well-preserved seal in New York is of unknown provenance but in the Jemdet Nasr style. It shows a similar scene with a figure seated beneath the arched canopy of a litter (pl. II*a*). The litter has legs and pole stops resembling those on the British Museum plaque. A driver stands immediately in front of the litter; a line from his right hand goes directly to the nose of the draught bovid, and his left hand holds what may be a goad. In front of him a second figure bends over the upturned "prow" of the sledge. The sledge is followed by two men on foot, the forward one again steadying the canopy with one hand while, with the other, he grasps a litter pole. These men seem clearly to be litter bearers.

These scenes are unusual and puzzling in the placing of two independently valid forms of early transport – the litter and the sledge – one on top of the other. A suggestion, however, from Mr. David Loggie, that the scene on the New York seal might have something to do with agriculture, immediately offers a plausible explanation for

---

[7] Brandes 1979, Index s.v. Menschen a) Priesterkönig; Collon 1987, 15.

Fig. 3. Stone plaque. London, BM 12885. After Littauer and Crouwel 1979, fig. 2.

the puzzling combination of litter and sledge. The combination of a seat (although not of a litter) and a sledge may sometimes be found in the Near East today in connection with the threshing sledge. This runnerless sledge, into the underside of which several hundred sharp-edged flints have been hammered, and which turns up at the front, has been described a number of times.[8] Dr. Sevim Buluç tells us that it is still used in many parts of Anatolia. When the grain is cut and has been stacked in a mound, the sledge, pulled by oxen or sometimes by horse, is driven over it in a circular path as it is gradually brought down from the mound. The threshing lasts for many hours and the sledge, in order to crush the grain effectively, must be weighted. This might be done with rocks but, since the draught animals need someone to control them during many hours of threshing, the driver either stands on the sledge or, if he so wishes, places a chair or stool on it on which to sit (pl. 150).

While it is not clear in our scenes whether the driver is actually standing on the sledge or just to the far side of it, a driver of oxen, when he goes on foot, normally walks by the head of his team – neither before or behind it. Hence here he seems more likely to be standing on the sledge. With a usual goods-carrying sledge he would walk, so as not unnecessarily to weight the draught load of a vehicle already hampered by a large frictional surface. This suggests that we have not to do here with the one type of sledge in which added weight is desirable: the threshing sledge.

---

[8] White 1966; Crawford 1935 and pls. I–III (Cyprus); Bordaz 1967, ill. 77; Wulff 1966, 274f. and fig. 384; Salonen 1968, pls. XXXIV, XXXVIII–XXXIX; Mantran 1959, pls. 70 (our pl. chair on sledge) and 71 (stool on sledge). In 1971 one of the present authors observed an ox-drawn sledge circling a mound of grain on a threshing floor within the walls of Boğazköy itself.

The Arslantepe seal impression, moreover, provides a striking clue: the enigmatic "fingered" objects carried by the figures at the rear of this sledge may now be seen as winnowing shovels, of which their appearance is extraordinarily reminiscent (pl. 151). Winnowing – the process that immediately follows threshing – is indicated here in its logical sequence.[9]

But how to explain the canopied litters instead of plain seats or chairs on the sledges, and the fact that their occupants are clearly not also the drivers? While Dr. Buluç tells us that some protection from the sun is often used – particularly in the hot season – these arched baldaquins are not simple sunshades: they are usually the prerogatives of important personages. A litter would fall into the same category. It was noted above that the figure on the British Museum plaque resembles in several respects that of the so-called Uruk priest king. Although the head of the figure on the Arslantepe seal impression is not complete or clearly defined and the New York seal, in its laconic Jemdet Nasr style, fails to differentiate the figures on it, we may assume that the canopied litter is a clear indication of the importance of whoever sits in it. Could these scenes represent a harvest ceremony at which a royal or priestly personage officiates, having been transported to the threshing floor on a litter?

Some "shorthand" pictograms of the Uruk period do indeed show sledges carrying box-like structures with peaked or rounded roofs. While there may have been a seat within these, they show neither legs nor litter poles, nor is any context indicated.[10] In the third millennium, however, we have archaeological evidence of perhaps two ceremonial sledges, both from tombs associated with female burials. These are the highly decorated, bovid-drawn sledge of Pu-abi of Ur (pl. 152)[11] and the remains of what may have been another bovid-drawn, wheelless vehicle found in a tomb in Susa.[12] Pu-abi's sledge

---

[9] White 1966, s.v. *Ventilabrum*, 32–35; Theocharis 1973, pl. 163 (our pl. IIc: four-fingered shovel almost identical in appearance with those on the Arslantepe sealing); Oates and Oates 1976, 69.

[10] ATU, nos. 741f.; Langdon 1924, pl. XXXI: 1–2; also Littauer and Crouwel 1979, 12f. with fig. 1.

[11] London, BM (from tomb PG 800). Woolley 1934 (Vol. II), 74, 78–80, 556 (no. UE 10438. Total height 1.15 m.; width across front 0.85 m.; depth of sides 0.52 m.) with pls. 122 (reconstruction), 123–126, also 36 (plan of tomb). For the identification of the draught animals as bovids, see Dyson Jr. 1960, 102–104. For Pu-abi see especially Moorey 1977b, 25–40.

[12] Tallon 1987, 297 (Donjon tomb A 32).

carried a rectangular box on legs, with three closed sides. Wickerwork that had fallen between the sides could possibly have supported a canopy. While there appears to have been no indication of litter poles, the material was in a very fragmentary condition, and the fact that the box as now displayed on the reconstructed runners has been recently replaced back-to-front would suggest that the original report left some options open.[13] No flints were found with either of these remains and the use was certainly ceremonial rather than functional. Moreover, as Steinkeller has noted below, the sledges in two of his Early Dynastic texts, although of a different type from those illustrated, were for princesses and were of exotic wood.

We must still try to account for the extra figure — neither driver nor officiant — bending over the prow of the threshing sledge in the scene on the New York seal (pl. 149). Can he be casting aside the cattle droppings so that they will not offend the nostrils of the personages on the sledge when they are crushed beneath it? This is a nicety dispensed today, when it is taken care of only on the next stage — the winnowing — but it might have been appropriate in the special circumstances.

The illustrations confirm the existence of this type of threshing sledge as early as Uruk times. This is not surprising for such a simple implement made of wood and flints and which, one would imagine, might even go back to Neolithic times. Sir Leonard Woolley suggested that the numerous small flint blades found on pre- and proto-historic sites in Iraq may sometimes have been erroneously identified as "sickle blades" when they might equally well have qualified as threshing sledge studs.[14]

The other type of threshing machine, the *plostellum poenicum* or Punic cart, was described by Varro as a "toothed axle running on low wheels"[15] and is still referred to as a "threshing wheel" or "threshing wain", despite the fact that the wheels have been abandoned for thick runners between which the "axles" revolve. It was in use in recent times in Egypt, Syria, the Lebanon, Transcaucasia, Iraq and Iran (pl. 153a–b).[16] The "axles", to the number of two or three, are

---

[13] See Woolley's "Ur of the Chaldees" as revised by Moorey 1982, ill. p. 100.
[14] Woolley 1955, 14; cf. McC. Adams 1975, 17–19 and figs. 1–2.
[15] White 1966, 152: 3, 153: h.
[16] White 1966, 155–156 with fig. 117; R. Mesnil du Buisson, L'éthnographie 25 1932, 112f. with pl. IV (Syria); Meissner 1920–25, I, fig. 83 (Iraq); Wulff 1966, 273 and figs. 381–383; also Desmet-Grégoire and Fontaine 1988, 3, figs. 5–6 and pl.

set with large wooden or iron "teeth". The "teeth" of ancient times could have been of wood or flints considerably larger than the flints of the true sledge. R. McC. Adams discusses a small set of large flints he found on a late Uruk-period site in Iraq and which, he suggests, might have been suitable for such a threshing machine.[17] Leather and bitumen, although not used to secure the teeth of the sledge (which are simply hammered into slots), might have been used with the rollers of the wain. This thresher, in constrast to the former, has no floor; its seat, the supports of which are attached to the runners, forms a kind of bridge over the "axles". To our knowledge, no representations of this form of threshing machine in the ancient Near East have come to light, but it appears to be mentioned in the cuneiform sources to be discussed in the second part of this paper.

Acknowledgements

We are greatly indebted to Professor E. Porada for calling our attention to the Jemdet Nasr cylinder seal and to Mr. J. P. Rosen for permission to publish it. Thanks are also due to Dr. J. E. Curtis of the British Museum, London, for checking and xeroxing Sir Leonard Woolley's fieldnotes of the excavation of the sledge of Pu-abi at Ur. We are also grateful to Dr. C. Kramer, Dr. P. R. S. Moorey and Dr. R. R. Knoop for their help.

---

[17] *Supra* n. 14.

25. EARLY METAL MODELS OF WAGONS
FROM THE LEVANT*

MARY A. LITTAUER** AND JOOST H. CROUWEL

This paper is concerned with a number of metal models of four-wheeled *wagons* (as distinguished from two-wheeled *carts*) from Syria and Anatolia that have been attributed to the late third or early second millennium B.C. These models, apart from quite summarily rendered terracottas, constitute our only three-dimensional representations of early four wheelers in the Levant and the Near East at large. It therefore seems worthwhile to examine them carefully to see whether they can shed any light on the history of wheeled transport, i.e. on early wagons, their construction and use. Comparison with other sources of information for vehicles and draught animals may also help to establish their relationships and ultimate origin, as well as their chronology.

From Syria we have two models that have long been in museums, one in the Louvre (our Syria no. 1) and one in Stockholm (our Syria no. 2). Details of their provenance are lacking: the first was said to come from Homs, the other from "north Syria". The models, which are closely related in technique, shape, and style, are certainly genuine, although some restorations have been made.

From Anatolia we have been able to bring together some dozen models – a figure that is certainly incomplete. This is because more and more examples have been appearing since the first were published in 1962 (New York, Pomerance Collection, our Anatolia no. 2) and 1964 (Boston, Museum of Fine Arts, our Anatolia no. 4). Thus far, none has been found in a controlled excavation. Some at least have come via Beirut[1] to be dispersed by dealers over public and private collections in Europe and the United States. Verifiable information about the find places is at present not obtainable. There

---

* *Levant* 5, 1973, 102–126.
** The editor of "Levant" is most grateful to Mrs. M. A. Littauer for a contribution towards the cost of illustrating this paper.
[1] Danmanville 1968, 60; letter from H. Seyrig to J. Crouwel (15.6.1971).

is a report of a number of metal models having been found together near Marash in southeast Turkey.[2] At least three of the examples listed among these, however, are described in their original publications as coming from "south central Anatolia", "south Anatolia" and from "a cache said to be near Alaca Hüyük" (central Anatolia), respectively.

This lack of provenanced and properly excavated material seriously hampers a systematic study of the Anatolian models. Neither do they form a wholly homogeneous group by their technique, shape, or style, but fall into a few related groups. Within the best represented group our numbers 1, 2, 5, and 6 are strikingly similar.

This raises the question of whether we may unhesitatingly accept all examples as genuine. The recent analysis of the so-called Hacilar ceramics[3] – also from Anatolia – shows that the appearance of a new class of finds may give rise to fabrications – often very good ones.

Thus at this point we state specifically that, as far as we are able to judge now, a certain number are probably basically genuine. We assume this for no. 1 (in the Metropolitan Museum of Art), no. 2 (in the Pomerance Collection), no. 3 (in the Adam Collection, London) and no. 4 (Boston, Museum of Fine Arts). Nos. 1 and 4 have been tested in their respective museum laboratories, and no. 3 in that of the British Museum, while nos. 2 and 4 were the first models from Anatolia to be published. These four examples have been examined by us personally. To these may be added two more: no. 5 (in the Staatliche Museen, Berlin), and no. 6 (in the Thierry Collection, France). These we have not examined, but information has been available to us thanks, in one case, to the museum authorities and, in the other, to a published description.

The majority of these models have been at least partly reassembled, and some details have been restored, subsequent to discovery. In one case (no. 3), the vehicle in its present state seems to have been composed of elements taken from more than one model.

In the catalogue we have also included a list, with illustrations wherever possible, of yet other models said to be from Anatolia, which we have neither seen nor about which we have been able to obtain detailed information. Hence we can only discuss them cursorily. These examples will be lettered rather than numbered.

---

[2] Piggott 1968, 273; see also Bittel 1970a, 21f.
[3] Aitken, Moorey and Ucko 1971.

Catalogue

I. *Syria*

1. Paris, Louvre AO 2773 (pl. 154a–e); reported to come from Homs (acquired in 1898).
Publication: Heuzey 1909, 17ff.; 1910, 117, with fig. C.
Material and technique: copper with traces of nickel (analysis, information P. Amiet). Floor and body cast in one piece; wheels cast separately.
Condition: front axle and two wheels modern. Corroded. Fragment of one side screen missing. (For pole see Note at end.)
Dimensions: Overall L. 0.218 m., W. 0.092 m., H. 0.064 m.
    Box, L. 0.067 m., W. 0.032 m., H. 0.044 m.
    Wheels, (diam). 0.04 m. (Information Miss A. Caubet).
Rectangular frame. Front axle set back from front edge of floor, rear axle close to rear edge. The original axle is mostly rectangular in section, flattened where it is attached to the floor centre by a single rivet, round where it takes the wheels; it is bent over at the ends to prevent the wheels slipping off. Wheels, revolving on axles, as solid disks with wide raised centres at either side.
Solid body, with higher vertical front. The latter has a deep depression in centre, from which each half of the top breastwork curves up and away. Near top of each half there is an obliquely placed oval aperture. Low side and rear screens with three vertical ridges at side and two at rear. Side screens extend full length of floor but rear screen is placed somewhat forward so as to leave a platform at back. Central and right-hand panels of rear screen do not reach all the way to the floor, but leave shallow, rectangular opening at bottom. At each side, two large, upward-curving hooks rise from floor level above or nearly above axles.
Note. Heuzey reported that the pole – a straight bar subrectangular in section – was found detached from the vehicle (as were the remaining axle and pair of wheels). At present one end of pole is fused to floor near its front edge. The "pole" appears to have forked at a short distance in front of the body. The left-hand fork remains; the right-hand one is broken off at its inception. The two parts would seem to have run straight forward parallel to each other almost to the yoke. There are good reasons for doubting such an arrangement,

which is almost unprecedented, despite Heuzey's interpretation as a pole (see below pp. 366–367).

2. Stockholm, Medelhavsmuseet (formerly Statens Historika Museet) 14305 (pl. 155a–d). Reported to come from north Syria.

Publication: Przeworski 1936, 88ff. with fig. 14.

Material and technique: said to be of bronze (no analysis reported). Technique as no. 1.

Condition: corroded. Front of box lost. Front axle and two left wheels modern. Wire original over right, rear, side hook. Wire over other three side hooks modern.

Dimensions: H. (total with wheels) 0.05 m.
    L. (total) 0.09 m.
    W. (floor) 0.04 m.
    Wheels, (diam.) 0.045 m. (information Miss G. Walberg).

Very similar to no. 1, except for the following points: floor terminates at front in three blunt projections, one in centre and one at either side. These are crossed on top by a flat bar at floor level, forming two apertures between it and front edge of floor. Vertical rivets through cross-bar, one at either side of central projection. Side screens project slightly beyond floor at rear. As on no. 1, there is an opening at the bottom of the rear screen, but this time on the left side and half-moon shaped. Side hooks smaller than on no. 1, placed directly over axles.

II. *Anatolia*

1. New York, MMA, acc. no. 66.15 (pl. 156). Reported to come from south central Anatolia.

Publication: Harper 1968, no. 5, 195.

Material and technique: Floor and railing cast together. Axles, wheels, sheet lining, pole, yoke animals, lines separate.[4]

Condition: corroded. Partly reassembled. Left-hand floor projection partly missing. Sheet-metal lining incomplete.

Dimensions: Overall L. 0.225 m.
    Floor, L. 0.082 m., W. 0.042 m.
    Railing, L. 0.065 m., W. 0.035 m., H. (front) 0.05 m., H. (rear) 0.022 m.

---

[4] See appendix for analysis.

Side hooks, L. 0.005 m., H. 0.007 m.
Axles, 0.097 m.
Wheels, (diam.) 0.06 m.
Pole (to fork) 0.125 m.
Animals, (height at withers) 0.076 m.

Rectangular floor with three tapering projections in front, one in centre and one at either side. These are crossed on top, somewhat back from their tips, by a thin, flat strip which ends at either side in an upward-curving hook; to this the axle is lashed by wire. There are two apertures between the projections and behind the transverse strip. A similar strip, with up-curved, hooked ends, crosses floor slightly in from its rear edge. The rear axle is similarly lashed to these hooks.

Axles rectangular in section and flat under body, round where they take the wheels and bent up at ends; attached to floor as described. Solid disk wheels with spool-like naves, revolving on axle.

Railwork box is made up of vertical and horizontal bars, round in section. Of these the front and rear uprights are seated in the flat transverse strips, the rear ones leaving a shallow platform behind. Front upright forms a double-headed hoop with depression in centre and is set on at a slightly forward cant. Side rails supported by corner verticals with two uprights between; rear rail rests on corner verticals and single central one. Inside the railing are remains of a sheet-metal lining, reaching in front to just below top, leaving two small apertures, stretching back along sides to first side verticals, and folded over upper part of railing. A slender, tubular object is set diagonally outside the right-hand railing and is lashed to front hoop by wire. Draught pole is straight rod, round in section, forking as it approaches vehicle. Two-pronged fork hooks over transverse strip and through two apertures described above. Pole runs obliquely up to yoke, under which it is lashed. Yoke rectangular in section and pinched to form upright in centre; now lashed to horns of two bovids by wire, but could have rested on necks. Animals crudely formed, with elongated bodies and legs, and clumsily balled-up feet. Eyes and ears indicated by holes. Noses vertically pierced to take a line. This is made of flattish wire, rectangular in section and twisted. At present it runs from the nose of one bovid back through the apertures in the front breastwork, and returns to the nose of the other bovid.

2. New York, Pomerance Collection (pl. 157a–e). Reported to come from south Anatolia. Publication: Terrace 1966, no. 26.

Material and technique: Said to be of bronze (no analysis reported). Technique similar to no. 1.

Condition: Partly reassembled (on photograph in original publication draught pole attached to rear of vehicle). Sheet-metal lining incomplete. Lashings and lines missing. Corroded. Axles apparently modern. Part of horn of one animal missing. (For attachment of pole see Note at end.)

Dimensions: Overall L. 0.235 m.

Floor, L. 0.0725 m., W. 0.035 m.

Railing, L. 0.06 m., W. 0.025–0.03 m.; H. (front) 0.045 m., (rear) 0.02 m.

Side hooks, H. 0.007 m., W. 0.004 m..

Wheels, (diam.) 0.055–0.057 m.

Pole (to fork) 0.142 m.

Animals, L. 0.095 m., H. 0.082 m., W. (between horns) 0.03 m.

Vehicle and animals very similar to no. 1 except for following points: three verticals along sides between corner posts. Remains of sheet-metal lining extend back to second vertical on right side. No definite signs of tubular object at right front, but possible traces of such. Loops in under side of floor near its edges hold axles. No wire preserved over side hooks.

Note. As reassembled, the prongs of the pole hook over the front axle. Originally they would probably, as on no. 1, have hooked over the transverse strip.

3. London, P. Adam Collection no. 358 (pl. 158a–e). No report on provenance.

Publication: None.

Material and technique: Copper (analysis). Technique related to nos. 1 and 2, but railwork made of separate members.

Condition: reassembled from elements belonging to different models (pastiche). Rear horizontal of framework too long in proportion to width of floor; side screens too high, rising above top of front breastwork; wheels and animals too small for vehicle. Front and side screens corroded and badly preserved; of front only one small fragment remains in lower right-hand corner. Axles, pole, and yoke modern. Animals well preserved (tip of one horn lost).

Dimensions: Floor, L. 0.16 m., W. 0.07 m.

Rail, H. (front) 0.095 m., (rear) 0.055 m.

Side screen (left-hand), H. 0.11 m., (rear) 0.08 m.

Wheels, (diam.) 0.08 m.

Animals, L. 0.125 m., H. 0.09 m., W. (over horns) 0.07 m.

Related to nos. 1 and 2, but box almost twice as large, and different in construction. Floor as in nos. 1 and 2, ending in front in three projections, outer ones blunt and central one tapering. Four holes pierce floor in line just inside front edge, presumably to take verticals piercing a flat, transverse strip similar to those on nos. 1 and 2. Such a strip, with three holes, is preserved just far enough inside rear end of vehicle to leave a shallow platform, its ends turned up to form low side hooks, as on nos. 1 and 2.

Box composed of railwork cage and front and side screens attached to outside railing. Latter made up of verticals and flattish top rail rectangular in section. The high front, with double arched top, has either end seated in a hole in one of outer floor projections. Behind this, four verticals along each side, their lower ends piercing floor, their upper ends piercing horizontals and bent back; one side vertical is set in transverse strip at rear, with another close by at very end. Single vertical supports at centre of rear horizontal.

Sheet-metal lining attached to outside railwork. Originally this must have been effected by wire (now lost) passing through holes (present on left-hand screen at front corners, top and bottom) and around verticals. Instead of folding over side rail as on nos. 1 and 2, screen has sharp, upstanding edge which becomes lower as it goes back.

Bovids differ from those on nos. 1 and 2, with shorter legs, defined elbow, hock, and fetlock joints, and inserted tails. Prominent horns curve forward. Eyes and ears (?) indicated by smaller and larger holes; slits for mouths. Noses pierced vertically for lines (now lost).

Note. Some scraps of metal not belonging to it were also acquired with this model (pl. 158b). Some may come from other, similar models. This would seem to be the case with a flat strip pierced in four places at regular intervals (L. 0.082 m.) which may have been a transverse horizontal of a railwork. What may be the remains of a very light, flat pole (if it *is* such) has been given a curve unique among the poles belonging to these models. The other three rods and pieces of sheet-metal lining are incomplete.

4. Boston, MFA no. 62.678 (pl. 159). Reported to come from a cache near Alaca Hüyük.

Publication: Terrace 1964, 56ff. with fig. 12.

Material and technique: Almost pure copper (analysis). Cast in one piece by lost-wax process except for triangular attachment at rear.

No thorough cleaning down after casting. (For male figures accompanying it see Note at end).

Condition: good.

Dimensions: Overall L. 0.19 m.

Floor, L. 0.085 m., W. 0.06 m.

Railing, H. (front) 0.058 m., (side) 0.026 m., (rear) 0.03 m.

Wheels, (diam.) c. 0.043 m.

Pole, L. 0.075 m.

Animals, L. 0.063 m.

Rectangular floor (no front projections). At centre, just behind front axle, a hole in floor 0.009 m. in diam. At rear, large triangular projection, made of single piece of bent metal irregular in section, welded on and projecting 0.027 m. beyond rear of floor.

Open, rail-work box; verticals and horizontals roughly round in section. High, double-arched front; side rails low and not extending fully to rear, leaving shallow platform behind. Single vertical in centre of each side and centre of rear.

"Axles" running under floor and cast solid with it, projecting little at either side. Solid disk wheels, with very small spool-like naves.

Pole, round in section, rises obliquely from front of floor. Roughly indicated yoke apparently supposed to be attached to horns of bovids. These modelled differently from all others, with very short, tapering legs and no indications of head features. A line from the nose of each runs in to the junction of pole and yoke; from here on they are twisted together and run back to lie in depression in front railing.

Note. Together with the wagon model were acquired two almost identical figurines of males, which were said to have been found with it, and which analysis proved were similar to it in metal content. Furthermore, it was said that, at the time of discovery, there had been a scrap of metal found with these objects. Terrace, in his publication, suggests that this may have had something to do with a platform for attaching the warriors in the vehicle by way of the hole in the floor. Unfortunately, it is impossible to verify this information. The men are flattish and modelled only crudely. Both stand upright, the legs separated only by a groove, the feet forming a kind of platform. No indication of dress. Their left arms are akimbo; their right hands hold similar medium-long objects (sticks or weapons?) upright before them at chest height. The heads, set on long necks, have round faces, with prominent, pinched noses, and holes for eyes.

5. Berlin, Museum für Vor- und Frühgeschichte (pl. 160). Cat. no. XLb 1874 A–C/1966. Reported to be from south central Anatolia.

Publication: none (mentioned by Danmanville 1968, 60).

Material and technique: said to be of copper (no analysis reported). Technique appears very close to that of nos. 1 and 2.

Condition: partly reassembled. Axles either cleaned or modern. Sheet-metal lining incomplete. Tubular sheath at side may not be at original angle; pole probably upside down. Yoke lashings missing.

Dimensions: Overall L. 0.223 m.

    Axles, (front) 0.066 m., (rear) 0.064 m.

    Wheels, (diam.) 0.058 m.

    Tubular attachment, 0.08 m.

    Pole, 0.137 m.

    Yoke, 0.084 m. (information Mrs. E. Nagel-Strommenger).

Vehicle, animals, and traction gear very similar to those of nos. 1 and 2. Special mention may be made of the following points: axles are held on by loops under floor at each side (as on no. 2). Remains of sheet-metal lining extend roughly halfway back on either side; at front more remains of part folded over outside than on nos. 1 and 2. Tubular object at side in vertical position (correct?) near first upright behind breastwork. Rather narrow arches of present yoke would indicate that, if original, it was always a neck yoke and never a horn one.

6. France, Collection Thierry IV (pl. 161). No reported provenance.

Publication: Danmanville 1968, 59ff.

Material and technique: said to be of bronze (no analysis reported). Technique presumably like that of nos. 1, 2, and 5.

Condition: partly reassembled. Pole seems too long and unusually curved to be original. It seems laid over yoke instead of lashed under it. Yoke not in original position but laid across bodies.

Dimensions: Overall L. 0.21 m.

    Vehicle H. (to top of front) 0.09 m.

    Axles L. 0.069 m.

Vehicle and animals very similar to nos. 1, 2, and 5. Special mention may be made of following points: three side verticals between corner posts, the one near rear very close to rear corner upright. Remains of sheet-metal extend about halfway along sides; at front a central strip extends over top of breastwork, leaving two apertures. The front breastwork itself does not seem to arch doubly as on nos. 1, 2, and 5. There is no sign of tubular object at side.

The following unpublished models have also come to our notice:

(a) Unpublished (pl. 165a–b). Overall L. c. 0.24 m. wheels (diam.) c. 0.05 m.

Vehicle, animals, and yoke very similar to nos. 1, 2, 5 and 6, although side rails extend further beyond corner posts at rear.

(b) Unpublished (pl. 166). Overall L. c. 0.21 m., wheels (diam.) c. 0.05 m.

Vehicle, animals, and traction elements similar to nos. 1, 2, 5 and 6, except for following points: screen is outside railwork as on no. 3, but differs from the latter's in being of a single piece and of equal height everywhere; there seems to be some sort of covering across the rear part of the box at rail height; bovids' legs straight and proportionately shorter, bodies proportionately longer and thinner.

(c) Unpublished (pl. 167a–c). Overall L. c. 0.50 m., wheels (diam.) c. 0.10 m.

Similar to no. 3 except for following points: both verticals and horizontals roughly rectangular in section. Bovids have longer, slenderer horns, curving inwards at tips, longer legs with lower-set knees and hocks.

(d) Unpublished (pl. 168a–b). Overall L. 0.39 m., H. (to top of front rail) 0.125 m.

Material said to be 99% copper. Screens, yoke, and lines missing. Vehicle similar to models 3 and c. Animals similar to those of c, but with higher articulations.

(e) Unpublished (pl. 169). Overall L. c. 0.51 m., wheels (diam.) c. 0.11 m.

Vehicle appears to be similar to models 3, c and d. Animals extremely leggy, with no articulations in front legs, hocks very high; necks rather elk-like.

Note. Models 3, d and e roughly twice as large as nos. 1, 2, 5 and 6; d is considerably larger also.

(f) Illustrated in *Galerie am Neumarkt*, Zurich, Auction XX (19. 11. 1970) lot 122. Said to be from southern Anatolia and to be of bronze rich in copper. Overall L. 0.26 m. Apparently similar in all respects to nos. 1, 2, 5 and 6, it has a tubular sheath placed diagonally at right side as on no. 1.

Note. We have been shown photographs of two other models offered for sale in the late sixties.

J. Danmanville (see no. 6) referred to a letter by W. Nagel of 27. 9. 1966 that mentioned a model on the market – perhaps the same as one seen by the Thierrys. (L. 0.25 m.).

The models described or listed above are related to each other in their material (copper, pure or alloyed), their technique (wholly or partly cast) and their design. All have rectangular frames directly over the axles, disk wheels, and a rectangular superstructure made up basically of a high front breastwork with double-arched top (lost on Syria no. 2), and low side and rear projections – although on Anatolia 3, b, c and e the front does not rise above the sides. Differences and variations can, however, be noted in both execution and design. The following groups may be noted:

A first group comprises the two Syrian models, which closely resemble each other. The frames and boxes are cast together and the latter have solid screens.

A second group is formed by the Anatolian models 1, 2, 5 and 6 (to which a and f may be added), which are closely related to each other. They have floors and boxes cast separately, the latter of railwork construction with sheet-metal screens *inside*. On these the side screens are lower than the front ones.

A second Anatolian "group" is represented by the single model, no. 4, which is unique in being cast – vehicle and animals – in one piece, in having no side screens nor signs of any, and in the style of its bovids.

To a third group belongs the *pastiche*, no. 3, which, however, as presently reassembled, probably cannot be read entirely literally. Its railwork is distinguished from that of the previous groups by being much slenderer and roughly rectangular in section, the verticals piercing both the floor and the horizontals. It differs also in having its sheet-metal screens placed *outside*, rather than inside, the railwork. Anatolian models c, d and a appear to be of similar fabric. It is to be noted that all examples of this group have high side screens. The animals of no. 3 resemble most closely those of model c. Anatolian model b seems to be a *pastiche* of a different sort, having the round-sectioned railwork of the first Anatolian group combined with the outside screens of the third.

Information on the early history of four-wheeled and two-wheeled vehicles in the Near East comes from four sources: figured documents, documents in the round, remains of actual vehicles, and textual references.

Representations begin in the late fourth millennium B.C. with the so-called "sledge-wagon" pictographs[5] and those of four-wheelers become extensive in the third millennium B.C., consisting then of pictorial evidence and models in the round. To the first type belong paintings on two scarlet-ware vases,[6] inlays, such as the famous "Standard" of Ur (ED III),[7] and fragments from Mari (ED III),[8] and the relief on one side of the Vulture stela from Lagaš (the "historical side"; ED III).[9] Further, there are various cylinder seals, some provenanced like the ones from Ur (ED II or III)[10] and Kiš (ED II or III),[11] Tell Chuēra (attributed to ED II),[12] and Brak (an impression, Akkadian);[13] others unprovenanced (dating to ED III and Akkadian);[14] with the latter go some cylinders thought to have been made in Syria under the influence of Early-Dynastic or Akkadian styles.[15] Still other representations in glyptic come from Anatolia. These were made locally and date to the beginning of the second millennium B.C., and they can be associated with finds from level II in the Assyrian merchant colony at Kültepe.[16]

Three-dimensional representations of wagons are, after our models, supplied by terracottas. Mostly fragmentary, these have been found at various sites, from Syria to Iran.[17] We shall illustrate, and use in the discussion to follow, some well preserved examples:

---

[5] ATU no. 743–745.

[6] From Khafajah, cf. Delougaz 1952, 69ff. with pls. 62 and 138, and Yadin 1963, 128; and from Susa, cf. Amiet 1966, 146ff., no. 106.

[7] Woolley 1934 (Vol. II), pl. 92; Strommenger and Hirmer 1964, pls. 72 and XI.

[8] Parrot 1956, 136–146, pl. LVI; 1967a, pl. LXV, especially nos. 2466, 2598, 2680; Calmeyer 1966, 161ff. with fig. 6; Pritchard 1954, pl. 305; Yadin 1963, 139.

[9] Strommenger and Hirmer 1964, pls. 66, 68; A. Moortgat, Die Kunst des alten Mesopotamien, pl. 119.

[10] Woolley 1934, pl. 196: 54 (U. 12461): Amiet 1961, pl. 92: 1216.

[11] Watelin 1934, pl. XXIV: 2, 32–34; Amiet 1961, pl. 92: 1217; Buchanan 1966, pl. 20: no. 255.

[12] Moortgat 1960b, 18 with fig. 23. The publication dated the cylinder to the second millennium. This was corrected to Early Dynastic II in a personal communication from U. Moortgat-Correns.

[13] Buchanan 1966, no. 292.

[14] Porada 1948, pl. XIX: 118E, 119; von der Osten 1934, pl. V: 41; Porada 1948, pl. XXXIV: 220 (Akkadian); Moortgat 1940, pl. 33: 240 (Akkadian).

[15] Porada 1948, pl. CLXIV: 1081f.; Amiet 1963, 70ff., with pl. VI, 5.

[16] Cf. Frankfort 1939a, pl. XL: m, n; Bossert 1942, nos. 409f.; Porada 1947, pl. XLVIII: 977; Porada 1948, pl. CXXXIV: 893E; Özgüç 1965, pl. III: 9.

[17] No systematic study of these has yet been made. A few examples from Syria

1. Oxford, Ashm 1925.291 (pl. 164). From Kiš, Mound A, dating presumably to ED III. Cf. Mackay 1925, pl. XLVI, 8, 9, no. 2015. (Information on dating, Dr. P. R. S. Moorey.) Rather coarse, pale buff clay, painted. H. c. 0.09 m., W. (box) c. 0.05 m., L. (box) c. 0.075 m. Part of top of breastwork with one aperture lost. Covered seat and rear platform. Sheath on left side with two tubular shafts.

2. From Tell Chuēra no. T. Ch. 57/1959 (pl. 163), attributed to ED II. Unpublished (information Mrs. U. Moortgat-Correns). Yellow clay. H. 0.045 m., L. (total) 0.05 m. Covered seat and rear platform.

3. England, Collection J. Bomford (pl. 162). Provenance unknown. Unpublished. Rather coarse, greenish-brown clay, knife-smoothed. H. c. 0.135 m., W. (box) c. 0.09 m., L. c. 0.11 m. Covered seat and rear platform.

Remains of actual wagons come from tombs at Ur (ED III),[18] Kiš (presumably ED II and not entirely distinguishable from carts),[19] and Susa (presumably ED III).[20]

Textual evidence is available from ED onwards. The exact interpretation of the terms is extremely problematical.[21]

In discussing the metal models use will also be made of remains of actual wagons and wheels found elsewhere, particularly in Russian Transcaucasia. These finds, often in remarkably good condition, have recently been discussed at length by Piggott. They range over a considerable period of time and all authorities are not agreed on their absolute dating, some placing the earliest as early as the later third millennium and others the latest as late as the early first millennium B.C.[22]

---

and Mesopotamia are described and illustrated below. For another piece from Tell Chuēra in Syria, cf. Moortgat 1960a, 44, with fig. 44 (attributed to ED II in letter from U. Moortgat-Correns, 3.2.1970). For Iran cf. de Mequenem 1943, fig. 91b: 8. 10.

[18] Woolley 1934, 64, 108f.; cf. Childe 1951, 179–183, for a discussion of vehicle remains.

[19] Watelin 1934, 30–34; Moorey 1966, 41ff.; McGuire Gibson 1968, 177ff.; Childe 1951, 179–183.

[20] de Mequenem 1943, 89f., 103f., 1922, 137f.

[21] Salonen 1951, 28–36.

[22] Piggott 1968. See particularly 281–286. 300–304 and Tables I and II. Piggott also places the Ciscaucasian burials of the Kalmyk steppe in the second half of the third millennium B.C. (297), while Gimbutas 1965, 207, suggests that the Tri Brata burial from this area was in the early second millennium B.C., and Hančar 1956, pl. III) would put this burial as late as c. 1000 B.C. Mnatsakanian 1957 and 1960 (in Russian).

Our models may be profitably compared with much of this material. Particularly striking are the parallels with the two- and three-dimensional representations from the Near East that, from ED times onwards, show disk-wheeled wagons with box-like superstructures incorporating a high front breastwork.

The limitations of the strict profile views, however, the summariness of the terracottas, the poor state of preservation of the earliest vehicles, and the difficulties in interpreting the texts have, so far, prevented us from understanding various elements of construction of ancient wagons. The metal models, in a material so much more appropriate than clay for rendering details, would seem, at first sight, capable of increasing our knowledge considerably – particularly of the frames and superstructures and the attachments of the axles and draught poles. We should, however, be careful to distinguish between those details that represent elements of actual wagons and those whose form may have been dictated rather by the exigencies of the medium or the convenience of the metallurgist. In the following discussion of individual parts we shall have to assess carefully the source of each.

Frame

In the case of these wagons, frames seem to have been synonymous with floors, there being no evidence at all of the "undercarriage", composed of a "forecarriage" and a "hindcarriage" that is typical of medieval and modern wagons and that we may find as early as the seventh-century B.C. Val Camonica rock carvings.[23]

All wagons have floors that are longer than they are wide. With one exception (Syria no. 2), the length is pronounced.

Representations of wagons in the Near East never show more than one man abreast. When a driver and a single passenger are shown – the maximum number of occupants – one is placed behind the other. That this is not a convention of the artist's for representing two people side by side, as on some Greek Geometric vases,[24] is attested by the widths of actual wagons found. The floors of two wagons from Ur and one from Kiš measured, respectively 0.50 m., 0.56 m., and

---

[23] Megaw 1967, pl. 1.
[24] Coldstream 1968, 30: no. 4, 31: no. 21, 59: nos. 21, 21a, with pls. 7a and 8a.

0.45 m. Moreover, a disk-wheeled four-wheeler, wide enough to carry two people abreast, would have been even more difficult to turn than a narrower vehicle – particularly without a swivelling fore-carriage. We must also consider that the added weight of a bigger vehicle would have been a liability for fast, equid draught under the then-obtaining pole-and-yoke system. It proved impossible, on the other hand, to determine the exact lengths of these wagons from their remains. We may only get an idea of something less than the *minimum* length by adding up the radii of rear and front wheels.

Ur, 0.30 m. + 0.40 m. = 0.70 m.

0.50 m. + 0.50 m. = 1.00 m.

From Kiš we have a scale drawing with a partial reconstruction of a wagon showing the distance of the two axles from each other, which yields a more accurate minimum of 0.80 m. It might be suggested here that, given the real absolute measurements in one direction, the relative proportions of our wagon models would be helpful in indicating real measurements in the other. But, although the vehicles at Ur at the time of burial were drawn, like our Anatolian models, by bovids,[25] we do not know that they were *designed* for them. As for the wagons at Kiš, they may also have been pulled by bovids. These tombs have been restudied,[26] and it seems that the original determination of the species was far from certain. At least three teams from two, and probably from three, different burials were combined. The one animal that was found in front of a vehicle, and with a terret ring by its head, was a bovid. The conformation of cattle is far better adapted to yoke-and-pole traction and they are not expected to show speed, hence bovid-drawn wagons of the period may have been wider than equid-drawn ones. Certainly, the wagons of which we have remains could hardly have been narrower and yet viable. Since all our models that show teams are bovid-drawn, it may be hazardous to extrapolate the dimensions of equid-drawn ones from them.

Two of our models (Syria no. 1 and Anatolia no. 4) have plain, solid floors (ignoring the hole in the latter) while all the floors of the others terminate in front in a special manner: three projections with a transverse piece on top, leaving two apertures between this member and the rest of the solid floor and at either side of the middle

---

[25] Woodley 1934, 48f, 64f.
[26] Gibson 1968.

projection. The three projections quite clearly represent the ends of the lengthwise timbers of the frame, which would have had a flooring of cross-laid planks on top of them. Wagon and cart floors are made on this principle or a variation of it today.

The failure of the Louvre model to show the ends of the three lengthwise beams in front may perhaps be attributed to the fact that the "pole" was soldered on after discovery. At that time the front edge of the floor may have been "evened off" to facilitate this.

The Boston model fails to give this detail of floor construction. Is it because, in an object that was cast in one piece, this would just add an extra complication? Moreover, as we shall point out when discussing the pole attachment, we believe the projecting floor-beam ends supported a cross-bar on which the pole could articulate vertically. Since no part of the Boston model articulates, it would have been unimportant to reproduce the beam ends and cross-bar.

As for the two unique details of this model's floor, the hole behind the front "axle" and the triangular appendage at the very rear, we cannot relate these to any features of actual wagons. And while we do not attempt to explain the purpose of the hole for this particular model, the added triangular element looks in shape and proportions like an attachment by which to hang the model on the wall. But this is pure conjecture.

Information on the frame construction of Near Eastern wagons is extremely scarce: we can only point to the partial reconstruction of a wagon found at Kiš,[27] (mentioned above) with two lengthwise beams and a small, semi-circular platform at the rear. Good evidence is, however, available from tombs in Russian Transcaucasia. One, at Trialeti, attributed to the later third millennium B.C., produced a wagon with two lengthwise beams and cross-laid planks nailed on top. Another, at Lchashen on the shores of Lake Sevan, and probably dating to the late second millennium B.C., yielded a wagon with five lengthwise floor timbers.[28]

Axles

We are obliged to distinguish here, as with other features of the models, between ancient elements in their original positions, ancient

---

[27] Watelin 1934, 30ff. with fig. 3 and pl. XXIII: 2
[28] Piggott 1968, fig. 12; Mnatsakanian 1960, fig. 9.

elements reassembled but still with their original vehicles, ancient elements that once belonged to other models, and modern elements. In assessing the shape and manner of attachment of the axles we must also take into account the role played by convenience of model manufacture. A patent example of this in the case of our axles is the small diameter of the wire in which they terminate and its bent back ends, which keep the wheels from slipping off. These form an easy substitute for a finished axle end pierced by a linch pin.

The two Syrian models appear to preserve the original construction of an axle, rectangular to round in section, bolted to the centre of the floor and further secured by wires lashed over hooks at the sides of the vehicle body. On Anatolia no. 4, at least the simulated front axle (bar cast with the floor) has a simulated attachment, which looks like a loop, in its centre; the rear one has no indications of an attachment.

Other Anatolian models vary: on Anatolia no. 1 the axle is held on only by the wire that passes over the side hooks. On nos. 2 and 5 the axles pass through loops that depend from the floor on either side near the edge; but the wire from the side hooks, if it existed, is missing. On no. 3 the ends of vertical elements of the rail work may have passed through the floor and been bent around the axle to hold the latter on. The wire that might also have lashed these to the side hooks is now gone.

What sources of information do we have for Near Eastern axles? The terracotta models are uninformative, since the tubular sheaths meant to carry a wire or wooden axle were clearly merely a convenience for the coroplast. The two-dimensional representations tell us no more than that the axle ends were round. Among the remains of actual wagons, information for axles is extremely limited; Wooley refers, in one case at Ur, to the axle or axle box (he was not sure which) being attached to the floor by two copper bolts.[29] He cautiously suggests that this and the other vehicles might have had fixed axles that did not revolve. *Two* bolts (provided these passed through the axle itself) would certainly prevent it both from revolving and from swivelling. If there was only a single central bolt, as on the Syrian wagons and perhaps on Anatolia no. 4, the axles would be inclined to swivel. While usually regarded as a desirable feature, the swivelling front axle is not unconditionally so. In the first place, pole,

---

[29] Woolley 1934, 64.

shafts, or other elements of draught must connect with the axle – not with the frame of the wagon – so that the axle turns *with* the draught animals and not differentially. For a pole, such as we have on the vehicles of this period, to be attached to the axle and still to clear the front edge of the floor as it swings, the axle would have to be placed lower than the wagon floor, in other words, we would need an undercarriage or at least a forecarriage. One of the Ur wagons might suggest this. It had front wheels 0.20 m. smaller in diameter than the rear ones, which would give a forward axle clearance of 0.10 m., assuming the rear axle were bolted directly to the floor. But would this be enough leeway for the *vertical* articulation of the *pole*, a more basic necessity on four-wheelers, and one that we shall discuss when we come to the pole? The other factor to be considered with a swivelling axle is the danger of the rims of the front wheels running into the edges of the floor on turns. This may be obviated in one of three ways: there may be a mechanism to limit the degree of turning, as on modern vehicles; the floor may be raised so high over the front wheels that it completely clears them; or the diameter of the wheels may be so small and the axles so long that there is little likelihood of the felloes running into the floor. There is no indication that any of these conditions existed on third- or second-millennium wagons, so we may discard the possibility of a swivelling axle here.[30]

At first glance, however, it might seem that, on the Syrian models, where the single, central bolt *would* permit the axles to swivel, the lashings between axle and side hook might constitute precisely the mechanism we are looking for to limit the play of the axle. We do not have reliable evidence on these two models of how the poles were originally attached, so we cannot entirely reject some direct connection with the axle. On the other hand, there is no evidence of the floors clearing the front axles and it seems unlikely that the poles would have been attached to the latter.

---

[30] Piggott 1968, 297 notes that under the framework of the wagon found in Lolinsky, barrow 4, grave 7 (on the Kalmyk steppe) "were two transverse beams, to front and rear, to which the axles were attached, that in front by a wooden coupling bolt through a perforated wooden disc 25 cm. in diameter, interpreted by the excavator as a device enabling the front axle to swivel." The scale drawing of this tomb, however, shows a vehicle with wheels of equal diameter front and rear, and axles so short that the wheels could turn very little before running into the wagon sides.

Moreover, we run into the side hooks on other models where the axles are not attached by a central bolt and where there would be no question of swivelling. For instance, these obtain on Anatolia nos. 2 and 5, where the axles are attached to the floor through two loops fixed in it at either side. Whether this means of attachment was a mere convenience for the metallurgist or whether it crudely represents an actual condition is impossible to tell.[31] Perhaps a pertinent light may be cast on this by the wagon mentioned above from Trialeti. On this, axles round in section revolved in rectangular recesses in the two lengthwise floor beams on either side of the floor.[32] On Anatolia 2 and 5 this system is roughly approximated. The rectangular recesses at Trialeti are very shallow, and while no side hooks are shown in the reconstruction of this vehicle, it is easy to see how binding the axles to the hooks might prevent the former from being jolted out of their shallow seats in rough going. In fact, some such arrangement would seem to be essential with this axle attachment. The hook lashings may therefore be vestigial from a time when all axles were attached in this elementary manner, and they would have continued usefully to reinforce the action of a central bolt when that was introduced. That they alone can have held the wheels on seems doubtful. Although rendered in wire on our models, the originals must have been of rope, which would have been rapidly strained by pressure and frayed by friction. Hence it would seem that in attaching the axles to Anatolia no. 1 by means of lashings alone, the metallurgist omitted another element – a bracket – if the axles revolved – or a bolt – if they did not.

Wheels

All models have wheels formed as plain disks with raised centres at either side. With the exception of Anatolia no. 4, they revolve on the axles. Certain variations occur in the size of the wheels relative to that of the raised centres.

These wheels clearly represent the disk type so well documented in Near Eastern art from the inception of wheeled transport onwards. The representations – like the actual finds – illustrate composite disk

---

[31] The copper model two-wheeler from Tell Agrab is also described as having an axle that "turned within bronze loops": Frankfort 1943, 13.

[32] Piggott 1968, fig. 11.

wheels, usually tripartite, but sometimes pentepartite,[33] made of planks held together by transverse slats. The central plank might have straight sides or it might be lenticular. The end of the nave is always shown as round and the nave looks as if inserted. On some representations the linch pin, intended to keep the wheels in position on the axles, is clearly marked. Actual pins of wood and metal have been found at Kiš and Susa.[34] Certain Near Eastern representations, as well as actual finds, evidence wheel rims studded with hobnails.[35] Others indicate smooth tyres, which could only have been of leather or metal. There is also figured and material evidence for a metal tyre made in segments.[36]

There is no indication of either smooth tyre or hobnails on any of our wheels and, indeed, the fabric seems too thin to carry either. It is impossible to say whether this was due to absence on the originals or to summariness of execution. It may be worth noting, however, that there seems to have been no indication of either nails or tyres on one of the wagons from Ur[37] or on the material remains from the Caucasus region.[38] The role of linch pin is played on all models, except the solid-cast Anatolian no. 4, by the turned-up ends of the wire axles.

We may wonder whether the lack of detail (except for the nicely modelled naves) on our wheels is significant. Does it really mean that they were solid disks such as have been found on the Pontic steppe and in Holland?[39] Or are they summary renderings of tripartite or pentepartite wheels? It should be noted that the fabric is so thin that it could not represent realistically either type of wheel, so that we do not feel justified in drawing any conclusions.

Superstructure

All models are enclosed on all four sides and the majority share a higher front, usually double-arched, with an aperture on either side

---

[33] Yadin 1963, 358; Orthmann 1971, pl. 41: f.; Piggott 1968, fig. 8.
[34] Watelin 1934, 30; de Mequenem 1922, 138, fig. 16.
[35] Watelin 1934, 33 with fig. 3; Childe 1951, 180, fig. 3; Frankfort 1943, pls. 58–60.
[36] Woolley 1934, 64; Frankfort 1943, pl. 65; de Mequenem 1922, 137f. with fig. 14; Salonen 1951, 114 with fig. 7; Childe 1951, 180 with fig. 4.
[37] Woolley 1934, 108f.
[38] Piggott 1968, pls. XXI–XXIII.
[39] van der Waals 1964.

at the top. The Syrian wagons, however, have solid walls, while the Anatolian ones are surrounded by an open railwork that may be closed by adding screens either inside or outside.

The most distinctive common feature – the high front – varies somewhat. On Syria no. 1 it rises vertically, its two oval apertures open diagonally on either side of the V-shaped depression in the middle. On Anatolian models nos. 1, 2, 3, 5, 6 (and also on a and c), it has a slight cant forward. On Anatolia no. 4 (and on b and e) it seems to be vertical. On the Anatolian models 1, 2, 4, 5, 6 (and on a, b, and f) it is made of a single bar of metal round in section, seated at either end in the floor, arching towards the centre and depressed there to greater or lesser degree so as to form a double arch (with the exception of Anatolia no. 6, where there is no depression in the front centre). On Anatolia no. 3 (also on c and d; e is too covered to tell), it is made of a thin strip of metal, roughly rectangular in section and pinched into a sharp depression at centre top. On all the Anatolian models the two apertures at the front are formed by the gaps between the arches of the railing and the horizontal top edge of the inside or outside screening, hence they are roughly lunate in shape.

We speak of a "high front", but on the group consisting of Anatolia no. 3 and the unexamined c and d, the top rails rise little above the side rails and the side screens appear to have been at the same level as the front one. These conditions probably obtain also on the otherwise seemingly similar b and e, where the photographs do not elucidate these features. Under these circumstances the apertures at the front are minimal. We shall discuss the significance of this difference when we examine the possible uses of the originals of these models.

A high front, either vertical or placed at a slight cant, is very common on Near Eastern representations of four- and two-wheelers from ED II to the Anatolian cylinder seals of the beginning of the second millennium B.C.[40] The terracottas offer many examples (see pls. 161–164). In most cases the top is double-arched, usually with two apertures just below. While these are often rendered negligently as merely two round holes in a solid front, a carefully made mould for the front of a two-wheeler, now in Yale[41] instructs us about their

---

[40] See representations cited *supra*, nn. 6–16.
[41] Buchanan 1962, 273 with ill. 272; Barrelet 1968, 46 with fig. 16.

detail. The trapezoidal front is made up of two slender side posts joined by five horizontals at irregular intervals, the area between filled with wicker work above and panels below. At the top centre, two antennae-like rails rise and curve away from each other, supported at *their* centres by two short uprights and near their outer ends by the ends of the side posts. Thus we see that the "holes" so often appearing on these clay fronts are not holes, but the coroplast's shorthand for an open railwork.

What was the purpose of this front? It offered protection, not, as has sometimes been suggested, against enemy missiles, but against gravel and stones struck up by the hooves of the team. The apertures at the top were not "spy holes" through which to look at the enemy,[42] but enabled the driver to grasp the rail. This provided a handhold in rough going or for moments when a sudden plunge forward of the team would unbalance the driver backwards or an abrupt stop throw him forwards. This type of front is, however, usually shown with equid draught, for which it was certainly originally designed, since bovid draught would not be lively enough to offer any of the inconveniences mentioned. It has also been suggested that the apertures were for the passage of the lines to the animals' noses.[43] This too would seem impractical, since they would interfere with the driver's handling of the lines. In fact, no representations other than our Anatolia no. 1 (with a and b) show lines passing through the apertures. The fact that on Anatolia no. 4, the only model where they must be in their original position, the lines lie together in the depression may not be as significant, however, as it seems at first glance, since there are no small apertures below, convenient for them to pass through. That on no representations where they are shown do they pass through the aperture is a sounder argument. The running of the lines through the apertures on the three models cited does not necessarily reflect actual practice; it could have been done either at the time of original assembly or at a secondary one, to prevent them from "floating".

Considering now the sides and rears of the superstructures, those on the Syrian models are very similar; they also compare well with

---

[42] Cf. van Buren 1930, 252, no. 1240. 254, no. 1245; Salonen 1951, 156; Gadd 1971, 31f. for protection and spy-holes.
[43] Cf. Salonen 1951 for use as line holes.

those on the "Standard" of Ur and certain other representations.[44] We seem to have here vertical, wooden struts, supporting what are probably wooden side panels. The rear screens on these two models are placed somewhat forward to leave a platform behind, still within the side walls. Platforms are apparent on many representations, including the Ur "Standard" and most terracottas (they can hardly be called "steps", since they are on the same level as the rest of the floor). The terracottas show the platform in combination with a seat, either as a solid lump of clay or as a covered part of the body (as on the ones illustrated here). The seat returns on many cylinder seals, including Anatolian ones.[45] The only one of the Anatolian models illustrated here that displays anything like it is Anatolia b, which we unfortunately have not examined.

We would suggest that the Early-Dynastic wagons such as those on the Ur "Standard" and the one on the Vulture stela had the rear walls that accompany the side walls of similar appearance to those on our Syrian models. They would certainly strengthen the side walls. In the lower register of the Ur "Standard" we see warriors standing on what might well be rear platforms; on the Vulture stela a figure once stood behind the king; we see his right hand carrying the shaft of a goad or lance. Was he too standing on such a rear platform? Salonen mentions a term that he translates as *Trittbrett* of a four-wheeled wagon and that might apply to such a feature.[46] The Syrian models may throw an extra light on this area. They display a feature hitherto unsuspected: a floor-level opening in the rear wall. The only purpose it occurs to us to ascribe to this is to give extra toe room on one side to the passenger standing behind. The stance of action is with one foot somewhat ahead of the other – it gives better balance. For wielding either a weapon or a goad and for keeping one's balance in a moving vehicle such a position would be desirable, yet, other possible dimensions taken into consideration, this rear platform must have been very shallow. Moreover, the sides

[44] Woolley 1934, pl. 92; Strommenger and Hirmer 1964, pls. 72 and XI; Parrot 1967a, pl. LXV, nos. 2598 and 2680.
[45] Buchanan 1966, no. 255; Porada 1948, pl. XXXIV: 220, CXXXIV: 893e; Frankfort 1939a, pl. XL: m, n; Bossert 1942, nos. 409 and 410; Özgüç 1965, pl. III: 9.
[46] Strommenger and Hirmer 1964, pls. 66a and 68; Moortgat 1967, pl. 119; Salonen 1951, 89.

of these vehicles seem low for grasping, and to clutch one's companion's shoulder, as the warriors on the "Standard" seem to be doing, might often disturb him. Was this opening an attempt to answer these problems? The difficulty is to account for a "toehold" on the left side of the platform on Syria no. 2. One must postulate either carelessness on the part of the artisan, or a left-handed warrior standing here, or a driver, since with the driver to the rear of the warrior (as he seems to have been on the Vulture stela) the lines would interfere less with the latter's freedom of action if they were carried back on his left side. An alternative explanation for these apertures that might come to mind is that the wagons might have been used for carrying some sort of saturated produce that needed to drain. But drainage holes would be along the side as well as at the rear, since a wagon cannot be tilted backwards like a cart. Moreover, an exclusively rear drainage outlet would not be confined to one side of the rear screen, but would run all along its base. Hence it seems to us that this aperture makes more sense as foot room than as anything else.

The Anatolian models, as said, have a superstructure of rails, with, except in the case of no. 4, additional screening. The rear posts of the railings are placed somewhat forward of the floor edge. Although, again, this rear "platform" is not a real step, it would offer foot-room to someone as he mounted the vehicle from the rear – the railing being low enough to step over. Otherwise, there would seem to be no way of mounting.

On one group of models – the smaller examples with rail work round in section, Anatolia 1, 2, 5, 6 (see also a and probably f) – the screening is placed inside, folded around the front posts and over the sides. Unfortunately, we do not know how far it originally extended backwards. Anatolia no. 3, belonging to the group of larger models, with lighter railwork rectangular in section, and proportionately higher side railings, shows a different arrangement: the screening is now attached on the outside, and not by being folded over the railings, but by wires passed through holes. On Anatolia no. 3 the upper edge of the screening is somewhat above the side rails and curves slightly upwards as it approaches the front. On Anatolia c and e, where the front screen is present, the latter reaches almost to the top, leaving mere slits of apertures. On e, the screens are of equal height all the way around, and on c they appear to be almost so. There is no indication on any of these of a rear screening.

No Near Eastern representations, with the possible exception of those on Anatolian cylinder seals show anything like the superstructures of the Anatolian models. The seals render what looks like a low side wall with very numerous verticals. While it is possible that these represent the struts of such boxes as we see on our Syrian models, or the uprights of the Anatolian models' rail work, their number suggests something else: either the multiple panel moldings of such boxes as are seen on the Mari "Standard" and the Vulture stela[47] or simply the transverse planks of a wagon bed, since these scenes are shown in different perspective from the Early-Dynastic representations.

The construction of our models indicates detachable screens on the originals, probably of wicker-work, as used on carts in Anatolia today.[48] The apparently total absence from the beginning, of screens on Anatolia no. 4, may suggest that these wagons were also used without them as one would surmise.

Some of the Anatolian models display a narrow, tubular sheath lashed to the right railing. These are reminiscent of similar accoutrements on Early-Dynastic representations (cf. the terracotta from Kiš, pl. 164, with two compartments). These are shown as javelin quivers, but the one on the Eannatum stela may also contain an axe and a whip.[49] We shall return to these sheaths when we discuss the uses of the originals of the models

We may now return to a device shared by both Syrian models and by Anatolian nos. 1, 2, 3, and 5 that we know of, and that may well be present on the others. This is the hook placed over each axle with, in some instances, remains of the wire by which it was lashed to the axle. The hooks on the Syrian models are prominent and extend from the sides, while on the Anatolian models they are small and are formed by the upturned ends of the flat strips that run across the floor. Neither of these methods can correspond exactly to actuality, since the hooks would probably have been of a different fabric from that of the sides or cross planks, yet that there were hooks on the originals seems undoubted. In only one instance – that of Anatolia no. 1 – do they serve the coroplast's convenience by

---

[47] Parrot 1956, pl. LVI; Pritchard 1954, no. 305; Yadin 1963, 138–9; Strommenger and Hirmer 1964, pls. 66 and 68; Moortgat 1967, pl. 119.

[48] Koşay 1951, pl. XXXIII: 221.

[49] Strommenger and Hirmer 1964, pls. 66 and 68; Moortgat 1967, pl. 119.

acting as the sole means by which the axles are attached to the frame. It has been suggested above that they performed the duty of auxiliary axle attachments either if the axle turned in recesses in the floor beams or if it was secured by a central bolt. They may also have served a different function that may, in some instances, have been the primary one. Not only the screens, but the entire railwork of the original wagons may have been removable, turning them at times into flat cars. If these vehicles served more than one purpose, and if the floor surface was as small as is indicated by the dimensions of the wagons from Ur and Kiš, there would have been occasions when it would have been desirable to convert them into floats. Side walls or railwork with hooks on either side might have been secured on top of the frame by lashings joining these hooks with the axle. This explanation has been suggested by the fact that the end verticals of the railwork on the Anatolian models are seated in the flat, cross strips to which the hooks may have been directly attached.

Draught Pole

Here too it is important to try to distinguish between ancient poles in their original positions, ancient but recently re-attached poles, and modern restorations.

As said above, we question whether the "pole" of Syria no. 1 is genuine, although it may represent a type experimented with at one time. This is suggested by a Cappadocian sealing in the Louvre originally published by J. Lewy and recently republished by P. Amiet.[50] However, the Metropolitan Museum of Art possesses a very clear imprint of the same seal on which no such forking is visible.[51]

Only on Anatolia no. 4 can we be positive that the pole is in its original position. It is straight and rises obliquely to the yoke. Beyond this, however, it tells us little, since, in the casting, it simply merges into the front edge of the floor, and there is no indication of how the pole on a real wagon would have been attached.

On Anatolia nos. 1, 2, 5 (and b) – about the others we cannot tell – the pole, a long, slender rod, forks just before it reaches the

[50] AO 8306. Lewy 1935–37, pl. CCXXXVII, no. 99; P. Amiet 1969, 1–3 with figs. 1 and 2.
[51] We are indebted to P. O. Harper for being able to examine this sealing.

wagon. On Anatolia no. 1 the prongs of the fork are curved, and now hook over the transverse bar that lies across the floor-beam ends, the hooks being accommodated by the apertures here that we have discussed. All models with removable poles have certainly been reassembled. On Anatolia no. 2 the prongs of the fork, which are partly broken off, have been hooked over the axle. This is possible because this axle is not tight against the wagon floor, which it would have been if attached in either of the two ways envisaged above. Attachment of the pole to such an axle would virtually preclude the pole's vertical articulation, whereas hooking over the transverse bar would permit it. Although the pole of a two-wheeler must be fixed and rigid, because it supports the vehicle, on a four-wheeler a pole with vertical play is essential. This is not only because a rigidly fixed pole would fit only one height of draught animals, but also because rigid attachment would turn the wagon and pole into a single, long, rigid body. Although this might perhaps function adequately on smooth and level going and at slow gaits, unevennesses in the ground would immediately create difficulties. Front and back wheels would be alternately suspended in the air, putting stress on the wagon frame, on the area of attachment of the pole and wagon and of the pole and yoke, and pressure on the necks of the animals. A wagon with vertically articulating pole, however, may tilt independently, at a different angle from the pole, and thus the entire equipage adapt itself better to the terrain.

We are therefore inclined to believe that the purpose of the extension of the three lengthwise beams and of the bar across them was to permit a vertical articulation of the pole. This belief is further supported by the fact that there seems to be no other *raison d'être* for this particular arrangement.

The exact original construction is not made clear by the models, however. Did the pole terminate in prongs that hooked over the transverse bar, or were the three beams proportionately heavier than on the models and the bar proportionately slenderer so that it passed as a pin through their ends and the two fork ends, as does the "shaft pin" or "draught bar" of a modern wagon? The former arrangement would necessitate a naturally-forking pole with heat-bent tines, or a pronged metal fork attached to the pole by a sleeve. The arrangement with the bar as a pin is documented among the remains of wagons from a later period in Transcaucasia. At Lchashen and probably elsewhere the pole did not merely fork near the wagon

front but was itself composed of two timbers of equal length forming an equilateral triangle, the apex of which lay under the yoke
and the legs of which were united with the two outer stringers of
the wagon bed (which had five stringers) by two pins, and which
articulated vertically.[52] The poles of our models are stronger too than
ones with single hooking ends would be. The two vertical rivets in
the cross bar of Syria no. 2 were probably a convenience of the
artisan for securing the forking ends of the now missing pole to the
former member.

We shall look in vain for other Near-Eastern evidence for such
an arrangement. The terracottas on the whole have a centrally
placed hole to take the pole. One such model, representing a tilt
wagon, which was found at Tepe Gawra and dated to the third millennium B.C.,[53] has been tentatively linked to the Russian material
by Piggott.[54] Its two vertically placed and horizontally pierced lugs,
however, almost certainly do not reflect the Russian composite poles,
but are simply a means of attaching the rope by which the *model*
was pulled.

Profile views of ancient Near-Eastern wagons illustrate two types
of pole, but never their attachment. One is straight, rising obliquely
from the level of the vehicle floor to the yoke;[55] the other rises almost
vertically at first, hugging the front breastwork of the vehicle, and
dropping eventually forward and away from it towards the yoke.[56]
This latter pole appears more frequently on two-wheelers. While the
curve it executed would have permitted some vertical play, a brace
that linked its highest point to the top of the breastwork would have
strictly limited this.[57] Thus, while this type of pole was suitable for
two-wheelers, it was not suitable for wagons, and we should not be
surprised that ours do not display it. The remains of actual wagons
from the Near East offer hardly any information on the poles and
their attachment, although the terret rings set on top of them tell
us that they were round in section.[58]

---

[52] Piggott 1968, fig. 12; Mnatsakanian 1960, fig. 9.
[53] Speiser 1934, 75, 192 with pl. XXXV: a 2; Salonen 1951, pl. VII.
[54] Piggott 1968, 295.
[55] Woolley 1934, pls. 92, 196: 54; Strommenger and Hirmer 1964, pl. XI;
Calmeyer 1966, 161 with fig. 2 (Shamash temple); 1964, 73, no. R with fig. 12.
[56] Strommenger and Hirmer 1964, pls. 66 and 68; Moortgat 1967, pl. 119;
CANES, I, pl. XXXIV: 220.
[57] Woolley 1934, pl. 181b; Moortgat 1967, pl. 43.
[58] Cf. Calmeyer 1964 for a comprehensive discussion of these.

We may at least suggest that the poles of such Early-Dynastic wagons as those seen on the "Standard" of Ur may have been attached by forking over a cross bar similar to that on our Anatolian models. Syria no. 2 also, with its projecting lengthwise beams crossed by a bar, seems to have been thus constructed to receive a vertically articulating pole.

Yoke

Where the draught animals are combined with the vehicle, they are harnessed to the pole by means of a yoke. Only on the solid-cast Anatolia no. 4 may we be sure that the latter is now in its original position. Here it is very summarily rendered and seems to be a horn yoke. On Anatolia nos. 1, 5, and 6 (and also on a, b, and c) it is rendered as a slender bar of metal, roughly rectangular in section. On nos. 1 and 5 – and perhaps on no. 6, but this is not clear – it is pinched in the middle, probably to simulate the pin at the junction of pole and yoke. This condition appears also on a and c, the yoke on the latter having been reassembled upside down.

About two-thirds of the way towards each end, the yoke is shaped into a bay of greater or lesser depth or sharpness. On no. 1 these parts of the yoke are presently lashed over the horns of the bovids, yet such sharp bays as those of no. 5 (and perhaps of no. 6) would have been more suitable for a neck yoke. Some yokes, on the other hand, as those of no. 1 and of a, b, and c, have such shallow bays that they could be horn yokes. On no. 3 the yoke is modern, and on no. 5 it has been laid across the backs of the animals. We wonder, however, if any of these yokes can be interpreted literally.

Rare comparative evidence is provided first of all by one example that may be close in time and place: a bronze "Standard" top in the Metropolitan Museum of Art, said to come from central Anatolia, perhaps from Horoztepe, just south of Ankara.[59] This represents a pair of yoked bovids. The yoke here is straight and roughly round in section and curves up at the end. We have seen that four equids were hitched to the Tell Agrab copper model two-wheeler; the two centre ones were under a yoke oval in section.[60] That bovids

---

[59] Özgüç and Akok 1958, 56 with pl. XVII: 4; Oliver 1960, 253 with fig. 14; Muscarella 1968, fig. 2.
[60] Frankfort 1943, pls. 58–60.

in ancient times were yoked by both horn and neck yokes is illustrated by Egyptian documents showing plough teams.[61]

Lines

Among the animals of the numbered groups those of Anatolia 1, 2, 3, 5, and 6 have their noses pierced vertically to take wire. (This seems also to be the case with a, b, c, d, and e.) On Anatolia no. 4, where the lines were cast with the whole, they merely begin at the nose. The wire, where it is well preserved, appears to form the two lines by which the animals were controlled. In reality, the lines would have been attached to nose rings permanently fixed to the bovids' noses in a *horizontal* position through the nostrils as are bulls' rings today. The vertical position of the perforation on the models recalls the position of the rings of bovids and equids alike on the "Standard" of Ur.[62] When we get to the wall paintings from Mari, we see that this was an awkwardly rendered representation of the nose ring.[63] The vertical ring, which would have had to be a lip ring, would have interfered with the animal's grazing, since the upper lip is used as a kind of proboscis for seizing and breaking off grass.[64] Nose rings in the correct, horizontal position and with double lines are seen on a pair of terracotta rhyta in the form of bulls or oxen found at Boğazköy in central Anatolia and dated to the Old Hittite Kingdom.[65] Significantly, a metal figurine of a bovid from Horoztepe to be discussed more fully later, has the remains of wire in a horizontal position through the nostrils too.[66]

There is something curious about these lines. While in Early-Dynastic times, single bovids are shown *led* by a line attached to a nose ring, and while equids are *driven* with lines to nose rings,[67] we have no representations of *bovids* driven with lines to nose rings. Our closest examples would be the second-millennium rhyta of

---

[61] Hayes 1953, fig. 173; Pritchard 1954, pls. 84, 91; Smith 1958, pl. 58b; Michalowski 1969, pls. 20, 295.

[62] Woolley 1934, pl. 92; Strommenger and Hirmer 1964, pls. 72 and X.

[63] Strommenger and Hirmer 1964, pl. 164; Parrot 1959, pls. V, VI; 1960, pls. 344f.

[64] Antonius 1938, 478.

[65] Published by Neve 1965, 48ff. with figs. 12a, b, 13, 14a, b.

[66] Özgüç and Akok 1951, 47ff. with pl. XI: 2.

[67] Woolley 1934, pl. 92; Strommenger and Hirmer 1964, pls. 72, X, XI.

bridled but unharnessed bovids from Boğazköy mentioned above. As a matter of fact, the representations of harnessed bovid teams – the great majority of them Egyptian plough teams[68] – that have come down to us show neither nose rings nor lines of any kind. Two exceptional scenes with bovids pulling wheeled vehicles – the relief at Abydos showing the Hittite baggage train before Kadesh (period of Ramses II) and that at Medinet Habu celebrating Ramses III's defeat of the Peoples of the Sea-depict four-wheeled wagons and two-wheeled carts, respectively.[69] In neither case is there any sign of nose rings or lines. Nor is there any on Neo-Assyrian scenes of bovids pulling carts.[70] The teams would have been driven by whip or goad, probably assisted by the voice, as in recent times.

If the lines of the models' bovids are original (and the holes in the noses can hardly have been made for anything else) they tell us of a time in the Near East when these animals were driven in lines. That such a practice existed would be more or less borne out by equid harnessing. This was under a yoke, like bovids, and with the bovid nose ring; presumably the line that ran to this ring was also in imitation of bovid bridling.

Material documents exist from the Early-Dynastic period. Silver rings were found in the noses of the bovids that pulled the wagons in the "King's Grave" (PG 789) at Ur, and the use of a single line is evidenced from the position of the beads that were attached to it.[71] The terret rings found in connection with bovid draught at Ur would also attest the same practice.[72]

We have used the term "lines" rather than reins in this discussion, since reins are always in pairs and go to either side of the head. It should be pointed out that single lines on either equids or bovids could only have exercised braking, not directional, control. Here is where the whip, goad, or voice, or a combination of them, would have been necessary.

In discussing the superstructure of the wagons we mentioned the placing of the lines in the trough of the breastwork, and the possible reason why on Anatolia no. 1 (and on a and b) the lines pass

---

[68] See *supra*, n. 61.
[69] Wreszinski 1935, pl. 22f., 113f.
[70] Gadd 1936, pls. 13, 35; Barnett (n.d.), pls. 36, 45.
[71] Woolley 1934, 65 with fig. 8.
[72] Woolley 1934, 48 with fig. 3. 64. 78, pls. 166 and 167; see also Calmeyer 1964.

through the apertures. We should here remark on the fact that the lines pass from the nose of one animal to that of the other, as a single wire. Does this too represent a convenience of the craftsman? It may. But a single line was indicated by the looping of the beads in the "King's Tomb" at Ur, cited above,[73] and this is what seems to be shown on the Ur "Standard", where a loop hangs from the driver's hands.[74] The arrangement of the two lines on Anatolia no. 4 is peculiar. It seems unlikely that this represents the twisting of actual lines rather than a measure facilitating casting. It is *possible*, however, in view of the fact that, as pointed out above, the lines would be only for braking and not for directional control, they sometimes might be twisted together. The twisting of the single line on Anatolia no. 1 may indicate the twisting of actual rope, since it would seem to serve little purpose on the model. We have, moreover, representations of rope headstalls and lines from the Early-Dynastic period, and there is textual evidence that lines were of Wool.[75]

Draught Animals

Most of the Anatolian models are provided with a pair of bovids yoked on either side of a pole. We cannot always be sure that they belonged originally to the particular model (cf. Anatolia no. 3).

Neither can we be certain what kind of bovid is meant. The lack of genitalia may be significant or may be due to the negligence of the craftsmen.

On the whole, the modelling of the animals is very poor. This applies particularly to Anatolia nos. 1, 2, 5, and 6 (to which a, b, and f may be added). These are very clumsily made. Those of Anatolia no. 4 show even less modelling, and a different style and proportions. Only the animals of Anatolia no. 3 (and those of c, d, and e) are more finely modelled and show some sense of style – even of abstraction – although here there are some differences between individual teams, particularly in the proportions of the legs and the position of their articulations. They differ from the first group also by their larger size and by the fact that they all seem to have inserted tails.

---

[73] Woolley 1934, 65.
[74] Woolley 1934, pl. 92; Strommenger and Hirmer 1964, pl. XI.
[75] Salonen 1956, 119.

These animals, showing stylistic differences among themselves, have no close parallels elsewhere. The well-known metal bulls from Alaca Hüyük and those that are perhaps from Horoztepe inevitably invite comparison.[76] They have been dated roughly to the later third millennium B.C. Basically of cast copper or bronze, these animals are technically superior to ours, with finer modelling and considerable sense of style. Often they are inlaid with more valuable metals, such as gold, silver, electrum or lead. The genitalia are commonly marked, identifying the animals as unaltered males. Stylistically speaking, only the bovids of Anatolia no. 3 (and of c, d, and e) come anywhere near these. Even they are not close, having consistently longer bodies, smaller heads, slenderer or shorter horns and differently or more sharply defined articulations of the legs.

The Alaca Hüyük or Horoztepe-related animals are set single on shafts to form the tops of "Standards" or, together with other animals (stags) and ornaments, they are found on the so-called "sun disks". Two pieces, both mentioned above, from Horoztepe or its vicinity, interest us here. One is a "Standard" top, made up of a pair of bulls with a neck yoke; the other is an incompletely preserved bull, its head, forelegs, and the fore part of the body plated with lead. The forehead has a triangular inlay of silver; in the nostrils traces of wire remain. It is uncertain whether this animal is another "Standard" terminal, or was meant to be free-standing – perhaps as part of a wagon group like ours.

Evidence for bovids put to four-wheeled wagons, as ours, in the ancient Near East, is available primarily from texts.[77] Representations are extremely rare; only two such are known to us. One of these is third millennium – on a scarlet-ware vase from Susa,[78] and the other is the already mentioned example of thirteenth-century wagons on the relief at Abydos.[79] All other depictions of bovids – and they are not numerous – show them hitched to carts or chariots. On the other hand, the two wagons in the "King's Grave" at Ur were each drawn by three bovids, a circumstance for which we have no parallels

---

[76] Bossert 1942, nos. 297. 298. 302. 306; Akurgal 1961, pls. II, 3–610; Özgüç and Akok 1951, pls. XI: 2–3. XVII: 4. One bovid "standard" top was actually found in the tomb at Horoztepe excavated by Özgüç and Akok 1951, pl. XI: 1a–c and fig. 28.

[77] Salonen 1956, 78ff.

[78] Childe 1951, 179 with fig. 2; Amiet 1966, 146ff., no. 106.

[79] Wreszinski 1935, pl. 22f.

among our models. Skulls of four bovids (Woolley considers the preservation of osteological material at Ur so erratic that the other bones may well have disappeared completely) were found in PG 580, associated with a terret ring.[80] The sledge of "Queen" Pu-Abi was drawn by a pair of bovids – not hemiones, as was originally believed.[81] This may be the correct identification also of two animals found in PG 1232 and never examined by a specialist.[82] They were associated with a wagon.

There seems, however, no reason to accept Orthmann's theory that the bovid remains found in the Alaca Hüyük tombs were those of draught animals belonging to vehicles with which the "Standards" or the "sun disks" would have been associated.[83] There is, in fact, no evidence for vehicles in or above the graves. Going further afield, we may point to the Caucasian material, where wagons (and carts) were found associated with the remains of cattle – clearly the draught animals.

Authenticity

Before discussing the chronology, origin, and possible use of these models, it might be well to try to weigh their authenticity. We have assumed that the numbered ones, which we have either inspected personally or which have been published, are basically genuine. We say "basically" since, as we have seen, most have been reassembled in modern times, leading to restorations and even to combinations of different ancient elements. We assume that a proportion of the others are too. The former assumption is based on the fact that several pieces have been tested in the laboratories of leading museums (one report is appended) and that no reasons have been found to suspect them. It is also based, in the cases of Anatolia nos. 1 and 2, on the fact that these were the first to appear in collections and that very few forgers initiate an entirely new type of artifact and one that, in this instance, is not even decorative.

About the Syrian models there seems to be no question, since these fragmentary objects are even less alluring than those with

---

[80] Woolley 1934, 64.
[81] Dyson 1960, 102ff.
[82] Woolley 1934, 48f.
[83] Orthmann 1967, 34ff.

animals, and since they entered the collections at a period prior to extensive forgeries.

Another reason for considering at least the first examples of these wagon models as genuine, is that they give details of construction of a type of four-wheeler that does not exist in Turkey today. The light, spoked-wheeled, horse-drawn wagons of the towns and cities have an undercarriage and swivelling pole or shafts; they are not harnessed to yokes. The only examples of oxen yoked to wheeled vehicles are those still pulling country carts. Hence it would be difficult for a forger familiar only with contemporary vehicles and the profile views of ancient ones to have arrived at some of the circumstantial detail that we have found. And part of this detail (the three lengthwise beams that protrude in front and the cross-bar) is supported by the evidence of Syria no. 2, and the side hooks by both Syrian examples, about which there can be little question.

As to the ability of late third- or early second-millennium B.C. metallurgists to produce objects of the complexity of our models, this is proven. We may, for example, cite the considerably earlier Tell Agrab model two-wheeler,[84] which was cast in copper by the *cire perdue* technique. Syrian metal work reached a high level too, as is shown, for instance, by the human figurines from Tell Judeidah in the Amuq[85] (bronze, cast by the *cire perdue* method) and various objects from the hypogaeum at Til Barsip.[86] In Anatolia, advanced metallurgical techniques are in evidence, particularly among the finds from Alaca Hüyük and the Horoztepe region already mentioned.

In construction, our wagons relate, in varying degrees, to wagons depicted in Near Eastern art of the third and early second millennia B.C.; the two Syrian models in particular can be closely paralleled.

The Anatolian models fall into three basic groups, some examples being closely related to each other. This in itself is not an argument against their authenticity, but may indicate that each group was made in a different workshop or in a different region, although the hybrid b might indicate that at least two workshops were situated closely enough to influence each other. No. 4 is closely related to neither group, but the figurines said to have been found with it and which have proved upon analysis to be of the same metallic struc-

---

[84] Frankfort 1943, 12f., pls. 58–60.
[85] Braidwood and Braidwood 1960, 300ff. with figs. 240–245 and pls. 56–64.
[86] Thureau-Dangin and Dunand 1936.

ture, are considered by Orthmann to show connections with Alaca Hüyük. Terrace, on the other hand, suggests resemblance to figurines from the Syrian coast but without being specific.[87]

The detailed analysis of such structural features as the three length-wise beams, front cross-bar, side hooks, and forking pole, makes such forgeries seem unlikely. This does not, of course, rule out the pos-sibility that, once the Anatolian models established themselves on the market and began to fetch large sums, imitations were not being forged.

As to the style of the models – one might ask whether some of the bovids could not have been inspired by the Alaca Hüyük and Horoztepe animals. It does not seem to us, however, that the sim-ilarities that can be detected are of a type that suggest imitation.

Connections with Actual Wagon

Since there are no other models with which to compare our Syrian and Anatolian ones, it may help in determining their chronology, origin, and purpose to try to assess when, where, and how the actual wagons that they could represent were used.[88]

All our wagons bear a basic resemblance to wagons illustrated in the Near East: they have the high front breastwork and the super-structure all around, with small platform at rear. Such vehicles are documented in Mesopotamia and Syria by Early Dynastic times and in Anatolia at the turn of the second millennium. There are no rep-resentations of similar wagons after this. When true wagons are shown, which, to our knowledge, is only twice in the second mil-lennium, they lack the high front and they are spoked-wheeled.[89]

The Syrian models seem crudely to reflect such wagons as those on the "Standard" of Ur, which were equid-drawn, and which carried two occupants.[90] The use of such four wheelers in war, however, is

---

[87] Orthmann 1967, 49; Terrace 1964, 56–58. Similarities can indeed be observed with such metal figurines as Akurgal 1961, pls. 21: below, left (Alaça Hüyük) and 23 (Horoztepe).

[88] Mellink 1971, 165, mentioned a "bronze wagon" found in the burnt palace level (i.e. Kārum Kaneš 1b period) at Acemhüyük, south of Ankara. Through the kindness of Professor N. Özgüç we were able to examine the fragments of this object and to determine that it was not a model, but must have been a small trol-ley for actual use, and quite unrelated to our models.

[89] Wreszinski 1935, pl. 22; Salonen 1951, pl. XXVII.

[90] Woolley 1934, pl. 92; Strommenger and Hirmer 1964, pls. 72, XI.

not evidenced after Early Dynastic times.[91] When we see wagons represented later, as on some Akkadian cylinders and some Anatolian cylinder-seal impressions, they seem to be cult cars, carrying deities or images of deities.[92] Although the four-wheeler possessed the advantage for warfare of being able to carry two people, its weight (particularly considering the disk wheels) and its lack of manoeuvrability must have outweighed this virtue, and it was discarded for military purposes. We are inclined to believe, however, that such vehicles continued to be used in the cult and that their later representation is not merely a matter of conservative iconography. On Anatolian sealings, for instance, their appearance in conjunction with cross-bar or spoked wheels depicts an innovation that would seem to reflect reality.[93]

Because of our ignorance of the dating, it is hard to say whether the originals of the Syrian models were still battle cars or whether they served another purpose. We may have one clue, and only one, in the pole of Syria no. 1 – if it is the pole – and if the Anatolian sealing in the Louvre referred to above does indeed show a pole that forks as it goes forward.[94] Then we might say that this feature is paralleled around the turn of the second millennium and at no other time *that we know of*. We cannot, however, even be certain that the models were made in Syria and not imported from further east. Neither can we be sure of the kind of draught animals that accompanied these models – assuming that there were any. Were they equids, as on most representations, or were they bovids, as on the Anatolian models?

The Anatolian models, on the other hand, have no close parallels among any examples appearing in Near Eastern art. Their superstructure is peculiar, with its rail work supports and removable screens. While it is possible that the Anatolian seal impressions showing wagons with striated sides above which the driver is fully shown represent some such thing, it seems more likely that they are trying to

---

[91] Nagel 1966, 10 comments correctly on this.
[92] Strommenger and Hirmer 1964, pl. 113; third row; Porada 1948, nos. 220, 893E; Frankfort 1939a, pl. XL: m, n; Bossert 1942, nos. 409f.; Özgüç 1965, pl. III: 9.
[93] Porada 1948, no. 893E; Frankfort 1939a, pl. XL: m, n; Bossert 1942, nos. 409f.; Özgüç 1965, pl. III 9.
[94] The New York sealing would argue against such a pole, see above pp. 361 with nn. 50 and 51.

depict the solid sides with panels or struts of such wagons as the Syrian models or those of the Ur or Mari "Standards".[95] Less likely, although not entirely to be excluded, is the possibility that sides are not intended to be shown at all, but the cross planks of the floor.

The forms of the Anatolian models are essentially those of farm or produce wagons, with the cage for transporting roughage and the dismountable screens for use in carrying sacks of threshed corn, or even loose chaff, as in the wicker-sided Anatolian carts of today.[96] In the latter case we should also envisage the original existence of a small separate screen to be used for closing the rear after the vehicle had been partly loaded. Bovid draught too would have been more appropriate for this purpose than equid draught, since it provided the slow, but strong traction required. The sheaths attached at the sides of Anatolia nos. 1 and 5 (and f) would then be explained as goad or whip holders, for which their extremely slender proportions would seem to fit them better than for javelin sheaths. We may ask, however, why, in this case, such a relatively high front would be necessary as that which appears on nos. 1, 2, 4, 5, 6 (and a and f) and one of a form that is reminiscent of that occurring on military and cult wagons? Another point to be considered is whether the models, which, by any standard, are complex pieces of metalwork, and must have been valuable, would reproduce simple farm or produce wagons.

A different problem is that we do not know what early bovid-drawn wagons intended primarily for transporting goods looked like in the Near East of the third and early second millennia B.C. The texts, which refer frequently to such vehicles, give no information. The only third-millennium representation of a bovid-drawn wagon – that on a Scarlet-Ware vase from Susa[97] – shows a very peculiar superstructure, with a single, apparently seated, occupant. The only second-millennium representations of bovid-drawn wagons show them being used for the transport of goods and, as mentioned above, without the high front and with spoked wheels.[98] We may note that a

---

[95] Woolley 1934, pl. 92; Strommenger and Hirmer 1964, pls. 72, XI; Parrot 1956, pl. LVI; Yadin 1963, 139.

[96] Koşay 1951, pl. XXXIII: 221.

[97] Childe 1951, fig. 2; Amiet 1966, 146ff., no. 106.

[98] We do not consider that the four-wheeled dolly used for transporting the funerary bark of Sebeknekht (Dynasty XIII; Smith 1965, fig. 34c) or the miniature one carrying a model of Queen Ah-hotep's boat (Dynasty XVIII; Smith 1958, pl. 84A)

few terracotta models of the later third millennium B.C. that show tilt wagons[99] probably represent vehicles that were pulled by bovids. Of course we do have evidence, as mentioned above, for bovid-drawn wagons from the tombs at Ur, Kiš, and probably from Susa. The evidence for the shape of the vehicles buried with these animals is, however, limited, and mostly circumstantial.

As far as the appearance of the Anatolian models goes, their chief resemblance to the Early-Dynastic war wagons of figured documents would seem to consist in a roughly similarly shaped front breastwork (although different in fabric) and in having a superstructure all around. They were probably similar in proportion too although, since they were bovid-drawn, hence not intended for fast going, they may have been somewhat larger than the battle cars. We mentioned this above in discussing the width of floor of the actual wagons found at Kiš and Ur. This also raises the question of whether the latter were strictly hearses, not war wagons, because they were bovid-drawn while the military vehicles were always equid-drawn. Both wagons in the "King's Grave" at Ur would hardly have been hearses, however, since there is no evidence that more than one important personnage was buried here.[100] Moreover, the width of at least one of the floors (0.50 m.), while allowing room for the legs of a standing man, would barely allow place for the shoulders of a lying one. Thus we cannot tell whether these wagons were permanently combined with bovid draught, or only temporarily. Were some of these battle cars that were normally pulled by equids?

Although the actual wagons found in Caucasia were bovid-drawn, they differed markedly in their superstructures and poles from our models and from the wagons of figured evidence from the Near East. They cannot safely be used to reconstruct bovid-drawn wagons in the latter area.[101]

There is a discrepancy in the evidence for bovid-drawn wagons in the Near East between the figured art on the one hand and the texts and actual finds on the other. As pointed out, it is very scarce

---

fall into the category of true wagons. For the latter see again Wreszinski 1935, pl. 22; Salonen 1951, pl. XXVII.

[99] Speiser 1934, 74 with n. 12, 192 with pl. XXV: a 2: de Mequenem 1943, 126, no. 10 with fig. 91: b 10; Childe 1951, 184; Piggott 1968, pl. XXIII (lower). The present authors are preparing a study of these models and others of tilt carts.

[100] Woolley 1934, 71.

[101] Piggott 1968, pls. XXII and XXIII (upper), fig. 12.

in the first type of documentation and amply established in the last. Military and cult themes dominate the art, with equids in the former scenes, and equids and mythical animals in the latter. More work-a-day subjects are not shown. How then to account for the cattle in the graves? We might explain their presence in one of three ways. As certainly predecessors of hemiones in draught, and therefore the more venerable, bovids might have been the more appropriate animals for a funeral ceremony. Again, the temperaments of hemiones might have been ill-suited to such purposes. Or they may have been (oddly enough) too valuable. In those Iron-Age burials with horses where remains are well enough preserved to be informative, we often find that it was crippled or diseased animals, hence less valuable ones, that the living felt readiest to part with to the dead.[102]

Piggott, who is the one thus far to discuss the Anatolian models the most extensively, suggested that the "Marash group", as he called the three examples known to him (Anatolia nos. 1, 2, and 4), reflected the introduction of a new type of vehicle from Mesopotamia in the context of the establishment of trade relations with Assyria in the first century of the second millennium B.C.[103] An ultimate origin, outside Anatolia, in Syria or Mesopotamia, would certainly be indicated by their general shape. As to their provenance from Marash – the lack of information, and the lack of properly excavated metalwork from the area of Marash in southeast Turkey, preclude any certainty at present about this (see above). As to the chronology proposed by Piggott, here too it is impossible to be specific. We have seen that high-fronted wagons are documented in the figured art of Mesopotamia and Syria by Early Dynastic times, and in Anatolia by the turn of the second millennium B.C. Independent evidence for the occurrence of any kind of wheeled vehicles in Anatolia before that time is very limited: we do not accept bovid-drawn-vehicle evidence at Alaca Hüyük as proposed by Orthmann,[104] but there is the Horoztepe bovid figurine with wire in its nose and the pair of yoked bulls perhaps from the same site. The two so-called "rein guides" from Anatolia[105] have been attributed to the later third or early second

---

[102] Bökönyi 1968, 50f.
[103] Piggott 1968, 273.
[104] Orthmann 1967, 52ff.
[105] Calmeyer 1964, 74, a, b; Bossert 1942, nos. 597–599, 601–604.

millennium B.C. Piggott's suggestion that the wagons reflect a type that came to Anatolia only at the beginning of the second millennium is not wholly satisfactory, since contacts with Syria and Mesopotamia were in existence before.[106]

As to the peculiar superstructure of our Anatolian models, this may reflect an Anatolian adaptation of Syrian and Mesopotamian forms, or it may represent a direct Anatolian borrowing of a Mesopotamian or Syrian type of vehicle, unrecorded in the countries of its origin by reason of its rustic character.

All things considered, however, we do not see the farm wagon interpretation as the complete one. As said, the models go back basically to Mesopotamian battle cars, later shown as cult cars, seen in art from Mesopotamia, Syria, and Anatolia, drawn by equids or (on Akkadian seals) by mythological animals. This would account for the sheath as a rendering of the quiver so often present on figured documents. On the other hand, this would give no satisfactory explanation for the removable screens. The bovid draught would then be for a special occasion, such as burial, for which we find precedence in the Ur, Kiš and perhaps Susa tombs. Or are the bovids, after all, meant to be sacred bulls? There are the probably sacred bulls on the Alaca Hüyük "Standards" and those from Horoztepe, as well as the separate animal from the latter site that might conceivably have been one of a pair pulling a model vehicle such as ours. In the second millennium B.C. we find the Weather God driving a vehicle drawn by bulls. Bittel indeed suggests that it is his bulls, Sheri and Hurri, that may be represented by the pair of unyoked but bridled bull rhytons from Boğazköy found in a 1700–1600 B.C. level.[107] This conception seems to have been of Hurrian origin, but became standard in Hittite mythology. There is an Anatolian stamp-cylinder seal in the Louvre, of the mid-second millennium B.C. showing a god driving a two-wheeler pulled by bovids;[108] a fragment of a relief vase from Boğazköy depicts what Bittel interprets as the Weather

---

[106] For early contacts between Anatolia and the Near East cf. a.o. M. Mellink 1965, 42ff., esp. 52ff.

[107] For references see *supra* n. 65, also Bittel 1970a, 72f. For these bulls in Hittite texts see a.o. von Brandenstein 1943, 71; Güterbock 1946, 98, no. 9; Laroche 1947, 49 and 59; Goetze 1958, especially 141 with n. 4.

[108] Parrot 1951, 180ff. with pls. XIII: 1. XIV: 1, and fig. 2; Porada 1957, 194 and n. 12 with pl. XXX, fig. 4; Beran 1965, 63, n. 19; Mellink 1966, 78; Vorys Canby 1969, 146 with n. 22. For earlier dating cf. a.o. Alp 1968, 271ff.

God mounting a bovid-drawn cart.[109] At the same time he calls attention to a thirteenth-century rock relief of a similar subject at Imamkulu in central Cappadocia.[110] Still later we find the Weather God mounting a bull-drawn cart on a tenth- or ninth-century B.C. relief from Malatya in southeast Anatolia.[111] Going further afield, we see what is perhaps the same subject on the thirteenth- or twelfth-century B.C. golden bowl from Hasanlu in Azerbaijan.[112] All these representations, however, have one thing in common besides bovid draught: the God always drives a two wheeler. This suggests that if our wagons pulled the Weather God they would at least have been prior to the middle of the second millennium B.C.

There is another argument against the originals of our models having served exclusively as farm or transport wagons: it is unlikely that models of purely work-a-day vehicles would ever have been anything more than toys. Yet the valuable material and rather fragile construction of most of the models would seem to preclude such a use; and unless the whole equipage, including the animals, had been mounted on wheels, it could not be pulled back and forth – something essential in a child's toy vehicle.

Function of the Models

Thus for the possible function of the models we are left with cult use of some kind, but the lack of information about the find contexts seriously hampers our drawing conclusions. The models could have been cult objects, ex votos, or grave gifts. Of the numerous terracotta models that have come down to us, most come from settlements, a few from tombs. Within the settlements the exact find circumstances have not been reported, often because they could not be established at all at the time of excavation. Of the few metal models surviving only one has a find context: the copper two-wheeler from Tell Agrab, which was in the temple of the Moon God, Sin, there, and which may well have been an ex voto.[113] We also know that

---

[109] Bittel 1970a.
[110] Bittel 1970a, 24, cf. Gelb 1939, pl. XLII.
[111] Bossert 1942, no. 778; Akurgal 1961, pl. 105 (above); Yadin 1961, 358f.; Orthmann 1971, pl. 41f. For discussion of Weather God driving a vehicle cf. a.o. Amiet 1965, 244ff.; also Mellink 1966, 72ff.
[112] Porada 1959, 19–22; 1964, 96–102 with pl. 23.
[113] Frankfort 1943, 13, with pls. 58–60.

vehicle models were kept in a later Hittite temple: an omen text, possibly from the thirteenth century B.C. mentions a model of unspecified material in the temple of a God of Vegetation, Sumuquan.[114]

Above, we discussed the metalwork from Alaca Hüyük and Horoztepe and saw that it came from tombs. This might well be true for the one bovid figurine that came from Horoztepe and that may have belonged to a model like ours, although it has no reported find context. We know that bovids were associated with actual vehicles in burials in the Early-Dynastic period. The association may have lingered in the burial rite (and its existence, still later, in Caucasia would indeed indicate such a thing). These models, then, might have been substitutes for those actual vehicles that once were buried with their owners — probably for use in another world.

Appendix

Approximate Composition of ANE cart 66.15 (see p. 104) as determined by semi-quantitative emission spectrography.

Location of Sample		Composition in percent						
	Cu	Sn	Pb	Zn	Fe	Ni	Sb	As*
Base	M	N.D.	N.D.	N.D.	1.1	0.05	0.05	0.07i
Upright (back)	M	N.D.	N.D.	N.D.	1.0	0.05	0.05	0.07i
Upright (side)	M	N.D.	N.D.	N.D.	3.0	0.06	0.06	0.17i
Bull	M	N.D.	N.D.	N.D.	0.5	0.05	0.06	0.15i
Wheel	M	1.4	0.03	N.D.	1.0	0.06	0.17	0.5i
Rein	M	1.4	0.03	N.D.	0.8	0.05	0.15	0.4i
Sheet	M	0.9	0.07	N.D.	0.4	0.06	0.18	0.3i

* Only the relative proportions of the Arsenic values are of significance.

Acknowledgements

The authors are indebted to all those private collections and museums that have given permission to publish the numerous photographs. Our especial thanks also go to individuals who have been personally helpful. First of all to Mrs. P. O. Harper, for permission to

---

[114] Goetze 1955, 498 (KUB V, 7); Ehelolf 1936, 192. Kümmel 1967, 136ff.

examine the model in the Metropolitan Museum of Art, and to publish it and the analysis of its metal composition; also for permission to examine related material. We are grateful to Mr. L. Pomerance for letting us study and photograph his model, and to Dr. Dows Dunham, who kindly allowed us to look at the Boston Museum of Fine Art's model. In London, Mr. P. Adam extended a similar courtesy, in connection with which Miss R. Ludovici was particularly helpful. We are obliged to Dr. P. Amiet for permission to publish the Louvre model and for information on the metal, as well as to Miss A. Caubet for its history and dimensions. Dr. O. Vessberg of the Medalhavsmuseet in Stockholm has kindly permitted us to publish that museum's model, and Miss G. Walberg has provided us with information concerning it. In Berlin, Mrs. E. Nagel-Strommenger of the Museum für Vor- and Frühgeschichte has graciously given us permission to publish the museum's model and has provided us with information relating to it. We are indebted to the late Mrs. J. Danmanville for allowing us to copy her photo of the Thierry IV model. We are particularly grateful to Mr. N. Schimmel for securing permission for us to publish photographs of models in anonymous collections. Our thanks go to Mrs. N. Özgüç for information concerning the bronze wagon from Acemhüyük and for the opportunity to examine it. Mrs. U. Moortgat-Correns has generously allowed us to illustrate the as-yet-unpublished terracotta model from Tell Chuēra, and has furnished us with information concerning a pertinent seal found at the same site. We are indebted to Mr. J. Bomford for permission to reproduce, and to Dr. H. W. Catling and Dr. P. R. S. Moorey for making available the photograph of the terracotta model in the Bomford Collection which we were allowed to study. Dr. Moorey has also arranged for us to examine a terracotta from Kiš in the Ashmolean and publish a new photograph of it. To him too, as editor of *Levant* go our especial thanks for his generosity and patience. For information of various kinds we wish also to thank Professor M. Mellink, Dr. H. Seyrig, Mr. J. Ternbach, Professors Ph. Houwink ten Cate, M. N. van Loon, and W. Orthmann.

26. TERRACOTTA MODELS AS EVIDENCE FOR WHEELED VEHICLES WITH TILTS IN THE ANCIENT NEAR EAST*

M. A. LITTAUER AND J. H. CROUWEL

In his important study of early wheeled vehicles from the Caucasus region, S. Piggott briefly considered two terracotta models of wagons with arched tilts from the Near East (Piggott 1968, 273). Following Speiser 1934, he argued that the actual wagons represented by these models had been introduced into the Near East from the Caucasus by the later 3rd millennium B.C. The present article aims at a more comprehensive review of the Near-Eastern evidence. It will be almost exclusively concerned with terracotta models of both four-wheeled wagons and two-wheeled carts, because these constitute practically all the documentation we have of vehicles with tilts. This material undoubtedly will be incomplete, since there must be more examples among the many models that have not been published, or published only inadequately. A full description will be possible only in the one case where we have personally examined the model (wagon A1).

Material

A. Four-Wheelers

1. From North Syria (pl. I above, and fig. i) (Childe 1951; Piggott 1968, 273, 294, pl. xxiii lower), at present in the Ashmolean Museum, Oxford (no. 1913, 183). The model was bought at Osheriyeh, near the confluence of the Euphrates and the Sajur, and almost certainly comes from a cemetery at Hamman in the same region.

    L (total): c. 0.19 m., H (with wheels): c. 0.15 m., H (without wheels): c. 0.13 m., W (over axle tubes): c. 0.10 m., W (over floor): c. 0.085 in. Greenish buff clay. Surface roughly smoothed, probably with a

* Proceedings of the Prehistoric Society 40, 1974, 20–36.

knife, before firing. Condition good, except for some incrustation on the back.

In order to accommodate the original wooden or metal axle (here restored in wood), the modeller fashioned tubular sheaths in terracotta beneath the front and back edges of the rectangular floor; these sheaths extend slightly beyond the floor at either side. Attached to the front axle sheath is a lug, vertically perforated. The U-shaped tilt is closed at the back and has a low breastwork at the front. A carelessly executed pattern of crosshatching is shallowly incised over the entire upper part of the tilt, except for the back, which is left plain. A narrow band of denser and more deeply incised crosshatching, framed by horizontal incisions, runs around the lower sides and rear of the wagon. The front breastwork is incised with three pairs of vertical lines. The wheels are plain, perforated discs (diam. c. 0.068 m.), which are not original, but which have been added to the model in recent times to make it more intelligible.

2. From Tepe Gawra, in northern Iraq (fig. 2) (Excavation no. 904.VI.620.D) (Speiser 1934). Now in Dropsie College, Philadelphia. This model is very similar to no. 1, but of much smaller dimensions. L (presumably with wheels): 0.062 m., H (presumably with wheels): 0.062 m. Greenish clay. From the published photographs, the axle sheaths appear to have been under the floor.

According to the description, both front and rear are open, with low breastworks at either end (Salonen 1951, pl. VII: 1; Pritchard 1954; Piggott 1968, pl. XXIII). Two horizontally perforated lugs project at either side of the front breastwork. Incision is present on the sides and front breastwork (no published information is available for the back); on the tilt, wide horizontal panels of cross hatching alternate with narrow plain ones; the front breastwork displays rows of verticals between horizontal incisions.

The wheels are plain perforated discs and are not original but, like those of A1, have been added subsequent to excavation.

3. From Susa in Elam (fig. 3) (de Mequenem 1943, 126, no. 10, with fig. 91b, 10). This fragmentary terracotta (existing L: c. 0.12 m.) has projecting axle sheaths and retains the lower part of the tilt. Like A1 and A2, this is incised with cross hatching.

These are the models indubitably representing wagons with tilts. As to their chronology, A2, although from a trial trench, may be attributed to Gawra level VI, which contained material of the Akkadian and post-Akkadian periods. A dating of c. 2350–2100 B.C. may

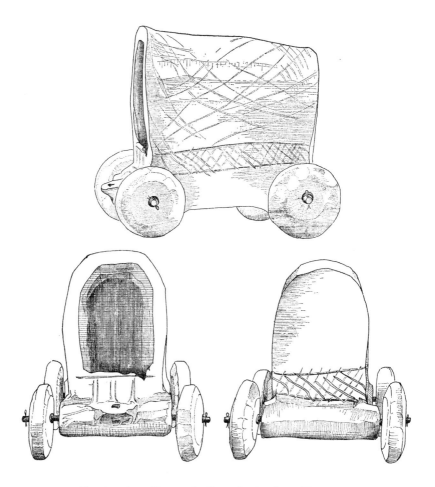

Fig. 1: a, b, c. Terracotta four-wheeler from Hamman.
(Oxford, Ashmolean Museum).

therefore be presumed (Porada 1965). This provides a clue to the
chronology of A1, which is so closely related, and quite possibly also
of A3, which has no registered find context. Also helpful in dating
A1 may be its possible relationship to some tomb groups from the
site of Hamman that are now also in the Ashmolean Museum
(Woolley 1914). These groups belong to the last quarter of the 3rd
millennium B.C. (P. R. S. Moorey, personal communication; Piggott
1968, 273).

These three models of baked clay represent one type of vehicle. Others, from a widespread area of the Near East, represent different types of four- and two-wheelers that may or may not have sometimes carried tilts but that are shown without them. No systematic study of these has yet been made, although some discussion can be found in van Buren (van Buren 1930, 252). These terracottas range in date from the Early Dynastic to the Old Babylonian periods. Among the remains of four-wheelers there are some fragmentary examples that might once have carried tilts. A wagon from Nippur, found in an Ur III context (McCown-Haines 1967), seems to have been open at the sides, but provided with fragmentary posts at each corner. Could this be an unparalleled case of the hoop posts without the covering? Two other fragmentary wagons that might be suspected of having carried tilts are from Hama in Syria – level J3 (late 3rd millennium B.C.) (Fugmann 1958, 72 with no. 6 and fig. 93), and Anau in what is now Soviet Turkmenistan (Pumpelly 1908; Bona 1960, 101 with fig. 6). Too little remains of either to justify

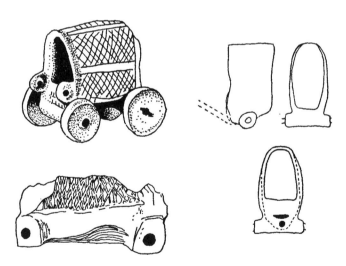

Upper Left: Fig. 2. Terracotta four-wheeler from Tepe Gawra. After Speiser.
Lower Left: Fig. 3. Terracotta four-wheeler from Susa. After de Mequenem.
Upper & Lower Right: Fig. 4. Terracotta two-wheeler from Homs region. After du Buisson.

drawing conclusions, although the open front of the Hama vehicle would be more appropriate to a tilt wagon than to an uncovered goods wagon.

B. *Two-Wheelers*

1. From the neighbourhood of Homs in Syria (fig. 4) (R. Mesnil du Buisson, Bulletin de la société nationale de antiquaires de France 1932, 143 with fig. 1; Forrer 1932) H: 0.115 m, W: 0.053 m. This model recalls A1 and A2 except that it has a single tubular axle sheath centrally located under the floor. At the front there is a low breastwork with a hole underneath it to take the metal or wooden draught pole. The side-view drawing shows that this must have projected at an oblique angle. There is no incision.

2. Unprovenanced; at present in Beirut (fig. 5) (Mackay 1951; Baramki 1967). H: 0.125 m. This model is very different from B1. Although it also has an unincised, U-shaped tilt, the front breastwork is high, narrow, complex, and seemingly not joined to the sides. Narrow in the lower part, it widens towards the top to form two loops. Over the depression between the loops a short clay strip is folded vertically; four pellets are applied on the face of the breast-

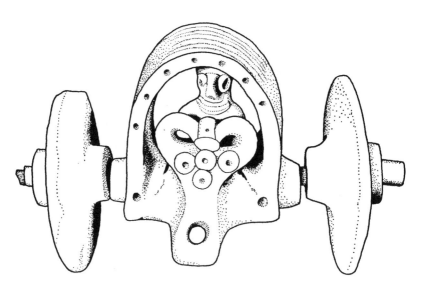

Fig. 5. Terracotta two-wheeler in Beirut. After Baramki.

work just below this. At the base of the breastwork is a hole for the draught pole. (From the illustration, the pole would appear to have come out at an oblique angle, as did the one on B1.) The plain tilt has shallow holes outlining its front edge, and seems to have been open at the back. Inside, partly hidden behind the breastwork, is the driver, with hollow pellet eyes, a prominent nose, and wearing a plastic 'necklace' with rows of short vertical incisions. For lack of a published description, some points cannot be ascertained, since the photograph does not tell us. For instance, are the wheels the original ones? These wheels, which are disproportionately large, have raised centres to represent the naves. Other points may perhaps be answered later on when we come to compare this with what seem to be similar vehicles without tilts.

3. From Tel Masin in Syria (fig. 6) (R. Mesnil du Buisson, Bulletin de la société nationale de antiquaires de France 1932, 145 with fig. 2; Forrer 1932). Size unknown. Unfortunately, the fragmentary state of preservation does not allow for a certain reconstruction. We see a floor with a roughly centrally-placed axle sheath projecting at the sides. The floor is somewhat concave at the sides and convex at the back. At the front it has a narrow extension at the centre, which is vertically pierced, perhaps to act as a lug. Along the sides there are the remains of a superstructure and, between them, vestiges of some object.

We wonder, however, if the broken-off sides are not the lower part of a tilt, and if the remains inside could not be those of a driver shielded behind a breastwork. If this were so, the model might come rather near to B2. Interestingly, there seems to be a hollow pellet at the front of the breastwork, with an impressed hole at either side below the areas where the tilt would start, which is also reminiscent of B2. This comparison and, in particular, the presence of a pellet, would suggest a date in the first half of the 2nd millennium B.C. for this model, which comes from Syria too, as we shall shortly see. Du Buisson, the excavator, called it 'Mitannian' but did not give his reasons for doing so.

No other indubitable models of covered two-wheelers, either complete or fragmentary, have come to our notice. Of the three examples to hand, B1 cannot be closely dated. R. Mesnil du Buisson, who published the object, assumed it to be of the 3rd millennium B.C. on the basis of its clay and firing. Comparison with the covered wagons might suggest a date in the later 3rd millennium B.C. but the earlier 2nd millennium B.C. cannot be excluded.

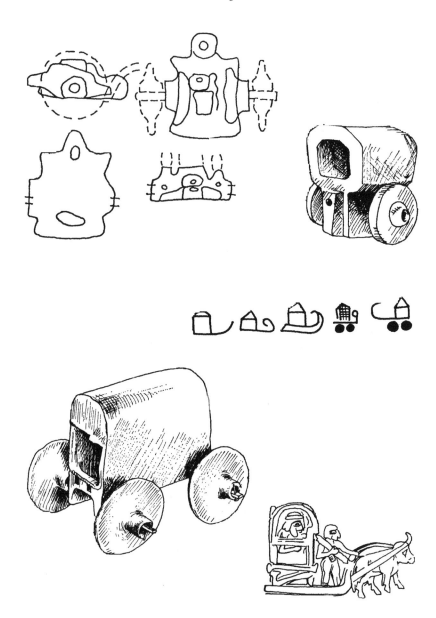

Upper left: Fig. 6. Terracotta two-wheeler from Tel Masin. After du Buisson.
Upper right: Fig. 7. Terracotta two-wheeler from Tri Brata. After Hančar.
Lower left: Fig. 8. Terracotta four-wheeler from Kerch. After Artamonov.
Centre right: Fig. 9. Uruk pictographs. After Falkenstein.
Lower right: Stone plaque in London. British Museum. After Nagel.

It is possible, on the other hand, to situate B2 quite firmly both chronologically and geographically. One closely similar model, with a driver, but without a tilt, comes from a tomb at Mourek in Syria, which is said to be contemporary with Hama, level H (Ingholt 1940; Bossert 1951). In it the driver stands, his arms stretched out towards the high breastwork, and he has no back support. Other fragmentary vehicle models of this type come from level H at the site of Hama itself (Fugmann 1958, fig. 110, no. 3A 214; fig. 132, no. 5A 475, fig. 139, no. 5A 602), which can be dated to the 20th–16th centuries B.C. (for beginning cf. also Dever 1970). Applied clay pellets and a 'necklace' are also found on the Mourek model and are, in fact, distinctive Syrian features of the first half of the 2nd millennium B.C. They appear on a variety of terracottas, including human and animal figurines (Hillen 1952; cf. a.o. Fugmann 1958, figs. 110–117, 120).

In conclusion, all three covered two-wheeler models come from Syria and, while B1 cannot be firmly dated, B2 clearly belongs to the first half of the 2nd millennium B.C., as does probably B3. (Mackay 1951 assigned B2 to the Early Bronze Age, Baramki to a period between Early and Middle Bronze, c. 2300–2200 B.C.).

Function

Since our models do not all fall into one category, but into at least three, it is the harder to ascertain what purposes they could have served. Were some or all of them no more than toys, or were there cult objects among them – funerary or otherwise? The same question is posed by most other wheeled terracottas from the ancient Near East. Few seem to have been found in tombs, as was probably the Ashmolean tilt wagon (A1) and certainly the Mourek open two-wheeler. The great majority comes from settlements, but the find contexts in these have rarely been reported, if they were established at all at the time of excavation. One class of platform cars with fronts moulded in low relief had a religious connotation (votive offerings?). (For illustrations cf. a.o. van Buren 1930, figs. 302–314; Barrelet 1968, pls. lvii: 549ff., lviii: 614ff., lix: 620ff., lxxi: 740ff.)

It is not unlikely that many of the terracottas could have served more than one purpose, including that of burial gift, according to the need.

The lugs on our wagons A1 and A2 and that perhaps on B3 would seem to indicate that these were used as toys that children could pull along by strings. A single lug appears also on a number of zoomorphic vessels in terracotta set on four wheels found in Early-Dynastic Iraq. There a cult function seems implicit, both because of the type of vessel (rhyton) and because of the occurrence of some pieces in sanctuaries (Woolley 1934; Delougaz 1952; Tuchelt 1962). The only other lugs that we know of are on covered two-wheelers of a much later period (10th–9th centuries B.C.), which were found at Mingetchaour on the right bank of the Kura river in the present Soviet Azerbaijan (Mongait 1959; Bona 1960, pl. lxviii: 2–3). In an evident effort to help these retain their equilibrium without a supporting pole, the wheels, which seem to be original, are placed so high on the sides that the vehicles virtually sit on the ground. More realistically, our two-wheelers, B1 and B2, have holes for the draught poles. The latter, however, do not rule out the possibility of their being toys, as a child could grasp the pole to run them back and forth.

Construction, Draught Animals, and Use

In the following discussion, comparative material for both categories – four-wheelers and two-wheelers – will be adduced when appropriate. Important among such material are the remains of actual wagons, both covered and open, and of open two-wheelers from the Caucasus region. These have been found both north and south of the greater Caucasus range in tombs that have been dated by Piggott to the later 3rd and to the 2nd millennium B.C. (Piggott 1968, Table I). In addition, from somewhat north of this region, from a kurgan at Tri Brata on the Kalmyk steppe, comes a clay model of a covered cart (fig. 7), dated by Piggott to the later 3rd millennium and by, others to various periods in the 2nd millennium B.C. (Hančar 1956; Piggott 1968, 300f.). Most of the other comparative evidence is considerably later: the cart models mentioned from Soviet Azerbaijan, terracotta and limestone model carts from Iron-Age Cyprus (Ohnefalsch-Richter 1893, Lorimer 1903 140f. with fig. 7; Bona 1960, pl. lxviii: 4), baked clay models of covered wagons and carts from tombs of the Greek colony at Kerch in the Crimea (Minns 1913; Bona 1960, pls. lxvii, 4, lxviii, 1; Artamonov 1969) and a terracotta model wagon from Alexandria (Lorimer 1903, 142; Hill 1897). Greek authors furnish us with literary references to covered vehicles used in Greece, in the Persian empire, and among the Scythians (Herodotus; Xenophon; Aristophanes; Plutarch). Going further afield, we find Etruscan and Roman reliefs showing four-wheelers with tilts (Zschietzschmann 1959; Tarr 1969). But the representations from the Mediterranean show spoked-wheeled,) horse- or mule-drawn vehicles. The same may well be true for most of those mentioned by Greek authors.

Evidence from the ancient Near East itself, apart from our models and the references in Greek texts, is rare and ambiguous pictographs on early Uruk clay tablets and the Idrimi text, both of which will be considered below. This is all the more striking in view of the considerable documentation – representations, actual finds, texts – of *open* vehicles from the Near East dating to the 3rd millennium B.C. and later. The disparity is not surprising, however, when one considers that the covered vehicles were probably primarily utilitarian, whereas the military, hunting, cult, or processional vehicles that were considered worthy of notice were all open ones.

Finally, comparative use can of course be made of the documentation for tilt vehicles in later and recent times in various parts of the world.

We illustrate here an unpublished example of a cart model from Cyprus, presently in the Ashmolean Museum, Oxford (pl. I, below); inv. 1950.18; formerly Rugby School; provenance unknown; H. (total): c. 0.095, L (total): c. 0.10, W (total) c. 0.055; also illustrated is a well-known wagon model from Kerch (fig. 8).

General Discussion

A. *Wagons*

The three models, A1–A3, all have rectangular floor plans and tubular axle sheaths. The latter, a feature also of numerous models of open vehicles, both four-wheeled and two-wheeled, do not reflect the construction of actual vehicles. They are no more than a convenient means for the coroplast to enable the vehicle to roll on wheels. In reality, the axles ran under the floor and may or may not have revolved. Both types of evidence come from the Caucasus, where the possibly covered wagon found in kurgan 5 at Trialeti had revolving axles (Piggott 1968, fig. 11) and the definitely covered ones found at Lchashen had fixed axles (Mnatsakanian 1960, 142). Woolley (1934, 64) suggested that the axles may have been fixed on the two open wagons found in PG 789 as well as that from PG 1232 at Ur. On the other hand, Childe (1957, 182) cites Miss Seton Williams as having seen in Turkey, as late as 1951, a solid-wheeled wagon with revolving axles. Once fixed axles had been invented, their presence or absence undoubtedly depended on the refinement of the primitiveness of the vehicle in question and the use to which it was destined. It is unlikely that the front axle could swivel. Although this ability has been claimed by the excavator for the wagon from Lolinsky kurgan 4, grave 7, on the Russian Kalmyk steppe (Piggott 1968, 297), this may be questioned (Littauer and Crouwel 1973b, 112, n. 30), and our first definite evidence of such an axle is only from the Iron Age. Considering the period of manufacture, the wheels would almost certainly have been of disc type. They may have been composite, like the originals from Kiš, Ur, Susa and the Caucasus (Watelin 1934; Woolley 1934, 64, 108; de Mequenem 1943, 122 p. with fig. 89, 1–2 and pl. x, lower; Piggott 1968, 278, 289 with fig. 7), and those on various representations from the Near East (cf. a.o. Salonen 1951, pls. xii, xiv, xviii, 1, xxi; Yadin 1963, 130, 132–133, 139).

The models themselves provide little information about the superstructure. We may, however, presume that there was a tilt composed of straw or reed matting or wickerwork or fabric on rigid hoops, strengthened sometimes by horizontals. The ends of the hoops must have been seated in the floor or attached to the side screens of the wagons (a float would hardly be furnished with a tilt). The models themselves offer no conclusive evidence as to whether the actual wagons were permanently equipped with tilts or might be covered only as the need arose. If the tilts of the wagons were of lattice or wickerwork, they are less likely to have been convertible than if the tilt were of matting or canvas. Wickerwork is what the excavator states was used on the wagon from kurgan 9 at Lchashen in Armenia and, since slots were cut in the numerous hoops themselves for passing the horizontals of the wickerwork, it would not seem to have been easily dismantled (Piggott 1968, 289).

To return to our models, the breastwork on A1 at the front and on A2 at both front and rear probably stands for the low screens of the original vehicles. Similarly, the narrow band of incision on the sides and rear of A1 undoubtedly represents such screens, the cross hatching perhaps denoting lattice or a heavier wickerwork than on the tilt. The vertical incisions at the front of that model may be skeumorphic too and indicate supports. For the incisions on the front screen of A2 no such explanation seems possible.

The models A1 and A2 could be pulled by strings tied to their lugs, as we have seen above. It was also pointed out there that all other baked clay models from this area, with the exception of B3 and the two ist-millennium Caucasian ones, whether of open wagons or of open or covered two-wheelers, have a single hole for a central draught pole. Such a pole, combined with a yoke, was an essential feature of all ancient traction everywhere. Therefore the single lug of A1 is already ruled out as reflecting the actual means of traction. As to the pair of lugs of A2 – Piggott has tentatively suggested a relationship with the triangular draught poles used on the Caucasian wagons (Piggott 1968, 295). The two legs of these triangles are attached at their bases to the front of the wagon bed in a manner permitting them to articulate vertically; as they run forward, they draw together, and the yoke lies across the apex of the triangle thus formed (Piggott 1968, fig. 12).

What is perhaps a modification of this arrangement is documented in the Near East on some metal wagon models from Syria and Anatolia dating presumably to the later 3rd millennium B.C. (Littauer and Crouwel 1973b). On these models the pole forks only as it approaches the vehicle, its arms being attached in such a way to a cross-wise element of the wagon bed as to make vertical articulation possible. It is just conceivable that the Gawra lugs were inspired by such actual practices. The position of the lugs, however, and the parallelism with A1 (and with zoomorphic wheeled vessels) strongly suggests that the lugs are an invention of the coroplast.

What kind of animals, and how many, were yoked to such tilt wagons? Both bovids and equids were in use at least from Early Dynastic II. That four-wheelers were drawn by teams of four equids in warfare in Sumerian times we know from such figured representations as the 'Standard' of Ur. These experiments, however, do not seem to have been very satisfactory: at least there is no evidence of them after Early Dynastic III. The pole-and-yoke hitch, well adapted to the conformation of bovids, was less suitable for that of equids, the throat strap tending to rise too high and press on the windpipe. Under these conditions, the wagon – particularly with the four disc wheels of the time – evidently proved too heavy in the long run for practical equid draught. Yet bovid draught would have been too slow for military purposes. Moreover, these four-wheelers, lacking a swivelling front axle, would have been difficult to manoeuvre at speed. Hence, towards the later 3rd millennium B.C. we find equid-drawn wagons only in cult, and perhaps parade, use. Such types of vehicles as ours, which are clearly utilitarian, would probably have always been pulled by pairs of bovids. Indeed the Caucasian wagons, both open and closed, were drawn by bovids (Mnatsakanian 1960, 142), and there is evidence for the same animals hitched to open wagons in Anatolia in the late 3rd or early 2nd millennium B.C. (Littauer and Crouwel 1973b).

The arched tilt must have been designed to give shelter against the weather: sun, wind, rain, and some cold. This type of hood sheds rain as a flat-roofed one would not, offers less wind resistance than would a flat-topped tilt with rectangular, curtained sides, and is in general easier to make weather-tight than the latter design. It is in wagons with this arched sort of covering that people have been known to live in historical times: the Scyths of the Pontic steppe, the American settlers who crossed the plains in 'Conestoga' wagons and, into recent days, the gypsies of the British Isles. This does not necessarily mean that our models represent permanent dwellings, but that they could have served as temporary ones during periods of transhumance. Ox-drawn, they would move at the same pace as the flocks and herds, and could carry women and small children, the elderly, the ailing, and even an animal too young to follow on foot. That they ever served able-bodied men for travelling distances seems doubtful; two-wheelers with equid draught, or the croup of an equid, would have been more suitable. For the transport of goods only they would have been slower and more costly than the ubiquitous pack animals.

The low breastworks at front, or front and rear, of the models would have helped to keep in goods or bedding on the originals and to tie the side screens together above the floor level.

Desire for protection from the elements when travelling was not something new even at the time of our models. We have already mentioned the pictographs from southern Mesopotamia of the late 4th millennium B.C. that were incised on clay or limestone tablets (ATU, nos. 743–746). These show wagons that still retain elements of the sledge. So much can be read in the simple profile views that combine what looks like a runner as base over two solid dots as wheels. The superstructure is shaped like a cabin – straight-sided, with pitched or rounded roof. Other pictograms show the same thing, but without the 'wheels' (Langdon 1924; ATU, nos. 741f.) (fig. 9). That these do not represent only portable shrines seems evidenced by a miniature stone plaque in the British Museum (no. 12885, formerly collection E. Herzfeld) of similar date, but unprovenanced (Amiet 1961, 92 with pl. 47: 662; Nagel 1964) (fig. 10). On this we see the wheelless sledge bovid-drawn, with a driver standing on the runner. The superstructure here has a rounded roof and, except for a single rail, is open at the sides, revealing a male figure seated within. There can be little doubt that this is a covered litter placed on runners. The legs are visible and what clearly seems to be a carrying pole extends beyond the lower part at front and rear. These poles, the passenger, and the litter bearers are plainly in evidence on a roughly contemporary sealing from Susa (Amiet 1961, pl. 17: 282). The same interpretation may be tentatively advanced for the crudely indicated superstructures of the sledges and sledge-type wagons of the tablets. The principle of the covered conveyance is attested for this period in Egypt also by the covered litter on the mace head of King Narmer (Moorey 1970). And at a later date we find a model of a covered litter with an arched roof in Mycenaean Greece (Cook 1955; French 1971).

While the tilt wagons we have been discussing can hardly be equated with the early mobile constructions of the tablets, which were used for conveying single, presumably important, persons (or figures of deities?), the principle of the tilt may well descend from the latter. It may also be suggested that such arched structures as the reed *mudhifs* of ancient and modern Iraq (Maxwell 1957; Delougaz 1968; Crawford 1972) might have inspired such coverings, which may even have been of similar materials. The Mesopotamian climate is one that requires as much protection from the sun as from the rains of the wet season, and there is no reason why the tilt should not have originated here as much as further north, as Speiser and Piggott have suggested (Speiser 1934; Piggott 1968, 273) – if it had to originate in only one place, which seems doubtful.

B. *Two-wheelers*

Since the three models B1, B2 and B3, although they are all from Syria, fall into two groups, the types will be considered separately.

It is impossible to tell whether the original of B1 had a fixed or a revolving axle. It seems more likely that it had the latter, as had the late 2nd-millennium carts at Lchashen (Piggott 1968, fig. 8), as had Greek country carts (Lorimer 1903, 134f.), as well as a cart found in Tomb 2 at Salamis in Cyprus (Karageorghis 1967a, 119 with pl. cxv), and as have carts in Anatolia today (Koşay 1951). The exact construction of the superstructure cannot be determined, but it, like the wagons, clearly had an arched tilt. The latter is marked by no incision. The actual cart may have been smaller than the wagons, but not necessarily. Indeed one of the 10th–9th-century B.C. clay models of tilt carts mentioned above as found on the right bank of the Kura river in Transcaucasia shows a vehicle very deep from front to rear. B1, as B2, as the model from Tri Brata on the Kalmyk steppe, and as the later models from Cyprus and the Pontic region, has a hole for a central draught pole. It was the pole also that, whether straight or curved, kept the real vehicle in balance when the pole's further end was held up by the yoke of the team or was supported by a stationary prop.

There can be no absolute certainty about the kind of wheels or the animals associated with the original cart, although, on balance, disk wheels and bovid traction seem to be the most likely by comparison with the wagon models. Internal evidence for wheels and animals is also lacking for the Kalmyk steppe model, but discs may probably be assumed there on the basis of the actual wheels found in the same grave (Piggott 1968, 297). If the wheels on the models from the Kura river are original, they would indicate discs too.

More can be said about B2, the original of which would seem to have been closely related to a frequently represented type of early tiltless two-wheeler. This we shall call a 'platform car' to distinguish it from the 'straddle car', another type of single-occupant two-wheeler in use also in Early Dynastic times (Littauer and Crouwel 1973a). In the latter, the driver might sit or stand astride the pole casing with his feet on two treads just in front of the axle (cf. a.o. Salonen 1951, pls. xi, xii, xiv). The former seems to have had a floor with a bench across the rear of it. This type appears in terracottas (cf. a.o. Salonen 1951, pls. x, xv, xvii–xix) from different parts of the Near East. While the possible prototypes go back to Early Dynastic II (Littauer and Crouwel 1973a, 326f.), the majority range from Ur III to the Old Babylonian period (Salonen as above; Barrelet 1968, figs. 304–314). Apart from terracottas, the type is also illustrated by two metal models, both presumably from Iran (of which one also belongs to the Ur III period or to no later than the Old Babylonian one) (Calmeyer 1964; Schlossmann 1968) and by a Syrian cylinder-seal impression on a tablet dated to the 14th year of Hammurabi (i.e. 1779 B.C. on the Middle Chronology) (Figulla 1967; Buchanan 1971), and at least one cylinder seal, also Syrian (Porada 1948).

Characteristic not only of the platform car, but of many straddle cars and of wagons, is the high, lectern-shaped breastwork at the front, which may have acted as a protection, not against the enemy, but against flying stones or gravel kicked up by the team's heels. From examples where this breastwork is more carefully rendered, one can see that this was made partly of bent wood and wicker-work (Buchanan 1962; Barrelet 1968, 46 with fig. 16). What the careless coroplast has often shown as mere holes at the top are the spaces, straight below and semi-arched above, between the upper rails and the beginning of the actual breastwork. The important thing here is the *railing*, not the *holes*. It must be stressed that to pass the lines of early equid nose rings or the reins of early cavessons or bits *through* these apertures would only have interfered with control, while the little valley in the middle of this top railing might have formed a convenient place to lay them at times. What this railing did pro-vide was a handgrip for a standing occupant, essential when the team suddenly swerved or plunged forward or when the going was rough.

Often there is what appears to be a step at the rear. If we are to judge by one of the metal models that is more carefully fashioned than many of the clay ones, the 'step' either represents the draught pole protruding at the rear or a covering for it (Schlossmann 1968). Some models have a high back support instead of a seat (du Buisson 1930, 145f. with fig. 3; de Borghegyi 1970). But these backs are peculiarly shaped, with 'wings' on either side at the top, and to fit a tilt over them would be difficult. We may assume that our B2 is the more common kind of platform car, with a standing driver.

The pellets on the front of B2 and the single one on B3, which reappear on the Mourek vehicle, cannot be very well explained except as decoration. The vertical clay strip that depresses the top railing in the centre was probably a convenience to the coroplast in pro-ducing this valley.

As on B1, the hole in the lower breastwork of B2 was for the draught pole. Whether this rose obliquely all the way or arched, we do not know. It is impossible to judge the exact profile of the original metal or wooden poles on clay models by the angles of the holes (which vary greatly) because the poles themselves may have been variously bent.

B2 and perhaps B3 seem to be our unique examples of platform cars fitted with tilts, and we do not know whether these tilts are supposed to rise from low side screens or from the floor. The holes framing the front edge of the tilt perhaps indicate the manner by which matting or fabric was lashed to the front arch.

If these were essentially platform cars, then they carried only single occupants. There seems to be no good reason to suggest that such a driver possessed special, even divine, status. The only possibly distinctive element, the 'necklace', returns on figurines of naked females and as a kind of breast strap on model animals, all categories being at home in Syria. On the animals this may have been a kind of charm, like the blue 'donkey beads' still seen in the Near East today (Wulff, Wulff and Koch 1968). The drivers preserved with a few of the other Syrian terracotta models, like the Mourek one, are similar to ours (Fugmann 1958; de Borghegyi 1970).

What kind of wheels was B2 supposed to have? The wheels presently associated with the model would, by the proportions of their naves, indicate disc wheels. But the wheels are so disproportionately large that they probably cannot be read seriously. Original model wheels, usually found separate from models themselves, are mostly plain with raised hubs, and seldom indicate spokes by either paint or incision. The probably original wheels on the two metal models are also plain discs (Calmeyer 1964; Schlossmann 1968). If the real wheels they represent had been spoked, it would not be difficult to cast them in metal. On the other hand, the Syrian seal impression (Figulla 1967; Buchanan 1971) and the cylinder mentioned above (Porada 1948) display an open version of the type of car we believe B2 to be, with four-spoked wheels. These representations seem to show vehicles that are transitional between the old, single-occupant, platform car, with seat, solid wheels and hemione (the more usual 'onager' is correctly applicable only to the Iranian subspecies) or mule draught, and the new *chariot*. This was horse-drawn, spoked-wheeled, and seatless, with low breastwork at front and sides and room for two to stand abreast. Whether B2 was entirely traditional, with disc wheels, or transitional, with spoked wheels, we cannot tell.

A similar question may be asked about the draught animals. Were they horses already, or were they other equids still? It is impossible to say. No terracotta models are definitely associated with any model animals, therefore no light is thrown on the subject by them. They were more likely to have been equids than bovids, considering the type of vehicle.

Some illumination may be cast on this problem by a passage in the famous text of Idrimi, king of Alalakh in Syria, inscribed on the statue of that king, who seems to have lived in the later 16th century B.C. (Drower 1970). In a recent translation by Oppenheim we read (11. 13ff.): "(So) I took with me my horse, my chariot, and my groom, went away and crossed over the desert country and even entered into the region of the Sutian warriors. I stayed with them (once) overnight in my . . . chariot, but the next day I moved on and went to the land of Canaan" (Oppenheim in Pritchard 1969; cf. also the original translation by Smith 1949). The 'horse' may have been for riding, although there is little evidence for important people riding horseback at this time, and what riders we do see are perched far back on a horse, in the position they would assume on a hemione, donkey, or mule, which would be unsatisfactory for long on horseback (Moorey 1970). More probably, the 'horse' stands for a team, in which case we may assume that the vehicle was light and for fast travelling, hence most likely spoke-wheeled, although the Sumerogram ^{GIŠ}GIGIR used twice above denotes only a two-wheeled vehicle without indicating the type of wheels. It was probably something with a larger floor space than our B2 seems to have had. The second time the vehicle is mentioned, it is modified by an adjective of irregular form and spelling, which Oppenheim did not feel sure enough to translate (*CAD* 1963 s.v. *salīlu* B). A *hapax*, it has, however, been connected with a word for shadow that, among its other meanings, includes those of awning or covering (*CAD* 1962 s.v. *sillu*). As such, it occurs in Old Babylonian texts, although not in connection with vehicles. If we may, in our text, translate this passage as 'covered chariot', we may suppose that Idrimi spent the night in his fast, horse-drawn two-wheeler after travelling during the day.

While the type of vehicle that we believe is represented by B2 and B3 would afford no place for lying down and sleeping, daytime travellers in these latitudes, at certain times of year, and particularly over stretches of shelterless country, might find some shade very welcome. It does not seem to us that such vehicles can have been tilted for more than this.

We have attempted to assemble documentation for vehicles with tilts in the ancient Near East. Unambiguous evidence has appeared to be forthcoming only in the form of a few terracotta models. Of these, three are wagons that, despite their wide distribution – Syria, northern Iraq, Elam – closely resemble each other. In dating too they appear to be contemporary, since at least two of them can be attributed to the later 3rd millennium B.C. Three other models, all from Syria, represent two-wheelers. B2 and perhaps B3 date to the earlier 2nd millennium B.C.; B1 may be contemporary with these, or somewhat earlier, like the wagon models.

All vehicles are covered according to the same principle, which has been a constant one throughout the ages and, it may be added, the most general: the arched tilt.

Origins

What now can be said of the origins of the combination of vehicle and tilt, its documentation being so limited yet so widespread geographically? Are these sources to be sought in the Near East itself, or do we have to look elsewhere, as some scholars have done? Indeed, Speiser, when publishing the Gawra model wagon (A2), considered it a stranger amidst the well-documented open wagons and carts of the Near East (Speiser 1935). He proposed northern influence, and linked it with a terracotta model from a tomb at U1 in the Maikop region of the Kuban (Tallgren 1929). This particular piece of comparative evidence may, however, be eliminated, as the model has been discarded, for instance, by Piggott, as not representing a covered vehicle, but a house or yurt (Piggott 1968, 301). But a northern origin has been proposed again by Piggott himself – this time on better evidence. As already mentioned at the beginning of this paper, he did so only for the wagons illustrated by the Ashmolean and Gawra models, and did not concern himself with two-wheelers except for the model from Tri Brata on the Kalmyk steppe (Piggott 1968, 297). Piggott presented evidence of actual covered wagons from both Ciscaucasia (the Kalmyk steppe) and Transcaucasia (Trialeti and Lchashen). The Ciscaucasian covered wagons were placed in graves dated by Piggott to the later 3rd millennium B.C., and the badly preserved but probably covered wagon from kurgan 5 at Trialeti was given a similar dating. It should be noted that these dates are based on a complete reappraisal of the evidence and are considerably higher than some of those previously given for this material. The other burials of wagons with tilts from Lchashen on Lake Sevan in Armenia seem to be almost 1000 years later.

Piggott suggests that the use of a tilt spread from Cis to Trans-caucasia, and thence to the Near East, where we have seen that the earliest models date again roughly to the later 3rd millennium B.C. In the Caucasus region, however, evidence of wheeled vehi-cles antedating those with tilts is ambiguous at present, since it con-sists only of terracotta wheels. On the other hand, we have already cited evidence not only of wheeled vehicles in Mesopotamia as early as the late 4th millennium B.C., but of covered ones (ATU). It is true that the roofs are of varying shapes and that the rounded ones happen to be illustrated on sledges rather than on wheeled vehicles, but the main point is that they existed. In fact, the idea of an arched tilt covered with matting would come very easily to people who were used to building *mudhifs*. And one needs protection from a powerful sun as well as from wind and rain. Thus we see that the initial impetus could have come from the south.

Speiser's argument, based on the rarity of the tilt vehicle among the many models of open ones in the Near East, may be answered by the observation that most tilt vehicles were utilitarian, and that the military, cult, parade, or hunting vehicle was always much more apt to be represented than the workaday one. This applies to all media. In Iron-Age Cyprus, for instance, where we find quite a few models of open and covered carts, these are still far outnumbered by the models of chariots (Young and Young 1955; Karageorghis 1962b; Gjerstad 1963). And although there were undoubtedly many more carts (of one kind or another) than chariots in the 6th-century B.C. Greece, one would hardly think so from the vases, as a glance at any survey of these will reveal (for specific studies see Lorimer 1903, and Moore 1971).

From grave gifts associated with vehicle burials in the Caucasus area, we know that some connections with the Near East existed at the time the covered wagons were built, and the idea of the tilt could have come north in the course of such contacts. In principle, how-ever, the tilt could have been developed in any place where people using vehicles needed protection from the weather, and where there was material suitable for a tilt. Both the Near East and the Caucasus region would have provided such conditions in different ways. It is also possible that the influence of the tilt is more apparent than real, since it may be argued that something as obvious could have developed independently in each area. We may stress that there is no evidence for a coinciding introduction of a *basically new* type of vehicle. On the contrary, the superstructure appears to have been adapted to the vehicles already existing in each area.

Note. Piggott, in passing, refers to Greek Attic Geometric vase representations of the 8th century B.C. (Piggott 1968, 295) and asks himself whether the vehicles shown there (Lorimer 1950) could not be tilt wagons and carts on which the material had been removed from the hoops. This is surely mistaken. Apart from the question of whether four-wheelers are shown on these vases, the superstructures are really those of open vehicles. The hoops seen at the front and often at the rear have nothing to do with a tilt framework, but belong to the front and side breastworks, as von Mercklin (1909, 1916) established. The side breastwork was apparently shown at the back by the artists so as not to cross the body of the rider. This convention is sometimes abandoned in later Geometric art, where the railing *does* cross the body (cf. a.o. Arias and Hirmer 1962; Snodgrass 1971; Ahlberg 1971a). Moreover, even where the hoops are shown at front and rear, in the majority of cases the rear hoop differs from the front one not only in being of smaller size but in being placed at an inclination, whereas the front one is vertical – conditions that would not exist were these the hoops of a tilt. The 'wickerwork' sides of the examples mentioned by Piggott (one of which does, misleadingly, have equal and vertical hoops front and rear) are not the sides, but represent the crisscross thong floor of the chariot, as Miss Richter has pointed out for the palls and bed frame on *prothesis* scenes on the same vases (Richter 1965). It may be added that representations in the round from the same period, in the form of bronze and terracotta model chariots (von Mercklin 1916; Sarian 1969) confirm the above interpretation.

Addendum. Since writing the above two new models of early vehicles have been called to our attention.

The first is a model of a wagon offered for sale 2nd March 1973 by Charles Ede Ltd. of Brooke Street, London (pl. II). It is of cream-coloured clay, and the only dimension given is 0.146 m., which may be either the length or the maximum height. Since, according to the photograph, there is no great difference between the two, this gives at least a rough idea of the size of the piece. In the catalogue the provenance is given as 'Syria', and the date as '2000–1900 B.C.'

It is stated that 'one pair of wheels and the axles are supplied in facsimile'. At the front are three horizontally pierced lugs. There is a small window 'at the back, under the roof'. The fabric of the tilt is indicated by repeated herring-bone pattern incisions running horizontally from front to rear and by a vertical herring-bone pattern on the lower part of the sides, beginning just a little below the top rims of the wheels. This model differs from A1 and A2 in the following respects: (1) the tilt seems to drop slightly towards the rear. This is probably due to carelessness on the part of the coroplast rather than to a faithful copying of a real condition, as such a form would be quite unusual for anything except the collapsible hoods of some relatively recent vehicles. (2) The herring-bone design on the tilt itself is more sophisticated than the rather simple cross-hatchings on A1 and A2 and the vestiges of such on A3. Although too large in scale, this actually crudely resembles a type of reed-matting pattern found in Iraq today (Maxwell 1957). (3) If one of the pairs of wheels is original, there seems to have been little effort made by the coroplast to indicate the thickening at the centre that is so characteristic of this type of solid wheel, and which the modellers often do try to show, no matter how summarily. (4) From what can be seen in the photograph, there would appear to be not even a low front screen. (5) The most interesting anomaly here, however, is the three lugs. These may be interpreted in one of two ways, and the authors are divided on this point. One explanation would be that these bear no relation to reality and that the coroplast has simply provided a number of lugs quite superfluous for pulling such a small object. The other explanation would be that, because coroplasts seldom seem to give themselves unnecessary work, the three lugs must have in some way corresponded to features of actual wagons. Since there appears to be evidence for such features from approximately the time and area to which this vehicle is ascribed, it is possible that the same thing is represented here. The three lugs would be the ends of the two side and one centre lengthwise beams of the floor, which are shown on some metal models as projecting out in front of the floor (Littauer and Crouwel 1973b, 110).

The second example is a two-wheeler. This was offered for sale at auction on 29th August 1961 by *Ars Antiqua*, Lucerne, Switzerland (lot 35). H: 0.115 m.; diam. wheels: 0.006 m. It is of light yellow clay. The suggested provenance is 'North Syrian' or 'Hurrian' and it is attributed to the end of the 2nd millennium B.C. The tilt and the figure seated within are remarkably similar to the same features on our B2. The tilt has similar holes on its front face, but its walls are described as covered with incisions, rather than plain, as those of B2. The face of the figure, called a 'woman', is extremely close in type and technique to that of B2, and it wears a similar, incised, triple, plastic necklace. Where the vehicle differs from B2 and the related open two-wheeler from Mourek (Ingholt 1940; Bossert 1951) is in having no comparable front breastwork – in fact it has no front breastwork at all. Instead, it is suggested that the figure holds in front of itself with both hands a 'vessel'. Such a pose in a vehicle is, to our knowledge, unparalleled, and it would be a peculiar thing for a driver to be doing. All things considered, we are not convinced that this is an original work.

Finally, excavations at Selenkahiyeh in Syria have produced evidence for terracotta tilt wagon models dating to the end of the 3rd millennium B.C. We owe this welcome information to the excavator, Prof. M. N. van Loon.

Acknowledgements

We are most grateful to Professor Stuart Piggott for calling our attention to the wagon model discussed in the *Addendum* and for providing us with a photograph. Our thanks are also due to Dr P. R. S. Moorey, who has not only drawn our attention to the same object, but who has given us help and information concerning the Ashmolean wagon model. We are indebted to Professor P. Houwink ten Cate for discussing the Idrimi text with us. The photographs in pl. I appear by courtesy of the Ashmolean Museum, Oxford, that on pl. II by permission of Mr C. Ede, London. The line drawings were prepared by Mrs J. Croxall (the Ashmolean Museum), Miss P. Cullen, and Mr G. Strietmann.

27. A TERRACOTTA WAGON MODEL
FROM SYRIA IN OXFORD*

M. A. LITTAUER AND J. H. CROUWEL

In a recent paper, Dr E. Özgen published a group of three terracotta models of four-wheeled wagons, said to come from the Şanhurfa
district in southeastern Anatolia.[1] The present note concerns a related
model, reportedly from Syria, but without further details of source
(pl. 173).[2] The model, in the Ashmolean Museum, Oxford (acc. no.
1975.326), was acquired on the London art market in 1975.[3] Its
authenticity has been confirmed by thermoluminescence testing in
the Research Laboratory for Archaeology and the History of Art at
Oxford.

Description

Hand-modelled. Rather coarse, gritty, greenish clay, fired dark in
several places. Surfaces and edges smoothed – probably with a knife –
before firing. Condition good, except for incrustations (limestone
pebbles) on front breastwork, on one horn-like projection at rear
and on wheels; one wheel hub chipped; rear half of body mended.
L. (total) 0.142 m.; Ht. (with wheels) 0.196 m.; W. (over axle tubes
only) c. 0.075 m.; Diam. wheels 0.082 m.

Body: Narrow, rectangular floor, with tubular sheaths beneath front
and rear to accommodate wooden axles (now restored, and with
modern wire linch pins); axle tubes project somewhat beyond floor

---

* *Levant* 22, 1990, 160–162.
[1] Özgen 1986.
[2] We are most grateful to Dr P. R. S. Moorey, Keeper of the Department of
Antiquities of the Ashmolean Museum, for permission to publish this object
and for providing the photographs and information on the thermoluminescence
analysis.
[3] See Sotheby's Auction Sale July 14th, 1975, lot 53 with ill. (line drawing by
Mr G. Strietman, our fig. 4a); Ashmolean Museum. Report of the Visitors for
1974–75, 14 with pl. III.

at either side. Box-like superstructure, with high, vertical front breast-work and lower side and rear screens; rear half covered over; small platform projects behind. Breastwork widens slightly towards double-arched top, with two obliquely placed oval apertures; two horizon-tally pierced lugs project at either side of lower breastwork. Upper edges of side screens curved; a horn-like projection at each upper rear corner; a small, seat-like projection rises above covered part of box.

Wheels: Centrally perforated discs, with projecting hubs; two of these, in view of their identical fabric and decoration, belong to the vehicle; other wheels probably not original.

Decoration (incised): Outer face of high front screen or breastwork has rows of oblique dashes in chevron pattern; dashes at edges; inner face shows two diagonally crossed lines; randomly distributed dots near and around the area of the arches. Side screens carry a hori-zontal herring-bone design. Two wheels show four herring-bone designs radiating from the hubs on both outer and inner faces.

Discussion

This terracotta belongs in a category of model wagon widely dis-tributed in time and space: examples are known from southeastern Anatolia, Syria, Mesopotamia and southwestern Iran, ranging in date from the early 3rd to the earlier 2nd millennium B.C. – from Early Dynastic II to Old Babylonian, in terms of Mesopotamian chronology.[4]

Along with bronze models and two-dimensional representations, the terracottas portray actual four-wheeled vehicles of a type some-times called a "battle car". The term derives from their depiction in explicitly military contexts – particularly on the "Standard of Ur". There we see four-wheeled vehicles, drawn by teams of four equids abreast, on a field of battle.[5] Apart from the driver behind the high front breastwork with its two handholds at the top, a warrior is

---

[4] For the "battle car" and its illustrations, including terracotta models, see Littauer and Crouwel 1979, 15–20. 32ff. 37ff. 44. 48ff. 61ff. For an interesting recent find, see Finkbeiner 1983, 29 with pl. 1 = Boehmer 1985, 104 no. 85 (vase fragment with seal impression of wagon scene from Uruk-Warka).

[5] Strommenger and Hirmer 1964, pls. 72 and XI. For a recent discussion of the identification of draught equids in Sumer, see Postgate 1986.

shown standing on the floor that projects at the rear, behind the side screening. At first represented mainly in warfare, this type of wagon appears after ED III only in cult or mythological scenes, where its draught team may consist of bovids or fabulous creatures as well as of equids. The relatively large and well-preserved Oxford model is noteworthy on several counts.

1. A striking anomaly is the incised wheel decoration. Wheels of terracotta models usually consist of plain, solid discs. From more detailed depictions, however, such as those on the "Standard of Ur" or on reliefs from Ur and Khafaje and from remains of actual wheels, we know that the disc wheels of the ancient Near East were usually of tripartite construction.[6] The four herring-bone motifs radiating from the naves of this model's wheels bear no relationship to such a technique. What they suggest far more is a playful rendering of four spokes. This is a possibility that should, we think, be considered. It would be consistent with a date in the early 2nd millennium B.C., at which time we find four-spoked wheels on an Anatolian cylinder seal that shows a similar type of four-wheeler, and on some representations of two-wheeled vehicles.[7]

2. Although the patterned incisions on the outer faces of the front and side screens are not unique,[8] they are not common. They tend to support the likelihood that wickerwork was often used for screens. Nor do the diagonal incisions crossing each other on the inner face of the front breastwork tell us anything new; they certainly represent the actual diagonal struts that were usually employed to brace this part.[9] They are, however, unusual in a terracotta model.

3. The small, raised seat, presumably intended as separate, is another unique feature in a terracotta model. The crosspiece or thwart that joins the sides of the vehicle and on which the seat is set, is found on some other four-wheeled models where it may have served both as a covering for objects stowed beneath it and also as

[6] See Littauer and Crouwel 1979, 18ff. 38 with figs. 5. 7. 8.
[7] See Porada 1948, 893 E in pl. CXXXIV; Littauer and Crouwel 1979, 48ff., 54ff. with figs. 25, 28–30; Littauer and Crouwel 1986.
[8] For patterned incisions, see the Şanhurfa vehicles (*supra* n. 1); Littauer and Crouwel 1979, fig. 16; Mesnil du Buisson 1947, 26 with fig. 15 and pls. XIIf. (Asharah). Cf. also Andrae 1905, fig. 1, no. 315 (model of two-wheeled "platform car" from Ashur).
[9] For other representations, in false perspective, of these struts, see Strommenger and Hirmer 1964, pls. 72 and XI ("Standard of Ur"), 66 and 68 ("Vulture stela"); Buchanan 1966, no. 255 (Ki,); Littauer and Crouwel 1979, figs. 24f.

a seat.[10] The high seat on the Ashmolean model, with its depressed center and slightly raised corners, suggests a stool with a hide or leather seat. Such an extra seat – if in a rather different form – appears to have been added at the rear of the four-wheeled vehicle on the Anatolian cylinder seal mentioned above.[11] A seat rises directly from the floor of numerous terracotta models of two-wheelers of "platform car" type.[12] On these, however, the lack of the side screens (necessary to steady and brace the front breastwork and the seat) should be attributed rather to their summary execution than to a faithful rendering of the construction.[13] The addition of an unusual, high seat on the more detailed and carefully made Ashmolean model suggests, on the other hand, an actual feature. Such an elevated position would indicate a desire to display the sitter prominently, and its precariousness would demand a slow-moving vehicle. These considerations, as well as the absence of a sheath for javelins at a corner of the front breastwork, would imply a civil or cult (i.e. processional) use rather than a military one for the original of this model.

4. The horn-like projections at the upper rear corners of the vehicle are unknown on other four-wheeled terracotta models, but some Anatolian bronze wagon models of the later third millennium B.C. may suggest their origin. On these vehicles, which have no seats or thwarts, the upper railings of the side screens often project beyond the rear screens; they would furnish convenient handholds for anyone standing on the rear platform of the vehicle the model represents – or even in reaching the seat.[14]

The two lugs at the front, although unique for a model in this category, cannot be considered as significant anomalies, since they do not represent features of an actual vehicle. They were for con-

---

[10] See Littauer and Crouwel 1973a, 108ff. with pls. XLIV: B, C (Tell Chuēra), D (Ki,).

[11] See *supra* n. 7.

[12] See Littauer and Crouwel 1979, 40. 49ff., Salonen 1951, pls. XV, XVII–XIX.

[13] Note that seal engravings may also show four-wheelers with an unsupported seat rising at the rear; in these the suppression of side screens may be attributed to the desire to show the complete figure of the sitter. See Littauer and Crouwel 1979, figs. 24, 25; also Buchanan 1966, no. 255. For a wagon model with such a seat, see Klengel-Brandt 1978, no. 761.

[14] Littauer and Crouwel 1973a, pls. XXXVII: A, XXXIX: B, XLI: A. Note that a seal impression from Sippar (Littauer and Crouwel 1979, 51ff. with fig. 31), dated to the 14th year of Hammurabi of Babylon, appears to show a modified "platform car" with projections at the top of its seat, which rises above low side screens.

venience in pulling the model along – either as a toy or, more probably, for use in cult.[15]

The possibility of spoked wheels, the elevated seat, the horn-like
projections at the rear are all features that would point to a later
third millennium or, perhaps rather, early second millennium B.C.
date for this important addition to the corpus of Near Eastern terracotta vehicle models.

---

[15] For such lugs – single or in pairs – on terracotta models of covered vehicles,
see Littauer and Crouwel 1974, 20ff. no. 2 with fig. 2 (Tepe Gawra), cf. 20 no. 1
with pl. 1 above and fig. 1 (probably from Hammam), also 25 (discussion). The
majority of Near Eastern models – whether two-wheelers or four-wheelers – have
a single hole centered near the bottom of the front breastwork to take the wooden
rod that represented the draught pole of the actual vehicle. Since all draught was
by paired animals under a yoke, the single pole was standard.

III. RIDING

28. RIDDEN HORSES IN IRON AGE CYPRUS*

J. H. CROUWEL AND VERONICA TATTON-BROWN

This paper is dedicated to Dr Vassos Karageorghis whose excavations of horse and vehicle burials at Salamis are among the
more significant of his many invaluable contributions to Cypriot
archaeology.**

In recent issues of *RDAC* one of us discussed evidence for the use
of different types of wheeled vehicles – the cart and the chariot –
in Cyprus during the Iron Age (Crouwel 1985; 1987). The present paper is concerned with another means of land transport – on
horseback.

What we know of ridden horses derives only from representations,
there being no other sources such as burials of horses identifiable
as mounts, or texts. The figured documents are mainly terracotta
models in the round, dating from the 11th/10th but mostly from
the 7th century B.C. onwards.[1] There are also several models made
of stone, dating to the later 6th and 5th century B.C.,[2] and two-

---

* *Report of the Department of Antiquities Cyprus* 1988, 77–87.

** We are most grateful to Dr A. Caubet, Dr E. Goring, Dr V. Karageorghis,
Mrs S. Lubsen-Admiraal and Dr J. R. Mertens for information and assistance
of various kinds. We are also much indebted to Mrs M. A. Littauer for comments upon most of a draft text, to Mr J. Morel for most of the drawings and Mr
M. Bootsman for assistance with the illustrations. The photographs appear by
courtesy of the British Museum (London), the Department of Antiquities (Cyprus),
the Musée du Louvre (Paris), the Metropolitan Museum of Art (New York), the
Royal Scottish Museum (Edinburgh) and the Allard Pierson Museum (Amsterdam).

[1] No list is attempted here but individual examples are mentioned in the text
when relevant. The largest collections from controlled excavations are from Kourion
(mainly the Apollo Hylates sanctuary; see Young and Young 1955, esp. 191–233;
Buitron 1983, 230f. Karageorghis 1983b, 933 with fig. 54) and Salamis (the settlement and the Cellarka necropolis; see Monloup 1984, nos. 149–243; Karageorghis
1970, pls. XXVII: Q. 24. XLII: 79. XCII: 16 = B: 4, left. CIX, 4 = B: 4, right.
CXI: 8. 9. CXXIX: 17). For discussion of these and many other examples, see
Monloup 1984, 37–46.

[2] Cesnola 1894, pl. LXXX, no. 512 (= Myres 1914, no. 1014; from Golgoi; our
pl. 175), no. 518 (from Kourion), no. 519 (= Myres 1914, no. 1015; from Kythrea;
our pl. 176b) nos. 521–522 (from Kourion), cf. no. 511 (= Myres 1914, no. 1013;
saddle horse, from Tamassos; our pl. XXV: 5); Myres and Ohnefalsch-Richter 1899,

dimensional representations, including the well-known fifth century stone sarcophagus with relief sculpture from Amathus[3] and vase paintings of the 10th/9th to 7th centuries but primarily of the latter.[4] (The time span covered by this material is known in local terms as Cypro-Geometric I–III, Cypro-Archaic I–II, Cypro-Classical I–II and Hellenistic).[5]

Throughout the main text the form of riding considered is astride. In an Appendix riding with both legs on one side of the mount is discussed. (For definitions of technical terms, see the glossary in Littauer and Crouwel 1979, 3–7).

The Rider's Seat

The riders are always male. On most of the more careful representations they are seated comfortably just behind their mount's withers and with their legs hanging naturally (pls. 174, 175, 176b, 177). On some stone and terracotta models, however, the riders have a more cramped seat, with their knees sharply bent back (pls. 176a, 179, 180).[6]

Riding may be bareback, on a saddle cloth or, occasionally, on an animal skin or saddle. While most terracottas illustrate a bareback seat, the Amathus sarcophagus and most stone models show saddle cloths. On the sarcophagus the saddle cloth is secured by a

---

no. 6013 (from Tamassos); Pryce 1931, nos. C 81 (from Tamassos; our pl. XXIV) and C 82 (our pl. 174), cf. no. C 83 (said to be a ridden horse, but, in point of fact, harnessed, with traces of a yoke on its neck); Blinkenberg 1931, pl. 75, no. 1802 (from Lindos, Rhodes); Young and Young 1955, 174f., esp. nos. St 211, 210, 213 with pl. 70 from Kourion); Karageorghis 1976, no. 156 with cover ill. (from Ayios Therapon, Famagusta district); Buchholz 1978, 233 with fig. 63. a (from Tamassos); Hermary 1981, no. 41 (= Ohnefalsch-Richter 1893, pl. CLXXXVIII; from Amathus); Caubet n.d., fig. 95.

[3] See esp. Myres 1909–11, 1f.; Tatton-Brown (née Wilson) 1972 and 1981 (our pl. XXIV: 5).

[4] Karageorghis and des Gagniers 1974, no. I. 1 (White Painted II bowl from *Vathyrkakas*), nos. 2–6 (Bichrome IV vases), cf. also no. III. 4 (led horse on Bichrome IV vase); 1979, no. SI. 1 (= Karageorghis 1973b; White Painted III amphora from Khrysokhou; our fig. 2); Karageorghis 1980, 132–5 with pl. XIX (another White Painted III amphora from same site, probably by same painter).

[5] For chronology, see Karageorghis 1982b, 9f., table A. At Kourion terracotta models of ridden – and chariot – horses continued to be made into Roman times, see Young and Young 1955, 230. 232f.

[6] See also Perrot and Chipiez 1885, pl. II, right.

breaststrap (pl. 177); a girth or a crupper to help keep it in place is nowhere clearly in evidence.

On these stone documents the saddle cloths were originally painted with solid colours or in patterns, but few traces now remain. On two models a rear border, with a zigzag design, is marked by incision (pls. 174, 176b). The saddle cloths seen on the Amathus sarcophagus and some of the stone models have straight or curved edges (pl. 177). Other stone and terracotta models depict the lower edge as toothed (pls. 178, 181, 182).[7] This feature recalls the saddle cloths with stepped edges shown, sometimes in considerable detail, on various Achaemenid figure documents. They are also illustrated on what is often called Graeco-Persian art, as well as in East-Greek art of the later 6th/early 5th century B.C.[8] Their appearance here, as well as on the Cypriot stone models which are of roughly similar date, must be due to Achemenid influence.

The toothed or stepped edges of these saddle cloths suggest felt. This material, unlike woven fabric, needs no binding and is stiff enough to lend itself to cut-out decoration. Indeed, a felt saddle cloth with stepped edges was found in barrow 5 at Pazyryk in southern Siberia (5th–4th century B.C.), where a Persian pile carpet depicting riding horses wearing such stepped cloths was also discovered.[9]

A Cypriot terracotta model from Kourion shows a rider on a saddle (secured by a breast strap) that appears to resemble some Roman cavalry saddles of a type also illustrated in early Sasanian Iran (fig. 1: 1).[10] These saddles, instead of having an arch fully across the front, had two small, backward-sloping projections at either side, in positions to press against the rider's thighs and help secure him in

---

[7] Stone models: see also Young and Young 1955, nos. St 210. 211. 305. 272. 306. cf. 305 (from Kourion); Buchholz 1978, fig. 63: a (from Tamassos). Terracottas: see Cesnola 1894, pl. LXIX, no. 637 (= Myres 1914, no. 2086; from Kourion); Young and Young 1955, no. 1480 with pl. 25, no. 3057 + 3058 with pl. 54, no. 1145 with pl. 20 and no. 3025 with ill. p. 164 (from Kourion).

[8] See esp. Goldman 1984; cf. Kramer 1986 (similar saddle cloth still shown on bronze equestrian statue of Marcus Aurelius on the Capitol in Rome). For ills. on East Greek vases and (Clazomenian) sarcophagi (not mentioned by Goldman), see Anderson 1961, 79f. with pls. 25: d. 26: a; Cook 1981, 126.

[9] Goldman, 1984, 10f.; Rudenko 1970, pls. 160. 174f.; Littauer and Crouwel 1979, 156.

[10] Young and Young 1955, 55. 216 no. 1053 with pl. 58, cf. 139, 216 no. 2951 with pl. 48 (fragmentary terracotta; 'pommel' and 'cantle' reversed in restoration drawing, p. 139).

a stirrupless saddle.[11] Roman saddles might have two similar supports at the rear or they might sometimes have what appear to be
low arches there, which may be what we see on the Cypriot terracotta. The latter, from the sanctuary of Apollo Hylates, has no well-
dated find context and was tentatively attributed to the 5th or 4th
century B.C. However, the comparative material mentioned above
suggests a date no earlier than the Roman period, when the sanctuary was still in use. At present this terracotta furnishes the only
evidence for the use of proper riding saddles in ancient Cyprus.

Mounts

The horses represented by many of the terracotta models have a
stiff crest-like mane, often ending in a prominent arching forelock
(pls. 184–185, fig. 1: 4).[12] Apart from this convention, which was
retained by Cypriot coroplasts from the 11th/10th to the 7th/6th
century B.C., the figured documents show no differences between
ridden and harnessed horses.

Information on the size of the animals is provided by some of the
horse skeletons found with the remains of actual vehicles in 8th–7th
century tombs at Salamis. Their dimensions show a wide range, from
1.32 to 1.53 m. at the withers.[13]

Control

Ridden horses appear to be controlled in the same way as harnessed
animals – by bridles, each composed of a headstall, usually with a
bit, and reins. *Bits.* Explicit illustrations of bits are on the 5th century Amathus sarcophagus, where both ridden and chariot horses
are shown with curved cheekpieces fastened at three points to the
cheekstraps (pl. 177). Similarly shaped cheekpieces with triple cheek-

---

[11] This passage owes much to Mrs M. A. Littauer. For the Roman saddles, see
esp. Schleiermacher 1984, 27 with many illustrations; Groenman-van Waateringe
1967, 106–120 (actual remains). For the Sasanian saddles, see Ghirshman 1962,
pls. 163. 165f. 168. 171 (rock reliefs); Shepherd 1966, 209f. with figs. 6, 8 (silver
rhyton).
[12] See Monloup 1984, 38, 42 and s.v. no. 180; Tatton-Brown 1982a, 177–80.
[13] Ducos 1967; 1980, esp. table I.

strap attachments can be seen on some of the stone models (pls. 175, 176b, 178, 182). In one instance the junction of the cheekstraps is masked by a roundel, decorated with a panther head in relief (pl. xxiv: 1); it may be noted that the sculptor of this model confused the cheekstraps with the reins.

The other representations of ridden horses – terracotta models and vase paintings – are usually too summary to give details of the bits. Several terracottas simply illustrate cheekstraps, sometimes with clay pellets to mark the ends of the mouthpiece of the bit (pl. 187).[14] In one such case a curved cheekpiece is also indicated (pl. 183).

The narrow curved shape of the cheekpieces and the three-point attachment of the cheekstraps seen on the more explicit representations of ridden – and chariot – horses suggest bits of a single, well-known type, which is documented chiefly by actual finds associated with the buried vehicles at Salamis, some of them lying *in situ* on the harnessed animals.[15] Made of iron and less often of bronze, these bits have jointed mouthpieces that pass through holes, sometimes collared, in the centres of the cheekpieces and end in loops or rings to take reins or rein attachments. The cheekpieces are usually long and flat with roughly rectangular ends but are sometimes curved, as on the figured documents, and carry three loops or apertures for attachment to the headstall. This type of snaffle bit goes back to the Late Bronze Age in the eastern Mediterranean. In the first millennium B.C. there is also evidence for it in Assyria.[16]

Headstall

Apart from cheekstraps, illustrated headstalls of ridden horses comprise a browband – occasionally in conjunction with a brow cushion – and often some kind of noseband.

One or two terracotta models show a quilted or padded object that lies across the brow and must have been attached to the

---

[14] See also esp. Cesnola 1894, pl. LXIX, no. 639 (= Myres 1914, no. 2094; from Dhali); Karageorghis 1978, pl. XLVIII, no. 196 (from Kazaphani).

[15] Crouwel 1987, 109 with nn. 78f. (refs.).

[16] Littauer and Crouwel 1979, 88 (type 4), 119 (type 2); Donder 1980, type I, variants C and D.

browband (pl. 180; cf. pl. 187). This so-called brow cushion is more often indicated for chariot horses of terracottas. In the Near East it appears on Assyrian reliefs of the 8th and 7th centuries and on some contemporary ivories.[17]

A noseband, encircling nose and jaw, is often in evidence. It may be shown at the level of the cheekpieces of the bit or just above, as on the detailed Amathus sarcophagus where the ridden horses have such a noseband, while the driven ones do not (pl. 177; cf. pls. 174–176a–b, 179, 183).

A few terracotta models of ridden – and harnessed – horses illustrate a different arrangement, with two straps running diagonally upwards across the nose from a point near the junction of the cheek-straps with the cheekpieces and joining at the browband (pl. 180).[18] In the Near East this form of half noseband appears on Assyrian reliefs of the 8th–7th centuries and there is an explicit illustration on a stone horse's head from Zinjirli where the area of crossing is covered by a decorative plaque.[19] In Cyprus such a plaque seems to be indicated on a terracotta model of a ridden horse from Kourion (fig. 1: 1).

The use of yet another headstall strap, the throatlash, is attested only on the Amathus sarcophagus – with both ridden and harnessed horses (pl. 188).

Some terracottas show clay pellets at the junctions of the cheek-straps with the browband or noseband (pl. 183).[20] These may well represent metal appliques or strap distributors, such as are known from the Near East where they are also illustrated on Assyrian reliefs of the 9th–7th centuries.[21] In Cyprus there is an explicit illustration of such objects on a stone horse's head, possibly of the 4th century B.C.[22]

On two of the stone models of ridden horses, tiers of tassels hang from the browband, one at either side of the head (pl. 174).[23] These

---

[17] Crouwel 1987, 109 with n. 83 (refs.).
[18] See also Cesnola 1894, pl. LXIX, no. 639 (= Myres 1914, no. 2094; from Dhali).
[19] Crouwel 1987, 109 with n. 84 (refs.); Littauer and Crouwel 1979, fig. 63.
[20] See also Cesnola 1894, pl. LXIX, no. 637 (= Myres 1914, no. 2086; from Kourion).
[21] Littauer and Crouwel 1979, 127, cf. 117 with n. 69 (refs.).
[22] Buchholz 1987, 209 with fig. 37 (from Trikomo).
[23] See also Blinkenberg 1931, pl. 75, no. 1802.

can also be seen with ridden and harnessed horses on Assyrian reliefs of the later 8th and 7th centuries and may have helped to keep flies away, if they were not purely decorative.[24]

Bridle Accessories

These include frontlets, possibly blinkers, and tassels.

1. *Frontlets.* They appear sometimes on terracotta models of the 7th–6th centuries and on stone models of the later sixth but no later (pls. 174, 176a–b).[25] For comparison, frontlets are often portrayed with chariot horses on contemporary terracottas, and bronze examples have been found *in situ*, lying over the forehead and nasal bone of harnessed animals at Salamis.[26]

The frontlets shown with models of ridden horses appear to be suspended from the browband and not to continue over it, like many actual ones and some of those illustrated on harnessed horses from Cyprus. At the lower end they may or may not be fastened to a noseband. Decoration is sometimes marked by incision (pl. 180). A terracotta of the 6th century from Meniko in addition shows two pairs of protuberances on either side of the frontlet, something unknown to the actual examples from the island but recalling a type of similarly hingeless, bronze frontlet from Urartu (pl. 183).[27]

Frontlets of varying design were widely used in the Near East during the 9th–7th centuries, viz. actual examples – of bronze, ivory and few of silver – and representations. The bronze examples are not hinged, unlike the actual frontlets of this material from Cyprus but similar to those illustrated with ridden horses on the island.[28]

---

[24] See Yadin 1961, ills. 420f., 427; Barnett 1975, pls. 61. 65. 127–129. 168.
[25] See also Karageorghis 1979, pl. XLVIII, nos. 192, 196 (from Kazaphani); Gjerstad 1935, pl. CLXXXII, no. 556 (from Idalion). Other terracottas seem to illustrate not a frontlet but a strap joining browband and noseband, see Cesnola 1894, pl. LXIX, no. 637 (= Myres 1914, no. 2086; from Kourion), cf. also our fig. 1: 1.
[26] Crouwel 1987, 111 with nn. 94–95 (refs.); Donder 1980, 85–94.
[27] A terracotta model from Kazaphani shows a frontlet with one pair of such protuberances, see Karageorghis 1978, pl. XLVIII, no. 196. For Urartu, see Özgen 1984, 92f. (type A).
[28] Littauer and Crouwel 1979, 125f. (with refs.); add Özgen 1984, 92–98 (Urartu).

2. *Blinkers.* Unlike frontlets, blinkers are rarely illustrated on ridden horses in Cyprus (cf. pl. 185).[29] In contrast, they are often shown with chariot horses and pairs of bronze examples have been found *in situ* on buried animals at Salamis.[30] This contrast between ridden and harnessed horses is well illustrated by the Amathus sarcophagus where the former have no blinkers and the latter do. Like frontlets, blinkers are again well-known from the Near East, by actual examples of bronze or ivory, and by representations.[31]

3. *Tassels.* Ridden ‒ and chariot ‒ horses in Cyprus are often shown with up to three or four decorative tassels, stacked in a tier, suspended from a neck strap (pls. 174–177, 180). Similar tassels appear frequently on Assyrian reliefs of the 9th–7th centuries and other contemporary representations from the Near East.[32] On one Cypriot stone model of a ridden horse the tassels are suspended from a roundel, with a panther head in relief similar to that shown with the cheekstraps (pl. 174).

4. *Poll decoration.* A terracotta model and a vase painting, both of the 7th century B.C., appear to show the same form of poll decoration (fig. 1: 4).[33] This can be interpreted in the light of the detailed Assyrian reliefs of the later 8th–7th centuries as an arching metal crest, running back-to-front and holding a fan of hair.[34] Many other Cypriot terracottas show what looks like another form of poll decoration but is more likely to have been a crest-like forelock (see s.v. Mounts).

---

[29] See also Gjerstad 1935, pl. CLXXXII, no. 556 (from Idalion).
[30] Crouwel 1987, 11 with nn. 90–91 (refs.); Donder 1980, 68–81.
[31] Littauer and Crouwel 1979, 125f. (with refs.); add Özgen 1984, 99f. (Urartu).
[32] Crouwel 1987, 112; Littauer and Crouwel 1979, 127.
[33] See Karageorghis and des Gagniers 1974, no. I. 2, cf. possibly also no. I. 4.
[34] Littauer and Crouwel 1979, 126 with figs. 56. 78. This type of crest is similar to the helmet crest worn by Assyrians as well as by the mounted rider of a Cypriot terracotta, see Törnqvist 1970, 44 with fig. 26.

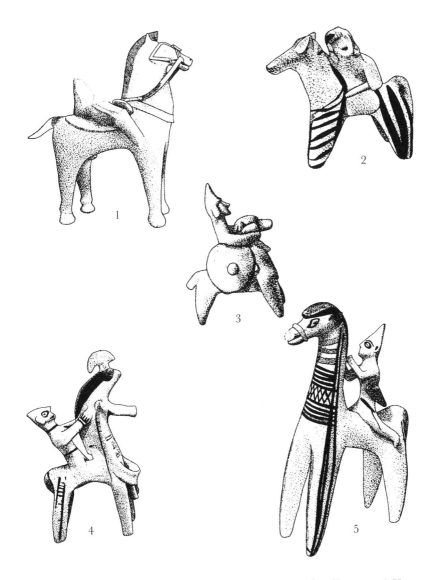

Fig. 1: 1. Terracotta model. From Kourion (no. 1053). After Young and Young 1955, pl. 58.

Fig. 1: 2. Terracotta model. Larnaca. Pierides Collection. After Karageorghis 1973c, no. 74, ill. p. 137 and colour pl.

Fig. 1: 3. Terracotta model. From Ayia Irini (no. 921). Nicosia, CM. After Törnqvist 1970, fig. 32.

Fig. 1: 4. Terracotta model. West Germany, private collection. After Hornbostel et al. 1977, no. 86, ill. p. 115.

Fig. 1: 5. Terracotta model. Nicosia, Cyprus Museum 1936–IV–15/1. After Tatton-Brown 1982b, ill. p. 84.

Whips and Sticks

Most of the vase paintings illustrate the use of a whip or stick.[35]

Use

The ridden horses represented by the terracotta models quite often have a military appearance. This is demonstrated both by the weapons carried and the protective gear of the riders themselves and sometimes of their mounts too.

Some terracottas of the 7th–6th centuries show a sword or dagger at the rider's waist, suspended from a baldric which is sometimes explicitly indicated (fig. 1: 5; pl. 185).[36] In one case the weapon is shown inside a shield at the rider's side (pl. 186). Similar round shields, with and without a central boss, are seen on other terracottas, carried again at the rider's side or on his back. They must have been suspended from slings too (pl. 184; fig. 1: 3).[37] All these armed riders wear conical headdresses. Sometimes there is a crest of varying design to identify them as helmets (pl. 186).[38] It should be noted that simple conical headdresses, without such additional identifying features, appear on many terracottas of otherwise unarmed horseback riders. Here it must remain uncertain whether helmets or caps were intended.[39]

None of these riders is shown as if in action, in contrast to a group of terracottas from Kourion, apparently dating from the 5th to the later 4th/early 3rd centuries B.C.[40] Often wearing crested helmets, these riders in some cases have their right arms raised, to bran-

---

[35] See Karageorghis and des Gagniers 1974, nos. I. 2f., 5f. Our fig. 2 shows a stick rather than a spear, as suggested by Karageorghis 1973b, 173.

[36] See also Karageorghis 1973c, no. 73.

[37] See also Cesnola 1894, pl. LXXXII, no. 656 (from Kourion); Winter 1903, ill. 4, p. 15 (= Ohnefalsch-Richter 1893, pl. CXXII, no. 15 = Gamber 1978, pl. VII; from Athienou); Walters 1903, no. A 167 and no. A 172 (= Smith 1900, fig. 164: 2, from Amathus); Young and Young 1955, no. 1069 with pl. 19 (from Kourion); Karageorghis 1966c, 315 with fig. 43 (= 1976–78, no. 151; from Palaepaphos).

[38] See also Törnqvist 1970, fig. 26; cf. Perrot and Chipiez 1885, pl. II, right (conical helmet with cheekpieces).

[39] See Monloup 1984, 39f., 46.

[40] See Cesnola 1894, pl. XXI, no. 261 (= Myres 1914, no. 2271); Young and Young 1955, 211–214, with pls. 23. 26. 29–33. For dating, see now Buitron 1983 (cf. pl. XXXVI: 2–3); Karageorghis 1983b, 933.

dish spears (now lost, since they were made of other material) or to throw stones, while holding up round shields with their left arms. The shields frequently have devices of Greek type and the group as a whole is clearly distinct from the terracottas discussed above.

An unprovenanced terracotta model, probably of the 6th century B.C., shows a helmeted rider who must originally have held a spear in his raised right arm (pl. 187); his mount wears chest armour, rendered in relief. The same form of horse armour is presumably indicated on some terracottas of the 7th–6th centuries, its straight lower edge marked in relief just above the forelegs (possibly fig. 1: 3).[41] A more explicit rendering can be seen on a stone model from Golgoi, dating to the later 6th or 5th century (pl. 179). By comparison, the horses of some Cypriot terracotta chariot groups of the 7th–6th century B.C. have a longer chest protection, sometimes with a fringe at the bottom.[42]

Several of the more elaborate terracotta models of armed riders, probably dating to the 7th century B.C., show a thick clay strip running horizontally or swag-like across the lower chest of the mount. The strip is sometimes decorated with three applied pellets, one at either side and one in the middle; the strip supports a fringe of tassels (pls. 184–186).[43] This element is probably not to be confused with the fringed, bib-shaped gorgets worn at the throat by ridden and harness horses on Assyrian reliefs of the 9th and 8th centuries (but no later) and on some other Near Eastern representations of the time. In Cyprus that type of chest armour is worn by some of the chariot horses represented by terracottas of the 7th–6th century B.C. Actual bronze examples of similar form, both plain and decorated, have been found with the 8th–7th century vehicle burials at Salamis and also at Hasanlu in N. W. Iran. Bronze gorgets of related type, with two hinged parts, are known from Urartu.[44] By contrast, on the Cypriot terracottas of ridden horses the clay strip is placed much lower than a gorget would, while the tassels that sometimes

---

[41] See also Cesnola 1894, pl. LXXVI, no. 656 (from Kourion); Walters 1903, no. A 218 (= Smith 1900 fig. 112; from Kourion); Young and Young 1955, 214f. and nos. 1060, 1083 with pl. 19.

[42] Crouwel 1987, 113 with pl. XXXVII: 1–3.

[43] See also Cesnola 1894, pl. LXXI, no. 646 (= Myres 1914 no. K 2079; from Ormidhia, Benson 1973, pl. 41, no. K 1148 (from Kaloriziki). Cf. Tatton-Brown 1982a, 178. 180 with pl. XXXVIII: 2–5 (terracotta group, probably from Kourion, showing an armed man leading two horses wearing such elements).

[44] See Crouwel 1987, 112f. with nn. 107f. (refs.) and pl. XXXIX: 4.

hang from the neck are entirely above. The clay element is much more reminiscent of the fringed or tasseled fly aprons worn in approximately this position by mounted horses on Assyrian reliefs of the 8th and 7th centuries.[45]

On balance, what we see on these Cypriot terracottas is better interpreted as a "fly apron" than as a gorget. This is supported by a terracotta found on Rhodes, where straps that support the apron can be seen on either side low on the neck, and by fragmentary terracottas from Kourion which clearly illustrate simple chest straps without a fringe.[46] The pellets seen on some of the models mentioned above may indicate decorative appliques, as seen on the Assyrian reliefs.[47]

It should be noted that the chest area of horses, with and without riders, represented by terracotta models ranging from the 11th/ 10th century B.C. onwards, is often painted with geometric patterns (pls. 184, 186; fig. 1: 1,5).[48] In the absence, however, of substantiating evidence, this cannot be assumed to represent armour. It is more likely to be simply the coroplasts' decoration.

None of the Cypriot figured documents considered so far provides explicit evidence – in relief or painting – to show that the riders themselves wore body armour of some kind. A (scale?) corslet may, however, be recognized on a vase painting of the 7th century, showing two men on foot – one drawing a bow, the other leading a horse.[49] The latter man, probably wearing a helmet and with a sword stuck at his waist, may well be a dismounted rider. Body armour – and helmets – cannot be entirely excluded for the horseback rider and chariot occupants seen on another vase painting, of the 8th century (fig. 2). While the chariot carries a pair of spears, fixed at the rear of the body, the rider has a quiver of arrows at his back. The lat-

---

[45] See Littauer and Crouwel 1979, fig. 77; Albenda 1986, pls. 29, 85; Barnett 1976, pl. XXV (slab 5); Paterson 1915, pls. 48. 57–58. 79; cf. Özgen 1983, fig. 11 (Urartu).

[46] Blinkenberg 1931, pl. 88, no. 1977; Young and Young 1955, 215 with ills. 1–3, cf. no. 1115 with ill. p. 61.

[47] See Yadin 1961, ill. p. 427; Barnett 1975, pls. 127–129.

[48] See also Benson 1973, pl. 41, no. K 1147 (Cypro-Geometric I; from Kaloriziki; Karageorghis 1974, 833, 835 with fig. 14 (similar date); Morris 1985, figs. 336–339, pls 235–238; cf. Karageorghis, Styrenius, Winblath 1977, 40 with pl. XXV: 2 (Ayia Irini no. 922; said to wear a "front cover").

[49] Karageorghis and des Gagniers 1974, no. III. 4, cf. p. 19 (vol. I).

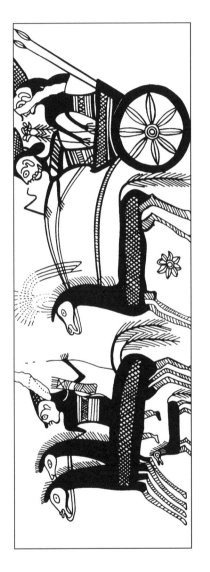

Fig. 2. Terracotta White Painted III amphora, detail. From Khrysokhou. After Karageorghis and des Gagniers 1979, no. SI. 1, ill. p. 10.

ter recurs on a vase, probably by the same painter, showing a man on horseback leading a bovid.[50]

These two vase paintings are the only – indirect – witnesses to the use of the bow and arrow by men on horseback in ancient Cyprus. In contrast, archers are often among the crews of the chariots represented by 7th–6th century terracotta models from the island.[51] In addition, these chariots carried close-range weapons (single spears or swords), the crews being protected by shields and helmets and the draught teams often wearing armour of varying forms. All this military equipment can be matched among chariots in the Near East during the earlier first millennium B.C., Assyrian reliefs of the 9th–7th centuries being our most detailed pictorial sources. In view of these striking similarities between the Cypriot chariots and those in the Near East, which extend to aspects of the vehicles themselves and the ways the horses were harnessed and controlled, a similar – military – use can be assumed. We know – primarily again from the Assyrian reliefs – that chariots in Assyria and other parts of the Near East were mainly used as elevated, mobile firing platforms for an archer standing beside the driver. The close-range weapons also carried were used should it be necessary to fight from slow-moving or immobilized chariots or on the ground.

Assyrian reliefs, from the 9th century B.C. onwards, show increasing numbers of *mounted warriors* operating side by side with the chariots.[52] At first the riders operate in pairs, consisting of an archer and a squire who controls both horses and also protects the warrior with a round shield. The reliefs demonstrate that by the late 8th and 7th century mounted troops had become more effective: practice had given the riders a more secure seat – on a saddle cloth, the proper riding saddle appearing only much later – while bits with greater braking powers permitted them to pull up their reins, and a special reining system finally freed both hands to wield their primary weapon – bow and arrow.[53] Their superiority over chariots in economy of materiel, in mobility in all types of terrain, and as a flanking and pursuing arm, their suitability for protecting infantry on the march and for use as scouts and messengers, would have made them invalu-

---

[50] Karageorghis 1980, 133 with pl. XIX: 3–4.
[51] For what follows, see Crouwel 1987, 112f.
[52] For what follows, see Littauer and Crouwel 1979, 130f., 137–139; Crouwel 1987, 112.
[53] See Spruytte 1983.

able. This development of military riding is reflected in the Assyrian reliefs where the light, mobile chariot is gradually seen turning into the bigger, less manoeuvrable vehicle, carrying as many as four men, of the later 8th and 7th century. The later scythed chariots of the Achaemenid and other armies represent the final and degenerate stage of the military chariot in the Near East.

In Cyprus the military function of the chariot seems to have been abandoned in the 5th century B.C., from which time representations show only civil vehicles. In a recent paper one of us suggested that this phenomenon may be explained as a parallel to the rise of mounted troops and the decline of chariotry in the contemporary Near East.[54] Unfortunately, in Cyprus we have no such large-scale and detailed scenes as the Assyrian reliefs which allow us to trace the development of chariot driving and horseback riding in warfare over a period of several centuries. Texts bearing on the role of riding in warfare in the island are also lacking. The figured documents available to us, illustrating ridden horses of a military character, are of limited value. Possibly beginning in the 8th century B.C. (the two vase paintings cited above), they increase in the 7th and 6th centuries with the terracotta models. However, no development in riding techniques can be observed and there is no significant increase in the number of representations from the 5th century onwards when the military chariot has disappeared.

The presence of horse armour, however, on terracotta and stone models of the 7th and 6th–5th centuries must indicate that the mounts were not only a means of transport for armed men but actually came within range of enemy fire, although the riders' weapons – swords or daggers – are for close-range fighting on the ground. Only the spear, associated with a number of terracottas, could have been used on horseback, as is illustrated in the Near East and also, for that matter, in Greece from the 6th century onwards.[55] And there are the two early vase paintings (of the 8th century) to suggest the use of the bow on horseback in the island. Nevertheless, the increasingly important role of mounted troops in warfare in neighbouring areas during the first millennium B.C. – in the Near East and to some extent also in Greece[56] – must have been reflected in Cyprus

---

[54] Crouwel 1987, 113.
[55] For Greece, see Greenhalgh 1973, index s.v. spears.
[56] See Littauer and Crouwel 1979, 137–19, 157f.; For Greece, see Anderson 1970, index s.v. cavalry; Greenhalgh 1973, index s.v. cavalry.

which enjoyed close cultural and, for long periods, political connections with east and west.

Ridden horses in ancient Cyprus were certainly also used for civil purposes. There is nothing military, for instance, about the riders represented on the 5th century Amathus sarcophagus (pl. 177). The same can be said of the stone models of the later 6th and 5th century, with the exception of the one where the mount seems to be wearing chest armour; the rider, however, is not equipped for war, wearing a short garment and a turban held by a chin strap (pl. 179). The riders on the Amathus sarcophagus, comfortably seated on saddle cloths, wear short-sleeved tunics reaching down to their knees and covered by short cloaks. Their conical headdresses are not helmets but soft caps of a well-known type.[57] The scene on this important document, which includes two men on horseback preceding two chariots, one with a parasol carried inside, suggests a procession of some kind.

The unarmed riders presented by the stone models and some of the terracottas may also wear short tunics and conical caps (pl. 180).[58]

A use of ridden horses in hunting seems to be illustrated by an incomplete stone model from Kythrea (pl. 181). The rider is seen attacking a lion, crouched under his mount's forelegs, with a spear. (Only part of the spear's shaft is preserved, lying alongside the horse's right foreleg). This document is a unique in Cyprus, there being no other evidence for lion hunting in the island. In fact, this may well be an artistic motive borrowed from the Near East. In Assyrian reliefs and other figured documents of the earlier first millennium B.C. and again in later Achaemenid and Graeco-Persian art, kings and aristocrats are often depicted on horseback spearing lions.[59]

The horseback rider, possibly carrying a quiver of arrows on his back and leading a bovine animal by a rope, seen on an 8th century vase painting from Cyprus, has been tentatively interpreted as a huntsman bringing home a bull.[60]

---

[57] See Pryce 1931, 29.
[58] See also Karageorghis 1977, 27 and 37f. no. 15 with pls. VIII–IX (head of horse is illustrated in our pl. XXV: 6).
[59] See Littauer and Crouwel 1979, 139, 158; Anderson 1985, 10, 67f.
[60] Karageorghis 1980, 134.

Concluding Remarks

Ridden horses are first attested in Iron Age Cyprus in the 11th/10th century B.C., by terracotta models.[61] From then on they are documented both by terracottas and other figured documents down to Hellenistic (and Roman) times. In addition, there seems to be a little evidence for their use at an earlier date, in the Middle and Late Bronze Age.[62]

The more detailed representations of the 7th century and later make clear that many harness elements were adopted from the Near East. These include saddle cloths of felt with toothed edges, tassels suspended from neck straps, fly aprons and most, if not all, parts of the bridles and their accessories. This is not surprising in view of Cyprus' proximity to and close connections with the east during most of the first millennium B.C., which included long periods of Assyrian and, later, Achaemenid domination. It is worth noting that strong influence from the orient can also be observed in the chariots and chariot horse harness in Cyprus at the time.

The evidence available for horseback riding in Cyprus does not allow us to trace a development in either riding techniques or use. We only catch a glimpse, probably of Roman date, of an early form of riding saddle. In the island and in the Near East alike, the treed saddle, with two lengthwise wooden stretchers on either side of the horse's spine to unite and support the front and back bows, and another important harness element, the stirrup, do not appear until well into the first millennium A.D.[63]

We may end by drawing attention to the distribution of the hundreds of terracotta models that constitute our main source of evidence for horseback riding in Iron Age Cyprus. While they have been found at settlement sites (chiefly at Salamis) and in tombs, the

---

[61] For models dating to Cypro-Geometric I, see Benson 1973, pl. 41, no. K 1141 (from Kaloriziki, Tomb 34); Karageorghis 1974, 833, 835 with fig. 14. Cf. Karageorghis and des Gagniers 1974, no. I. 1 (the earliest vase painting, dating to Cypro-Geometric II).

[62] Buchholz and Karageorghis 1971, no. 1562 (= Morris 1985, 85 with fig. 329 (attachment to Middle Bronze Age vessel from Vounous, tomb 64), cf. no. 1725 and also Karageorghis 1974, 847 with fig. 43; 1980, 135 with pl. CVIII (Late Bronze Age terracotta figurines). In no case is the modelling explicit enough to rule out other kinds of equids.

[63] See Littauer 1981.

great majority derive from sanctuaries (especially at Kourion).[64] They clearly enjoyed great popularity as ex-voto's, even more so than terracottas representing chariot groups.

Appendix

A different manner of transportation on animal back is illustrated by some terracotta models, which show riders with both legs on one side of their mount (fig. 1: 2; pl. 188).[65]

This sideways seat, which is much more precarious than one astride and gives the rider much less control over the animal, is not for fast riding. Traditionally it has been used by the elderly or the infirm, by important dignitaries as well as by women, whose long garments would have precluded their sitting astride anyway. Asses and mules would have been more suitable than horses for a sideways seat (at least before the introduction of the true riding saddle), since they have smoother travelling gaits and are less apt to shy or bolt, thereby requiring less firm control.[66]

The Cypriot terracottas of this type are mostly too summarily rendered or too fragmentary to shed light on the identity of the mounts and their riders. In a few cases apparently male figures are seen holding on to the animal's neck or tail. Of particular interest is a terracotta from a 9th/8th century tomb at Palaepaphos-*Skales* (pl. XXVI: 5).[67] The animal here was presumably meant to be a horse, as it has the crest-like mane ending in a forelock typical of many

---

[64] See Monloup 1984, 41, pointing out the curious fact that there are only two terracottas illustrating ridden horses among the numerous published examples from the sanctuary at Ayia Irini (Ayia Irini nos. 921 and 922, see our fig. 1: 3 and Karageorghis, Styrenius, Winblath 1977, pl. XXXV: 2), whereas there are many of chariot groups.

[65] Cesnola 1885, pl. LXIX, no. 636 (= Myres 1914, no. 2086; from Dhali); Winter 1903, ill. 6, pl. 15; Young and Young 1955, 65. 216 nos. 1221f. with pl. 22 (Kourion); Karageorghis 1970, 368 with fig. 74; 1973a, no. 74 (our fig. 1: 2; rider holding a stick or goat to help control mount); Monloup 1984, nos. 305f. (from Salamis); see also *infra* nn. 67–68. On most vase paintings (listed *supra* n. 4) the riders are shown as if seated sideways or standing on their mount. These positions cannot be taken seriously but reflect the painters' unfamiliarity with the motif of ridden horses.

[66] Littauer and Crouwel 1979, 46; Crouwel 1981, 51f.

[67] Karageorghis 1983a, 90 no. 2 with pl. LXXXII (Tomb 52, dating to Cypro-Geometric III); also 1980, 129 with pl. XVII: 4f.

terracottas showing horses ridden astride. The male rider, originally apparently holding a lyre, is seated not directly on the back of the animal or on a cloth, but on a saddle with a rigid wooden frame. The latter can be seen again on a fragmentary terracotta figurine from Kourion-*Bamboula*, its painted decoration suggesting a 11th/10th century date.[68] Here we have, in fact, not a true riding saddle but a pack saddle with arched bows for and aft – a type never shown with riders seated astride.[69]

The use of rigid-framed pack saddles of this type to facilitate this form of riding is well-documented in Greece, from the Late Bronze Age to modern times: one may still observe the sideways seat on pack saddles among men or women going to or returning from the fields. In some cases it is the so-called chair-saddle, an adaptation of the pack saddle in which a backrest or footboard were added to give the rider a firmer and more comfortable seat.[70] In Cyprus it is documented too, but only during the Late Bronze Age. A hollow terracotta figurine, probably of the 13th century B.C., shows an apparently male figure with both his hands resting on the bows of the saddle, which also has a backrest (pl. 189).[71] The animal, an equid of uncertain species, wears a headstall and there is a strap going around its chest, possibly reflecting one that helped to secure the saddle. A chair-saddle, held by a breast strap and a crupper, is seen on a related terracotta figurine.[72]

---

[68] Yon and Caubet 1985, 17 no. 53 with figs. 16. 18 (Cypro-Geometric I, in view of the White Painted I decoration).

[69] A pack saddle may perhaps be identified on some (incomplete) Cypriot Iron Age terracottas, see Gjerstad 1937, pl. LXXVII, no. 130 (from Vouni); Monloup 1984, no. 295, cf. 74–76 and nos. 295–304 (models of pack animals from Salamis and elsewhere).

[70] Crouwel 1981, 51f. with n. 42 (refs.); Voyatzis 1985, 160f.; cf. Jantzen 1972, 83f. no. B 452 (bronze figurine from Samos, thought to come from the Caucasus region).

[71] Karageorghis 1980, 128–32 with pl. XVII: 1–2.

[72] Cesnola 1894, pl. LXXVI, no. 691 (from Alambra); Catling 1976, 67f. no. 5, cf. 73f. (discussion of chronology of this and related terracottas); Karageorghis 1980, 129 with fig. 1; Morris, 1985, 205. Note that an animal rhyton of the 11th century B.C. illustrates a male figure, apparently seated sideways directly on his mount's back, Catling 1974, 95–111 with pls. XVI–XVII.

29. A TERRACOTTA HORSE AND RIDER IN BRUSSELS*

VERONICA TATTON-BROWN AND JOOST CROUWEL

We are pleased to dedicate this paper to our colleague and friend, Dr Vassos Karageorghis, whose own work on Cypriot terracottas will enhance the subject.**

The terracotta model of a rider on horseback discussed in this paper has for long been in the collection of the Musées Royaux d'Art et d'Histoire, Brussels (Inv. A 1323; Pl. 190a–e). It was acquired in Paris in 1906 and reportedly comes from Byblos.[1] Though illustrated in the catalogues accompanying three recent exhibitions on the Phoenicians,[2] the model has so far not received the attention it deserves for the elaborate detail of its mount and rider. Another problem is its place of manufacture, the candidates being Phoenicia or Cyprus, the source of many terracotta models of horseback riders made in the first millennium B.C.

Our model has a total height of 0.325 m. and a length of 0.24 m. Its hind legs are supported on a flat base, which is broken at the front and may have run under its entirety;[3] alternatively, each pair of legs could have had a separate base.[4] Missing too are the animal's right ear and the rider's right arm, as well as most of the

* In: ΑΦΙΕΡΩΜΑ ΣΤΟ ΒΑΣΟ ΚΑΡΑΓΙΩΡΓΗ (Studies in Honour of Vassos Karageorghis). Nicosia 1992, 291–295.

** We are most grateful to Professor D. Homès-Fredericq for facilitating this study in every possible way. We are also indebted to Professor J.-C. Balty for help, and to Dr P. R. S. Moorey and Dr L. Burn for their comments.

[1] *Catalogue de la vente Philip* (Paris 1905), no. 569.

[2] *Les Phéniciens et le monde méditerranéen* (Brussels 1986), no. 41; *I Fenici* (Venice 1988), no. 30; *Die Phönizier im Zeitalter Homers* (Hannover 1990), no. 53. See also Cumont 1926, 271 with fig. 59; Bisi 1989, 257.

[3] The plaster restoration of such a base and of the horse's forelegs, seen in earlier photographs (such as our), has recently been removed.

[4] Such separate bases, though unusual, appear with another large horse-and-rider terracotta, excavated from Meniko in Cyprus (Karageorghis 1977, 27, 37f. no. 15 (56 + 29 + 766) with pls. VIII–IX); cf. also an incomplete terracotta found at Tell Sukas in Phoenicia (Riis 1963, 218 with fig. 18; tentatively but probably incorrectly identified as a handle).

horse's forelegs. The model has been mended in some places, particularly where the – separately made but clearly belonging – rider
was attached to the horse's rump.

The clay is medium coarse with some medium-sized black grits
and varies in colour from light red (2.5 YR 6/8)[5] at the core to
light reddish brown (5 YR 6/4) at the surface. The horse's head
and the rider's face are mould-made; the rest is hand-modelled, with
rather roughly finished surfaces, except for the horse's front. The
body of the animal is hollowed out underneath but the rest of the
model is solid; the animal's hind legs lean somewhat to one side.
The original paint is best preserved on the rider's quiver of arrows
and headdress, while traces of similar (black) paint can be made out
on the saddle cloth, the horse's tail, headdress and tassel pendant.

The Rider and his Seat

The male rider is seated astride, just behind the mount's withers
with his legs hanging slightly forwards. Riding is on a saddle cloth, its
straight edges marked below and – by a rough knife-made groove –
at the rear. It is sufficient here to note that in the Near East saddle cloths of different kinds are illustrated – on Assyrian reliefs and
other documents – from the 9th cent. B.C. onwards.[6] In Cyprus, on
the other hand, they are rarely indicated on terracotta models but
they do appear on stone models of the later 6th and 5th cent. B.C.
and on a 5th-century sarcophagus from Amathus.[7]

The rider has his arms bent forward and is holding onto the
horse's neck. This is a convenience of the coroplast: in reality, the
rider would have held reins, fastened to his mount's bit (see below).

The man's well modelled face is clean-shaven and shows almond-
shaped eyes, one being larger than the other. The eyelids are indicated in relief, as are the eyebrows and ears; the small mouth has
slightly V-shaped lips. A fringe of hair with oblique incisions is visible below his tall headdress. The later is completely preserved, with
ridges down the centre and sides, which suggest fabric or leather
rather than metal. The tassel-ended elements seen depending from

---

[5] Munsell Soil Color Charts. Baltimore 1973.
[6] Littauer and Crouwel 1979, 134. 156.
[7] Crouwel and Tatton-Brown 1988, 77f.

behind the ears on the rider's shoulders are best explained as "lappets", by which the headdress may have been tied under the chin.[8] It is uncertain whether this headdress, for which we have no exact parallels, should be classified as a helmet.

The rider is barefoot and wears a knee-length tunic or mantle with long sleeves, apparently over an undergarment since two incised borders are visible at the hem and also faintly at the end of the surviving full-length sleeve.[9] The undergarment has in addition a decorated border at the neck. Quite deeply incised patterns, noticeable in particular on the left upper arm and right leg of the rider, probably indicate folds of the outer tunic or mantle. They are visible too on the top part of the now mostly missing right arm, but are partly obscured by the quiver on the left leg. These folds together with the outer garment's sleeves and its length suggest that it is made of linen. The lacing at the neck occurs too for the tunics worn by the triple-bodied warrior (?Geryon) of the late 7th cent. B.C. from Pyrga in Cyprus,[10] but there it is combined with obviously metal arm bands and neckguards, missing for our figure.

The quiver at the rider's left side identifies him as an archer, the only terracotta model of a Cypriot or Levantine horseback rider to play this role known to the authors. The quiver must have been suspended from a sling (not shown). In the Near East, horse-borne archers with quivers of arrows, carried on their back rather than at their side, can first be seen on Assyrian reliefs of the 9th–7th cent. B.C. and on contemporary figured documents.[11] In Cyprus, evidence for the use of bow-and-arrow by men on horseback is confined to one or two vase paintings of the 8th cent. B.C.[12] In contrast, archers are often shown among the crews of the chariots represented by

---

[8] Note that the "lappets" seem to have been painted in the same colour (black) as the headdress.

[9] Cf. the Cypriot terracottas discussed by Törnqvist 1973, 9f.

[10] Tatton-Brown 1979, especially 284f. with pl. XXXII; for identification as Geryon, see Karageorghis 1989. The lacing recurs with an unprovenanced terracotta shield-bearer from Cyprus, Karageorhis 1973d, 606 with fig. 17.

[11] Littauer and Crouwel 1979, 135. 137f. with figs. 76. 78.

[12] Karageorghis and Des Gagniers 1979, no. SI.1; possibly also Karageorhis 1980c, 133f. with pl. XIX: 3f.; Crouwel and Tatton-Brown 1988, 81f. Note the decorated quiver, containing both arrows and a – broken off – bow, slung at the left side of the kneeling archer (Heracles ?), represented by a fragmentary limestone sculpture from Golgoi (di Cesnola 1885, pl. CXXVIII, no. 932; Myres 1914, no. 1409; on display in New York, Metropolitan Museum of Art 74.51.2500).

7th–6th century terracotta models from the island, the quivers here attached to the vehicle body or placed inside it.[13] Interestingly, where our terracotta horseback rider has a quiver at his left side, others – from Cyprus – may have a round shield, in the same place and similarly suspended from a sling.[14]

High on the back of our rider is a small projection, pointing downwards and with a groove down its upper part. Apparently completely preserved and surrounded by rough knife(?) marks, the projection again is not readily explained as a hook to support a sling for a bow, or as a shieldboss or another part of the rider's equipment;[15] neither does it seem to have to do with the process of manufacture of the terracotta.[16]

The Mount and its Harness

The animal with its short ears, impressed nostrils, half open mouth, roughly marked knee-joints and fetlocks must be a horse. Its long tail, applied against the left hind leg, bears incisions. These may possibly suggest braiding, something not illustrated on other terracottas.[17]

The mount is controlled by a bitted bridle, the cheekstraps dividing into two strands for the attachment of the cheekpieces of the bit. The junction of the two strands is covered by a clay pellet, such as is seen on other figured documents from the Near East and Cyprus and quite probably indicating a metal appliqué or strap divider.[18] Just above the cheekpieces, which appear to be of rectangular shape, there is a noseband, apparently encircling nose and jaw.

There is also a browband, running across the forehead from cheekstrap to cheekstrap and overlying the horse's forelock, and just above,

---

[13] Crouwel 1987, 112f.

[14] Crouwel and Tatton-Brown 1988, 81 with fig. 1: 3 and pls. 184, 186.

[15] Horseback riders with shields in this position are seen on Assyrian 9th century reliefs (Littauer and Crouwel 1979, 137 with fig. 76) and, later, on Cypriot terracottas (Crouwel and Tatton-Brown 1988, 81 with pl. XXVI: 1; also Gamber 1978, pl. VII).

[16] There is a slight boss in a similar position on a terracotta model of a horseback rider, probably from Cyprus; (Lubsen-Admiral and Crouwel 1989) no. 178 with ill. p. 77: Allard Pierson Museum 1881. Height 0.165 m.).

[17] Cf. the incised, free-hanging tail of the terracotta mounted horse from Meniko, supra n. 4.

[18] See Crouwel and Tatton-Brown 1988, 78f.

a so-called brow cushion. This padded or quilted object, somehow attached to the browband, is indicated for ridden and more often chariot horses of other terracottas, mainly from Cyprus and dating to the 7th–6th cent. B.C. It also appears on Assyrian reliefs of the 8th and 7th cent. B.C. and on contemporary figured documents from the Near East.[19]

Bridle accessories include a frontlet a pair of blinkers and tassels – a combination which can be paralleled on other terracottas, mainly of chariot horses found in Cyprus, and dating to the 7th–6th cent. B.C.

The frontlet is probably suspended from the browband; at the lower end it may or may not be fastened to the noseband. As on other terracottas, decoration is marked by incision. It recalls the highly decorated bronze frontlets found associated with the late 8th–7th cent. B.C. burials of vehicles and their harness teams at Salamis and elsewhere in Cyprus. Actual frontlets of bronze and other materials, with and without decoration, are also known from different parts of the Near East, while they are illustrated on Assyrian reliefs and other representations of the 9th–7th cent. B.C.[20]

The blinkers, fastened in the corner between cheekstrap and browband and actually shielding the eye, are rendered in more detail than those shown with other terracottas.[21] Like actual examples of bronze or other materials from the Near East and Cyprus, the blinkers are spade-shaped.[22] The incised oval in the centre recalls both the inlaid eyes of certain bronze blinkers found with harness animals at Salamis, and the bosses of ivory specimens from Nimrud.[23]

The three tassels, stacked in a tier, are suspended from a neckstrap, with loops on either side marking their attachment. The neckstrap bears chevron-like incisions, suggesting cord. Single or multiple decorative tassels are a common feature of riding and harness horses

---

[19] Crouwel 1985, 109; 1987, 109; Crouwel and Tatton-Brown 1988, 79.

[20] Donder 1980, 85–94 (Salamis); Littauer and Crouwel 1979, 125f. (with refs.); Crouwel 1987, 111; Crouwel and Tatton-Brown 1988, 79.

[21] For another detailed rendering, from Cyprus, see the broken-off chariot horse's head, Karageorghis 1967, 48 with fig. 10; Crouwel 1987, pl. XXXIX: 1.

[22] Donder 1980, 68–81; Littauer and Crouwel 1979, 125f.; Crouwel 1987, 11; Crouwel and Tatton-Brown 1988, 79. 81.

[23] Donder 1980, 72–74, nos. 152–156 (Salamis, Tomb 3), also nos. 158–162 (Tamassos and Idalion) and 163 (Lindos in Rhodes); Orhard 1967, especially nos. 71–83 (Nimrud; cf. Donder 1980, nos. 168–177 for similar examples of bronze from Salamis).

in the Near East and Cyprus. They are illustrated, for instance, on Assyrian reliefs of the 9th to the 7th cent. B.C.[24]

The tassels hang over a deep, bib-shaped gorget or breastplate with thick upper and lower edges and a fringe of tassels at the bottom. The gorget may have been of boiled leather or bronze, like the actual specimens of similar shape that have been found with the burials of draught animals at Salamis and also at Hasanlu in northwest Iran, the latter in a context dating to ca. 800 B.C.[25] This type of chest armour is seen worn by riding and draught horses on Assyrian reliefs of the 9th and 8th cent. B.C. but no later, and on other Near Eastern representations of the time. It is also illustrated with some of the chariot horses of 7th–6th century terracottas, mainly from Cyprus.[26]

Two features of our model are of special interest. One is the attachment of the fringe – not directly to the lower edge of the gorget, as is seen in other representations, but by means of five short, cord-like straps. The fringe itself, its lower end at the start of the forelegs, may well have been to keep flies away, recalling the "fly apron" apparently worn by the mounts represented by several 7th–6th cent. B.C. terracottas from Cyprus.[27] The other feature is the small, rather crescent-shaped object with a small pendant at the centre, worn over the gorget and suspended from a separate neckstrap. This object, its incised decoration partly masked by the three-tiered tassel pendants, does not appear on other representations, but is somewhat reminiscent of certain elements of actual bronze horse gear found in the destruction level of ca. 800 B.C. at Hasanlu.[28] These consist of plaques with straight upper edge, rounded corners and curved lower edge, and were found together with the bib-shaped

---

[24] Littauer and Crouwel 1979, 127; Crouwel 1987, 112; Crouwel and Tatton-Brown 1988, 81.

[25] Crouwel 1987, 112f.; Crouwel and Tatton-Brown 1988, 82. For Hasanlu, see especially De Schauensee and Dyson 1983, 72 with fig. 21; De Schauensee 1988, 48 with fig. 15; 1989, 46f. with figs. 27. 29: left. Bronze breastplates of related type, with two hinged parts, are known from Urartu, see Haerinck and Overlaet 1984, 56f. with pl. I; Seidl 1986a and 1986b.

[26] Littauer and Crouwel 1979, 129; Winter 1980, 3–5; Crouwel 1987, 112f.

[27] Crouwel and Tatton-Brown 1988, 81f.

[28] Winter 1980, especially 3–6; De Schauensee and Dyson 1983, 72 with fig. 20; De Schauensee 1988, 48 with fig. 16; 1989, 46f. 50 with figs. 26f. (cf. 47 with figs. 28f.: two decorated, crescent-shaped objects with end loops, said to be too small to have served as "breastplates" and reconstructed as having been suspended from a browband; cf. also Winter 1980, 22f. with figs. 58f.: blue paste-inlaid "gorgets").

gorgets. Apart from apparently plain examples, there is one with highly elaborate decoration. Though described as breastplates, their protective function will have been limited, in view of the published dimensions of the highly decorated example: 0.428 by 0.202 m. These objects from Hasanlu may rather have had some symbolic meaning or indicated a particular army unit. The same may be true of the object that is worn in conjunction with the bib-shaped gorget by our terracotta riding horse.

Our horse preserves, on the right side of its neck well below the traces of the rider's lost hand, remains of an object. With rounded edges and central groove to its preserved forward end, and with two lines depending from it, this object may perhaps have been part of the bib-shaped gorget.[29]

Use

Most of the elaborate horse gear − breastplate, frontlet and blinkers − associated with our model is basically a protection against enemy missiles, while presumably also enjoying an ornamental purpose. The presence of a quiver of arrows too points to a potentially military role for the rider, as may the tall cap or helmet.

The archers on horseback depicted on Assyrian reliefs of the 9th–7th cent. B.C. are often actually engaged in warfare. They frequently wear metal helmets and armour. It may be noted that on other reliefs horse-borne archers are shown in hunting scenes.[30]

Our rider is not shown as if in action. This and his elaborate, presumably non-military dress suggest he is an important officer or dignitary, engaged in some peaceful activity.

---

[29] The remains of this object are somewhat reminiscent of the loop marking the place where the harness straps are tied to the yoke of chariot horses on some Cypriot terracottas (e.g. Littauer and Crouwel apud Karageorghis 1977, 71 with pl. XXV: model from Meniko). There being no other indications, however, it is most unlikely that our horse was first used as a harness animal and subsequently converted into a mount.

[30] See Littauer and Crouwel 1979, 134–139; Crouwel and Tatton-Brown 1988, 83f.; also Spruytte 1983.

Chronology and Place of Manufacture

General dating information may be yielded by the accoutrements of the mount. Several of these – breastplate, frontlet and blinkers – have close parallels among the actual metal finds from the burials of vehicles and their harness teams of the late 8th and 7th cent. B.C. in Cyprus, notably at Salamis. Figured documents illustrating such objects range from the 9th to the 7th century in the Near East, while in Cyprus they extend into the 6th cent. B.C. However, the particular combination of this and other horse gear, illustrated by our terracotta model, cannot be matched by any of the mounts depicted on the Assyrian reliefs or other well-dated figured documents.

Be that as it may, the tassel in front, suspended from the cord-like neckstrap, along with the frontlet, blinkers and possibly the bib-shaped breastplate, recur on a terracotta model of a horseback rider reportedly from Tyre (Pl. 191).[31] By the style of his mould-made head this rider belongs to a well-known class of terracottas, widely distributed over the eastern Mediterranean (Cyprus, Rhodes, Samos, Caria, Naucratis in the Nile Delta, as well as Phoenicia, albeit not from controlled excavations) and roughly dating to the later 7th–earlier 6th cent. B.C.[32] These terracottas, which include mainly chariot occupants or men on foot, have very similar facial features and beards, a fringe of hair visible below their cap-like headdress, and often wear a mantle with fringed border over a tunic. The representatives of this class of terracottas have recently been described as "personnages barbus de type assyrien" because of their eastern appearance.[33] However, most of their characteristics have excellent parallels in Cyprus where the class may well have originated.[34] The distribution of finds may then reflect export from one or more production centres in the island or local manufacture with the help of imported moulds or copies of these for the men's faces. A programme of chemical and petrological analyses of the clays, against the background of a large database, would obviously be helpful, though it cannot be ruled out that the clays travelled from one area to another.

---

[31] Crouwel 1991, 123 with pl. 4, g: London, British Museum WA93092 (1884.10–29.3). Ht. ca. 0.145 m.; L. (base) 0.078 m.

[32] See, most recently, Hermary 1990, 361; Crouwel 1991.

[33] Monloup 1984, 174f.

[34] Bisi 1982; 1989; Crouwel 1991, 123.

Our horseback rider, with his rather different facial features and headdress, does not belong to the class, while at the same time it displays the use of moulds in combination with hand-modelling. Though reportedly from Byblos in Phoenicia, a detail like the lacing at the front of the rider's tunic is again best paralleled in Cyprus.[35] In addition, the relatively large size of the model (height 0.325 m.), while contrasting with that of the general run of Cypriot terracotta riders on horseback, brings to mind an example from the 6th century B.C. shrine at Meniko, its height restored as 0.42 m.[36]

The detailed rendering of the rider's facial features, dress and equipment and of the mount's accoutrements cannot as yet be matched in Archaic Cypriot coroplasty. All the same, the fine model in Brussels, like the "personnages barbus de type assyrien", is in the tradition of terracotta production of the later 7th and 6th centuries B.C. in the island. An origin further east is unlikely: admittedly, the archaeology of Phoenicia is still poorly known, but there is as yet no good evidence to suggest a production of terracottas of such elaboration at this time.

[35] Controlled excavations at the site have produced some fragments of terracotta riding or chariot horses, again reminiscent of Cyprus, gee Dunand 1958, nos. 12655. 13211. 13261. 13311 with fig. 681.

[36] Supra n. 4. Cf. also an incomplete, limestone example from Tamassos (height 0.46 m.): Price 1931, no. C 81; Crouwel and Tatton-Brown 1988, pl. xxiv: 1 (here pl. 174).

30. EARLY STIRRUPS*

MARY AIKEN LITTAUER

The stirrup helped a more heavily armoured rider to mount a bigger horse; it is considered to have permitted the shock encounter with couched lance and, by offering lateral support, to have encouraged the development of the sabre; it provided a top-heavy armoured warrior with more stability in the saddle, and it gave archers the possibility to rise and turn in the saddle, as well as furnishing them with a firmer base from which to shoot.

Except among scholars keeping up somewhat with Far-Eastern discoveries, the most generally accepted opinion still seems to be that of Bivar 1955. He sees the original stirrup as basically the metal one we still know and as an invention of the southern Siberian or Altaic nomads, probably during the fifth century A.D., and diffused soon afterwards to China, Korea and Japan. Its earliest appearance west of the Altai would have been in late sixth-century A.D., or later, graves in Hungary, where its form points to the Chinese and where it was brought by the invading Avars. New material from the Far East, however, has pushed back the date for this type of stirrup, and a re-examination of some familiar documents as well as a reconsideration of other theories and of recent ethnographic parallels may show a more complex picture.

For the genesis of this seemingly simple invention has proved elusive. A proto-stirrup of rope or thong and/or wood has been suggested by some scholars, but strenuously rejected by others. Because it is only under exceptional conditions that such materials survive in the archaeological record, the likelihood of being able to settle the matter has seemed remote.

A treed saddle (i.e. a saddle with a tree: the two lengthwise wooden stretchers that unite and support the front and back bows) has also sometimes been considered a prerequisite for the secure attachment

* *Antiquity* 55, 1981, 99–105.

of a stirrup and that it would be futile to look for the latter before the former had made its appearance.

The roots of the word 'stirrup' have been cited as proof that the object's origin was in a rope to assist mounting, but this etymology has been seriously questioned.

The hanging strap in the horse-hobbling scene on the Chertomlyk vase was advanced by Arendt 1934, 206–208) in a well-known paper as evidence of an original strap stirrup. The fact, however, that this feature has turned out to be merely the loose end of the girth (Ambroz 1973, 81; Weinstein 1966, 63; autopsy by author) still need not eliminate the possibility of such a form of early stirrup. Nor need the objections raised that, were the rider thrown, it would tend to drag him necessarily do so (White 1962 19), since there is other evidence, both ancient and modern, for the use of strap stirrups. And it has the further disadvantage that, unless the rider is wearing stiff-soled boots, it can tighten up on the foot when much pressure is put on it, hence interfere with the circulation of the blood (Lázló 1943, 158).

Such considerations, however, did not stop the invention and use of a 'soft' big-toe stirrup, which would have had similar defects, as well as tending to dislocate the toe during violent action. The early existence of such a stirrup is documented at Sanci, in northwest India in the first century A.D. (des Noëttes 1931, pl. 261; White 1962, 14, 140, n. 7), and supposedly on a vase from the Kulu valley on the border of Kashmir, perhaps to be dated to the first/second centuries A.D. (des Noëttes 1931, pl. 263; White 1962, 15, n. 1). The latter actually looks more like a whole-foot stirrup. The big-toe stirrup has been in use in recent times in Ethiopa and the Sudan (des Noëttes 1931, pl. 397–399) and is acknowledged even by those who consider a 'soft' whole-foot stirrup impractical.

Moreover, figured evidence for the latter is to be found even earlier. At Mathura, between Agra and Delhi, c. 50 B.C., we find a rider with his naked foot in such a stirrup (pl. 192). This is not a 'girth stirrup', with the foot merely tucked under a 'loose surcingle' (White 1962, 14), as we do see once at Sanci (Zimmer 1955, pl. 12), but a separate element. It is forward of the real girth, indented just above the rider's foot, as a loose girth would not be, and has its own tab hanging free beneath it. An indented strap over the foot suggests the same thing on a less well-preserved first-century B.C. relief at Bhaja near Poona (Zimmer 1955, pl. 40). Stirrups in such forward locations are not unusual, even much later.

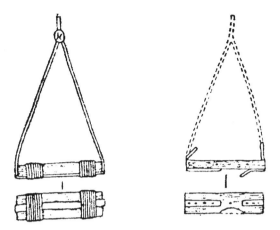

Fig. 1. (a) Recent thong and wood stirrup as used in central Russia; (b) stirrup from Rim Gori, 10th–12th centuries A.D., northern Caucasus. After Rounitch 1973 (a), Fig. 1: 20; (b), Fig. 1: 19.

A whole-foot rope or strap stirrup is sometimes used even today in Siberia and Central Asia (Kyzlassov 1973, 30 (pls. 193–194)). This suggests that the 'soft' stirrup, aside from its obvious role as a mounting aid (for which only one stirrup would be needed), may have had another use which, because not directly connected with the military, has been overlooked. Anyone who, not in training, has attempted to ride without stirrups for any considerable length of time will find that dangling feet get very tired and that hanging toes do not improve circulation – particularly in cold weather. The strap stirrup, as a mere support for the foot, could give relief here. For long hours of herding or travel, with the weight primarily on the riding pad or saddle and little pressure in the stirrup, such simple rope or leather loops might have provided comfort, as well as better lateral security – especially to the infirm or elderly (pl. *xxiia*).

Nevertheless, the problem of dragging a thrown rider or of squeezing the foot when too much weight was placed in such a stirrup would remain. The most obvious remedy could have been to set a rigid tread in the soft loop. A stirrup of this kind was employed not long ago by the peasants of central Russia (Rounitch 1973, 167). The pliable loop was spread to sufficient width by a wooden tread, the latter secured by lashing (fig. 1*a*). In a cemetery of the tenth-twelfth centuries A.D. at Rim Gori, near Piatigorsk in the northern Caucasus, where organic material was partly preserved, the remains of two strap stirrups with wooden treads were found (Rounitch 1973,

166). These treads had been secured to the straps with little nails (fig. 1*b*).

Because of their perishability, it would be hard to tell how far back in time such stirrups extended. A pair of iron rods, looped at either end, which were found in a cairn-pit burial with a bridle bit at Nagpur in central India and attributed to the 'early centuries B.C.' [*sic*], have been tentatively identified as metal stirrup treads (Leshnik 1971, 147, fig. 2:21). In the absence of similar finds or of figured evidence, this identification must remain in abeyance, yet even if correct, it is easy to see how barefooted riders in a hot climate would have been slow to put metal treads into general use.

Whether a wooden tread was a step in the direction of a complete wooden stirrup or not, wooden stirrups are not to be lightly dismissed as too fragile, as White has done (1962, 19). Although their material may make them less enduring than metal ones, they are well documented in recent times. They are to be found in Kazakhstan, Yakutia, Bashkiria and Tuva (Kyzlassov 1973, 33) (fig. 2). The stirrups of the American Plains Indians were made of wood and rawhide (Ewers 1955, 93), and stirrups of similar materials were for long the only type in use with the cowboy's saddle of the American Far West. In the latter two cases, at least, we know that they sustained considerable pressure under very active riders. The earliest entirely wooden examples known to me, however, date only from the eighth–ninth century A.D. in Mongolia (Kőhalmi 1968, 356) (fig. 3) and from the eleventh–twelfth centuries A.D. in Khakasia (Kyzlassov 1973, 34, fig. 6:1). Again, their material would discourage preservation, although, had they been in use in the Altai at the period of the Pazyryk tombs, we should expect to find them there. We shall return to this subject.

Moreover, we seem now to have evidence that the earliest preserved stirrups of roughly modern type had a wooden base, which may point to a yet earlier stirrup made entirely of wood: metal-sheathed wooden stirrups have been found in fourth-century A.D. tombs in northeastern China, as we shall see later.

The treed saddle as a prerequisite for the stirrup (Weinstein 1966, 67), or at least for its wider diffusion (Ambroz 1973, 94) may also be discarded. The Mathura stirrup (pl. 192) was clearly in use with only a flat pad. Pl. 194 shows a rope stirrup (of flat-braided camel and horse hair) used with a 'soft' saddle on the Iranian Turkoman steppe. In central Russia a peasant might ride with his rope or rope-

and-wood stirrup hung from a surcingle thrown over an old piece of blanket (Rounitch 1973, 167). The Blackfoot Indian of the North American prairies when fighting or hunting used a pad saddle constructed in a manner remarkably similar to that of the simplest Altai saddles – the fifth-century B.C. ones from Tuekhta. The first Indian pad saddles had no stirrups, and such saddles continued often to be ridden without stirrups but, by the early nineteenth century, they began to be used also with stirrups (Ewers 1955, 81–85). And these were rigid wooden stirrups – not merely 'soft' ones.

The roots of some of the words for stirrup may also be a more reliable source of information than is often conceded. Although the OED's derivation of stirrup from the Anglo-Saxon *stigan* (to climb) plus *rap* (rope) has been questioned and attributed to 'folk etymology' after the fact (Bivar 1955, 7; White 1962, 142, n. 1), there appears to be other etymological support for an original 'soft' stirrup. While the meaning of the word in other western European languages (French: *étrier*; Italian: *staffa*; Spanish: *estribo*) still seems uncertain and debatable, the root of the Russian word (*stremja*) and of the word in eleven other Slavonic languages, all deriving from the same root, means cord or strap, according to Russian etymologists (Kyzlassov 1973, 31f., n. 69). The function as an aid in mounting is found again, far to the east, in a completely unrelated language – Chinese – where it is made up of the word for horse (*ma*) and to climb or mount (*den*) (Ambroz 1973, 83).

While the earliest recognized evidence for rigid stirrups points to the East, it is not China, but southern Siberia that is suggested by Kyzlassov (1973, 30, fig. 5) for their first recorded appearance. His claims; however, of a third-century A.D. dating for chance finds of miniature bronze stirrups on the middle Yenissei, based on the assumption that the making of miniatures ceased after the Tashtyk period, have been denied by Weinstein (1966, 64f.). The latter states categorically that miniatures – as votive objects or toys – continued to be made in this region right into recent times, and his argument seems supported by the fact that this type of stirrup has not been found in normal-sized examples before another 300 years.

Moreover, experiments with a metal stirrup of quite different form may be traced to a much earlier date and far to the West. One of the terminals of a torque from a fourth-century B.C. Kurgan at Kul Oba in the Crimea shows a rider with a hook stirrup (pl. 195). We can see the small, bulbous, outer end, designed to protect the rider

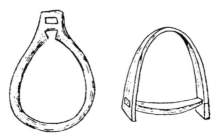

Fig. 2. Contemporary wooden stirrups from Khakasia and Yakutia. After Kyzlassov 1973, fig. 6: 3, 4.

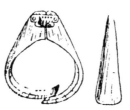

Fig. 3. Wooden stirrup from Khovd Sum in western Mongolia, 8th–10th centuries A.D. After Kőhalmi 1968, fig. 6: 12a.

from jabbing his foot, the inner shank, reaching to the upper calf, and four links of the chain by which the stirrup is suspended. M. J. Spruytte very generously offered to reproduce such a stirrup, in order to find out by experiment if it would be practical. The first essay was made with an inside shank no higher than the outside one. The resulting shallow, U-shaped element would not stay horizontal and was very unstable. A lengthening of the inner shank, to correspond with the proportions on the torque, however, produced a hook that would hang by itself (pls. 195, 196). It would be no more apt to drag a fallen rider (White 1963, 15) than would many normal metal stirrups. Its chief defect would have been that the high metal shank could rub against the rider's shin bone and the chain interfere with his knee. We must envisage at least some sort of small pad beneath the rider, and a girth – the latter presumably concealed by his leg.

The carefully rendered bulbous end of the tapering hook stirrup, as well as the shank and chain, differentiate this rider's equipment from that of the rider facing him on the opposite end of the torque. The strap that crosses the latter's instep is of equal width through-

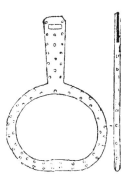

Fig. 4. Wooden stirrup covered with gilt bronze, from Kirin provinces in north-eastern China. First half of 4th century A.D. After Kaogu, 1977 (2), 124.

out and disappears beneath the trouser bottom; there is neither shank nor chain. The instep strap corresponds to similarly placed straps seen on dismounted Scythians (*e.g.* Artemonov 1974, pls. 45, 48), the function of which seems to have been to keep a rider's trousers down in place, in a manner similar to straps used for this purpose in Europe and America in the early nineteenth century.

The small scale of the figures, the general similarity between the outer part of the hook on the Kul Oba torque and the normal Scythian instep strap, and the absence of shank or chain in front of the other rider's leg, are undoubtedly responsible for the failure hitherto to recognize the feature as a hook stirrup. And why was it not repeated under both riders? Was the execution of this fine detail on so minute an object too troublesome to repeat? Or was the naturally realistic Greek artist of the time told for some reason not to repeat it?

This stirrup still might be dismissed as representing a merely abortive experiment, were it not for the fact that a Kushan gem of c. A.D. 50 in the British Museum (pl. 197a–b) shows what also appears to be a hook stirrup, although the tread is wider and there is no third, outer part to the hook. This seems to indicate a widespread and an enduring acquaintance with, if perhaps only a sporadic use of, a metal hook stirrup. The main problem is to account for the paucity of documents, but I hope to be able later to suggest an explanation that would fit the circumstances.

The next evidence is from the Far East. It is plentiful, and consists of rigid stirrups of already roughly modern form. At Wan-pao T'ing in Chi-an county of Kirin province in north-eastern China, stirrups have recently been found, together with metal saddle-bow plaques, in a tomb (no. 78) dated to the first half of the fourth century A.D. At Yu-shan, in the same region, tomb no. 41, of the mid fifth century A.D., contained saddle plaques and stirrups of the same type (*Kaogu* no. 2, 1977, 124–145. pls. 8–9). In 1979, *Kaogu* (no. 1, 27–32) again reported similar finds from a tomb at Kao-kou-li in the same area (fig. 4).

These are closely matched by numerous stirrups (fig. 5) and saddle-bow plaques found in fourth-sixth century A.D. tombs of the Silla kingdom in Korea (Ito 1971, 82–86, 139–142, pl. 3, 5, 15 and Abb. 56, 91), whence they went to Japan (fig. 6) (Onoyama 1966, 1f.). The fourth- and fifth-century examples of these are composed of a wooden base (in some cases heat-bent) covered with iron (sometimes silvered) and/or gilt-bronze sheeting. Those from the late fifth or early sixth century are of cast iron. These stirrups are not merely mounting aids. The fact that they are paired, that the treads soon show a tendency to widen from front to back and that these treads are frequently given small blunt studs (as modern treads are roughened or rubber-padded) to prevent the foot slipping in them, all point to an active use. It is interesting that Ito's 'Type 3', which is of cast iron and which he places in the A.D. 470–550 period, is very reminiscent, in its pear-like shape, of the well-known Chinese cast bronze stirrups in the Ashmolean Museum, Oxford (Bivar 1955, figs. 5a–b) and the Field Museum, Chicago (Rostovtzeff 1929, pl. XXIII: 4.), although in the Korean example the tongue for the stirrup leather could not be reconstructed from the remains. It is to this form of stirrup that the first examples found in Europe – those from late sixth- or (more probably) seventh-century Avar graves in Hungary – are considered to be related (Bivar 1955, 4).

The absence of firm evidence for a true metal stirrup anywhere west of China before this time is the more surprising. It is very difficult to understand why there is no trace of its use by Sarmatians, Parthians or Sasanians, although it seems to have been known (at least in its hook as well as its 'soft' form) in more than one region with which they would have been in contact.

Many of the new developments in the arms, armour and tactics of mounted warfare employed by these peoples (Bivar 1972) would have made such an aid desirable – if, apparently, not indispensible. The long, armoured trapper, reaching to below the horse's belly, would have impeded the rider's use of grip to secure his position on

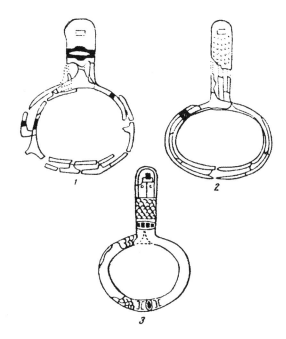

Fig. 5. Korean stirrups, 4th–6th centuries A.D. Nos. 1 and 2 with metal sheathing over wood base, no. 3 of cast iron. After Ito 1971, fig. 56.

the horse while, at the same time, his own increased body armour and the wielding of a long lance would have made him more top-heavy and susceptible to loss of balance than ever before. At least one Sarmatian grave stela of the first or second centuries A.D. at Kerch in the Crimea shows a horse wearing lamellar armour (Dessiatchikov 1972, fig. 3), as do some of the tomb paintings that survive from that site in only somewhat unreliable copies (Bivar 1972, fig. 2). Parthian Dura-Europus provides not only the well-known grafitto (Bivar 1972, fig. 5), but actual horse trappers of scale armour in both iron and bronze (Rostovtzeff 1936, 448, pls. xxi–xxiii) from the first century A.D. These show that it was only the horse's back immediately beneath a narrow saddle that was not covered with metal, and that the trapper hung free and straight, offering only a hard surface to the rider's legs. Also for the Parthian period we have the relief from Tang-i Sarwak (Ghirshman 1962, fig. 69). At Firouzabad the Sasanian king's horses wear long, leather housings with what seem to be metal appliqués (Ghirshman 1962, figs. 165f.). The type of direct attack with lowered lance – not spear or javelin – illustrated

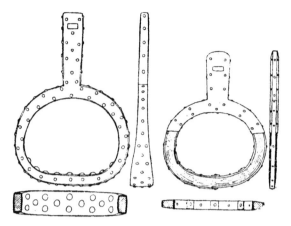

Fig. 6. Early Japanese stirrups, showing development towards widening of tread and studs on tread. After Onoyama 1966.

here was bound to have an unseating effect. While this may have been primarily fore-and-aft, such actions as the 'squire's' attempt to drag his opponent off his horse would clearly also threaten lateral balance – especially when the rider had neither stirrups nor the possibility of gripping with his calves.

Contemporaries of the Sasanians, the Huns, although their primary weapon was the bow rather than the lance, might also have used the stirrup to good advantage (Lázló 1943, 158). Although no trace of stirrups has been found even in those Hun burials that contained what were considered to be metallic saddle-bow plaques, this negative evidence has not been entirely conclusive, since such plaques had never been found with horse skeletons, hence the certainty of the presence of a complete set of saddle accessories. Just recently this question, as well as that of the form of the Hun saddle, seems to have been answered by the finding of 16 horse burials near Novorossiisk in the northern Caucasus (Dmitriev 1979; Ambroz 1979). These have been provisionally dated to the fifth century A.D. In four of the graves, saddle plaques (three of gold, one of silver) of a shape and decorated with a scale motif associated with Hun burials (Werner 1956, 50–53; pl. 52:13; 62:4, 5; Maenchen-Helfen 1973, 208–210) were found in situ over the animals' backs. Nothing remained of the organic parts of the saddle but, by careful deduction, Dmitriev has shown that these plaques could only have decorated the upper surfaces of the two parallel wooden planks that formed the saddle tree, in the area where they extended ahead of the front saddle bow. The plaques had previously presented a dilemma, because they did not fit any known shape of saddle bow. Ambroz (1979), in an appendix to Dmitriev's article, has reversed his former opinion that the treed saddle did not yet exist at this time and has shown that some other, small, motif-related elements would fit the *rear* projections of the tree. Something similar to the Avar saddle, with its nearly vertical front bow and its raking rear bow, has been suggested (Dmitriev 1979, fig. 5). The important thing for us here, however, is that *no stirrups were found*, although such metal fittings as the buckles belonging to girth, breastplate and crupper were still in place. If stirrups were indeed used, they must have been entirely of organic (and perishable) materials. They clearly were not objects to be enhanced with precious metals or, if of metal, to be considered appropriate as grave goods.

The majority of the saddle plaques of the Novorossiisk type show a scale pattern that is reminiscent of scale armour, and that is also found on the scabbards of Hunnic swords. This pattern recurs on some gilded bronze saddle-bow plaques and stirrup casings (fig. 5) found in fifth-century tombs in Korea (Ito 1971, 83, 89). This common motif only emphasizes the apparent absence of stirrups among the peoples we have just been discussing. One may hazard an explanation for the difference in practice between peoples, all of whom were ultimately of a steppe background, and those to the Far East. Early domestic horses were pony-sized. The Scythian horses of the Pontic steppes, for instance, according to Tsalkin (1960, 44) averaged 1.35 m. (13 hands 1"). Men must have been strong, agile and light. It may be assumed that all able-bodied men in a traditionally mobile, horse-breeding society could mount easily without stirrups. That same society, however, would have members – the infirm, the elderly, pregnant women – who would need assistance in mounting, and there might not always be someone present to 'give them a leg up'. A hanging strap would be a logical solution, and two stirrups of some kind would help them preserve their balance, once mounted (pl. 193). In a society with a strong riding tradition, this association with the feeble and infirm could make the stirrup seem unmanly and even disgraceful for a warrior. Even if it may sometimes have been used, it was not an object to be adorned, represented in art or included among grave goods. Such an attitude would help to explain a peculiar form like the hook, which would be less obvious than a full stirrup. On the Kushan stirrup even the outer vertical of the hook, which in actuality would have been useful in taking the outward pressure of the foot, seems to have been suppressed. Was this in an attempt to make the object as inconspicuous as possible?

The very different situation in the Far East may have been due to the fact that the *ridden* horse (as opposed to the *chariot* horse) began to be used in China only very late – 307 B.C. is the traditional date. The tomb of the First Emperor of Ch'in (Dien 1979, 45, fig. 1; Hearn 1980, 191f., pls. 101f.), near Sian in Shensi, has shown that at least at the time of his burial (206 B.C.) cavalry was still inferior in importance to chariotry and that it still showed a strong foreign (nomad) influence. The saddles, although undecorated, are identical in construction to some of those from the Pazyryk kurgans and the horses' tails are braided in a manner known only from those burials. The cavalrymen are considered to have been archers, which again suggests the nomad background.

Needless to say, there are no stirrups. But as China began to follow the example of southwest Asia in the use of the lance on horseback and of barded horses, she rapidly developed a rigid saddle, with high and unusually vertical back and front arches, in order to give more security to cavalrymen from a sedentary background (Ambroz 1973, fig. 5:2). The Chinese were not 'born in the saddle'; they had no long-held horsemen's traditions; a high-arched saddle or a stirrup would not be for them a symbol of womanish weakness; the national reverence for age would preclude any prejudices due to its infirmities. The stirrup could easily here be a legitimate and respected part of the equipment of a cavalryman's or an official's horse, hence of his grave goods.

The stirrup, as it first appears in the West in seventh-century A.D. Avar graves in Hungary, so close in form to that of contemporary Chinese examples, seems to be an indication that all-metal stirrups of this type came fairly directly from China. This does not rule out the possibility, however, that stirrups of other form – indistinguishable from ordinary hooks, or of organic materials – had long been in use in the areas between, even if not granted a respectable place among horse gear. Kyzlassov (1973, 36) indeed suggests that the stirrup probably did not originate in one single place or in one single form or material. Present evidence, however, appears to indicate that it had first assumed its approximately final form in northeast China by the fourth century A.D.

Acknowledgements

I am greatly indebted to Dr J. Clutton-Brock for calling my attention to the hook stirrup of the Kul Oba torque and for generously allowing me to publish her discovery, and to M. J. Spruytte for his reconstruction and practical testing of such a stirrup. My thanks also go to Dr W. Zwalf for supplying me with photographs of the Kushan gem and its impression under different lightings, to Dr A. Soper who interpreted the recent Chinese textual material, and to Mrs Emma Bunker, for enabling me to study detailed photographs of the Bhaja and Sanci material.

31. HOW GREAT WAS THE "GREAT HORSE"? A REASSESSMENT OF THE EVIDENCE*

MARY AIKEN LITTAUER

Was the knight's "great horse" all that the term "great" sometimes implies of stature, power and mass? Or was he simply the big horse of the time? For the *magnus equus* of the medieval documents can be translated today as well by "big horse" as by "great horse". Our ancestors used the term "great" more frequently than we do when all they meant was big and nothing more. And if the knight's horse was big, how big was he? Everything is relative, and a big horse in say, the 14th century would only have to be bigger than the rounceys and palfreys and pack horses around him. But would he have looked even big to modern eyes? The horses ridden by the military of ancient and postclassical times were small. Without a stirrup it was more difficult to mount, easier to lose one's balance (particularly when wielding weapons), and harder to rein in an excited horse. A small horse would have been preferable to a large one in any one of these circumstances. Cavalry was a lightly mounted, skirmishing, flanking, pursuing arm. With the possible exception of the cataphracts (and even these are shown mounted on very light horses on the Column of Trajan – the chief source of information about them). There was nothing to change this picture before the appearance of the stirrup. Thus it is useless to look for a heavy warhorse in very early Middle Ages.

The first evidence of the stirrup in western Europe is found in Swedish Vikings' graves of the 8th century A.D., but a series of mss. illuminations reveal that it was not immediately universally adopted and that its full possibilities were not realised for another 400 years. During this time stirrups were affixed to a saddle with outward curving pommel and cantle, the leg hung vertically, light spears continued to be *cast*, and the only hand-to-hand fighting on horseback

* *Light Horse*, Vol. 13 (no. 144, 2/6), 1963, 350–352.

occured when swords were drawn or maces raised. There was little reason to increase the size or weight of the horse. We have material proof of this in skeletal evidence from 9th century Norway. The horse remains from the Oseberg and Gökstad Viking ship burials reveal animals averaging 14 hands. Since the Vikings were the "tall-men" of their day, since they prized their chargers highly, and since all the coasts of Europe were open to their trading or pillaging, they would surely have taken their pick of the sizes available. In fact, the horse remains from the Danish port of Hedeby (destroyed by fire in the 11th century) show such a variety of types as to indicate wide importation. These horses range from 13 hands 2 ins. to 14 hands 2 ins.

If the Bayeux tapestry is to be trusted – and it must be remembered that it was produced by the winning (and horsy) side, and that few horsemen care to see themselves glorified at the expense of their animals – then the steeds that the Normans (who were supposed to have lost some stature themselves after two centuries of French living) rode to the conquest of England were even smaller than the horses used in Scandinavia. And the same size of horse appears on continental art. Since this is a time of vertical-leg riding it is true that every inch of rider's leg possible shows below the belly of the horse. On the other hand, when we look at these horses and men we unconsciously measure them by our own scale. Although there are more suits of armour (from the 15th and 16th centuries, that is) for big men than is generally believed, and although we may safely assume that the privileged classes of the Middle Ages who lived on a rich (if not necessarily balanced) diet, were consistently bigger than the general population, it has been established by anthropologists that modern man in the more advanced parts of the western world (and particularly of the English-speaking world) is substantially larger than his forbears of even only 100 years ago. We must keep this in mind when measuring horse against man in early representations. The full potential of the combined stirrup and saddle and the changes this permitted in armament and tactics (which in turn called for a bigger horse) was realised only in the first half of the 12th century. The saddle now acquired a high, embracingly curved cantle, against which the knight could brace himself by "putting his feet on the dashboard" and both *thrust* with a couched lance and receive the shock of his opponent's thrust. As a result, stronger defensive armour became desirable and its weight was increased. Even so, horses do not seem to have increased greatly in size to meet the new conditions of warfare.

The 14th and 15th centuries saw the development of plate armour continually increasing in coverage and weight as first the clothyard arrow and then crossbow began to pierce mail, and then as gunpowder started to play its unchivalrous role. Finally, even the horse is clad in plate (in France from about the middle of the 15th century). Although with the strength added to plate by the invention of fluting, armour took on no more weight after the end of the 15th century, it continued to be used for both horse and man right through the 16th century. It is in these centuries that the horse was called upon to bear his heaviest burden and here it is that we must most seriously look for the Great Horse. Luckily for us, the 15th century is one of enormous artistic energy and greatly improved draughtsmanship. The products of this confirm the emergence of an undoubtedly robust type of charger, yet not necessarily one of great stature. With various devices in the saddle to secure the rider, the pendulum of the leg is beginning at times to swing back towards the vertical again. It is a good bit higher up the horse's side than it was in the 11th century, with the rider's sole now only a few inches below the girth or just even with it. But not all chargers are heavy, even now.

Fig. 1. "It was not until the first half of the 12th century that a high, supporting cantle permitted a strongly braced seat. This led to changes in warfare, armour and, ultimately, in the knight's horse."

Fig. 2. Warriors of the 10th century, with long straight stirrup outward sloping cantle, and light cast spears. (Cod. Peris. 17, Library of the University of Leyden).

The Metropolitan Museum of Art in New York City displays a cortege of horsemen in full panoply of plate covering the period 1490 to 1575. The horse models are in plate armour or tilt trappings. These animals are suitably scaled to their appointments and when measured (through the courtesy of the curator of the Arms and Armour Department) they were found to stand two of them at 14 hands 2 in., and four at 14 hands 3 in. The weight of the horse equipment alone ranged from 64 to 92 lb. In the Musee de l'Armee at les Invalides in Paris, similar models for the same time were measured by kind permission of the guard. The following dates and dimensions were obtained: 1480–1490, 14 hands 2 ins.; 1533, 15 hands 1 1/2 ins.; 1540, 15 hands 2 ins. It was noticed that on these French models the armour did not descend quite so far on the horse's chest as that on the Metropolitan Museum ones. It afforded less protection, and corresponded less to the fitting of horse armour as evidenced in the art of the period. The disparity was not great – a matter of 1 in. to 3 ins., yet this would be enough to reduce by that much the heights of the horses listed above. It should also be noted that the 1540, 15 hand 2 ins. horse carried Francis I, the tallest monarch of his time and a man well over six feet. And now at last we come upon written evidence, a 1534 edict of Francis I confirms the retention of the gendarmerie, the first regular cavalry corps an elite body founded by Charles VII at the end of the 100 Years War. The edict stipulates that of the 100 mounted men and 150 archers who composed each company, the 25 "most robust" horsemen, wearing complete plate armour, should be mounted on horses bearing head, chest, and flank armour, and that these steeds should not be less than 15 hands. This accords very well with Henry VIII's edicts of the '40s. These were enacted for the "encrease of stronger horses" as a help to the "defence of the realm", yet only in one instance, that of the Depasturing of Stallions on Commons, is a height of as much as "15 handfulls" required. Oddly enough, the stoned horses that are to be kept by noblemen are put at "14 handfulls". It is further illuminating that, by the time of Elizabeth, it was found that certain areas of "marishes and fenne gronndes" were not able to sustain such "great breeds" (i.e. the 15-hand horses) as were stipulated by Henry VIII, and the size was reduced to 13 hands. Will the reader kindly note the use of the adjective "great" in the previous sentence, and to what size it was applied.

It is in the early 16th century that we find an illustration that has so frequently been presented to us as the prototype of the Great Horse that it dominates our imaginations. Dürer's "Great Horse" was engraved in 1505 along with a companion piece, the "Little Horse". It has always seemed curious to this writer that, although Dürer depicted at least two perfectly plausible warhorses *under armoured knights*, that in the "St George", and that in the "The Knight, Death, and the Devil", this unsaddled creature, whom no rider except a ploughboy used to sitting sideways could possibly contemplate with pleasure, was chosen to represent the *destrier*. It seems to have been first selected for this purpose by Sir Walter Gilbey in his "The Old English War-Horse or Shire-Horse" in 1884. Sir Walter in his "Great Horse" of 1899 did yeoman's work in ransacking early documents relative to the horse in England, and everyone interested in the subject must be grateful to him (even when not agreeing with all of his conclusions). Yet why did he again in 1899 choose this animal as an example of the typical knightly steed, and write that the "Shire Horse is the purest survival of the type described by medieval writers as the Great Horse"? The answer seems to be that, as a breeder of Shires himself and a prime mover in the Shire Horse Society, he took a perhaps excessively romantic view of the heavy draft type.

He may have felt his assumption justified too in this particular case by the fact that the groom is in armour, as is the groom in the pendant engraving, the "Little Horse". The armour and helmet are, however, of a fantastic, parade sort, not battle dress. Dr Franz von Juraschef, in his "Albrecht Dürer", says that this pair of pictures are simply studies in extremes of proportion, which fascinated Dürer, as they did so many sons of the Renaissance. Thus this creature may represent the exceptional rather than the usual aspect of the large horse of the time and there is nothing at all to prove that he was a riding horse.

Even this animal, when analysed, turns out to be not so big as he at first appears. It is peculiar that, although the horse is standing still, the groom is striding along with bent knees, and so is not drawn up to his full height. Even so, his head and neck are fully above the withers. Let us grant the man a height of six feet, which would be very generous for a member of the under-privileged classes at this time, and take off only an inch for the flexed knees. Even a small man's head and neck will add up to 10 in. Take 11 in. from 72 ins. and you are left with 61 ins., or 15 hands 1 in., for the most

Fig. 3. Dürer's 16th century armoured knight shows clearly the proportions between mount and man at that period.

Fig. 4. Dürer's "Großes Pferd", 1505 A.D., often used to illustrate the knight's
        "great horse" but with seemingly little justification.

massive candidate for the role of Great Horse. This is beside the
fact that Sir Walter made a basic error in evidently assuming that
the conformation best adapted for weight *pulling is* the same as that
most suitable for weight *bearing*. Perhaps he believed that the Great
Horse was modified in the direction of draft by selective breeding
in the intervening centuries. But it could have been modified also
in the direction of size – and then we do not have much of the
original left.

Thus we have come to the end of the the Middle Ages, and a
little beyond, for good measure. If there ever was a formidably great
horse by modern standards he seems to have slipped through our
fingers. Is this possible? Size and weight beyond those essential for
any task follow the law of diminishing returns. Again and again we
see the smaller animal able to carry a greater weight in proportion
to his size than the larger one; we see him staying sound longer.
Before the days of scientific feeding and modern veterinary practices
there was even less chance of the overlarge individual reaching healthy
maturity – or staying workable if he did. While there must constantly

have been the temptation to have a warhorse who would impose by his mass and height this must have been frustrated in practice by the limitations of nature – barring those exceptions that always occur. Perhaps our conception of the knight's Great Horse is due to be revised – downwards.

32. AFTER SEEING THE SPANISH RIDING SCHOOL*
A CLASSICAL HERITAGE?

MARY AIKEN LITTAUER

The recent performances of the Spanish School of Vienna in this country displayed a nice combination of colour and precision. They were of especial interest to the amateur of dressage, for they enabled him to compare some movements (the collected trot and canter, the passage, two tracks, and pirouettes) executed in the manner of traditional (17th and 18th century) manege riding with the same as performed in modern international dressage. To the breeder it was enlightening to observe a horse that has changed little in 200 years, and that represents a strain which was one of the most highly prized of its time. To the horseman who is a lover of history it was a delight to see one phase of the equestrian past recreated with an accuracy beyond the capacity of movie-makers, no matter how spendthrift. And, for us all, it was a privilege to be able to witness the old dramatic airs of High School, which are no longer performed by anyone else with the splendor and dignity that are their rightful accompaniment. The Spanish School is a conservatory in the truest sense of the word.

For all this we are very gratetul. But the visit has been stimulating in another way too: it has made us ask once more "how?" and "why?" What are the real origins of High School? Disregarding for the moment whether the rearings and prancings of the horses of Greece and Rome were executed in a manner to deserve the term High School, was the manege riding of the 16th, 17th, and 18th centuries set consciously upon an antique plinth? One frequently runs across the assertion that manege riding was based upon Xenophon, with a few contributions from the Middle Ages – put there to account for those "airs" (the capriole, croupade, etc.) not faintly resembling

* *The Chronicle of the Horse*, Vol. 37 (no. 24), February 5, 26–27 (Part I), *The Chronicle of the Horse*, Vol. 37 (no. 25), February 12, 22–25. (Part II).

anything to be found in ancient art. The place to look for an answer to these questions is among the articulate and influential masters of the art of High School in the days of its growth (16th century) and of its fullest flowering (17th and 18th centuries). If anyone consciously imitated precepts or examples, or shaped its course, it was these men. And there were strong reasons why they should be drawn to do so. In the period of the Revival of Learning there was a profound reverence for antiquity, and a prevalent (and often correct) belief that the ancients had done things much better. Men were familiar with the doings of antiquity; education meant a classical education. Those who did not know Greek at least knew Latin, and Greek authors were rapidly being translated into the latter tongue. The 16th century produced no less than nine editions of three separate Latin translations of Xenophon containing his equestrian writings, the "Horsemanship" and the "Cavalry Commander." Three of these had appeared by 1545. The first French translation was to come out in 1613.

Fig. 1. A 17th century master of High School writes of the riders of antiquity: "I say that the most part of the Postures they have given to the horse should not be imitated. . . . The Horses of the Ancients were in no ways managed and but little under Subjection." (Marburg Art Reference Bureau).

Renaissance Masters of Equitation

The first Renaissance master of equitation to write on his subject
and to mention High School airs was Federico Grisone, a Neapolitan
gentleman who flourished in the middle of the 16th century. He was
one of the most famous horsemen of his day, and did much to make
the reputation of the School of Naples. The admired Neapolitan
strain of horses contained some of the same blood as the Lipizzaners.
Naples was then a dominion of the King of Spain, with a viceroy
and court in residence. Andalusian horses (the finest of Spain) went
to southern Italy as well as to Austria in this century.

Grisone's historic work, "Gli Ordini di Cavalcare", was first published in 1550. At the beginning of his first chapter the author is
anxious to display his familiarity with antiquity; he speaks of the
horses of Alexander and Caesar, those who "danced" for the Sybarites,
and others enshrined in classical literature. But not a single reference is made to Xenophon or to any "principles" inherited from the
great past. If Grisone was not already familiar with Xenophon's
works himself, his attention would have at least been called to them
by some of his pupils – especially in an age and a country where
learning was an adornment of courtly life. The translator of the first
French edition of Grisone (1559) is also eager to cite the classics.
He names no fewer than eleven Greek Hippiatrists (horse anatomists
and veterinarians), but not Xenophon.

A contemporary of Grisone's, Caesar Fiaschi, a gentleman of
Ferrara, founded a school in that north Italian town. The nobility
of northern Europe flocked there, as they flocked to Naples, to learn
the horsemanship. He was the teacher of the famous Pignatelli who,
in his turn, taught la Broue and Pluvinel. Fiaschi's "Trattato" appeared
in 1556. This work on schooling, bitting, and shoeing contains no
mention at all of classical riding. It too was translated into French
(in 1564) and a different translator again spent a good deal of his
preface in references to the horses of antiquity, but he nowhere connected the equitation of the remote past with that of his own day.

The French Writers

The next important work to appear was in French. La Broue was
a well-known horseman and an equerry to the King of France; his

"Cavalrice Francois" first came out in 1594. This long and thorough book contains no mention of Greek or Roman horsemanship. A teacher of great fame and influence was Pluvinel. With royal patronage he founded a school in Paris for the sons of the nobility. This was not only a riding school; mathematics, literature, painting, and music were also taught there. Pluvinel, who was one of the tutors of the dauphin, was a cultivated gentleman quite capable of giving his subject a historical background. He does not do so, however, in his writings, "Le Maneige Royal" (1623) or "L'Instruction du Roy" (1625).

The Duke of Newcastle, whose formidable work, "La Methode nouvelle and Invention extraordinaire de dresser les Chevaux" (1657) first appeared in French because he was at the time a royalist exile on the continent, fails to recognize any debt to antiquity. In the next century the extremely influential de la Gueriniere (to whom the Spanish School looks consciously back) also ignores the ancients in his "Ecole de Cavalerie" (1733). These men, Grisone, Fiaschi, la Broue, Pluvinel, Newcastle, and de la Gueriniere, were the acknowledged pillars of High School in the period when it played its greatest role. If they believed they were reviving the glories of Greece or Rome, they kept a strange silence on the subject. Another, less known, but highly qualified horseman did express himself, however. He still did not refer to Xenophon directly or to any early "principles", but he did tell what the educated 17th-century rider thought of the way antiquity rode.

Jacques de Solleysel (1617–1680) was the pupil of Menou, Pluvinel's friend and favorite pupil. When he accompanied a diplomatic mission to Germany, he also studied German schooling and veterinary methods. On his return to France he founded two schools, one in Paris and one in the provinces. His "Parfait Mareschal" (1664) was the first regular veterinary work to appear in the French language. It reveals a familiarity with the Greek and Roman authors on the subject. He made a second French translation of Newcastle in 1677, and was the champion of many of the latter's methods on the continent. Besides this, he is known to have had a talent for music, for painting, and for making friends. The fact that his work came out in 10 editions and 31 reprints in France (the last in 1782), and also in English and German translations, testifies to its extensive popularity and influence.

De Solleysel Deprecates Classical Influence

It was his interest in art that led de Solleysel to discuss the manner in which men rode in classical times. He felt very strongly about the fact that contemporary artists were too much under the influence of classical art in their equestrian subjects, and that they misrepresented the horses and riding they saw around them. I give his words in Sir William Hope's translation, which appeared in the latter's "Compleat Horseman" (1696).

> It is certain that all the famous Painters and excellent Carvers, design and aim at nothing so much as to imitate Antiquity ... to give you a few instances of it I shall discourse of the Attitude or Situation, which is properly the Postures in which they put the Horses they represent; and, I say, that the most part of the Postures they have given to Horses should not be imitated in this Age wherein we live. The Horses of the Ancients were no ways Managed, and but little under Subjection; and all the Actions they represented them performing under a Man appeared Desperate and Furious, because the Riders themselves did not know what to require of them. Their Bitts, which were badly chosen, and capable to render a horse desperate, might contribute much to it, especially the Riders being not at all Horsemen ... they caused their Horses ... to perform such Actions as would appear to us now a Days so strange and extravagant ... and contrary to all the Rules of Art (the art of High School) ... Moreover, since the Art of Bitting Horses is arrived at its greatest Perfection, the Bitts which are made use of now a Days, besides that they place a Horse's Head right, give also his Neck the most beautiful Turn and Situation it is capable of, without forcing him to open his Mouth as the Bitts of the Ancients did, which cut and spoil'd the Barrs and were of no other use but to torment a Horse and make him show a Pair of wide frightful Jaws. I ask any Man of Sense if we should imitate the Ancients in those Things, wherein they were wrong and erred; if they have represented Horses in Postures of Rage and Despair, they could not do otherwise because they knew no better; but now a Days to represent under a King, great Prince or General of an Army, a Horse in such Actions ... would be enough to make the Spectators believe, that either the Rider knows not how to Govern him or that the Horse is altogether disobedient, which would be thought ridiculous; because Persons of that Condition and Quality mount no Horses but such as are ... under a perfect Subjection, their Heads and Necks exactly well placed, and performing some fine Pesade or becoming Passage, which make them appear Brisk and Stately, without seeming in the least to deny that perfect Obedience which they should give to their Masters. And much more of the same. ("The Compleat Horseman", edition of 1717, pages 14, 15).

Making due allowance for Baroque exaggeration, there is truth in what de Solleysel writes. We know that the ancient riding bits (in contrast to the driving snaffles) were severe. But they did not, until later Roman times at least, have a curb action, and the horse was able to fight the bit with his head in the air. The often seemingly equally diabolic bits of the Renaissance all had curb action, which brought the head in and gave the riders greater control over the horse. And the better riders of the period, using milder forms of these bits, were able to make a horse go on contact. The stimulated movements and raised airs were so familiar to the 17th century horseman that anything irregular in their execution would strike him sooner than they would us. This is perhaps why the eyes of few in modern times have been caught by the obvious defects in ancient riding. It seems clear that the great masters of High School consciously adopted neither the "principles" nor the practices of antiquity. It remains to be seen whether they owed any debt to the medieval war-horse. There has long been a romantic inclination to find a military origin for the more spectacular airs of High School. They are supposed to have been based on movements the horse was taught to make to defend himself or his rider, or to discomfit the enemy. The Spanish Riding School's visit, by giving us a renewed glimpse of elevated airs, has once more raised this stubborn and entertaining ghost. The only way to go about laying it is to examine the early witnesses once more.

Four high airs were demonstrated here: the levade, pesade, capriole, and courbette. The levade is a low rear off bent hocks, with hind legs and forelegs lined up and forelegs bent under the body; the pesade is the same thing at a higher (45 degree) angle; the capriole is an air above the ground, with body horizontal, forelegs lined up and bent together under the body, and hindlegs out together in a horizontal kick; at the courbette the animal assumes a pose similar to the pesade, but advances with a series of leaps off the hocks, without lowering the forehand. To the masters of the 16th and 17th century schools the levade and pesade were lumped together under the term posade, of which there were high or low variations. In those days the courbette was a less difficult movement than the modern Spanish School's version of it; Newcastle and la Gueriniere develop it from a short high gallop in two beats – that is, with both forelegs striking the ground approximately together, and both hindlegs striking it approximately together and almost immediately after the forelegs have come down, so that these can go right up again. Garsault in "Le Nouveau Parfait Marechal" (1746), defines it as an "air where the horse, lowering the quarters, raises the forehand, and lowering the forehand, raises slightly the hindlegs." The old engravers usually show it at its moment of greatest elevation, when it is indistinguishable from the levade. I shall here use the term courbette only in this earlier sense, and I shall call all formalized rears posades. There are other dramatic High School airs but they are all based either on the horse's ability to rear or his ability to spring forward and/or kick.

Fig. 2. The same teacher of High School writes of the properly schooled horses of his own time that they are "under a perfect Subjection, their Heads and Necks exactly well placed." (Illustration from Baron Eisenberg's "Description du Manege Moderne", 1727).

Airs Based on Rearing

Those airs based on the rear have the most venerable ancestry. That horses were made to rear at the rider's will in antiquity is clear, both from the writings of Xenophon and from classical art. What is not so clear is whether these movements were executed according to any strict standards and may justifiably be called High School. And it is safe to say that many of the rearing horses in classical (as well as later) art are not executing a formal rear at their rider's behest. Some are rearing over an object on the ground, some are rearing to indicate a (clumsily rendered) phase of the gallop, some are placed in this position by the artist simply to convey the terror and excitement of battle, or to make an individual figure more dramatic. It is a commonplace of artistic composition that, while a horizontal line is static, a diagonal one is dynamic. A rearing horse was a good strong diagonal ready to hand for any artist depicting a battle scene. It has been a common prop through the centuries.

This artistic value of the rearing horse has been misleading. Taken together with some lines from the 5th-century B.C. historian, Herodotus, in which he describes a horse who had been trained to rear and strike infantrymen with his feet and savage them with his teeth (V,3), it has led to the assumption that horses were taught to rear for this purpose in battle. It may be suggested that Herodotus would not have bothered to make a special thing of it had it been common practice. And the most famous horseman of antiquity, Xenophon himself, bears witness against it. He not only does not recommend any such practice in either the "Horsemanship" or the "Cavalry Commander", but in the "Anabasis" (111,2) he writes "No one yet died in battle from having been bitten or kicked by a horse; it is men who do what is done in battle."

If the rear was not practical for fighting when horses were unarmed, it would have made even less sense in the later Middle Ages, when they were covered with long boiled-leather or mail housings, or plate armour. To expose a charger's unprotected belly to the blade of any dismounted man in front of him would have made little sense. But processions and triumphs, the very occasions for which Xenophon suggests a dramatic rear to impress the multitude, went on wending their colourful way right through the Middle Ages. All the Renaissance manege had to do was to take the dutiful rear out of the parade, give it stricter rules, and call it a posade.

Kicking and Leaping

It seems clear why the movements based on kicking and "leaping", of which the capriole is the most difficult, were never popular in antiquity. The horses were ridden without saddles and had little "front." The movements would not have been pleasant to sit, and they were more a display of skill than of dignity or grace. Riders would probably have had little taste for them before the saddle came into use, which in the western world would mean after the late 4th century A.D. But was their purpose – except for the ruade, or plain kick – military? Again the factor of heavy armour (on both horse and man) enters the picture – from the 13th century on, anyway. It is hard to see how a horse could have executed such movements under a cumbrous and weighty load, even had the rider been in a position during the heat of battle to give the proper signals or the horse to receive them. It was quite clear, for instance, to those who watched

Fig. 3. Even the unique teacher who recommended that the horse assist his master in the manner here shown suggests no connection between this action and any High School Movement. (From V. Trichter's edition of Lohneisen, 1729).

the Spanish School here that even under proper manege conditions every raised air required an interval of preparation, during which the animal was being highly collected etc.

Regarding these leaps, it is significant that Fiaschi, the second author after Grisone to mention them, writes ("Traicte" French edition of 1564, page 90) that the rider should not use for them a saddle with long straight quards in front such had been used in the past to protect the rider's knees in a press or shock with other horses. These prevent the rider from bending his knees to give the proper signals, other details of the old war saddle make it insecure for "leaps", and the rider may even be pitched off! Hardly a desirable thing in the fighting line. As to the difficulty of obtaining the capriole even on an unburdened manege horse, Pluvinel has the following to say in his "Instruction du Roy"; (Frankfort edition of 1628, page 81),

> There are in truth so few horses capable of naturally, executing caprioles well that I have known only four in your Kingdom (he is addressing the king of France) who, with a combination of strength and lightness executed this air" and (page 83) "Few horses are proper for executing caprioles, in that in the first place they must have great strength, be very light, nervous, and well founded on their legs and feet, because the shock (of this movement) ruins them more than any other.

It sounds as though we might safely eliminate the capriole from the average knight's repertoire.

There is one very valuable piece of figured evidence from the very late medieval period, valuable because it is not just an artist's conception of how he thinks a knightly fracas should look, but a serious illustration of a manual executed under the direction supervision of the author. King Rene of Anjou (1409–1480) longed to revive the dying age of chivalry. He was the acknowledged authority of the period on everything to do with knighthood, and he wrote a treatise on the proper way to hold a tournament, the "Traictie de la Forme et Devis d'un Tournoi." The large illumination in this manuscript that depicts the climax of the tournament, the grand melee, with the Queen of Beauty looking on, shows no horse doing anything more elaborate than pushing and showing.

Evidence Against the Fighting Horse

But although we may feel that we have swept the high airs from the medieval battlefield we still have to answer those people who believe that they were used on unarmoured horses by the Renaissance or Baroque cavalryman – presumably after the enemy had run out of bullets. For this period there is a lot of contemporary evidence – some of it at least seemingly for the opposition. In 1570 William Blundeville translated Grisone (the first author to mention airs) into English, and added a few words of his own among them these (referring to the courbette and the capriole):

> Unless your horse be naturally light of his body and nimble of his legs, it is impossible by Art to make him do any of these things well; and to say the truth, they be things that may be very well spared, and specially in horses of service (military horses), which being once used to such delighting toies, do forget in time of need their necessary feats. For when they are spurred to go forward . . . they fall a hopping and dancing up and down in one place. Likewise, when in their manege they should make a speedy round, and just turn . . . they will not turn but leisurely with the Corvetti: and therefore I would wish none of the Queens Majesties Horses to be used for the Corvetti but such as are only left for pleasure. ("The Art of Riding," edition of 1609, page 36).

This not only confirms what we suspected about horse and rider getting their signals mixed in the heat of battle, but clearly implies that the "delighting toies" had no place in serious warfare. In 1594 la Broue, an old soldier, was saying something similar in France;

> It is almost as great a mistake to wish to use a horse for war who is born for leaping as it is to make one leap who is suitable only for low airs . . . it is very unpleasant for a completely armed rider who is on a nervous horse with natural leeping ability, from whom he cannot obtain four passades or war voltes without suffering the discomfort to his spine of such leaps as to put him out of breath and hors combat. ("Le Cavelrice Franscois", edition of 1646, page 133).

That this particular shoe was still pinching 60 years later we know from the Duke of Newcastle, who loudly disclaims any difficulties:

> Some wagg perhaps will ask, what is a horse good for that can do nothing but dance and play tricks? . . . if those gentlemen were to fight a duel, or to go to the wars, they would find their error, for these horses perform a journey as well as they do the high airs; and the

long marches occasionally make them soon forget those airs which are calculated merely for pleasure; moreover they are much fitter for galloping, trotting, whealing or anything else which is necessary." "Horsemanship," edition of 1743, page 14).

In trying to sell High School to his pragmatically minded fellow countrymen, Newcastle, who had known war intimately as one of Charles I's generals, would surely have cited any positive application of the high airs in battle, instead of protesting that those airs "calculated merely for pleasure" could be avoided, and defending them only by claiming that they made the horse fitter.

In 1696 another military man, Sir William Hope, Deputy-Lieutenant of the Castle of Edinburgh, who was also looking for incentives to make British horsemen study manege riding, writes:

> Curvets and other Ayres, settle a Horse mightily upon the Hand, make him light before, and put him upon his Haunches, which is very useful, especially for a man in armour; for did his Horse stop upon the Shoulders, he would give his rider (being armed) such a shock as would make his Bones ake were he never so found ... But, says a Gallant, when I should have Use for him in the Field, then he would be playing his Tricks: But this is a great Mistake for the Helps to make Horse go in Ayres, and to make them go upon the Ground, are vastly different ... so that if you let them alone they will not trouble you; besides, two or three Days March will make them that they will not go in Ayres if you would have them. ("The Compleat Horseman", edition of 1717, Part 1, page 246).

Again, there is not only no suggestion of using elevated airs in warfare, but the author feels obliged to reassure his readers that there is no danger of the horse going inadvertently into them.

La Gueriniere is another manege rider who endeavors to defend manege schooling for the war horse. But even he does not go so far as to claim that any of the high airs are useful in battle. In his "Ecole de Cavalerie", 1733, page 78 he writes:

> There are, according to ordinary usage, two sorts of manege, that of war and that of the cariere or school.... The war manege means the developement of a sensible horse, comfortable and obedient to both hands, who springs forward swiftly, stops and turns easily on the haunches, who is used to gunfire, drums and banners and who is afraid of nothing.... By the cariere or school manege one should understand all the airs invented by those men who have excelled in this art. And on page 150: The passage ... makes the action of a horse that is at the head of a troup high and noble. By means of Voltes (in this

Fig. 4. Did the theory of the military origin of High School "airs" grow out of something like this imaginative illustration, which may have misled unwary readers? (From a chapter added to a translation of Grisone, Augsburg, 1608).

Fig. 5. The Ruade, seldom displayed today and infrequently mentioned by the old masters, is still the most likely candidate for an "air" that might have had some practical use in battle. (From Trichter's edition of Lohneisen, 1729).

case a circle on two tracks) one attains the croup of one's enemy and surrounds him diligently . . . Pirouettes and Half-pirouettes make it easier to turn around more swiftly in combat . . . And if the raised airs have no advantage of this nature, they at least have that of giving a horse the lightness that he needs to negotiate hedges and ditches.

Evidence to the Contrary

All the evidence quoted is supported by yet other passages in these and other authors. Whence, then, comes the theory of the fighting horse? At least two plates in early books may be partly responsible for it. The first adorns the third of four apocryphal "books" to a German translation of Grisone (Augsburg 1608). This particular book is devoted to tricks of single combat – or How to Get the Better of your Enemy in Twenty Unchivalrous (and often quite unrealistic) Ways. One of these, for instance, is to seize your enemy's reins and throw them over his neck! The one plate of interest to us, that showing a horse throwing himself at the croup of another, is accompanied by the following text.

> The Thirteenth Combat Trick – with Spear and Dagger. If you ride against someone and meet or miss him, turn quickly, drop your spear, spring from your horse, seize your enemy with one hand and with the other draw your dagger, and thus you will easily be able to overcome and injure him. We may add, If your enemy hasn't had the sense to get away in the meantime or turn and seize you himself.

It is interesting that nothing at all is said in the text about the nicely cooperative horse. Fifteen years earlier la Broue, writing on the warhorse, had advised the horseman that

> Whatever the horse, if it is inclined or accustomed to throw itself on other horses to bite them (we must remember that these were stallions), that he avoid as far as possible finding himself astride it in war, particularly in a melee, not only because this vice is very dangerous and may lose a good man but because it is very difficult to punish.

Another example comes from 1729, from Valentin Trichter's edition of Baron von Lohneisen's "Hof-Kriegs- und Reitschul" (p. 74; original edition 1609). These illustrations show a horse throwing itself on the neck of another horse and biting it or kicking back at a horse behind it. These are accompanied by a note to Lohneisen's text by Trichter: "A warhorse must also assist his rider before and behind,

fighting his enemy, and defend him from being struck or bitten in
the back if he has lost his advantage." Superficially this text and
these illustrations could be interpreted as meaning that horses were
generally trained to behave thus in battle. But closer analysis will
reveal that

1. Lohneisen himself when he wrote in 1609 made no other rec-
ommendations for the training of a charger than that it be exercised
at all kinds of turns and be accustomed to gunfire;

2. Trichter himself does not suggest that what the horse should
use to help his rider is any of the proper High School airs – a fact
borne out by the plates which, with the possible exception of the
ruade, depict no true manege air;

3. The actions clearly would have made no sense on armoured
horses in earlier times, and by 1729 it is too late to ascribe to them
any influence in the formulation of already long-established manege
airs.

But the mention of the ruade does bring up one possible militant
use of an air. The ruade, or kicking back with the legs straight out
and high, is an old movement not on the program of the modern
Spanish School, and practiced recently only by the Cadre Noir of
Saumur, unless I am much mistaken. Although Grisone recommends
this air only "to lighten the quarters" it is, in its simplest form, the
most natural defense of the horse. It would not be difficult for an
animal unencumbered by armour to execute. In certain types of
fighting it might have had value. But its popularity must always have
been limited by the fact that in war one at least hopes to have
friends rather than foes on one's heel most of the time, and a horse
encouraged to kick too readily might turn out to be more of a liability than an asset.

Ancestry of the High School Airs

But if such elaborate airs as the capriole and its first cousins, the
ballotade and the croupade, did not originate in battle, or as "pro-
cessionals" like the posade and the courbette, if they did not start,
like the volte or pirouette, as turns at either end of the jousting ring
(probably once accomplished with little more formality than a polo-
pony or a cutting-horse turn), what was their real ancestry? It is
clear from the way in which Grisone refers to "leaps" in 1550 that

his readers must already have been familiar with them for some time. Perhaps something mentioned by Fiaschi in 1556 will give a clue. Speaking of the posade, he remarks casually that it used to be called "orsade" from the fact that in it the horse holds his legs bent together the way a walking bear (Latin *ursus* = bear) does. Now the only place where the people of 16th or 15th century Italy saw walking bears was in the acts of itinerant animal trainers. This even makes one suspicious that the first posades executed with true precision might have been in the circus. At any rate, it reminds us that medieval animal trainers did exhibit unridden horses performing airs reminiscent of the ruade, posade, and capriole, as evidenced by at least two 14th century manuscripts.

Just how the capriole and other "leaps" entered polite society we shall probably never know, but it is significant that they first appeared in Renaissance Italy, among a people curious, lively, quick to appreciate "art" in any field, and socially more flexible than their conservative cousins of the feudal north. Man's response to the challenge of what's difficult has brought him the best (as well as perhaps the worst) things he has. His desire to display his ability is surely as ancient as the wish to slay his fellow men, and definitely more constructive. This is an ancestry of which High School need not be ashamed.

IV. HARNESS AND CONTROL

33. THE FUNCTION OF THE YOKE SADDLE IN ANCIENT HARNESSING*

M. A. LITTAUER

Dr Watson's review of Dr von Dewall's *Pferd und Wagen im Frühen China* in your June issue [Watson 1968] raised a very interesting question, a hitherto unexplored aspect of which is indicated, if never developed, in the book.**

Dr Watson writes that the author "Rather surprisingly, sees no problem in the perennial question of the place – chest or neck – on which the yoked horses took the load, and assumes that the system of traces kept the point of draught low and protected the horses from the choking effects of a band around the neck." Dr von Dewall referred to a girth (*Bauchgurt*)[1] rather than to traces (which did not then exist) as performing this function, but was over-optimistic in believing it could be successful. But she does assign a role, although a not entirely correct one, to the yoke saddle: "Die Jochgabel auf dem Nacken der Pferde, an der ein Brustblatt angesetzt haben muss, das von Brust und Schulter die Zugkraft abnahm, war damit ein wichtiges Verbindungsglied in diesem Zugsystem."[2] The saddle is an element of the harness long neglected in the literature and, although it could never completely have removed the pressure from the throat ("breast" is a euphemism), I hope to demonstrate that it would permit the withers and particularly the upper shoulder to absorb some of this – at least when the horse was in certain positions.

In the numerous Chinese chariot graves abundant evidence has been found of these objects and of their position, "stets auffallend hoch auf dem Nacken der Pferde",[3] and it is impossible to overlook

---

* *Antiquity* 42, 1968, 27–31.
** (= von Dewall 1964). I am indebted to Professor J. K. Anderson, with whom I first discussed this matter, for his interest and for his helpful comments.
[1] von Dewall 1964, 147.
[2] von Dewall 1964, 133.
[3] von Dewall 1964, 208. 210. 212f. 215. 218f. 220. 224. 227f. 232. 235. 239. 244–246. 147.

them. There is ample evidence of them in the west too, but they seem never to have been seriously considered – perhaps because Lefebvre des Noëttes does not take them into account, mentioning them only three times in passing as "fourchons de garrot".[4] His failure to understand their purpose and his statements that the equid yoke was "posé au-dessus du garrot"[5] have led to an exaggerated conception of the undeniably, at times, throttling effect of the ancient harness.

Des Noëttes did not describe his practical experiments in detail and illustrated them merely with drawings of maquettes that show a yoke but no saddles. Hilzheimer even misunderstood these so far as to assume that the yoke rested on the back and protested, "das Joch lag nicht, wie Lefebvre annahm, hinter dem Widerrist, sondern vor dem Widerrist in dem Einschnitt zwischen diesen und den Hals" – in other words, on the nape: but he did not develop this.[6] On the other hand, the effects of the yoke itself, were it placed directly over the withers, were so little discussed by des Noëttes that Needham and Lu, using him as an authority, were able to call the ancient system merely a "throat-and-girth harness". They write that it "consists of a girth surrounding the belly and the posterior [sic] part of the coastal region, at the top of which the point of traction is located. In order to prevent the girth being carried backwards, the ancients combined it with a throat-strap"; and "The throat-and-girth harness of horses was nothing but a makeshift alternative [sic] for the yoke of the ox." The yoke saddles in Chinese graves are yokes themselves in "vestigial forms", living on with the "throat-and-girth harness, for reasons perhaps of symbolism, perhaps of ornament".[7] Haudricourt too accepted the idea of a yoke on the withers.[8]

Potratz does consistently speak of a "Nackenjoch" and not a "Widerristjoch" but, curiously, he recognizes a yoke saddle and its function only on the chariots of Ashurnasirpal II,[9] and considers it an innovation of the period. And the frequently illustrated Rosellini chariot in Florence still has its yoke saddles hung upside down, while

---

[4] des Noëttes 1931, 38. 49. 68.
[5] des Noëttes 1931. 12. 13. 46.
[6] Hilzheimer 1931, 6.
[7] Needham and Lu 1960, 122f., 126.
[8] Haudricourt 1948, 61, n. 1; fig. 2d.
[9] Potratz 1966, 17–45, esp. 44.

H. A Shelley

Fig. 1. Yoke saddle from Chariot of Tut'ankhamūn.

Botti, in a fairly recent paper discussing it, still calls them "sotto gole".[10]

The yoke saddles are wishbone- or chevron-shaped wooden objects, usually with finials, by which they were lashed to the yoke. In China the finials were of bronze and the outer sides of the saddle legs frequently had a bronze half-sheathing. Saddles were found in Egypt with the Rosellini chariot, and with those of Tuthmosis IV and Tut'ankhamūn (fig. 1).[11] The western Asiatic ones, being small and narrow, tend to be obscured among the other trappings of harnessed

---

[10] Botti 1951, 197.
[11] Botti 1951; Carter and Newberry 1904, 34, fig. 21; Carter 1927, pl. xlii.

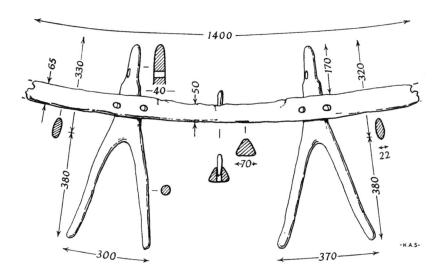

Fig. 2. Yoke saddles found with the 4-wheeled carriage in Kurgan V at Pazyryk, showing dimensions. This is the only scale drawing of yoke saddles found intact in position on the yoke known to the author (after Sorokin, Hermitage, St Petersburg).

horses on figured documents, and are more clearly seen on some Egyptian representations of horseless chariots or in chariot-workshop scenes, where they hang on the wall or are being shaped over stands.[12] They depend from the antennae-like yokes of chariots on some Knossos tablets.[13] They seem to have gradually diminished in size in the west, for on their last appearances they look very small indeed. These are on chariots being ferried across a river in the reign of Ashurnasirpal II and on the necks of a team under Tiglath-Pileser III in Assyria, and in a 7th-century B.C. tomb in Egypt.[14] To the east, large ones were found from as late as the 5th century B.C., in Kurgan V at Pazyryk (fig. 2) in the Altai[15] and at Liu Li Ko in Honan (pl. 199).

---

[12] Davies 1943, pl. xxii; Wreszinski 1923, pls. 17. 137. 227.
[13] Evans 1935, fig. 763 b and d; fig. 764 a. c. d.
[14] Barnett (n.d.), pls. 16. 17. 18. 20; Wreszinski 1923, pl. 36; Potratz 1966, pl. xlv, 101.
[15] Talbot Rice 1957, fig. 30.

The yoke saddle clearly originated in an attempt to adapt the yoke, designed for the broad necks of oxen, to the narrow necks of equids. (It is tempting to associate these objects with the adoption of the light, spoke-wheeled, horse-drawn chariot – particularly since there is no material or figured evidence from Sumerian times. But Salonen 1955, 105, interprets a Sumerian term as "'Halsstück', eigentlich 'Fledermaus'", which sounds very much like a saddle pad. Another Sumerian term is interpreted as "Kralle des 2-rädrigen Wagens des Halsstückes". Thus these objects may originally have been designed for other equids than horses.) The ox yoke is either lashed to the horns or, more commonly, rests across the short, strong necks, which are admirably suited to either method of harnessing. The ox carries his head and neck low and, in the case of the neck yoke, his withers rise prominently behind it, keeping it forward and exerting pressure against it. Equids have long slender necks, set on at a different angle. Horses, especially when excited, may carry their heads high, and small horses and ponies tend to have low withers. On the basis of these well-known facts, on the vagueness of much of the figured evidence, and on the actual absence of a yoke saddle in later antiquity, des Noëttes evidently concluded that the only pressure the horse could exert on the pole was through his trachea, by way of the strap that held him under the yoke.

But this was to neglect other facts of equine anatomy. The withers, even when these are relatively low, are the area where the bones of the spine are most prominent and come closest to the surface. It would be difficult to attach a yoke so that it would sit securely over this highest and very short stretch of back; it would require that both the neck strap, keeping it forward, and the girth, keeping it back and down, remain taut at all times, so that a constant and equal tension was exerted. But a horse, depending upon his gait and his degree of relaxation or excitement, lowers or raises his head and neck. When he raised and brought them back the throat band would slacken, permitting the yoke to slip behind the withers; when he lowered and extended them, drawing the band taut, it would have a tendency to pull the yoke ahead of the withers.

Even had it been possible to keep the yoke satisfactorily in position over the withers, it would hardly have been desirable. Because of the closeness of the bones to the surface, the withers are particularly susceptible to chafing; under a rigid yoke beam they would be subject to bruising also, from the banging of the yoke when the chariot went over rough ground or when the team was out of step. On the other hand, the roll of muscle or "crest" on the neck of an unaltered male equid (who seems to have been in almost exclusive use as a chariot animal) gives the cervical vertebrae protection.

Yoke saddles represent an effort to prevent the equid yoke from slipping back over the withers when the head and neck were raised and thrown back, and to keep the pull of the yoke *in front* of the withers and thus take some of it off the throat. Ancient drivers cannot have been so blind as is often assumed to the disadvantages of traction by the windpipe alone, and would have done what they could to ameliorate it, within the limits of the pole-and-yoke system. The narrow yoke saddles were of a shape to fit more comfortably and to stay more firmly in place than the plain yoke beam itself; there would be less rubbing, and the upper parts of the team's shoulders, pressing against the "legs" of the saddles, would be able to exert some forward pull on the yoke. (It may be added that in no modern method of harnessing does anything rest on the withers; the collar lies directly in front of them and the girth directly behind.)

When it comes to figured evidence, it is the position of the saddle pad and of the girth, attached to the ends of the saddle, rather than the slender, practically invisible yoke saddle itself, that reveals the location and angle of the latter. On Egyptian monuments the saddle pad is pictured as a rectangular or thumbnail-shaped object. This rests almost vertically on the nape of an animal with lowered head and neck, as it is seen on that farthest from the viewer on a relief from the tomb of Kha-em-het (pl. 200) or on the horse nibbling his foreleg on an Amarna relief (pl. 201). As the head and neck are raised the pad assumes an oblique angle, as on the near animal of the first relief (pl. 202) and, finally, on a horse with high and retracted head and neck, such as that on the chest of Tutʿankhamūn (pl. 200), the pad lies almost horizontally. From the unusually carefully rendered Kha-em-het relief, it is clear that not only the throat band but also the girth is attached to the lower ends of the yoke saddle. This girth on a horse with lowered head and neck stretched forward assumed an oblique position (pl. 201), slanting forward across the horse's shoulder; it progressively changes to the vertical as the horse raises and brings back his head and neck (pl. 200). Were the pad really fixed over the withers (assuming such a thing were possible) and not the neck, the pad and girth would remain in much the same position in relation to each other no matter what the head and neck were doing. [The present writer has experimented with model saddles of the proportions of those found in Egypt (in so far as the dimensions are ascertainable from the literature) and the opening between the legs is too narrow (even without a pad) to permit them to lie anywhere except ahead of the shoulders – even on ponies.]

The fact that the girth was attached to the ends of the yoke saddle, rather than higher up, at the junction of the yoke with the saddle finial, indicates that its aim was not only to permit backing but to keep the saddle, hence the neck band, as low as possible. (The Chinese yoke saddles seem usually to have had longer legs than the western Asiatic ones, and it would hardly have been feasible to attach the girth to their ends. In the absence of figured evidence one can only suggest that the girth may have been attached to the yoke itself. The longer legs alone would ensure a greater purchase area for the shoulders.) But in order not to cut the horse under the elbows when his head and neck were advanced and lowered, it had to be slack; and a vertically hanging girth is often shown as slack and looping (pl. 200). This slackness sometimes assumed proportions that must have been exaggerated, and it seems to have become rather an artistic cliché. Yet there is no question but that it had its origins in actuality. [des Noëttes 1931, 48 believed this very loose girth was the fault of a copyist who "ne comprenant pas le harnachement antique a réuni en un seul organe la sangle et la courroie accessoire qui la relie au collier". But on good modern photographs the same appears, and it is often quite clear (on pl. ivb, for instance) that this looping girth does not represent a "courroie accessoire".]

With the yoke resting essentially on the neck, which is not the strongest area for weight-bearing, it is clear that a central-axled chariot still possessed certain advantages, advantages which, *depending on the conditions of its use*, outweighed, or did not outweigh, certain other advantages of the rear-axled chariot. But, as Kipling used to say, 'that is another story'.

That the yoke saddle was never completely successful in accomplishing its aim is indicated by the fact that from the 8th century B.C. onwards it began to disappear in the west, where, in some areas at least, a new type of yoke was adopted.

It seems a little unfair of Dr Watson to have suggested that, had Dr von Dewall included Salonen in her bibliography, she could not have overlooked one of the 'historical points' mentioned by the latter – namely that "At the turn of the 14th century B.C. the axle of chariots in Western Asia was moved from the centre of the rider's box to the back edge, the change coinciding with the replacement of 4-spoke by 6-spoke wheels" – and would have come to the supposedly inevitable conclusion that 1400 B.C. provides a *terminus post quem* for the beginning of the diffusion of the western Asiatic chariot towards China. The first evidence of the chariot in China is 12th century B.C. Yet Dr von Dewall lists Wiesner,[16] on whom Salonen largely drew for his brief historical sketch of the development of the chariot,[17] as well as other sources (Nuoffer 1904; Schachermayr 1951; Lorimer 1952; Hančar 1956) in which this rather well-known point (to which there are, however, exceptions) is to be found. She may merely not have found the logic inescapable. If 14 spokes were added to the chariot wheel in its long journey across Asia (the Shang chariot at Ta-ssu-k'ung-ts'un had 18 spokes as opposed to the four on 15th-century western chariots), the rear axle might easily have been shifted from an already rear position back to a central one – to suit a different set of circumstances. And then it could have been post-1400 B.C. – and only 12 spokes would have had to be added!

Dr Watson questions whether "linked harness-bits; appeared earlier in Western Asia than in China", and adds, "Those from the Caucasus and Urartu are roughly of the same age as the specimens of the early Chou period – the 10th–9th centuries B.C." This is to overlook the Bronze Age bits with jointed mouthpieces found in Egypt and Palestine. And is the one from Mycenae too far away to count?[18]

---

[16] Wiesner 1939.
[17] Salonen 1951, 164f.
[18] Potratz 1966, 107.

34. BITS AND PIECES*

M. A. LITTAUER

A number of relatively recent works concerned entirely or incidentally with early horse gear call attention to the fact that various features of this are still imperfectly understood. At the same time, new
discoveries have shed new light (Anderson 1961; Childe 1954; Hančar
1955; Jope 1956; Karageorghis 1962, 1965, 1967; Nagel 1966; Potratz
1966; Salonen 1956). J. A. H. Potratz, notably, despite great familiarity with bit material, fails to recognize the functional or genetic
implications of some of its details.

The studded cheekpiece

Blunt spikes on the inside of cheekpieces appear already on our earliest Oriental and Mediterranean examples from the Late Bronze
Age figs. 1*a* and 1*b*) (Childe 1954, 722, fig. 521). These have frequently been explained as the means of attaching a leather backing – the purpose ascribed to them by Potratz (1941, 3ff.). Despite
the fact that J. K. Anderson (1961, 48f., 195, n. 23) pointed out
that the studs tapered *away* from the cheekpiece, hence in the wrong
direction to hold anything on, Potratz continued in 1966 to prefer
his original interpretation (1966, 104f., 138, 144). Anderson was further correct when he suggested that these spikes were for coercive
effect, only he did not have the modern evidence with which to back
up his suggestion. It is unfortunate that it may take someone who
knows something of the 'seamy side' of the horse world to interpret
certain elements of its early gear. Plates 203a–b, 204a show a 'run-
out bit' and a bristled bit 'burr' or 'brush pricker' (Edwards 1963, 88);
pl. 204b shows a tack 'burr', now happily illegal. The purpose of these
objects is to exert lateral persuasion – on horses 3,300 years further

* *Antiquity* 43, 1969, 289–300.

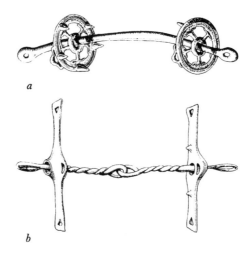

Fig. 1 (a) 'Run-out bit' from Gaza. Bits of similar type are known from Tell el Amarna and Ras Shamra.
(b) 'Run-out' bit from Mycenae. Bits with similar cheek-pieces and plain or twisted jointed mouthpieces are known from Egypt, Palestine, Asia Minor and Assyria. After Potratz 1966.

removed from their wild state than were those on which the earliest bits in question were used. The 'run-out bit' is especially for race horses (either ridden or driven). Since many horses resist primarily on one side, this is a one-sided affair, which is, however, reversible. It is advertized as 'the most effective bit for horses that tend to bear either in or out. Rein pressure causes retracting prongs to bear on cheeks of horse'. (In pl. 203b the spring is under invisible pressure.) The leather 'burr' with bristles (or its nailed prototype) is an accessory that may be added at will to either or both sides of the mouth. Its leather backing with radial slit is flexible enough to be fitted around the mouthpiece inside the cheekpiece. The bristled 'burr' is used today not only on the race track, but in the hunting field or show ring – either singly, on a horse that pulls to one side, or doubly, on a horse that resists control in either direction. The *comparative* mildness of early studded cheekpieces may be ascribed to the fact that the horse would be wearing one over a longer period of time than the duration of a race or show-ring round, and that too much irritation could cause infection.

The problem of directional control of ancient chariot animals was probably more acute than that of simple checking or braking. From

18th-dynasty Egypt to 9th-century Assyria, Near Eastern reins passed through terret rings located at or near the ends of the yoke saddle, a few centimetres down on the horses' shoulders (Pritchard 1954, pls. 314, 332; Barnett 1960, pls. 26f.). These rings broke the line of the reins and the pulley effect thus created was in favour of the charioteer, since by far the longest part of the line was on his side. Directional control was not so easy; the pull could only be directly backwards, and not outwards, as was later possible on the ridden horse; nor could the shifting of the rider's weight, feasible on the latter, act here as influence or signal. It must have been particularly difficult to enforce obedience on horses moving at speed in the excitement of battle. The spiked cheekpiece which, when a single rein was pulled, pressed against the opposite side of the mouth, would have been an obvious answer. It may not be mere coincidence that these began in an age of light, manouevrable chariotry, that they declined in the 8th and 7th centuries with the heavy, cumbersome, straight-moving Assyrian chariot. They were later adopted by the riding peoples of the steppe apparently after the Scythians' tour of the Near East, and by the 6th-century Greeks, who needed strong directional control for chariot racing. In these two late cases, however, spikes are the exception, not the rule, and they appear on a 'burr', rather than as an integral part of the bit (Potratz 1963, figs. 40–42, 45, 50).

The Scythian 'burr' is a metal rectangle or St Andrew's cross with a hole in the centre and a prong at each corner (fig. 2). The ends of the mouthpiece must have passed through the holes when the bit was made. Hence, although the 'burr' was separate, it was a permanent part of the bit complex. The use of a 'burr' here, rather than a spiked cheekpiece, is probably explained by the slender, rod-like Scythian cheekpiece (which may derive its form from an antler prototype), which would neither lend itself to spikes nor hold them as flatly and firmly against the corners of the mouth as did the oriental cheeks of rectangular or discoid shape. (Luristan finds illustrate this graphically: the spikes appear only on the inside of the plaque-like cheeks which, despite their elaborate carving, are in the tradition of the early Oriental bits, while the rod-like cheeks found here never show spikes (Goddard 1931, 77f.).

While the Scythian 'burr' was used mainly on the ridden horse, there is evidence of something similar on chariot animals much further afield and at an earlier date. A pair of small (7 cm.), bronze, U-shaped objects found near a chariot horse's head in a Western

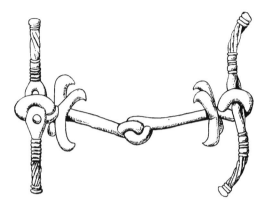

Fig. 2. Scythian bit with claw-like 'burrs'. After Potratz.

Chou burial (c. 1000 B.C.) (pl. 205).[1] These have three studs on either arm and a hole at either end. These seem to have been true 'burrs' that could be added at will, being passed over the mouthpiece inside the cheekpiece, and held up in place by attachments to the forks of the cheekstrap.

In Greece, where the evidence is exclusively figured, we find the 'burr' from the 6th century on. It was of a still different type, and might be used on either driven or ridden animals.[2] It is usually a rectangular plaque strewn with dots, which may represent the heads of tacks – if it was of leather, or the reverse side of punched holes – if it was of cheese-grater construction in metal (Anderson 1961 pls. 20–22; Beazley 1956, 145, no. 13; 1942, 427, no. 1, 672, no. 11, 678, no. 15, 724, no. 2).

The use of the 'burr' in Greece, as in Scythia, may be explained by the shape of the Greek cheeks, which were not plaques, like the earlier oriental ones, but were bars, slender crescents, etc. The fact that the 'burr' appears at least once used selectively, on the outside

---

[1] I am most grateful to Mrs Barbara Stephen of the Royal Ontario Museum, Toronto, for permission to reproduce these hitherto unpublished objects.

[2] Miss Mary Moore, who has been making a study of horses on Greek 6th-century vases, tells me that she knows of very few examples in Black-Figure on a *ridden* horse, and that in Red-figure the ridden horses wearing 'burrs' are usually Amazons' mounts. The predominant use of this feature on chariot animals would accord with its directional function, and the apparently more severe (because more extensive and more densely studded) Greek 'burr' may indicate racing use (strenuous but brief).

horse of a chariot team, but not on the other horses of the same team, may indicate that here it was an optional addition (Beazley 1956, 330, no. 2). If the 'burr' was of leather, this would conveniently explain its complete absence from the archaeological record – although the scarcity of finds of Greek horse gear and the sparing use of the 'burr' itself might be sufficient to account for this.

A broad, low, studded noseband, appearing on a fifth-century Attic vase (Anderson 1961, pl 23; Beazley 1942, 405, no. 60) almost certainly was of leather. Anderson has called attention to a similar device, described by Arrian (*Indica*, xvi, 10ff.) and Strabo (xv, 1, 66) as in use in India, apparently sometimes in conjunction with a straight bar bit and sometimes without. The general use in India of a noseband is of particular interest, because it was in this country that the *hemione* was still being driven at the time of Herodotus (vii, 86). I shall later suggest a direct relationship between these.

Dropped Noseband Control

These nosebands belonged to the same large family as the simple halter, the cavesson in its different forms, the various hackamores or 'bitless bridles', and the American 'bosal'. The basic elements of these are a noseband, and the strap that holds it in place, passing over the horse's head just behind the ears (Edwards 1963, figs. 13, 71f., 174f.). While most of these may be used in conjunction with a bit, they are also used without it. All of them achieve control through pressure on the nose. The pressure may be high up, on the nasal bones or, when the noseband is 'dropped', on the sensitive, soft tissue below the end of the nasal bones. Pressure here may not only be painful but may, since the horse breathes entirely through his nose, impair breathing. Hence this type of bridle has strong, if not entirely satisfactory, braking powers[3] (see p. 292).

---

[3] Hančar is incorrect in his statement that control by cavesson is based on an artificially *permanently* closed mouth, and control by bit on an artificially *permanently* open mouth (Hančar, 1955, 499). The control by one is achieved by pressure on the nose and by the other (depending upon its type) by pressure on the bars of the mouth, on the corners of the lips, or even on the roof of the mouth. The mouth may be open or closed in either case, depending upon the type of cavesson or bit, its adjustment, the emotional state of the animal, the condition of its mouth, the hands of the rider, etc.

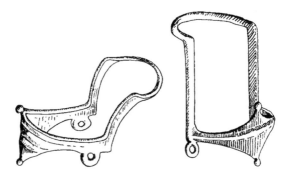

Fig. 3. The true psalia. After Potratz.

While Childe and Anderson recognized the possibility of driving a horse without a bit, others have overlooked or rejected such a likelihood (Childe 1954, 722f.; Anderson 1960a; Potratz 1938, 195). This is convenient doctrine, because if no bits are present one need not waste time looking for other evidence of draught. Unfortunately it is not so. Horses are both driven and ridden in 'bitless bridles' of one kind or another in Mediterranean and Near Eastern countries today. In America horses are sometimes broken by being put in a cart and driven on a dropped noseband. This or some form of hackamore may be used for breaking, so as to avoid spoiling the mouth of a young horse; they are also used on animals whose mouths have been so badly treated that they are either insensitive or hypersensitive. There are even horses of a size and power undreamed of in ancient times that are ridden over international jumping courses in this gear.

Although it is a fact that intact bridles without bits (some even with the reins still attached directly to the noseband) have been found in Egyptian tombs, this is often overlooked, or it is explained away on the grounds that tomb robbers had made off with all metal objects (Carter and Newberry 1904, 25; Carter 1927, 113). Anderson, however, not only noted the bit's absence, but suggested a direct relationship between this fact and the very low-placed Egyptian nosebands, which must have exerted pressure on the sensitive part of the nose (1961, 45). While the open mouths of horses, and what look like cheekpieces on many Egyptian reliefs, indicate that the bit was already in use at the same time as the noseband (and we have bits from this period) these very open mouths *in conjunction* with a low noseband prove that the noseband was still the primary braking element.

When the dropped noseband is used as *accessory* to a bit today, its purpose is to keep the mouth closed, so that the animal cannot 'get away from the bit'.[4] On numerous reliefs from Egypt, however, which show open mouths, there is no evidence of cheekpieces or of mouthpiece ends, and the horses seem to be driven on the noseband alone. Either they had acquired the habit of opening the mouths from being sometimes bitted or (more likely) the artist, having sometimes seen open mouths, found them more 'spirited'.

New light is shed on this bridling by details of Amarna reliefs recently published (Cooney 1965, pls. 27–34). These clearly show not only the low position of the noseband, but the practice of slitting nostrils (pl. 207). The usual explanation of this ancient custom, which is found in some areas today, has been that it is a means of improving the breathing of animals (de Solleysel 1685 II, 11; Chardin 1927, 170; Youatt 1868, 198; Littauer 1969, 185). But in the horse, breathing is normally restricted by the upper nasal passages, not by the nostrils. Hence it seems likely that the practice originated in an attempt to compensate for the impaired breathing caused by the use of the very low noseband, which did press on the nostrils. It may be significant that when the low noseband disappears in ancient times, the slit nostrils disappear with it, and that they often seem to reappear in times and places where the animal is controlled by a noseband (the ass in parts of the Near East (pl. 209) or where a low-placed cavesson was used extensively and severely in training, as in Europe in the 15th to 17th centuries, and nasal tissues may have been damaged (Hill 1965, pls. xvii, xxii, xxiv, xxxi) (fig. 4).

---

[4] The classical and Sasanian bridle accessories often called 'muzzles' or 'cavessons' (pl. 208) played a role similar to that of the modern dropped noseband used with a bit; they were not braking elements, but 'gadgets' designed to prevent the horse from opening his mouth and 'getting away from the bit'. These are called 'cavessons' by Potratz (who illustrates them upside down) (fig. 3). Anderson does the same (1961, pl. 37b), but recognizes their correct function as accessories, and identifies them as the true *psalia* (1960, 3–6). Neither author evidently knew the proportions; the diameter of the decorated segment is greater than that of the plain one, which fits under the chin, the bays where it joins the verticals being designed to accommodate the ends of the bit. I am indebted to Mr Andrew Oliver of the Metropolitan Museum of Art, New York for the dimensions of the *psalion* shown in pl. 206. The loops (swan-headed here, but often plain) are *not* for reins, but for attachment to the headstall. A similar function has been tentatively attributed by Kossack 1954, 120, pl. 14a to the long, curved and sometimes widened upper ends of many Central European early Hallstatt cheekpieces. There is evidence that these were sometimes attached so that the upper, curved part would press inward on the nostrils if the horse tried to fight the bit.

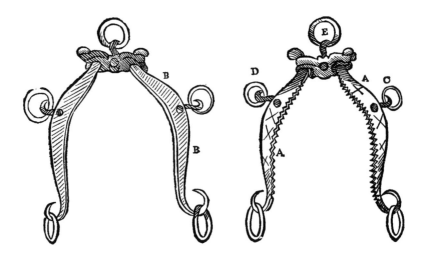

Fig. 4. The 17th-century cavessons. Reins and headstall were attached to the two
forward rings; rear rings were for chin strap. After Fouquet.

The toothed cavesson reminds us again of spikes, the use of which
in the ancient Orient may well have preceded that of the bit. One
of the drawbacks of the noseband type of control in driving is its
weak lateral effect – a fact noted by those using it today. It seems
possible that spikes, first used on the insides of nosebands, as described
by Arrian and Strabo for later India, were transferred to the cheekpieces of bits as these were introduced. The unusually wide, flat form
of ancient oriental cheekpieces, which have few modern parallels (the
'run-out bit' in pl. xl*a* is an exception) may have been occasioned
by the necessity of continuing to provide a surface for studs already
in use in the noseband. Although we have no early figured evidence
to support this suggestion, it may be noted that modern leather
'burrs' are made of two pieces of leather, with the tack heads in
between, and that these are not apparent on the outside.

Moreover, once reins are attached to the noseband of a halter, it
is essentially a cavesson. Many cavessons have rigid components, and
it would be natural to place a metal reinforcement in the area where
the reins were attached. This would not only strengthen the attachment but would increase and harden the area of lateral pressure
when the opposite rein was pulled. If these two reinforced sections
were joined by a bar through the mouth (in this area the horse's
lower teeth are conveniently missing), their lateral effectiveness would

be further increased, without increasing the checking on the nose (one problem with the noseband). Here was the early bar bit.[5]

This would also eliminate the tendency of the entire headstall to skew around on the horse's head when one rein was pulled strongly. Now, when a single rein was pulled, it worked primarily through the bit, against the opposite cheek; it was directional; when both reins were pulled, they still worked primarily on the low noseband which, otherwise, would have been eliminated – as it was later, when the full potential of the bit was recognized.

Phases in the Development of the Snaffle

Anderson does not believe that the cheekpieces of early bits that had 'broken' mouths were connected with the noseband, because "the jointed mouthpiece when both reins are pulled, folds in the middle, and herein lies a good part of its effect" (1961, 48). Quite true, therefore the use of the low noseband in Egypt into the 12th century may indicate continued reliance on its braking powers and an unawareness of certain properties peculiar to the jointed snaffle, whose form may originally have been accidental rather than calculated – as I shall suggest later. There is, unfortunately, a hiatus of almost 300 years in both material evidence and circumstantial figured documents. When both reappear, in 9th-century Assyria, the snaffle is attached rather differently, *without* any noseband, and its proportions may denote a new understanding and enthusiastic exploitation of its special potential. The extremely long canons (260.4 mm. as compared with a maximum of 152.4 mm. today) of a 9th-century bit from Assyria in Berlin (VA 7284) (Hančar 1955, 494f., fig. 18; Potratz 1941, 5f., fig. 2; 1966, pl. 105), whose working value has sometimes been questioned, appear, in the light of recent Cypriot discoveries, not to have been eccentric for their time. Bits with similar straight cheeks and jointed, twisted mouths of unusually great length (c. 184 mm. c. 304 mm.) have been found in the *dromoi* of

---

[5] Hermes 1936, 379–382 postulates such a metallic reinforcement to the noseband as marking the early stage of the bit but, like Hilzheimer 1931 she accepts the early Mesopotamian equid muzzle as already a cavesson. Moreover, she does not recognize the importance of the noseband's position, and the tight one she suggests is nowhere evidenced by Egyptian horses, which have open mouths.

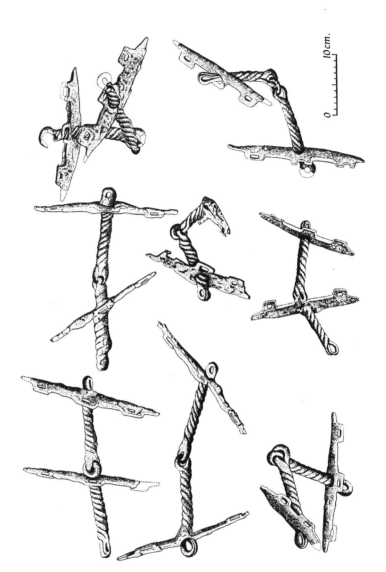

Fig. 5. Bits found in *dromos* of Tomb 47 at Salamis. After Karageorghis 1967, pl. CXLI.

8th–7th century chamber tombs at Salamis (Karageorghis 1967a = fig. 5). These bits are undecorated, they were found *in situ* in mouths; their functional status is unquestionable. In 1941 Potratz suggested that the Berlin bit's proportions might be for exaggerated snaffle action, i.e. pressure on the corners of the lips (1941, 5f.). Such bits would have another effect: when both reins were pulled on such long canons a considerable angle would be formed by their joint, and one that would be high enough to press painfully against the roof of the horse's mouth.

Another look may be taken, too, at the straight-barred elaborate-cheeked Luristan bit with a long mouthpiece, whose functional properties have often been questioned. Although the lack of signs of wear and the elaborate design may indicate that this type of Luristan bit's use was primarily ceremonial (Godard 1931, 77f.), the object may well have been modelled on a working prototype, and one in which such a long mouthpiece served a purpose, pl. 203a shows a 'run-out bit' in which one end of the mouthpiece permanently extends 76 mm. beyond the check on its side. This extension would be placed on the opposite side from that on which the horse would tend to run out; on this bit this adds leverage to pain as a persuader. pl. 206 shows a simpler bit with the same feature – but 101 mm. long. Here the horse is controlled by reins attached to the two large rings which lie in normal position on either side of the mouth; when extra leverage is needed, a third rein; attached to the smaller ring at the end of the mouthpiece extension, is pulled. These are for horses that tend to pull only to one side. In the modern 'slip-mouth bit' a hollow, tubular mouthpiece carries a bar longer then itself; the reins are attached to either end of this bar. When a single rein is pulled, the bar is extended on that side, producing a leverage similar to that of the bit in pl. 209. The Luristan bits with exaggeratedly long bar mouthpieces are also leverage bits designed to work in either direction.

The Genesis of the Oriental Bit?

Because insufficient consideration has been given to the evidence of a stage of low-placed noseband control in the Orient, the possibility of the bit developing thus out of it has been largely overlooked or rejected (Hančar 1955, 498f.; Nagel 1966, 11, 23; Potratz 1966,

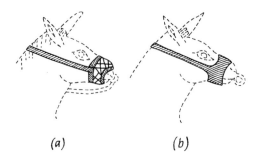

(a)   (b)

Fig. 6. Onagers wearing nose rings and muzzles. Left: from the 'Standard of Mari': right: from that of Ur. After Schaeffer 1935, fig. 40.

82). And the likelihood that cavesson control of this type might have evolved naturally in southwest Asia out of the onager *muzzle* seems entirely overlooked. Schaeffer 1935 suggested that the equids of the Ur and Mari 'standards' were controlled by a line to a 'lip ring', and that they were wearing muzzles, not cavessons (fig. 6). This was far closer than Hilzheimer's suggestion that the animals were controlled by (invisible) reins to 'cavessons', and that the rings were for attaching only the two centre animals to a transversal bar in front of their noses (Hilzheimer 1931). Schaeffer based his 'lip ring' on the difference in the way the equid rings and the ox's nose ring was rendered on the same 'Standard'. But the artist's attempt to distinguish between the shapes of the two animals' noses might be enough to account for this. Moreover, O. Antonius, for many years Director of the important Vienna Zoological Garden, pointed out, in a much-neglected article, that since equids use their upper lips in eating, rings cannot be placed in these (1938, 478). This therefore keeps early equid harnessing, with its yoke-and-pole hitch, consistently within the pattern of bovid. My stress on the difference between cavesson and muzzle here may seem to be splitting hairs, but the importance is this: the noseband of the ordinary halter or headstall lies much further up – not over the sensitive part; it is more comfortable this way, and much more secure than it would be lower down, unless it were carefully adjusted and quite tight. But to achieve a muzzling effect and still permit a line to reach a nose ring, this wide, low-placed, strap muzzle, reminiscent of one type still in use on dogs, was devised. Moreover, when we see unharnessed equids on the 'Peace' side of the Ur 'Standard', they are without any kind of headstall and led, like a bull, by a ring; thus the halter does not seem to have been used here even for its primary purpose – that of controlling an animal in hand. A bone plaque from Nippur (Crawford 1959, 79) with the heads of a team of four equids with nose rings shows what may look like a mere halter, but its low, tight noseband indicates a muzzle.

That this muzzle could exert advantageous pressure on sensitive areas must have been evident from the beginning, but a stubborn addiction to the bovid nose ring continues into the early 2nd millennium. This behaviour, however, is not inconsistent with a disregard of equine anatomy that kept horses under the yoke for millennia. Whoever thought of eliminating the ring and attaching a line to either side of the noseband was on the way to achieving the graded braking effect and the at least partial directional control impossible with a single-line nose ring. If we put studs on the inside of the band it is even more effective. With this, man could already manoeuvre horses in fast chariots, even if with less refinement than with the bit. It may be significant also that it could be achieved by a means arising directly out of ancient Near Eastern harnessing; it did not have to be introduced from outside, as is almost unanimously assumed. The idea of slit nostrils, too, would come easily to men whose fathers had used nose rings on their equids.

Our earliest Oriental and Mediterranean cheekpieces differ from most early (and many later) ones in the north. The former are flat on the inside face, symmetrical, often incorporate studs, and their holes lie all in one plane. The latter are rod-like, sometimes asymmetrical, unstudded and, in some categories, have holes in different planes (Mozsolics 1953, 69–109; Gallus and Horvath 1939, pls. 6, 8–10, 12f., 18, 20, 41, 45, 54, 59–60, 66, 73; Kossack 1954, fig. 14a). This circumstance has before now suggested the possibility of a different genesis for the cheeks. Hančar (1955, 532f.) postulates this, but would derive both types from an *Urtrense*, which has never been found, but which he believes had a mouthpiece. As everyone else, he would see behind the twisted, jointed snaffle a rope prototype. The existence of such a stage in the Orient is postulated because this type appears early – soon after the straight bar.

The early bit in these regions, however, differed from early bits and from most later ones down to this day in another respect: the ends of the mouthpiece passed through holes in the cheekpieces. While it is possible to envisage a rope mouthpiece the ends of which were fastened around rod-like cheekpieces, or even through holes in bone ones, a rope passing through a hole in a metal plate would seem highly impractical. Even if there were large knots in the rope on the outside of each cheekpiece, so as to prevent the rope slipping right through when a single rein (presumably more of the same rope) was pulled, the metal edge of the hole would fray and cut it rapidly. (Nor would a rope be 'jointed'). These are, at least, arguments for a different genesis of the jointed, twisted, metal mouthpiece in the Orient. We may suggest it as a modification of the solid bar passing from rein to rein through the two cheekpieces – an arrangement designed, as we have seen, to improve directional control of the driven horse. That this construction created extra pressure and wear on the cheekpiece is testified to by the raised tubular reinforcement that surrounds the central holes of ancient bronze cheekpieces of this type (Potratz 1966, figs. 45b–g). No such reinforcement existed, or could exist, on the mouthpiece proper, the bronze of which was equally soft. But if one 'broke' the mouth in its centre and linked it, the ends of the two sections (canons), when pulled, would slant somewhat backward and there would be less severe pressure on them and the cheekpieces in the area of friction. Jointed mouths are not always twisted – even in early days (Potratz 1966, 110, fig. 45f). The twisted form may have started when replacing damaged mouthpieces, or making cheap ones, which did not need to be welded. A slenderer piece of metal could be handled more easily, and might even be replaced in the field in an emergency. Two pieces of wire could be crossed in the centre and returned on themselves, twisted to give them the proper thickness and strength. Thus, the better-made twisted canons may have had a simpler *wire* prototype, rather than a rope one. As the extra effectiveness of the twisted ones was recognized, they would become popular. Twisted snaffles are used today when a 'stronger' snaffle is needed (Edwards 1963, fig. 40). A still stronger modern bit is the wire snaffle.

This design of bit, with the ends of the canons passing through the cheeks, is unsound from the point of view of wear and tear on both elements (particularly since it was in bronze) and it must have had compensatory virtues: It may be seen as an attempt to separate directional control from braking, in a bridle on which the cheekpiece was still a part of, or was still connected to, the low noseband. The other possibility – that it was designed so as to exert extra leverage on the jaw, would be eliminated so long as the noseband connexion was present, but would play a role when that was abandoned – as on the Assyrian and Luristan bits.

We have perhaps for too long assumed the rope mouthpiece prototype in all our thinking, which has undoubtedly been coloured by the American Indian's frequent use of a rope in the horse's mouth. We should not forget that this rope was really tied *around* the lower jaw – not placed as a bit. There are peoples today in the Near East who have known and used the horse for millennia and these, when they do not have or are not using a metal bit, do not replace it with a rope in the mouth, but with a rope or chain around the nose.

This hypothesis would not only help to explain the basic differences between Oriental and other early cheekpieces, but would go further. We would now see the southwest Asian *mouthpiece* originating in a metal bar, the original role of which was to improve directional control.

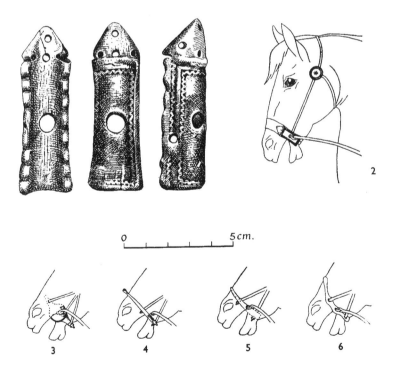

Fig. 7. Bone and horn bits from the Volga-Ural region. After Gimbutas 1965.

Here is where India's studded noseband control and her continued use of the *hemione* in the chariot may shed a backward light.
She may still be using a form of bridling that corresponds to the
transitional stage in the early 2nd millennium Near East. Such bits
as those described by Arrian are straight bars, like the first Oriental
ones – to the Greeks they are mere 'spits'. It would be extremely
interesting if practices (including the continued use of the *hemione* in
the chariot) that seem closer to 2nd millennium southwest Asia than
to the steppe still obtained in this 'Aryan' culture.

Admittedly, this is only a model, which remains to be proven, but
since the old ones are imperfect, it is perhaps time to examine some
of the evidence in the light of a new one.

Addendum

Since writing the above, K. F. Smirnov's very important article on
early Russian bits has come to my notice (Smirnov 1961). This discusses finds of small bone objects in the Timber-Grave and Andronovo
cultures of southeastern Russia and Kazakhstan. A pair of these
found *in situ* by the jaw of a buried horse at Komarovka (Smirnov
1961, 50) confirmed them as cheekpieces; They are half-tubular in
form, cut from lengths of long bones, with a large hole in the centre, a small one close to one edge, and an upper projection with
several small holes. The long edges (facing in) are toothed. Although
these cheekpieces were used with a 'soft' mouthpiece, and are neither flat nor symmetrical, Smirnov compares them to early Oriental
long-plate cheeks, with which they do have features in common: the
mouthpiece ends passing *through* the cheekpieces, and the studded
inner face. The disposition and number of holes suggest that they
lay at right angles to the jaw, as did the Oriental ones (and as
Smirnov has reconstructed one) (fig. 7, 2), and that they were attached
to a widish noseband.

Smirnov 1961, 57 would place the cheekpieces between 1500 and
1100 B.C. but, since the chronologies of the cultural contexts are
not well established, this dating is based only on a comparison with
Hungarian and Oriental pieces. Thus the question of which way the
influence flowed is still open. The Russian cheekpieces may be viewed
as primitive prototypes of the more advanced Asian bronze ones, or
as rough attempts to copy in bone and sinew the bits of more

advanced regions. The early teeth here might indicate the latter. Teeth, as noted, are primarily associated with the problem of directional control of the horse in draught. While a few paired horse burials have been found in the Timber-Grave culture (Smirnov 1961, 46), there is no other evidence of the driven horse here, and Smirnov considers this gear was used by riders. A derivation from southern driving bits may be supported by the fact that, after the early period, teeth are abandoned in these regions. They return only with the Scythians, who had had intimate experience of studded cheekpieces in the Near East, and who *sometimes* added bit 'burrs', but never incorporated them in their cheekpieces.

From the same cultures there are three examples of smooth-faced discoid cheekpieces, which Smirnov 1961, 60–63 sees as related to the Oriental wheel-shaped ones and to Hungarian ones. Leskov 1964 noted five more, even earlier, very crude examples, probably from settlement debris of the Late Catacomb and Abashevo cultures. These have a large central hole, one or two small ones on the side, and three or four pyramidal studs on one face. Once again (if all these *are* cheekpieces), studs are confined to the earlier pieces. Moreover, this form is soon modified (for better attachment) by various appendages (fig. 7, 3), which tended to break off. The small numbers (four possible examples among the many Hungarian Bronze-Age cheekpieces (Mozsolics 1963, 83f., fig. 20; Potratz 1966, 115, figs. 46h–i) besides the Russian ones) and the often fragmentary condition of this type would indicate that bone or horn was ill-adapted to it, although in bronze it was practical enough to yield examples to a late period. (They still appear among Luristan bits: Potratz 1966, pls. 116–119.) These circumstances again suggest northern attempts to copy a workable southern model, rather than the other way around. The problem here is complicated by the fact that the disposition or number of holes on some discoid pieces argues against their attachment to any of the types of bridles we know from figured evidence. The areas of wear, for instance, on one Hungarian example illustrated by Bökönyi 1953, fig. 2, would place the line of pressure of the 'reins' vertically, towards the apex of the divided cheekstrap, i.e. towards the top of the horse's head.

It is usually assumed that horse gear developed first on the northern steppe, whence came the horse. This is to forget that onagers (and wild true asses) are known for their speed and spirit. To drive four of these stallions abreast must have required skill and training;

and it was being done when the steppe peasant was still herding horses only for meat. When the horse came south he was harnessed as onagers had been – by yoke and pole; his jaws are like those of other equids. There is as much reason to believe that a late technique of onager control, developed by people used to handling onagers in teams, was *applied* to him as that he *brought* it with him. Moreover, the late use of bone and sinew bits (Smirnov 1961, 46, 72) in cultures already practising metallurgy (Gimbutas 1965, 554, 556, 562–565) implies a far less exacting use of the horse among them than in the ancient civilizations.

Note. Mrs Littauer would like to record her special thanks to Dr Karageorghis for permission to measure the mouths of two bits from Tomb 2 and eight bits from Tomb 47 at Salamis (see p. 47, fig. 5 above); and also to Mr Joost Crouwel for calling her attention to the article by A. M. Leskov, which led to the discussion of Smirnov's article in the Addendum.

35. A NEAR EASTERN BRIDLE BIT OF THE SECOND MILLENNIUM B.C. IN NEW YORK*

M. A. LITTAUER AND J. H. CROUWEL

In a recent issue of this Journal we published a bronze horse bit with a solid bar mouthpiece and circular checkpieces, presently in the Israel Museum, Jerusalem.[1] Although the provenance and history of the object are unknown, it was presumably made during the second half of the second millennium B.C., somewhere in the Near East, and possibly in the Levant. Since then another cast bronze bit of related type has come to light in the collection of the Department of Classics of New York University (pl. 210a).[2]

Although the provenance of this bit is also unknown, it is suggested that it came from the Cesnola coll. It may have been among the "Nine small objects, implements etc." of bronze acquired among other (identified) items by the University from the Cesnola coll. in the Metropolitan Museum of Art, New York, in 1925. They are listed under "Cypriot duplicate sales" in the Museum's records,[3] Since Cesnola was collecting during the second half of the nineteenth century, when no bits of this type had been published, it is most unlikely that it is a forgery or a pastiche. Moreover, its utilitarian character with only simple decoration would not be apt to tempt a forger. Autopsy appears to show that the piece is genuine and as originally

* _Levant_ 18, 1986, 163–167.
[1] Littauer and Crouwel 1982, 178 with pl. XVII.
[2] The bit is now on loan to the Department of the Ancient Near East of the Metropolitan Museum of Art, New York. It was first identified by Dr. E.-W. von Hase and was subsequently brought to our attention by Dr. T. Kawami, to whom we are most grateful, as we are to Prof. L. Bonfante for permission to examine and publish it and for arranging for its metal analysis. We are also indebted to Dr. S. Heming (MASCA, University Museum, Philadelphia for the analyses, to Dr. Mertens of the Metropolitan Museum of Art, New York for checking the Museum's records, to Dr. P. R. S. Moore, for commenting on the bit, and to Mr. D. Kawami for taking the photographs.
[3] Their number corresponds rather neatly with that of the nine small metal objects that we saw in the New York University Collection. These are of mixed origin and date and include, apart from the bit, mainly weapons.

assembled. The analysis (see Appendix) indicates that both cheek-pieces and the mouthpiece are low tin bronzes; this is a standard second millennium B.C. bronze composition.

The bit is composed of a solid-bar mouthpiece and two circular cheekpieces. The mouthpiece (overall L.: c. 0.19 m., within cheek-pieces: c. 0.135 m.; Diam. at centre: c. 0.006 m.) is round in sec-tion and relatively thick. It displays a slight curvature in the same direction as that in which the ends are rolled.[4] Its ends pass through holes in the centres of the cheekpieces and are hammered out flat and rolled back on themselves, forming small loops that may have carried rings for the attachments of the reins.

The circular cheekpieces (pl. 210b; Diam.: c. 0.05 m.; Ht., includ-ing loop on rim: c. 0.07 m.) are of pierced design and present the appearance of four-spoked wheels. The central openings, or "naves", through which the ends of the mouthpiece pass, have thin flanges on the outside. They show traces of the type of wear on their lower edges that would be caused by the mouthpiece of a bit. The "spokes" of the cheekpieces are grooved lengthwise on the exterior, but not on the interior. At the outer ends of the two sections of each spoke formed by this groove there is a small nub lying on the surface of the rim. Each cheekpiece has a rectangular loop on its upper rim to take the cheekstrap of a horse's headstall. The top section of one loop, where the cheekstrap would have been fastened, shows shine – probably from friction. The loops, although cast together with the cheekpieces, end in hands shown as if grasping the rims of the cheek-pieces. The incised fingers are placed on the outside of the rims and the thumbs on the inside. Two incised lines cross the wrists. The flat, inner faces of the rims carry five, pointed studs (Ht. max.: c. 0.008 m.) at roughly regular intervals. The loops still show the casting spouts at their tops, where the molten metal was poured in. One of the cheekpieces is less well cleaned down and finished than the other: some metal still adheres to the rim, while the fingers of the hand grasping the rim are barely delineated by incision.

The object belongs in a well-known category of ancient copper/bronze bits with solid-bar mouthpieces and "wheel-shaped" cheek-pieces.[5] These, relatively few, bits have been found in the Levant,

---

[4] This arching is a functional feature, common on solid bar bits today, which allows room for the tongue.

[5] See Potratz 1966, 110ff. (type 2); Littauer and Crouwel 1979, 86ff. (type 1).

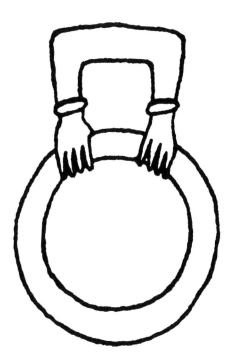

Fig. 1. Metal buckle from Susa. After Crouwel, 1972, 30, fig. 1a.

Egypt and Mycenaean Greece, as well as (probably eastern) Anatolia; there are also unprovenanced examples that have been attributed to "Luristan". Most, if not all, can be dated in the second half of the second millennium B.C.

The cheekpieces of the New York bit go with those (the majority) that carry suspension loops on their rims, and many of these are also studded on their inside faces. But its mouthpiece, with rolled ends, falls, rather, with the heavy, somewhat shorter mouthpiece of

Published material: Petrie 1934, no. 558 with pls. XXIII and XXXV = Potratz 1966, fig. 46: b – Littauer and Crouwel 1979, fig. 48 there fig. 4: complete example from I 830, Tell el Ajjul); Petrie 1933, 10, no. 221 with pls. XVII and XXXV (pain of cheekpieces from KS 998 at same site); Schaeffer 1938, 319 with fig. 46 = Potratz 1966, fig. 46: a (complete bit, with two suspension loops on each solid,* cheekpiece, from Ras Shamra); Borchardt 1912, 35ff. with figs. 26–27 = Potratz 1966, pl. 115 (complete pair of bits from Tell el Amarna); Crouwel 1981, nos. B 1–2 5–6 with pls. 1, 5 (fragmentary examples from Mycenae and Thebes); Bittel 1975, 303ff. with figs. 3–5 and pl. 56:1–2 (six complete or fragmentary examples, reportedly from Sarkişla, eastern Anatolia); Potratz 1966 112 with pls. 118–119 ("Luristan" bits, which have been dated to the end of the second millennium B.C. by Moorey 1971, 110 s.v. nos. 110–111).

the bit now in Jerusalem (L. overall: 0.145 m.). The cheekpieces of the latter, however, have no suspension loops and are more heavily studded on their inner faces.

The New York bit possesses two unique features:
(1) the lengthwise grooves down the centres of the "spokes" of the cheekpieces, with the nubs at their ends on the rim;
(2) the hands where the suspension loops join the rim.

The grooves do not occur on the reverse faces of the "spokes" and do not appear to be explained by any necessity of casting. They seem to be intentional – as decoration or in imitation of an actual type of spoke. We are reminded here of a type of wheel construction materially documented in Egypt, and very possibly in use in other parts of the Near East in the second half of the second millennium B.C.[6] In wheels of this construction the spokes are composite, each spoke sharing a longitudinal half with its neighbouring spoke, the outer ends of the "spoke" being morticed into the rims. The nubbins at the ends of the sections of "spoke" on the cheekpieces appear to be simply where the flow of metal was stopped. In view of this, we wonder if the cheekpieces were cast entirely in one piece or if the "spokes" and "nave" were added in a second stage: The suspension loops and the studs on the inner faces of the cheekpieces, however, were certainly cast simultaneously with the rim.[7]

The rectangular suspension loops are made to appear as if they were attached by means of hands that grasp the rims between fingers and thumbs. The incisions on the wrists suggest bracelets or the cuffs

---

[6] See Littauer and Crouwel 1979, 78ff.

[7] That the cheekpieces of this bit may represent wheels should not surprise. The form of the earliest known three-dimensional representations of spoked wheels (from an eighteenth-century B.C. copper/bronze vehicle model found in central Anatolia, Mellink 1971, 165) are closely echoed in metal cheekpieces of the later second millennium B.C. from Mycenae and Thebes (cf. Crouwel 1981 B1, B2, B3). And other ancient bits in the Near East at different times carried motifs related to their function. The same little hands that hold our cheekpieces in the headstall often held the rein rings at the ends of the mouthpieces (cf. *infra* n. 8) and quite possibly symbolized, and may even have been supposed to enhance, human control. The phallus (upper) and horse-hoof (lower) endings of the rod-like cheekpieces of bits of the Persian period that symbolized the fertility and swiftness desirable in the mount are other examples (*e.g.* Potratz 1966, pl. 124a, where the object is shown upside down). Equally symbolic are the galloping horse cheekpieces of the sixth-fifth centuries B.C. from southern Siberia and Mongolia (*e.g.* Moorey, Bunker, Porada and Markoe 1981, no. 871). Such an association of ideas is a ubiquitous human trait.

of long sleeves. These hand-ended rectangular loops are closely paralleled by a number of rectangular loops attached in similar fashion, not to the rim of a cheekpiece,[8] but to the ring of a buckle or
a roller. The former were probably used on belts; the latter may
have been connected with weaving.[9] The buckles can be dated on
the basis of the find contexts of examples from Susa (an Old Babylonian
tomb) and from the Assyrian merchant colony at Kültepe in central
Anatolia (a tomb in Kārum level II). The loops on the belt buckle
from Susa (fig. 1; dimensions not given) and on two others (presumably also from Iran) wear bracelets or cuffs too – not incised but
rendered in relief. The realistic conception of the thumbs around
the inside of the rims of our cheekpieces is repeated on the Kültepe
buckle (fig. 2; L. total: c. 0.08 m.; Diam. ring: c. 0.06 m.) and on
one from Iran. One loop with a roller is reported from the same
level at Kültepe as the buckle and clearly shows the grasping, hands,
although neither thumbs nor bracelets nor cuffs are visible in the
published illustration.[10] An object quite similar to the latter was found
at Gezer in Israel, "in an area of domestic occupation, probably in
levels of the local Late Bronze Age";[11] here the thumbs are present
although they are misplaced on the outside of the hands (fig. 3;
dimensions not given).

A rectangular suspension loop attached as if by grasping hands is
thus seen to be a type of loop that goes back to the beginning of the
second millennium B.C. and that remains in use until the later part
of the millennium, assuming that the roller from Gezer was made

---

[8] The motif of grasping hands is found on number of other bits in, however, a
different position – at one or both ends of the mouthpiece, to hold a rein ring, see
supra n. 5 (pair of "wheel" bits from Tell el Amarna); Potratz 1966, fig. 46: d, (bits
with openwork, circular cheekpieces, but jointed mouthpieces, from Transcaucasia,
probably of the later second millennium B.C.) figs. 59: a and b and pls. 126–131
("Luristan" bits with rod-like cheekpieces and jointed mouthpieces); Ghirshman 1939
(Vol. II), pls. XXV: 1 and LXXVI (pair of similar bits from Sialk B, tomb 74, in
central Iran, dating to the earlier first millennium B.C.).

[9] For buckles, see Crouwel 1972, 49ff. with figs. 1a (Susa; here fig. 1), 3 (Kültepe;
here fig. 2), 2 ("Luristan") and pl. XXI: 1a–b (acquired on art market, Teheran).
For rollers, see Moorey 1977a, 146ff. with figs. 6 (Kültepe) and 7 (Gezer). These
simple rollers are related to elaborately decorated openwork frames, without recorded
provenances but datable to the Old Babylonian period, two of which, from "Luristan,"
also have rollers, although without well-defined hands, ibid. 137ff. with figs. 2–4.

[10] T. Özgüç, H.N., October 6th 1951, ill. p. 547 (traced off by Moorey 1977a,
fig. 6); Özgüç 1952–53, 150 with fig. 15: right.

[11] Quoted from Moorey 1977a, 147. Original publication in Macalister 1912,
268ff., fig. 416 (= Moorey 1977a, fig. 7).

at that time. As something connected with small and utilitarian objects, the motif evidently travelled far and wide in the Near East.

Does this feature shed any light on the origin and date of the bit in New York? Although we have no bits with secure find contexts that can be dated before the fifteenth century B.C., and although there is no other evidence, such as representations or texts, it may be argued that it is most likely that the metal bits we know had more primitive metal antecedents, which have not been found or which have perished utterly. Our earliest bit with a (roughly) datable context, from Tell el Ajjul (ancient Gaza), is already a fairly sophisticated instrument and can hardly demonstrate the first attempt in metal (fig. 4. L. mouthpiece, overall: 0.265 m., within cheekpieces: c. 0.22 m.; Diam. cheekpieces: 0.07 m.).[12] Driving with fast, horse-drawn chariots appears to have been developed in the Near East in the earlier second millennium B.C., at a period when the mounted horse in this area still played an insignificant role.[13] We may assume that this and other early metal bits were driving bits and indeed their form would correspond to this necessity. The studs on the inner faces of the cheekpieces were for enforcing effective directional control, so essential for the war chariot and something more difficult on driven than on ridden horses. The long mouthpiece of the bit from Tel el Ajjul makes it correspond to the modern "run-out" bit, where the extension of the mouthpiece also provides extra leverage for enforcing direction.[14]

These features, to which may be added the decorative treatment of the five "spokes" of the cheekpieces – as lotus blossoms – indicate a certain degree of sophistication.[15]

---

[12] *Supra* n. 5. The drawing of this bit in Potratz 1966, fig. 462b, which has unfortunately been widely copied, is inaccurate: the "spokes" are actually lotus-shaped and the suspension loops are giving more room for the cheekstraps. For the dating of the other bits from the site, see Stewart 1974; also Littauer and Crouwel 1979, 87, n. 59 (using supplied by Moorey).

[13] See Littauer and Crouwel 1979, 50ff.

[14] See Littauer 1969, 289ff.

[15] Other evidence to support the premise of Near Eastern metal bits antedating the fifteenth century B.C. may be offered by the bone and antler cheekpieces found over a wide area from the Carpathians to the Urals, some of which have been given a sixteenth century B.C. dating. These objects were use with "soft" mouthpieces of rope or thong and appear to derive from metal prototypes in the Near East. They have been most recently exhaustively discussed by Hüttel 1981 (see esp. p. 178) and 1982, 39ff.

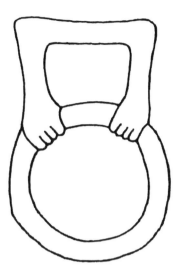

Fig. 2. Metal buckle from Kültepe. After Crouwel 1972, 51. fig. 3.

Fig. 3. Metal roller from Gezer. After Moorey 1977, 146. fig. 7.

Fig. 4. Metal bridle bit from Tell el-Ajjul. Jerusalem, Rockerfeller Musem 37.3271.
After Littauer and Crouwel 1979, fig. 48.

The New York bit, despite the close resemblance of its grasping
hands to motifs on objects going back to the beginning of the second millennium B.C. is probably not to be regarded as one of the
early prototypes postulated above. Although heavier in fabric than
the metal bit from Tell el Ajjul, it seems no more elementary in its
workmanship or its functioning. The most primitive feature – the bar
mouthpiece with flattened and rolled ends – is unfortunately unhelp-
ful in pinpointing date or place of manufacture. Similar mouthpieces
were associated with "wheel-shaped"cheekpieces of Anatolian bits
attributed to the fifteenth-fourteenth centuries B.C., with the Jerusalem
bit, the Ras Shamra bit with discoid cheekpieces, and with "Luristan"
bits with circular (but mainly zoomorphic) cheekpieces occurring into
the next millennium. The only differences are that one of the ends
of the Anatolian and Ras Shamra mouthpieces terminates in a flat
button (like one end of the Tell el Amarna "wheel-shaped" bits in
Berlin) while, with a few exceptions, the "Luristan" mouthpieces show
ends that are almost always rolled in opposite directions.[16]

---

[16] See Bittel 1975 (Anatolia), Schaeffer 1938 (Ras Shamra) and Potratz 1966,

The cheekpieces of the New York bit, although also wheel-shaped, like the Tell el Ajjul, Jerusalem, Egyptian, Anatolian, and Mycenaean ones, differ considerably from all these in design. The bit's closest parallel seems to be provided by an example said to be from "Luristan," that was seen on the German art market in 1954.[17] Unfortunately, its documentation is limited to a brief notice and a none-too-clear photograph published twelve years later. The one dimension recorded is the small diameter of the cheekpieces – 0.03 m. and 0.04 m. – which would seem to impair its efficiency as a working bit. Each cheekpiece has four simple "spokes", a relatively large rectangular suspension loop, without hands, and a very similar disposition of pointed studs. There are two additional studs where the thumbs appear on the New York bit, at the junctions of rim and loop. The mouthpiece of this bit, however, unlike the one in New York, has its ends rolled in opposite directions, in the usual manner of bits attributed to Luristan.

The New York bit is another important addition to the still small corpus of Near Eastern metal bits of the second millennium B.C., and certain details of its cheekpieces make it unique in its own category.

133ff. with pls. 118–119; Moorey 1971, nos. 116f., 119. 121. 124f.; also Littauer and Crouwel 1979, 118ff. (type 1). The "Luristan" bit with circular cheekpieces, shown in Potratz pl. 118 (London, BM), is exceptional in that the ends of the mouthpiece are rolled in the same direction, as on the New York and Jerusalem bits.

[17] Potratz 1966, 112, no. IV. 11 with pl. 119 (attributed to the end of the second millennium B.C., by Moorey 1971, 110).

Appendix

Elemental Composition (<, BY WT)*

Elements	End of mouthpiece	Loop of cheekpiece A	Loop of cheekpiece B
Cu	95.5	90.3	92.8
Sn	2.4	6.7	4.8
As	0.67	0.99	0.81
Pb	0.30	0.76	0.55
Zu	<0.081	<0.089	<0.075
Fe	0.086	0.062	0.072
S	0.13	0.14	0.098
Si	0.078	0.038	0.055
Ni	0.23	0.39	0.30
Ag	0.17	0.083	0.057
Sb	0.071	0.14	0.11

* Detection limits for trace elements here are: Pb (0.030%), Fe (0.015%), S (0.0070%), Si (0.0038%), Ni (0.013%), Ag (0.019%), and Sb (0.027%).

36. A PAIR OF HORSE BITS OF THE SECOND MILLENNIUM B.C. FROM IRAQ*

M. A. LITTAUER AND J. H. CROUWEL

This note concerns a pair of copper/bronze horse bits from recent excavations at Tell al-Haddad, a site in the region of the Hamrin Dam project in eastern Iraq.[1] The bits were found in 1980 by Iraqi archaeologists in the course of the removal of a grave belonging to a modern cemetery that covered the whole of the mound. Nothing was found with the bits to fix their date, but pottery described by the excavators as Kassite was found over the tell, below the surface, but above Old Babylonian levels. The bits were assigned to the Kassite period.[2]

The nearly identical bits clearly form a pair and show no sign of wear. They have solid bar mouthpieces and circular cheekpieces (fig. 1; pl. 211a–b). The mouthpieces (overall L.: c. 0.227 m., within cheekpieces: c. 0.168 m.) are round in section and relatively thick (0.011 m.). Their ends pass through the centres of the cheekpieces and are hammered out flat and rolled back on themselves, forming small loops that may have carried rings for the attachment of the reins.

The circular cheekpieces (Diam.: c. 0.07 m.; Ht., including loop on rim: c. 0.086 m.) are flat and of pierced design, with eight roughly triangular openings evenly disposed around the central hole (Diam.: 0.014–0.016 m.), while the area directly opposite the suspension loop is solid. The loops on the rim (broken off on both cheekpieces of one bit) were to take the cheekstraps of the horses' headstalls. The flat, inner faces of the cheekpieces carry eight pointed studs

* *Iraq* 50, 1988, 169–171.

[1] For this site, see Hanoon 1984, 70f.; also Iraq 43, 1981, 177f.; Iraq 47, 1985, 220f." (with bibliography). From textual evidence it seems clear that Tell al-Haddad, along with two mounds at neighbouring al-Sib, was called Me-Turan in the Old Babylonian period and Me-Turnat in Neo-Assyrian times.

[2] The preliminary report in Hanoon 1984 is slightly inaccurate in that the bronzes shown on p. 79, fig. 21 do not come from Old Babylonian tombs at al-Sib but represent a selection of objects from this site and Tell al-Haddad.

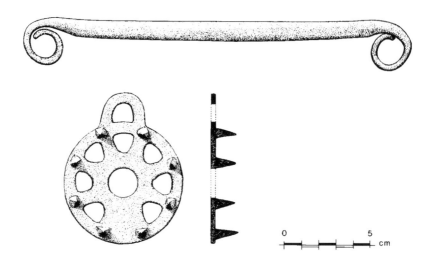

Fig. 1. Mouthpiece and cheekpiece, Tell al-Haddad.

(L.: 0.01–0.014 m.; one broken off on two checkpieces of separate bits) arranged at regular intervals along the circumference.

The bits belong in a well-known category of ancient copper/bronze bits with solid bar mouthpieces and "wheel" cheekpieces. Such bits have been found in the Levant, Egypt and Mycenaean Greece, as well as in (probably eastern) Anatolia.[3] There are also unprovenanced examples, some of which have been attributed to "Luristan".[4] Most, if not all, can be dated to the second half of the 2nd millennium B.C.

The bits from Tell al-Haddad would fall in the same time range and are the first to have been found in Iraq. Their cheekpieces go with the majority, which carry suspension loops, while studded cheek-pieces are also common.

Mouthpieces that have both ends rolled in the same direction are unusual, but they occur on two unprovenanced bits, in Jerusalem and New York (pl. 212), as well as on a "Luristan" bit in London.[5]

---

[3] See Potratz 1966, 110ff. (type 2); Littauer and Crouwel 1979, 86ff. (type 1). Published material assembled in Littauer and Crouwel 1986b, 164, n. 5.

[4] Littauer and Crouwel 1982, 178 with pl. XVII (Jerusalem) and 1986b, 163ff. with pls. XLII and XLIII (New York bit); Potratz 1966, 112 nos. 10f. with pls. 118f. ("Luristan" bits).

[5] Littauer and Crouwel 1986b, 163ff.; Potratz 1966, pl. 118 (British Museum).

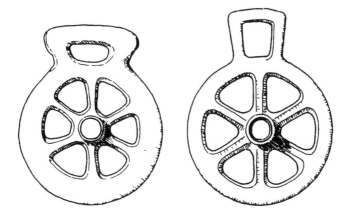

Fig. 2. Cheekpieces of horse bits from Anatolia. After Bittel 1975, figs. 4–5.

(The ends of the mouthpieces of the great majority of "Luristan" bits are rolled in directions *opposite* to each other.)[6]

In the form of their piercings the al-Haddad cheekpieces most closely resemble those of the circular cheekpieces from (probably eastern) Anatolia (fig. 2), although the latter have only six openings and no blank space.[7] In one respect, however, the Haddad bits differ from all known bits of this period: in the absence of flanges or collars reinforcing the exterior edges of the central holes of the cheekpieces.

The bits from Tell al-Haddad, if they are indeed from the Kassite period, help to date those in Jerusalem, New York and London with similar mouthpieces, mentioned above.[8] They also extend the area of distribution of Near Eastern Bronze Age bits.

The most important role of the horse in 2nd millennium B.C. – and particularly during the second half – was as a member of a chariot team.[9] The type of bit described here was a driving bit. Directional control is more difficult to exert on the driven than on the ridden horse. The studded cheekpieces would press against the horse's cheek

---

[6] See amongst others Littauer and Crouwel 1979, 118f.; Potratz 1966, 107, 138ff.; Moorey 1971, 106ff.

[7] Bittel 1975, 303ff. with figs. 3–5 and pl. 56.

[8] It should be noted that "Luristan" bits with circular cheekpieces were already attributed to the 2nd rather than to the 1st millennium B.C. by Moorey 1971, 110, because of their similarity to bits from the Levant.

[9] See Littauer and Crouwel 1979, 90ff.

and lips on the opposite side from that on which the rein was pulled. This persuasion was often reinforced by a long mouthpiece, as in the case of the Tell al-Haddad bits, which would have somewhat the leverage effect of a modern "run-out" bit.[10] It is therefore not surprising that these bits formed a pair. It so happens, however, that only one other *pair* of bits in this category has thus far come to light – that from Tell el Amarna.[11]

Acknowledgements

We are most grateful to Mrs. Rasmiya Rashid and the State Organization for Antiquities and Heritage of Iraq for permission to illustrate the bits from Tell al-Haddad, which are now in the Iraq Museum at Baghdad, and to Mr. Doni George for providing a photograph of them. Many thanks are also due to Dr. J. Black for much help and information, to Dr. P. R. S. Moorey for advice and to Professor E. Porada for first calling our attention to these horse bits. The photograph in pl. 212 appears by courtesy of the Classics Department of New York University and the Metropolitan Museum of Art.

---

[10] See Littauer and Crouwel 1986b, 166; Littauer 1969a, 289ff.
[11] Borchardt 1912 with figs. 26–27 = Potratz 1966, pl. 115.

37. SLIT NOSTRILS OF EQUIDS*

M. A. LITTAUER

The practice of slitting the nostrils of equids, which still obtains today in Iran for asses (pl. 213), is very ancient. It is first evidenced on chariot horses in 18th-dynasty Egypt. Fig. 2 shows a relief from Tel el Amarna (2nd quarter of the 14th century B.C.) with horses whose nostrils are slit. Egyptian bridles show a noseband placed very low. In the tomb of Tuthmosis IV (died 1402 B.C.) the excavators found bridles with "reins fixed to the nose-strap", and state "We believe that the command of the horses was obtained simply by the nose-strap" (Carter and Newberry 1904, 25f.). And no bits were found with the bridle material from the tomb of Tutʿankhamūn (Carter and Mace 1923, 173).

These nosebands were adjusted so low as to have exerted a painful pressure on the soft part of the nose – a condition of their effectiveness, then as today. But one of the disadvantages of this type of control is that it interferes with breathing. It is therefore possible to suggest that the original slitting of the nostril was in an attempt to compensate for the impairment in breathing caused by the "dropped noseband". The more so, since with the universal adoption of the bit in the Near East, the practice disappears. Assyrian and Persian horses show neither "dropped nosebands" nor slit nostrils – nor do Greek or Roman.

Slit nostrils are next documented from a very different time and area. In 786 A.D. two Italian bishops, George and Theophylact, were sent by Pope Hadrian to attend the Synod of Chelsea in Anglo-Saxon England. Among other local practices of which they disapproved was the slitting of horses' nostrils (Dent 1962, 70f.).

But at least by the 15th century A.D. this custom obtained in Italy itself (pl. 215). And the horse in Sodoma's painting of St. George and the Dragon (in the National Gallery in Washington, D.C.) shows

---

* *Zeitschrift für Säugetierkunde* 34, 1969, 183–186.

it in the first half of the 16th century. Powerful bits, rather than "dropped nosebands" were in use at the time, and the practice cannot be attributed to an effort to overcome the effects of the latter. It seems as if there may have been simply a general belief that it would improve breathing.

In the 17th century, the practice of slitting the nostrils is discussed by Jacques de Solleysel (1617–1680), the first Frenchman to write a regular veterinary work. Accompanying a diplomatic mission to Germany in 1645, he profited by the occasion to learn the language and to study German horsemanship and veterinary methods. In his *Parfait Marechal* (6th edition, Paris 1685, Tome Second, 11) he wrote, "The nostrils should be wide open, so that the carmine inside is seen when they are distended; nostrils thus open contribute not a little to the ease with which a horse breathes".

"It is for this reason that the Spaniards and many other peoples slit the nostrils . . . Slit nostrils serve another purpose besides easing the breathing of horses, which is that they are very practical because they prevent the horse from whinnying, which is very convenient for those who go on a scouting party, because then the whinnying does not betray them. This is why they slit the nostrils, because they rarely whinny thereafter".

"In Germany and in the north almost all crop-eared horses [military horses] have slit nostrils, even when their wind is good. In France, on the contrary, they only slit the nostrils of wretched horses with broken wind."

Ease of breathing was the alleged reason for this practice in Iceland into the 2nd half of the 19th century, and in North Africa at least as late as the turn of the century. It was still used in Mongolia in the nineteen twenties, as it had been in 17th-century France – in an effort to heal brokenwinded horses (Hill 1965, 34, 35). Mrs. Louise Laylin Firouz informs me it that the purpose of slitting donkeys' nostrils today in Iran is the supposed aid it gives to breathing.

38. AN ELEMENT OF EGYPTIAN HORSE HARNESS*

M. A. LITTAUER

In 1923 a curious object was found by Newton and Griffith in the excavation of a private house – probably that of the steward Akhetaten – at Amarna.** This consisted of a slender rod, made from the wood of a deciduous tree, topped by a spindle-whorl-like disk; short bronze spikes protruded from the edge of the latter. The disk and rod were inlaid with coloured bark in patterns (Rieth 1957, 148f.). At the centre top of the disk was what appeared to be a small, round, sunken hole. Although the German excavators in the previous decade had identified sites of stables and carriage houses and found fragments of leather harness and a pair of bronze bits at Amarna (Borchardt 1911, 16f., 26 with Abb. 7; 1912, 35f.), no one would have guessed that the 'mace' was in fact an element of harness, had not similar objects been discovered soon afterwards in the tomb of Tutʿankhamūn (pl. 217). It was then recognized as part of what, in representations, could be taken for a second rein running back from the bit to the yoke saddle, with an unexplained diamond-shaped object placed in the centre of it (pl. 218). This shape was evidently an awkward attempt to show a centrally thick disk edge-on. Carter described these rods with disks as 'goads', 'to prevent the horses from breaking from the line of draught' (Carter 1927, 112f.).

In 1957 A. Rieth published the Amarna fragment and one complete pair of the Tutʿankhamūn 'goads' as *Halssporen* (Rieth 1957). There were seven more examples of these from the tomb of Tutʿankhamūn, two pairs and three odd ones.[1] They varied in overall length from 0.185. to 0.565 m., with the majority being 0.53 m.

* *Antiquity* 48, 1974, 293–295.
** I am greatly indebted to Dr P. R. S. Moorey for his help with this note. He not only examined the Ashmolean fragment for me, but provided me with a copy of H. W. Fairman's transcript of Griffith's field notes for 30.12.1923. This was Griffith's only mention of this object, and it was Fairman who deduced that the find place must have been the house of Akhetaten.
[1] I owe this information to Howard Carter's notes, which are preserved in the

or over. The diameters of the rowels (without the spikes) ranged from 0.055 m. to 0.085 m. The Amarna ones, with an extant length of c. 0.33 m. and a rowel diameter of 0.092 m. must have been even bigger. Does this indicate that these bridle accessories were still in an experimental stage, or did it simply result from the preferences of individual drivers? The sizes of the chariot animals would not vary in anything like a corresponding degree.

A small hole pierced the shaft near either end, and in some of these are still traces of the leather thongs that attached them to headstall and yoke, respectively. Even the longest examples would probably fall short of the entire distance between these two areas; they must have been extended by the attachment thongs, which would thus allow the play necessary for the movements of the neck and head. Since the disks on the Cairo 'goads' revolved on the rods and were held in position by circular flanges apparently slipped over the latter and glued, the rods must have been continuous. This would be a stronger construction than if made in two pieces, one end of each being sunk into either face of the disk with no apparent adhesive except glue, as postulated by Rieth 1957, 149f. Tension would tend to pull these apart, unless the whole element were very slackly attached. Yet the fact that the Amarna example seemed definitely to have a fixed rowel and a socket for the other piece of rod was puzzling. Dr Moorey has kindly examined the fragment for me in the Ashmolean and states that he believes that this disk, too, once freely revolved on a continuous rod. "The hole in the disk is now partly obscured by the wax/glue used to restore it; but it looks to me as if the rod broke off in the hole . . .".

Carter believed that the 'goads' were purely for keeping the animals in the line of draught, but Rieth added to this the suggestion that they helped to spur the horses on at faster gaits, when the movement would particularly animate the rowels (Rieth 1957, 151). Neither of these explanations seems satisfactory. If the 'goads' prevented the horses from moving out of a straight line, one wonders how it would have been possible to turn the team. And, if their action became accentuated at faster gaits, they would have been a hindrance in slowing the animals down or stopping them. In reality, a horse moves

Griffith Institute, and to the courtesy of Dr G. E. Mouktar and Dr H. Riad. Through them I was able to examine the Cairo material, together with J. H. Crouwel, with whom I am collaborating on the publication of the Tut'ankhamūn chariots for the Griffith Institute (see Littauer and Crouwel 1985).

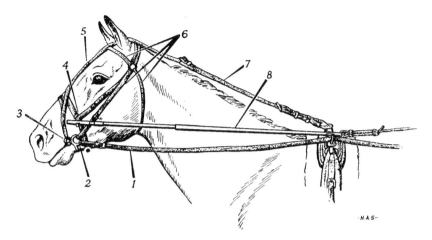

Fig. 1. Head pole on harness horse (drawn by H. A. Shelley, after J. C. O'Brien in Harrison 1968).

his head and neck up and down most at the walk and, were it movement that activated the effect of the *Halssporen*, the charioteer would
have had particular difficulty in keeping the horses down to this slow
gait when it was necessary.

A modern parallel to these rods suggests their real purpose. On
the trotting-horse track today – that is, where horses are raced at a
trot, hitched to light, two-wheeled vehicles, there is an object known
as a 'head pole' (fig. 1). This extends from the bridle near the bit
to the harness saddle behind the withers and, since the most modern examples are telescopic in construction, they need no slack line
at either end. The purpose of this pole is to keep the horse from
carrying his head crookedly, a fault that may spoil his gait or even
slow him down a fraction. This would not matter in chariot usage,
but where seconds count it is important. The pole does not, however, prevent him from making a normal turn. "If a horse is turning his head to the right . . . the head pole is placed on the left
side. . . . If the horse wants to carry his head to the left, the head
pole goes on the right side." When the horse bends his head
sharply in one direction, the middle of his neck (particularly thick
in stallions, of which chariot teams were composed) bulges out in
the opposite direction. With stubborn cases, a 'burr' or a 'ball' (fig.
2) – which between them divide the honours of the Egyptian disk –
is placed on the pole. When the horse turns his head sharply in the

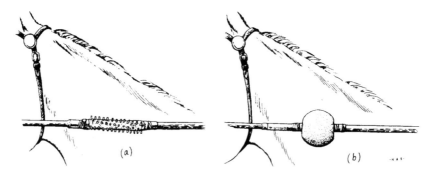

Fig. 2. 'Burr' and 'balls' on head poles (drawn by H. A. Shelley, after O'Brien in
Harrison 1968).

opposite direction from the pole, his neck is pressed by one of these
'gadgets', and he tends to straighten it quickly to avoid discomfort.

The Egyptian poles were not more than two to a team, and they
were placed on the outside of the horses. Hence their purpose would
have been to prevent the animal turning his head sharply towards
his team mate; in other words, it had nothing to do with keeping
him in the line of draught. The chief reason that would cause him
to make this movement would be the natural intolerance of one stallion for another and their considerable disposition to bite; a bickering chariot team would hardly have been desirable. The difficulty
encountered in this respect with earlier onager teams is well evidenced by the muzzles in which they were driven (Littauer 1969,
296 with fig. 6). Even Greek horses 800 years later still wore muzzles when led, even if these were removed in the bridling (Buschor
1969, pls. 132, 151).

Rieth has a note to the effect that Vienna fiacre drivers attached
thick knobs to the outer traces of their horses on the level of their
flanks to keep them from breaking from the line of draught (Rieth
1957, 153 n. 11). It is with his relatively freer hindquarters that the
animal *is* able to swing out, but in ancient harnessing, in particular,
the yoke would have kept the forehand quite rigidly in place.

The head poles are first depicted in Egypt in the Amarna period,
and there is no evidence of them later than the Ramessides, although
the latter circumstance may be due to paucity of figured documents.
There is no evidence for them outside Egypt and, so far as we know,
even Egyptian artists never illustrate them on foreign teams.

39. NOTE ON PROMETOPIDIA*

M. A. LITTAUER AND V. KARAGEORGHIS

A passage in E. Kunze's article on "Prometopidia" in the Olympia-
bericht VIII (1967) 194f., calls attention to the fact that both the
purpose and the manner of attachment of the bronze hinged horse
frontlets found in Cypriot 8th and 7th century B.C. tombs over the
past few years are not generally understood. In the *drómoi* of four
royal tombs excavated during recent years at Salamis skeletons of
horses have been found with bronze frontlets in situ on their fore-
heads (pl. 219).[1] The upper section of these frontlets was as a rule
found curved to fit exactly on the cushion which lay underneath it
(pl. 220). The hinge of the frontlet was always above the level of
the eyes, allowing the upper curved part to be attached to the strap
behind the ears. The top of the upper part of the frontlet terminates for this purpose in a hook. Near the top of the upper part of
the frontlet there was often a curving crest for feathers, as are often
seen on reliefs appearing between the ears of the horses. Evidence
in the round, provided by terracotta figurines from Cyprus, has now
not only established the manner of attachment, and the reason for
the two-piece format, but may explain another piece of puzzling
horse gear from the Near East. A 6th century chariot model from
Tamassos, now in the British Museum (pl. 223)[2] and another from
Ayia Irini, now in the Medelhavsmuseet, Stockholm show clearly the
use of frontlet and cushion. It is even more clearly seen and in detail
on a terracotta head of a horse probably of late 6th century B.C.
date, again from Cyprus, now in the Metropolitan Museum of Art,
New York (pl. 224).[3]

* *Archäologischer Anzeiger* 1969, Heft 2, 152–160.
    [1] The Salamis material has already been published: see mainly Karageorghis,
1967a; 1969c, 57ff.
    [2] Photo British Museum.
    [3] Fig. 5 by Courtesey of the Metropolitan Museum of Art, New York, The Cesnola
Coll. no. 74. 51. 1805; purchased by subscription 1874–76. – For the Tamassos

There is a slight difference in the lengths of the two sections of these frontlets, the upper one being always somewhat shorter than the lower. The upper end of this top section was attached to the crownpiece of the headstall, i.e. the strap that went over the horse's poll behind the ears. In some cases a half-tubular channel for a horse-hair crest curved forward directly over it, rising from the plate just in front of the area of attachment. This upper section of the frontlet, starting over the poll and running forward between the ears, would have protected the occiput and part of the parietal bones. The lower and slightly longer section of the frontlet, depending by a hinge from the upper one, would have protected the remainder of the parietals and the frontal and nasal bones. Because these parts of the horse's head do not lie in the same plane but form an angle, it was necessary to make the frontlet in two sections joined by a hinge.

A wide, thick cushion, which appears from the Assyrian reliefs to have been of quilted material (pls. 224, 225),[4] lay under the hinged part of the frontlet. It crossed the brow from cheekstrap to cheekstrap, just under the ears. This would not only have prevented the metal from resting directly upon the animal's head in the area immediately beneath it, but appears to have been thick enough to have held the plate somewhat up from the areas above and below it. In all this area the bone is very thinly covered and there would be no natural cushioning. Moreover, the direct rays of the noonday sun in these latitudes, striking a metal plate, would generate considerable heat, hence this type of padded browband would be effective as insulation as well as a cushion.

In looking for figured documents outside Cyprus to illustrate this further, one naturally turns to Assyrian reliefs, both because of the quantity of fine detail and because Cypriot harnessing of this period possesses more Near Eastern features than Greek.

The earliest Assyrian evidence of protective frontlets is 9th century B.C., under Ashurnasirpal II. It is very hard to tell from the reliefs whether these frontlets, which appear to be flat and undecorated, cover any more than the forehead and nasal bones of the

---

terracotta figurine see recently Masson 1964, 235f. fig. 20; for the Medelhavsmuseet specimen see Gjerstad 1963, 11 fig. 10 and cover; the Metropolitan Museum terracotta head has already been illustrated in Karageorghis 1967, 47 fig. 10.

[4] London, BM no. 124875. Photos BM. – Schäfer and Andrae 1925, pl. 33; Barnett (n.d.) pl. 84; Yadin 1963, 427; Strommenger and Hirmer 1964, pl. 458.

horse. In some cases they seem to continue upwards and backwards to form part of the arch that holds a crest of feathers over the poll, but in other cases no connection is visible. The first type, in which the crest holds a number of feathers together, may run from front to back, rather than transversally.[5] On the second type, the arched crests appear to hold three small distinct feathers transversally across the horse's polls.[6] In neither case is the brow cushion present, and the horse's normal forelock hangs free. On some renderings of the first type it looks as though the frontlet arched up and away from the forehead from the area of the eyes on back, but this may be due to the artist's inability to foreshorten. The second type seems to have been entirely separate from the crest and to have been suspended from an ordinary browband, the forelock hanging over it to shade it.

The latter seems to have been the way in which the majority of the ivory frontlets found at Nimrud were attached. Although these, because of their material, may have been primarily for ceremonial purposes, and are usually too short to have afforded much protection, they were probably modeled after more functional prototypes.[7] The manner of their attachment, as well as that of similarly proportioned bronze pieces, is indicated by a row of holes along their upper edges, and established by the stone horse head from Zinjirli.[8] This also demonstrates that the browband (a simple strap) and the upper part of the attached frontlet lay under the forelock, although in this case the latter is parted to show the design. A wide frontlet, however, that ran back between the ears to the poll to form also a poll plate would have to lie over rather than under the forelock, or it would be obstructed by the latter's roots. Of one 9th century type, noted above, that may have avoided this problem by arching over the forelock, there is no material evidence; of a later hinged type

---

[5] Barnett (n.d.) pl. 25; Yadin 1963, 387; Strommenger and Hirmer 1964, pl. 206 above.

[6] Barnett (n.d.) pl. 24; Yadin 1963, 386; Strommenger and Hirmer 1964, pl. 206 above.

[7] Orchard 1967, figs. 128–187. Similarly proportioned ivories were found at Gordion: Young 1965, 166f.; Kohler 1965, 198, pl. 46. We wish to thank Miss Kohler for the estimated dimensions of these, which have not yet been published. For a discussion of this type of frontlet in bronze as well as ivory, see Kantor 1962, 93ff.

[8] Bossert 1942, pl. 905; Barnett 1957, pl. 63.

there is. This is not only attested in bronze in Cyprus, but in ivory at Nimrud.[9]

A metal plate, however, even if hinged, would not lie very well over the forelock; it would tend to rub and break the hair, and if the forelock were thin or it parted under the plate, there would be almost no protection for the poorly padded bone here, not only from rubbing, but from the heat of the metal plate. Even under natural conditions, one of the functions of the horse's forelock is to shade his brow;[10] it also helps to keep the insects away.[11] With this normal protection damaged or inefficient, and with possibly at times greatly increased heat in this area, a substitute would have been desirable. It seems extremely likely that the brow cushion placed beneath these hinged Cypriot frontlets was devised especially for this purpose.

It is tempting to draw further conclusions and to suggest that a similar hinged frontlet was responsible for the introduction of the quilted brow cushion in Assyria — an object that has puzzled students of horse gear. Unfortunately, the only material evidence here consists of a few plates from hinged ivory frontlets.[12] The figured evidence is inconclusive. In it the cushion first appears in the 8th century B.C., under Tiglath-Pileser III, in conjunction with a three tiered poll crest, but no apparent frontlet.[13] If the latter were a thin plate, however, the artist might not have attempted to show it in strict side view. Neither should we overlook the fact that there is a lacuna of eighty years or more in the Assyrian reliefs — from the time of Shalmaneser III to that of Tiglath-Pileser III. This is a period long enough to have witnessed the introduction of a hinged frontlet and a brow cushion to go with it. Horses that sometimes wore such frontlets and had had their forelocks accordingly shaved (to accommodate the brow cushion) might have worn this cushion even when unprovided with a frontlet of any kind. This would have shaded the

---

[9] Orchard 1967, figs. 191–197.

[10] One of the authors remembers from her childhood delivery-wagon horses, which would be out in the sun all day, wearing men's old straw hats in summer. These had been pierced on either side with holes, so that the horses' ears would not only be free but would serve as pegs to keep them in place.

[11] Wolff and Opitz 1935–36, 326 suggested that the special purpose of the brow cushion in Assyria was to act as a fly screen, but for this alone it would be less effective than the longer and more freely hanging natural forelock.

[12] Orchard 1967, figs. 191–197.

[13] Barnett and Falkner 1962 pls. 14, 16, 67.

forehead, afforded some protection against insects, and counteracted the 'naked' look a shaven forelock produces – particularly among animals usually provided with one, as were the Assyrian horses. It may be significant that there is no instance in all these reliefs of a horse with a completely naked brow. Under Sargon II we find clear cases of the brow cushion without the frontlet.[14] Under Ashurbanipal we most frequently find the natural forelock present when the horse is without a frontlet and the brow cushion in use when there is a frontlet.[15] Unfortunately, there is nothing to indicate that the frontlet extends above the browband – rather the contrary. The most explicit document of all – a relief in Berlin, showing a quilted riding cloth and a bridle of Ashurbanipal's lying on a table – seems to prove that at least the type of frontlet always depicted under this king did not extend above the eyes, and depended from a regular browband, the cushion being extra, and that the crest is separately attached to a double crownpiece.[16] This type extended down to just above the nostrils, it was probably of bronze, and appears to have had a raised midrib, which would make it easier to depict in strict profile. Actual specimens of this type seem never to have been found. The rather prominent projecting knob at its junction with the browband finds a parallel only among a certain type of Scythian frontlet, which is, however, much shorter, and of decorative rather than utilitarian function.[17] But while we feel we should call attention to this negative evidence, it does not seem sufficient to refute conclusively the suggestion that the brow cushion began as an accessory to a hinged frontlet – and may have continued as a fashion even when the latter was not present.

[14] Barnett (n.d.), pl. 43; Yadin 1963, 427.

[15] Paterson 1915, pls. 42, 66 (top right); Barnett, (n.d.), 64, 84, 85, 87, 89, 96; Strommenger and Hirmer 1964, pls. 252, 256–258.

[16] Paterson 1915, pl. 100; Gadd 1936, pl. 41. The best photo is in Meyer 1965, pl. 160. We wish to thank Miss E. Porada for calling our attention to the recent work by Hrouda 1965, 93ff. 134ff. 150ff. Although Hrouda discusses the figured evidence for Assyrian bridling in some detail, he does not recognize the frontlet of which we seem to have evidence under Ashurnasirpal, nor that of which we do have incontrovertible evidence under Ashurbanipal.

[17] Minns 1913, figs. 45, XIII 6, 7; 61; Artamonova and Formana 1966, figs. 128, 132.

40. THE TRUNDHOLM HORSE'S TRAPPINGS: A 'CHAMFREIN?' REASONS FOR DOUBTING*

M. A. LITTAUER AND J. H. CROUWEL

In Antiquity 63 (1989) 539–546, P. Ashbee suggested a re-interpretation of the punched and incised pattern on the head and neck of the horse of the famous "sun carriage" from Trundholm, Denmark (fig. 1). In his view these patterns should no longer be regarded as mere decoration, but as representing a stud-ornamented leather chamfrein and the elements holding it in place. Such a possibility would be of prime importance to the history of horse equipment and requires fuller consideration.

As the Trundholm model is attributed to Bronze IIb or IIc on the Montelius system (i.e. to the 13th century B.C.), we would here have not only much the earliest example in western Europe, as Ashbee points out, but the earliest anywhere from the Atlantic coast to the Caspian Sea. By comparison, the hitherto known chamfreins are young. A number of bronze examples come from 9th- and 8th-century B.C. Urartu (Özgen 1984, 92–98, plates 6–15); an unusual chamfrein was found at Hasanlu in northwest Iran, dates c. 800 B.C. (de Schauensee and Dyson 1983: 67, 68; Littauer and Crouwel 1984, fig. 7 and pl. VIII; for most recent dating see Dyson and Muscarella 1989). Numerous bronze chamfreins were found in 8th- and 7th-century B.C. Cypriot burials with horses (Donder 1980, nos. 201–244 with plates 20–28) as well as ivory parade examples in 9th–7th-century B.C. contexts from Nimrud (Orchard 1967, nos. 138–191, plates XXVI–XLI; for a discussion of the figured evidence from this period see Littauer and Karageorghis 1969).

While none of these, with the exception of the Hasanlu example, have eye-holes or are as extensive as the Trundholm one would have been, the bronze ones lined with leather were undoubtedly designed

* Antiquity 65 1991, 199–122.

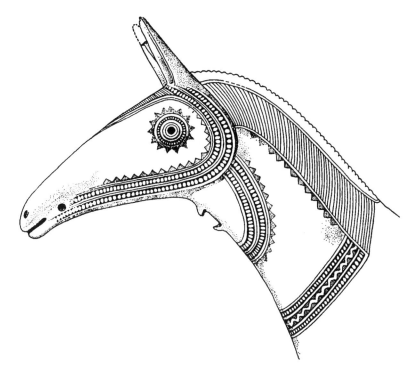

Fig. 1. Head of the Trundholm horse. After Sandars 1968: 185, figure 69A; used as Ashbee 1989: 543, figure 2b.

to furnish protection as well as decoration in areas where we know military chariot horses and mounts were in use.

It is generally assumed that a ceremonial object had a functional prototype, rather than the opposite. The Trundholm chamfrein appears in a clearly cultic context, implying a predecessor of practical intent. The use of the chariot, however, was still very limited in Late Bronze Age northern Europe and its design, illustrated primarily in rock art (Piggott 1983, 16–19), points to the southeast. Ashbee suggests this area for the type of horse. Despite its considerable schematization, the figure seems to indicate a light, gracile type of animal, unlikely to be native. The four-spoked wheels of the carriage, moreover, unless they are pure convention (Piggott 1983, 115), point to a dryer climate (Littauer and Crouwel 1985, 102). The authors know, from having worked with both the Near Eastern and the Egyptian documentation, that there is no evidence for any

Fig. 2. Reconstruction of horses with mane covers found in Barrow 1 at Pazyryk, Siberia. After Jettmar 1964: figure 87.

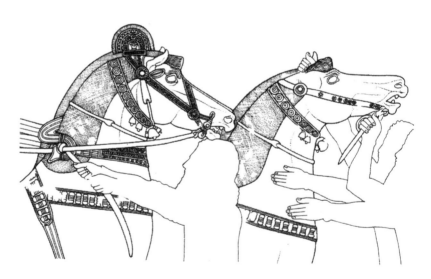

Fig. 3. Details of harnessing scene on relief of Ashurbanipal, Nineveh. British Museum, 1223339. After Littauer and Crouwel 1979: figure 62.

type of chamfrein in that direction at such an early date, nor is the Trundholm chamfrein formally related to the examples that appear there later.

We therefore query Ashbee's interpretation of the decoration. It is related to that on the sun disk that the horse pulls and could as well be a manner of emphasizing the line of the mandible, while the narrow triangle depending from between the ears suggests a forelock. Ashbee's "pierced eye guard" could similarly emphasize the orbits. Faint lines in the drawing (fig. 1) – now apparently badly worn – indicate that the chamfrein extended to the end of the horse's muzzle. But all full chamfreins of any period are cut back here to allow room for the bit, which Ashbee places in the hole *above* the corner of the horse's lips. If the hole were for a cord to pull the model along this would account also for the wear.

Ashbee suggests that the upper part of the chamfrein was "anchored to a broad, line-ornamented mane-cover or perhaps sidelong bands", and finds his parallels as far away in time as place as the 4th-century B.C. frozen burials at Pazyryk in Siberia (fig. 2). But these mane covers do *not* lie along the side of the neck as do Trundholm's vertical lines, but are entirely above it. What we see at Trundholm is far more reminiscent of the manes in many Assyrian reliefs of the 7th century B.C. (fig. 3). This seems to be a way of showing a parted mane, such as we sometimes see again in illustrations of European horses in the 17th century A.D. (Ridgeway 1905, fig. 91).

The swag of decoration across the throat was, Ashbee suggests, to help hold the chamfrein in position, but a strap at such an angle would only fall forward and away. If we suppose that the decoration may represent artefactual as well as anatomical features, this swag could stand for a chaplet on the neck of a cultic animal. The lower band of decoration across the neck, Ashbee suggests, was for securing the supposed mane-cover. More realistically, it could be intended for the strap that held a yoke in place. All draught in antiquity was by paired animals under yoke, and it has been suggested that there was a second horse here, as there was with a fragmentary sun chariot found at Halsingborg in Skane (Kühn 1935, 90f., fig. 315: Davidson n.d., 52). There should then have been a yoke, as well as the second horse, among the elements known to be missing at Trundholm.

41. ANCIENT IRANIAN HORSE HELMETS?*

M. A. LITTAUER AND J. H. CROUWEL

A small number of metal objects, of homogeneous but distinctive and unusual form, some allegedly from northwestern Iran, appeared on the antiquities market in the late 1960's. A few examples have subsequently been acquired by museums in Europe and the United States, and one of these has been published (catalogue no. 4).[1]

The objects did not come from controlled excavations, their exact origin is not certainly established and, since they are completely lacking in any form of decoration, their date and provenance cannot even be suggested indirectly by art-historical methods. After waiting for other, similar, examples or for more reliable information to appear, we have decided to publish the ones of which we know now, in the hope that this may lead to recognition of some affiliation hitherto unsuspected.

Precisely because these objects have no decorative attraction and belong in a thus far unknown category, it is reasonable to suppose that they are genuine and not fakes.

The material – copper/bronze (in no case has the metal been subjected to scientific analysis), the technique – hammered – the dimensions, and the form are so similar that the examples discussed here undoubtedly form a closely related group. At the same time; no one is entirely identical to any other.

Catalogue

1. London. British Museum, inv. no. 135437; pl. 226.
Provenance: "Northwestern Iran (Urartian), 8th–7th c. B.C."
Condition: Excellent.
Dimensions and disposition of holes: see schematic drawing fig. 1.

---

* *Iranica Antiqua* 19, 1984, 41–51.
[1] Moorey 1981, no. 700 p. 119.

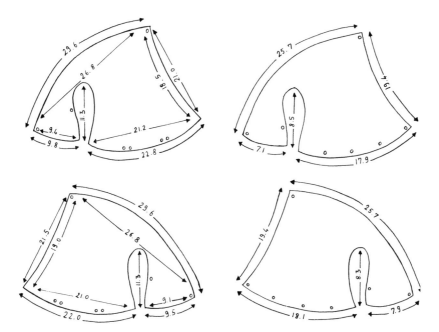

Fig. 1. Dimensions of helmet no. 1. Schematic drawing by Catherine Gorainoff.

Fig. 2. Dimensions of helmet no. 2. Schematic drawing by Catherine Gorainoff

2. Edinburgh, Royal Scottish Museum, inv. no. 1969.395; pl. 227a–b.

Provenance: "Northwestern Iran (Amlash region), c. 1000–800 B.C."

Condition: Generally good; small break in rear right-hand corner, probably site of a hole; the whole object has been under lateral pressure, which has reduced the distance between the lower sides. *Dimensions and disposition of holes*: see schematic drawing fig. 2.

3. Hamburg, Museum für Kunst and Gewerbe, inv. no. 1969. 249; pl. 228a–b.

Provenance: None given.

Condition: Generally good; two long dents across centre a little above ear holes, with a horizontal break along line of left side of lower dent, and vertical break in centre between upper and lower dents.

Dimensions and disposition of holes: see schematic drawing fig. 3.

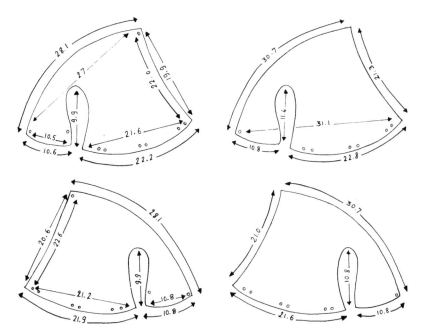

Fig. 3. Dimensions of helmet no. 3.
Schematic drawing by Catherine
Gorainoff.

Fig. 4. Dimensions of helmet no. 4
Schematic drawing by Catherine
Gorainoff.

4. Los Angeles, Los Angeles County Museum of Art., inv. no. M. 76.174; pl. 229a–b.

Provenance: "Iran, Sasanian period, 250–650 A.D. or earlier".

Condition: Generally good; small cracks at centre rear and at left-hand hole in centre front; lower right side bent inwards.

Dimensions and disposition of holes: see schematic drawing fig. 4.

5. Formerly Amsterdam, "Ancient Art"; 230.

Provenance: "Persia, Amlash, 1200–800 B.C."

Condition: Fair; small crack at rear near upper part of right side; apparent perforated break in fabric slightly above right earhole; lower sides apparently slightly pressed inwards. Small nick in central ridge just above earholes.

Dimensions: The only dimension given, seeming to correspond to the chord from front to back at top in the schematic drawings of figs. 1 and 3, is 0.25 m.; two holes at front and back edges on either side of ridge; holes on inner sides of earholes, in locations similar to those on Edinburgh helmet (no. 2); other holes not visible.

Fig. 5. Modern leather "head bumper" for transporting horses by van. Drawing by Catherine Gorainoff.

6. Formerly Amsterdam, "Ancient Art"; pl. 231.
Provenance: "Persia, Amlash (?), 1200–800 B.C."
Condition: Fair; small rectangular area at centre rear seems to have been broken off or removed and repaired (in antiquity?) by similar sized piece of different material, now apparently much corroded.
Dimensions: The only dimension given, seeming to correspond to the chord across the top in the schematic drawings of figs. 1 and 3, is 0.25 m.; two holes in front on either side of ridge; two holes along bottom edge of left side panel; other holes not visible, except for one apparently larger one to right of "mend" at rear.

The shape of these objects has primarily suggested their location on a pony's head. An exact replica[2] seems to support this supposition (no. 1, pl. 226), as does the fact that a padded leather accessory of fairly similar form is actually in use today as a head "bumper"

---

[2] We are greatly indebted to Dr. John Curtis and to the Department of Western Asiatic Antiquities of the British Museum for providing us with an exact replica of its helmet in fibre glass.

for horses being transported by van (fig. 5). Our objects have usually been called "horse helmets" or "chamfreins", but before seriously considering their suitability for this purpose we should mention
an alternative use that has been proposed. This would be on pit
(mine) ponies, as head protection against rocks or falling debris.[3] Pit
ponies' heads in recent times, however, have been protected by
leather padding with only a wide strap passing over the poll between
the ears and with the emphasis on protecting the eyes from above –
sometimes with iron fittings.[4] This our helmets would not do, although
pl. I indicates that normal side blinkers could have been used in
conjunction with them. Moreover, hand-hammered bronze would
seem to be too costly a material to be used on pit ponies.

Lacking the information that might have been provided by decorative motifs and finding no exact parallels illustrated in ancient
figured documents, we shall first approach the question from a negative point of view. By what kind of horses would these objects *not*
have been worn? The British Museum replica fitted (taking the nec-
cessary padding beneath it into consideration) a small Dartmoor pony
stallion, standing 1.07 m. at the withers (see pl. I), but it was too
large for the slenderer neck and smaller head of a mare of the same
breed and size. On the other hand, it was too small for a cross-bred
pony mare standing 1.27 m.[5]

This clearly rules out animals large enough to be practical military mounts. It suggests, rather, the chariot teams of the ancient
Near East, which are also consistently depicted as stallions. While
almost all early domestic horses were "ponies" by modern standards
(the official horse-show pony limit is 1.47 m.), chariot teams in the
first millennium B.C. are frequently shown as even smaller than
mounts. But in Iran in later antiquity we cannot even look for pony

---

[3] We are indebted to Hofrat Dr. Ortwin Gamber, Director of the *Waffensammlung*
of the Kunsthistorisches Museum in Vienna, for this interesting suggestion.

[4] Personal communication of F. Atkinson, Director of the North of England Open
Air Museum at Beamish.

[5] Athough individual animals standing up to 1.50 m. at the withers have been
found in Egypt, those suitable in height for the chariots of Tutʿankhamūn could
not have stood more than 1.28 m. (Spruytte 1983, 39f.) or 1.35 m. (Littauer and
Crouwel 1979, 82); for other discussions of the sizes of harness teams see Littauer
and Crouwel 1979, 56f., 110f. and 148f.; also Littauer 1971, 24–30 with pls. VI–IX.
There is also osteological evidence for a "miniature horse" among larger ponies in
northwestern Iran in the Median period (pers. comm. S. Bökönyi, 20.6.1977).

Fig. 6. Tell el Amarna relief. After Davies 1903, pl. XVII.

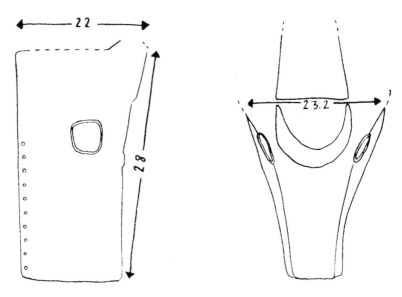

Fig. 7. Hasanlu fragmentary chamfron with dimensions. After de Schauensee and
Dyson 1983, 67, fig. 10.

teams, since there is no evidence of wheeled vehicles in Sasanian
times.[6]

Chariot teams ofter wear some kind of headpiece – i.e. plumes,
crests or chamfrons. The earliest illustrations, however, of anything
in shape resembling the "helmets" seem to occur in 14th century
B.C. Egypt – on a relief at Tell el Amarna, on Tuʿtankhamūn's
painted box and bowcase (pl. 232) and on other objects from the
latter's tomb.[7] This headgear is worn by royal chariot horses in a
variety of situations: processional, military and hunting (fig. 6). It not
only covers, as do the objects discussed here, the occiput and parietal bones, but also the first and perhaps even the second cervical
vertebrae, as ours would not. The "helmets" illustrated give no evidence of being of metal, but appear as of real (or imitation?) spot-
ted hide or of patterned or decorated cloth, and they are usually
crowned with the pharaonic plumes. The hide or cloth could, of
course, have covered metal, and in contemporary Nuzi protective

---

[6] Bulliet 1975, 16.
[7] Smith 1965, fig. 201; Davies 1962, pls. 1–4; Carter 1933, pl. XXVIII (bowcase), and vol. II (London 1927), pls. LXI a and LXII (gold fan – too garbled to
be informative); Desroches-Noblecourt 1963, pl. XXIIa (gold openwork plaque).

headpieces of metal or leather lamellae were worn by non-royal chariot horses.[8] The type of headpiece illustrated in Egypt is followed by a long line of Assyrian, Syrian, Iranian, Urartian, Cypriot, Italic and Scythian frontlets and/or crest holders in metal or ivory, numerous, actual examples of which have been found.[9] Although these vary a good deal in form and dimensions, none of them extends to the rear beyond the occiput to cover the first cervical vertebra and the upper ends of the lower jawbone, nor, with the probable exception of some Urartian examples, do they spread so widely over the parietal bones between the ears as do the examples discussed here. The most extensive head protection known to us from the ancient Near East is represented by a fragmentary copper/bronze piece found in Burnt Building II of level IV B at Hasanlu, in northwestern Iran, dating to the late 9th century B.C. (pl. 233 and fig. 7).[10] It appears to be unique for such an early period in having eyeholes and extending over the upper cheeks of the horse. Only in Roman Imperial times do we find metal parade chamfrons that cover the front and sides of the head completely, extending much further than ours in these areas, yet not reaching beyond the ears in the upper parts and, since these are for mounts, they would be too large for the small ponies that our helmets fit.[11]

The only known late object that covers a similar – if more limited – area of the animal's head is the "Torrs chamfrein" (fig. 8). This unique piece of Celtic bronzework was found in southern Scotland and is attributed on stylistic grounds to the second half of the 3rd century B.C. Careful examination confirmed that it had been tampered with – probably in antiquity – and that the horns that it carried when found had been added.[12] It is here shown with the horns removed and with a poll plume, as it was most likely originally designed and as it must have fitted at one time, over a small

---

[8] Kendall 1978, 192f. (with fig. 5); Zaccagnini 1977, 32ff. Much of this detail on Egyptian monumental reliefs seems to have been in colour – if one is to trust the 19th century copyists – that has almost entirely disappeared today; see, however, Nelson 1930–32 (Vol. I), pls. 23, 24 (royal teams of Ramesses III).

[9] E.g. Orchard 1967, pls. XXVI–XLI; Özgen 1982, 113ff. gives a summary of Near Eastern chamfrons, with stress on Urartian examples; Donder 1980, pl. 20–28; Berger 1982; Artamonov 1969, fig. 31, pls. 146. 186. 187; Murzhin and Chernenko 1980.

[10] de Schauensee and Dyson 1983, 67f. with fig. 10.

[11] Garbsch 1978, pl. 4–6, 13, 46f.

[12] Atkinson and Piggott 1955, 197.

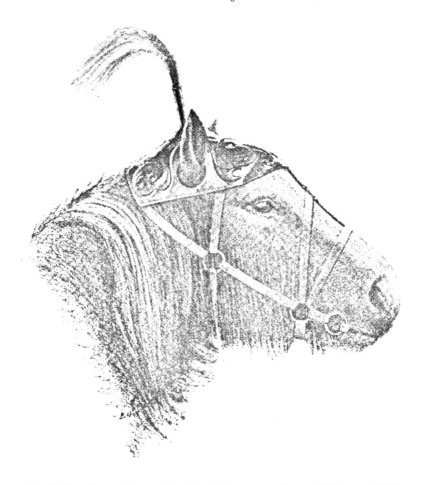

Fig. 8. The Torrs "chamfrein". After Atkinson and Piggott 1955, pl. LXXIX.

pony's head. This particular example appeared to be purely decorative, but whether it may be the sole survivor of a type that might
have served a more utilitarian purpose is unknown. It may or may
not be significant that Britain was one of the last areas to abandon
the military use of the chariot.[13]

Nos. 2, 4 and 5 and perhaps the left side of no. 3 seem to show
the effects of lateral pressure, suggesting that they lay on their sides

---

[13] Anderson 1965, 349ff.

in the earth. This is the position in which chariot teams were buried.[14] Moreover, the long transverse dents made by some sharp instrument on the top of no. 3 would appear, rather, to have been caused by a blow from above – as would the nick in the same area of no. 5 – making them less likely to be the traces of the digging spade than of a weapon's blade.[15]

The holes along the edges of the helmets seem most obviously intended for the attachment of a lining – probably padded – and from which straps could have secured the headpiece either to the headstall or independently. It is possible that the helmets were also covered with something like a patterned fabric or hide.

These copper/bronze objects, several of which are reported to have come from northwestern Iran or neighbouring regions, form a highly homogeneous group. By their shape they seem more suitable to be used as horse helmets than for any other purpose. Their dimensions indicate that they would only have fitted the heads of quite small ponies – too small for normal adult riding purposes.[16] Unfortunately, we still do not have enough secure information to confirm their use on chariot teams as suggested above, but what evidence there is appears to point more in this direction than in any other.

---

[14] E.g. Ghirshman 1964, figs. 131 (Hasanlu) and 133 (Scythian Kostramskaya); Artamonov 1969, pls. III, IV, VII and VIII (These are riding rather than chariot horses, but their positions follow the usual harness-horse burial formula); Vermeule 1964, pl. XLVII B (Marathon); Watson 1961, pl. 11 (Shang China). The well-known harness teams in the *drómoi* of the Salamis tombs in Cyprus are not "laid out" formally, as in many team burials, but apparently were left to lie in a disorderly fashion, as they fell in their death struggles; they were, moreover, sometimes disturbed by secondary burials, Karageorghis 1969a, figs. 6. 7. 10. 15. 19.

[15] We are much indebted to Dr. Wilhelm Hornbostel, Director of the Museum für Kunst and Gewerbe, Hamburg, for helpfully answering our inquiries as well as for supplying us with detailed photographs, and to Dr. Helmut Nickel, Curator of the Arms and Armor Department of the Metropolitan Museum of Art, New York, for discussing these matters with us.

[16] This is not to deny the fact that equally small ponies can carry grown men, as they have carried farmers on the moorlands and islands of Great Britain until recently, but to stress that such animals would not be chosen for mounts in warfare were anything larger available (as it was in most areas in antiquity, barring perhaps Britain).

Acknowledgements

We are very grateful to the Museum Curators, Dr. J. E. Curtis (London), Miss J. Scarce (Edinburgh), Dr. W. Hornbostel (Hamburg) and Miss S. Candy (Los Angeles), as well as to Messrs. J. Möger and G. Turner (Amsterdam) for helping with information and supplying photographs; to Miss M. de Schauensee for answering our queries about the horse helmet from Hasanlu and to her and Dr. R. H. Dyson for permission to publish a photograph of it; to Miss C. Gorainoff for making the drawings in figs. 1–5.

42. NEW LIGHT ON PRIAM'S WAGON?*

MARY AIKEN LITTAUER AND JOOST H. CROUWEL

ἐκ μὲν ἄμαξαν ἄειραν ἐΰτροχον ἡμιονείην
καλὴν πρωτοπαγέα, πείρινθα δὲ δῆσαν ἐπ᾿ αὐτῆς,
κὰδ δ᾿ ἀπὸ πασσαλόφι ζυγὸν ᾕρεον ἡμιόνειον
πύξινον ὀμφαλόεν, εὖ οἰήκεσσιν ἀρηρός·
ἐκ δ᾿ ἔφερον ζυγόδεσμον ἅμα ζυγῷ ἐννεάπηχυ.
καὶ τὸ μὲν εὖ κατέθηκαν ἐϋξέστῳ ἐπὶ ῥυμῷ,
πέζῃ ἔπι πρώτῃ, ἐπὶ δὲ κρίκον ἕστορι βάλλον,
τρὶς δ᾿ ἑκάτερθεν ἔδησαν ἐπ᾿ ὀμφαλόν, αὐτὰρ ἔπειτα
ἑξείης κατέδησαν, ὑπὸ γλωχῖνα δ᾿ ἔκαμψαν.
ἐκ θαλάμου δὲ φέροντες ἐϋξέστης ἐπ᾿ ἀπήνης
νήεον Ἑκτορέης κεφαλῆς ἀπερείσι᾿ ἄποινα,
ζεῦξαν δ᾿ ἡμιόνους κρατερώνυχας ἐντεσιεργούς,
τούς ῥά ποτε Πριάμῳ Μυσοὶ δόσαν ἀγλαὰ δῶρα.

Iliad xxiv 266–278

brought out the light-running mule wagon, fair and newly made, and bound on it the wicker box; and down from its peg they took the mule yoke, a boxwood yoke with a knob on it, well fitted with guiding rings; and they brought out the yoke band of nine cubits, and with it the yoke. The yoke they set with care on the polished pole at the upturned end, and cast the ring on the peg; and they bound it fast to the knob with three turns to left and right, and then made it fast to the post, and bent the tongue underneath. Then they brought out from the treasure chamber and heaped on the polished wagon the countless ransom for Hector's head, and yoked the strong-hoofed mules that toil in harness, which once the Mysians had given to Priam, a glorious gift.

(Wyatt. Jr 1999, 583)

Homer's description of the harnessing of a wheeled vehicle has puzzled commentators since antiquity because of the unusual technical

* Journal of Hellenic Studies 108, 1988, 194–196.

terms used.[1] This note concentrates on one of these, drawing upon archaeological evidence.

The mule-drawn *apēnē* – somewhat later described as four-wheeled (line 324) – is being prepared on Priam's orders for the purpose of carrying the ransom to Achilles in exchange for Hector's body, which is then brought back to Troy by the same conveyance. The wagon is driven by Priam's herald, Idaios, but the old man himself drives a horse-drawn chariot behind it. Clearly, a wagon is not the proper equipage for a king. And indeed, the heroes of the *Iliad* and the *Odyssey* commonly used chariots – fast two-wheelers pulled by horses – for ceremony and travel, as well as in racing and as conveyances to and from the battlefield.[2] But the *apēnē* and *amaxa* (obviously synonymous in the epic poems)[3] are more mundane vehicles, used as carriers (for timber, stone, laundry) and may be pressed into service to carry the dead.[4] Apart from the passage under discussion, there is another, in the *Odyssey* (ix 241f.) where the number of wheels is explicitly stated as four. In the other cases it is not clear whether four-wheeled wagons or two-wheeled carts are intended.[5]

The term with which we are here concerned, however, was only used in the Homeric poems in connection with a specifically four-wheeled vehicle. It is *zugodesmon*, which in Homer occurs only in *Iliad* xxiv 270: ἐκ δ᾽ ἔφερον ζυγόδεσμον ἅμα ζυγῷ ἐννεάπηχυ 'and they (Priam's sons) brought forth the *zugodesmon*, nine cubits long, together with the yoke'. Taken in its literal sense of 'yoke binding' *zugodesmon* may be interpreted as meaning the lashing by which the yoke was secured to the pole. It would be quite natural to mention it in this passage, since the yoke had been stored separately from the vehicle and the binding is often a feature of ancient yoke-and-pole harnessing. A problem arises, nevertheless, when the apparently excessive length

---

[1] We are most grateful to Mrs I. J. F. de Jong for her help with the textual material and to her and Professor Dr C. J. Ruijgh for comments upon a draft text. For discussion of the passage in recent times, see esp. Helbig 1887, 147–155 with fig. 44; Leaf 1884 with fig. 3; Reichel 1901, 128–142 with fig. 69; Wiesner 1968, 6-9, 16f.; cf. Delebecque 1951, 178, 180.

[2] For Homeric chariots, see esp. Wiesner 1968 and Delebecque 1951.

[3] See *Lexikon des frühgriechischen Epos I*, s.v. ἀπήνη: the choice between ἀπήνη and ἅμαξα depends on metrical criteria.

[4] Passages collected in Wiesner 1968, 5-11. We are not convinced that the amaxa, referred to by Hesiod (*Op.* 421–31) is a wagon rather than a cart, cf. Richardson 1982, 227.

[5] Note that explicit representations of wagons in Iron Age Greece are rare, in marked contrast to those of carts, see Crouwel 1981, 57.

(9 cubits or c. 4 meters) is considered. Commentators have rightly found it difficult to accept so long a binding for one small area. Some, in order to explain it, have turned to chariot-harnessing in mainland Greece during the iron Age. By adding the yoke-and-pole binding to the so-called pole-end support – a thong running out horizontally from the top of the front rail of the chariot box to the upward-curving forward end of the pole – they have attempted to find sufficient length to account for Homer's *zugodesmon*.[6]

Now the pole of a four-wheeler must articulate vertically in order to permit vehicle and draught team to adapt differentially to uneven-ness in the terrain, in contrast to the pole of a chariot or other two-wheeler which must be rigidly fixed so as to prevent it from collapsing. A pole-end support on Priam's *apēnē* would only eliminate the nec-essary flexibility.

There was, however, another type of lashing on ancient poles and yokes that would have been considerably longer than even the pole-end-support-cum-yoke binding and that should be taken into con-sideration as a possible candidate for the *zugodesmon*. This was the lashing that was wound around the pole and protected it from split-ting or breaking and that branched at some point before the pole end to run forward diagonally to either yoke arm. These 'yoke braces' prevented the yoke from swivelling on the pole, which could have squeezed the inside draught animal on a turn and caused him to kick the pole; they kept the team level and helped to distribute the pull along both pole and yoke. Yoke braces were a regular feature of Near Eastern and probably Aegean chariot harnessing of the Late Bronze Age. They also appear with ninth-century Assyrian chariots and seventh-century mule carts on Assyrian reliefs.[7] Although not illustrated on the few representations of four-wheelers that we have, they would in no way have interfered with their functioning, as would the pole-end-support. And they would have been appropriate on a vehicle drawn by 'powerful-footed mules'. In mainland Greece the binding of the pole is often illustrated on Black-figure vases show-ing chariots in side view, while the actual yoke braces are visible in some frontal views, branching out from the pole quite near the yoke.[8]

---

[6] See Helbig 1887 and Leaf 1884; cf. Stubbings 1962, 540f.
[7] See Spruytte 1983, 25 and n. 5; Littauer and Crouwel 1979, 85, 113, 101 with fig. 52 (mule cart); 1985, 79f.; Crouwel 1981, 97f.
[8] See Crouwel 1981, 98, cf. 93 (profile views showing the binding from the side).

The whole is well illustrated by the pole and yoke which are all that remain of a full-sized bronze chariot of Selene from third-century B.C. Etruria (pl. 234a–b).[9]

Were the ends of the yoke braces then brought inward to form the binding of the pole-and-yoke area, as the latter stage is described in Homer? We simply do not know.[10] But if they were, it would account for both the length of the *zugodesmon* and its use here as a pole-yoke binding. The wooden peg that pierced both the Yoke and the underlying pole and was often used in antiquity in conjunction with yoke lashings, may also have been present on Priam's wagon, as suggested by the word *hestōr* – 'pin' (line 272).

Is it possible to reconcile this interpretation of Homer's *zugodesmon* with the term when it appears again almost a millennium later in Arrian and Plutarch? In the former's *Anabasis of Alexander*, ii 3, we find the story of how Alexander solved the riddle of the 'Gordian knot'. The question was 'who could untie the binding of the yoke of the wagon/cart?' (τοῦ ζυγοῦ τῆς ἁμάξης τὸν δεσμόν). The vehicle is described as having been ox-drawn and the binding as made of cornel bark; neither the beginning nor the end of the lashing could be seen. Arrian gives two versions of Alexander's solution. In the first, he simply cut the knot with his sword. In the second version 'he took out the pin (ἕστωρ) of the pole, a wooden peg which was driven right through the pole, holding the binding together, and so removed the yoke from the pole'. Both versions are repeated by Plutarch (*Life of Alexander* xviii), who actually uses the word *zugodesmon*.

It would seem as if the sense of *zugodesmon* was by now restricted to mean simply pole-and-yoke binding. The vehicle, an ox-drawn *hamaxa*, was certainly not for fast driving and pole bindings and yoke braces would have been quite superfluous. Cornel bark seems a peculiar material for binding and would be difficult to tie, but it seems possible that the ends had been slipped under the binding when the material was wetted, to be pliable when applied. When it dried, the end would be invisible.

---

[9] Reichel 1901, 131f. with fig. 70; Piccardi 1950–51 with figs. 1–2; Littauer 1977d, 254 with pl. 19; Spruytte 1983, pl. 2: 1.

[10] Lines 273–4 are hard to explain in detail, but they suggest that the zugodesmon was wound around both the yoke, which was fitted with a knob (τρὶς δ'ἑκάτερθεν ἔδησαν ἐπ' ὀμφαλόν), and the pole (αὐτὰρ ἔπειτα ἐξείης κατέδησαν). Cf. Reichel's reconstruction (1901, fig. 69), and also Wiesner 1968, 16–18.

The same meaning may well obtain in the few other instances in which the term *zugodesmon* appears (either in the singular or the plural, diminutive or in the variant *zugodesmos*).[11] Two papyri from Egypt are of special interest. The relevant passage in one of these, a letter from a certain Sabinus to Geminus dated c. 100 ad, reads: "Kindly give Vestinus for his yoke a new, strong *zugodesmon*, which you will carefully grease, from those in the box of skins which you have with you ... for his own is cut."[12] The other passage, also in a letter, reads: 'Send to me at Aphroditopolis a *zugodesmon* for the oxen, strong and broad, as the one they have is cut.'[13] Leather or hide would be a normal material for any kind of harness bindings and it is not clear from the first passage what type of vehicle or draught animals were intended. But in the case where oxen are mentioned, the binding would certainly have been restricted to the yoke and pole.

It is possible to suggest that the word *zugodesmon* changed its meaning over the centuries or was used very loosely, the *zugodesmon* of a chariot or a fast mule team being more elaborate and including much more than that of a simple ox-drawn vehicle.

---

[11] LSJ s.v. 'ζυγοδέσμιον' etc.
[12] P. Fayum 121, 5; edited by Grenfell, Hunt and Hogarth 1900.
[13] P. Fayum 115, 15.

BIBLIOGRAPHY

Abbott, H.
1862   *The Abbott Collection of Egyptian Antiquities* (part of the catalogue of the
        Museum and Gallery of Art of the New York Historical Society). New
        York.
1915   *Catalogue of the Egyptian Collection in the New York Historical Society.* New York.
Ahlberg, G.
1971a   *Prothesis and Ekphora in Greek Geometric Art.* Studies in Mediterranean
        Archaeology 32. Göteborg.
1971b   *Fighting on Land and Sea in Greek Geometric Art.* Skrifter utgivna av Svenska
        institutet i Athen 4; 16. Stockholm.
Aitken, M. J., Moorey, P. R. S. and Ucko, P. J.
1971   "The authenticity of vessels and figurines in the Hacilar style", *Archaeometry*
        13 (2), 89–141.
Åkerström, Å.
1953   "Some pictorial vase representations from the Mainland in Late Helladic
        times", *Opuscula Atheniensia* 1, 9–28.
1978   "Mycenaean problems I. On the Mycenean chariot", *Opuscula Atheniensia*
        12, 19–37.
Akurgal, E.
1962   *The Art of the Hittites.* New York.
Alapfy, I. and Török, A.
1971   *Du cheval arabe au cheval hongrois.* Librairie des Champs-Élysées. Paris.
Albenda, P.
1986   *The Palace of Sargon, King of Assyria. Monumental Wall Reliefs at Dhur-
        Sharrukin, from Original Drawings Made at the Time of Their Discovery in
        1843–1844 by Botta and Flandin* Synthèse 22. Paris. (Editions Recherche
        sur les Civilisation). [in English (pp. 1–188); translation into French
        by A. Caubet (pp. 190–280)].
Alberti-Parronchi, G. and Piccardi, G.
1950–51 "Sui bronzi sacri del Bagno di Sellene", *Studi Etruschi* 21, 249–260.
Aldred, C.
1954   "Fine wood-work", in: Singer, Holmyard and Hall 1954, 684–703.
1961   *New Kingdom Art in Ancient Egypt During the Eighteenth Dynasty 1570–1320
        BC.* London.
Alexiou, S.
1964   "Neue Wagendarstellungen aus Kreta", *Archäologischer Anzeiger 1964*,
        785–804.
1973   "New ship representation on a Minoan larnax", *Acts of the Third Cretological
        Conference, Rethymnon, 18–23 September 1971*, vol. 1. Athens, 3–12. (in
        Greek).
Alp, S.
1968   *Zylinder- und Stempelsiegel aus Karahöyük bei Konya.* Ankara.
Amadasi, M. G.
1965   *L'iconographia del carro di guerra in Siria e Palestina.* Centro di studi semitici,
        17. Roma.
Ambroz, A. K.
1973   "Stirrups and saddles of the early Middle Ages as an indicator of

chronology (4th–8th century)", *Sovetskaja Arkheologija* 1973 (2), 81–98. (in Russian).

1979 "(Remarks) On the article by A. V. Dmitriev", *Sovetskaja Arkheologija* 1970 (4), 229–231. (in Russian).

Amiet, P.

1961 *La glyptique mésopotamienne archaïque*. Paris.

1963 "Notes sur la diffusion de la civilisation mésopotamienne en Syrie du nord", *Syria* 40, 57–83.

1965 "Un vase rituel iranien", *Syria* 42, 233–251.

1966 *Elam*. Auvers-sur-Oise.

1969 "Quelques ancêtres du chasseur d'Ugarit", *Ugaritica* 6, 1–8.

1972 *Glyptique susienne des origines à l'époche des Perses achémédides*. Mémoirs de la Délégation archéologique en Iran 43. Paris.

1987 "Nouvelle acquisitions du Départment des Antiquités orientales", *La Revue du Louvre* Février (1), 13–25.

Anati, E.

1960 "Bronze Age chariots from Europe", *Proceedings of the Prehistoric Society* 26, 50–63.

Anderson, J. K.

1960 "Notes on some points in Xenophon's ΠΕΡΙ ΊΠΠΙΚΗΣ", *Journal of Hellenic Studies* 80, 1–9.

1961 *Ancient Greek Horsemanship*. Berkeley.

1965 "Homeric, British, and Cyrenaic chariots", *American Journal of Archaeology* 69, 349–352.

1970 *Military Theory and Practice in the Age of Xenophon*. Berkeley and Los Angeles.

1973 "Review of Greenhalgh 1973b", in: *Antiquity* 69, 335.

1975 "Greek chariot-borne and mounted infantry", *American Journal of Archaeology* 79, 175–187.

Andrae, W.

1905 "Zusammenfassender Bericht über die Grabungen in Assur", *Mitteilungen der Deutschen Orientgesellschaft zu Berlin* 27, 4–28.

1943 (ed.) *Ausgrabungen in Sendschirli von Felix von Luschan (Herausgegeben und ergänzt von Walter Andrae)*. V. *Die Kleinfunde*. Mitteilungen aus den altorientalischen Sammlungen, 15. Berlin.

Andrews, R. C.

1932 *The New Conquest of Central Asia*. New York.

Andronikos, M., Chadzedakis, M. and Karageorghis, V.

1975 *The Greek Museums and Archaeological Sites of Cyprus*. Athens.

Anonymous

1823 *Vues de St. Petersburg*. St. Petersburg.

Antonius, O.

1938 "Zur Frage der Zähmung des Onager bei den alten Sumerern", *Bijdragen tot de Dierkunde* 27, 477–484.

Anthony, D. W.

1994 "The earliest horseback riders and Indo-European origins: new evidence from the steppes", in: Hänsel and Zimmer 1994, 185–195.

1995 "Horse, wagon & chariot: Indo-European languages and archaeology", *Antiquity* 69, 554–565.

—— and Vinogradov, D.

1995 "Birth of the chariot", *Archaeology* 48, 36–41.

—— and Wailes, B.

1988 "Review of Renfrew 1987", in: *Current Anthropology* 29, 441–445.

—— Telegin, D. Y. and Brown, D.

1991 "The origin of horseback riding", *Scientific American* 265 (6), 94–100.

Arendt, W. W.
1934 "Sur l'apparition de l'étrier chez les Scythes", *Eurasia Septentrionalis Antiqua*, 206–208.
Arias, P. E. and Hirmer, M.
1962 *A History of 1000 Years of Greek Vase Painting*. New York. (translated and revised by B. Shefton).
Artamonov, M. I.
1969 *Treasures from Scythian Tombs in the Hermitage Museum, Leningrad*. London.
1974 (ed.), *The Dawn of Art. Palaeolithic, Neolithic, Bronze Age, and Iron Age Remains Found in the Territory of the Soviet Union*. The Hermitage Collection. St. Petersburg.
Artamonova, M. and Formana, V.
1966 *Sokrovischa Skifskich Kurganov*. Leningrad. (in Russian).
Ashby, P.
1989 "The Trundholm horse's trappings: a chamfrein?", *Antiquity* 63, 543–546.
Astour, M. C.
1965 "New evidence on the last days of Ugarit", *American Journal of Archaeology* 69, 253–258.
1988 "The geographical and political structure of the Ebla empire", in: Waetzoldt, H. and Hauptmann, H. (eds.), *Wirtschaft und Gesellschaft von Ebla. Akten der internationalen Tagung Heidelberg 4–7. November 1986*. Heidelberger Studien zum alten Orient. Heidelberg, 139–158.
Atkinson, J. A. and Walker, J.
1803 *A Picturesque Representation of Manners, Customs and Amusements of the Russians* I. London.
Atkinson, R. J. C. and Piggott, S.
1955 "The Torrs chamfrein", *Archaeologia* 46, 197–235.
Babelon, E.
1893 *Les Perses achéménides, les satrapes et les dynastes tributaires de leur empire Chypre et Phénicie*. Paris.
Baramki, D.
1967 *The Archaeological Museum of the American University in Beirut*. Beirut.
Barfield, L.
1971 *Northern Italy Before Rome*. London and New York.
Barnett, R. D.
1939 "Phoenician and Syrian ivory carving", *Palestine Exploration Quarterly* 1939, 4–19.
1957 *A Catalogue of the Nimrud Ivories with other Examples of Ancient Near Eastern Ivories in the British Museum*. London.
n.d. *Assyrian Palace Reliefs*. London. (2nd edition with a supplement by L. G. Davies 1975).
1964 "The gods of Zinjirli", Compte rendu de l'onzième Rencontre assyriologique internationale. Leiden, 59–87.
1969 "Anath, Ba'al and Pasargadae", *Mélanges de l'Université St. Joseph* (Beirouth) 45, 407–422.
1975 *Assyrian Sculpture in the British Museum*. London.
1976 *Sculptures from the North Palace of Ashurbanipal at Niniveh (668–627 B.C.)*. Toronto.
—— and Falkner, M.
1962 *The Sculptures of Assur-Naṣir-Apli II (883–859 B.C.), Tiglath-Pileser III (745–727 B.C.), Essarhaddon (681–669 B.C.) from Central and South-West Palaces at Nimrud*. London.
1976 *The Sculptures of Tiglath-Pilesar III*. London.
Barrelet, M.-T.
1968 *Figurines et reliefs en terre cuite de la Mésopotamie antique*. Institut français d'Archéologie de Beyrouth. Bibliothèque archéologique et historique 85. Paris.
1970 "Peut-on remettre en question la 'restitution materiélle de la 'Stèle des Vautoures'"?, *Journal of Near Eastern Studies* 29, 233–258.

Basch. L.
1987   *Le musée imaginaire et la marine antique*. Athens.
Bates, O. and Dunham, D.
1927   *Excavations at Gammai*. Harvard African Studies 8. Cambridge, Mass.
Baud, M.
1935   *Les dessins ébauchés de la nécropole thébaine au temps de Nouveau Empire*. Mémoirs de l'Institut français d'archéologie orientale du Caire 63. Cairo.
Beal, R. H.
1992   *The Organisation of the Hittite Military*. Texte der Hethiter 20. Heidelberg.
Beazley, J. D.
1942   *Attic Red-Figure Vase Painters*. Oxford.
1951   *The Developement of Attic Black-Figure*. London and Berkeley.
1956   *Attic Black-Figured Vase-Painters*. Oxford.
Benson, J. L.
1961   "Observations on Mycenaean vase-painters", *American Journal of Archaeology* 65, 337–347.
1973   *The Necropolis at Koloriziki*. Studies in Mediterranean Archaeology 36. Göteborg.
Berg, G.
1935   *Sledges and Wheeled Vehicles. Ethnological Studies from the View-Point of Sweden*. Nordiska Museets Handlingar 4. Stockholm-Copenhagn.
Berger, E.
1982   "Etruskische Bronzebeschläge vom Kopfschutz eines Pferdegespannes", in: Berger, E. (ed.), *Antike Kunstwerke aus der Sammlung Ludwig. Terrakotten und Bronzen* II. Veröffentlichungen des Antikenmuseums Basel 42. Basel, 264–290.
Betts, J. H.
1967   "New light on Minoan bureaucracy. A re-examination of some Cretan sealings", *Kadmos* 6, 15–40.
Bisi, A. M.
1982   "Su una terracotta di tipo cipriota di Amrit", *Rivista di Studi Fenici* 10, 189–196.
1989   "Le rayonnement des terres cuites chypriotes au Levant aux premiers siècles de l'âge du Fer", in: Peltenburg, E. J. (ed.), *Early Society in Cyprus*. Edinburgh, 56–265.
Bissing, F. Freiherr von
1900   *Ein thebanischer Grabfund aus dem Anfang des Neuen Reiches*. Berlin.
Bittel, K.
1970a   "Fragment einer hethitischen Reliefvase von Boğazköy", in: Kuschke, A. and Kutsch, E. (eds.), *Archäologie und Altes Testament. Festschrift für Kurt Galling zum 8. Januar 1970*. Tübingen, 19–25.
1970b   *Hattusha. The Capital of the Hittites*. New York
1975   "Altkleinasiatische Pferdetrensen", *Istanbuler Mitteilungen* 25, 301–311. (= Studies in Honour of G. Kleiner).
Bivar, A. D. H.
1955   "The stirrup and its origins", *Oriental Art N. S.* 1 (2), 3–7.
1972   "Cavalry equipment and tactics on the Euphrates frontier", *Dumbarton Oaks Paper 26*, 273–291.
Blinkenberg, Chr.
1931   *Lindos* I. Berlin.
Boehmer, R. M.
1972   *Die Kleinfunde von Boğazköy-Ḫattuša*. Wissenschaftliche Veröffentlichungen der Deutschen Orientgesellschaft 87. Berlin.
1985   "Uruk-Warka XXXVII. Survey des Stadtgebietes von Uruk IV. Glyptik", *Bagdhader Mitteilungen* 16, 99–108.

Bökönyi, S.
1953 "Reconstruction des mors en bois de cerf et en os", *Acta Archaeologica Academiae Scientiarum Hungaricae* 3, 113–121.
1968 *Data on Iron Age Horses of Central and Eastern Europe.* American School of Prehistoric Research, Bulletin 25. Cambridge, Mass.
Boese, J.
1975 in: Orthmann, W. et al. (eds.), *Der Alte Orient.* Propyläen Kunstgeschichte 14. Berlin, 199–209.
Bona, I.
1960 "Clay models of Bronze Age wagons and wheels in the Middle Danube basin", *Acta Archaeologica Hungarica* 12, 83–111.
Bonomi, J.
n.d. *Catalogue of a Collection of Egyptian Antiquities, the Property of Henry Abbott, Esq., M.D.* Cairo. [According to Williams 1920 written in 1843, not published before 1846].
Borchardt, L.
1911 "Ausgrabungen in Tell-el Amarna 1911", *Mitteilungen der Deutschen Orientgesellschaft zu Berlin* 46, 13–27.
1912 "Ausgrabungen in Tell-el Amarna 1911/12", *Mitteilungen der Deutschen Orientgesellschaft zu Berlin* 46, 1–40.
1935 *Studien and Entwürfe altägyptischer Künstler,* Kunst und Künstler 8 (1910). Leipzig.
Bordaz, J.
1967 "Flint flaking in Turkey", *Natural History* (Feb. 1967), 73–77.
Borghegyi, S. F. de
1970 "Wheels and man", *Archaeology* 23, 18–25.
Bossert, H. Th.
1937 *The Art of Ancient Crete. From the Earliest Times to the Iron Age.* The Earliest Cultures of Mediterranean Countries 1. London.
1942 *Altanatolien. Kunst und Handwerk in Kleinasien von den Anfängen bis zum völligen Aufgehen in der griechischen Kultur.* Berlin.
1951 *Altsyrien. Kunst und Handwerk in Cypern, Syrien, Palästina, Transjordanien und Arabien von den Anfängen bis zum völligen Aufgehen in der griechisch-römischen Kultur.* Unter Mitarbeit von R. Naumann. Die ältesten Kulturen des Mittelmeer-kreises 3. Tübingen.
Botta, P. E. and Flandin, M. E.
1849–60 *Monuments de Niniveh* I–V. Paris.
Botti, G.
1951 "Il carro del sogno", *Aegyptus* 31, 192–198.
Braidwood, R. J. and Braidwood, L. S.
1960 *Excavations in the Plain of Antioch.* Oriental Institute Publications 61. Chicago.
Brandenstein, C. G. von
1947 *Götterbilder in hethitischen Texten.* Mitteilungen der Vorderasiatisch-ägyptischen Gesellschaft 46(2). Leipzig.
Brandes, M. A.
1979 *Siegelabrollungen aus den archaischen Bauschichten in Uruk-Warka.* Freiburger altorientalische Studien 3. Wiesbaden.
Braun-Holzinger, E.
1984 *Figürliche Bronzen aus Mesopotamien.* Prähistorische Bronzefunde 1.4. München.
Breasted, J. H.
1927 *Ancient Records of Egypt* II. Chicago.
—— and Allen, T. G.
1930–32 *Medinet Habu* II. *Later Historical Records of Ramses III.* University of Chicago. Oriental Institute. Chicago.

Breitenstein, N.
1941 *Catalogue of Terracottas (Cypriote, Greek, Etrusco-Italian)*. Copenhagen. (Danish National Museum. Department of Oriental and Classical Antiquities).

Broue, S. de la
1646 *Le cavalrice françois*. Paris.

Bronson, R. C.
1965 "Chariot racing in Etruria", in: Beccati, G. (ed.), *Studi del onore di Luisa Banti*. Roma, 89–106.

Brown, A. C.
1974 "Etrusco-Italic terra-cottas in the Ashmolean Museum, Oxford", *Archaeological Reports for 1973/74*, 60–65.
—— and Catling, H. W.
1980 "Additions to the Cypriot collection in the Ashmolean Museum, Oxford, 1963–77", *Opuscula Atheniensia* 13, 91–137.

Brunner-Traut, E.
1956 *Die altägyptischen Scherbenbilder (Bildostraka) der deutschen Museen und Sammlungen*. Wiesbaden.

Brunton, G. and Engelbach, R.
1927 *Gurob*. British School of Archaeology in Egypt 41. London.

Buchanan, B.
1962 "Ancient Near Eastern seals in the Yale Babylonian collection", *Archaeology* 15, 267–275.
1966 *Catalogue of Ancient Near Eastern Cylinder Seals in the Ashmolean Museum* I. Oxford.
1971 "A snake Goddess and her companions", *Iraq* 33, 1–18.

Buchholz, H.-G.
1973 "Tamassos, Zypern, 1970–72. 1. Bericht", *Archäologischer Anzeiger 1973*, 295–388.
1974 "Tamassos, Zypern, 1973. 2. Bericht", *Archäologischer Anzeiger 1974*, 554–614.
1978 "Tamassos, Zypern, 1974–76. 3. Bericht", *Archäologischer Anzeiger 1978*, 155–230.
1987 "Tamassos, Zypern, 1977–1986. IV", *Archäologischer Anzeiger 1987*, 165–228.

Budge, E. W.
1914 *Assyrian Sculptures in the British Museum*. London.

du Buisson, R. Le Comte du Mesnil
1947 *Le sautoir d'Atargatis et la chaîne d'amulettes*. Documenta et Monumenta Orientis Antiqui; Studies in Near Eastern Archaeology and Civilization 1. Leiden.

Buitron, D.
1983 "Excavations in the Archaic precinct at Kourion", *Report of the Department of Antiquities, Cyprus* 1983, 228–231.

Bulliet, R. W.
1975 *The Camel and the Wheel*. Cambridge, Mass.

Buren, E. D. van
1930 *Clay Figurines of Babylonia and Assyria*. Yale Oriental Series (Researches 16). New Haven, Conn.

Buschor, E.
1969 *Griechische Vasen*. München.

Calmeyer, P.
1954 *Altiranische Bronzen der Sammlung Bröckelschen*. Berlin.
1964 Archaische Zügelringe, in: Bittel, K. et al. (eds.), *Vorderasiatische Archäologie. Studien und Aufsätze. Anton Moortgat zum fünfundsechszigsten Geburtstag gewidmet von Kollegen, Freunden und Schülern*. Berlin, 68–84.
1967 "Zur Rekonstruktion der 'Standarte' von Mari", in: *La civilization de Mari*. XVe Rencontre d'assyriologie. Liège, 161–169.
1969 *Datierbare Bronzen aus Luristan und Kirmansha*. Untersuchungen zur Assyriologie und vorderasiatischen Archäologie 5. Berlin.

1984   "Zur Genese altiranischer Motive VII. Achsnägel in Form von Betenden", *Archaeologische Mitteilungen aus Iran N.F.* 13, 99–111.

Cameron, M. A. S.
1967   "Unpublished fresco fragments of a chariot composition from Knossos", *Archäologischer Anzeiger* 1967, 330–344.

Carter, E. and Stolper, M. W.
1984   *Elam. Surveys of Political History and Archaeology.* University of California Studies 25. Berkeley-Los Angeles-London.

Carter, H.
1927   *The Tomb of Tut.ankh.Amen* II. New York.
1933   *The Tomb of Tut.ankh.Amen* III. London.
—— and Mace, A. C.
1923   *The Tomb of Tut.ankh.Amen* I. London.
—— and Newberry, P.E.
1904   *The Tomb of Thoutmôsis IV.* Catalogue général des antiquités égyptiennes du Musée du Caire; no. 46001–46529. Westminster.

Cassimatis, H.
1976   "Un rapt de Perséphone à Chypre", *Report of the Department of Antiquities, Cyprus* 1976, 178–184.
1986   "Terres cuites chypriotes à Dublin", *Report of the Department of Antiquities, Cyprus* 1986, 173–182.

Catling, H. W.
1968   "A Mycenaean puzzle from Levkandi in Euboea", *American Journal of Archaeology* 72, 41–49.
1971   in: Moorey, P. R. S. (ed.), *Ancient Glass, Jewellery and Terracottas from the Collection of Mr and Mrs James Bomford* (catalogue of the exhibition at the Ashmolean Museum). Oxford, 34–70. (catalogue of terracottas).
1971–72   "Archaeology in Greece, 1971–72", *Archaeological Reports 1971–72*, 3–26.
1974   "The Bomford horse-and-rider", *Report of the Department of Antiquities, Cyprus* 1974, 95–111.
1976   "Prolegomena for a study of a class of Late Cypriote terracotta figurines", *Report of the Department of Antiquities, Cyprus* 1976, 66–74.
—— and Karageorghis, V.
1960   "Minoika in Cyprus", *Annual of the British School of Athens* 55, 109–127.

Caubet, A.
1984   "Aux origines de la collection chypriote du Louvre: le fonds Guillaume-Rey (1860–1865)", *Report of the Department of Antiquities, Cyprus* 1984, 221–229.
n.d.   *Les Âge du Antiquités de Chypre: âge bronze.* Départment des antiquités oriental du Musée du Louvre. Paris. (Catalogue by A. Coubet, V. Karageorghis and M. Yon).

Cesnola, L. Palma di
1885   *A Descriptive Atlas of the Cesnola Collection of Antiquities in the Metropolitan Museum of Art* I. Boston.
1894   *A Descriptive Atlas of the Cesnola Collection of Cypriot Antiquities in the Metropolitan Museum of Art* II. New York.

Chamoux, F.
1975   "Triges chypriotes", *Report of the Department of Antiquities, Cyprus*, 93–95.

Chardin, Sir J.
1927   *Travels in Persia.* London.

Chase, G. H. and Vermeule, C. C.
1973   *Greek, Etruscan and Roman Art. The Classical Collections of the Museum of Fine Arts in Boston.* Boston.

Childe, V. G.
1951   "The first waggons and carts. From the Tigris to the Severn", *Proceedings of the Prehistoric Society* 17, 177–194.

1954a   "The diffusion of wheeled vehicles", *Ethnologisch-Archäologische Forschungen* 2, 1–17.

1954b   "Wheeled vehicles", in: Singer, Holmyard and Hall 1954, 716–729.

Chouchoud, P. L.

1928   *Mythologie asiatique illustrée.* Paris.

Christopoulos, G. A.

1974   (ed.) *A History of the Hellenic World* I. *Prehistory and Protohistory.* Athens.

Civil, M.

1968   "Išme-Dagan and Enlil's chariot", *Journal of the American Oriental Society* 88, 3–14.

1994   *The Farmer's Instructions. A Sumerian Agricultural Manual.* Aula Orientalis, Supplementa 5. Barcelona.

Cline, E. H.

1994   *Sailing the Wine-Dark Sea. International Trade and the Late Bronze Age Aegean.* British Archaeological Reports International Series 591. Oxford.

Coldstream, J. N.

1968   *Greek Geometric Pottery. A Survey of Ten Local Styles and Their Chronology.* London.

1985   "The Geometric and Archaic periods", in: Karageorghis, V. (ed.), *Archaeology in Cyprus 1960–1985.* Nicosia, 47–59.

1993   "Mixed marriages at the frontiers of the early Greek world", *Oxford Journal of Archaeology* 12, 89–107.

1996–97   "The Dypylon krater, Sidney 46.11: context, style and iconography", *Mediterranean Archaeology* 9–10, 1–11.

Cole, S. M.

1954   "Land transport without wheels. Roads and bridges", in: Singer, Holmyard, Hall and Williams 1954, 704–715.

Collon, D.

1972   "The smiting god: A study of a bronze in the Pomerance collection in New York", *Levant* 4, 111–134.

1975   *The Seal Impressions from Tell Atchana/Alalakh.* Alter Orient und Altes Testament 27. Neukirchen-Vluyn.

1987   *First Impressions, Cylinder Seals in the Ancient Near East.* London.

Contenau, G.

1931   *Manuel d'archéologie orientale depuis les origines jusqu'à d'Alexandre* II. Paris.

1947   *Manuel d'archéologie orientale depuis les origines jusqu'à d'Alexandre* IV. Paris.

Cook, J. M.

1955   "Terracotta model of a Mycenaean litter", *Kretika Khronika* 9, 152–154. (in Greek).

Cook, R. M.

1981   *Clazomenian Sarcophagi.* Kerameus 3. Mainz.

Cooney, J. D.

1965   *Amarna Reliefs from Hermopolis in American Collections.* Brooklyn.

Crawford, O. G. S.

1935   "A primitive threshing machine", *Antiquity* 9, 335–339.

Crawford, V.

1959   "Nippur, the holy city", *Archaeology* 12, 74–83.

1972   "Excavations in the Swamps of Sumer", *Expedition.* (University Museum of Pennsylvania), Philadelphia 14(2), 12–20.

Crielaard, J. P.

1998   "Het aristokratische karakter van de vroege Griekse koloni satie", Spiegel Historicel 33(3), 114–120.

Crouwel, J. H.

1972   "Early belt-buckles from western Iran and central Anatolia", *Iranica Antiqua* 9, 49–59.

1981   *Chariots and Other Means of Land Transport in Bronze Age Greece.* Allard Pierson Series 3. Amsterdam.

1987   "Chariots in Iron Age Cyprus", *Report of the Department of Antiquities, Cyprus 1987*, 101–118.

1991a   "A group of terracotta chariot models—Cypriote or Phoenician?", in: Vandenabeele, F. and Laffineur, R. (eds.), *Cypriote Terracottas. Proceedings of the First International Conference of Cypriote Studies, Bruxelles-Liège-Amsterdam, 29 May–1 June, 1989.* Bruxelles and Liège, 115–129.

1991b   *Well Built Mycenae 21. The Mycenaean Pictorial Pottery.* Oxford.

1992   *Chariots and Other Wheeled Vehicles in Iron Age Greece.* Allard Pierson Series 9. Amsterdam.

—— and Tatton-Brown, V.

1988   "Ridden horses in Iron Age Cyprus", *Report of the Department of Antiquities, Cyprus* 1988 (Part 2), 77–87.

Culican, W.

1975–76 "Some Phoenician masks and other terracottas", *Berytus* 24, 47–87.

Cumont, F. V. M.

1926   *Fouilles de Doura-Europos (1922–1923) avec une appendice sur la céramique de Doura.* Paris.

Curle, J.

1911   *A Roman Frontier Post and its People. The Fort at Newstead.* Glasgow.

Dakoroneia, F.

1987   "Kynos", *Archaeologikon Deltion* 42:B1, 234. (in Greek).

1990   "War-ships on sherds of LH IIIC kraters from Kynos", in: Tzalas 1990, 117–122.

1996a   "Kynos. . . . fleet", in: Tzalas 1996, 159–171.

1996b   "Mycenaean East Lokris", in de Miro, E. Godart, L. and Sacconi, A. (eds), *Atti e memorie del secundo congresso internazionale di Micenologia 3.* Incunabula Graeca 98:3. Roma, 1167–1173.

Dalton, O. M.

1964   *The Treasure of the Oxus* (3rd edition). London.

Danmanville, J.

1968   "Collection Thierry IV.—char votif anatolien", *Revue d'Assyriologie* 62, 59–61.

Dattari, G.

1901   *Numi Augustei Alexandrini. Catalogo della collezione G. Dattari.* Cairo.

Davidson, H. R. E.

n.d.   *Pagan Scandinavia.* London.

Davies, N. de Garis

1903   *The Rock Tombs of El Amarna I. The Tomb of Meryra.* London.

1922   *The Tomb of Puyemrê at Thebes* I–II. Metropolitan Museum of Art. Robb de Prysters Tytus Memorial Series 2. New York.

1943   *The Tomb of Rekh-mi-Rē' at Thebes.* I.–II. Publications of the Metropolitan Museum of Art. Egyptian Expedition. New York 11. New York.

—— and Gardiner, A. H.

1962   *Tutankhamun's Painted Box.* Oxford.

Davies, N. M.

1963   *Scenes from Some Theban Tombs. (Nos. 38, 66, 162 with Excerpts from 81).* Private Tombs at Thebes 4. Oxford.

Davison, J. M.

1961   *Attic Geometric Workshops.* Yale Classical Studies 16. New Haven, Conn.

Decaudin, A. J.

1987   *Les antiquités chypriotes dans les collections publiques françaises.* Nicosia.

Déchelette, J.
1910   *Manuel d'archéologie. Préhistoire celtique et gallo-romaine* II. Archéologie celtique et protohistorique. Prèmiere partie: Âge du bronze. Paris.

Decker, W.
1994   "Pferd und Wagen im alten Ägypten", in: Hänsel and Zimmer 1994, 259–270.

Deger-Jalkotzy, S.
1983   (ed.) *Griechenland, die Ägäis und die Levante während der "Dark Ages" vom 12. bis zum 9. Jh. v.Chr.* Akten des Symposions von Stift Zwettl (NÖ), 11.–14. Oktober 1980. Sitzungsberichte der Österreichischen Akademie der Wissenschaften 418. Wien.
1994   "The post-palatial period of Cyprus: An Aegean prelude to the 11th century B.C.", in Karageorghis, V., *Cyprus in the 11th Century.* Nicosia, 11–30.
1991   "Die Erforschung des Zusammenbruchs der sogenannten mykenischen Kultur und der sogenannten dunklen Jahrhunderte", in: Latacz, J. (ed.), *Zweihundert Jahre Homer-Forschung.* Colloquium Rauricum 2. Stuttart, 127–154.

Delebeque, E.
1951   *Le cheval dans l'Iliade suivi d'un lexique du cheval chez Homère et d'un essai sur le cheval pré-homèrique.* Paris.

Delougaz, P.
1952   *Pottery from the Diyala Region.* Oriental Institute Publications 63. Chicago.
1968   "Animals emerging from a hut", *Journal of Near Eastern Studies* 27, 184–197.
——— and Lloyd, S.
1942   *Pre-Sargonid Temples in the Diyala Region.* Oriental Institute Publications 58. Chicago

Dent, A. A. and Godall, D. M.
1962   *The Foals of Epona. A History of the British Ponies from the Bronze Age to Yesterday.* London.

Denzer, J.-M.
1982   *Le motif du banquet couché dans le Proche-Orient et le monde grec du VIIe au IVe siècle avant J.-C.* Paris.

Desmet-Grégoire, H. and Fontaine, P.
1988   *La région d'Arak et de Hamadân. Cartes et documents éthnographiques.* Leuven. (Studia Iranica Cahier, 6).

Desroche Noblecourt, C.
1963   *Tutankhamun.* London.
1976   et al. (eds.), *Ramsès le Grand.* Galerie du Grand Palais, Paris. (catalogue of the exhibition at the Louvre). Paris.

Dessiatchikov, Y. M.
1972   "A cataphract represented on the Stela of Afenios", *Sovetskaja Arkheologija* 1972 (4), 68–77. (in Russian).

Dever, W. G.
1970   "The 'Middle Bronze I' period in Syria and Palestine, in: Sanders, J. A. (ed.), *Near Eastern Archaeology in the Twentieth Century Essays in Honour of Nelson Glueck.* Garden City, New York, 132–163.

Diamant S.
1988   "Mycenaean origins: infiltration from the north?", in: French, E. and Wardle, K. A. (eds.), *Problems in Aegean Prehistory.* Bristol, 153–159.

Dickinson, O. T. P. K.
1977   *The Origins of Mycenaean Civilisation.* Studies in Mediterranean Archaeology 49. Göteborg.
1994   *The Aegean Bronze Age.* Cambridge.

Dien, A. E.
1979.   "Excavations of the Ch'in Dynasty pit containing pottery figures of warriors and horses at Ling-T'ung, Shensi province", *Chinese Studies in*

Archaeology 1 (1), 8–55. [Originally published in *Wen Wu* 1978 (5), 1–19; translation by A. E. Diem; cf. also translator's note p. 8f.].

Dikaios, P.
1963   "A "Royal" tomb at Salamis", Cyprus, *Archäologischer Anzeiger 1963*, 126–206.
1969–71   *Enkomi Excavations 1948–58* I. *The Architectural Remains: The Tombs*. II. *Chronology, Summary and Conclusions, Catalogue Appendices*. IIIa–b. *Plates* Mainz am Rhein.

Dewall, M. von
1964   *Pferd und Wagen als Kulturgut im frühen China*. Saarbrücker Beiträge zur Altertumskunde 1. Bonn.

Dietz, S.
1991   *The Argolid at the Transition to the Mycenaean Age. Studies in the Chronology of the Shaft Grave Period*. Copenhagen.

Dittmann, K.-H.
1941   "Der Segelwagen von Medinet Madi", *Mitteilungen des Deutschen Archäologischen Instituts Abteilung Kairo* 10, 60–78.

Dmitriev, A. V.
1979   "Burials of horsemen and war horses in the cemetery on the Dyurso River near Novorossiisk", *Sovetskaja Arkheologija* 1979 (4), 212–231. (in Russian).

Döhl, H.
1980   "Mykenische Kampfdarstellungen: Bild und Deutung im prähistorischen Griechenland", *Beiträge zur Archäologie Nordwestdeutschlands und Mitteleuropas. Materialhefte zur Ur- und Frühgeschichte Niedersachsens* 16, 21–33.

Donder, H.
1980   *Zaumzeug in Griechenland und Zypern*. Prähistorische Bronzefunde 16.3. München.

Drews, R.
1988   *The Coming of the Greeks. Indo-European Conquests in the Aegean and the Ancient Near East*. Princeton, New Jersey.
1993   *The End of the Bronze Age. Changes in Warfare and the Catastrophe ca. 1200 B.C.* Princeton, New Jersey.

Drioton, E.
1949   *Le Musée du Caire*. Paris.

von den Driesch, A.
1993   "'Hausesel contra Hausonager'. Eine kritische Bemerkung zu einer Untersuchung von J. Bollweg und W. Nagel über die Equiden Vorderasiens", *Zeitschrift für Assyriologie* 83, 258–267.

Drower, M. S.
1973   "Syria c. 1550–1400 B.C.", in: *The Cambridge Ancient History* (3rd edition) II.1, 417–525.

Ducati, P.
1910   "Le pietre funeraire felsinée", *Monumenti Antichi* 20, 360–727.

Ducos, P.
1967   "Les équides des tombes royales de Salamine", in: Karageorghis 1967a, 154–181.
1980   Remarques comparatives sur les chevaux de Salamine, in: *Salamine de Chypre. Histoire et archéologie. Colloque internationale du Centre national de la recherche scientifique*. Paris, 161–167.

Dunand, M.
1958   *Fouilles de Byblos* II. Paris.

Dunbabin, T. J. and Boardman, J.
1957   (eds.), *The Greeks and Their Eastern Neighbours. Studies in the Relations Between Greece and the Countries of the Near East in the Eighth and Seventh Centuries B.C.* London.

Dyson, Jr., R. H.
1960   "A note on queen Shub-ad's 'onagers'", *Iraq* 22, 102–104 (= *Ur in Retrospect. In Memory of Sir C. L. Woolley*. Edited by Mallowan, M. E. L. and Wiseman, D. J.).
1965   "Problems in the relative chronology of Iran, 6000–2000 B.C.", in: Ehrich, R. W. (ed.), *Chronology in Old World Archaeology*. Chicago, 215–226.
1973   "The archaeological evidence of the second millennium B.C. on the Persian Plateau", in: *The Cambridge Ancient History* (3rd edition) II.1, 686–715.
——— and Muscarella, O. W.
1989   "Constructing the chronologies and historical implications of Hasanlu IV", *Iran* 27, 1–7.

Ebeling, E.
1951   *Bruchstücke einer mittelassyrischen Vorschriftensammlung für die Akklimatisierung und Trainierung von Wagenpferden*. Deutsche Akademie der Wissenschafen zu Berlin. Institut für Orientforschung 7. Berlin.

Edwards, E. Hartley
1963   *Saddlery. Modern Equipment for Horse and Stable*. London.

Eggenhofer, N.
1961   *Wagons, Mules and Men. How the Frontier Moved West*. New York.

Ehelolf, H.
1936   "Hethitisch-akkadische Wortgleichungen", *Zeitschrift für Assyriologie* N.F. 9, 170–195.

Emery, W. B.
1938   *The Royal Tombs of Ballana and Qustul*. Mission archéologique de Nubie 1929–1934. Cairo.
1965   *Egypt in Nubia*. London.

Evans, Sir A.
1921–35   *The Palace of Minos at Knossos* I–IV. London.

Evers, J. C.
1955   *The Horse in the Blackfoot Indian Culture*. Washington.

Fakhry, A.
1944   *The Siwa Oasis. Its History and Antiquities*. Cairo.

Felsch, R.
1981   "Mykenischer Kult im Heiligtum bei Kalapodi", in: Hägg and Marinatos 1981, 81–89.

Fenton, A.
1973   "Transport with pack horse and slide car in Scotland", in: Fenton, A., Podolak, J. and Rasmussen, H. (eds.), *Land Transport in Europe*. Copenhagen, 121–171.

Fiaschi, C.
1556   *Trattato dell'imbrigliare, maneggiare, et ferrare*. Bologna.

Figulla, H. H.
1967   *Cuneiform Texts from Babylonian Tablets in the British Museum* 47. *The Old-Babylonian naditu Records*. London.

Finkbeiner, U.
1983   "Uruk-Warka XXXV: Survey des Stadtgebietes von Uruk. Vorläufiger Bericht über die erste Kampagne 1982", *Bagdhader Mitteilungen* 14, 14–31.

Foltiny, S.
1967   "The ivory horse bits of Homer and the bone horse bits of reality", *Bonner Jahrbücher* 167, 11–37.

Forrer, R.
1932   *Les chars cultuels préhistoriques et leurs survivances aux époques historiques*. Préhistoire 1(1). Paris.

Fortenberry, C. D.
1990   *Elements of Mycenaean Warfare.* (doctoral dissertation,, University of Cincinnati, Ohio).
Fox, C.
1931   "Sleds, carts and wagons", *Antiquity* 5, 185–199.
Fox, P.
1951   *Tutankhamun's Treasure.* London.
Franke, P. and Hirmer, M.
1964   *Die griechischen Münze.* München.
Frankfort, H.
1939a   *Cylinder Seals.* London.
1939b   *Sculpture of the Third Millennium B.C. from Tell Asmar and Khafâjah.* The University of Chicago Oriental Institute Publications 44. Chicago.
1943   *More Sculpture from the Diyala Region.* The University of Chicago Oriental Institute Publications 60. Chicago.
1958   *Art and Architecture of the Ancient Orient.* Harmondworth.
French, E.
1971   "The development of Mycenaean terracotta figurines", *Annual of the British School of Athens* 66, 101–187.
Fugmann, E.
1958   *Hama. Fouilles et rércherches de la Fondation Carlsberg, 1931–1938* II. L'architecture des périodes préhéllénique. Copenhagn.
Furumark, A.
1941   *The Mycenaean Pottery. Analysis and Classification.* Stockholm.
1953   "A scarab from Cyprus", *Opuscula Atheniensia* I, 47–59.
Furtwängler, A.
1886   (eds.) *Mykenische Vasen. Vorhellenistische Thongefäße aus dem Gebiete des archäologischen Instituts in Athen.* Berlin.
Gadd, C. J.
1936   *The Stones of Assyria. The Surviving Remains of Assyrian Sculpture their Recovery and their Original Positions.* London.
1971   "The cities of Babylonia", in: *The Cambridge Ancient History* (3rd edition) I.2, 93–144.
Gallus, S. and Horvath, T.
1939   *Un peuple cavalier préscythique en Hongrie. Trouvallies archéologiques du prèmier âges du fer et leurs relations avec l'Eurasie.* Dissertationes Pannonica 2. Leipzig.
Gamber, O.
1978   *Waffe und Rüstungen Eurasiens. Frühzeit und Antike.* Bibliothek für Kunst- und Antikenfreunde. Braunschweig.
Gamkrelidze, T. and Ivanov, V. V.
1995   *Indo-European and Indo-Europeans. A Reconstruction and Historical Analysis of a Proto-Language and a Proto-Culture.* Berlin-New York. [translation of the Russian original, Tblissi 1984].
Garbsch, J.
1978   *Römische Paraderüstungen.* Münchener Beiträge zur Vor- und Frühgeschichte 38. München.
Garelli, P. and Collon, D.
1975   *Cuneiform Texts from Cappadocian Tablets in the British Museum* VI. London.
Gegeschidze, M. K.
1956   *Georgian People's Transport.* Tblissi. (in Georgian and Russian; with a German summary, pp. 177–188.)
Gelb, I. J.
1939   *Hittite Hieroglyphic Monuments.* Oriental Institute Publications 45. Chicago.
——— et al.
1958ff.   (eds.), *The Assyrian Dictionnary of the Oriental Institute of the University of Chicago.*

Gening, V. F.
 1977   "Burial grounds of Sintashta and problems of early Indo-European
          tribes", *Sovetskaja Arkheologija* 1977 (4), 53–73. (in Russian).
—— and Ashichmina, L. J.
 1975   "A cemetery of the Bronze Age on the Sintashta river", Arkheologicheskie
          Otkritisya 1974, 144–177. (in Russian).
——, Zdanovich, G. B. and Gening, V. V.
 1992   *Sintashta. Archaeological Sites of Aryan Tribes of the Ural-Kazakh Steppes.*
          Chelyabinsk. (in Russian with an English summary).
Genouillac, H. de
 1909   *Tablettes sumériennes archaïques. Matériaux pour servir à l'histoire de la société
          sumérienne.* Paris.
Ghirshman, R.
 1938–39 *Fouilles de Sialk près de Kashan 1933, 1934, 1937* I–II. Musée du Louvre.
          Department des antiquités orientales et de la céramique antique. Series
          archéologique IV. Paris.
 1962   *Iran. Parthes et Sassanides.* Paris.
 1964   *Persia, from the Origin to Alexander the Great.* The Arts of Mankind 5.
          London.
Gibson, M.
 1968   *The City and Area of Kish.* (Doctoral thesis, University of Chicago, Illinois).
          [Published as *The City and Area of Kish*; with an appendix by McCormick
          Adams, R.; edited by H. Field and E. M. Laird. Coconut Grove,
          Miami, Florida 1972].
Gimbutas, M.
 1965   *The Bronze Age Cultures of Central and Eastern Europe.* The Hague-New
          York-London.
Gjerstadt, E.
 1935   "Ajia Irini", in: *The Swedish Cyprus Expedition* II. Stockholm, 642–824.
 1957   "Vouni", in: *The Swedish Cyprus Expedition* III. Stockholm, 76–339.
 1963   "Supplementary notes on finds from Ajia Irini in Cyprus", *Medelhavsmuseet
          Bulletin 3*, 3–40.
Godard, A.
 1931   *Les bronze du Luristan.* Ars Asiatica 17. Paris.
 1950   *Le trésor de Ziwiyè.* Haarlem.
Goetze, A.
 1955   "Hittite omen", in: Pritchard, J. B. (ed.), *Ancient Near Eastern Texts Related
          to the Old Testament* (2nd edition). Princeton, New Jersey, 497–498.
 1957   *Kulturgeschichte des Alten Orients. Kleinasien.* (2nd edition). München.
Goldman, B.
 1984   "The Persian saddle blanket", *Studia Iranica* 17, 7–18.
Gray, D.
 1974   *Seewesen.* Archaeologica Homerica G. Göttingen.
Graziadio, G.
 1991   "The process of social stratification at Mycenae in the Shaft Graves
          period. A comparative examination of evidence", *American Journal of
          Archaeology* 95, 403–440.
Graziosi, P.
 1942   *L'arte rupestre della Libia.* Napoli.
Green, M. W.
 1987   "The sign list", in: Green, M. W., Nissen, H. et al. (eds.), *Zeichenliste
          der archaischen Texte aus Uruk.* Berlin, 167–345.
Greenhalgh, P. A. L.
 1973a   *Early Greek Warfare. Horsemen and Chariots in the Homeric and Archaic Ages.*
          Cambridge.

1973b   "How are the mighty fallen", *Acta Classica* 21, 1–38.
1980   "The Dendra charioteer", *Antiquity* 54, 201–205.
Grenfell, B. P., Hunt, A. S. and Hogarth, D. G.
1900   *Fayûm Towns and thier Papyri*. Graeco-Roman Memoirs 3. London.
Griffith, F. Ll.
1922   "Oxford excavations in Nubia", *Liverpool Annals of Arts and Archaeology*
          9, 67–124.
Grisone, F.
1550   *Gli Ordini di Cavalcare*. Napoli.
Groenman-van Waateringe, W.
1967   *Romeins lederwerk uit Valkenburg Z. H.* Groningen. (in Dutch with English
          summary).
Groslier, B. and Arthaud, J.
1952   *The Arts and Civilization of Angkor*. New York.
Grunwaldt, C.
1983   "Frühe attische Kampfdarstellungen", *Acta Praehistorica et Archaeologica*
          15, 155–204.
Güterbock, H. G.
1946   *Kumarbi. Mythen vom churritischen Kronos*. . . . Istanbuler Schriften 16. Zürich.
1967   "The Hittite conquest of Cyprus reconsidered", *Journal of Near Eastern
          Studies* 26, 73–81.
Gurney, O.
1954   *The Hittites*. (3rd edition 1990). Harmondsworth.
Gutsch, G.
1898–99   "The terracottas", in: Hogarth, D. G. et al. (ed.), Excavations at
          Naukratis. *Annual of the British School of Athens* 5, 67–97.
Haddon, A. C.
1898   *The Study of Man*. London.
Hagen, A.
1967   *Norway*, London.
Hägg, R and Marinatos, N. (eds.)
1981   *Sanctuaries and Cults in the Aegean Bronze Age. Proceedings of the First International
          Symposium at the Swedish Institute in Athens, 12–13 May, 1980.* Skrifter
          utgivna av Svenska institutet i Athen 28. Stockholm.
Hänsel, B. and Zimmer, S.
1994   (eds.) *Die Indogermanen und das Pferd. Akten des Internationalen Interdisziplinären
          Kolloquiums Freie University of Berlin, 1.–3. Juli 1992.* Archaeolingua. Main
          Series 4. Budapest. (= Studies in Honour of B. Schlerath).
Haerinck, E. and Overlaet, B. J.
1984   "Zur Funktion einiger urartäischer Gegenstände", *Iranica Antiqua* 19,
          53–70.
Häusler, A.
1984   "Neue Belege von Rad und Wagen im nordpontischen Raum", *Ethno-
          graphisch-archäologische Zeitschrift* 25, 629–682.
Haller, A. and Andrae, W.
1955   *Die Heiligtümer des Gottes Assur und der Sin-Šamaš-Tempel in Assur.* Wissen-
          schaftliche Veröffentlichung der Deutschen Orientgesellschaft 67. Berlin.
Hančar, F.
1955–56   *Das Pferd in prähistorischer und früher historischer Zeit.* Wiener Beiträge zur
          Kulturgeschichte und Linguistik 11. Wien and München.
Hanoon, N.
1984   "Baradan, Al-Seib and Haddad Tells", *Sumer* 40, 70–71.
Hansen
1983   *Carmina epigrahica graeca: saeculorum VIII–V a.Chr. n.* Texte und Kommentare
          12. Berlin and Novi Eboraci.

Haudricourt, A. G.
    1948   "Contribution à la géographie et à l'ethnologie de la voiture", *Revue de géographie humaine et d'ethnologie* 1, 54–64.
Hauptmann, H.
    1982   "Lidar Höyük, 1982", *Anatolian Studies* 33, 254–256.
    1987   "Recent archaeological research in Turkey", *Anatolian Studies* 37, 203–206.
Hawkins, J. D. and Morpurgo Davies, A.
    1978   "On the problem of Karatepe: the hieroglyphic text", *Anatolian Studies* 28, 103–119.
Hayes, W. C.
    1953   *The Scepter of Egypt From the Earliest Times to the End of the Middle Kingdom.* Cambridge, Mass.
    1959   *The Scepter of Egypt.* II. *The Hykos Period and the New Kingdom.* New York.
Head, B. V.
    1887   *Historia Numorum. A Manual of Greek Numismatics.* Oxford.
Helbig, W.
    1887   *Das homerische Epos aus den Denkmäler erläutert.* (2nd edition) Leipzig.
Hearn, M.
    1980   "The terracotta army of the first emperor of Qin (221–206 B.C.), in: O'Neill, J. P. (ed.), *Treasures from the Bronze Age of China. An Exhibition from the People's Republic of China.* New York, 44–48. (objects nos. 98–108 in the catalogue; pp. 191–192).
Hermary, A.
    1981   *Amathonte* II. *Testimonia deuxième partie. Les sculptures découvertes avant 1975.* Recherches sur les grande civilisations, Memoires 10. Paris.
    1990   "Petite plastique archaïque de Cnide", *La Revue du Louvre et des Musées de France (Decembre, no. 5),* 359–369.
Hermes, G.
    1936   "Das gezähmte Pferd im alten Orient", *Anthropos* 31, 364–394.
Herzfeld, E.
    1934   V. Formenwelt und geistiger Gehalt, *Archaeologische Mitteilungen aus Iran* 6, 187–223.
Heuzey, L.
    1883   *Les figurines antiques de terre cuite du Musée du Louvre.* Paris.
    1909   *Restauration matérielle du Stèle des Vautours. (restitution archéologique (par L. Heuzey, restitution epigraphique par F. Thurau-Dangin).* Paris.
    1923   *Catalogue des figurines antiques de terre cuite du Musée du Louvre.* Paris.
Hill, G. F.
    1897   "Notes on additions to the Greek coins in the British Museum, 1887–1889", *Journal of Hellenic Studies* 17, 78–91.
    1932   *A Guide to the Principal Coins of the Greeks from ca. 700 B.C. to A.D. 270 based on the Work of Barclay V. Head.* (2nd edition 1959). London.
    1969   *The Drawings of Pisanello. A Selection with Introduction and Notes.* New York.
Hillen, C.
    1952   in: "Reis in Irâq en proefgraving in Syrië in 1951", *Jaarbericht van het vooraziatisch-egyptisch Geneootschap. Ex Oriente Lux* 12, 191–202.
Hiller, S.
    1981   "Pax Minoica versus Minoan Thalassocracy: military aspects of Minoan culture", in: Hägg and Marinatos 1981, 27–31.
Hilzheimer, M.
    1931   "Die Anschirrung bei den alten Sumerern", *Prähistorische Zeitschrift* 22, 1–18.
Höckmann, O.
    1970   *Lanze und Speer. (Kriegswesen 2. Angriffswaffen).* Archaeologia Homerica E 2. Göttingen, 275–319.
    1987   "Lanzen und Speere der ägäischen Bronzezeit und des Übergangs zur Eisenzeit", in: Buchholz, H.-G. (ed.), *Ägäische Bronzezeit.* Darmstadt, 329–358.

Hofmann, U.
1989   *Fuhrwesen und Pferdehaltung im Alten Ägypten*. Bonn.
Hoffner, H.
1992   "The last days of Khattusha", in: Ward and Joukowski 1992, 46–52.
Holland, Th. A.
1993–94 "Tall as-Sweat 1989–1992", *Archiv für Orientforschung* 40–41, 275–285.
Hooker, J. T.
1989   "The coming of the Greeks—III", *Minos N.S.* 24, 55–68.
Hornbostel, W. et al.
1977   (ed.), *Kunst der Antike. Schätze aus norddeutschem Privatbesitz*. Mainz. (exhibition catalogue Museum für Kunst und Gewerbe Hamburg).
Houwink ten Cate, Ph. H. J.
1984   "The history of warfare according to the Hittite sources: the Annals of Ḫattušili I. (Part II)", *Anatolica* 11, 47–83.
Hrouda, B.
1963   *Kulturgeschichte des assyrischen Flachbildes*. Saarbrücker Beiträge zur Altertumskunde 1. Bonn.
Hüttel, H.-G.
1977   "Altbronzezeitliche Pferdetrensen", *Jahresbericht des Instituts für Vorgeschichte der Universität Frankfurt am Main* 1977, 75–86.
1979   "Zur westlichen Komponente des chinesischen Pferd-Wagen-Komplexes der Shang- und frühen Chou-Zeit", *Beiträge zur Allgemeinen und Vergleichenden Archäologie* 1, 1–29.
1981   *Bronzezeitliche Trensen in Mittel- und Osteuropa. Grundzüge ihrer Entwicklung*. Prähistorische Bronzefunde 16.2 München.
1982   "Zur Abkunft des danubischen Pferd-Wagen-Komplexes der Altbronzezeit", in: Hänsel, B. et al. (eds.), *Prähistorische Archäologie in Südosteuropa zwischen 1600 und 1000 v.Chr.* Berlin, 39–63.
1994   "Zur archäologischen Evidenz der Pferdenutzung in der Kupfer- und Bronzezeit", in: Hänsel and Zimmer 1994, 197–215.
Huish, M. B.
1900   *Greek Terracotta Statuettes. Their Origin, Evolution and Use*. London.
Humphrey, J. H.
1986   *Roman Circuses*. Berkeley and Los Angeles.
Immerwahr, S. A.
1985   "Some pictoral fragments from Iolkos in the Volos Museum, *Archaeologiki Ephemeris* 1985, 85–94.
1990   *Aegean Painting of the Bronze Age*. Philadelphia.
Ingholt, H.
1940   *Rapport préliminaire sur sept campagnes de fouilles à Hama en Syrie (1932–8)*. Copenhagn.
Ito, A.
1971   *Zur Chronologie der frühsillazeitlichen Gräbern in Südkorea*. Bayerische Akademie der Wissenschaften. Philosophisch-historische Klasse, Abhandlungen N.F. 71. München.
Izbitser, E.
1993   *Wheeled Vehicle Burials of the Steppe Zone of Eastern Europe and Northern Caucasus, 3rd to 2nd Millennium B.C.* (unpublished doctoral dissertation, University of St. Petersburg; in Russian with English abstract).
James, F.
1974   "Stone knobs and chariot tracks", *Expedition* 16, 31–39.
Jacob-Felsch, M.
1987   "Kalapodi-Bericht 1987–1982. Bericht zur spätmykenischen und submykenischen Keramik", *Archäologischer Anzeiger* 1981, 26–35.

Jacobs, B.
1984–85 "Wagenfahrt im Alten Orient", *Acta Praehistorica et Archaeologica* 16–17, 153–158. (review article on Littauer and Crouwel 1979).
Jantzen, U.
1972 *Ägyptische und orientalische Bronzen aus dem Heraion von Samos*. Samos 8. Bonn.
Jettmar, K.
1964 *The Art of the Steppes*. Baden-Baden.
Jope, E. M.
1957 "Vehicles and Harness", in: Singer, Holmyard, Hall and Williams 1957, 537–562.
Kadyrbaev, M. K. and Marjaschev, A. N.
1972 "The third season of work in Karatau", *Arkheologicheskie Otkrytie*, 499–501. (in Russian).
1972 "Karatau chariots", *Arkheologicheskie issledovanie v Kazakhstane* (Alma-Ata), 128–145. (in Russian).
Kammenhuber, A.
1961 *Hippologia hethitica*. Wiesbaden.
Kantor, H. J.
1947 *The Aegean and the Orient in the Second Millennium*. Archaeological Institute of America Monograph 1—Monographs on Archaeology and Fine Arts. Bloomington, Indiana.
1962 "A bronze plaque with relief decoration from Tell Tainat", *Journal of Near Eastern Studies* 21, 93–117.
Kapera, Z.
1981 "The Amathus gold plaques from the Old Goluchow collection", *Report of the Department of Antiquities, Cyprus* 1981, 106–114.
Karageorghis, V.
1962a "Chronique des fouilles . . . à Chypre en 1961", *Bulletin de Correspondence Héllenique* 86, 317–414.
1962b *Treasures in the Cyprus Museum*. Nicosia.
1962c "A "Homeric" burial discovered in a royal tomb of the 7th century B.C.", *Illustrated London News*, 894–896.
1963a "Une tombe de guerrier à Palaepaphos", *Bulletin de Correspondence Héllenique* 87, 265–300.
1963b "Chroniques des fouilles . . . à Chypre en 1962", *Bulletin de Correspondence Héllenique* 87, 325–387.
1965 "Horse burials on the island of Cyprus", *Archaeology* 12, 282–290.
1966a "À propos de quelques représentations de chars sur des vases chypriotes", *Bulletin de Correspondence Héllenique* 90, 101–118.
1966b "Recent discoveries at Salamis (Cyprus)", *Archäologischer Anzeiger 1966*, 210–255.
1966c "Chroniques des fouilles . . . à Chypre en 1965", *Bulletin de Correspondence Héllenique* 90, 297–389.
1967a *Excavations in the Necropolis of Salamis* I. Nicosia.
1967b "Chroniques des fouilles . . . à Chypre en 1966", *Bulletin de Correspondence Héllenique* 91, 337–348.
1967c "Nouvelles tombes de guerriers a Palaepaphos", *Bulletin de Correspondence Héllenique* 101, 202–247.
1967d "Chronique des fouilles . . . à Chypre en 1967", *Bulletin de Correspondance Hellénique* 91, 275–370.
1969a *Salamis in Cyprus*. London.
1969b "Chronique des fouilles . . . à Chypre en 1968", *Bulletin de Correspondence Héllenique* 93, 431–569.

1970   *Excavations in the Necropolis of Salamis* II. Nicosia.
1973a   *Excavations in the Necropolis of Salamis* III. Nicosia.
1973b   "A Cypro-Geometric III chariot krater", *Report of the Department of Antiquities, Cyprus* 1973, 167–178.
1973c   *Cypriote Antiquities in the Pierides Collection, Larnaca, Cyprus.* Larnaca.
1973d   "Chronique des fouilles . . . à Chypre en 1972", *Bulletin de Correspondence Héllenique* 97, 601–689.
1974   "Chronique des fouilles . . . à Chypre en 1973", *Bulletin de Correspondence Héllenique* 98, 821–896.
1975   "Kypriaka II", *Report of the Department of Antiquities, Cyprus* 1974, 58–68.
1976–78   *Treasures of the Cyprus Museum. An Exhibition of Cypriot Art.* Baltimore.
1977   *Two Cypriot Sanctuaries of the End of the Cypro-Archaic Period.* Roma.
1978   "A "Favissa" at Kazaphani", *Report of the Department of Antiquities, Cyprus* 1978, 156–193.
1980a   "Chypre: dernieres découvertes", *Archéologia* 146, 38–51.
1980b   "Chronique des fouilles . . . à Chypre en 1979", *Bulletin de Correspondence Héllenique* 104, 776–822.
1980c   "Kypraika V", *Report of the Department of Antiquities, Cyprus* 1980, 128–135.
1981   "Chronique des fouilles . . . à Chypre en 1980", *Bulletin de Correspondence Héllenique* 105, 967–1024.
1982a   "A Late Mycenaean IIIB chariot krater from Cyprus", *Report Department of Antiquities Cyprus, 1981,* 77–82.
1982b   *Cyprus. From the Stone Age to the Romans.* London.
1988   *Palaipaphos-Skales. An Iron Age Cemetery in Cyprus.* Ausgrabungen in Alt-Paphos auf Cypern 3. Konstanz.
1989   "A new "Geryon" terracotta statuette from Cyprus", *Eretz-Israel* 20, 92–97.
1994   (ed.) *Cyprus in the 11th Century.* Nicosia.
——— and Gagniers, J. des
1974   *La céramique chypriote de style figure. Âge du Fer (1050–500 av. J.-C.).* Roma.
1979   *La céramique chypriote de style figure. Âge du Fer (1050–500 av. J.-C.). Supplement.* Roma.
———, Styrenius, C.-G. and Winblath, M.-L.
1977   *Chypriote Antiquities in the Medelhavsmuseet, Stockholm.* Memoir 2. Stockholm.
Karakhanian, G. O. and Safian, P. G.
1970   *The Rock Carvings of Syunik (Erevan).* Erevan (in Armenian and in Russian).
Karo, G.
1930–33   *Die Schachtgräber von Mykenai.* München.
Kayser, H.
1969   *Ägyptisches Kunsthandwerk.* Braunschweig.
Kendall, T. B.
1978   *Warfare and Military Matters in the Nuzi Tablets.* (doctoral dissertation, Brandeis University, Ann Arbor, Michigan).
Kenna, V. E. G.
1960   *Cretan Seals, with a Catalogue of the Minoan Gems in the Ashmolean Museum.* Oxford.
Kilian, K.
1980   "Zur Darstellung eines Wagenrennens aus spätmykenischer Zeit", *Mitteilungen des Deutschen Archäologischen Instituts Athenische Abteilung* 95, 21–31.
1982   "Mycenaean charioteers again", *Antiquity* 56, 205–206.
Kirk, G. S.
1949   "Ships on Geometric vases", *Annual of the British School at Athens* 44, 93–153.
1975   "The Homeric poems as history", in: *The Cambridge Ancient History* (rd edition) II.2, 820–850.

Kirwan, L. P.
1939   *The Oxford Excavations at Firka*. Oxford.
Klengel-Brandt, E.
1978   *Die Terrakotten aus Assur im Vorderasiatischen Museum*. Berlin.
Knauer, E. R.
1986   "The Persian saddle blanket. Gleanings", *Studia Iranica* 15, 265–266.
Kőhalmi, K. U.
1968   "Two saddle finds from western Mongolia", *Acta Archaeologica Academiae Scientiarum Hungaricae* 20, 349–358.
Kohler, E. L.
1964   "Phrygian animal style and nomadic art", in: Mellink, M. J. (ed.), *Dark Ages and Nomads*. Istanbul, 59–60.
1965   "Review of Kalicz, N., *Die Péceler (Badener) Kultur und Anatolien*. Budapest 1963", in: *American Journal of Archaeology* 69, 71–72.
Korres, G. S.
1989   "New observations on the ship representations on the LH IIIC:1/2 pyxis from Traggana, Pylos", in: Tzalas 1989, 177–202. (in Greek).
Koşay, H. Z.
1951   *Alaca-Höyük. Das Dorf Alaca-Höyük. Materialien zur Ethnographie und Volkskunde Anatoliens*. Ankara. (in Turkish and German).
Kossack, G.
1954   "Pferdegeschirr aus Gräbern der älteren Hallstattzeit Bayerns", *Jahrbuch des Römisch-Germanischen Zentralmuseums Mainz* 1, 111–178.
1971   "The construction of the felloe in Iron Age spoked wheels", in: Boardman, J., Brown, M. A., Powell, T. G. E. (eds.), *The European Community in Later Prehistory. Studies in Honour of C. F. C. Hawkes*. London, 141–163.
Kozhin, R. M.
1968   "The Gobi Quadriga", *Sovetskaja Arkheologija* 1968 (3), 35–42. (in Russian).
Kramer, S. N.
1963   *The Sumerians. Their History, Culture, and Character*. Chicago.
Kübler, K.
1950   *Altattische Malerei*. Tübingen.
Kühn, H.
1935   *Die vorgeschichtliche Kunst Deutschlands*. Propyläen Kunstgeschichte. Ergänzungsband 8. Berlin.
Kümmel, H.-M.
1967   *Ersatzrituale für den hethitschen König*. Studien zu den Boğazköy-Texten 3. Wiesbaden.
Kuz'mina, E. E.
1994   *Where did the Indo-Aryans come from? The Material Culture of the Andronovo Tribes and the Origins of the Indo-Iranians*. Moskva. (in Russian with English abstract).
Kyzlassov, I. M.
1973   "On the origin of the stirrups", *Sovetskaja Arkheologija* 1973 (2), 25–36. (in Russian).
Lang, M. L.
1969   *The Palace of Nestor at Pylos in Western Messenia* II. The Frescoes. Princeton, New Jersey.
1991   "The Greek alphabetic impact on Archaic Greece", in: Buitron-Oliver, D. 1991. (ed.), *New Perspectives in Early Greek Art*. Hannover and London, 65–79.
Langdon, S.
1924   *Excavations at Kish. The Herbert Weld (for the University of Oxford) and Field Museum of Natural History (Chicago) Expedition to Mesopotamia* I. Paris.
Laroche, E.
1947   *Recherches sur les noms des dieux hittites*. Paris.

Lázló, G.
1943   *Der Grabfund von Koroncó und der altungarische Sattel.* Budapest. (pp. 5–106
              in Hungarian; pp. 107–191 translation into German).
Leaf, W.
1884   "The Homeric chariot", *Journal of Hellenic Studies* 15, 185–194.
Leclant, J.
1960   "Astarté à cheval d'après les répresentations égyptiennes", *Syria* 37,
              1–67.
Lefebvre, G.
1923–24   *Le Tombeau de Petosiris.* I–III. Cairo.
Legrain, L.
1951   *Seal Cylinders.* Ur Excavations X. London and Philadelphia.
Lehmann, G. A.
1985   *Die mykenisch-frühgriechische Welt und der östliche Mittelmeerraum in der Zeit
              der 'Seevölker-Invasionen' um 1200 v.Chr.* Opladen.
Lenz, D.
1995   *Vogeldarstellungen in der ägäischen und zyprischen Vasenmalerei des 12.–9.
              Jahrhunderts v.Chr.* Leidorf.
Lepsius, R.
1897–1913   *Denkmäler Aegyptens und Aethiopiens . . .* I–V. Leipzig.
Leshnik, L.
1971   "Some early Indian horse bits and other bridle equipment", *American
              Journal of Archaeology* 75, 141–150.
Leskov, A. M.
1964   "Ancient horn cheekpieces from Trakhtimirov", *Sovetskaja Arkheologija*
              1964 (1), 299–303. (in Russian).
Lewy, J.
1935–37   *Tablettes cappadociennes. Textes cunéiformes* XXI. Paris. (Musée du Louvre,
              Départment des antiquités orientales).
Lhote, Henri
1953   "Le cheval et le chameau dan les peintures et gravures rupestres du
              Sahara", *Bulletin de l'Institut français de l'afrique noire* 15, 1138–1228.
Limet, H.
1955   "Documents économiques de la IIIᵉ Dynastie d'Ur", *Revue d'Assyriologie*
              49, 69–93.
1960   *Le travail du métal aus pays de Sumer au temps de la IIIᵉ Dynastie d'Ur.*
              Bibliothèque de Faculté de Philosophie et Lettres de l'Université de
              Lièges 155. Paris.
Linder, E.
1973   "Naval warfare in the El-Amarna Age", Blackman, D. J. (ed.), *Marine
              Archaeology.* Colston Papers 23:9. Bristol, 319–322.
Littauer, M. A.
1968a   "The function of the yoke saddle in ancient harnessing", *Antiquity*
              42, 27–31.
1968b   "A 19th and 20th dynasty heroic motif on Attic black-figured vases",
              American Journal of Archaeology 72, 150–152.
1969a   "Bits and pieces", *Antiquity* 43, 289–300.
1969b   "Slit nostrils on equids", *Zeitschrift für Säugetierkunde* 34, 183–186.
1971a   "The figured evidence for a small pony in the ancient Near East?",
              Iraq 33, 24–30.
1971b   "V.O. Vitt and the horse of Pazyryk", *Antiquity* 45, 293–294.
1972   "The military use of the chariot in the Aegean and the Late Bronze
              Age", *American Journal of Archaeology* 76, 145–157.
1976a   "New light on the Assyrian chariot", *Orientalia* 45, 217–226.

1976b "Reconstruction questioned", *Archaeology* 29, 212.
1977a "Rock carvings of chariots in Transcaucasia, Central Asia and Outer Mongolia", *Proceedings of the Prehistoric Society* 43, 243–262.
1977b "Review of Greenhalgh 1973a", *Classical Philology* 72, 363–364.
—— and Crouwel, J. H.
1973a "The Vulture Stela and an early type of two-wheeled vehicle", *Journal of Near Eastern Studies* 32, 324–329.
1973b "Early metal models of wagons from the Levant", *Levant* 5, 102–126.
1973c "The dating of a chariot ivory from Nimrud considered once again", *Bulletin of the American Schools of Oriental Research* 209, 27–33.
1973d "Evidence for horse bits from Shaft Grave IV at Mycenae?", *Praehistorische Zeitschrift* 48, 207–213.
1974 "Terracotta models as evidence for wheeled vehicles with tilts in the ancient Near East", *Proceedings of the Prehistoric Society* 40, 20–36.
1977a "The origin and diffusion of the crossbar wheel", *Antiquity* 51, 95–105.
1977b "Chariots with Y-poles in the ancient Near East", *Archäologischer Anzeiger 1977*, 1–8.
1977c "Terracotta chariot model", in: Karageorghis, V. (ed.), *Two Cypriote Sanctuaries of the End of the Cypro-Archaic Period*. Rome, 67–73.
1979a *Wheeled Vehicles and Ridden Animals in the Ancient Near East*. Handbuch der Orientalistik 7.1 (2–1). Leiden and Köln.
1979b "An Egyptian wheel in Brooklyn", *Journal of Egyptian Archaeology* 65, 107–120.
1982 "A bridle bit of the second millennium B.C. in Jerusalem", *Levant* 14, 178.
1983 "Chariots in Late Bronze Age Greece", *Antiquity* 57, 187–192.
1984 "Ancient Iranian horse helmets?", *Iranica Antiqua* 19, 41–51.
1985 *Chariots and Related Equipment from the Tomb of Tutʿankhamūn*. Tutʿankhamūn Tomb Series 8. Oxford.
1986a "The earliest known three-dimensional evidence for spoked wheels", *American Journal of Archaeology* 90, 395–398.
1986b "(Archaeological Notes): 1. A Near Eastern bridle bit of the second millennium B.C. in New York", *Levant* 18, 163–167.
1996a "A note on the origin of the true chariot", *Antiquity* 70, 934–939.
—— Crouwel, J. and Collon, D.
1976 "A Bronze Age chariot group from the Levant in Paris", *Levant* 8, 71–79. (Littauer, M. A. and Crouwel, J. H., "A. The chariot", pp. 71–79; Collon, D., "The figures", pp. 79–81).
—— and Karageorghis, V.,
1969 "Note of prometopidia", *Archäologischer Anzeiger* 1969, 152–160.
Liverani, M.
1994 "History as a war game", *Journal of Mediterranean Archaeology* 7, 241–248.
Longperier, A. de
1871 *Musée Napoleon* III. *Choix de monuments antiques*. Paris.
Lorimer, H. L.
1903 "The country cart in ancient Greece", *Journal of Hellenic Studies* 23, 132–151.
1950 *Homer and the Monuments*. London.
Loud, G.
1936 *Khorsabad* I. *Excavations in the Palace and at the City Gate*. The University of Chicago Oriental Institute Publications 28. Chicago.
Lubsen-Admiral, St. and Crouwel, J. H.
1989 *Cyprus and Aphrodite*. (catalogue of the exhibition at the Allard Pierson Museum.) Amsterdam.
Lucas, A. T.
1952 "A block-wheel car from Co. Tipperary", *Journal of the Royal Society of Antiquaries of Ireland* 82, 135–144.

Lucas, A. and Harris, J. R.
  1962 *Ancient Egyptian Materials and Industries*. (4th edition revised by J. R. Harris).
         London.
Macalister, R. A. S.
  1912 *The Excavation at Gezer* II. London.
Mackay, A.
  1925 *Report on the Excavations of the "A" Cemetery at Kish, Mesopotamia* I.2. Chicago.
  1929 "Note on a bas-relief found in Ur", *Antiquaries Journal* 9, 26–29.
Mackay, D.
  1951 *A Guide to the Archaeological Collections in the University Museum*. American
         University in Beirut.
Maclean, F.
  1975 *To the Back of Beyond. An Illustrated Companion to Central Asia and Mongolia*.
         Boston.
Madhloom, T. A.
  1970 *The Chronology of Neo-Assyrian Art*. London.
Maenchen-Helfen, O.
  1973 *The World of the Huns. Studies in their History and Culture* Berkeley. (edited by
         M. Knight).
Mallowan, M. E. L.
  1966 *Nimrud and its Remains* I–II. London.
—— and Hermann, G.
  1974 *Furniture from S.W. 7, Fort Shalmaneser. Ivories from Nimrud (1949–1963)* 3.
         London.
Mantran, R.
  1959 *Turkey*. London.
Mariette, A.
  1889 *Monuments divers recueillis en Egypte et en Nubie*. Paris.
Marinatos, S. and Hirmer, M.
  1960 *Crete and Mycenae*. New York.
  1973 *Kreta, Thera und das mykenische Hellas*. München.
Markoe G.
  1985 *Phoenician Bronze and Silver Bowls from Cyprus and the Mediterranean*. Berkeley.
Markle, M.
  1977 "The Macedonian sarissa, spear and related armor", *American Journal of
         Archaeology* 81, 232–239.
Maspero G.
  1889 *Catalogue du musée égyptien de Marseilles*. Paris.
Marstander, S.
  1963 *Ostfolds Jordbrukristninger Skeijberg*. Oslo.
Masson, O.
  1961 *Les inscriptions chypriotes syllabiques. Recueil critique et commentaire*. Paris.
  1964 "Kypriaka I. Recherches sur les antiquités de Tamassos", *Bulletin de Cor-
         respondence Héllenique* 83, 199–238.
Maxwell, G.
  1957 *People of the Reeds*. New York.
McAdams, R.
  1975 "An ancient threshing sledge or harrow", *Sumer* 31, 17–19.
McCown, D. E. and Haines, R. G.
  1967 *Nippur I. The Temple of Enlil, Scribal Quarter, and Soundings*. Oriental Institute
         Publications 78. Chicago.
McDonald, W. A.
  1964 "Overland communications in Greece during LH III with special refer-

ence to southwest Peloponnese", in: Bennett, E. L., Jr. (ed.), *Mycenaean Studies. Proceedings of the Third International Colloquium.* Madison, 217–240.

—— and Hope Simson, R.

1961 "Prehistoric habitation in the southwestern Peloponnese", *American Journal of Archaeology* 65, 221–260.

Meadow, R. H. and Uerpmann, H.-P.

1986 (eds.), *Equids in the Ancient World.* Beihefte zum Tübinger Atlas des Vorderen Orients, Reihe A (Naturwissenschaften) 19/1. Wiesbaden.

1991 (eds.), *Equids in the Ancient World* II. Beihefte zum Tübinger Atlas des Vorderen Orients, Reihe A (Naturwissenschaften) 19/2. Wiesbaden.

Mecquenem, R. de

1922 "Fouilles de Suse (campagnes 1914–21, 1922)", *Revue d'Assyriologie* 19, 109–140.

1924 "Fouilles à Suse (campagnes 1923–24)", *Revue d'Assyriologie* 21, 105–108.

1943 *Fouilles de Suse, 1933–39.* Mémoirs de la Mission archéologique en Iran 29. Paris.

Megaw, A. H. S.

1954 "Archaeology in Cyprus", *Journal of Hellenic Studies* 74, 172–176.

1955 "Archaeology in Cyprus, 1955", *Archaeological Reports 1955*, 41–46.

1967 *The Art of the European Iron Age. A Study of the Elusive Image.* Bath, Somerset.

Meissner, B.

1920–25 *Babylonien und Assyrien* I–II. Kulturgeschichtliche Bibliothek 1. Reihe: Ethnologische Bibliothek. Heidelberg.

Mellink, M. J.

1966 "The Hasanlu Bowl in Anatolian perspective", *Iranica Antiqua* 6, 72–87.

1967 "Anatolian chronology", in: Ehrich, R. W. (ed.), *Chronologies in Old World Archaeology.* Chicago, 101–131.

1971 "Archaeology in Asia Minor", *American Journal of Archaeology* 75, 161–181.

1983 "Archaeology in Asia Minor", *American Journal of Archaeology* 87, 427–442.

Mendel, G.

1908 *Catalogue des figurines grecques de terre cuite.* Constantinople. (Musées imperiaux ottomans).

Mercklin, E. von

1909 *Der Rennwagen in Griechenland. Erster Teil.* Leipzig.

1916 "New representations of chariots on Attic Geometric vases", *American Journal of Archaeology* 20, 397–406.

Messerschmidt, W.

1988 "Der ägäische Streitwagen und seine Beziehungen zum Nordeurasischvorderasiatischen Raum", *Acta Praehistorica et Archaeologica* 20, 31–44.

Meyer, G. R.

1965 *Altorientalische Denkmäler im Vorderasiatischen Museum zu Berlin.* Leipzig.

Michalowski, K.

1969 *Art of Ancient Egypt.* New York. (translated and adapted from Polish and French by N. Guterman).

Mieroop, M. van de

1987 *Crafts in the Early Isin Period. A Study of Isin Craft Archive from the Reigns of Isbi-Erra and Su-Ilisu* Orientalia Lovaniensia Analecta 24. Leuven.

Minns, E. H.

1913 *Scythians and Greeks. A Survey of Ancient History and Archaeology on the North Coast of the Euxine from the Danube to the Caucasus.* Cambridge.

Mnatsakanyan, A. O.

1957 "Excavations of kurgans on the shores of Lake Sevan in 1956 (preliminary report)", *Sovetskaja Archeologija* 1957 (2), 146–153. (in Russian).

1960   "Ancient vehicles from the kurgans of the Bronze Age on the littoral of
        Lake Sevan", *Sovetskaja Archeologija* 1960 (2), 139–152. (in Russian).
Mötefindt, H.
1918   "Die Entstehung des Wagens und des Wagenrades", *Mannus* 10, 1–63.
Mollard-Besques, S.
1954   *Catalogue raisonné des figurines et reliefs en terre-cuite grecs, étrusques et romaines.*
        Paris.
Mongait, A.
1959   *L'archéologie en U.R.S.S.* Moskva.
Monloup, T.
1980   "Figurines de terre cuite à roulettes", in: *Salamine de Chypre. Histoire et
        archéologie. Lyon, 13–17 mars 1978.* Centre Nationale de la Recherche 578.
        Paris, 169–176.
1984   *Les figurines de terre cuite de tradition archaïque.* Salamine de Chypre 12. Paris.
Moore, M. B.
1971   *Horses on Black-Figured Greek Vases of the Archaic Period.* (doctoral disserta-
        tion, Institute of Fine Arts, New York University).
Moorey, P. R. S.
1966   "A reconsideration of the excavations at Tell Ingharra (East Kish)
        1923–1933", *Iraq* 28, 18–51.
1968   "The earliest Near Eastern spoked wheels and their chronology", *Proceedings
        of the Prehistoric Society* 34, 430–432.
1970a   "Pictoral evidence for the history of horse-riding in Iraq before the Kassite
        period", *Iraq* 32, 36–50.
1970b   *Ancient Egypt.* Oxford. (Ashmolean Museum).
1971   *A Catalogue of Ancient Persian Bronzes in the Ashmolean Museum.* Oxford.
1977a   "Bronze rollers and frames from Babylonia and Western Asia: Problems
        of date and function", *Revue d'Assyriologie* 71, 137–150.
1977b   "What do we know about the people buried in the Royal Cemetery?",
        Expedition 20 (1), 24–40.
1981   "Persian Art", in: Markoe, G. (ed.), *Ancient Bronzes, Ceramics and Seals.
        The Nasli M. Heeramaneck Collection of Ancient Near Eastern, Central Asiatic
        and European Art.* Los Angeles, 13–137. (Los Angeles County Museum of
        Art).
1982a   "Archaeology and pre-Achaemenid metalworking in Iran: a fifteen year
        retrospective", *Iran* 20, 81–101.
1982b   "The archaeological evidence for metallurgy and related technologies in
        Mesopotamia, c. 5500–2100 B.C.", *Iraq* 44, 13–38.
1986   "The emergence of the light, horse-drawn chariot in the Near East
        c. 2000–1500 B.C.", *World Archaeology* 18, 196–215.
1989   "The Hurrians, the Mitanni and technological innovation", in: de Meyer,
        L. and Haerinck, E. (eds.), *Archaeologia Iranica et Orientalis. Miscellanea in
        Honorem Louis Vanden Berghe.* Gent, 273–286.
Moortgat, A.
1940   *Vorderasiatische Rollsiegel. Ein Beitrag zur Geschichte der Steinschneidekunst.* Berlin.
        [3rd edition 1983].
1960a   *Tell Chuẹra in Nordost-Syrien. Vorläufiger Bericht über die Grabungskampagne 1958.*
        Wiesbaden.
1960b   *Tell Chušra in Nordost-Syrien. Vorläufiger Bericht über die Grabungskampagne 1959.*
        Wiesbaden.
1967   *Die Kunst des alten Mesopotamien.* Köln.
Moretti, M. and Maetzke, G.
1970   *The Art of the Etruscans.* London.

Morgan, J. de et al.
1900   *Fouilles à Suse en 1897–1898 et 1898–1899*. Mémoirs de la Délegation en Perse. 1. Paris.
Morgan, L.
1988   *The Miniature Wall Paintings of Thera*. Cambridge.
Morris, D.
1985   *The Art of Ancient Cyprus. With a Check-List of the Author's Collection*. Oxford.
Morrison, J. S. and Williams, T. T.
1968   *Greek Oared Ships 900–322 B.C.* Cambridge.
Mozsolicz, A.
1963   "Mors en bois de cerf sur le territoire du bassin des Carpathes", *Acta Archaeologica Academiae Scientiarum Hungaricae* 3, 69–109.
Mountjoy, P.
1993   *Mycenaean Pottery: An Introduction*. Oxford University Committee for Archaeology monograph 36. Oxford.
1997   "The destruction of the palace of Pylos reconsidered," *Annual of the British School in Athens* 92, 109–137.
Müller, V.
1929   *Frühe Plastik in Griechenland und Vorderasien. Ihre Typenbildung von der neolithischen bis in die griechisch-archaische Zeit (rund 3000 bis 600 v. Chr.)*. Augsburg.
Muhly, J.
1980   "On the Shaft Graves of Mycenae", in: Powell, Jr., M. A. and Sach, R. H. (eds.), *Studies in Honor of Tom B. Jones*. Alter Orient und Altes Testament 203. Neukirchen-Vluyn, 311–323.
Murzhin, V. U. and Chernenko, E. V.
1980   "Means of protecting war horses in Scythian times", *Sbornik Skifia i Kawkaz (Kiev) 1980*, 155–167. (in Russian).
Muscarella, O. W.
1968   "Anatolia", The Metropolitan Museum of Art Bulletin 26 (5) [January]. (objects 1–4).
1981   (ed.) *Ladders to Heaven. Art Treasures from the Land of the Bible*. Toronto. (catalogue of the exhibition at the Royal Ontario Museum).
Musti, D.
1990   (ed.), *Le origine dei Greci. Dori e mondo egeo*. Roma-Bari.
Myres, J. L.
1909–11   in: *Antike Denkmäler* III.1. Berlin, 1–4. [edited by Kaiserlich-Deutsches Archaeologisches Institut].
1914   *Handbook of the Cesnola Collection of Antiquities from Cyprus*. New York.
—— and Ohnefalsch-Richter, M.
1899   *Catalogue of the Cyprus Museum with a Chronicle of Excavations Undertaken since the British Occupation and Introductory Notes on Cypriote Archaeology*. Oxford.
Nagel, W.
1964   *Zum neuen Bild des vordynastischen Keramikums in Vorderasien*. Berliner Jahrbücher zur Vorgeschichte 15. Berlin.
1966   *Der mesopotamische Streitwagen und seine Entwicklung im ostmediterranen Bereich*. Berliner Beiträge zur Vor- und Frühgeschichte 10. Berlin.
1984–85   "Zwei Kupfermodelle eines Kultwagens mit Rinderzweigespann vom zweiachsigen Gatterkanzeltyp aus der Alacahüyük-Kultur im Museum für Vor- und Frühgeschichte Berlin", *Archaeologica Praehistorica et Archaeologica* 16–17, 143–151.
1987   "Indogermanen und Alter Orient. Rückblick und Ausblick auf den Stand des Indogermanenproblems", *Mitteilungen der Deutschen Orientgesellschaft zu Berlin* 119, 157–213.

1992   "Das Aufkommen des Klassischen Streitwagens *w* . . . *ta-* in Syrien und Ägypten", in: Nagel, W. and Eder, C., "Altsyrien und Altägypten", *Damaszener Mitteilungen* 6, 1–108 [The quoted chapter "Das Aufkommen des Klassischen Streitwagens". . . = chapter 9 in Eder's and Nagel's "Altsyrien und Altägypten" pp. 67–81; see Raulwing 1994].

Naville, E.
1870   *Textes relatifs au mythe d'Horus. Recueillis dans le Temple d'Edfou.* Genève and Basel. (Reprinted Wiesbaden 1982).

Needham, J.
1965   *Science and Civilisation in China* IV. *Physics and Physical Technology* Part II. *Mechanical Engeneering.* Cambridge.

—— and Lu, G.-D.
1960   "Efficient equine harness: the Chinese inventions", *Physis. Revista di storia della scienza* 2 (2), 121–162. [cf. also "A further note on efficient equine harness: the Chinese Inventions", *Physis. Revista internazionale di storia della scienza* 7 (1), 1965, 70–74].

Nelson, H. H.
1930–32   *Medinet Habu* I. *The Earlier Records of Ramses III.* Chicago. University of Chicago, Oriental Institute, Epigraphic Survey.
1954   "The naval battle depicted at Medinet Habu", *Journal of Near Eastern Studies* 2, 40–55.

Neve, P.
1965   "Die Grabungen auf Büyükkale im Jahre 1963", *Mitteilungen der Deutschen Orientgesellschaft zu Berlin* 95, 35–68.

Newberry, P. E.
1906   *Scarabs. An Introduction to the Study of Egyptian Seals and Signets.* London.

Newhall Stillwell, A.
1948   *Corinth. Results of Excavations Conducted by the American School of Classical Studies at Athens* XV.1. *The Potter's Quarter.* Cambridge, Mass.

Noëttes, L. des
1931   *L'attelage, le cheval de selle à travers les âges.* Paris

Nuoffer, O.
1904   *Der Rennwagen im Altertum. Erster Teil.* Leipzig.

Oates, D. and Oates, J.
1976   *The Rise of Civilization.* Oxford.

O'Brien, J. C.
1968   "Bits, boots and bridles", in: Harrison, J. C. (ed.), *Care and Training of the Trotter and Pacer.* Columbus, Ohio, 419–526.

Ohnefalsch-Richter, M.
1893   *Kypros, die Bibel und Homer. Beiträge zur Cultur-, Kunst- und Religionsgeschichte des Orients im Alterthume mit besonderer Berücksichtigung eigener zwölfjähriger Forschungen und Ausgrabungen auf der Insel Cypern.* Berlin.
1915   "Kyprische Bildwerke", *Athenische Mitteilungen* 40, 53–70.

Okladnikov, A. P.
1964   *Stag—Golden Horns.* Moscow and Leningrad, 206–11. (in Russian).

Oliver, P.
1960   "The second millennium B.C.", *The Metropolitan Museum of Art Bulletin (April)*, 241–252.

Onoyama, S.
1966   "Early horse equipment discovered in Japan", *Kokogaku-Zasshi* 52, 1–2.

Oppenheim, A. L.
1969   "The story of Idrimi, King of Alalakh", in: Pritchard, J. B. (ed.), *The Ancient Near East. Supplementary Texts and Pictures.* Princeton, New Jersey, 121–122.

Orchard, J. J.
1967   *Equestrian Bridle-Harness Ornaments. Catalogue and Plates.* Ivories from Nimrud
          (1949–1963) I.2. Aberdeen.
Ormerod, H. A.
1924   *Piracy in the Ancient World.* London.
Orthmann, W.
1967   "Zu den Standarten aus Alaca Hüyük", *Istanbuler Mitteilungen* 17, 34–54.
1971   *Untersuchungen zur späthethitischen Kunst.* Bonn.
von der Osten, H. H.
1934   *Ancient Oriental Seals in the Collection of Mr. E. T. Newell.* The University
          of Chicago Oriental Institute Publications 22. Chicago.
Owen, D. I.
1991   "The 'first' equestrian: an Ur III glyptic scene", *Acta Sumerologica* 13, 259–273.
Özgen, E.
1982   *The Urartian Bronze Collection at the University Museum.* (doctoral disserta-
          tion, University of Pennsylvania).
1984   "The Urartian chariot reconsidered I", *Anatolica* 10, 111–131.
1985   "The Urartian chariot reconsidered II", *Anatolica* 11, 91–154.
1986   "A group of terracotta wagon models from southeastern Anatolia",
          Anatolian Studies 36, 165–71.
Özgüç, N.
1952–53 "Ausgrabungen in Kültepe", *Archiv für Orientforschung* 16, 149–150.
1965   *The Anatolian Group of Cylinder Seal Impressions fröm Kültepe.* Ankara.
1980   "Seal Impressions from the palaces in Acemhöyük", in: Porada, E.
          (ed.), *Ancient Art in Seals.* Princeton, New Jersey, 61–100.
Özgüç, T. and Akok, M.
1958   *Horoztepe. An Early Bronze Age Settlement and Cemetery.* Ankara.
Palmieri, A.
1981   "Excavations at Arslantepe (Malatya)", *Anatolian Studies* 31, 101–119.
1985   "Scavi ad Arslantepe (Malatya) 1976–1979", *Quaderni della 'Ricerca Scientifica'*
          112 (CNR, Roma), 75–114.
——— and Frangipane, M.
1986   "Assetto redistributivo di una società protourbana della fine del 4° mil-
          lennio", *Dialoghi di Archeologia* 3rd Series 4, 35–44.
Parrot, A.
1951   "Cylindre hittite nouvellement acquis (AO 20138)", *Syria* 27, 180–190.
1953   *Mari.* Paris.
1956   *Le temple d'Ischtar.* Mission archéologique de Mari 1. Paris.
1959   *Le palais: Peinture murales.* Mission archéologique de Mari 2. Paris.
1960   *Sumer.* Paris.
1961   *Assur.* Paris.
1967a   *Les temples d'Ishtarat et de Ninni-Zaza.* Mission archéologique de Mari 3. Paris.
1967b   "La collection De Clerq entre en Louvre", *Syria* 44, 449–450.
1968   "La donation de Clercq—M. de Boisgelin, *La Revue du Louvre* 18, 4–5,
          299–300.
Paterson, A.
1915   *Assyrian Sculpture. Palace of Sinacherib.* The Hague.
Perrot, G. and Chipiez, Ch.
1885   *Histoire de l'art dans l'antiquité* III. Paris.
Petrie, W. F.
1933   *Ancient Gaza III. Tell el Ajjul.* Publications of the Egyptian Research Account
          and British School of Archaeology in Egypt 55. London.
1934   *Ancient Gaza IV.Tell el Ajjul.* Publications of the Egyptian Research Account
          and British School of Archaeology in Egypt 56. London.

Philipp, H.
    1981   "Ein archaischer Pferdebehang aus Zypern", in: Mallwitz, A. (ed.), *X.
            Bericht über die Ausgrabungen in Olympia 1966–1976*. Berlin, 91–108.
Piggott, S.
    1952   "Celtic chariots on Roman coins", *Antiquity* 102, 87–88.
    1957   "A tripartite disk wheel from Blair Drummond, Perthshire", *Prehistoric
            Society of Antiquity Scotland* 90, 238–241.
    1968   "The earliest wheeled vehicles and the Caucasian evidence", *Proceedings
            of the Prehistoric Society* 34, 266–318.
    1974   "Chariots in the Caucasus and in China", *Antiquity* 48, 16–24.
    1979   "The first wagons and carts: twenty-five years later", *Bulletin of the Institute
            of Archaeology, University of London* 16, 3–17.
    1983   *The Earliest Wheeled Transport. From the Atlantic Coast to the Caspian Sea.*
            London.
    1992   *Wagon, Chariots and Carriage. Symbol and Status in the History of Transport.* London.
Plath, R.
    1994a   *Der Streitwagen und seine Teile im frühen Griechischen. Sprachliche Untersuchungen
            zu den mykenischen Texten und zum homerischen Epos.* Erlanger Beiträge zur
            Sprache, Literatur und Kunst 76. Nürnberg.
    1994b   "Pferd und Wagen im Mykenischen und bei Homer", in: Hänsel and
            Zimmer 1994, 103–114.
Pluvinel, Antoine de
    1623   *Le maneige royal ou l'on peut remarquer la defaut la perfection du chevalier.* Paris.
    1625   *L'instruction du roy en exercise de monter à cheval.* Paris.
Popham, M.
    1987   "An early Euboean ship", *Oxford Journal of Archaeology* 6, 353–360.
—— Touloupa, E. and Sackett, L. H.
    1982   "The hero of Lefkandi", *Antiquity* 56, 169–174.
Porada, E.
    1947   *Seal Impressions of Nuzi.* Annual of the American Schools of Oriental
            Research 24. New Haven, Conn.
    1948   *Corpus of Near Eastern Seals in North American Collections* I. *The Collection of
            the Pierpont Morgan Library.* Catalogued and edited by E. Porada—in col-
            laboration with B. Buchanan—I (Text), II (Plates). New York.
    1957   "Syrian seal impressions of tablets dated in the time of Hammurabi and
            Samsu-Iluna", *Journal of Near Eastern Studies* 16, 192–197.
    1959   "The Hasanlu Bowl", *Expedition* 1959, 19–22.
    1964   *Art of Ancient Iran. Pre-islamic Cultures.* New York.
Porter, B. and Moss, R. L. B.
    1964   *Topographical Bibliography of Ancient Egyptian Hieroglyphic Texts, Reliefs and
            Paintings* I.2. (2nd edition). Oxford.
Postgate, J. N.
    1986   "The equids of Sumer again", in: Meadow and Uerpmann 1986, 194–206.
Potratz, J. A.
    1938   *Das Pferd in der Frühzeit.* Leipzig.
    1941   "Die Pferdegebisse des zweistromländischen Raumes", *Archiv für Orientforschung*
            14, 1–39.
    1963   *Die Skythen in Südrussland. Ein untergegangenes Volk in Südosteuropa.* Basel.
    1966   *Die Pferdetrensen des alten Orient.* Analecta Orientalia 41. Roma.
Pottier, M. H.
    1984   *Matériel funéraire de la Bactriane méridionale de l'âge du bronze.* Mémoirs,
            Recherche sur les civilisations 36. Paris.
Poulsen, F.
    1912   *Der Orient und die frühgriechische Kunst.* Leipzig and Berlin.

Powell, T. G. E.
  1963   "Some implications of chariotry", in: Foster, J. L. and Alcock, L. (eds.),
          Culture and Environment. Essays in Honour of Sir Cyril Fox. London, 153–169.
Pritchard, J. B.
  1954   (ed.) *The Ancient Near East in Pictures Relating to the Old Testament.* Princeton,
          New Jersey.
  1955   *Ancient Near Eastern Texts Relating to the Old Testament.* Princeton, New Jersey.
Pryce, F. N.
  1931   *Catalogue of Sculpture in the Department of Greek and Roman Antiquities in the
          British Museum* I.2. *Cypriote and Etruscan.* London.
Przeworski, S.
  1928   "Notes d'archéologie syrienne et hittite", *Syria* 9, 273–287.
  1936   Altorientalische Altertümer in skandinavischen Sammlungen, *Eurasia Septen-
          trionalis Antiqua* 10, 71–128.
Pullen, D. J.
  1992   "Ox and plow in the Early Bronze Age", *American Journal of Archaeology* 96,
          45–54.
Pumpelly, R.
  1908   (ed.) *Explorations in Turkestan. Expedition of 1904. Prehistoric Civilisations of Anau.
          Origins, Growth, and Influence of Environment* I. Carnegie Institution of Washington
          Publication 73. Washington.
Pyne, W. H.
  1806   *Microcosm or, a Pituresque Delineation of the Arts, Agriculture and Manufactures of
          Great Britain in a Series of above a Thousand Groups of Small Figures for the
          Embellishment of Landscape.* London. (reprinted New York 1971).
Quibell, J. E.
  1908   *The Tomb of Yuaa and Tuiu.* Catalogue générale des antiquités égyptiénnes
          du Musée du Caire. Cairo.
Raban, A.
  1995   "The Sea Peoples and Thera ships", in: Tzalas 1995, 353–366.
Raulwing, P.
  1994   "Ein indoarischer Streitwagenterminus im Ägyptischen?—Kritische Bemer-
          kungen zur Herleitung der Wagenbezeichnung *wrrjj.t* aus einem für das
          indoarische Sprachcorpus erschlossenen Nomen *wṛta-* 'Streitwagen'", *Göttinger
          Mizellen* 140, 71–79.
  1995   "Review of Hänsel and Zimmer 1994", in: *Kratylos* 40, 109–118.
  2000   *Horses, Chariots, and Indo-Europeans. Foundations and Methods of Chariotry-Research
          from the View of Comparative Indo-European Linguistics.* Archaeolingua. Series
          Minor 13. Budapest.
Reade, J. E.
  1975   "Aššurnasirpal I and the White Obelisk", *Iraq* 37, 129–150.
Reichel, W.
  1901   *Homerische Waffen. Archäologische Untersuchungen.* (2nd revised edition). Wien.
Reinach, S.
  1901   *La répresentation du galop dans l'art ancien et moderne.* Paris.
  1914   *Répertoire de la statuaire grecque et romaine* V. Paris.
Renfrew, C.
  1987   *Archaeology and Language. The Puzzle of Indo-European Origins.* London.
Reisner G. A. and Smith, W. S.
  1955   *A History of the Giza Necropolis* II. *The Tomb of Hetep-Heres, the Mother of Cheops.
          A Study of Egyptian Civilization in the Old Kingdom.* (completed and revised by
          Smith, W. S.) Cambridge, Mass.
Richardson, E.
  1966   *The Etruscans. Their Art and Their Civilization.* Chicago.

Richardson, N. J. and Piggott, S.
  1982 "Hesiod's wagon: text and technology", *Journal of Hellenic Studies* 101, 225–229.
Richter, G. M. A.
  1949 *Archaic Greek Art Against its Historical Background. A Survey*. New York.
  1965 "The furnishings of ancient Greek houses", *Archaeology* 18, 29–32.
  1969 *A Handbook of Greek Art*. London.
Ridder, A. de
  1905 *Collection de Clerq* III. *Les bronzes*. Paris.
  1909 *Collection de Clerq* VI. *Les terres cuites et les verres*. Paris.
Ridgeway, W.
  1905 *The Origin and Influence of the Thoroughbred-Horse*. Cambridge. (reprinted New York 1972).
Riet, A.
  1957 "'Halssporen' am Pferdegeschirr des Neuen Reiches", *Mitteilungen des Instituts für Orientforschung* 5, 148–154.
Riis, P. J.
  1963 "L'activité de la mission archéologique danoise sur la côte phénicienne en 1961", *Annales archéologiques en Syrie* 13, 211–224.
Rintschen, B.
  1968 *Les designs pictographiques et les inscriptions sur les stèles en Mongolie. Recueillis par Rintschen*. Ulan Bator. (in Mongolian).
Rodenwaldt, G.
  1911 "Fragmente mykenischer Wandgemälde", *Mitteilungen des Deutschen Archäologischen Instituts Athenische Abteilung* 36, 221–250.
  1912 *Tiryns. Die Ergebnisse der Ausgrabungen des Instituts*. II. *Die Fresken des Palastes*. Athen.
  1921 *Der Fries des Megarons von Mykenai*. Halle.
Roeder, G.
  1956 *Ägyptische Bronzefiguren*. Berlin.
Rossi, F.
  1970 *Mosaics. A Survey of their History and Techniques*. London.
Rostovtzeff, M.
  1929 *The Animal Style in South Russia and China being the Material of a Course of Lectures Delivered in August 1925 at Princeton University under the Auspices of the Harvard-Princeton Fine Arts Club*. Princeton Monographs in Art and Archaeology 14. Princeton, New Jersey.
  1936 *The Excavations at Dura-Europos. Preliminary Report of the Sixth Season of Work, October 1932–March 1933*. New Haven, Conn.
Rounitch, A. D.
  1973 "Saddlery from the region of Piatigorsk", *Sovetskaja Arkheologija* 1973 (1), 163–170. (in Russian).
  1976 "The burial of a warrior of the early Middle Ages in the Kislovodsk basin", *Sovetskaja Arkheologija* 1976 (3), 255–266. (in Russian).
Rutter, J. B.
  1975 "Review of Slenckza, E., *Tiryns* VII. *Figürlich bemalte mykenische Keramik aus Tiryns*. Mainz", in: *American Journal of Archaeology* 79, 377–378.
  1992 "Cultural novelties in post-palatial Aegean world: indices of vitality or decline?", in: Ward and Joukowski 1992, 61–78.
  1993 "Review of Aegean prehistory II: the Prepalational Bronze Age of the southern and central Greek mainland", *American Journal of Archaeology* 97, 745–797.
Sakellarakis, J. A.
  1992 *The Mycenaean Pictorial Style in the National Archaeological Museum of Athens*. Athens.

Sakellariou, A.
1957   "New light on ancient objects in the National Archaeological Museum",
         Archaiologike Ephemeris, Chronika 1–8. (in Greek).
Sandars, N. K.
1968   *Prehistoric Art in Europe.* Harmondsworth.
1978   *The Sea Peoples. Warriors of the Ancient Mediterranean.* London.
Salonen, A.
1951   *Die Landfahrzeuge des alten Mesopotamien nach sumerisch-akkadischen Quellen* . . .
         Suomalaisen Tiedeakatemian Toimituksia/Annales Academiae
         Scientiarum Fennicae, Series B, Tom. 72.3. Helsinki.
1955   *Hippologica Accadica* . . . Suomalaisen Tiedeakatemian Toimituksia/Annales
         Academiae Scientiarum Fennicae, Series B, Tom. 100. Helsinki.
1968   *Agricultura mesopotamica nach den sumerisch-akkadischen Quellen* . . . Suomalaisen
         Tiedeakatemian Toimituksia/Annales Academiae Scientiarum Fennicae,
         Series B, Tom. 149. Helsinki.
Sarian, H.
1969   "Terres cuites géometriques d'Argos", *Bulletin de Correspondence Héllenique*
         93, 664–672.
Schachermeyr, F.
1951   "Streitwagen und Streitwagenbild im alten Orient und bei den mykeni-
         schen Griechen", *Anthropos* 46, 705–753.
Schäfer, H. and Andrae, W.
1925   *Die Kunst des alten Orients.* Berlin.
Schaeffer, C. F. A.
1935   "Neues zur sumerischen Anschirrung", *Prähistorische Zeitschrift* 26, 202–208.
1938   "Contribution à l'étude de l'attelage sumérien et syrien aux IIIième et
         IIième millénaires", *Préhistoire* 6, 49–63.
Schauensee, M. de and Dyson R. H.
1983   "Hasanlu horse trappings and Assyrian reliefs", in: Harper, P. O. and
         Pittman, H. (eds.), *Essays on Near Eastern Art and Archaeology in Honour of
         Charles Kyle Wilkinson.* New York, 59–77.
1988   "Northwest Iran as a bronzeworking centre: the view from Hasanlu",
         in: Curtis, J. (ed.), *Bronzeworking Centres of Western Asia c. 1000–539 B.C.*
         London, 45–62.
1989   "Horse gear from Hasanlu", *Expedition* 31, 2–3, 37–52.
Scheil, V.
1914   Recueil de travaux relatifs à la philologie et à l'archéologie égyptiennes
         et assyriennes 36, 179–180.
Schleiermacher, M.
1984   *Römische Reitergrabsteine. Die kaiserzeitlichen Reliefs des triumphierenden Reiters.*
         Bonn.
Schliemann, H.
1885   *Tiryns. The Prehistoric Palace of the Kings of Tiryns. The Results of the Latest
         Excavations.* New York.
1886   *Tiryns. Der prähistorische Palast der Könige von Tiryns. Ergebnisse der neuesten
         Ausgrabungen.* Leipzig.
Schlossmann, B. L.
1968   *Animal Art from the Ancient Near East* (catalogue of the exhibition at the
         Queens College, New York). New York.
Schmidt, E. F.
1937   *Excavations at Tepe Hissar Damghan, 1931–1933.* Philadelphia.
1953   *Persepolis* I. Oriental Institute Publications 68. Chicago.
Schulman, A. R.
1962–63 "The Egyptian chariotry: a reexamination", *Journal of the American Research
         Center in Egypt* 2, 75–98.

   1979   "Chariots, chariotry, and the Hyksos", *Journal of the Society for the Study of Egyptian Antiquities* 10 (2), 105–153.

Schweitzer, B.
   1955   "Zum Krater des Aristonotos", *Römische Mitteilungen* 62, 78–106.

Seeden, H.
   1980   *The Standing Armed Figurines in the Levant*. Praehistorische Bronzefunde I.1. München.
   1983   "Introduction", *Berytus* 31, 9–26.

Seidl, U.
   1980   "Einige urartäische Bronzezylinder (Deichselkappen?)", *Archaeologische Mitteilungen aus Iran N.F.* 13, 63–82.
   1982   "Corrigendum zu 'Einige urartäische Bronzezylinder'", *Archaeologische Mitteilungen aus Iran N.F.* 15, 101–103.
   1986   "Ein Pferde-Pektorale", in: Kelly-Buccellati, M. (ed. in collaboration with P. Matthiae and M. van Loon), *Insight Through Images. Studies in Honor of Edith Porada*. Bibliotheca Mesopotamica 21. Malibu 229–236.

Sethe, K.
   1961   *Urkunden der 18. Dynastie* III. Berlin.

Seyrig, H.
   1953   "Statuettes trouvées dans les montagnes du Libanon", *Syria* 30, 24–50.

Sheperd, D. G.
   1966   "Two silver rhyta", *Bulletin of the Cleveland Museum of Art (October)* 289–317 [with technical notes by J. Ternbach].

Sherratt, S. E.
   1981   *The Pottery of Late Helladic IIIC and its Significance.* (unpublished doctoral dissertation, University of Oxford).

Siedentopf, H.
   1991   *Alt-Aegina IV. Mattbemalte Keramik der Mittleren Bronzezeit.* Mainz am Rhein.

Singer, C., Holmyard, E. J. and Hall, A. R.
   1954   (eds.), *A History of Technology* I. *From Early Times to Fall of the Roman Empire.* Oxford.
—— Holmyard, E. J., Hall, A. R. and Williams, T. I.
   1957   (eds.), *A History of Technology* II. *The Mediterranean Civilizations and the Middle Ages c. 700 B.C. to c. A.D. 1500.* Oxford.

Smirnov, K. F.
   1961   "Archaeological data on ancient riders of the Volga-Ural Steppes", *Sovetskaja Arkheologija* 1961 (1), 46–72. (in Russian).

Smith, A. H.
   1900   "Excavations at Amathus", in: Murray, A. S. et al., (ed.), *Excavations in Cyprus.* London, 87–126.

Smith, S.
   1928   *Early History of Assyria.* London.
   1934   "An early painted vase from Khafaji", *British Museum Quarterly* 8, 38–41.
   1949   *The Statue of Idrimi.* British Institute of Archaeology Occasional Publications 1. London.

Smith, W. S.
   1958   *The Art and Architecture of Ancient Egypt.* Baltimore.
   1965   *Interconnections in the Ancient Near East. A Study of Relationship Between the Arts of Egypt, the Aegean, and Western Asia.* New Haven and London.

Snodgrass, A. M.
   1964   *Early Greek Armour and Weapons from the End of the Bronze Age to 600 B.C.* Edinburgh.
   1965   "The Linear B arms and armour tablets—again", *Kadmos* 4, 96–110.
   1967   *Arms and Armour of the Greeks.* Ithaca, New York.

1971 "The first European body armour", in: Boardman, J., Brown, M. A., Powell, T. G. E. (eds.), *The European Community in Later Prehistory. Studies in Honour of C. F. C. Hawkes.* London, 35–50.

Soden, W. Freiherr von
1965–81 *Akkadisches Handwörterbuch....* I–III. Wiesbaden.

Solleysel, J. de
1685 *Le parfait marechal.* Paris.

Speiser, E. A.
1934 *Excavations at Tepe Gawra* I. Philadelphia.

Spiteris, T. F.
1970 *L'art de Chypre des origines à l'époque romaine.* Formes et couleurs 2. Paris.

Spruytte, J.
1977 *Études expérimentales sur l'attelage. Contribution à l'histoire du cheval.* Paris.
1978–79 "Le véhicule à un essieu, à brancards ou à deux timons, dans l'antiquité", Almogaren (Jahrbuch des INSTITUTUM CANARIUM und der Gesellschaft für interdisziplinäre Sahara-Forschung, Hallein, Austria) 9–10, 53–76.
1983a *Early Harness Systems.* London.
1983b "La conduite du cheval chez l'archer assyrien", *Plaisirs Équestres* 129, 66–71.

Starr, R. F. S.
1937–39 *Nuzi. Report on the Excavation at Yorgan Tepe near Kirkuk, Iraq, Conducted by Harvard University in Conjunction with the American Schools of Oriental Research and the University Museum of Philadelphia, 1927–1931* I–II. Cambridge, Mass.

Stenberger, M. n.d.
1962 *Sweden.* Ancient Peoples and Places 30. London.

Stewart, J. M.
1974 *Tell el 'Ajjūl. The Middle Bronze Age Remains.* Studies in Mediterranean Archaeology 38. Göteborg.

Stoop, M. W.
1975 "A Cypriot charioteer", *Bulletin Antieke Beschaving* 50, 16–17.

Strommenger, E. and Hirmer, M.
1964 *5000 Years of the Art of Mesopotamia.* New York.

Studniczka, F.
1907 "Der Rennwagen im syrisch-phönikischen Gebiet", *Jahrbuch des Archäologischen Instituts* 22, 147–196.

Sürenhagen, D.
1975 "Einige kulturelle Kontakte zwischen Arslantepe VIA und den früh-sumerisch-hochprotoelamischen Stadtkulturen", in: Liverani, M., Palmieri, A. and Peroni, R. (eds.), *Studi di paletnologia in onore di S. M. Puglisi.* Roma, 230–232.
1986 "Ein Königssiegel aus Kargamis", *Mitteilungen der Deutschen Orientgesellschaft zu Berlin* 118, 183–190.

Suffern, C. and Hemp, W. J.
1929 "Primitive carts", *Antiquity* 3, 340–341.

Tait, G. A. D.
1963 "The Egyptian relief chalice", *Journal Egyptian Archaeology* 49, 93–139.

Talbot Rice, A.
1957 *The Scythians.* London.

Tallgren, A. M.
1929 "Études sur le Caucase du nord", *Eurasia Septentrionalis Antiqua* 4, 22–40.

Tallon, F.
1987 *Metallurgie susienne* I. *De la fondation de Suse au VIIᵉ avant J.-C.* Notes et documents des musées de France 15. Paris.

Tarr, L.
1967   *The History of the Carriage.* New York.
Tatton-Brown, V. (née Wilson)
1972   *The Cesnola Sarcophagi. Studies in Cypriote Iconography and Sculpture* (unpublished doctoral dissertation,, University of Oxford).
1979a   (ed.). *Cyprus B.C. 7000 Years of History* (catalogue of the exhibition at the British Museum). London.
1979b   "A terracotta "Geryon" in the British Museum", *Report of the Department of Antiquities, Cyprus* 1979, 281–288.
1981   "Le sarcophage d'Amathonte", in: Hermary 1981, 74–83.
1982a   "Two finds alledgedly from Rantidi", *Report of the Department of Antiquities, Cyprus* 1982, 174–182.
1982b   "The Archaic period", in: Hunt, D. (ed.), *Footprints in Cyprus.* London, 73–91.
1985   "Archaeology in Cyprus 1960–1985: Classical to Roman periods", in Karageorghis, V. (ed.), *Archaeology in Cyprus 1960–1985*, 60–72.
Televantou, C. E.
1990   "New light on the West House wall paintings", in: Doumas, C. (ed.), *Thera and the Aegean World* III.1. London, 309–326. (in Greek).
1994   *Akrotiri on Thera. The Wall Paintings of the West House.* Athens. (in Greek)
Terrace, E. B. L.
1962   *The Art of the Ancient Near East in Boston.* Boston (Museum of Fine Arts).
1964   "Recent acquisitions in the Department of Egyptian Art", *Bulletin of the Museum of Fine Arts* 62 (328), 49–64.
1966   *The Pomerance Collection of Ancient Art.* (catalogue of an exhibition held at the Brooklyn Museum). Brooklyn.
Theocharis, D.
1973   (ed.), *Neolithic Greece.* Athens.
Thureau-Dangin, F.
1931   (et al. eds.), *Arslan Tash.* Paris.
—— and Dunand, M.
1936   *Till Barsip.* Paris.
Törnqvist, S.
1970   *Arms, Armour and Dress of the Terracotta Figurines from Ajia Irini, Cyprus* (unpublished doctoral dissertation,, University of Lund).
Tsalkin, V. I.
1960   *A History of Stock Raising in the North Pontic Area.* Moskva. (in Russian).
Tuchelt, K.
1962   *Tiergefäße in Kopf- und Protomengestalt. Untersuchungen zur Formengeschichte tierförmiger Gießgefäße.* Istanbuler Forschungen 22. Berlin.
Tuke, D. R.
1965   *Bit by Bit. A Guide to Equine Bits.* London.
Tylor, J. J.
1896   *Wall Drawings and Monuments of El Kab. The Tomb of Sebeknekht*, in: Quibell, J. E. (ed.) *El Kab.* British School of Archaeology in Egypt and Egyptian Research Account 3. London.
Tzalas, H. E.
1989   (ed.), *Tropis I. Proceedings of the Second International Symposium on Ship Construction in Antiquity* (Piraeus, 1985). Piraeus.
1990   (ed.), *Tropis II. Proceedings of the Second International Symposium on Ship Construction in Antiquity* (Delphi, 1987). Athens.
1995   (ed.), *Tropis III. Proceedings of the Third International Symposium on Ship Construction in Antiquity* (Athens, 1989). Athens. (also "Editor's note", 147–148).

1996   (ed.), *Tropis* IV. *Proceedings of the Fourth International Symposium on Ship Construction in Antiquity* (Athens, 1991). Athens.

Unger, E.
1932   *Der Obelisk des Königs Assurnassirpal I. aus Ninive.* Mitteilungen der altorientalischen Gesellschaft 6 (1–2). Wiesbaden. (reprint Osnabrück 1972).

Vandenabeele, F.
1977   "Some aspects of chariot representations in the Late Bronze Age of Cyprus", *Report of the Department of Antiquities, Cyprus* 1977, 97–109.
1985   "L'influence phénicienne sur la coroplastie chypriote", in: Gubel, E. and Lipinski, E. (eds.), *Phoenicia and its Neighbours. Proceedings of the Colloquium Held on the 9th and 10th December 1980 at the "Vrije Universiteit Brussel"*. . . . Studia Phoenicia 3. Leuven, 203–211.
1986   "Phoenician influence on the Cypro-Archaic terracotta production and Cypriot influence abroad", in: Karageorghis, V. (ed.) *Acts of the International Symposium "Cyprus between the Orient and the Occident".* Nicosia, 351–360.

Vanderpool, E.
1963   "Newsletter from Greece", *American Journal of Archaeology* 67, 279–283.

Vandier, J.
1952   *Manuel d'archéologie égyptienne* I. Paris.

Ventris, M. G. F. and Chadwick, J.
1971   *Documents in Mycenaean Greek.* (2nd revised edition by Chadwick, J.). Cambridge.

Verdelis, N. M.
1967   "Neue Funde von Dendra", *Mitteilungen des Deutschen Archäologischen Instituts Athenische Abteilung* 82, 8–53.
1977   "The metal finds", in: Åström, P. et al. (eds.), *The Cuirass Tomb and Other Finds of Dendra* I. Studies in Mediterranean Archaeology 4. Göteborg, 28–65.

Vermeule, E.
1964   *Greece in the Bronze Age.* Chicago.
1968   "The decline and end of Minoan and Mycenaean culture", in: *A Land Called Crete. A Symposium in Memory of Harriet Boyd Hawes, 1871–1954, Smith College, Northampton, Mass., October 1967.* Northampton, Mass., 81–98.
—— and Karageorghis, V.
1983   *Mycenaean Pictorial Vase Painting.* Cambridge, Mass.

Vernier, E.
1927   *Bijoux et orfèvriers.* Catalogue génèral des antiquités égyptiennes du Musée de Caire I–II. Cairo.

Vigneron, P.
1968   *Le cheval dans l'antiquité gréco-romaine (des guerres mediques aux grandes invasions). Contribution à l'histoire des techniques* I–II. Nancy.

Volkov, V. V.
1972   "Ancient Chariots of the Mongolian Altai", Studia Archaeologica Instituti Historiae Academiae Scientiarium Republicae Populi Mongolici 5, Fasc. 6 (Ulan Bator), 75–80. (in Russian)

Vorys Canby, J.
1965   "Early Bronze Age 'trinket' moulds", *Iraq* 27, 42–61.
1969   "Some Hittite figurines in the Aegean", *Hesperia* 38, 141–149.

Voyatsis, M. E.
1985   "Arcadia and Cyprus. Aspects of their interrelationship between the twelfth and eight centuries B.C.", *Report of the Department of Antiquities, Cyprus* 1985, 155–163.

Waals, J. D, van der
1964   *Neolithic Disc Wheels in the Netherlands.* Groningen.

Wace, A. J. B.
1949   *Mycenae.* Princeton, New Jersey.

—— and Stubbings, F. H.
1962 *A Companion to Homer*. London and New York.
Wachsmann, S.
"Bird-head devices on Mediterranean ships", in: Tzalas 1996, 539–572.
Waetzold, H. and Bachmann, H. G.
1984 "Zinn- und Arsenbronzen in den Texten aus Ebla und aus dem Mesopotamien des 3. Jahrtausends", *Oriens Antiquus* 23, 1–18.
Wang, P., Chung, S. and Chang, C.
1959 "Short report on the excavations in the area west of the river Feng, district of Ch'ang-an, Shensi in 1955–57, *K'ao ku* (Beijing), 516–530.
Walters, H. B.
1903 *Catalogue of Terracottas in the Department of Greek and Roman Antiquities, British
Museum*. London.
1912 *Catalogue of the Greek and Etruscan Vases in the British Museum* I.2. *Cypriote,
Italian and Etruscan Pottery*. London.
1926 *Catalogue of Engraved Gems and Cameos, Greek, Etruscan and Roman, in the British
Museum*. (revised and enlarged edition). London.
Ward, W. A. and Joukowski, M.
1992 (eds.), *The Crisis Years. The 12th century B.C. from beyond the Danube to the
Tigris*. Dubuque, Iowa.
Ward, W. H.
1910 *The Seal Cylinders of Western Asia*. Carnegie Institution of Washington pub-
lication 100. Washington, D.C.
Warren, P. M. and Hankey, V.
1989 *Aegean Bronze Age Chronology*. Bristol.
Watelin, L. Ch. and Langdon, S.
1934 *Excavations at Kish. The Herbert Weld (for the University of Oxford) and Field
Museum of Natural History (Chicago) Expedition to Mesopotamia, 1925–1930*. Kish
Excavations 4. Paris.
Watson, W.
1961 *China before the Han Dynasty*. London.
1967 "Review of von Dewall 1964", in: *Antiquity* 41, 156–158.
Weber, C. D.,
1966 "Chinese pictorial bronze vessels of the Late Chou Period, Part II", *Artibus
Asiae* 28 (4), 271–302.
1968 "Chinese pictorial bronze vessels of the Late Chou Period, Part IV", *Artibus
Asiae* 30 (2–3), 145–214.
Weber, W.
1914 *Die ägyptisch-griechischen Terrakotten*. Berlin.
Wedde, M.
1996 "Rethinking Greek Geometric art: consequences for the ship representations", in: Tzalas 1996, 573–596.
1998 "War at sea: the Mycenaean and Early Iron Age oared galley, in: Laffineur,
R. (ed.), *POLEMOS. Le contexte guerrier en égée à l'âge du bronze*. Actes de la
7e Recontre égéenne internationale Université de Liège, 14–17 avril 1998.
AEGAEUM 19. Annales d'archéologie égéenne de l'Université de Liège
et UT-PASP. Université de Liège (Histoire de l'art et archéologie de la
Grèce antique) and University of Texas at Austin (Program in Aegean
Scripts and Prehistory), vol. II, 465–478.
Wees, H. van.
1992 *Status Warriors. War, Violence and Society in Homer and History*. Amsterdam
1992.
1994 "The Homeric way of war: the Iliad and hoplite phalanx (I and II)",
Greece and Rome 41, 1–18 and 133–155.

Wegener Sleeswyk, A.
1987   "Pre-stressed wheels in ancient Egypt", *Antiquity* 61, 90–96.
Weinstein, S. I.
1966   "Some problems in the history of ancient Turkish culture", *Sovjetskaja Etnografija* 1966 (3), 61–81. (in Russian).
Wells, B., Runnels, C. and Zangger, E.
1990   "The Berbati-Limnes archaeological survey. The 1988 season", *Opuscula Atheniensia* 18, 207–238.
Werner, J.
1956   *Beiträge zur Archäologie des Attila-Reiches.* Bayerische Akademie der Wissenschaften. Philosophisch-historische Klasse, Abhandlungen, N.F. 38. München.
Western, A. C.
1973   "A wheel hub from the tomb of Amenophis", *Journal of Egyptian Archaeology* 59, 91–94.
Westholm, A.
1937   "Mersinaki", in: *The Swedish Cyprus Expedition* III. Stockholm, 340–398.
White, K. D.
1966   *Agricultural Implements of the Roman World.* Cambridge.
White Jr., L.
1962   *Medieval Technology and Social Change.* Oxford.
Wiesner, J.
1939   *Fahren und Reiten in Alteuropa und im Alten Orient.* Leipzig. (Der Alte Orient, 38, 2–4, reprinted in the series "Documenta Hippologica. Darstellungen und Quellen zur Geschichte des Pferdes". Hildesheim and New York 1971).
1968   *Fahren und Reiten.* Archaeologia Homerica, F. Göttingen.
Wilkinson, J. G.
1878   *Manners and Customs of the Ancient Egyptians. Including their Private Life, Government, Laws, Arts, Manufactures, Religion, Agriculture, and Early History.* London. (1st edition 1837–1841).
Williams, C. R.
1920   "The place of the New York Historical Society in the growth of American interest in Egyptology", *New York Historical Society Quarterly Bulletin* 4, 3–20
1923   "Material bearing on the new discoveries in Egypt", *New York Historical Society Quarterly Bulletin* 7, 7–9.
Winter, F.
1903   *Die antiken Terrakotten* III.1. *Die Typen der figürlichen Terrakotten* I. Berlin and Stuttgart.
Winter, I.
1976   "Carved ivory furniture from Nimrud. A coherent subgroup of North Syrian style", *Metropolitan Museum Journal* 11, 25–54.
1980   *A Decorated Breastplate from Hasanlu, Iran.* University Museum Monograph 39. Philadelphia.
Wiseman, D. J.
1962   *Catalogue of the Western Asiatic Seals in the British Museum.* London 1962.
Woldering, I.
1958   *Ausgewählte Werke der aegyptischen Sammlung.* Bildkataloge des Kestner-Museums 1. (2nd revised edition). Hannover.
1961   *Meisterwerke des Kestner-Museums zu Hannover.* Hannover.
1967   *Gods, Men and Pharaohs. The Glory of Egyptian Art.* New York.
Wolff, M. and Opitz, D.
1935–36 "Die Jagd zu Pferde in der altorientalischen und klassischen Kunst", *Archiv für Orientforschung* 10, 219–240.

Woolley, C. L.
1914   "Hittite burial customs", *Liverpool Annals of Art and Archaeology* 6, 87–96.
1934   *The Royal Cemetery. A Report on the Predynastic and Sargonid Graves Excavated between 1926 and 1931. Vol.* I *(Text)*—II *(Plates).* Ur Excavation Reports, 2. London and Philadelphia.
1955   *Ur Excavations* IV. *The Early Periods.* London and Philadelphia.
1982   *Ur of the Chaldees.* (revised and updated edition by P. R. S. Moorey). New York.
—— and Barnett, R. D.
1952   *Carchemish* III. London.
Wreszinski, W.
1923–38 *Atlas zur altägyptischen Kulturgeschichte* I–III. Leipzig. (Vol. I. 1923, Vol. II. 1935, Vol. III. 1938; reprinted Gèneve 1988).
Wriedt Sørensen, L.
1978   "Early limestone statuettes in Cypriote style. A review of their chronology and place of manufacture", *Report of the Department of Antiquities, Cyprus* 1978, 111–121.
Wulff, H.
1962   *The Traditional Crafts of Persia.* Cambridge, Mass.
Wulff, H. E., Wulff, H. S. and Koch, L.
1968   "Egyptian faience, a possible survival in Iran", *Archaeology* 21, 99.
Wyatt, W. F., Jr.
1970   "The Indo-Europeanization of Greece", in: Cardona, G., Hoenigswald, H. and Senn, A. (eds.), *Indo-European and Indo-Europeans. Papers Presented at the Third Indo-European Conference at the University of Pennsylvania*, 89–111. (The Nineth Publication in the Haney Foundation Series University of Pennsylvania).
Xenaki-Sakellariou, A.
1964   *Die minoischen und mykenischen Siegel des Nationalmuseums in Athen.* Corpus der minoischen und mykenischen Siegel I. Athen.
Yadin, Y.
1955   "Hyksos fortifications and the battery ram", *Bulletin of the American Schools of Oriental Research* 137, 23–32.
1963   *The Art of Warfare in Biblical Lands in the Light of Archaeological Discovery* I–II. New York-Toronto-London.
Yon, M.
1992   "The end of the kingdom of Ugaritt", in: Ward and Joukowski 1992, 111–122.
Yon, M. and Caubet, A.
1985   *Kition-Bamboula* III. Paris.
Youatt, W.
1846   *The Horse. With a Treatise on Draught.* London.
Young, J. H.
1969   "Review of Folsom, R. S., *Handbook of Greek Pottery: A Guide for Amateurs.* New York Graphic Society Greenwich Connecticut. (n.d.)", in: *American Journal of Archaeology* 73, 385.
Young, J. M. and Young, S. H.
1955   *Terracotta Figurines from Kourion in Cyprus.* Philadelphia.
Zancani, M. and Montaoro, P.
1953   "La teogamia di Locri Epizefiri", *Archivo storico per la Calabria e la Luccania* (Roma) 24, 283–308.
Zaccagnini, C.
1977   "Pferde und Streitwagen in Nuzi. Bemerkungen zur Technologie", *Jahresbericht des Instituts für Vorgeschichte der Universität Frankfurt am Main* 1977, 21–38.

Zarins, J.
1976 *The Domestication of Equidae in Third Millennium B.C. Mesopotamia* I–II. (doctoral dissertation, University of Chicago).
1986 "Equids associated with human burials in third millennium B.C. Mesopotamia: Two complementary facets", in: Meadow and Uerpmann 1986, 164–193.
Zhukov, V. A. and Ranev, V. A.
1972 "Petroglyphs on the Northern Akdzilgi River (Eastern Pamirs)", *Arkheologicheskie Otkrytie*, 540–541. (in Russian).
Ziegler, C.
1962 *Die Terrakotten von Warka*. Ausgrabungen der Deutschen Forschungsgemeinschaft in Uruk-Warka 6. Berlin.
Zschietzschmann, W.
1959 *Hellas and Rome. Eine Kulturgeschichte des Altertums in Bildern*. Tübingen.
Zimmer, H.
1955 *The Art of Indian Asia, its Mythology and Transformations*. (completed and edited by J. Campbell) I. (Text)—II. (Plates). Bollingen Series 39. Princeton, New Jersey.

INDEX OF NAMES

1. *Historical persons*

Ahotep, 293, 373[98], 304
Alexander the Great, 462
Amenophis III, (composite nave and spoke), 320f.; (pair of wheel of), 302
Ashurbanipal II, 32–35, 205, 215[7], 311; (equipment for royal or other hunters), 230[48]; (four-man chariots), 198, 198[29], 203; (harnessing scene), 532; (high-sides and toggle-fastened strap on Assyrian chariots), 252f.; (lion hunt), 257; (natural forelock/chariot horse without frontlet), 529, 529[16]; (rear doors on Assyrian chariots), 193[7]
Ashurnasirpal II, 32, 238**, 252; (balance and harnessing of chariots), 258; ('bibs' shown on horses), 249f.; (bronze gate from Balawat), 216[10]; (equipment for royal or other hunters), 230[48]; (frontlets), 526, 529[16]; (reins), 252; (river crossing scene), 246, 256, 482; (scale model of a chariot of), 241f.; (shields in conjunction with Assyrian chariots), 80[17], 194; (small, low chariots), 254f.; (soft handgrips), 180[24]; (yoke saddle), 480; (Y-pole and three-man chariots), 182, 242

Caesar, 462
Cheops, 330[5]

Darius Codomannus, 56

Esarhaddon, 311

Gudea of Lagaš, 267; (stela of), 264f., 268f.

Hammurapi, 17, 317; (seal with chariot of the 14th year of), 395, 406[14]
Hattušili, 315
Hetepheres, 330, 330[5]

Idrimi of Alalaḫ, 397; (text), 389, 402

Kamose, 293
Kuzi-Teššup, 316f.

Narmer, (macehead), 330f., 393

Ptolemy XVI, (*quadriga* from the reign of), 309. *See also* Astarte, *Quadriga*.
Pu-abi, (sledge of), 10, 333, 335, 369

Ramses II, (battle of Kadesh), 57, 366; (conquering Sabat and Akat), 136; (siege of Tabor), 86[39]. *See also* 'Foot-on-the-Chariot-Pole' Motif.
Ramses III, 69, 103; (hunting the white bull), 82[22]; (fighting the Libyans and storming a city), 136, 138[23]; (royal teams) 541[8]. *See also* 'Foot-on-the-Chariot-Pole' Motif, Sea Peoples.
Rene of Anjou, 469

Sargon II., 35; (bow cushion without frontled), 529; (chariots in conjunction with shields), 194; (four-man chariots), 198, 198[29], 203; (two-wheeled platform), 216; (unharnessed four-horse fitted yoke), 252f., 256
Sennacherib, (invasion of Palestine), 311[64]; (shoulder disk), 250; (unharnessed four-horse fitted yoke), 52f.; (unharnessed chariot), 256
Sethos I, (charging the Libyans), 136, 307–309. *See also* 'Foot-on-the-Chariot-Pole' Motif.
Shalmaneser III, 32, 528; ('bibs' shown on horses), 249f.; (squire motif with war chariots), 240[11]; (Y-pole and three-man chariots), 182
Shamshi-Adad I., (tyre fragments from the reign of), 264
Shoshenk IV, (scarab of), 308
Šuppiluliuma I., 316f.
Šuppiluliuma II., 317

Talmi-Teššup, 316f.
Thutmosis III, (seizing two ships and their cargo), 103[10]; (cross-bar wheel on Scarab of), 282
Thutmosis IV, 56, (body of the chariot of), 291; (bridles with reins fixed to nose strap), 519; (yoke saddle of chariot of), 481
Thuiu, See Yuaa.
Tutʿankhamān, (bowcase), 540; (chariots), 125, 246f.; (element of harness), 521ff.; (engraved disk) 249; (felloes of chariot of), 320; (goads [Halssporen]), 521f.; (painted box)

121, 291, 484, 540; (wheels), 266, 302, 312; (yoke saddle of chariots of), 418, 522[1]
Tiglath-Pilesar I, 317
Tiglath-Pilesar III, 32, 34f., 257; (four-man chariots), 198[29]; (first appearance of the cushion under), 528; (raised handgrip), 180; (yoke saddle), 248, 482; (breastplates), 252
Tukulti-Ninurta II, ('bibs' shown on horses), 249; (shoulder disk), 250

Yuaa, (preserved Egyptian chariots of Y. and Thuiu), 178, 300[6], 320[14]

2. Scholars

(Modern and classical authors' names only appear when their views are specifically mentioned, discussed in the articles or if their contributions are valuable for the history of research.)

Alexiou, S., 84
Amiet, P., 40, 185, 185[52], 188
Anderson, J. K., 60, 486, 491f., 493[4], 495
Andrae, W., 261
Anthony, D., 45ff.
Antonius, O., 498
Arendt, W. W., 440
Ashbee, P., 530–533

Barrelet, M.-T., 38ff. See also Vulture Stela.
Berg, G., 4
Bivar, A. D. H., 439ff.
Botti, G., 480f.
la Broue, S., 462f., 470, 473
du Buisson, R. Mesnil, 385, 395
Buluç, S., 332f.

Cameron, M. A., 84
Carter, H., 249[15], 302[44], 305[33], 307[34], 521, 521[1], 522
Catling, H. W., 75, 83f., 98
di Cesnola, P., 505. See also Collections.
Childe, G., 273, 283, 492
Civil, M., 44[23]
de Clercq, L., 188. See also Collections.
Clot, A.-B. (Clot Bey), 303
Collon, D., 185ff.
Contenau, G., 39[6]

von Dewall, M., 127, 132, 479ff.
Dittmann, K. H., 304f.

Firouz, L. L., 520
Fiaschi, C., 462f., 469, 475

Greenhalgh, P. A. L., 53ff., 62ff.
Grisone, F., 462f., 469f., 474
de la Gueriniere, F., 463, 465, 471
Guillaume-Rey, A. E., 191, 206

Haller, A. (see Andrae)
Hančar, F., 348[22], 491[3], 499
Harris, J. R. (see Lucas, A.)
Haudricourt, A., 4, 6f., 479
Hauptmann, H., 291[13], 314–317
Höckmann, O., 231[53]
Hood. M. F. S., 64

Isbitzer, E., 50

Karageorghis, V., 525ff.
Kenna, V. E. G., 83[30]
Kilian, K., 58f.
Kossack, G., 266
Kozhin, R. M., 119, 122, 128, 132, 135
Kunze, E., 525
Kyzlassov, I. M., 450

Lang, M. L., 84, 89
Layard, H. A., 247, 249

Liverani, M., 71[21]
Loggie, D., 331
Löhneisen, G. E., 473f.
Lorimer, H., 76f. 77[11], 272f.
Lucas, A. (and Harris, J. R.), 302
Lucas, A. T., 7, 287

McC. Adams, R., 335
Mace, A., 307[34]
von Mercklin, E., 63, 82, 400
Moore, B., 490

Nagel, W., 38f., 97, 255, 346
de Noëttes, L., 11, 20, 38, 480, 483, 485

Özgen, E., 293, 403
Özgüç, N., 289ff.
Okladnikov, A. P., 119, 128
Orthmann, W., 369, 371, 376

Piggott, S., 14, 51, 182, 184, 277, 348, 348[22], 353[30], 363, 375f., 380, 388f., 391, 393, 398–400
Potratz, J., 41, 480, 487, 493[4], 497
Pottier, M. H., 261, 269f.
Powell, T. G. E., 92[59], 93[66], 95

Reinach, S., 86[40]
Richter, G. M. A., 400
de Ridder, A., 174
Rieth, A., 521ff.
Rodenwaldt, G., 63, 84ff., 101[3]

Rosellini, I., 480f. *See also* Florence Chariot.
Rudenko, S. I., 131f.
Rutter, J., 58

Salonen, A., 39[6], 40, 358, 484–486
Schachermeyr, F., 97,
Schaeffer, C. F. A., 498
Schliemann, H., 82[22]
Schulman, A. R., 64
Seyrig., H., 186
de Solleysel, J., 463ff., 520
Snodgrass, A. M., 53
Spruytte, J., 20, 23, 124, 241f., 267, 324, 444, 451
Smith, W. S., 86, 307
Smirnov, K. F., 50–504
Speiser, E. A., 380, 393, 398f.

Tallon, F., 261

Volkov, V. V., 108f., 113ff., 128ff., 254
van der Waals, J. D., 275, 286

Watson, W., 479, 485f.
White, L. Jr., 440, 442
Wilkinson, J. G., 296, 298
Williams, C. R., 296, 298f., 301[8], 305
Woolley, L., 7, 12, 275–277, 334, 369, 390

Yadin, Y., 61, 63f., 65, 90, 254

INDEX OF PLACES, AREAS AND COUNTRIES

Acemhüyük, 17, 289ff., 321, 326, 371[88], 379
Akrotiri, 103, 103
Alashiya, 103
Amrit. *See* Marathus.
Angkor Wat, 140
Ankara, 253, 289, 364, 371[88]
Anatolia, 28, 45f., 67, 69, 74, 134, 188f., 229, 274, 280ff., 289ff., 314f., 329, 332, 336ff., 344ff., 391ff., 403ff., 507, 507[5], 508[7], 509, 512ff.
Akat, 136
Akdzilgi river, 108, 125, 134
Akrotiri, 103, 103[9]
Altai, 108, 113, 114, 115ff., 254, 439, 442f., 482
Argos, 91
Armenia, 106, 118, 135, 243, 275, 278, 322f., 390, 399
Arslan Tash, 248
Arslantepe, 329f., 330[5], 333, 333[9]
Ashur, 160, 160[80], 261–264, 269, 405[8]
Assyria, 35, 124, 128, 149, 154[53], 161f., 166, 168, 171f., 180, 182, 198, 202, 218, 242f., 246, 248, 250, 252, 257, 308ff., 375, 415, 424, 482, 488f., 495, 528, 528[11]
Athens, 75, 100[2], 104, 136f., 199[32], 235, 313[73]
Attica, 63
Avd
Avdu, 94, 96f.
Ayia Irini, 141[2], 142[7], 149[30], 150[34], 158[72], 161, 162[88], 164, 164[97], 166[101–101], 169[118], 199[30], 246**, 249, 251, 251[28], 255, 419, 422[48], 428[64], 525
Ayios Therapon, 412

Babylonia, 41, 383, 394f.
Baghdad, 44[20], 330
Balawat, 216[10]
Balkan, 14
Bashkiria, 442
Beit-el Weli, 136, 139
Berekeij, 120
Byblos, 189, 207, 430, 438

Carkemiš, 314
Caucasus, 131, 274, 355, 380, 388ff., 399, 429[70], 441, 448, 486
Cerveteri, 104, 137, 137[9], 137[17]
Chiang-chia-po'o, 132
China, 66, 118, 120, 122ff., 172, 231[52], 255f., 272, 274, 286, 325, 439ff., 478ff., 543
Ciscaucasus, 348[22], 398
Crete, 67[4], 70, 94, 102, 105, 115[18]
Cycladic Islands, 70
Cyprus, 33, 35ff., 71, 80, 83[30], 103, 105, 105[18], 118, 123, 125, 141ff., 180[23, 25], 181, 184f., 190, 192ff., 202ff., 211ff., 239f., 244, 249, 258, 284, 332[8], 389, 394, 399, 411ff., 430ff., 525ff., 542[14]
Cyrene, 60, 239

Dadja, 192, 200, 202
Darvy Somon, 109, 118
Dzhambulsk region, 109

Egypt, 29, 32, 46f., 54ff., 61, 66, 68, 68[10], 69, 71, 77, 84[30], 90, 95, 97, 98, 101, 103[10], 118, 121, 123, 125, 138, 144, 172, 177[2], 182, 185, 188, 247, 285, 290f., 295, 295[296ff.], 318ff., 330, 334, 393, 481ff. 506, 508, 516, 518, 524, 540f., 549
Elam, 6, 10, 172, 277f., 325, 381, 398
Elis, 91
Enkomi, 86[40], 105[18], 178[9]

Farmagusta, 199[32]
Fezzan, 239
Frangissa, 161[83], 199[32]
Frænnarp, 118, 133

Gaza (*see* Tell el Ajjul)
Gazi, 105, 105[18]
Gezer, 509, 509[9], 511
Golgoi, 142[3,4], 150, 155, 155[59], 160f., 202[43], 313[41], 411[2], 421, 432[12]
Gordion, 221, 221[24], 253, 527[7]

Hagia Triada, 97
Horoztepe, 364f., 368, 368[76], 370f., 371[87], 375f., 378

Idalion, 142[7], 162, 162[51], 417[25], 418[29], 434[23]
Iceland, 20, 520
Iran, 6, 15, 16, 167, 180[23], 196, 261f., 266[10], 269f., 270, 323, 334, 347, 348[17], 395f., 404, 413, 421, 435, 442, 509, 509[8], 518, 520, 530, 534ff.
Italy, 119, 217[11], 221, 224, 226, 226[37], 231, 232[258], 272, 283, 462, 475, 519

Jamani Us, 108f., 113ff., 125, 129, 132f.
Jaxartes, (Syr Darya), 108

Kadesh. See Battle of Kadesh.
Kalapoidi, 100[2]
Kalmyk Steppes, 273, 348[22], 353[30], 388, 390, 394, 398, 398
Karatau, 108, 111f., 122
Khafajah. See Tell Agrab.
Khovd Sum, 444
Knidos, 192
Knossos, 66, 75, 84, 89f., 92, 97, 322, 482
Kobdo Somon, 109, 117, 131, 133
Kojbaga, 108f., 111, 122f.
Kokbulaka, 111
Kolonna, 103[9]
Kopala, 109
Krivoe-Ozero, 45ff.
Kültepe, (Kārum kaneš), 15f., 45f., 280, 289, 347, 509, 509[9], 511
Kourion, 141[2f.], 142[8], 154[52], 157, 160[79], 164[100], 176, 181, 239, 242, 411[1f.], 412[5], 413, 413[7], 416, 416[20], 417[25], 419f., 420[37], 421[41,43], 422, 428, 428[65], 429
Korea, 439, 446f., 449
Kynos, 102[6]

Lake Balkash, 109
Lake Sevam, 323, 325, 351, 399
Lapithos, 142[7]
Lebanon, 334
Lefkandi, 98, 100[2], 104f., 172[124]
Levant, 29, 32f., 71, 94, 95, 98, 172, 174ff., 202, 206, 238–240, 322, 336ff., 505f., 516, 517[8]
Lidar Höyük, 314ff.
Livanates, 101ff.

Lchaschen. See Chariot.
Luristan. See Bronze.
Lydos, 136

Marathus (Amrith), 80[17], 148[24], 180[25], 191, 202, 204, 206, 209f., 215, 215[6], 251f.
Mari, 347, 360, 365, 373, 498
Medinet Habu, 69, 103, 366
Meniko, 37, 148[26], 150[34f.], 166[103], 417, 430[4], 433[17], 436[29], 438
Meroë
Messenia, 70, 91
Mexiko, 286
Miner el-Beida, 189[64]
Mongolia, 106ff., 272, 442, 444, 508[7], 520
Mycenae, 63, 69ff., 84ff., 100, 295[22], 486, 488, 507[5], 508[7]. See also Shaft Grave, Warrior Vase.

Nauplion, 75
Nimrud, 33, 148, 150, 151[38], 180, 194, 198, 198[29], 203, 259, 434, 434[23], 527f., 530
Nippur, 44[20], 383, 499
Nubia, 136, 302, 304

Olympia, 92, 158[71], 221, 221[24]
Oughtasar, 106, 110, 120, 133

Palaepaphos, 142, 142[5f.], 142[11], 156, 156[62], 160ff., 420[37], 428
Pamir, 108, 111, 113, 125, 133–136
Pazyrik, 110, 123, 129, 131f., 413, 442, 450, 482, 532f.
Peloponnes, 67[4], 70, 90
Persepolis, 151, 159, 179f., 180[24], 310, 311[60]
Phoenicia, 143, 148f., 174, 181, 190ff., 214f., 223ff., 309, 430, 437f.
Phocis, 100[2]
Pylos, 90

Ras Shamra, 178[9], 189, 189[64], 448, 507[5], 512, 512[16]
Rhodes, 167[109], 200, 205f., 412[2], 422, 434[23], 437

Sabat, 136
Sakçagözü, 180[23], 310
Salamis, 80[17], 141[2], 142, 142[6], 143f., 148ff., 181, 193ff., 249, 250f. 258,

394, 411, 414ff., 421, 427f., 434f., 496f., 504, 525ff., 543
Samos, 200, 205f., 205[27], 429[70], 437
Sanam, 304
Sintashta, 45ff., 292, 323
Sippar, 406[17]
Slavokambos, 97
Sparta, 91
Steppes, 10, 14, 17, 20, 21, 45ff., 66, 448
Syunik region, 106f., 110f., 122, 129f., 133
Syr Daja. *See* Jaxartes.
Susa, 6, 10, 39, 261ff., 268f., 277ff., 330, 333, 347[6], 348, 355, 368, 374, 376, 381, 383, 390, 393, 506, 509, 509[9]
Syria, 28, 50, 67, 80[17], 311, 314ff., 322, 334, 334[16], 336ff., 380ff., 403ff.

Tadzhikistan, 106, 108
Tamassos, 142, 142[5,11], 152[42], 156, 156[62], 161ff., 235, 411[2], 413[7], 434[25], 438[36], 525, 525[3]
Tamgaly, 109
Tang-i Sarwak, 447
Tbilisi, 134
Tell Agrab, 6, 9, 13, 27, 39, 49, 260, 278, 354[21], 364, 370, 377
Tell el Ajjul, 488, 507[5], 510, 512f.
Tell el Amarna, 24, 488, 507[5], 509[8], 512, 518, 539f.
Tell Chuēra, 347f., 347[17], 379, 406[10]
Tell al-Haddad, 515, 515[1f.], 316–318
Tell Halaf, 64
Tell Judeidah, 370
Tell-el Rimah, 189
Tell Sukas, 430[4]
Tell es-Sweyhat, 50

Tepe Gawra, 363, 381,383, 408
Tepe Hissar, 15, 28, 279, 323. *See also* Cross-Bar Wheel.
Thebes, 30, 86, 293, 295[22], 303, 321f., 507[5], 508[7]
Thera, 103, 105
Thessaly, 69, 100[2], 102[7]
Til Barsip, 216, 216[10], 220, 212[48], 232, 370
Tiryns, 57, 59, 63, 72, 75, 77, 82, 84ff., 101[2]
Tragana, 105[17]
Transcaucasus, 67, 106ff., 155[33], 171[123], 182, 239, 242, 273, 295[22], 334, 348, 351, 362, 394, 398f., 509[8]
Trialeti, 275
Tuva, 442
Tyre, 202, 205f., 208f., 215

Ur, 10–12, 267, 269, 273, 277, 333; tombs, 269[23], 277f., 348ff., 366f., sealing with two-wheeler, 42. *See also* 'Standard of Ur'.
Urals, 45, 121, 135, 285, 292, 323, 510[15]
Urartu, 151, 159, 162[92], 163[95], 164[100], 167, 167[108], 172, 417, 417[27f.], 418[31], 421, 422[45], 435[25], 486, 530
Uruk, 17, 45f., 48, 329ff., 386, 389, 404[4]

Val Camonica, 119, 130, 439
Vaphio, 57, 62, 82, 97
Volos, 100[2]
Vulci, 137[7], 137[10f.], 137[15f.], 137[19], 229[46], 283

Yakutia, 442, 444

Zinjirli, 159, 161, 180, 416, 527

INDEX OF SUBJECTS

Achilles, 546
Amorites, 67
Antler [= tine], 31, 489, 510[15]. *See also* Cheekpieces.
Agriculture, 331
appliqués, 416, 422, 433, 447, 161[83]
Archer, 32, 35–37, 56, 68, 72, 78, 83, 83[30], 88, 101–103, 101[4], 102[8], 138[28], 164, 166, 200, 203f., 204[48], 244f., 424, 432, 432[12], 436, 439, 450, 456. *See also* Armour.
Aristophanes, 389
Armour, 167, 424, 446, 453; 15th and 16th century AD, 453ff.; late 17th century AD, 471; of Assyrian archers, 436; body 72, 101, 422, 447; body and leg, 72; defensive 90[53]; heavy (13th century AD), 468; horse, 425; horse and crew, 203; horse chest, 421f., 426, 435; metal, 60; neck, 56, 58; plate, 456, (later Middle Ages), 467; protective, 34f., 166; scale, 68, 447, 449; (in connection with stirrups), 439. *See also* Helmet.
Armoured Knight. *See* Knight.
Arrian, 37, 491, 494, 502, 548
Arrow, in Angkor Wat reliefs, 140, 140[1]; bombarding of ships with arrows, 103; chariots forced to an abrupt halt by Egyptian arrows, 86; chariot teams vulnerable to, 58; clothyard, 454. *See also* Bow, Quiver Weapons.
Arrowhead, 166, 166[104], 262
Asia(tic). *See* Near East(ern).
Ass, Donkey, domestication, 47f., 50; introduction of, 27; 'Irish', 287; osteological evidence, 156; representational evidence, 229, 223, 237, 493. *See also* Equid, Hemione, Slit Nostrils.
Astarte, (lion-headed driving a quadriga. *See* Ptolemy XVI)
Axe, from Susa (Donjon tomb A 89), 262; in 4-wheeled 'battle cars', 27; of *Attaḫušḫu* (or *Addaḫušḫu*) type, 264;

in Assyrian chariots, 34; in Cypriote chariots, 166; in the vehicle of the Eannatum stela, 360. *See also* Weapon.
Axle, 3rd millennium BC Mesopotamia, 26; 2nd millennium BC Mesopotamia, 30; 1st millennium BC Mesopotamia, 35; arm, 51; block (*see* Axle Brackets); central, 39, 92–94, 110f., 114, 121f., 150, 218–220, 385, 485; driver's/rider's position on the, 39, 41; ends, 259, 275, 281; fixed, 218f., 221, 274f., 283, 285, 290, 390, 394; front, 238, 381, 390; hole, 277; from Iron Age Cyprus, 150f.; of models from Iron Age Cyprus, 194f., 218–220; iron, 293; in Linear B texts, 66f.; of metal wagon models, 338ff., esp. 351ff., 380f.; position of, 97, 120f., 125, 131, 150, 153, 176f., 194f., 390, 486; projected, 54, 68f., 381; rear, 30, 32, 35, 36, 39, 80, 84[30], 92–94, 109, 111, 113f., 119f., 121, 133, 139, 144, 150f., 194f., 216, 218–220, 307, 485f.; rotating, 150; revolving, 142, 218f., 221, 268, 274f., 281, 286, 334, 390, 394 (*see also* Wheel); rod, 218; scythed, (on Persian chariots), 36f.; size of, 319; terracotta model from Susa, 268; "toothed" of *plostellum poenicum*, 334; tubes, 403; "truned within bronze lops" (Tell Agrab straddle car), 354[32]; wooden, 54, 151, 191, (of a threshing mashine. *See plostellum poenicum*) 334f., 352; (axle reconstruction of a wagon model), 381, 403. *See also* Chariot, Nave, Hub, Wheel.
Axle Brackets, 212, 217, 219, 219[14], 232
Axle Caps, 151[131], 154[49], 170, 325

Backing element, 224
Baldachin, 131, 329, 331, 333 *See also* Cart.

'Battle Car(s)', 404, 404[1]; Anatolian metal wagon models in comparison with, 374; Mesopotamian (ED III), 27f., 376; and Syrian metal wagon models, 372
Battle of Kadesh, 57, 63, 78, 82, 86, 178, 282, 304[19], 366
Battlefield, Greek, 52, 546; medieval, 470; Pharaoh on the, 138[23]; role of chariots on the, 72; role of the triga on the, 258
battue, 71[19]. *See also* Hunting.
Bayeux Tapestry, 453
Bell, 162, 164[99]; parallels and function, 164. *See also* Tassel.
bigae, Bronze Age chariot teams, 90; Cypriote, 143, 148, 153, 155f., 161[85], 169, 172, 240; depicted on Pamir petroglyphs, 111; in the Mongolian Altai mountains, 114
Bier, 229
Birch (*Betula* sp.), Birch Bark; provenience of, 322f.; properties of, 291, 322; use of, 323, 325
Bit(s), 28, 37, 50, 159f., 161[85]; 232, 244, 295, 295[22f.]; 395, 416, 433, esp. 487ff.; Aegaean, 293, 295, esp. 505ff. and 515ff.; assecoirs (from Iron Age Cyprus), 417ff.; of Assyrian mounted warriors, 42; from Assyria, 160[80]; 495, 501; bar, 495, 506[4]; bitless bridle, 491; bitted bridle, 33, 36, 46, 50, 433, 442; bridle, 224, 414; bronze, 505f.; in China, 486; copper/bronze horse bits from eastern Anatolia and the cheekpieces of, 35; on Cyprus, 159f., 170, 224, 227, 232, 255, 496f., 504, (of ridden horses), 414f., 431, 433; driving a horse without a bit, 492; driving bit, 503, 510, 517; Egyptian/Hyksos, 98[85], 513; on Egyptian reliefs, 492 (*see also* Tell el Amarna below); end, 255; from Gaza (*see* Tell el Ajjul); genesis of the oriental bit?, 497ff.; Greek, Mycenaean, 98[85], 513; horn (from the Volga-Ural region), 501; iron, 170, 172[124], 227; from Jerusalem, 512f.; linked harness-bits, 486; in India, (described by Arrian), 502; from Luristan, 497, 501, 503, 512f.; metal, 31, 142, 197[23], 224, 232, 495–497, 501, 505ff., 515ff.; Ras

Shamra, 512; 'run-out' bit from Gaza and Mycenae, 487f., 494, 497, 510, 518; early Russian, 502–505; Sassanian bridle accessoirs, 49[34]; Scythian, 490; sinew, 504; 'soft-mouthed', 46; snaffle, 160; in Solleysel's "Complete Horseman", 464f.; straight bar, 491; from Tell el Ajjul, 510, 512f.; from Tell el Amarna, 512f.; from Tell el Haddad, 515–518; on terracotta models from the Levant, 197. *See also* Antler, Bone, Burr, Cheekpiece, Harnessing, Nose-Band.
Bit Burr. *See* Burr.
Black-Figured Vases. *See* Vase Painting.
Blanket, 443
Blinkers, 162f., 162[90], 162[91], 167, 170, 197, 202f., 232, 244, 417f., 434, 436f., 538; bronze from Cyprus, 152[42], 227; bronze and ivory from Assyria, 198, 418, 434; covered with gold foil, 162; spade-shaped, 434
Boat, wooden model on wheels (Gurob Egypt), 304[25]
Body (of vehicle), 51, 56, 68, 80, 91, 99, 138; of carts in Iron Age Cyprus, 212ff.; of the chariot model from the Oxus Treasure, 171[123]; of chariots in Iron Age Cyprus, 143ff.; of the chariot of Tuthmosis IV, 290f.; of the horse, 465, 470; lower 41; of metal wagon models from the Levant, 338ff.; quivers attached to the vehicle, 433; series of modifications in the construction of, 67; spears fixed at the rear of a chariot, 422; of terracotta chariot models from the Levant, 192–194; of a terracotta models from the Levant in Oxford, 403f.; of the two-wheelers from Lake Sevan, 325
Body-armour. *See* Armour.
Bone, cheekpieces, 499f., 502ff., 510[15]; found in King's Grave at Ur, 368f.; in equine anatomy (importance for harness), 483, 526, 528, 540f.; objects of the Timber-Grave and Andronovo cultures, 502; osteologial remains of horses, 152[42], 156, 162f., 197, 417, 526; plaque from Nippur, 499; pressure on the nasal bone of horses, 491; rider's shin, 444

Bovid, Cattle, adaption of pole and yoke for bovid anatomy, 278; bovid as top on "Standard", 368[76]; bronze models, 340ff.; burial of 333, 333[11], 369, 375; cattle 98, 132, 334, 350; harnessing, 498f.; in ceremonies, 286, 375. *See also* Bull, Draught, Ox.

Bow, composite 247; crossbow, 454; in the ancient Near East and Egypt, 28, 33f., 64, 79, 82, 136, 166, 169, 203, 230, 244, 257; in Mongolia, 117; of the Huns, 448; on Greek ships, 102[8], 104ff.; relationship between bow and chariot: in the ancient Near East, 83; (in Homeric and Mycenaean Greece), 58, 61, 71, 71[19], 88, 166, 422, 424f., 429, 432f., 432[12]; supposedly on Mycenaean wall paintings, 88f.; volleys of arrows, 56. *See also* Arrow, Armour.

Bowcase, 32, 83, 116, 166, 204[48], 307, 540, 540[7]; misinterpretations of, 308

Bowknot. *See* Yoke.

Bowmen, in chariots, 57, 138[23]; mounted, 35, 424f., 432f., 432[12]

Box, of chariot. *See* Chariot.

Bridle. *See* Bits.

Bronze, Assyrian Bronze reliefs from Til Barsip, 216; bells, 164; bit, 159, 415, 521 (*see also* Horse Bit); blinker, 152[42], 162, 162[92], 197, 227, 418, 434, 434[23] (*see also* Blinker); breastplate, 170, 227, 249, 435[25]; 'burr', 489f.; caps on axle end, 151, 170; celtic bronzework, 541; cart, Levantine bronze model, 222[26]; chamfrein, 530ff. (*see also* Chamfrein); chariot group, 154, 174ff.; from Gordion, 253; from the Iberian pensinsula, 288; from Trundholm, 128; 430ff.; (life size) in Florence, 256; from Bolsena, 283; three models found in Lchaschen tomb, 120; cheekpieces, 500, 502f., 505ff., 515ff.; chest armour for horses found *in situ*, 421; corselet (*see* Corselet); disks, ovoid, 154; equestrian statue of Marcus Aurelius on the Capitol in Rome, 413[8]; fan-shaped object (appearing in the yoke area of Assyrian chariots), 159; fibula with illustration of a ram, 104; figurine (charioter from the Levant), 185ff., 240; finials (of yoke saddles) from China, 481; frontlet, 152[42], 162f., 170, 197, 227, 417f., 434, 525, 527[7] (*see also* Frontlet); garment (*see* Garment); gate of Ashurnasirpal II from Balawat, 216[10]; gildet bronze saddle-bow plaques, 449; gilt-bronze sheeting, 446; gorget, 167, 421, 435; harness elements (so-called shoulder pendant), 158; horse gear, 435, 525ff.; horse trappers, 447; linch pin, 149, 151[38]; lion heads with sockets (chariot decoration), 218; loop, 80[17], 147, 149, 180[25], 251, 354[31]; model, Elamite, 39; *prometopidia*, 525ff.; reins made of bronze wire, 187; sheet, 260[4]; shoulder disk made of, 250; spikes, 521; standards, 227; stirrups, miniature bronze stirrups (middle Yenissei), 443; Chinese cast bronze stirrups, 446 (*see also* Stirrups); straps, 164[99]; terminals of the yoke, 157, 223[30]; textual evidence of 265f.; tyres, 261f., 278, 287; Urartian 36, 154[49]; vessel (in chariot burial from Cyprus), 170; from late in the Eastern Zhou period, 256; wagon models, 337ff.; trolley (and wheels) from Acemhöyük, 289, 291–295, 371[88], 508[7]; Weather-god's divine charioteer, 188[56]; wheel (*see* Wheel); wire binding/thongs on spokes, 290, 306; yoke ends (Shang and Zhou) with bronze leaf-shaped or lanceolate terminals, 123

Browband, 160f., 161[83], 162[90], 163, 197, 415–417, 417[25], 433f., 435[28], 526f., 529

buckle, 449, 505ff.

Building material, 231

Burial. *See* Chariot.

Bull(s), as top of "Standard", 368, 376; ring, 365, 498; in Hittite texts, 376[107]; metal figurines, 368 (metal analysis 378); sacred, 376; team of yoked, 188f., 375–377; terracotta rhyta in form of, 365. *See also* Draugh, Hunt, Hunting.

Burr, 487ff.; on Amazon mounts in Red-figured vase painting, 490[2]; bit 'burr' (or 'brush picker'), 487f.; bristled 'burr', 488; in Greece, 490, 490[2]; leather, 488, 494; Scythian 'burr', 489; tack 'burr', 487. *See also* Draught, Hunt, Hunting.

Caesar, 140[24]
Cadre Noir of Saumur, 474
Calabré Allongé, 311
Camel, Bactrian, 111; draught, 124, 134; hair of, 442; light two-wheelers drawn by, 108
Canon, 160, 495f., 500
Canopy. *See* Baldachin.
Canter, 259f., 460. *See also* Canter, Gallop, Gait, Trot.
Carriage, 117; -building practise of wagon models, 290; covered, 226; forecarriage, 131, 349f., 353; 'carriage houses', 48; head-and-neck, 48; hindcarriage, 349; houses, 521; Kurgan V at Pazyryk and Late Zhou China, 123, 129, 131f., 482; neck, 64; travelling in, 226; undercarriage, 130f., 349, 353, 370; women and grandees travelled in carriages (Achaemenid empire as reported by Greek authors), 196, 232
Cart, 94; 151, 190, 238, 301, 359, 380, 411; A-frame, 4f. 117, 133, 134, 182; absence of scenes of bovids pulling carts, 366, 547; Alexander the Great and the 'Gordian knot' (description of the vehicle), 548; in (modern) America, 492; in Anatolia, 133f., 360, 373, 394; A-pole, 183, 243; in Assyria, 282, 547; on Assyrian reliefs, 282; bovid-drawn (with cross-bar wheels), 281, 368, 377; bronze model from Bolsena, 283; bull-drawn, 377; burials in Cyprus, 172, 211ff.; in the Caucasus, 368; in China carrying baldachins or parasols, 131; clay model (from the Kalmyk steppe), 388; construction, 211ff.; country, 370; in Cypriot cart models, 211ff.; in Cyprus, 141f.; 153[46], 156–163; 169f., 208–210, especially 211ff.; 388, 394, 399; Cypriot cart wheels, 153; definition, 141, 211; distinction between cart and chariot, 109, 122, 128, 303; distinction between cart and wagon, 336, 348, 546; in Egypt, 303f.; Elamite carts (on Assyrian reliefs)

215[7], 325f.; Etruscan (covered carts in late Etruscan and Roman Italy derive from the east, Höckmann), 232[58]; farm carts, 93; floor, 351; from the Greek colony at Kerch in the Crimea, 388; on Greek Attic Geometric vases 400; horse-drawn, 116, 209; from Lchaschen, 243, 394; light, 286; from Marathus (Amrith), 204, 206; as 'missing link' in the development of wheeled vehicles (Piggott), 184; models, from Iron Age Cyprus, 211, 388; in Mongolia, 116; mule carts on Assyrian reliefs, 547; mule-drawn, 68; origin of the two-poled chariot in the A-frame cart, 243; 282; ox-drawn, 68; on Panathenaic vase 284; passengers, 209; primitive, 274; pulling country carts 370; Punic, 334 (*see also plostellum peonicum*); 'Red-River cart', 300[6]; of the Sea-Peoples, 282, 366; terracotta and limestone carts from Iron Age Cyprus, 388f.; in Transcaucasia, 182; from Tyre, 202; wheelmarks on, 231[53]; wheels of, 394; Yemeni, 282; Y-pole developed out of Transcaucasian A-frame cart (Piggott), 182, 222[25]. *See also* pp. 141ff. and 211ff. for Iron Age Cyprus.
Cartwright, 239
Cattle. *See* Bovid.
Cavalry, replacement of the chariot, 21ff.
Cavesson, 28, 31, 395, 491, 491[3], 493f., 498
Ceremony, ceremonial, 170. *See also* Treshing.
Chamfrein, 531ff.
Chariot
Achaemenid (Persian), 36f., 169, 193[7], 310–312; chariot group from Levant (models manufactured during Achaemenid domination), 174ff., esp. (date and origin), 184f., 240; closed Achaemenids Chariots (as described by Xenophon), 252; on cylinder seals, 179; golden chariot models (from the so-called Oxus Treasure), 147, 154, 169, 195f., 310f.; at Persepolis, 151, 153, 159, 169, 180, 310; influence on Egyptian drawing of a chariot, 180 (*see also* under

Scythed below in this entry);
Anatolian, (Kārum Kaneš/Kültepe),
15–17, 28f., 46,f., 289; early metal
models of wagons, 339ff., 406;
stamp cylinders and seal
impressions, 280, 284, 289, 356,
358, 360, 372f., 376f., 405f.
Ancient British
Assyrian, 35ff., 66ff, 75ff.; body (*see*
Body); box, 'quartered' by the pole
and the axle on rock carvings, 114,
117, 119, 122; in Bronze Age
Greece, 53ff., 62ff., 66ff., 75ff.;
burial, 27, 45, 48, 52, 126f., 132ff.,
142[33], 151, 153, 160, 167, 169ff.,
184[34], 196, 212, 249, 323, 348[22], 375,
399, 411, 421, 434ff., 490, 543[14];
Celtic, 139; in Central Asia, 106ff.;
Chinese, 118f., 120, 122f., 125, 127,
129, 131ff., 150, 172, 172[52], 255f.,
272, 274, 280, 325, 543[14]; Celtic,
139, 140[25]; charioteer (*see* driver
below in this entry); combat, 10, 61,
64f.; construction, 94, 96, 106,
143f., 171, 195, 232, 246, 251, 282
(*see also* Axle, Cart, Pole, Spoke,
Wheel, Wagon); cult (*see* Cult); 32,
35ff., esp. 141ff., 190ff., 326[32];
decoration, 68, 159, 162f., 164,
170f., 355, 404; definition, 28f., 45,
51, 66, 141, 238 (*see also* the
Glossary above); driver 26f., 32,
36f., 57, 63f., 78, 88, 92, 99, 111ff.,
138[23], 161, 164, 168, 200, 203f.,
213, 241, 244f., 250, 255f., 280,
289f., 308, 311; Dual Chariot (*see*
s.v.); Egyptian, 29, 32, 47, 54ff., 61,
63f., 66ff., 77, 82, 83[29f], 86, 90, 93,
95, 97f. 118, 121, 123, 125, 136ff.,
144, 177f., 180, 246f., 317, 320,
326, 482 (*see also* Egypt, Wheel);
equipment, 56, 70, 72, 98, 100ff.,
166, 168, 170f., 249, 424; floor, 34,
76; floor frame, 31, 35, 144, 154,
178; frame, 34; Florence (*see*
Florence Chariot); front, 30ff., 54,
80, 133; funerary (*see* Funeral);
Gallic, 139; Hittite, 30f., 57, 63, 67,
78, 82 (*see also* Kadesh, Hittites; and
Neo-Hittite below in this entry);
Homeric, (manner) 88f.; (practise)
84, 84[31], (use of) 62ff. (*see also*
Homer); hunting (*see* s.v.); in Iron
Age Cyprus, 79, 82, 141ff., 243,

281, 323; in Kazakhstan, 45ff.; from
Lchaschen, 119ff., 131, 133f.;
logistic, 68[12], 69; massed, 53, 60, 62,
68, 71, 98, 101[4]; Mesopotamian,
28ff., 47f.; Minoan (*see* Bronze Age
Greece above in this entry); models
from the Levant, 174ff., 180ff.,
190ff., 337ff.,; origin of, 4ff., 45ff.,
54, 67; as mobile firing platform, 27,
32, 34f., 37, 56, 58, 68, 72, 83, 101,
168, 203, 424; Mycenaean (*see* under
Bronze Age Greece above in this
entry); Neo-Hittite, 36, 78, 80, 80[17],
82, 98, 150, 194, 248[10], 286, 310,
Persian (see Achaemenid above in
this entry); pole (*see* Draught Pole);
prestige symbol, 48, 51, 68, 70, 97,
257; procession (*see* s.v.); progress vs.
invention, 48ff.; *quadriga*, 37, 113,
115, 117, 127ff., 132, 143, 148, 151,
153, 153[48], 155, 157, 161, 161[85],
167, 169, 172, 181, 195, 221, 252,
252[37], 253, 255, 258[1], 260, 309f.;
racing, 45, 52, 57, 62f., 92, 96[72],
172, 251[25], 255, 258, 326[3], 489, 546;
Etruscan, 255; Rail, 72[23], 101, 290;
rock carvings, see s.v.; Shang
pictographs (*see* Chinese); 'scythed',
36f., 56, 169, 425; status symbol
(*see* prestige symbol above), of
the Sun (bronze model of the
so-called Chariot of the Sun from
Trundholm), 128, 530ff.; terms for,
(Indo-European), 66f.; textual
evidence, 29, 32, 36f., 48, 60, 64f.,
67, 67[8], 72; two-man, 32, 56, 77f.,
82, 309; three-man, 32, 67, 78,
80, 82, 178, 182, 199[32], 204;
unharnessed, 11, 133, 157, 246, 248,
252, 310[52], 366; warrior, 63, 136 (*see
also* driver above in this entry)
Chariot-Borne, infantry, 64; lancers,
60; opponent, 57, 62; pharao
(Tuthmosis IV), 56; spearman, 54,
57; warfare, 56f., 72,
77[11]; (on Greek vases), 64
Chariot Racing, Race, 46, 52, 258;
Etruscan, 254; Driver, 57, 138[23]; in
Greece, 96[72], 172, 489, (use of
Greek 'burr' [s.v.] indicating chariot
use), 490[2], 546, Roman, 251[25];
scene, 57, 59, 254; use of *trigae* in,
258; wheels, 96[72]. *See also* Chariots.
Charioteer. *See* Chariot.

Chariotry, esp. 66ff.; ancient Near Eastern, 66ff., 90; Assyrian, 79f., 98; avoiding confrontation, 56; and cheekpieces, 489; Chinese cavalry inferior in importance to, 450; Egyptian, 83[28], 90; enemy, 53; goddess of, 188 (Anath); Greek, 53ff., 66ff., 75ff., 89; importance of petroglyphs for, 106ff.; impracticality of attacting fortified cities with, 98[87]; later 2nd millennium, 32; massed, 98; migration and, 69; military role of, 32; mounted troops as important arm alongside, 64, 255; mounted troops taking over role of, 35, 37, 169, 326, 425; movements of (limitations in Greece), 69; Mycenaean opposing, 54; as primary force in late Bronze Age warfare?, 68; protective armor and, 89; "realistic use of", 62; reserve horses accompanied, 90, 254; Roman; speeding, 53. See also Chariot, Warfare.

Cheekpiece, 487ff. See also Antler, Bits, Bone, Bronze, Horn.

Cheekstraps, 160, 197, 244, 414ff., 433, 510[12], 515

Clamp, 35, 152, 152[42], 195, 266–268, 271, 325

Cloth, Costume, Dress, 155, 244; as horse helmet decoration, 541; cloth backing (as material for fastening to breastplates), 249; mummy-cloth painting, 304; riding cloth, 529; saddle cloth, 412f., 413[8], 424, 426f., 429, 431. See also Garment, Tunic.

Coins, 140[24], 179, 217[11], 283f., 305, 309

Collar. See Harnessing.

Collections, Abbott, 296; Adam, 337, 341; Bomford, 190, 348, 379; Borowski, 189; Cesnola, 214[5], 234, 236, 505, 525, 525[3]; Chester, 206; de Clercq, 148[24], 174, 188, 190f., 240; Clot (Clot-Bey), 303; Colonna-Ceccaldi, 237; Forrer, 237; Herzfeld, 329[4], 393; Lunsingh-Schuerleer, 192; Morgan, 280; Newell, 29; Nretié, 206; Pierides, 235, 237, 419; Pomerance, 336f., 340; Pozzi, 192; Rosen, 329; Thierry, 337, 344

Collision, (of vehicles), 54

Column of Trajan, 452

Combat. See Chariot.

Controll. See Harnessing.

Copper, 27, 39, 44, 49, 174, 186, 261, 264–266, 271, 278, 289, 293, 338, 341f., 344–346, 352, 354[31], 364, 368, 370, 377, 506, 508[7], 515f., 534, 541, 543

Corselet, of chariot-borne warriors, 58, 91; of the Dendra charioteer, 60, 90f.; Egyptian, 56; on LH IIC krater from Pyrgos Livanates, 102, 104; in Linear B tablets, 89; on the Warrior Krater from Mycenae, 100; on a warrior krater from Volos, 102[7]

Costume. See Cloth.

Craftsmen, 324, 367

Crossbow. See Bow.

Crownpiece, 526, 529

Cult, 389, 399; car, 372, 376; 11, 14; funerary, 135; military, 375; models, 377, 406f.; objects, 377, 387; practices, 246, 253; scenes, 28; solar, 122; sun, 128; trolley, 293; wagon, 373, 388, 392, 405.

Cult car. See Cult.

Dagger, 61, 70, 86, 262, 420, 425, 473; (Lion-Hunt), 53f., 88

Deity, 140[25], 188, 237, 281, 303; god, 48, 134, 188, 206, 206[55], 210, 218, 264, 281, 376–378; goddess, 43, 143, 185[52], 188

Dendra, equipment of the tomb, 59f., 90f.; panoply, 53, 56, 60, 94. See also Driver.

Donkey. See ass. See also Equid, Hemione, Horse.

'Donkey Beads', 396

'Donkey Seat'. See Seat.

Draught, 50, 93, 110f., 116, 129, 134f., 142, 154, 156f., 170, 172, 184, 203, 205, 208, 212, 324, 336, 353, 362, 364, 366ff., 388ff., 435, 547; animals, 93, 111, 129, 134f., 143, 154ff., 170, 172, 184, 203, 208, 211f., 217, 223, 227, 227, 231f., 240, 251[35], 324, 332, 333[11], 336, 353, 362, 364, 367, 369, 374, 388, 396, 435, 547, 549; ass, 223; bovid, 67[4], 122, 280; burial, f., 292, 330f., 333[11], 350, 357, 367ff., 373ff., 377, 388ff., 525ff.; bull, 376 (see also

Bovid, Cattle); camel, 108, 124; donkey, 223, 233; equid, 28, 45, 50, 67, 218, 275, 278, 286, 350, 357, 371, 373f., 376, 389, 391f., 404; horse, 28, 45, 45[1], 66ff., 129ff., 134, 208f., 233ff., 270, 281, 310, 320, 324, 370, 396f., 483, 510; goat, 96; mule, 15, 17, 23, 64, 68, 133, 223f., 284, 304, 324, 326, 389, 546ff.; ox, 48, 67, 106, 110f., 116ff., 122, 129, 223, 326, 230, 332, 389, 392, 396, 428, 545ff.; paired, 184; single, 170; team, 27f., 34f., 37, 47, 67, 111, 142, 150, 159, 164, 168f., 172, 202, 205, 211, 219, 224, 227, 229, 405, 424, 547

Draught Pole, 27, 31, 33, 54, 66, 131, 143, 153f., 176, 192, 195, 202, 212, 215, , 218f., 222, 241, 340f., 349, 361ff., 388; Y-pole, 182, 238ff.

Draught System, 27, 33f.

Dress. See Cloth.

Driver, Charioteer, see Chariot. (See also Terracotta Figurines, Models)

Dual Chariot, 63, 72[23], 96, 101

dvoika (Russian), 258ff.

Eannatum Stela, 360

Economy, 37, 74, 121, 169, 324, 424

Elm Wood (Ulmus sp.), 320–322

Equestrian Studies, 460ff.

Equid, 27, 42f., 45, 48, 127, 372, 405, 427[62], 429, 504; control, 225; domestication of, 47, 404[5]; draught, 28, 45, 50, 67, 218, 223, 275, 278, 286, 289f., 350, 357, 371, 373–377, 392, 397; four, 27f., 44, 127f., 289, 364, 391, 404, 499; neck, 132, 483f.; skeletons, 156, 261; yoke, 27, 48, 122–124, 223f., 247, 391f., 480; See also Ass, Draught, Hemione, Horse, Hybrid, Nose Ring, Riding, Slit Nostril.

Equitation, 462

Equus. See Horse.

Felloe, bent-wood, 266; construction 33, 35f., 94, 152, 220f., 267[15], 272, 277, 281ff., 290f., 292[14], 293[20], 297ff., 320, 353; original findings, 296ff.

Fighting, on land and sea in Greek art, 10ff.

Fledermaus. See Yoke Saddle Pad.

Flying Gallop, 86, 86[40]

Flying Stones, (protection against), 97, 150, 395

Florence Chariot, 177[2], 246f., 256, 309, 309[48], 312, 480f.

'Foot-on-the-Chariot-Pole' Motif, 136ff.

Forelock, 414, 418, 428, 433, 527–529, 533

Four-Wheeled Wagon. See 'Battle Car', Wagon.

Frame, floor, 31, 35, 144, 154, 178, 192, 214, 239, 242; rectangular, 338, 346; of wagon models, 349ff., 361f.

Framework, 131, 212, 214, 216, 341, 353[30], 400

Fresco. See Wall Paintings.

Frontlet, from Ion Age Cyprus, 162, 417

Funeral, context, 142, 162; cult, 135; funerary function of carts in Iron Age Cyprus, 226f.; funerary function of chariots in Cyprus, 169f., 227, 250; Graeco-Persian funerary represenatations from Anatolia and Phoenicia, 229; funerary procession (12th dynasty in Nubia), 304

Gait, 64, 128, 259f., 311, 483, 523. See also Canter, Gallop, Gait, Trot.

Gallop, 54, 64, 84[31], 86, 101[3], 259f., 311, 467, 471; bounding, 98, 257; high, 465. See also Flying Gallop.

Games. See Funeral Games.

Garment, 38, 40, 90, 187, 188, 199, 208f., 426, 428, 432; robe, 57

Gauge, Wheel Track, 45

Girth, 87, 93, 158, 196, 224, 253f., 274, 413, 440, 444, 449, 454, 479f., 483–485

Glyptics, 347

Goad, 38, 43, 57, 113, 225, 330f., 358, 366, 373, 521f.

'Gobi' Quadriga, 106, 109, 117, 128ff.

God, Goddess. See Deity.

Gold, Goldwork, Gold Foil, 162f., 170; bowl from Hasanlu, 180[23], 377; fan, 540[7]; inlay, 368; leaf, 162[90], 163[93]; plaques, 142, 155, 155[59], 167, 448, 540[7]; plating, 189; sheet, 325. See also Oxus Treasure, Shaft Grave IV.

Gorget, 167, 167[108], 196f., 421f., 435f., 435[28]. See also Bronze.

Greaves, Leggings, 59, 85, 89, 90, 90[53], 100

Greek. See Chariot.

Half ass. *See* Hemione.

Half Noseband, 161, 416

Halssporen. See Tutʿankhamān.

Halsstück. See Yoke Saddle Pad.

(h)amaxa, 546ff.

Handgrip, 32f., 35f., 77, 96, 149, 178, 193, 252, 395; of Achaemenid chariots, 180; of chariot (from metal wagon model from the Levant), 180

Handhold, 80, 80[17], 96, 251, 286, 311, 357, 404, 406

Harnessing, 68, 70, 86, 92f., 94, 110, 121, 124, 132–134, 143, 150, 156ff., 170–172, 196–198; 223f., 227, 232, 238, 258, 260, 260[4], 275, 366, 414ff., 424, 427, esp. 476ff.; in Assyria, 246ff., 532; asymmetrical, 258; in burials, 162, 164, 211f., 227, 543[14]; in China, 231[52]; in Cyprus, 433ff., 526; collar, 27, 56, 128, 132, 231, 260, 484, 517; from Egypt, 521ff.; in the Iliad, 545ff.; muzzle, 50, 493[4], 495[5], 498f., 524, 533; nose ring, 27f., 50, 365f., 395, 498f.; pole-and-yoke system, 34, 44, 85, 124, 256[60], 241, 278, 350, 364, 391, 484, 548; *prometopídia*, 525ff.; reins, 20, 28, 34f., 56f., 64, 78, 83[30], 85–89, 97, 97[80], 111, 113, 124, 138–140, 159f., 161, 187, 197f., 222, 224, 229, 244, 246ff., 254f., 273, 310[52], 310[54], 366, 395, 414f., 424, 431, 473, 489, 492ff., 506, 515, 519; scene, 85, 124; shaft, 116, 181, 181[39], 184, 231, 259f., 299, 301[8], 348, 352f., 358, 362, 368, 370, 522; straps, 97, 99, 111, 124f., 127, 143, 158, 161f., 164, 164[99], 167, 196f., 202, 224, 244, 252, 255f., 260, 324, 391, 396, 413–418, 422, 426f., 429, 433, 436[29], 437, 442ff., 480, 483, 491, 498, 519, 525ff., 533, 538, 543; stirrup, 60, esp. 439ff., 452f.; (10th century AD), 455; (of American Plain Indians), 442; (in Avar Graves), 450; (big-toe) 440; (in China), 445f., 450; ('girth'), 440; (earliest preserved), 442; (etymology of), 442; (hook), 443ff., 451; (of the Huns), 448f.; (Iron Age Cyprus), 427; (in Japan), 448; (Kushan), 450; (Mathura), 442; (metal), 443f., 450; (miniature bronze), 443;

(Mycenaean), 105[18]; (Novorossiik type), 448f.; (proto-), 439; (rigid), 443, 445; (rope), 442; (from the Silla kingdom in Korea), 446f.; ('soft'), 443; (stirrupless saddle), 441; (strap), 440f.; (in Swedish Vikings's graves), 452; (treads), 442; (whole-foot), 440; (wooden), 441ff.; yoke, 127f., 256[60]. *See also* Antler, Bit, Bone, Cheekpiece, Collar, Yoke, Yoke Saddle.

Harnessing Scene. *See* Harnessing.

Headstall, 159f., 197, 224, 244, 255, 367, 414–416, 493[4], 494f., 498, 506, 508[7], 515, 522, 526, 543

Hearse, 217, 226–229, 233, 249f., 374

Hector, 98, 545f.

'Helladic' Chariot. *See* Chariot.

Helmet, 70, 85; for charioteers, 59, 77, 80–82, 89, 100f., 166, 203, 244f.; for foot soldiers, 59, 72, 85, 102, 104f.; for horses, 534ff. (*see also* chamfrein); metal, 203, 436; parade (in a drawing of Dürer), 457; for riders, 420ff., 436; 'spiked', 102, 102[7]

Hemione, 27, 47, 369, 375, 396f., 491, 502

hemione-ass hybrid, 10, 47, 253

Herakles, 136–138

Hero, Heroic, 89, 136ff., 546

Herodotus, 104[14], 168, 389, 467, 491

Herring-Bone Pattern, 401f., 404f.

High School, 460ff.

High School Airs. *See* High School.

High School Movements. *See* High School.

Hittite(s), (three-man) chariots of the, 30–33, 57, 63, 67, 67[8], 78, 82, 103, 280f.; cuneiform records, 317; empire, 47, 71, 314–317; four-wheeled baggage wagon, 282, 366; language, 67; mytholgy, 376; Sekundogenitur, 314; spears, 63f.; terracotta rhyta found in zattuša, 376, 376[107]; vehicle models kept in a later Hittite temple, 378. *See also* Battle of Kadesh, zattušili, Šuppiluliuma I., Šuppiluliuma II.

Homer, Homeric, 58, 62ff., 71, 84, 88f., 102[6]; description of the binding of the pole-and-yoke area, 548; description of harnessing, 545; description of three-horse hitches,

254; *hippeēs*, 63; poems, 546. *See also* Chariot, Iliad, *Zugodesmón*.

Hoplite, 104, 137f. *See also* Shield, Warrior.

Horn, 186f., 341f., 345, 368, 503, 514; bits, 501; bovid, 340, 343, 346; ibex, 316; horn, 344, 364f., 483

Horse, bones (osteological evidence), 152[42], 156, 197, 223, 414, 448, 524; breeding, 191, 449, 456, 458, 538; four yoked, 34ff., 48, 63, 127ff., 131, 147[21], 153, 156f., 159, 161f., 164, 166, 168f., 172f., 172[124], 181, 183[48], 184f., 195f. 203, 223, 227, 239, 241, 243, 252f., 255ff., 289f., 310, 310[52], 310[52] (*see also quadriga*, Yoke); 'Great Horse', 452ff., hair, 442; history of, 18ff., 452ff., 460ff.; in medieval times, 452ff.; training, 460 (in medieval times). *See also* Chariot, Cheekpiece, Equid, Draught, Harnessing.

Horse Bit, 32, 37, 159, 161[85], 293, 487ff., 505ff., 515ff.

Horse Burial. *See* Chariot, Horse.

Horse Shoe, 260

Housing. *See* Trapper, Trapping.

Hub. *See* Nave.

Hunt, Hunting, 28, 46, 57, 68, 85, 89, 93, 150, 169, 224, 229f., 240[11], 258, 260, 270, 307, 389, 399; 488, 540; Blackfoort Indian of North America, 443; Boar Hunt mural at Tiryns, 86; bulls, 82[22], 136, 249f., 426; scene, 61, 71[19], 108, 203, 316; lion, 203, 250, 257, 426, 436; hunters on foot, 57; Pharaoh as hunter, 136; ridden horse in, 426; trophies, 169. *See also battue*.

Hurrians, 67, 376, 401; building, 315f.

Hybrid. *See* Ass, Hemione, Mule.

Hyksos, 29

Iliad. *See* Homer.

Indo-European(s), 66ff.; critical examination of their role in chariotry, 67; in eastern Anatolia, 69; in Greece, (and the introduction of the chariot), 66f.; invasion hypothesis; Hittites, 67; and their so-called homeland, 66f.; (supposed), invention of the chariot, 66; terms for wheeled transport, 66

Inlay, 43f., 189, 347, 368

Iron, 142, 152[42], 153, 159, 161[85], 170, 172[124], 212, 214, 217, 219, 221, 223[29], 227, 232, 233, 274, 278, 293, 302, 324, 335, 415, 442, 446f., 538

Iron Age Greece Chariot. *See* Chariot.

Ivory, 86[40], 148, 162, 162[90], 163[93], 170, 180, 198, 198[29], 203, 417f., 434, 527, 527[7], 528, 530, 541

Javelin. *See* Spear.

Knight, armoured, 456f.; Medieval 82[22]

Knight. *See* Medieval. *See also* Armour, Parthian Cataphract.

Land transport. *See* Transport.

Leather, 91, 111, 125, 127, 143, 150, 156, 158, 167, 196, 202, 249, 253[41], 267, 277, 298[5], 300[6], 306, 320, 335, 355, 406, 431, 435, 441, 446f., 467, 487f., 490f., 494, 521f., 530, 537f., 541, 549. *See also* Harnessing, Oxhide, Rawhide.

Leather Backing, 487f.

Leggings. *See* Greaves.

Linch Pin, 221, 352, 355, 403; construction, 51, 355; original findings, 151, 151[38], 170, 261, 268, 268[21]

Linear B, 66; term for saddle, 247; terms for chariot and its elements, material or organization, 67, 67[3], 70, 322[20]

Linen, 91, 98, 432

Lines, of metal wagon models, 365–367; made of wool, 367

Lion. *See* Hunt, Hunting.

Lip Ring. *See* Nose Ring.

Litter, 330ff., 393; -pole terminal, 329

Mane, 110, 414, 428, 532f.

Manege, 460ff.; air, 474; conditions, 469; horse, 469; Modern, 466; riding, 460, 471; Renaissance, 467; schooling, 471

Mare, 538

Medieval, animal trainers, 475; horse, 452, 465; knight, 82; (in Nestor's description), 60; wagons, 349. *See also* Battlefield.

Metal, 27, 31[33], 35, 42, 51, 53, 56, 60, 111, 123, 142, 150[33], 151f., 152[43],

153, 154–156, 161, 161[83], 163f.,
   167, 174, 176, 180[23], 187f.,
   194–197, 203, 205, 212, 219, 219[14],
   224, 232, 238f., 242, 249, 260,
   261ff., 278, 289f., 292f., 298ff., 313,
   336ff., 381, 384, 391, 395f., 401,
   416, 418, 431ff., 439, 442ff., 444ff.,
   489f., 492, 494, 495[5], 500f., 504,
   505ff., 515ff., 526, 528, 534, 540f.
Metalwork, 261, 373, 375, 378
Military, accoutrements, 168; action,
   98, 168; campaigns, 322; chariots,
   26ff., 32, 36f., 53ff., 71f., 74, 75ff.,
   164, 169f., 172, 202, 225, 249, 425,
   542; context, 26, 47f., 63, 67, 84f.,
   88f., 92, 109, 225, 325, 375, 389,
   399, 404, 420, 441, 468, 470f., 540;
   equipment, 70, 72, 101, 166, 168,
   424; origin of High School, 465,
   472; riding, 64, 425f., 436, 452,
   520, 531, 538; transport, 60, 70;
   use, function, practice, purpose, 28,
   100f., 105, 168, 171f., 203f., 325f.,
   372, 425; value, 140; vehicles, 68,
   278, 373, 374, 392, 424
Minoan. See Chariot.
Mobile Firing Platform. See Chariot.
Mould, 191f., 199, 205f., 205[59], 207,
   209, 356, 431, 437f.
Mount, 46–48, 50, 91, 133, 202, 218,
   411f., 414, 421, 426, 428, 428[62], 429[72],
   430f., 433, 436[29], 437f., 439, 443,
   449, 452, 457, 464, 508[7]. See also Ass,
   Donkey, Equid, Horse, Mule.
Mounted hoplite/warrior. See Hoplite.
Mounted troops, 35, 37, 72, 74[26], 169,
   255, 309, 326, 424f.
Mouthpiece, 31f., 35, 159f., 414f.,
   486, 488ff., 505ff., 515ff.
Mule. See Draught, Riding.
Mule Cart. See Cart.
Muzzle, 50, 493[4], 495[5], 498f., 524,
   533
Mycenaean. See Chariot.
Myth, Mythical, Mythology, 38, 40,
   43, 230, 251, 375f., 405

Nackenjoch. See Yoke.
Nails (for tyres), 152, 152[43], 153,
   153[46], 186, 195, 214, 219, 219[14],
   267, 298, 299, 309, 351, 355, 442,
   488; hobnail, 27, 36, 268f., 278,
   355
Nave, 26, 45, 51, 54, 151f., 152[41],

176, 194, 220f., 268, 272ff., 284f.,
   290ff., 296ff., 317, 319ff., 340, 343,
   355, 385, 396, 405, 506, 508; Hub,
   244, 396, 403, 404
Naveless. See Wheel.
Neckstrap, 224, 244, 434f., 437
Nestor, 60, 63
Noseband, 160f., 224, 414, 416f.,
   417[25], 433f., 491ff., 519f.
Nose Ring, 365, 395, 498f.; lip ring,
   498

Onager. See Hemione.
Osteological Evidence. See Ass, Horse.
Outrigger, 27, 34, 48, 258–260, 260[2];
   trace horse, 113f., 117, 124, 132,
   181, 241, 247f.
Ox, 183, 483; cart, 224, 230, 282,
   370; -drawn, 48, 67, 68, 106, 110,
   129, 230, 243, 332[8], 324, 332, 365,
   392, 548f.; harnessed, 122; -yoke,
   122, 124, 132, 134, 157, 158[68], 184,
   223, 247, 251[25], 480, 483. See Bovid,
   Draught, Nose Ring.
Ox Cart. See Ox.
Oxus Treasure. See Chariot s.v.
   Achaemenid.

Pace, 84[30], 94, 96[72], 128, 225, 257,
   392
Pack Animal, 47, 68, 94, 108, 392,
   429[69]
Pack saddle. See Saddle.
Painted Box of Tut'ankhamān. See
   Tut'ankhamān.
Parasol, 131. See also Cart.
Parade, chariots, 170, 291; decoration
   of Dürer's horse, 457; equid-drawn
   wagons, 392; ivory parade
   chamfreins, 530; metal parade
   chamfreins, 541; in Renaissance,
   467; and tilt vehicles, 399; uniform
   for chariot horses, 250
Persian War Chariot. See Chariot.
Plane Wood (*Platanus orientalis*),
   320; car
'Platform Car', 27f., 41, 387, 394–396,
   405[8], 406, 406[14]
Plutarch, 389, 548
plostellum punicum, 329, 334. See also
   Cart.
Pole. See Draught Pole.
Pole Binding, 547
Pole Braces, 222

Pole Horse, 113f., 117, 124, 132, 181, 248, 253, 253[44], 254, 256, 260
Pole Stay, 87, 97
Pole-End, 114, 144
Pole-End-Support, 547
Poll Decoration (from Iron Age Cyprus), 163f., 419
Pony, cross-bread, 538; Dartmoor, 538; head, 537, 542; horse-show, 538; polo, 474; size, 449
Prestige Symbol. *See* Chariot.
Priam, 545ff.
Processsion, Processional, 11, 36, 48, 50, 68, 113, 131, 134, 168, 218, 304, 389, 406, 426, 467, 474, 540
Prometopidia, 525ff.
Prothesis, 400
Psalia, 492, 493[4]

quadriga, 37, 113f., 127ff., 143, 148, 151, 153, 153[48], 155, 157, 161, 161[85], 167, 169, 172, 181, 195, 221, 252, 252[36], 253, 255, 258[1], 260, 309f. *See also biga*, 'Gobi Quadriga', *dvoika, triga*.
Quiver, as equipment of chariots, 166, 307, 422, 426; as equipment for riders, 431, 436; decorated containing arrows, 432[12]

Race, Racing, 45, 52, 57, 59, 62f., 92, 96, 96[72], 138[28], 172, 251[25], 254f., 258, 326[33], 488ff., 546
Race Track, 488
Rail Chariot. *See* Chariot.
Ram (war machine), 104, 104[13]
Ramesseum, 82, 86[39], 304[19]
Rawhide, 27, 30, 144, 152, 152[43], 194, 267, 278, 291, 298ff., 322, 324f., 442
Reins. *See* Harnessing.
'Rickshaw', royal in Assyria, 216, 218, 228
Ridden Horses, 50, 110, 163[95], 167, 169, 197, 197[22], 205, 249, 411ff., 443, 450, 452, 468, 475, 488ff., 509, 517
Rider, mounted, 116, 64, 190, 202, 204, 204[50], 206f., 397, 400, 439ff.; in Iron Age Cyprus, 411ff.; in medieval times, 452ff.; Phoenician(?), 438ff.; in a chariot (*see* Driver). *See also* Riding, Stirrups.
Riding, 94, 397, 411ff.; astride, 39, 48, 64, 244, 394, 412, 428f., 431,

473; in a chariot, 72, 94, 100, 138, 187, 199, 204[50]; on domestic donkey, 47f.; history of modern riding, 460ff.; horseback, 64, 190, 196, 202, 204, 204[50], 206f., 397, 411, 420, 422, 424ff., 430, 432f., 436ff., 450, 452; in medieval times, 452ff.; people of the steppe, 489; techniques, 169, 427, 438[35]; tradition, 449; in warfare, 425. *See also* Rider, Stirrups.
Road, 70, 70[17], 94, 259
Roadster, nineteenth-century England and America, 93
Robe. *See* Garment.
Rock-Carvings, 106ff.; Altai, 108, 113ff., 254; Central Asia, 107f.; chariot representations, 109ff.; comparison with other chariot evidence, 118ff.; Outer Mongolia, 109; Scandinavia, 118, 129, 133; Transcaucasia, 106ff.; Val Camonica, 119, 130, 349
Rock-Painting, Sahara, 147, 154, 157, 239
Roman. *See* Chariot, Chariot Racing.

Saddle, 60, 412, 414, 424, 427f., 439, 441, 448, 450, 452, 454, 469; accessoirs, 448; Altai, 443; Avar, 449; 'chair', 429; cowboy's, 442; high-arched, 450; Hun, 448; old war, 469; pad, 443; pack, 429, 429[69]; rigid framed, 429, 450; Roman cavalry, 413, 414[11]; Sassanian, 414; seat, 40f., 48; 'soft', 442; stirruples, 414; treed, 427, 439, 442, 449
Saddle Cloth. *See* Cloth.
Sassanian Cataphract, 82[22]
Scyths, 20, 128, 389, 392, 425, 445, 489, 503
Sea Peoples, 71, 103, 282, 317
Seals, 28f., 40, 42ff., 45f., 57, 94ff., 123, 178ff., 188, 262, 279f., 282, 284f., 287, 289f., 292[14], 311[60], 323, 329ff., 347, 356ff., 372, 376, 393, 395f, 404f. *See also* Glyptics.
Seat, astride (from Iron Age Cyprus), 412–414, 431ff.; 'donkey', 64, 397; sideways, 428
Shaft Graves of Mycenae, 53f., 61f., 66, 66[1], 67, 69f., 74, 82, 86f., 98, 102

Shaft Harness. *See* Harnessing.
Shield, 32, 35, 56, 58, 59, 70, 72, 77, 77[11], 78, 80ff., 100ff., 149, 166, 190, 193f., 194[9], 198, 198[28], 202f., 244f., 241, 424, 433ff.; bearer, 32, 36f., 58, 77ff., 102, 102[6], 138[23], 164, 166, 204, 244f., 251, 251[30f.], 252, 432[10]
Siege, 85, 86[39], 88, 102
Silver, 102, 143, 163, 209, 214f., 217[11], 226, 232, 336, 368, 411[11], 417, 446, 448
Slashing Weapon, 54
Sledge, 329ff.
Slit Nostrils, 17th century France, 520; Anglo-Saxon England, 519; disappearing of, 493; Germany, 520; Iceland, 520; Iran, 519f.; Mongolia, 520; Spain, 520; Tell el Amarna, 519
Snaffle, 35, 159, 160, 145, 465; development, 495–497; wire, 500
Spanish Riding School, 460ff.
Spear, 32, 35, 53ff., 62ff., 82, 88f., 91, 102[7], 136, 166, 169, 204[48], 420[35], 421, 425f., 473; throwing (javelin), 40, 53, 63, 78, 82f., 103, 307, 360, 373, 406, 447; thrusting, 52ff., 62f., 70, 71[18], 82[22], 83, 203
Spearman, 32, 54, 56f., 60, 83, 101f.
Spoke, Egyptian nave-and-spoke construction four-spoked wheels, 96, 123, 230, 280, 285, 289, 292f., 307, 309, 321, 396, 405, 506, 531; six-spoked wheels, 96, 176, 177, 273, 279, 290ff., 304, 307, 317f.; eight-spoked wheels, 152f., 194f., 220, 220[21], 304, 304[19], 307ff., 323; over eight spoked wheels, 120, 152f., 171, 220, 285, 305, 323, 326[32]. *See also* Wheel, Spoked Construction.
Squire, 62f., 240, 240[11], 424, 448
'Standard of Ur', 11, 26, 29, 38, 40, 83, 347, 358, 364ff., 391, 404f., 498f.
Status Symbol. *See* Chariot.
Stallion, 50, 133, 456, 473, 503, 523f., 538
Stick, 64, 225, 343, 420, 420[33], 428[65]
Stirrups, 439ff. *See also* Bronze.
Strabo, 491, 494
'Straddle Car', 27, 39, 41–43, 48, 136, 139, 268, 268[20], 394f.

Superstructure. *See* Wagon Models.
Sword, 59, 61, 70, 72, 82, 100, 101, 136, 166, 166[104], 420, 422, 424f., 449, 453, 548

Tassels, 158, 162, 164, 164[97f.], 167, 196, 197, 203, 208, 250, 252, 307, 416, 417, 418, 421, 422, 427, 431, 434, 435, 437. *See also* Bell.
Technology, 274
Terracotta Figurines, Models, bronze figurines of chariot drivers from the Levant, 185ff.; bovid metal figurines, 368; (metal analysis), 378; chariot models, from Cyprus, 190ff.; from Greece, 198ff.; from the Levant, 174ff., 380ff., 393ff.; 'horse-and-rider', 411ff., 430ff.; use of, 420ff.; traction system, 114, 143, 147, 153, 177, 181–183, 195, 212, 219, 222, 240f., 258
Threshing, 325ff.; ceremonial, 327ff.
Thucydides, 104[14]
Tilt, 213, 216, 216[9], 218ff., 228, 232, 234, 236, 238, 363, 374, 374[99], 380ff.
Timber, 144, 147, 154, 178, 192, 212, 215, 219, 222, 222[25], 230, 266, 274f., 322, 322[20], 325, 351, 363, 546
Tine. *See* Antler.
Trace Horse. *See* Outrigger.
Transport, 3f., 47, 109, 231; ancestor of, 184; early, 331; military, 60, 70; on animal back, 411; wheeled, 50, 60, 68, 219, 325f., 336, 354, 373, 377, 392; for warriors, 71, 425
Trapper, Trapping, Housing, 83, 447, 467
tribulum, 329
triga, 114, 116, 127, 128, 153, 181, 24, 258ff.
Trittbrett, 358
troika, 259
Trolley. *See* Bronze
Trot, 84[30], 128, 259, 460, 522. *See also* Canter, Gallop, Gait, Trot.
Tunic, 90, 199, 202, 432, 437f.,
Tyre, copper and bronze, 261f., 278, 287

Ulmus sp. See Elm Wood.

Vase Painters, 136ff., (manner of) Antimenes painter, 137; Ellbow Out Painter, 137; (manner of) Exekias, 137; Lysippides Painter, 137; Nikosthenes, 137; Painter of the vatican, 137

Vase Painting, Attic Black-figured, 84, 92, 229, 253, 490[2], 547; 19th and 20th dynasty heroic motiv, 136ff.; Red-figured, 218, 490[2]; Mycenaean. See Warrior Vase.

Vehicles (Wheeled). See 'Battle Car', Cart, Chariot, 'Straddle Car', Wagon.

ventilabrum, 333[9]

Vulture Stela, 38ff.

Wagon, 27ff.; Standard of Ur', Vehicle construction of, 27ff.; connection wit actual wagons, 371ff.; function of, 380ff.; textual evidence, 348, 348[21]; superstructure, 355ff. See also 'Battle Car.'

Warfare, Anatolian, 372; Assyrian, 203, 257, 436; Bonze Age, 83; Bronze Age Greece, 57ff., 62ff., 66ff, 75ff., 139, 172; Celtic, 139; on Cyprus, 168; Egyptian, 56, 326; and horseback riding, 425; land and sea, 100ff.; medieval, 470f.; mounted, 446, 454, 543[16]; Near Eastern, 56, 89, 90, 96, 326, 391, 405; on the steppes, 47

Warrior. See Charioteer. Hoplite

Warrior Vase, Mycenae, 58, 77, 83

Weapons, defensive, 58, 72, 90[53], 101, 453; offensive, 58, 72, 101. See also Axe, Dagger, Javelin, Shield and Spear.

Wheel, disk, 26f., 76ff., 152, 220, 230, 239, 272ff., 292, 323; in Bronze Age Greece, 92ff.; construction, 28, 41f., 51, 296ff.; cross-bar, 28, 151, 218, 220f., esp. 272ff., 323, 339, 351, 370ff.; earliest three-dimensional, 289ff., 508[7]; H-spoked, 221; on Iron Age Cyprus, 151–153; models, 236ff., 394; original findings, 141ff., 296ff., spoked, 45ff., 289ff., 317ff.

(see also Spoke); track (See Gauge); tripartite, 14, 26, 267, 269, 272ff., 323, 355, 405

Wheel Track. See Gauge.

Wheeled Vehicle. See Vehicle.

Wheelmarks, on Cypriot carts or chariots, 231[53]

Whip, 113, 224f., 229, 311, 360, 366, 420; in the vehicle of the Eannatum stela, 360

White Obelsik, 247

Wickerwork, as decoration on terracotta wagon models indicating, 391; as protection on vehicles, 395; shield, 198, 198[28]; in Pu-abi's sledge, 334; on hoops, 216, 390; on wagon from kurgan, 9; in Lchashen (Armenia), 390; on wagon model from Syria in Oxford, 405; supposedly on Greek Attic Geometric vase representations, 400; tilts made of, 390

Widerristjoch. See Yoke.

Withers, 48, 64, 118, 156, 157, 223, 260, 340, 412, 414, 431, 457, 479ff., 523, 538, 538[5]

Wood. See also Birchbark, Elm Wood, Plane Wood.

Xenophon, 37, 81[19], 252[35]; on chariots in Persian times, 252, 389; on Horsemanship, 461–463, 467

Yoke, 27, 31ff., 48, 53f., 67, 93, 97, 110ff., 154, 157ff., 161, 168, 170ff., 181, 184, 190, 196, 219, 222ff., 233, 239, 240ff., 258ff., 260ff., 292, 310, 336ff, 360ff., 364f., 376, 391, 521ff.; 545ff.

Yoke Braces, 31, 111, 114, 124f., 127, 256, 256[60], 257, 547f.

Yoke Peg, 158, 159

Yoke Saddle, 31, 34f., 97, 111, 123f., 132, 158, 158[69], 223[30], 241, 247ff., 479ff., 489, 521

Yoke Saddle pad

Y-Pole. See Draught Pole.

Zugodesmón, 545ff.

PLATES

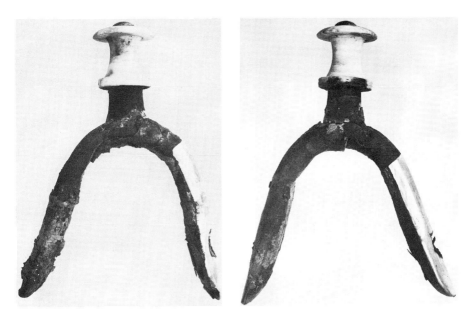

Pl. 1. Yoke saddles from the tomb of Tutʿankhamūn. Littauer and Crouwel 1985, pl. 33 [= pair of Yoke Saddles **B 1** (Obj. nos. 165, 169)]. Photograph by H. Burton, Griffith Institute, Oxford.

Pl. 2. Ur seal impression, U.13963 (photograph University Museum Philadelphia).

Pl. 3. Inlay fragment from Nippur 6N-169 (photograph Oriental Institute, University of Chicago).

Pl. 4. Sintashta, burial 28, imprints of spoked wheels (after Gening 1977, fig. 3).

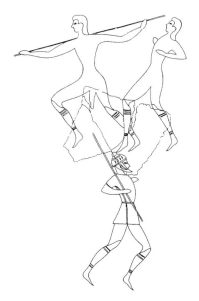

Pl. 5. Wall painting from the Megaron of the palace of Mycenae. After Rodenwaldt 1921, Beilage III, no. 11.

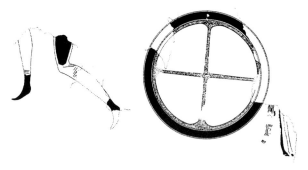

Pl. 6. Wall painting, same provenance as 4:1a. After Crouwel 1981, pl. 85, no. W8.

Pl. 7. Wall painting, same provenance as pl. 5-6. After Crouwel 1981, pl. 174.

Pl. 8. Krater fragment from Livanates. After F. Dakoroneia, in: Tzalas 1996, 147, fig. 1.

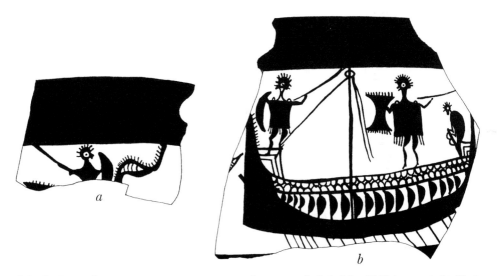

Pl. 9a–b. Krater fragments, same provenance as fragment of pl. 8. After F. Dakoroneia in: Tzalas 1995, 148, figs. 2–3.

Pl. 10. Detail of so-called Aristonothos krater from Cerveteri. After Crielaard 1998, ill. p. 119.

Pl. 11. Krater fragment from the Dipylon cemetery, Athens. After Grünwaldt 1983, 169, fig. 22, no 19.

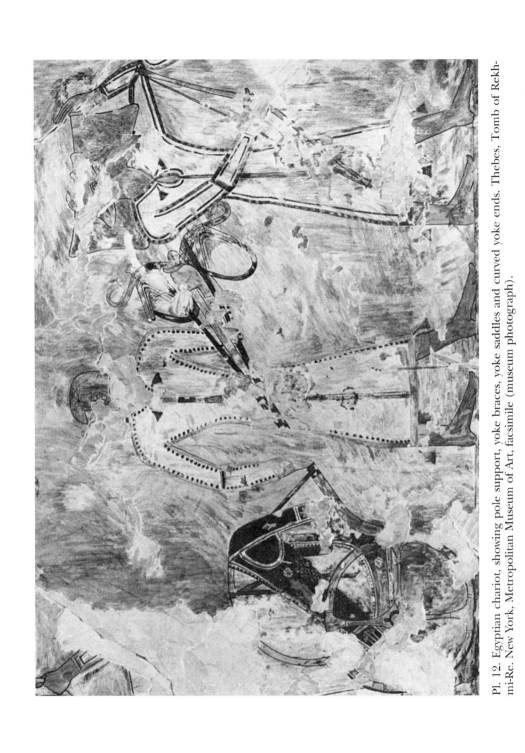

Pl. 12. Egyptian chariot, showing pole support, yoke braces, yoke saddles and curved yoke ends. Thebes, Tomb of Rekh-mi-Re. New York, Metropolitan Museum of Art, facsimile (museum photograph).

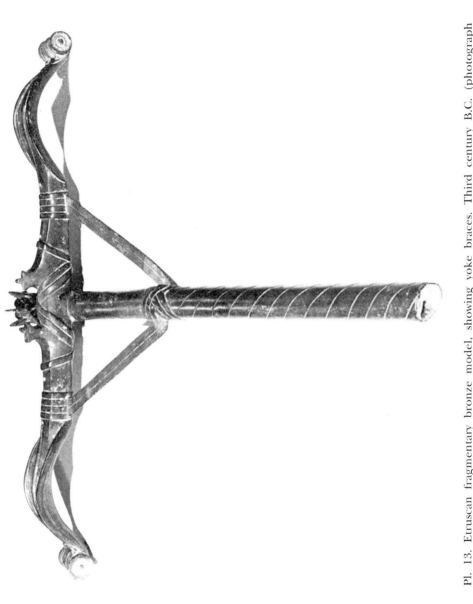

Pl. 13. Etruscan fragmentary bronze model, showing yoke braces. Third century B.C. (photograph Soprintendenza alle antichità, Firenze).

Pl. 14. Detail of a relief of Ramses III from Medinet Habu (drawing Oriental Institute of the University of Chicago).

Pl. 15. Neck amphora showing Ares in a Gigantomachy. London, British Museum. (museum photograph).

Pl. 16. Panathenaic amphora by the Lysippides Painter, showing Herakles fighting the giants. London, British Museum. (museum photograph).

Pl. 17. Type B amphora attributed to the Princeton Painter depticting a hoplite, New York, Metropolitan Museum of Art 56.171.9, Fletcher Fund 1956 (museum photograph).

Pl. 18a–b. Stone model from Kourion. New York, Metropolitan Museum of Art 74.51.2687. (museum photograph).

Pl. 19. Stone model. No provenance. New York, Metropolitan Museum of Art 74.51.2845. (museum photograph).

Pl. 20. Stone sarcophagus, detail from Golgoi. New York, Metropolitan Museum of Art 74.51.2451. (museum photograph). ←

Pl. 21. Stone sarcophagus, detail from Amathus. New York, Metropolitan Museum of Art 74.51.2453. (museum photograph). →

a   b

Pl. 22a–b. Terracotta model from Ayia Irini. Nicosia, Cyprus Museum 2000. (museum photographs).

a   b

Pl. 23a–b. Terracotta model from Ayia Irini. Nicosia, Cyprus Museum 1780. (museum photographs).

Pl. 24. Terracotta model from Ayia Irini. Nicosia, Cyprus Museum 1781+798. (museum photograph).

Pl. 25. Terracotta model from Ayia. Nicosia, Cyprus Museum 1170. (museum photograph).

a

b

Pl. 26a–b. Terracotta model from Meniko. Nicosia, Cyprus Museum. (museum photographs).

Pl. 27a–b. Terracotta model from Amrit/Marathus(?). Louvre, AO 25985. (museum photographs).

Pl. 28. Terracotta model from Ovgoros. Nicosia, Cyprus Museum 1955/IX-26/1. (museum photograph).

Pl. 29. Terracotta model from Kition. Larnaca District Museum. (museum photograph).

Pl. 30. Fragmentary terracotta model. New York, Metropolitan Museum of Art 74.51.1805. (museum photograph).

Pl. 31. Terracotta model. Nicosia Cyprus Museam 1968/V-30/635. (museum photograph).

Pl. 32. Terracotta model. Oxford, Ashmolean Museum 1968.488. (museum photograph).

a

b

Pl. 33a–b. Terracotta model. Oxford, Ashmolean Museum 17376. (museum photograph).

Pl. 34. Bronze horse bit from Amathus. Nicosia, Cyprus Museum. (museum photograph).

Pl. 35. Chariot B (our A3), plaster cast of pole support/breastwork brace from Salamis, Tomb 3 (photograph V. Karageorghis).

a

b

Pl. 36a–b. Bronze chariot model. Paris, Louvre 22265. (museum photographs).

c   *d*

Pl. 36c–d. Bronze chariot model. Paris, Louvre 22265. (museum photographs).

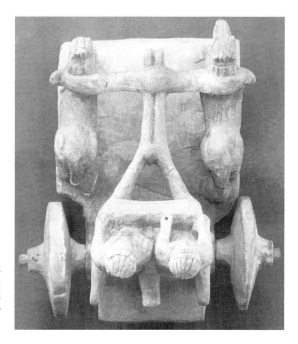

Pl. 37. Limestone chariot model from Kourion. New York, Metropolitan Museum of Art 74.51.2687. (museum photograph).

a   b

Pl. 38a–b. Figures from the bronze chariot model. Paris Louvre 22265. (museum photographs).

a   b

Pl. 39a–b. Terracotta model no. 1. Oxford, Ashmolean Museum 1974.349. (museum photographs).

a

b

c

Pl. 40a–c. Terracotta model no. 2 from Marathus (Amrit). Paris, Louvre AO 25985. (museum photographs).

a   b

Pl. 41a–b. Terracotta model no. 3. Paris, Bibliothèque Nationale D 3734. (photographs Bibliothèque Nationale).

a   b

Pl. 42a–b. Terracotta model no. 4 from Dadja. Amsterdam, Allard Pierson Museum 1364. (museum photographs).

Pl. 43. Terracotta model no. 4
from Salamis (Sal. 3518). (photograph T. Monloup).

a   b

Pl. 44a–b. Terracotta from Salamis (Sal. 3439). (photographs T. Monloup).

Pl. 46. Terracotta from Cyprus. Paris, Louvre AM 163. (museum photograph).

←

Pl. 45. Terracotta model from Oygoros. Nicosia, Cyprus Museum 1955/IX-26/1. (museum photograph).

a   b

Pl. 47. Terracotta from Cyprus. Paris, Louvre AM 3510. (museum photograph).

Pl. 48a–b. Terracotta from near Beirut. London, British Museum 136841 (1889. 18-17.13). (museum photograph).

Pl. 49. Terracotta from Naucratis. Oxford, Ashmolean Museum G.70. (museum photograph).

Pl. 50. Terracotta, Amsterdam Allard Pierson Museum 6212. (museum photograph).

Pl. 52. Terracotta from Helalieh. Paris, Louvre AM 1334. (museum photograph).

Pl. 51. Terracotta model from Tyre. London, British Museum 93092 (1884.10-24.3). (museum photograph).

Pl. 53. Terracotta from Helalieh. Paris, Louvre AM 1335. (museum photograph).

a   b

Pl. 54a–b. Terracotta from Marathus (Amrit). Paris, Louvre AM 3738. (museum photographs).

→

Pl. 55. Terracotta model. Holland, Private collection (after *Klassieke Kunst uit particulier bezit*, Leiden 1975, illustration no. 243).

a   *b*

Pl. 56a–b. Terracotta model from Tyre. London, British Museum 91567. (museum photographs).

a   *b*

Pl. 57a–b. Terracotta from Marathus (Amrit). Paris, Louvre AO 25986. (museum photographs).

a   b

Pl. 58a–b. Terracotta model no. 3. Paris, Bibliothèque Nationale, D 3735. (photographs Bibliothèque Nationale).

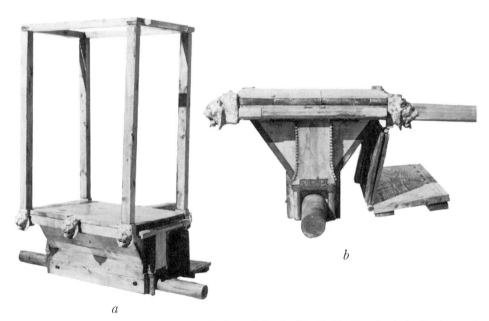

b

a

Pl. 59a–b. Cart ("cart/hearse Gamma") from Salamis, Tomb 79 (first burial). Catalogue A 4. (photographs V. Karageorghis).

Pl. 60. Terracotta model from Amathus. (British) Tomb 83. London, British Museum A 200. Catalogue TM 5. (museum photograph).

Pl. 61. Terracotta model from Alambra, tomb. New York, Metropolitan Museum of Art 74.51.1792. Catalogue TM 1. (museum photograph).

Pl. 62. Terracotta model from Alambra, tomb. New York, Metropolitan Museum of Art 74.51.1794. Catalogue TM 2. (museum photograph).

Pl. 63. Terracotta model from Amathus, (British) tomb 83. London, British Museum A 201. Catalogue TM 6. (museum photograph).

Pl. 64. Terracotta model from Alambra, tomb. New York, Metropolitan Museum of Art 74.51.1795. Catalogue TM 3. (museum photograph).

Pl. 65. Terracotta model from Alambra, tomb. New York, Metropolitan Museum of Art 74.51.1793. Catalogue TM 4. (museum photograph).

Pl. 66. Terracotta model from Amathus, (British) tomb 83. British Museum A 197. Catalogue TM 7. (museum photograph).

Pl. 67. Terracotta model from Amathus (British) tomb 88. British Museum A 199. Catalogue TM 8. (museum photograph).

Pl. 68. Terracotta model from Amathus (British) tomb 89. British Museum A 198. Catalogue TM 9. (museum photograph).

Pl. 69. Terracotta model from Amathus. (Cypriot) Tomb 159. Limassol, District Museum M. 652/2. Catalogue TM 11. (museum photograph).

Pl. 70. Terracotta model from Amathus. (Cypriot) Tomb 189/3. Limassol, District Museum M. 703/31 Catalogue TM 12. (museum photograph).

Pl. 71. Terracotta model from Nicosia, acropolis tomb. Cyprus Museum CS 2415/14. Catalogue TM 15. (museum photograph).

Pl. 72. Terracotta model. Nicosia, Cyprus Museum C 36 from Tamassos-*Chomazoudia*, Tomb II. B.C. Catalogue TM 18. (museum photograph).

Pl. 73. Terracotta model. Nicosia, Cyprus Museum D.106. Catalogue TM 21. (museum photograph).

Pl. 74. Terracotta model from Amathus, (British) tomb 83. British Museum A 201. Catalogue TM 22. (museum photograph).

Pl. 75. Terracotta model. Nicosia, Cyprus Museum B 252. Catalogue TM 23. (museum photograph).

Pl. 76. Terracotta model. Nicosia, Cyprus Museum C 48. Catalogue TM 24. (museum photograph).

Pl. 77. Terracotta model. Nicosia, Cyprus Museum C 37. Catalogue TM 25. (museum photograph).

Pl. 78. Terracotta model. Nicosia, Cyprus Museum C 42. Catalogue TM 26. (museum photograph).

Pl. 79. Terracotta model. Nicosia, Cyprus Museum C 11.742. Catalogue TM 27. (museum photograph).

Pl. 80. Terracotta model. Nicosia, Cyprus Museum C 40. Catalogue TM 28. (museum photograph).

Pl. 81. Terracotta model. Nicosia, Cyprus Museum C 46. Catalogue TM 29. (museum photograph).

a

b

Pl. 82a–b. Terracotta model. Nicosia, Cyprus Museum C 43. Catalogue TM 26. (museum photographs).

Pl. 83. Terracotta model. Nicosia, Cyprus Museum C 98. Catalogue TM 33. (museum photograph).

Pl. 84. Terracotta model. Nicosia, Cyprus Museum C 45. Catalogue TM 32. (museum photograph).

Pl. 85. Terracotta model. Nicosia, Cyprus Museum C 41. Catalogue TM 31. (museum photograph).

Pl. 86. Terracotta model. New York, Metropolitan Museum of Art 74. 51.1802. Catalogue TM 34. (museum photograph).

Pl. 87. Terracotta model. New York, Metropolitan Museum of Art 74. 51.1796. Catalogue TM 35. (museum photograph).

Pl. 88. Terracotta model. Oxford Ashmolean Museum 1958.18 (formerly Rugby School). Catalogue TM 36. (museum photograph).

Pl. 89. Terracotta model. Paris, Louvre N 3305 (formerly Colonna-Ceccaldi collection). Catalogue TM 37. (museum photograph).

Pl. 90. Terracotta model. Paris, Louvre AM 223. Catalogue TM 38. (museum photograph).

Pl. 91. Terracotta model. Paris, Louvre N 3306 (formerly Colonna-Ceccaldi collection). Catalogue TM 39. (museum photograph).

a

b

Pl. 92a–b. Terracotta model from Amrit (Marathus). Paris, Louvre AO 25986. (museum photographs).

a   b

Pl. 93a–b. Terracotta model from Tyre. London, British Museum 91567. (museum photographs).

Pl. 94. Bronze model. Nicosia, Cyprus Museum 1952/VII-19/2. (museum photograph).

Pl. 95. Limestone chariot model from Kourion. New York, Metropolitan Museum of Art 74.51.2687. (museum photograph).

Pl. 96. Bronze chariot model from the Levant. Paris, Louvre 22265. (museum photograph).

a

b

Pl. 97a–b. Terracotta model from Ovgoros (no. 1781+798). Nicosia, Cyprus Museum 1955/IX-26/1. (museum photographs).

c   d

Pl. 97c–d. Terracotta model from Ovgoros (no. 1781+798). Nicosia, Cyprus Museum 1955/IX-26/1. (museum photographs).

Pl. 98. Relief of Ashurnasirpal II. Staatliche Museen, Berlin Vorderasiatisches Museum 959. (museum photograph).

Pl. 99. Layard's interpretation of the Assyrian yoke (after Hrouda 1963, pl. 28, 6–9).

Pl. 100. Chariot of Ashurnasirpal II, showing yoke end, yoke-saddle finial, sun disk, and shoulder tassel (after Barnett and Falkner 1976, pl. 117).

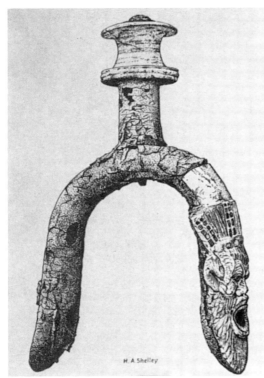

Pl. 101. Yoke saddle from a chariot of Tutʿankhamūn. After Carter 1927, pl. XLII.

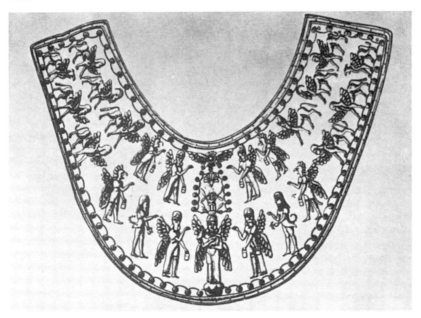

Pl. 102. Bronze breastplate from Salamis. After Karageorghis 1969, fig. 22.

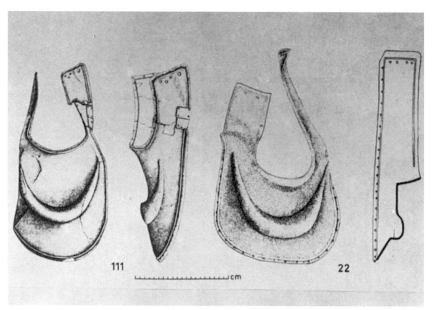

Pl. 103. Bronze breastplates from Salamis (after Karageorghis 1973, pl. 128).

Pl. 104. Chariot horses of Tukulti-Ninurta II (after Hrouda 1963, pl. 28:10).

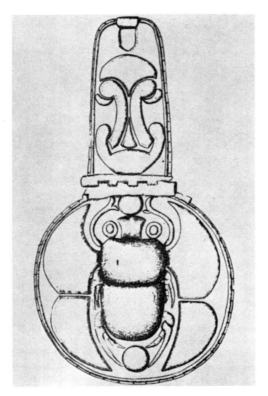

Pl. 105. Bronze shoulder pendant from Salamis. After Karageorghis 1969, fig. 21.

Pl. 106. Chariot of Sennacherib. After Gadd 1936, pl. 13.

Pl. 107. Chariot of Tiglath-Pileser III. After Barnett and Falkner 1976, pl. 15.

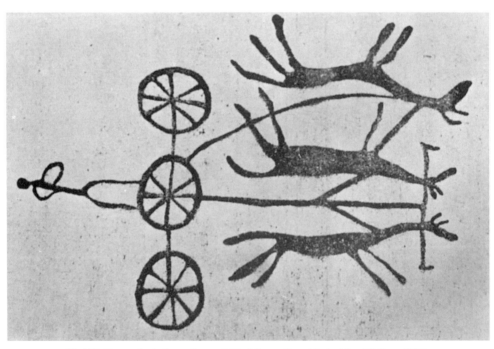

Pl. 108. Petroglyph from Jamani Us, Mongolian Altai. After Volkov 1972.

a

b

Pl. 109a–b. Wall paintings from Til Barsib. After Parrot 1961, pl. 345.

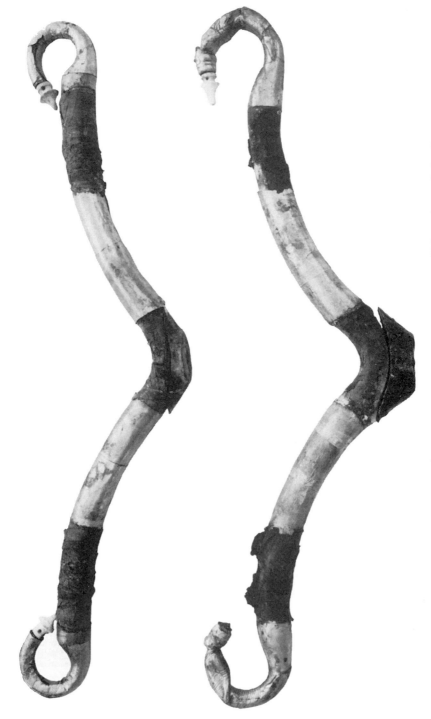

Pl. 110. Yokes from Tutʿankhamūn's chariots. (photograph Griffith Institute, Oxford).

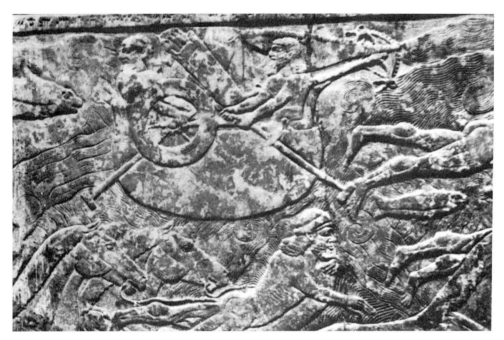

Pl. 111. Pole and yoke of Ashurnasirpal II's chariot on ferry. (photograph London, British Museum).

Pl. 112. Standard bearers of Ashurnasirpal II. (photograph London, British Museum).

Pl. 113. Fitted yoke of Ashurbanipal's chariot curving over neck. (photograph London, British Museum).

Pl. 114. Relief from Arslan Tash, showing breast plates, yoke saddles and six reins. After Potratz 1966, pl. 45, p. 101.

Pl. 115. Terracotta model from Ajia Irini. Nicosia, Cyprus Museum 2000. (museum photograph).

Pl. 116. Terracotta model from Ajia Irini Nicosia, Cyprus Museum 1780. (museum photograph).

a

Pl. 117a–b. Terracotta model from Marathus (Amrit). Paris, Louvre AO 25985. (museum photograph).

b

Pl. 118. Sargon's four-horse fitted yoke. Paris, Louvre. (museum photograph).

Pl. 119. Sanherib's four-horse fitted yoke. (photograph London, British Museum).

Pl. 120. Modern Hungarian harnessing, three-a-breast. After Alapfy and Török 1971.

Pl. 121. Fragmentary bronze model of quadriga with two pole horses under yoke. (photograph Philadelphia University Museum).

Pl. 122. Russian *dvoika* showing two gaits. After Anonymous 1823.

Pl. 123. Russian dvoika, showing attachment of to outrigger. After Atkinson and Walker 1803.

Pl. 124. Tyre segments A 1–3. Susa, Apadana area. Paris, Louvre Sb 6829. (photograph F. Tallon).

Pl. 125. Tyre segments B 1–6 Susa. Donjon tomb A 89, originally called 98b. Paris, Louvre Sb 14672–14677 and one unnumbered fragment; Teheran, Iran, Bastan Museum (four segments). (photograph F. Tallon).

Pl. 126. Tyre segments C 1–2; Tyre segments C 3–5. Holland, private collection. (photograph G. Strietman).

Pl. 127. Metal linch pin. Susa. Paris, Louvre (photograph F. Tallon).

Pl. 128. Cross-bar wheel in modern Spain.

Pl. 129. Cylinder seal from Tepe Hissar IIIB. Iran, Bastan Museum. (photograph Philadelphia University Museum).

Pl. 130. Cylinder seal impression. Paris, Louvre (Collection de Clerq 284). (museum photograph).

Pl. 131. Cylinder seal. Paris, Louvre AO 20.138. (museum photograph).

Pl. 132. Sarcophagus from Vulci, Italy. Boston, Museum of Fine Arts 1975.799. (museum photograph).

Pl. 133. The four wheels from Acemhöyük, with fragmentary axles and lugs. (photograph E. Özgen).

Pl. 134. Face of one wheel. (photograph E. Özgen).

Pl. 135. View of wheel from tread, showing slightly protruding naves and axle, rectangular in section where it ran under body of vehicle. (photograph E. Özgen).

Pl. 136. Pierced lugs, broken off at one end, one with part of axle in place. (photograph E. Özgen).

Pl. 137. T-shaped attachment with loop, arms bent out of position. (photograph E. Özgen).

Pl. 138. Fragments of sheet bronze body; lower piece riveting as well as part of T-shaped attachment in lower right-hand corner. (photograph E. Özgen).

Pl. 139. Egyptian wheel. New York E. 37.1700, Brooklyn Museum (museum photograph).

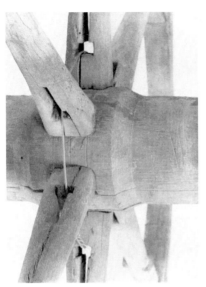

Pl. 140a–c. a. Egyptian wheel. Detail; b. Egyptian wheel. Detail; c. Egyptian wheel. Detail. (museum photographs).

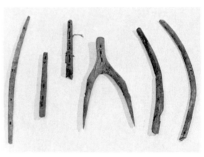

Pl. 141. Pieces of wood accompanying wheel in Brooklyn Museum. (museum photograph).

Pl. 142. Fragmentary wheel of Amenophis III. Oxford, Ashmolean Museum 1923.663. (museum photograph).

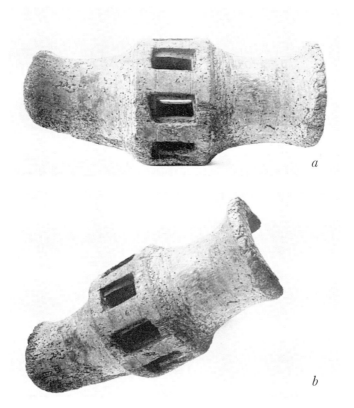

a

b

Pl. 143a–b. Nave of Egyptian wheel. Paris, Louvre E 109. (museum photographs).

Pl. 144. Wheels of a chariot of Tutʿankhamūn. (photograph H. Burton, Metropolitan Museum of Fine Art, New York).

Pl. 145. Painted wooden chest of Tutʿankhamūn. (photograph H. Burton, Metropolitan Museum of Fine Art, New York).

Pl. 146. Fragment of Tûna bowl. Boston, Museum of Fine Arts 59.422. (museum photograph).

Pl. 147. Fragment of a trial relief. Berlin Ägyptisches Museum, 3425. (museum photograph).

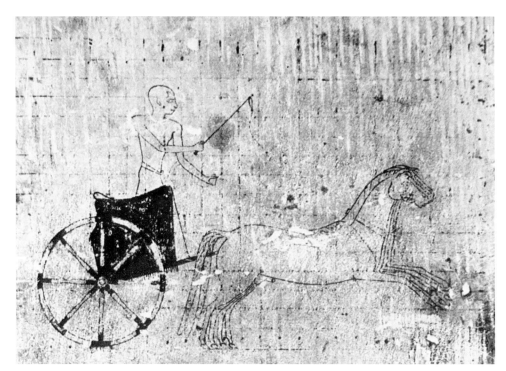

Pl. 148. Drawing on limestone. Hanover, Kestner Museum 2952. (museum photograph).

Pl. 149. Cylinder Seal. New York, J.P. Rosen Collection. (photograph courtesy of the owner).

Pl. 150. Threshing sledge (*tribulum*) in Turkey. After Mantran 1959, pl. 70.

Pl. 151. Winnowing shovel in use in northern Greece After Theocharis 1973, pl. 163.

Pl. 152. Pu-abi's sledge from Ur. London, British Museum. (museum photograph).

a

b

Pl. 153a–b. Threshing wain (*plostellum poenicum*) in eastern Kermanshaw, western Iran. (photograph C. Kramer).

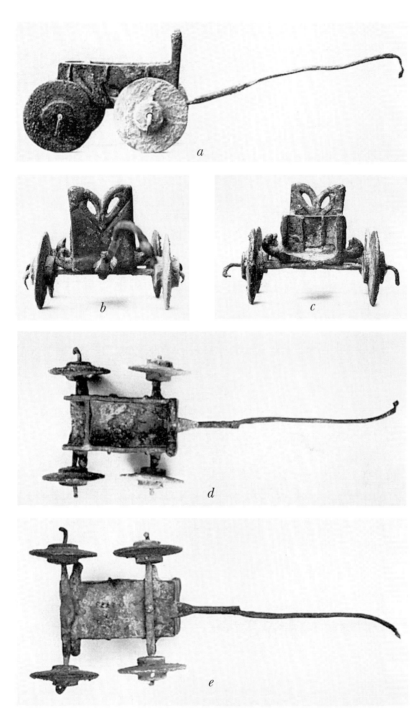

Pl. 154a–e. Syria no. 1. Bronze wagon model. Paris, Louvre AO 2773. (museum photographs).

Pl. 155a–d. Syria no. 2. Bronze wagon model. Stockholm, Medelhavsmuseet (formerly Statens Historika Museet) 14305. (museum photographs).

Pl. 156a. Anatolia no. 1. Bronze wagon model. New York, Metropolitan Museum of Art (formerly Edith Perry Chapman Fund 1966) 66.15. (museum photograph).

Pl. 156b-e. Anatolia no. 1. Bronze wagon model. New York, Metropolitan Museum of Art (formerly Edith Perry Chapman Fund 1966) 66.15. (museum photographs).

Pl. 157a–e. Anatolia no. 2. Bronze
wagon model. New York (formerly
Pomerance Collection).
(L. Pomerance photograph).

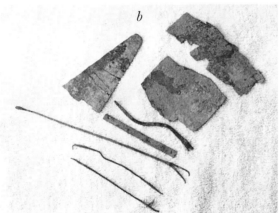

Pl. 158a–b. Anatolia no. 3. a. Bronze wagon model. London. (formerly London, P. Adam Collection 358; b. Scraps of metal acquired with this model. Some may come from other, similar models. (P. Adam photographs).

Pl. 159a. Anatolia no. 4. Bronze wagon model. Boston, Museum of Fine Arts 62.678. (museum photograph).

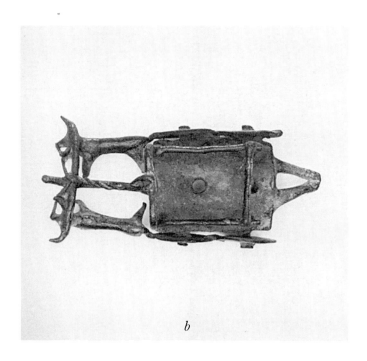

b

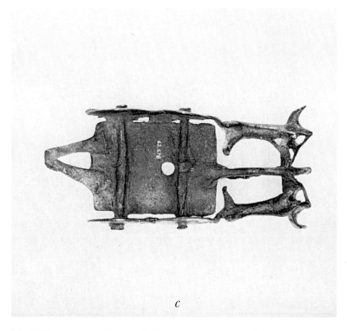

c

Pl. 159b-c. Anatolia no. 4. Bronze wagon model. Boston, Museum of Fine Arts 62.678. (museum photographs).

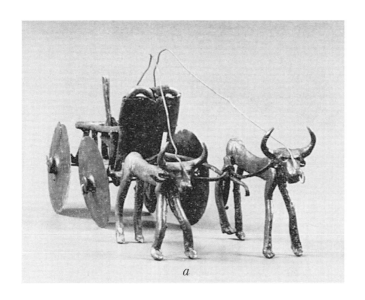

Pl. 160a-b. Anatolia no. 5. Bronze wagon model. Berlin, Stiftung Preussischer Kulturbesitz, Staatliche Museen, Museum für Vor- und Frühgeschichte XLb 1874 A–C/1966. (museum photographs).

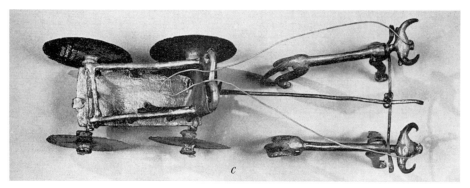

Pl. 160c. Anatolia no. 5. Bronze wagon model. Berlin, Stiftung Preussischer Kulturbesitz, Staatliche Museen, Museum für Vor- und Frühgeschichte XLb 1874 A–C/1966. (museum photograph).

Pl. 161. Anatolia no. 6. Bronze wagon model. France, Collection Thierry IV (after Danmanville 1968, 59ff.).

Pl. 162. Anatolia no. 6. Terracotta four-wheeler. Oxford, Ashmolean museum. Formerly Collection of Mr. and Mrs. James Bomford. (photograph Oxford, Ashmolean museum).

Pl. 163. Anatolia no. 6. Terracotta four-wheeler from Tell Chuēra T. Ch. 57/1959. (photograph U. Moortgat-Correns).

Pl. 164. Anatolia no. 6. Terracotta four-wheeler from Kish, Mound A. Oxford, Ashmolean Museum 1925.291. (museum photograph)

a

b

Pl. 165a–b. Anatolia a. Bronze wagon model. Private collection. (photographs D. Widmer).

a

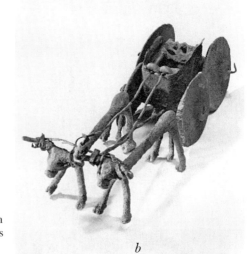

Pl. 166a-b. Anatolia b. Bronze wagon model. Private collection. (photographs D. Widmer).

b

a

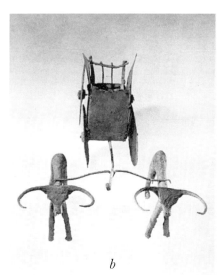

b

Pl. 167a–c. Anatolia d. Bronze wagon
model. Private collection. (photographs D.
Widmer).

c

Pl. 168a-b. Anatolia d. Bronze wagon model. Private Collection. (photographs D. Widmer).

a

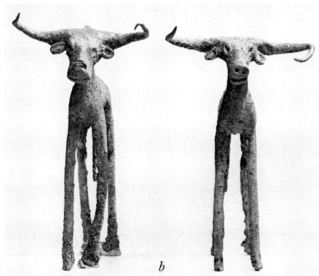

b

Pl. 169a-b. Anatolia e. Bronze wagon model. Private collection. (photograph D. Widmer).

Pl. 170. Terracotta four-wheeler from Hammam. Oxford, Ashmolean Museum 1913.183.

Pl. 171. Terracotta two-wheeler from Cyprus. Oxford, Ashmolean Museum 1950.80 (formerly Rugby School). (museum photograph).

Pl. 172. Terracotta four-wheeler from Syria (courtesy Mr C. Ede, London).

a

b

c

d

Pl. 173a-d. Terracotta four-wheeler from Syria. Oxford, Ashmolean Museum 1975.326. (a. drawing F. Strietman, b-d museum photographs).

Pl. 174. Stone model from Tamassos. London, British Museum C 81. (museum photograph).

Pl. 175. Stone model. London, British Museum C 82. (museum photograph).

a   *b*

Pl. 176a–b. Stone model. Nicosia, Cyprus Museum C 218. (museum photograph).

Pl. 177. Detail of sarcophagus from Amathus. New York, Metropolitan Museum of Art 74.51.2453. (museum photograph).

Pl. 178. Stone model. Paris, Louvre AM 210. (museum photograph).

Pl. 179. Stone model from Golgoi. New York, Metropolitan Museum of Art 54.51.2581. (museum photograph).

Pl. 180. Terracotta model. Amsterdam, Allard Pierson Museum 1881. (museum photograph).

Pl. 181. Stone model from Kythrea. New York, Metropolitan Museum of Art 74.51.2609. (museum photograph).

Pl. 182. Stone model from Tamassos. New York, Metropolitan Museum of Art 74.51.2581. (museum photograph).

Pl. 183. Terracotta model (detail) from Meniko. 56+29+77 Nicosia, Cyprus Museum. (museum photograph).

Pl. 184. Terracotta model. London, British Museum 1876.4.9.91. (museum photograph).

Pl. 185. Terracotta model. London, British Museum 1876.4.9.92. museum photograph).

Pl. 186. Terracotta model from Kurion. New York, Metropolitan Museum of Art 74.51.1778. (museum photograph).

Pl. 187. Terracotta model. Edinburgh, Royal Scottish Museum 1921.354. (museum photograph).

Pl. 188. Terracotta model from Palaepaphos-*Skales*, Tomb 52. Kouklia Museum. (museum photograph).

Pl. 189. Terracotta model. Nicosia, Cyprus Museum 1970/XII–8/2. (museum photograph).

a   *b*   *c*

d   *e*

Pl. 190a–d. Terracotta model of horseback rider. Brussels, Musées Royaux d'Art et d'Histoire A 1323. (museum photographs).

Pl. 191. Terracotta model of horseback rider reportedly from Tyre. London, British Museum WA93092 (1884.10–29.3). (museum photograph).

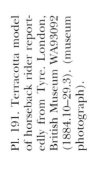

Pl. 192. 'Soft' foot stirrup, Mathura (between Agra and Delhi), India. (photograph Boston Museum of Fine Arts).

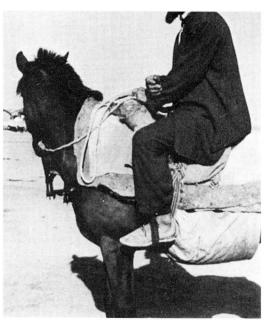

Pl. 193. Rope stirrup, Bokhara. After Fitzroy Maclean 1975.

Pl. 194. Rope stirrup, Northeast Iran, of flat-braided camel and horse hair used with a 'soft' saddle on the Iranian Turkoman steppe. (photograph L. L. Firouz).

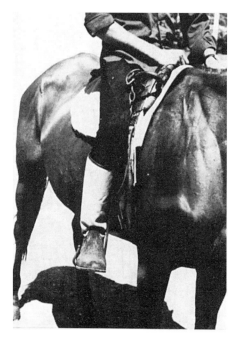

Pl. 195. Hook stirrup in use (photograph L. L. Firouz).

Pl. 196. Hook stirrup reconstructed. (photograph J. Spruytte).

a   *b*

Pl. 197a–b. Kushan gem and cast, ca. A.D. 50, width 2.5 cm (photograph London, British Museum).

Pl. 198. Terminals of torque from Kul Oba Crimea (photograph St. Petersburg Hermitage Museum).

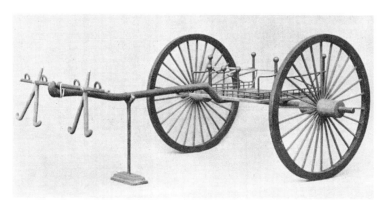

Pl. 199. Reconstruction of chariot found in horse burial No. 6 at Liu Li Ko in Honan, China.

Pl. 200. Detail of wooden chest from Tomb of Tutʿankhamūn (photograph H. Burton, Metropolitan Museum of Art, New York).

Pl. 201. Amarna relief. Formerly collection of Mr and Mrs N. Schimmel. (photograph O.E. Nelson).

Pl. 202. Relief from Tomb of Kha-em-het (photograph Egyptian Expedition of the Metropolitan Museum of Art, New York).

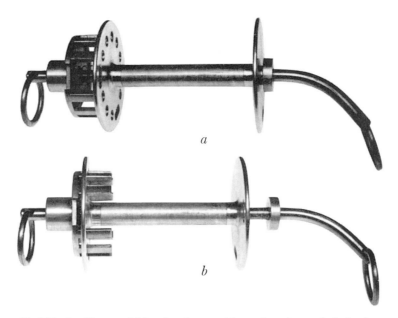

Pl. 203a–b. 'Run-out' bit, showing position when horse is behaving. Mouthpiece width between the cheeks: 11.4 cm. 'Run-out' bit, showing position if horse is pulled to left.

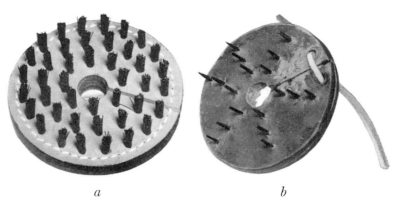

Pl. 204a–b. Brush 'burr' or 'picker'. Diameter 9.2 cm. Tack 'burr'. Diameter 8.8 cm. (photographs De Lilo).

Pl. 205. Bronze harness fittings (probably 'burrs') from China. Western Zhou, c. 1000 B.C. Length 6.9 cm. (photograph Royal Ontario Museum, Ontario).

Pl. 206. 'Run-out' bit on simple leverage principle. Mouthpiece between rings 11.4 cm. (New York, Metropolitan Museum of Fine Art, formerly Rogers Fund).

Pl. 207. Detail of stone relief from Amarna, Metropolitan Museum of Fine Art, New York, formerly Collection of Mr and Mrs N. Schimmel). (photograph Mr and Mrs N. Schimmel).

Pl. 208. Bronze bridle acessory, often called 'muzzle' or 'cavesson'. (photograph De Lilo).

Pl. 209. Slit nostrils on a donkey in Iran (photograph L. L. Firouz).

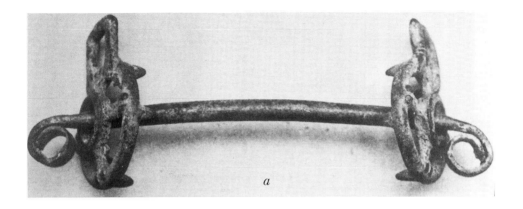

Pl. 210a–b. a. Metal bridle bit. New York University, Department of Classics, now on loan to the Department of the Ancient Near East of the Metropolitan Museum of Art, New York. L. 1984.85; b. Details of the cheekpieces of the bronze bridle bit. (photographs D. Kawami).

Pl. 211a–b. Pair of metal bridle bits from Tell a-Haddad, Iraq. (photograph D. George).

Pl. 212. Metal bridle bit. New York Metropolitan Museum of Fine Art L. 1984.85 lent by the Classics Department of New York University. (museum photograph).

Pl. 213. Donkey with slit nostrils, in Iran (photographs L. L. Firouz).

Pl. 214. 14th century B.C. Egyptian chariot team showing slit nostrils. Detail from a relief. New York, Metropolitan Museum of Art (formerly collection of Mr and Mrs Schimmel). (photograph courtesy of N. Schimmel).

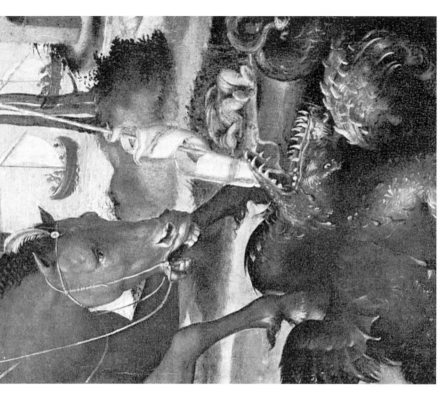

Pl. 216. St. George and the dragon, by Sodoma (1477–1549) (Photo: National Gallery of Art, Samuel H. Kress Collection 1947, Washington, D.C.)

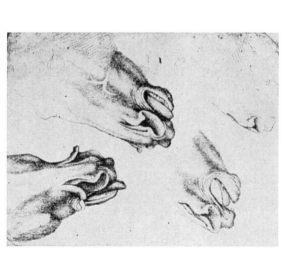

Pl. 215. Four studies of horses' muzzels, with slit nostrils by Pisanello (1395–1455). (photograph after Hill 1965).

Pl. 217. Pair of head poles from tomb of Tutʿankhamūn. Ashmolean Institute, Oxford. (photograph H. Burton, Griffith Institute, Oxford).

Pl. 218. Egyptian horse with 'head pole' from Tell-el Amarna. New York, Metropolitan Museum of Art. (museum photograph).

Pl. 219. Salamis Tomb 2. Head of an ass skeleton with bronze gear *in situ*.

Pl. 220. Salamis Tomb 2. Head of a horse skeleton with bronze gear *in situ.*

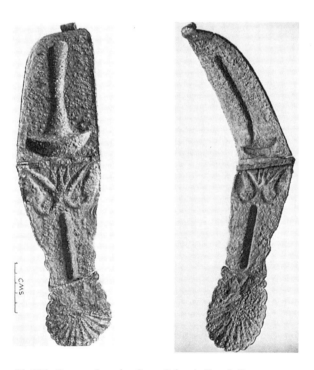

Pl. 221. Bronze frontlet from Salamis Tomb 2.

Pl. 222. Terracotta horse head. New York, Metropolitan Museum of Art 74. 51.1805. (museum photograph)

Pl. 223. Terracotta chariot group from Tamassos. London, British Museum. (museum photograph).

Pl. 224. Assyrian stone relief with Ashurbanipal shooting at lions. London, British Museum. (museum photograph).

Pl. 225. Assyrian stone relief with Ashurbanipal spearing a lion from the saddle. London, British Museum. (museum photograph).

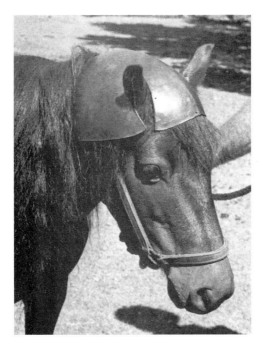

Pl. 226. Replica of helmet, from northwestern Iran on pony stallion's head. London, British Museum 135437. (photograph, M.A. Littauer).

Pl. 227a–b. Helmet from northwestern Iran (Amlash region). Edinburgh, Royal Scottish Museum 1969.395. (museum photographs).

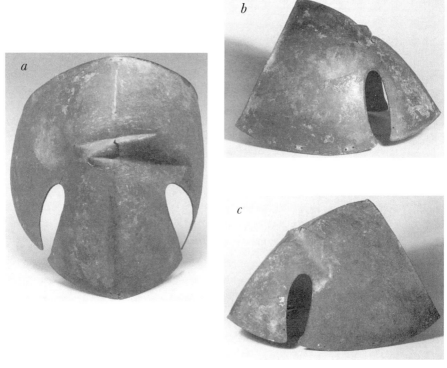

Pl. 228a–c. Helmet. Hamburg, Museum für Kunst and Gewerbe 1969.249. (museum photographs).

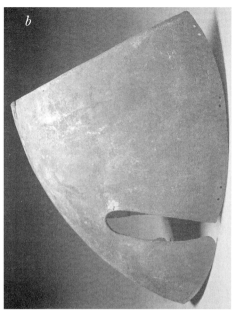

Pl. 229a–b. Helmet from Iran. Los Angeles, Los Angeles County Museum of Art M. 76.174. (museum photographs).

Pl. 230. Helmet from Amlash, Iran. Formerly Amsterdam. (photograph "Ancient Art").

Pl. 231. Helmet from Amlash (?). Formerly Amsterdam. (photograph "Ancient Art").

Pl. 232. Detail of Tutʿankhamūn's bowcase. (photograph H. Burton, Griffith Institute, Oxford).

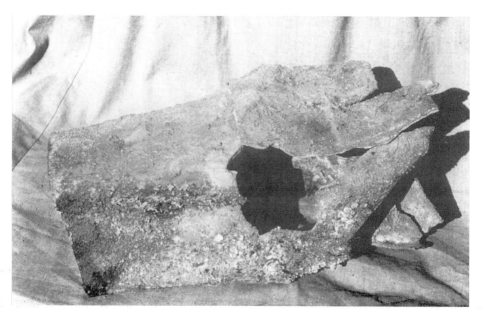

Pl. 233. Fragmentary chamfron from Hasanlu (photograph Philadelphia, University Museum).

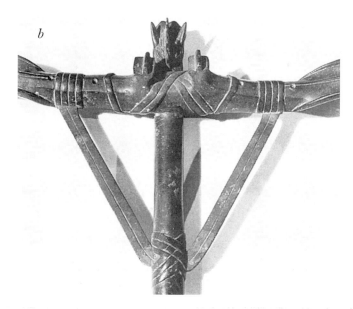

Pl. 234a–b. a. Fragmentary bronze chariot from Chianciano. Florence, Museo archeologico 76525 (photograph Alinari); b. Detail of the yoke and pole. (photograph Soprintendenza alle Antichità d'Etruria).

CULTURE AND HISTORY
OF THE ANCIENT NEAR EAST

ISSN 1566-2055

1. Grootkerk, S.E. *Ancient Sites in Galilee*. A Toponymic Gazetteer. 2000. ISBN 90 04 11535 8
2. Higginbotham, C.R. *Egyptianization and Elite Emulation in Ramesside Palestine*. Governance and Accommodation on the Imperial Periphery. 2000. ISBN 90 04 11768 7
3. Yamada, S. *The Construction of the Assyrian Empire*. A Historical Study of the Inscriptions of Shalmanesar III Relating to His Campaigns in the West. 2000. ISBN 90 04 11772 5
4. Yener, K.A. *The Domestication of Metals*. The Rise of Complex Metal Industries in Anatolia. 2000. ISBN 90 04 11864 0
5. Taracha, P. *Ersetzen und Entsühnen*. Das mittelhethitische Ersatzritual für den Großkönig Tuthalija (CTH *448.4) und verwandte Texte. 2000. ISBN 90 04 11910 8
6. Littauer, M.A. & Crouwel, J.H.and P. Raulwing (ed.) *Selected Writings on Chariots and other Early Vehicles, Riding and Harness*. 2002. ISBN 90 04 11799 7
7. Malamat, A. *History of Biblical Israel*. Major Problems and Minor Issues. 2001. ISBN 90 04 12009 2
8. Snell, D.C. *Flight and Freedom in the Ancient Near East*. 2001. ISBN 90 04 12010 6
9. Westbrook, R. & R. Jasnow (ed.) *Security for Debt in Ancient near Eastern Law*. 2002. ISBN 90 04 12124 2
10. Holloway, S.W. *Aššur is King! Aššur is King!* Religion in the Exercise of Power in the Neo-Assyrian Empire. 2002. ISBN 90 04 12328 8
11. Daviau, P.M.M. *Excavations at Tall Jawa, Jordan*. Volume 2: The Iron Age Artefacts. 2002. ISBN 90 04 12363 6